MAN'S CONQUEST OF THE PACIFIC

Peter Bellwood

MAN'S CONQU

*The Prehistory of Southeast
Asia and Oceania*

EST OF THE
PACIFIC

Collins
AUCKLAND
SYDNEY LONDON

FIRST PUBLISHED 1978
WILLIAM COLLINS PUBLISHERS LTD.
P.O. BOX No. 1, AUCKLAND

Dedication: FOR TANE

© 1978 PETER BELLWOOD
ISBN 0 00 216911 8
Printed in Hong Kong by
Dai Nippon Printing Co. (H.K.) Ltd.

Preface

This book is an attempt to describe and explain the prehistoric past of a region; a region of lands and islands under a tropical sun; a region which is at present the home of an indigenous population numbering almost 300 million souls. It is a region of new nations, and of nations still unborn. It is my hope that this book will assist in the realisation of cultural identity wherever it is sought for peaceful reasons, and I hope also that it will be of interest to students and professionals within the discipline of prehistory.

Acknowledgements are due to the Department of Anthropology, University of Auckland, and the Department of Prehistory and Anthropology, Australian National University, for providing typing services, and the essential environment for productive research. Many of the illustrations were prepared by Mrs Joan Goodrum, and the Visual Aids Unit, both of the Australian National University, and I am deeply indebted to them. Discussions with many scholars have taken place during the course of preparation, but actual sections of the manuscript have been read and commented upon by the following: Mr G. Barnett, Dr R. Blust, Dr B. Egloff, Professor J. Golson, Dr C. Groves, Dr A. Hooper, Professor D.J. Mulvaney, Dr A. K. Pawley, Dr A. Thorne, and Mrs B. van Wierst. I must also thank my wife, for helping me through a period of seemingly interminable preparation.

Peter Bellwood
Canberra, October 1975.

CONTENTS

PREFACE   5

1. Introduction   19
   Southeast Asia and Oceania   19
   Races, Languages, Ethnic Groups and Prehistory   21

2. Human Populations – Past and Present   25
   Present Populations of Southeast Asia and the Pacific   25
   Genetic Studies on Pacific Populations   32
   Evolutionary Processes in Oceania   33
   Natural Selection, Clines and Gene Flow   34
   Genetic Drift and Genetic Distances   34
   The Prehistoric Record of Man in Southeast Asia and the Pacific   38
   Homo Erectus and Modern Man in Eastern Asia   43
   The Racial History of Oceania   47

3. Cultural Foundations   53
   The Pleistocene Epoch in Southeast Asia   54
   Industries of the Middle Pleistocene   55
   The Upper Pleistocene Period   58
   Australia   62
   New Guinea   63
   The Hoabinhian Technocomplex of the Southeast Asian Mainland   64
      North Vietnam   66
      Malaya   67
      Thailand   69
      Laos and Cambodia   69
      Sumatra   70
      South China and Taiwan   70
      The Hoabinhian Sequence – a Summary   70
      Hoabinhian Economy   71
   The Earlier Holocene in Island Southeast Asia – the Flake and Blade
   Technocomplex   71
   Summary   79

4. The Cultures of Southeast Asia and Oceania   83
    The Southeast Asian Mainland   85
    Island Southeast Asia   88
    The Peoples of Oceania   92
    Melanesia   92
    The New Guinea Highlands   93
    Island Melanesia   96
    Trade Networks in Melanesia   102
    Melanesian Material Culture   104
    Micronesia   104
    Polynesia   107
    The Ethnohistory of Island Southeast Asia and Oceania   112

5. The Linguistic History of the Pacific Area   117
    The Language Families of the Pacific   119
    The Papuan Languages   119
    The Austronesian Languages   121
    The Major Austronesian Subgroups   121
    The Western Austronesian Languages   123
    The Eastern Austronesian and Oceanic Subgroups   124
    The Languages of Polynesia   126
    The Polynesian Outliers   128
    The Languages of Nuclear Micronesia   130
    A Problem of Correlation   130
    Dyen's Lexicostatistical Classification of the Austronesian Languages   131
    The Problem of Austronesian Dominance in Indonesia   132

6. Subsistence Patterns and their Prehistoric Implications   135
    The Origins of Cultivation   136
    Indigenous Major Food Plants of Southeast Asia and Oceania   136
    Cultivation Systems and their Development   142
    Cultivation in New Zealand   148
    The Wet-Field Cultivation of Rice   148
    Domesticated Animals   149

7. Neolithic and Early Metal Age Cultures on the Southeast Asian Mainland   153
    The Earliest Pottery in Southeast Asia   153
    The Prehistory of China   156
    Thailand – an independent focus of innovation?   161
    Lungshanoid Influences in Thailand and Malaya? The Ban Kao Culture   166
    The Adze Types of Southeast Asia   170

An Adze-based Migration Theory   173
The Neolithic Sites and Cultures of Indochina   175
   Cambodia   175
   Vietnam   176
Metal Age Cultures in Southeast Asia   180
The Dong-Son Style of Bronze Metallurgy   183
The Metal Age Jar Burial Tradition – South Vietnam and Laos   191
Stone Burial Jars and Megaliths of Northern Laos   194
Summary   198

8. Neolithic and Metal Age Cultures of Island Southeast Asia   203
The Neolithic Cultures of Taiwan   203
Neolithic and Metal Age Cultures in the Philippines   207
The Late Neolithic and Metal Ages in the Central Philippines   213
The Neolithic of Niah Cave, Sarawak   216
Neolithic Sites in Eastern Indonesia   217
Neolithic Sites in Western Indonesia   220
The Metal Age of Western and Southern Indonesia   222
Megaliths in Indonesia   225
The Problem of Beads in Southeast Asian Metal Age Sites   228
Summary   231

9. The Prehistory of Melanesia   233
Preceramic Settlement in Western Melanesia   233
Ceramic Assemblages in Melanesia   244
   The Lapita Culture   244
Major Sites of the Lapita Culture   249
Who were the Lapita Potters?   254
Lapita-like Assemblages in Melanesia   255
The Incised and Applied-Relief Ceramics of Melanesia   258
The Non-Lapita Prehistory of New Caledonia and Fiji   260
Southeast Asian Metal Age Influences in Western Melanesia   266
Comb-Incised Pottery in Melanesia   269
Human Sacrifice in the New Hebrides   270
Stone Structures and Rock Art in Melanesia   272
The Melanesian Past   275

10. The Prehistory of Micronesia   281
Western Micronesia – the Marianas Islands   282
The Island of Yap   285
The Palau Islands   286
Eastern Micronesia – the Caroline Islands   289

Eastern Micronesia – Nukuoro Atoll   293
Summary   295

11. The Prehistory of Polynesia: Part One   297
    Canoes and their Navigation   297
    The Whence of the Polynesians: Theorists Galore   303
    The Prehistory of Western Polynesia   311
    The Early Eastern Polynesian Culture (c.A.D. 300–1200)   317

12. The Prehistory of Polynesia: Part Two   329
    Later Eastern Polynesian Prehistory (c.A.D. 1200–1800)   329
    The Marquesas Islands   331
    Central Polynesia – the Society, Tuamotu, Austral and Southern Cook
      Islands   337
    The Society Islands   337
    The Tuamotu Archipelago   343
    The Austral Islands   344
    The Southern Cook Islands   346
    The Isolated Mystery Islands   352
    The Hawaiian Islands   353
    Easter Island   361

13. The Prehistory of New Zealand   381
    The View from Tradition   382
    The Coming of Archaeology   384
    The New Zealand Prehistoric Sequence   385
    The Origins of the Maoris   385
    Man and the Moas   386
    The Archaic Phase in the South Island   387
    Economy, Settlements and Trade in the South Island   391
    The Rock Art of the South Island   393
    The Archaic Phase in the North Island   395
    The Classic Maori Phase   399
    The Classic Maori Artefact Assemblage   400
    Classic Maori Settlements and Economy   406
    The Chatham Islands   416
    Summary   416

14. Some Problems for the Future   421
GLOSSARY   424
BIBLIOGRAPHY   425
INDEX   453

ILLUSTRATIONS

Note 1. The letter (c) indicates that the illustration appears also in the colour section.

Note 2. Sources of illustrations will be found on page 452. Where no credit is given the photograph or illustration is the property of the author.

CHAPTER 2	Page
1a. Batek Negritos of the Aring River, Malaya	26
1b. A Mendriq Negrito of the Lebir River, Malaya	26
2. New Guinea Highlanders in ceremonial dress	28
3. New Hebridean children, Efate (c)	28
4. Fijian women, Viti Levu (c)	29
5. Indonesian street scene, Borneo (c)	30
6. Polynesian family, southern Cook Islands (c)	31
7. Micronesian man of Truk	32
8a. Descent group lineage of the Murapin phratry	36
8b. Evolutionary tree for seven clans of the Murapin phratry	36
9. Zoogeographical divisions and Pleistocene sites	37
10. Cast of the lower jaw fragment of *Meganthropus*	38
11. Front and side view of a skull of *Homo erectus*	39
12. The skull of Peking Man (cast)	41
13. Skull V from Solo (cast)	43
14. Skull of *H. sapiens sapiens* from Niah Cave	45
15. Diagram of Polynesian skeletal relationships.	49

CHAPTER 3	
1. Pleistocene men and stone-tool industries	55
2. Stone tools of Pacitanian type	56
3. Tools from Tabon Cave	61
4. Pleistocene tools from Australia	62
5. Waisted tools from Southeast Asia and the New Guinea Highlands	63
6. Hoabinhian tool types from North Vietnam	65
7. Blade tools, Talaud Islands	72
8. Bone points from Paso, northern Sulawesi	73
9. Toalean tools, South Sulawesi	74
10. Flake and blade tools, eastern Timor	75
11. Tools from the Gua Lawa Cave, Java	77
12. Late Pleistocene and Early Holocene cultural developments	79

CHAPTER 4   Page

1. Major ethnolinguistic groups of Southeast Asia   86
2. Verandah of a Land Dayak longhouse, Sarawak   90
3. Ifugao rice terraces, northern Luzon   91
4. Ethnolinguistic map of New Guinea   93
5. Contrasting settlement patterns in the New Guinea Highlands   95
6. A northern Abelam ceremonial house (c)   97
7. A village on Kiriwina, Trobriand Islands (c)   99
8. Map of Micronesia   105
9. Diagrammatic representation of tribute and exchange system   107
10. A *bai* or lodge on Yap   107
11. The structure of a Polynesian chiefdom   108
12. Circular houses in a Samoan village (c)   111

CHAPTER 5

1. The distribution of the Austronesian languages   116
2. The distribution of the Papuan languages   120
3. A tentative family tree for Austronesian   122
4. A tentative family tree for the Oceanic languages   125
5. A family tree for the Fijian and Polynesian languages   127
6. The Polynesian Outliers   129
7. Dyen's family tree for the Austronesian languages   131

CHAPTER 6

1. Some major Pacific food plants   137
2. The breadfruit   138
3. The Pacific bananas   138
4. A yam store-house on Kiriwina (c)   140
5. A fenced swidden plot in New Ireland   143
6. Sweet potato cultivation, New Guinea Highlands   144
7. Swamp cultivation of taro, Cook Islands (c)   146
8. Terracing for taro cultivation, Rarotonga (c)   146
9. Feeding domestic pigs on coconuts in New Ireland   150

CHAPTER 7

1. Neolithic and Metal Age sites in Mainland Southeast Asia   154
2. Artefacts of the Taiwanese Corded Ware Culture   155
3. Stone adze of rectangular-cross-section from Spirit Cave   156
4. Bone points from Feng-pi-t'ou   159
5. The Lungshanoid assemblage from Feng-pi-t'ou   160
6. Fine red ware of Lungshanoid type from Feng-pi-t'ou   158

7. Cultural developments in Mainland and Island Southeast Asia 161
8. Non Nok Tha Early Period burial 162
9. Non Nok Tha pottery, Early Period 163
10. Moulds and bronze axes from Non Nok Tha, Middle Period 164
11. Ban Chiang painted pottery, north-eastern Thailand 165
12. Ban Kao grave-goods 166
13. Ban Kao vessels 167
14. Cord-marked and incised pottery from Gua Cha 169
15. Southeast Asian stone adzes 171
16. Bark-cloth beaters of stone from Southeast Asia 174
17. Artefacts of the Indochinese Neolithic 177
18. Somrong Sen: pots; ceramic decoration; pottery earplugs 178
19. Geometric pottery from Lamma Island, Hong Kong 181
20. Artefacts from the Geometric horizon on Lamma Island 182
21. Bronze drum of Heger type I 183
22. Rubbing of the tympanum of a Heger type I drum 184
23. Boat with warriors, Ngoc-Lu drum, North Vietnam 185
24. Artefacts of the Dong-Son Culture 186
25. Bronze dagger handle from Dong-Son 187
26. Cord-marked pot from Dong-Son 188
27. The distribution of Dong-Son drums of Heger type I 188
28. The Mlu Prei assemblage 190
29. The Sa-Huynh assemblage 192
30. Underground burial chamber, northern Laos 194
31. A part of the Plain of Jars 195
32. Mushroom-shaped stone at San Hin Oume 196
33. Stone disc with quadruped, at Keo Tane 196
34. Figurine from Thao Kham and schist pendant from Keo Hin Tan 197
35. The Ban Ang assemblage 199

CHAPTER 8

1. Neolithic and Metal Age sites in Island Southeast Asia 202
2a. Artefacts of the Yüan-shan Culture 204
2b. Artefacts of the Yüan-shan Culture 205
3. The Duyong Cave preceramic assemblage 208
4. Jar from Manunggul chamber A 209
5. Artefacts from the Tabon Caves 210
6. Vessel forms of the Tabon pottery complex 211
7. Vessels of the Tabon pottery complex 212
8. Sherds from the Batungan Caves, Masbate 213
9. Pottery of Kalanay type, central Philippines 214

10. Metal Age pottery, Talaud Islands   215
11. Vessel from Niah Cave, Sarawak   216
12. Tanged point 13 cm long, Indonesian Timor   217
13. Stone adzes and points, west-central Sulawesi   218
14. Ceramic decoration, west-central Sulawesi   219
15. Anthropomorphic flask from Melolo urnfield   221
16. Ceremonial bronze axe with Dong-Son ornament from Roti   222
17. Panel from the Sangeang drum   223
18. The drum from Salayar Island   223
19. Bronze flasks of possible Dong-Son affinity   224
20. Moving a megalith, South Nias   225
21. Excavated stone cist, South Sumatra   226
22. Man astride a buffalo, South Sumatra   227
23. Man flanking an elephant, Batugajah, South Sumatra   227
24. Stone vats and other monuments in Indonesia   229
25. Beads of the Early Metal Period, Talaud Islands (c)   230

CHAPTER 9

 1. Map of Melanesia showing archaeological sites   233
 2. Flaked stone tools, New Guinea Highlands   234
 3. The Kafiavana sequence, New Guinea Highlands   236
 4. Stone axe from the Jimi River   237
 5. Large drainage ditch, Kuk plantation, Mt. Hagen   239
 6. Bossed stone mortar, Papua New Guinea   240
 7. Bird-shaped stone pestle, Papua New Guinea   241
 8. Pestles and mortars in New Guinea and the Bismarck Archipelago   241
 9. Human head from Papua New Guinea   242
10. Flaked tools of chert, south-western New Britain   243
11. The Toiminapo axe, Bougainville   243
12. Lapita sherd, Santa Cruz Islands   245
13. Examples of Lapita pottery decoration   246
14. Flakes of Talasea obsidian from Ambitle Island   248
15. Flat-based vessel, Santa Cruz Islands   249
16. Late Lapita pottery from Sigatoka, Fiji   251
17. Decorated and plain vessel forms from Fiji, Tonga and Samoa   252
18. Non-ceramic artefacts of Lapita affinity from Tongatapu   254
19. Decorated sherds from Oposisi, Papua   256
20. Stone adzes from Apere Venuna, Papua   257
21. Sago storage jar, East Sepik District   257
22. Pottery manufacture by coiling, Talaud Islands (c)   258
23. Incised and applied-relief pottery in Melanesia   259

24.	Early Mangaasi handles from the central New Hebrides	261
25.	Paddle-impressed pots from Sigatoka, Fiji	263
26.	Bronze objects from Kwadaware, Lake Sentani	265
27.	Sherd from Wanigela, Collingwood Bay, Papua	266
28.	Pedestalled vessel of possible Novaliches affinity	267
29.	Incised *Conus* shell from Collingwood Bay	267
30.	Comb-incised pottery in Melanesia	269
31.	The collective burial of Roy Mata, central New Hebrides	271
32.	Male and female pair in the collective burial of Roy Mata	272
33.	Burial enclosure in Museu village, Trobriand Islands	274
34.	Rock engravings in Melanesia	276

CHAPTER 10

1.	Incised and lime-infilled sherds of Marianas Red pottery	283
2.	A *latte* on Tinian	284
3.	Standing *latte* pillars with capstones	284
4.	Palauan money of glass beads and bracelet segments	286
5.	A terraced hill in the Palau Islands	287
6.	Head of andesite at Aimeong, Babeldaob Island	287
7.	Hambruch's plan of Nan Madol	288
8.	Nan Douwas – outer wall at west corner	289
9.	Nan Douwas – inner gallery	291
10.	Nan Douwas – the roof of the tomb	291
11.	Shell artefacts from Nan Madol	292
12.	Stonework at Pot Falat, Kusaie	293
13.	Stylistic change in fishhooks from Nukuoro	293
14.	Shell adzes from Nukuoro	294

CHAPTER 11

1.	Outrigger canoe from the Caroline Islands	296
2.	A Fijian *drua*	298
3.	New Zealand war canoe	299
4.	Tahitian double canoe (*pahi*)	299
5.	Polynesian cultural divisions	308
6.	Island groups and archaeological sites in Polynesia	310
7.	The Ha'amonga-a-Maui, Tongatapu Island (c)	312
8.	A *langi* faced with coral slabs, Tongatapu (c)	313
9.	Dressed coral blocks, Tongatapu (c)	313
10.	Fenced gardens on Tongatapu	314
11.	Early adze assemblages from Fiji, western and eastern Polynesia	315
12.	Star mound at Vaito'omuli, Savai'i.	316

13. The Pulemelei mound, Savai'i   317
14. Fishing gear from eastern Polynesia   319
15. Manufacture of one-piece hooks of pearl-shell   320
16. Fishhooks of pearl-shell from the Hane site, Ua Huka   322
17. Early Eastern Polynesian artefacts from the Hane site   322
18. Ornaments from eastern Polynesia   323
19. Artefacts from Maupiti, Society Islands   324
20. Part of round-ended house, Halawa dune site   325
21. The pattern of Polynesian settlement   326

CHAPTER 12

 1. Adze types of eastern Polynesia   330
 2. Rock-cut ditch of fort, Marquesas (c)   331
 3. Types of house platforms in the Marquesas Islands   332
 4. A Marquesan *tohua*   333
 5. Lower terrace walling, Nuku Hiva (c)   334
 6. Marquesan stone statue, Nuku Hiva (c)   335
 7. Map of central Polynesia   336
 8. The *marae* Mahaiatea   339
 9. *Marae* of Tahitian inland type   340
10. Two-tiered *marae* platform, Huahine (c)   341
11. A *marae* scene observed on Tahiti during Cook's third voyage   341
12. Horned archery platform in the Papenoo Valley, Tahiti   342
13. *Marae* Mahina-i-te-ata, Takaroa Island   343
14. Wooden carving of A'a, Rurutu   345
15. Reconstruction of a Rapan terraced fort   347
16. Miniature *marae* in the Morongo Uta fort   347
17. Wooden fisherman's god from Rarotonga   348
18. The pattern of prehistoric settlement on Aitutaki   349
19. Excavated T-shaped house platform in the Maungaroa Valley   351
20. Basalt uprights, part of large *marae*, Aitutaki (c)   351
21. Stone monument on Penrhyn Island, northern Cooks   353
22. Sketch of a typical Necker Island *marae*   355
23. *Heiau* at Waimea, Kauai   357
24. The reconstructed Hale-o-Keawe, Hawaii   358
25. The reconstructed *heiau* Kaneaki, Oahu   359
26. Map of Easter Island   362
27. An Easter Island scene   364
28. *Ahu* Akivi: a restored Middle Period structure (c)   366
29. Drilled house kerbs re-used in the Middle Period *Ahu* Heki'i   367
30. Shaped and fitted facing blocks at *Ahu* Vinapu I (c)   368

31. Re-erected statues at *Ahu* Akivi 369
32. 20-tonne statue restored with topknot at *Ahu* Ko te Riku 370
33. Partially buried statues, Rano Raraku (c) 371
34. Restored houses in the village at Orongo 371
35. Carved birdmen and large-eyed human face, Orongo (c) 372
36. Obsidian *mataa* 373
37. *Tupa* near *Ahu* Heki'i (c) 374
38. *Rongorongo* script on a piece of European ash 375

CHAPTER 13
1. Archaeological and traditional map of New Zealand 380
2. The Tairua pearl-shell lure shank 386
3. A reconstruction of the large moa (c) 386
4. Reconstruction of burial 2 at Wairau Bar 387
5. Part of burial 29 at Wairau Bar 388
6. The New Zealand Archaic assemblage 389
7. Stages in the manufacture of New Zealand one-piece hooks 390
8. One of a pair of chevroned amulets, Kaikoura 391
9. The Opihi 'taniwha' charcoal drawing, South Canterbury 393
10. Various designs in South Island rock drawing 394
11. Meat weights and energy equivalents, Mount Camel 397
12. Archaic campsite at Tairua, Coromandel Peninsula 398
13. Artefacts of Classic type 401
14. Tattooed Maori man 402
15. Weapons drawn by Sydney Parkinson 403
16. A masterpiece of Classic Maori carving 404
17. Wooden lintel from Kaitaia, Northland 405
18. The Lake Hauroko Burial (c) 405
19. One Tree Hill, Auckland 407
20. View inside a New Zealand *pa*, drawn by J. Webber 407
21. Plan and side view of a promontory *pa* in the Bay of Islands 408
22. The ring ditch *pa* at Kauri Point, Bay of Plenty 409
23. Two fighting stages, Otakanini *pa*, South Kaipara Harbour 411
24. Excavated swamp *pa* by Lake Mangakaware, Waikato 412
25. Reconstructed house from the Lake Mangakaware excavations 413
26. Sweet potato storage pit at Taniwha *pa*, Waikato 414

Colour plates (also reproduced in black and white in text) Following page 384.
Fig. 2.3 New Hebridean children, Efate
2.4 Fijian women, Viti Levu
2.5 Indonesian street scene, Borneo
2.6 Polynesian family, southern Cook Islands
4.6 A northern Abelam ceremonial house
4.7 A village on Kiriwina, Trobriand Islands
4.12 Circular houses in a Samoan village
6.4 A yam store-house on Kiriwina
6.7 Swamp cultivation of taro, Cook Islands
6.8 Terracing for taro cultivation, Rarotonga
8.25 Beads of the Early Metal Period, Talaud Islands
9.22 Pottery manufacture by coiling, Talaud Islands
11.7 The Ha'amonga-a-Maui, Tongatapu Island
11.8 A *langi* faced with coral slabs, Tongatapu
11.9 Dressed coral blocks, Tongatapu
12.2 Rock-cut ditch of fort, Marquesas
12.5 Lower terrace walling, Nuku Hiva
12.6 Marquesan stone statue, Nuku Hiva
12.10 Two-tiered *marae* platform, Huahine
12.20 Basalt uprights, part of large *marae*, Aitutaki
12.28 *Ahu* Akivi: a restored Middle Period structure
12.30 Shaped and fitted facing blocks at *Ahu* Vinapu I
12.33 Partially buried statues, Rano Raraku
12.35 Carved birdmen and large-eyed human face, Orongo
12.37 *Tupa* near *Ahu* Heki'i
13.3 A reconstruction of the large moa
13.18 The Lake Hauroko burial

CHAPTER 1

Introduction

That vast portion of the earth's surface which extends from eastern Asia right across the Pacific Ocean to Easter Island has been the scene of an absorbing complexity of human activity for a very long time. Concerning the prehistory of its inhabitants, speculations and theories of equally absorbing, indeed often confusing, variability have been put forward for two hundred years or more. On the Asian mainland and the adjoining islands of western Indonesia, evidence for remote ancestors of man projects the interested scholar back almost two million years in time. In the eastern islands of the Pacific, on the contrary, the evidence points to settlement by horticultural peoples as recently as 1500 years ago.

The major aim of this book is to give some coherence to the overall prehistory of the area, as seen in the light of modern archaeological, anthropological and linguistic discoveries. It need hardly be said that it will not give the last word on any matter of real importance. Modern archaeology has only been applied in the greater part of Southeast Asia and Oceania since the Second World War, yet it has the towering task of writing the prehistory of an area said by some to sport an amazing total of 25,000 islands[1]. The whole area demonstrates exceptional cultural and linguistic complexity today, and probably has done so for many millennia.

The term 'prehistory', as used in this book, refers to the period before the earliest written records. In Southeast Asia these go back to Chinese reports and inscriptions of Indian inspiration which commence at around the time of Christ. In Oceania prehistory ends much later, and the earliest historical records belong to the period of European discovery between 1521 and recent decades. This definition means that indigenous traditions are taken to refer to the prehistoric period, even though some have undoubted historical validity.

SOUTHEAST ASIA AND OCEANIA[2]

Our area of interest, with the exception of New Zealand, is humid and tropical. It comprises two main geographical divisions; Southeast Asia, with mainland and island divisions; and Oceania, with the divisions of Melanesia, Micronesia and Polynesia. Figure 5.1 is a basic map giving details of the Oceanic divisions.

Mainland Southeast Asia comprises China south of the Yangtze River, and the countries of Thailand, Laos, Cambodia, Vietnam and West Malaysia. Southern China is a dissected region of hills and river plains, while the countries to the south are built from mountain ranges with a general north-south trend, separated by plateaux and four major rivers; the Mekong, Chao Phraya, Salween and Irrawaddy. Rainfall in this region is well distributed throughout the year in equatorial latitudes, but north of the Malay Peninsula the regime is monsoonal, with a summer peak and a winter dry season. Native vegetation under these general conditions, prior to widespread land clearance by man, would have been mainly a mosaic of different kinds of evergreen rainforest. However, in the drier inland regions of Thailand and southern Indochina there are deciduous forests and savanna grasslands, the latter perhaps being partly caused by burning by man during hunting and horticultural activities.

Island Southeast Asia consists of Indonesia, the Philippines, and Taiwan. Despite its fragmentation, a glance at a map will show that Indonesia alone, with the huge islands of Sumatra and Borneo, is just about equal in area to the whole of Mainland Southeast Asia. At the present time, Indonesia is the fifth most populous country in the world, with over 120 million souls. Just how many separate islands make up Indonesia and the Philippines is debatable, but the total, counting every speck of water-girt rock, could be around 15,000[3].

Geologically, the islands of Southeast Asia are grouped around the Sunda platform, which has apparently been stable since Miocene times, and which now supports the islands of Sumatra, Java, Bali, Borneo and Palawan. Around the edge of the platform, through southern Sumatra and Java, and on through the islands of Nusatenggara into the Banda Sea, are young fold mountains with many active volcanoes. These volcanoes can at times erupt with great explosive force, spreading ash and devastation for miles around. Conversely, the ashes can bring great soil fertility to areas of moderate rainfall and leaching, such as Java and Bali, and it is these areas which have such colossal populations based on wet-rice agriculture at the present time. As an acute Dutch observer noted many years ago: 'In the Netherlands Indies the population density is a function of the nature of the soil, and this is a function of the presence of active volcanoes'[4]. More active volcanoes continue up through the Philippines to Japan, and on right around the Pacific Basin into the Americas.

In eastern Indonesia and the Philippines, between the Sunda and Sahul platforms, the geological picture is complicated by a rather spectacular belt of crustal instability. The Sahul and Sunda shelves have never been joined by land during the Tertiary Era, and some of the oddly shaped islands in between, such as Sulawesi and Halmahera, owe their forms to recent fracturing and vertical movement. This area, including the Philippines, has been too unstable in the past to allow much coral formation, and the island of Timor actually has Quaternary corals uplifted to a height of 1400 m above sea-level. The area between the two shelves is known to zoologists as Wallacea[5], and here, by crossing a multitude of water barriers, have met and mixed the placental faunas of Eurasia and the marsupials of Australasia. The water barriers also posed a challenge to man, as we will see

in chapter 3.

Climatically, Island Southeast Asia is hot, allowing for the usual amelioration caused by topographical relief, and wet for most of the year. Monsoonal climates with marked summer rainfall peaks and winter dry seasons occur in the northwestern Philippines and the islands of Nusatenggara, and here again, as in Indochina, we find the tropical rainforests giving way to savannas and open parklands. The areas outside the equatorial belt, particularly north of the equator, are also subject to devastating periodic hurricanes.

Moving now into Oceania, we find ourselves in an island zone of increasing geographical fragmentation. We begin in the west with New Guinea – second largest island in the world – but then we move eastwards into zones of increasingly smaller islands with increasing distances between them. The ultimate is of course Easter Island, 4000 kilometres from the South American coast, and 2500 kilometres from Pitcairn Island, its nearest inhabited neighbour in prehistoric times.

Geologically, Oceania is divided by the 'andesite line', which runs to the east of New Zealand, Tonga, and Fiji, round to the north of the Solomons, Bismarcks and New Guinea, and up again to the east of Yap and the Marianas Islands of Micronesia. To the west of this line are islands with varied continental rocks in the volcanic, metamorphic and sedimentary classes. A line of active vulcanicity of the explosive ash type runs from New Zealand up through the New Hebrides, Solomons and Bismarcks, and even in prehistoric New Zealand we can see the effects of fertile volcanic soil on population size, although on a much lesser scale than that noted above for Java.

East of the andesite line the islands consist of basaltic rocks which have upwelled from the sea bed to produce lava rather than ash. The only active volcanoes in this truly oceanic region are on the island of Hawaii, but many of the other volcanic islands are geologically young and of spectacular relief. In addition to the volcanic islands there are the necklace-like coral atolls, which in general provide the poorest habitats for man owing to small size and poor soil development. In the Marshall Islands alone, which are all atolls, there are 1156 separate islets averaging 16 hectares in size, and covering a total area of only about 180 square kilometres[6].

Faunally, there is a marked diminution of

species in Oceania as one moves eastwards from New Guinea[7]. As an example, New Guinea has over 550 species of land birds, while Henderson Island, near Pitcairn, has only four. The Polynesian islands have no endemic land mammals apart from bats, and floras also become increasingly impoverished. Apart from a decrease in the number of species, the atolls with their poor coral soils would have supported very little vegetation, and generally the Oceanic islands of Micronesia and Polynesia would have been very poor habitats for unequipped human settlers. They simply had to take their domesticated animal and food resources with them.

Climatically, Oceania is tropical, apart from New Zealand and a few southerly specks such as Rapa and Easter Island. Rainfall can vary surprisingly, being very low in the equatorial belt from the Gilberts eastwards, yet very high (up to 4000 mm per annum) in parts of Melanesia and the Caroline Islands. Relief also has its effects, with high islands in the trade wind belts of the open Pacific having wet windward and dry leeward sides.

Yet basically, the small islands of Micronesia and Polynesia reveal little of the natural or cultural complexity of Melanesia or Southeast Asia. As anthropologists have stressed for many years, they may be regarded as laboratory situations, with cultural and environmental homogeneity, small size, isolation, and short-lived human occupation. We know how and why Tahitians differ from Maoris much better than we understand cultural differentiation in, for instance, New Guinea or the Solomon Islands.

RACES, LANGUAGES, ETHNIC GROUPS AND PREHISTORY

Many archaeologists, such as those studying some of the more ancient cultures and civilisations of the Old World, are trying to reconstruct societies which have no recognisable existing lineal descendants, whether one talks of culture, language, or perhaps even racial type. The justly famous and elaborate civilisation of the Indus Valley of Pakistan may be such a society, wherein the discipline of archaeology with its modern scientific aids must provide the main answers.

In the Pacific, on the contrary, direct descendants of prehistoric peoples and societies live on almost everywhere. Languages survive intact, apart from recent borrowings, and racial and cultural identities survive in a similar way. This is particularly true of an area such as the New Guinea Highlands, although the picture is naturally not so clear in the older civilised areas of Southeast Asia. Nevertheless, the meaning of all this for the prehistorian is clear; he ignores the findings of linguists, physical anthropologists, and social and cultural anthropologists at his peril. Furthermore, as the development of modern archaeology in the area proceeds apace, the prehistorian can make a lot more sense of the results of the sister anthropological disciplines without resort to the more primitive of the migration and racial-stratum theories of the earlier part of the century.

Since I am an archaeologist by trade, I make no apologies for elevating archaeology as the central discipline of this book. It is, with the important backing of skeletal anthropology, the only one which delves into the past in what we may describe as concrete terms. Linguists, geneticists and social anthropologists working in the Pacific can often make very useful inferences about the past, but they must, in the absence of written records, make these inferences from the patterns of present phenomena.

Let us look briefly at these present phenomena – linguistic, racial and cultural. The languages of Southeast Asia and the Pacific are grouped into a number of high-order entities variously designated families or phyla (see chapter 5). The most widespread family is Austronesian, which covers the vast region comprising Malaysia, Indonesia, the Philippines, and all of Oceania with the exception of some western parts of Melanesia (particularly New Guinea). Austronesian outliers also occur in South Vietnam and Madagascar. The languages of the Southeast Asian mainland generally belong to other families, specifically Mon-Khmer, Vietnamese, Thai-Kadai, Miao-Yao, and, at the present time, Chinese (see chapter 4). The languages of New Guinea and adjacent parts of Melanesia belong to yet another major group, known variously as Papuan or non-Austronesian.

Racially, the area very clearly does not break up in the same way. Melanesia (and Australia) are settled by Australoids, who are surrounded, albeit with very fuzzy boundaries, by Mongoloid peoples who stretch right through Southeast Asia, and on through Micronesia into Polynesia (see chapter 2). It goes without saying that for the high-order entities under discussion, races and languages do not correlate in any one-to-one fashion.

Cultures, as defined by social customs and material culture, are far more difficult to classify on a broad scale. Most prehistoric societies in the area were small-scale, kinship based, and perhaps rather conservative in the absence of the anonymity provided by urbanisation. Descent systems vary widely, and while it seems to me that material culture could be used to separate the peoples of such geographical areas as Indonesia, Melanesia and Polynesia, I would hesitate to commit myself to an offer of proof. On the other hand, one can see in Polynesia a trend towards a complexity of political organisation which might lead us to a concept of 'semi-civilisation', although this is a little imprecise. We might as well face facts and acknowledge that most ethnic groups (the self-conscious units of cultures) define themselves principally on the basis of language. We might also acknowledge that races, languages and cultures do not reveal ideal correlations, as anthropologists have of course realised for many years.

I make these points because the first chapters of this book are mainly on these topics; race, languages and cultures, as studied apart from archaeology. They each provide information about the past, but it is simply not possible to mix this information as in a soup, and to expect to produce the right flavour. Physical anthropologists have their races, and they divide them into populations of varying degrees of inclusiveness right down to the individual, who represents, after all, a population of genes in a unique combination. Linguists divide their language families into successive groupings down to the dialect, and social anthropologists can run from tribes down through individual settlements to nuclear families and the individual. All these disciplines have boundary problems behind their taxonomies; physical anthropologists have clines, linguists have dialect chains, and ethnologists (whom we may regard as the taxonomic branch of social and cultural anthropology) have their cultural gradations. For sharp differences between geographically contiguous entities one generally requires long isolation or some other process such as conquest and expansion resulting in juxtaposition of two unlikes. Failing such processes, human beings will tend to communicate, and races, languages and cultures will evolve in a complex reticulate fashion which not even the best of computers will untangle.

The smaller islands of the Pacific do help us to overcome some of these problems, because

they provide isolation. And it is because of isolation that the Polynesians have developed their homogeneity in linguistic, racial and cultural terms (see chapters 11 and 12). They have, as it were, evolved from a small founder population situated in a geographical bottleneck, although even in the Polynesian case some three thousand years of subsequent development have produced some major variations. Nevertheless, it would in theory be possible to use selected examples from Polynesia to investigate the rates at which languages and cultures in particular can differentiate, when time and place of common origin and length of subsequent isolation are known. The only snag is that one would have to consider environmental factors and a whole range of rather intractable random variables as well, so the result could easily be valueless. I will not try the reader with such abstruse matters further.

My final task in this introduction is to outline the major prehistorical themes to be covered. These are:–

1. Early human settlement in eastern Asia and western Indonesia from about 2 million years ago, and the penetration of Australoid populations across water gaps to New Guinea and Australia about 40,000 years ago. This topic is covered mainly in chapter 3.

2. The origins of horticulture in Southeast Asia, and the subsequent development of Neolithic and Metal Age societies down to the commencement of Indian and Chinese influences. These developments fall in the general period from 10,000 to 2000 years ago, and are discussed mainly in Chapters 6, 7 & 8.

3. The prehistories of the various areas of Oceania, which are related in chapters 9 (Melanesia), 10 (Micronesia), 11 and 12 (Polynesia), and 13 (New Zealand).

In presenting these themes I have tried to extract as much information as possible from the multitudinous sources pertaining to Southeast Asia and Oceania. Needless to say, many of these sources are poorly presented and difficult to use (especially some of the older ones), but I have attempted to fit them together into a narrative held together by my own interpretations. I have not been especially concerned to use any of the voguish models to which archaeologists now gleefully resort, mainly because the data are not always very sound, and I do not wish to waste time trying to make my subject matter run before it can walk.

On the other hand, to those who would see this book as premature, I would only say that I am certainly not going to wait another twenty years in the hope that all will suddenly be made clear. This is defeatism. Furthermore, my experience in teaching undergraduate courses over the past nine years at Auckland University and the Australian National University indicates to me the need for this book, which has no comparable predecessor. And if the man in the street still puts his faith (as many do) in astronauts or a white master race hot-footing it to the four corners of the earth, then the academic ivory-tower needs to take some steps at least to preserve its credibility. If this book can make some contribution to a new era of world prehistory, the author will be deeply gratified.

Footnotes

1. Thomas 1967. This total of course far exceeds the number of individually habitable islands, which possibly do not exceed 1500. I have no figures for Southeast Asia, but Oceania has 789 island units; 287 in Polynesia, 161 in Micronesia, and 341 in Melanesia (Douglas 1969).

2. The background information for this section comes mainly from Dobby 1961; Robequain 1954; Ho 1960; Thomas 1963, 1967.

3. e.g. Bryan 1963: 38.

4. Mohr 1945: 262.

5. Mayr 1945.

6. Thomas 1963: 11.

7. Zimmerman 1963; Usinger 1963.

CHAPTER 2

Human Populations - Past and Present

For the physical anthropologist, the myriad geographical complexities of Southeast Asia and Oceania provide homes for some of the most varied human populations in the world. We do not have to look very hard in order to suggest that some of this variation reflects very complex migration patterns, as well as the effects of genetic drift and natural selection on small isolated breeding populations over a very long time. In this chapter we can examine some of these processes, firstly through a comparative study of modern populations, and secondly from the skeletal record.

Perhaps it is ironic that it is much more difficult to provide an ordered chronological perspective for human beings than it is for languages or archaeological assemblages. Man is simply so much more complex than any of his creations, and the races of man are perhaps the most complex and most controversial entities which can be studied by anthropologists. Races cannot be viewed as a series of discrete pigeon holes, because the human species as a whole is a single continuum with intergrading nodes of variation. So the definition of any race will always tend to be an abstraction, or an ideal, because of the large numbers of people who will fall into a very hazy and very broad half-way zone.

While I do not wish to involve myself in a theoretical consideration of the concept of race[1], there are a few matters which the general reader should bear in mind. Races exist because relatively isolated geographical populations have shared common developing gene pools for tens, perhaps hundreds, of thousands of years. But it will probably still be many tens of years before the statistics of any race can be written down in full, because the human genetic code is so complex. Geneticists today can identify simple genetic characters, such as the blood groups, which are determined by one or a few genes, but characters of this type can fluctuate in frequency so much that they are of limited value for racial taxonomy. The more important phenotypic characters such as stature, skin colour or facial shape, which are determined by many genes and affected by environmental parameters, are still beyond the reach of modern genetic identification techniques. In ideal terms, a racial taxonomy which has phylogenetic validity (and any acceptable one must have) should be based on frequencies of all genes within human populations. This may be an impossible ideal.

At this stage of research, much caution is needed in applying the results of physical anthropology to the prehistory of Southeast Asia and the Pacific. But there are many grounds for optimism, as I hope this chapter will show.

PRESENT POPULATIONS OF SOUTHEAST ASIA AND THE PACIFIC

The major races which are now enshrined in the literature of physical anthropology have been defined by phenotypic characters only; hair form, skin colour, nose shape, and so forth. On such grounds, most authorities recognise the presence of two or more major races in the Pacific. For instance, for R. Biasutti[2] the two major races are Australoids and Mongoloids, each with subdivisions. The Australoids comprise two branches – the Australidi (Australians, Tasmanians and New Caledonians), and the Papuasidi (the peoples of Melanesia generally). The

Mongoloids are a widespread race in eastern Asia, and their Pacific representatives are the Indonesians. The Micronesians and Polynesians are grouped together into a hybrid race, the Polinesidi, thought by Biasutti to be mainly of Caucasoid and early Mongoloid derivation.

Carleton Coon[3] similarly favours the view of two major races for the area, these being again Australoids and Mongoloids. The Australoids include the Australian Aborigines, the extinct Tasmanians, the Melanesians (who have in many cases exchanged genes with Mongoloid populations), the Negritos of the Philippines, the Semang of Malaya, and the Andamanese. The Mongoloids are represented by Polynesians, Micronesians and Indonesians, although these groups have interbred with the Australoids to some extent in the past.

Coon and Biasutti differ on some points, particularly the placing of Polynesians and New Caledonians, and these viewpoints are only two selected from quite a number[4]. In this chapter I have adopted Coon's basic stance, because a primary division between Australoids and Mongoloids, allowing for clinal groups, does correlate

most economically with the present evidence from linguistics and archaeology.

(1) THE AUSTRALOID POPULATIONS
(A) DWARF POPULATIONS

The Negritos of the Andaman Islands, central Malaya (Semang), the Philippines, and the Pygmies of highland New Guinea are all dwarf Australoid populations. In the Andamans, Malaya and the Philippines they are fairly distinct phenotypically from neighbouring Mongoloids, and represent ancient populations which have survived absorption owing to their remote geographical situations. In New Guinea, on the contrary, there has been no massive immigration of Mongoloids, and here the Pygmies intergrade with surrounding Australoid · populations of greater stature.

The Semang, the Andamanese and the Philippine Negritos are mostly non-agriculturalists[5], and the latter, who live in pockets on the islands of Luzon, Panay, Negros and north-east Mindanao, have a mean stature for men of 147 centimetres, dark brown to almost black skin

Fig. 2.1a. Batek Negritos of the Aring River, Ulu Kelantan, Malaya.

Fig. 2.1b. A Mendriq Negrito of the Lebir River, Ulu Kelantan, Malaya.

colour, tightly curled hair, and facial features resembling those of Australian aborigines[6]. In New Guinea, the Pygmies are horticulturalists like their taller neighbours, and intergrade with surrounding Papuans physically, genetically and culturally[7]. Not all members of Pygmy groups are necessarily of pygmy size, and the average heights of the groups themselves vary in a continuum from below 150 centimetres to about 157 centimetres[8]. In fact, the concept of 'Pygmy' is rather arbitrary, and there is no distinct gap in the distribution of stature which separates Pygmies from normal statured Papuans. Sometimes there are local boundaries; for instance, the Pygmies of the Lake Paniai region of Irian Jaya are markedly shorter than some neighbouring groups[9], but such a situation may reflect local population movements leading to a break in an earlier continuum.

These dwarf populations present physical anthropologists with some of the most daunting phylogenetic problems of the Pacific area. Was there once an ancient Negrito continuum from Africa right through Southeast Asia which has now been swamped, or have the dwarf populations evolved in several places independently? Some anthropologists take the viewpoint of independence on the grounds that small size has increased survival value in a mountainous tropical forest environment with poor nutritional resources[10], and some have suggested localised mutation to be the answer[11]. But by no means all agree, and Birdsell[12] has recently reiterated the case for phylogenetic links between the dwarf populations of Southeast Asia, New Guinea, Australia and Africa. The Andamanese, with their well developed female steatopygia and peppercorn hair, possibly can be linked directly with Africa through a continuum which may once have existed through India. But for the other populations, we may need to look more towards a hypothesis of independence.

For instance, the New Guinea Pygmies do look like one end of a local continuum in stature, although they do have a higher incidence of brachycephaly than their taller neighbours. Other populations of small stature are also found in inland areas in New Britain, Bougainville, Espiritu Santo and Malekula, and since the last two islands have probably not been settled for more than five· thousand years, it does look as if small size in Melanesia has evolved independently, and perhaps fairly quickly. If we have a fairly small Australoid population in the

area to begin with, then inland forest situations with few proteins and steep terrain may have been the key factors favouring dwarfism. In the Philippines and Malaya the same factors have been at work, and here the Negritos have survived because of their secluded locations, while the larger sized Australoid populations which may once have existed around them have been absorbed and replaced by the more recently arrived Mongoloids.

(B) THE MELANESIANS

The Melanesians are a very diverse population phenotypically, as befits their multiple phylogenetic origins. They occupy all of Melanesia, apart perhaps from some of the Polynesian outliers, and extend westwards into some of the islands of eastern Indonesia. The Pygmies of New Guinea, discussed separately in the previous section, are also Melanesians.

The Melanesians are characterised by dark skin colour, which seems to be the result of natural selection operating in a hot humid environment over a long period of time. But there is a good deal of variation in skin colour from light to very dark[13], and even reddish in the Bismarck and Solomon Islands. Hair is generally black or brown, and is frequently woolly in New Guinea, with increasing proportions of frizzly, wavy and curly hair in island Melanesia. Stature is varied, averaging around 160 centimetres in the west, with taller populations approaching the Polynesian norm of about 170 centimetres in Fiji, New Caledonia and the New Hebrides. There seems to be a tendency towards dolichocephaly (long narrow headedness) in the west, but Fijians, and also rather interestingly some of the dwarf populations, approach the broader-headed norm (meso- or brachycephaly) more characteristic of Polynesians. Traits commonly found in Mongoloid populations, such as shovel-shaped upper incisor teeth, and the epicanthic, or 'Mongoloid' eyelid fold, are not found in high frequency[14].

The people of New Guinea Highlands are probably the most direct descendants of the original Australoid settlers of western Melanesia, and they generally have tightly curled hair, and a high frequency of high bridged convex noses. These may be adaptations to cool mountain air, involving a lengthening of the nasal passages to allow more efficient warming of inhaled air. The Melanesians of coastal New Guinea and

Fig. 2.2. New Guinea Highlanders in ceremonial dress, Kere tribe, Sinasina, Chimbu District.

Fig. 2.3. New Hebridean children at Ebao village, Efate. (See also colour plate.)

Fig. 2.4. Fijian women at Sigatoka village, Viti Levu. (See also colour plate.)

the islands are generally darker and taller than the Highlanders, and have less rugged facial features[15]. However, it has never been shown that there are any widespread phenotypic discontinuities which differentiate Austronesian from Papuan speakers (see chapter 5) in Melanesia, and the frequency of intermarriage would make survival of such discontinuities unlikely. But a few localised cases of differentiation have been reported; for instance, as early as 1876 the English missionary W. W. Gill observed that the Austronesian speakers whom he visited (and called 'Malays') in south-east Papua had much lighter skins than the Papuan speakers around the Fly Delta to the west[16]. As some of the Austronesian speakers who entered Melanesia some 4000 years ago had a high degree of Mongoloid inheritance, it is not hard to find a historical basis for Gill's observation.

The New Caledonians and Fijians are each slightly distinctive populations – some of the former because of their phenotypic similarity to Australian aborigines[17], the latter because of their intermediate status between Melanesians and Polynesians[18]. Gabel's study of Fijians[19] showed that the interior part of Viti Levu is inhabited by short, dark peoples who most closely resemble the Melanesians to the west, while the coastal populations of Viti Levu are taller and overlap more with the Polynesian phenotype. The Lau Islanders of south-eastern Fiji are in fact partially Polynesian, as a result of intermarriage and settlement from Tonga since prehistoric times. But apart from these, Fijians do differ from Polynesians in having generally darker skins, higher percentages of woolly and curly hair, and in certain other traits. Other Polynesian-like populations are also found in Tanna in the southern New Hebrides, and in southern New Caledonia[20].

(2) THE MONGOLOID POPULATIONS
(A) INDONESIA

Racial history in Indonesia has been undoubtedly very complex, owing to the tremendous time depth of human occupation in the west, and to the pattern of gene flow from Indian, Chinese, Arab, and European sources at various points through the past 2000 years. However, the presence of later gene flow has not drastically altered the basic Indonesian pattern, which may be viewed as a cline running from Mongoloid populations in the west to populations of Melanesian type in the east. The cline has no very sharp breaks, and may have attained almost its present form by 2000 years ago.

The peoples of Java, Sumatra, and Borneo are for the most part true Mongoloids, of medium stature, with yellowish-brown or brown skin and straight black hair. In older literature they are referred to as 'Deutero-Malays', and the assumption is very frequently made that they were preceded in the area by a migration of 'Proto-Malays', who now survive phenotypically as the Bontoc and Ifugao of northern Luzon, the Punans of interior Borneo, the Kubu of central Sumatra, the Batak of northern Sumatra, the Tenggarese of eastern Java, the Toala and Toraja of Sulawesi, and some of the peoples of Nias, western Sumba and western Flores[21]. Phenotypically these groups reveal a higher proportion of what appear to be Australoid traits, such as darker skins and curlier hair, and it has also been claimed that major elements of a Negrito phenotype survive in western Timor, western Sumba, central Flores, and southern Sulawesi[22]. It may well be that these groups do represent survivals of an early

stage of gene flow from a primarily Mongoloid Asian mainland into a primarily Australoid island world, but whether one can really speak of two separate 'Malay' migrations is another matter. It may be far more likely that population movement was continuous, and that the so-called 'Deutero-Malay' phenotype has been emphasised in the west by gene-flow resulting from the increased maritime activity of the Indianised Kingdoms over the past 1500 years.

To state the situation for Indonesia simply, if this is possible, it is clear that a Mongoloid phenotype predominates in the west, and gradually fades in the islands of Wallacea. In Maluku and eastern Nusatenggara, a population which is quite clearly a part of the Melanesian physical and cultural world predominates. This is a logical picture which fits well with the culture history of the area, and one can possibly neglect earlier theories about migrations of Veddoids and Caucasoids. A model of Mongoloid expansion into an Australoid sphere, allowing for considerable variation within each group, should suffice to explain the picture. The intricate details may always escape us, for of course the terms 'Australoid' and 'Mongoloid' themselves

Fig. 2.5. Indonesian street scene at Banjarmasin, Kalimantan Selatan (Borneo). (See also colour plate.)

Fig. 2.6. Polynesian family at Vaipae village, Aitutaki, southern Cook Islands. (See also colour plate.)

are ideal models, and the Southeast Asian area may have been a clinal zone between these ideal types for several thousands of years.

(B) POLYNESIANS

Compared to the Melanesians, Polynesians form a very homogeneous racial group, with the greatest degree of variation in the west, where gene flow from Fiji has been most marked. Unfortunately, Polynesian populations are usually small, and they have been in contact with Europeans for over 200 years in most cases, so that the degree of intermarriage has made great inroads into the original phenotype. The total population before European contact may have been in the vicinity of 3–400,000, but there was a marked decline after contact resulting mostly from introduced diseases, and the flow of European genes into a depleted Polynesian gene pool makes generalisation from twentieth century populations difficult.

Polynesians are generally tall, with males averaging between 169 and 173 centimetres. Skin colour is lighter than that of most Melanesians, and there is a much higher incidence of brachycephaly and straight and wavy hair. Features which indicate affinity with Mongoloid populations include scarcity of body hair, and the fairly high frequencies of shovel-shaped incisors and the epicanthic eyefold[23].

When European voyagers first discovered the islands of Polynesia, many reported the existence of individuals with light skins or red hair in their journals. Since then, the theory of a Caucasoid element in the Polynesian phenotype has appeared repeatedly (as in Biasutti above), although it has consistently failed to find scientific support[24], and light skins and red or fair hair colour are widely reported amongst the Australoid populations of Australia and New Guinea. The present Polynesians in fact demonstrate characteristics of both Mongoloid and Melanesian Australoid phenotypes – the former perhaps predominating – and in some of the more remote islands of Polynesia today one can see a whole range of physical types stretching between these two norms.

(C) MICRONESIANS

The Micronesians are again of basically Mongoloid phenotype, although gene flow from Melanesia has occurred in some areas, especially in parts of the Palau, Caroline and Marshall

Islands. In fact, a recent computer study of phenotypic characters by W. W. Howells[25] has shown that Micronesian populations fall closer to Melanesian than they do to Polynesian, but this is a rather surprising conclusion which even Howells himself seems reluctant to accept. In general, the Micronesians are shorter in stature than the Polynesians and tend more towards mesocephaly, but otherwise there are no very distinctive and widespread differentiating features. Micronesian populations are fairly diverse, how-

ever, and as we will see later, the Micronesians, unlike the Polynesians, are not necessarily of single origin.

GENETIC STUDIES ON PACIFIC POPULATIONS

The Australoids and Mongoloids share geographical proximity to each other, as well as relative isolation from the races west of the Himalayas. Accordingly, they do reveal genetic characteristics in common, such as an absence of the gene A_2 in the ABO blood-group system (apart from recent mutations in New Guinea[26]), absence or rarity of the Rhesus genes R^0 and r, and high frequency of Rhesus R^1. Recent computer analyses[27] have also shown how Australoids and Mongoloids fall close together on overall blood-group frequencies when compared to the rest of the world. But genetic differences at the blood-group level are not sufficient to rule out fairly ancient phylogenetic links, such as those which may have existed between Australoids and African Negroes[28], because natural selection could in theory produce the differences over a fairly short period of time.

When individual populations in the Pacific, at the level of the geographic races, are brought into focus, a number of significant similarities and differences can be observed. Blood-groups B and S are absent in Australia, although there are populations with group B around the Gulf of Carpentaria who may have been in contact with Indonesian traders or Melanesians in the recent past[29]. Both these blood-groups are present in New Guinea, but S is absent in a few Highland groups, and absent or rare in the Baining and surrounding groups in the Gazelle Peninsula of New Britain[30]. Australia and New Guinea do share some genetic markers, however, which are absent elsewhere in the Pacific[31], and the gene n in the MNSs blood-group system has very high frequencies in Australia and southern New Guinea. If we accept Coon's inclusion of the New Guineans (in general) and the Australians in his Australoid subspecies, then it should be of no surprise if it were discovered that both groups share a high degree of common origin. Kirk has analysed frequencies for a number of genetic systems detectable in blood samples, and he concludes that the Australian Aborigines are most closely related to the New Guineans, more closely at least than they are to the Ainu of Japan and the Bushmen of Africa[32]. There are, of course, differences, but these are to be expected

Fig. 2.7. Micronesian man of Truk, photographed early this century. His ornaments are suspended from perforated ear lobes, and those in the left ear alone weigh 230 gms. The white rings are of shell, the black ones of coconut shell. He also wears a necklace of pig or dog teeth. From Matsumura 1918.

if it be accepted that Australia and New Guinea have been mutually isolated gene pools for almost 10,000 years.

However, racial variation in New Guinea cannot be explained simply by a sibling relationship with Australia combined with separation. New people with Austronesian languages have arrived there within the past 5000 years, and some geneticists have attempted to see if there are overall genetic differences between the earlier-established Papuan speakers and the Austronesians. Interesting differences have been reported in the Markham Valley region[33] in the frequencies of certain gammaglobulin (Gm) factors in blood cells, and the Austronesian speakers here fall closer to some Southeast Asian Mongoloid populations. It has recently been claimed that differentiations in Gm factors separate Austronesian and Papuan speakers in New Guinea as a whole, although the pattern is, as might be expected, blurred by considerable gene flow[34]. In Bougainville[35] the Gm distinction is not present at all, and an Austronesian versus Papuan differentiation within New Guinea has not so far been supported from other genetic systems[36]. There is an inkling of support here, however, for the powerful linguistic hypothesis that the Austronesian and Papuan languages, and therefore probably their speakers in the final resort, are of different origin, although over 5000 years of co-existence in New Guinea have blurred any original genetic differences to a great extent.

At the present time, geneticists are undertaking fairly intensive research in Australia and Melanesia; hence the results related above. For Indonesia, Micronesia and Polynesia there is less to report, and the only overall summary of blood-groups and gene frequencies for these three areas is that by R. T. Simmons[37], which was undertaken with the specific aim of determining Polynesian origins. His conclusions suggest that points of broad serological similarity may be drawn with Polynesians as follows:

American Indians: No <u>B</u>, high <u>M</u>, high <u>R</u>², moderate Fyª (a Duffy blood-group).
Australians: No <u>B</u>, high <u>A</u>
Melanesians: Nil
Micronesians: Nil
Indonesians: High <u>M</u>
Ainu: Nil

These conclusions are interesting and surprising, because they point to more similarity

with Australia and America, which are both areas which would not be considered important in the settlement of Polynesia from other sources of evidence. The problem here is that average frequencies of genes in large populations do not necessarily reflect true phylogenetic affinity between those populations, and the populations considered do in fact show considerable internal diversity. Simmons is fully aware of this, and he and other geneticists are aware of the roles of natural selection and genetic drift in an area such as Oceania[38], which can cause fairly rapid fluctuations in gene frequencies. Simmons' conclusion is that the Polynesians are perhaps derived from a common gene pool composed of elements from Tonga, Samoa, Indonesia, and America. This conclusion may contain a good deal of truth, but Simmons himself is dubious about the validity of even a cautious conclusion such as this, for he states:

> I believe that the blood grouping percentage variations demonstrate the impossibility of equating a component of one racial group, with the possible component of another some thousands of miles away. If the gene frequencies as calculated do hold the clues, then posterity alone will provide the proof and the answers.

The reasons for Simmons' caution really stem from an increasing knowledge of the effects of the various evolutionary processes on gene frequencies, and to these we now turn.

EVOLUTIONARY PROCESSES IN OCEANIA

We have seen above how each of the major geographical races of the Pacific has genetic pecularities which serve to differentiate it from the others. The same observation could be applied to populations of lesser size, and in fact even those of two hamlets within a single culture could be expected to show significant genetic differences. The processes which give rise to these different genetic configurations in populations are mutation, natural selection, gene flow, and genetic drift. Mutation operates mainly at the individual level and will not be discussed here, but the effects of the other three can be revealed from the study of whole populations, particularly the small-scale isolated populations of the Pacific Islands.

The peoples of Oceania, and especially western Melanesia, are of great interest because of the small size of breeding populations and their relative breeding isolation. Genetic isolates in New Guinea and Australia may frequently contain fewer than 100 persons, if we adopt a definition of a genetic isolate as the smallest breeding population within which over 50% of matings are endogamous[39]. With isolates of this size the effects of random genetic drift and the founder effect are particularly emphasized, and this kind of situation probably resembles that in which man has evolved for the greater part of his prehistory. A number of studies on Oceanic populations, particularly in Melanesia, have revealed some aspects of the operation of the evolutionary processes listed above, and in the following sections some examples are given.

NATURAL SELECTION, CLINES AND GENE FLOW

Natural selection is the main non-random directive process behind evolution, and operates by means of differential rates of reproduction on the constantly occurring fresh genetic variation in human populations. New characters or combinations of characters which endow an individual with a superior breeding ability will have greater chances of survival in a population than those characters which endow a lesser breeding ability. The overall results of natural selection can probably be recognised through such factors as skin colour, stature, hair colour and form, and other anthropomorphic traits which are thought to undergo adaptive changes in differing environments.

The dark skin colour of the Melanesians may provide a good example of the results of natural selection, for these people appear to have been adapting to a hot humid environment for a very long time. The concentration of melanin in the epidermis helps to absorb harmful ultra-violet radiation, and it may also be that the high ability of dark-skinned people to absorb infra-red radiation gives them protection against the humid chill air of the tropics, when air is saturated and temperature drops below the sweating point[40]. This, at least, is one possible explanation; another, suggested by Loomis[41], is that skin colour relates to the human need to synthesise vitamin D from sunlight, with fair skins being an advantage in high latitude regions and vice-versa in the tropics. Another example of natural selection is the apparent selection for small stature in certain tropical forest regions, as discussed above for the Negritos, and a further well-known case is the selection for abnormal hemoglobin genes in

malarial areas of Africa, Southeast Asia and New Guinea[42].

Natural selection also appears to operate on the blood-group genes, because there are many instances where they tend to demonstrate clines, or regular geographical gradients in frequency of occurrence[43]. Such gradients may relate to the changing importance of a selective factor through different environmental zones. Genetic drift alone is most unlikely to lead to any such regularity, and although clines are difficult to explain, they are probably due to a combination of natural selection and patterns of gene flow resulting from intermarriage. In spite of the degree of genetic heterogeneity in New Guinea, there are recorded clines in some areas[44], although they are of rather uncertain significance for population history.

Perhaps the most important series of clines in Oceania runs all the way from New Guinea, through Bougainville, the British Solomon Islands, the New Hebrides, New Caledonia, Fiji, Tonga, and to New Zealand. Along this line there are definite gradients for a number of genes, albeit rough in places. $\underline{A}$ gradually increases, while $\underline{B}$ decreases; $\underline{M}$ and $\underline{R}^2$ increase, while $\underline{R}^1$ decreases. The conclusion drawn by Simmons and Gajdusek from the presence of these clines is of great interest:

> It seems fair to say that between the Melanesian of Papua New Guinea and the Polynesian (Maori) of New Zealand, the native populations of Bougainville, the British Solomon Islands, New Hebrides, New Caledonia, Fiji and Tonga can be arranged broadly according to gene frequencies in that order, and each intermediate population possesses a blending of Melanesian and Polynesian blood in varying amounts[45].

This is a most interesting situation and would appear to be due to the effects of natural selection and gene flow in tending to reduce the differences between two originally more distinct populations, namely the Australoids of western Melanesia and the more recent and partly Mongoloid settlers of eastern Melanesia and Polynesia.

GENETIC DRIFT AND GENETIC DISTANCES

Random genetic drift occurs in all human populations, and involves random fluctuations in gene frequencies from generation to generation[46]. In Oceania, it is possible that random drift of this type could give rise to considerable differences in gene frequencies between isolated but related populations, although the effects may be partially rectified by natural selection, which in this context acts as something of an equaliser.

However, Pacific anthropologists have recently become especially interested in a specific type of genetic drift, which is non-random, and which may lead to considerable genetic variations between colonising populations. This is the founder effect[47], which occurs when a breeding population splits and one part moves into a new territory to become a new isolate. The founders of the new group will be most unlikely to mirror the pooled gene frequencies of the total population from which they were drawn, and it seems fairly certain that the founder effect has been a factor causing a high degree of genetic difference amongst Pacific populations. Furthermore, a founder population may often be of related persons, and if either men or women are in short supply amongst the colonisers then a small number of people may make a disproportionately large contribution to the gene pool of the next generation. It has been shown in Venezuela how such events could lead to new genetic configurations as small founder groups expand in isolation[48], and the same process has undoubtedly been of great importance in Oceania.

Realisation of the importance of genetic drift has dealt a blow to those who once thought that overall gene frequency comparisons between large populations could automatically determine phylogenetic relationship. Simmons has pointed this out for Polynesia, as we have seen above. For instance, the virtual absence of blood-group B in Polynesia and South America is much more likely to reflect independent genetic drift and natural selection than it is to reflect Polynesian origins[49]. The realisation of such difficulties has caused geneticists to move away from gross comparisons of lumped gene frequencies between large populations, and towards the detailed analysis of gene frequencies in much smaller groups, such as villages or hamlets. The results have been surprising.

It has been found in both Melanesia and amongst South American Indians that even neighbouring villages with a common ancestry have gene frequencies which are significantly different in statistical terms[50] (i.e. there is a very low chance that both are random samples of a single population). The reasons for these variations seem to revolve around genetic drift, and

also round patterns of intermarriage which affect the nature of gene flow into a population[51]. Of course, this degree of divergence may not necessarily apply to polygenically inherited characters such as skin colour or hair form, but at present, gene frequency analyses are confined to characters of simple inheritance, which are unfortunately very subject to rapid time and space variations. So the crux of the matter for the anthropologist is that similarities or differences in gene frequencies cannot necessarily be used as direct indicators of historical relationship between populations.

The pessimist might now say that the matter is closed and genes can tell us no more. But this is where computers come in. By analysing a lot of data at once, they can sometimes spot relationships which would otherwise not be obvious to the human eye alone. In order to test whether genetic distances can actually be used for historical inferences, a number of physical anthropologists have experimented mathematically to see if coefficients for genetic distances correspond to linguistic and cultural differences between small populations. A number of these experiments have not achieved notable success, but a very interesting picture for the island of Bougainville has recently been claimed by Friedlaender and his colleagues[52], and it looks here as though genetic variation does relate partially to geographic, linguistic and migrational differences. One of the problems with these analyses is that the sheer complexity of the data makes it difficult to see the exact significance of the correlations in historical terms, but the experimental mathematical techniques which are now being used seem to hold great promise for the future.

Indeed, a recent analysis of genetic distances by Booth and Taylor[53] for the New Guinea Highlands suggests that information of this kind could be used to give approximate time depths for separations between related populations, rather like the linguistic technique of glottochronology (see page 119). The possibility of this kind of approach could be illustrated by a study by Sinnett and his colleagues[54] on seven clans which belong to the Murapin phratry in the Enga language group of the Western Highlands of Papua New Guinea. These seven clans have preserved genealogical information concerning their common origin from a single population six to seven generations ago. It was therefore possible to construct a descent 'tree' on the basis of these verbal accounts. A multivariate cluster analysis was then performed on the

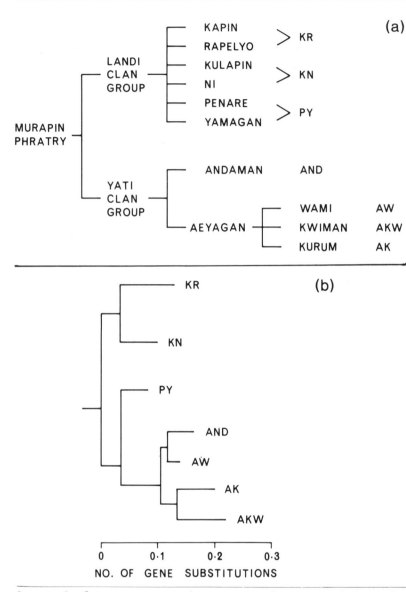

Fig. 2.8. (a) Descent group lineage of the Murapin phratry based on contemporary verbal accounts. (b) 'Minimum path' evolutionary tree for seven clans of the Murapin phratry based on gene frequencies for five genetic systems. After Sinnett *et al.* 1970.

frequencies for up to 12 genetic systems, and an evolutionary 'tree' computed from these. The result turned out to be a surprising correlation between both independent sets of data (see figure 2.8).

All these experiments bode quite well for the future, although it must be recognised that not all physical anthropologists agree on the validity of genetic distance analyses[55]. My own inclination is to retain an open mind, and to refrain from drawing conclusions at the present time.

Where, finally, does the study of the genetic evidence take us in a study of Pacific prehistory? We have examined the evidence for the long isolation of Australia and the possible ancient links between Australians and New Guineans. It is possible that there are significant genetic differences between Austronesian and Papuan speakers in New Guinea, but the differences are now masked by complex clines, as are the differences that may once have existed between incoming ancestral Polynesians and long-estab-

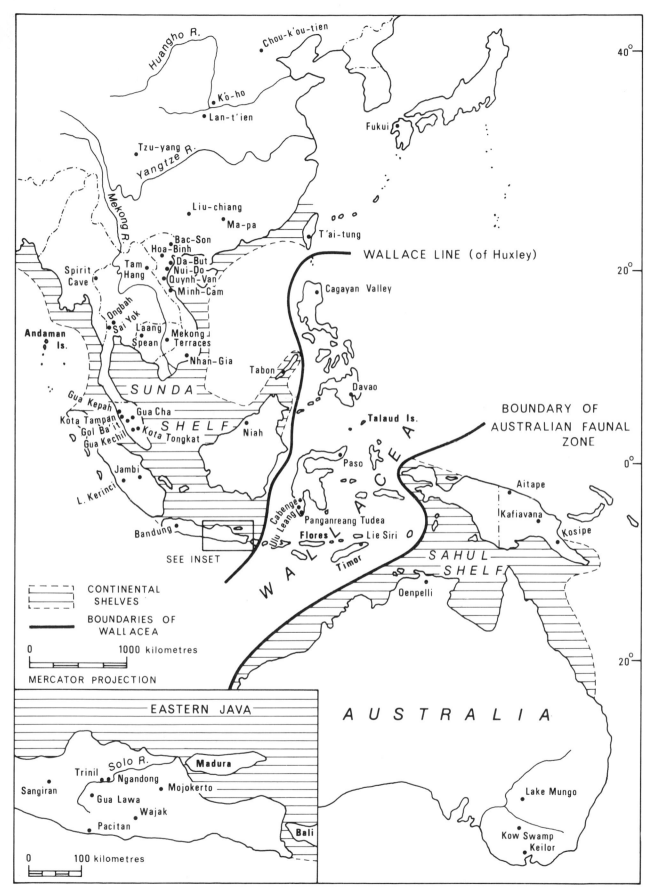

Fig. 2.9. Map of Southeast Asia showing zoogeographical divisions and Pleistocene sites mentioned in chapters 2 and 3.

lished Melanesian Australoids. The complex patterns resulting from genetic drift and natural selection make it very hard to generalise about ancient migrations on the basis of genetics alone, but the study of these processes in living populations can tell a good deal about human evolution, and how radically different gene pools can originate from the same ancestral population. Despite the promise of genetic distance analyses, the historical picture still remains sketchy, and must now be filled out by an examination of archaeological skeletal material.

THE PREHISTORIC RECORD OF MAN IN SOUTHEAST ASIA AND THE PACIFIC

From present-day populations we turn to dead ones, and firstly, to the great fossil discoveries made in Java and China since 1890. Man is the only living member of the primate family Hominidae, since the great apes belong to a separate family – the Pongidae. The origins of the Hominidae may be traceable to an extinct ape-like genus *Ramapithecus*, of which jaw fragments have been found in east Africa and north-west India dating from somewhere between 8

and 14 million years ago[56]. After this, we know little until the appearance of the genus *Australopithecus* in south and east Africa from about 6 million years ago, and it is most probably from a branch of the Australopithecines that the first tool-making populations of the genus *Homo* evolved. The exact course of man's ancestry in this period is still unclear, but very early remains of *Homo* have been found from almost 2 million years ago in east Africa, and the first crude pebble tools make an appearance with them. Some authors refer to this earliest tool-making ancestor as *Homo habilis*, and by 1.5 million years ago *H. habilis* had evolved into the larger brained form *H. erectus*, to which group the earliest fossils from Java and China belong.

From this brief resume arise two matters. Firstly, as far as we know, the earliest stages of human evolution are found only in Africa. It looks as though this is the homeland, and that early man began to spread from here across Asia about 2 million years ago. Future discoveries could of course upset this interpretation, particularly if definite remains of *Homo habilis* are ever found in Java or China. The second matter concerns tools; it is now common knowledge that apes can and do make tools under certain conditions, but in man's case, tool-making has been subject to increasingly complex modification for some 2 million years. No ape has ever flaked pebble-tools in the wild (even if they can make them in the laboratory[57]), and it seems that the African *H. habilis* was the first to make this crucial grade.

The earliest hominid finds in Java have been found with the Jetis mammalian fauna, which is of Upper Pliocene and Lower Pleistocene age (see figure 3.1). The beds which contain this fauna and its human fossils appear to date to between perhaps 3 and 1 million years ago, but it is not certain just where the finds fall within this range[58]. The earliest, which may be more than 1.5 million years old, is the skull of a child, referred to as *Homo erectus*, from Mojokerto in eastern Java. A little later than this may come three (or perhaps four) mandible fragments of a very large-jawed creature who was originally named *Meganthropus palaeojavanicus* (figure 2.10). These were found at Sangiran in central Java, and one at least came from a very late stage of the Jetis fauna. With *Meganthropus* we could have a problem of classification.

The evolution of the genus *Homo* appears to have been a continuum with no really marked

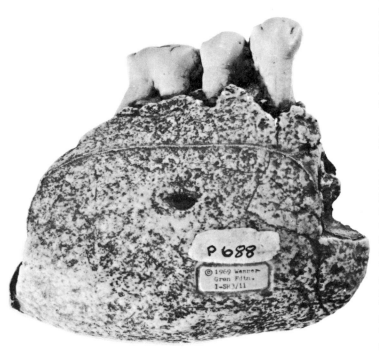

Fig. 2.10. Cast of the lower jaw fragment of *Meganthropus* found at Sangiran in 1941.

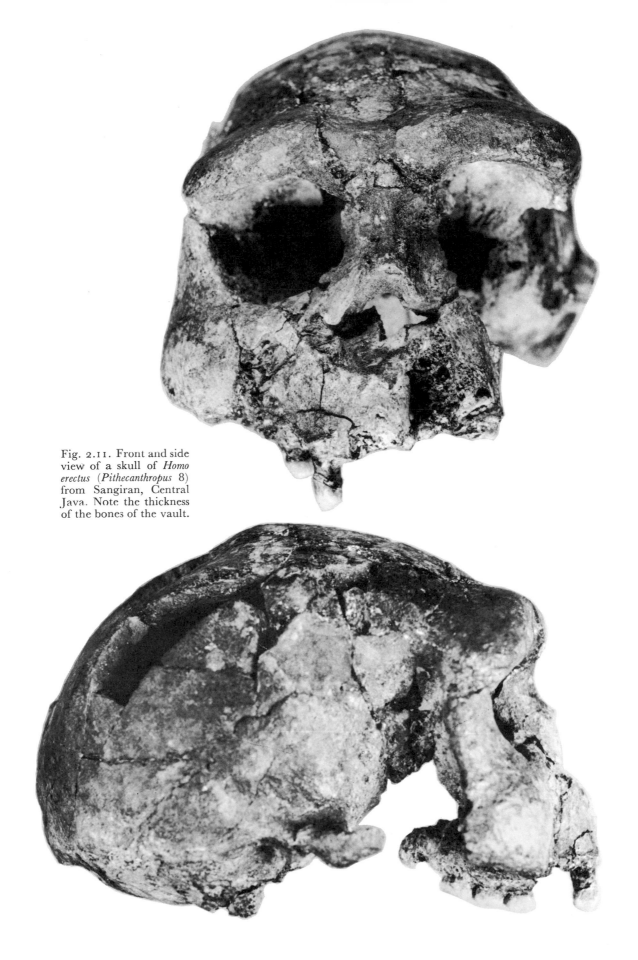

Fig. 2.11. Front and side view of a skull of *Homo erectus* (*Pithecanthropus* 8) from Sangiran, Central Java. Note the thickness of the bones of the vault.

jumps. This means that the borderlines between the *habilis* and *erectus* grades, and also between the *erectus* and *sapiens* grades, are defined more by scholastic agreement than by any sudden break. Massive-jawed *Meganthropus* has in fact been equated with the African Australopithecines, and in 1964 Tobias and von Koenigswald[59] equated him with *H. habilis* from Olduvai Gorge in Tanzania, who has an age of about 1.5 to 2 million years. However, it has been more recently suggested that the mandibles, while massive, are within the expected range for Javanese *H. erectus*[60], and here the matter seems to have come to rest. Only more discoveries will solve the problem conclusively, although we may note that there are other fossils of late Jetis age from Sangiran which are certainly *H. erectus*, so the whole group may eventually be agreed to be in this category.

On the other hand, however, there is one piece of evidence which suggests that hominids may have reached Java before the *erectus* stage. An upper jaw from Sangiran, which is of Jetis age and certainly *H. erectus*, has retained a definite simian feature in the form of a gap (or diastema) between each of the upper lateral incisors and canines. The diastema is absent in all the African Australopithecines, and because it is not an African feature, it does suggest that *H. erectus* in Java may have a separate Australopithecine heritage in Southeast Asia. But this is still only a tenuous possibility at present.

The majority of the undisputed *H. erectus* remains from Java come from the Middle Pleistocene Trinil faunal zone, which may date to between approximately 1 million and perhaps 3–400,000 years ago. The most important remains include a virtually complete skull from Sangiran (Pithecanthropus 8), two other calvaria, and a number of teeth and other fragments[61]. Estimates of cranial capacity range between 750 and 1125 ccs for the whole group (including the Jetis finds), and reconstructions reveal a long, low keeled skull with its greatest width at the base, heavy brow ridges with marked post-orbital constrictions, an angular nuchal area, and a rather prognathous face with a large jaw lacking a true chin (figure 2.11). The dental arcade is parabolic, and the teeth, particularly the molars, are considerably larger than in modern man, although morphology is similar.

The skull of *H. erectus* is obviously very archaic when compared to that of modern man, but the position of the foramen magnum at the base of the skull does suggest an almost upright body stance. A complete femur with a rather malignant looking bony growth, or exostosis, was found by Dubois at Trinil in 1892, and this is of completely modern form. For many years it was thought that this and several other fragments of femora belonged to *H. erectus*, and fluorine tests published in 1952 seemed to confirm this view[62]. However, more recent analyses have thrown doubt on their provenance[63], and it can only be regarded as suspicious that unequivocal femora of *H. erectus* from Olduvai Gorge in Tanzania and from Chou-k'ou-tien near Peking are considerably more archaic in appearance. But even if we reject the Javanese femora as evidence, it is still fairly clear that both *Australopithecus* and *H. erectus* had attained a near-erect posture, and it certainly appears that the evolution of the skull prior to this time had progressed at a different and slower rate from the evolution of posture and the dentition.

One other point of interest about Java Man is that he, or at least his mainland relations, may have been contemporary with a population of giant pongids, labelled *Gigantopithecus blacki*, who are estimated to have stood 3 metres high[64]. Remains of *Gigantopithecus* have been recovered from Hong Kong apothecaries' stores, and between 1956 and 1958 over 1000 teeth and 3 lower jaws were recovered from the region of southern Kwangsi in China. No post-cranial remains have come to light but the enormous teeth point to a seed and plant-eating ape who may have inhabited fairly open environments in Southeast Asia from the Pliocene through into the Middle Pleistocene epoch. In 1946 a rather interesting book was written by Franz Weidenreich, in which he suggested that these giants were the ancestors of man, from whom he evolved through a series of diminishing forms represented by *Meganthropus* and *Pithecanthropus* (*Homo erectus*)[65]. A few hominid traits in the *Gigantopithecus* dentition suggest that his lineage may in some way be connected with that of man at a very ancient remove, but he himself now appears to have been a highly specialised adaptation who was overtaken by extinction.

The fossil record in China is basically equivalent to that of Java, and we may begin with a mandible and braincase found in 1963 and 1964 respectively at Lan-t'ien in Shensi Province[66]. The braincase is on the same archaic grade as the Jetis specimens from Java, and has an estimated cranial capacity of 780 ccs. It was found

Fig. 2.12. The skull of Peking Man
(cast).

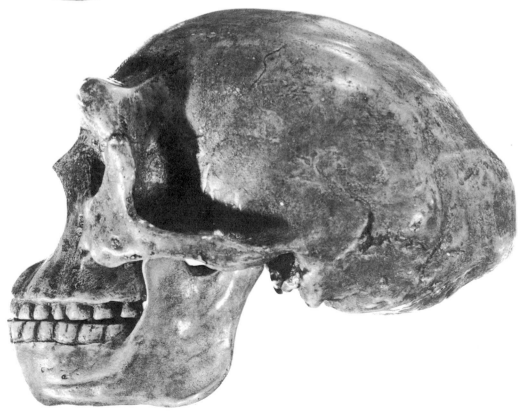

with some flake tools and a Lower or early Middle Pleistocene fauna, and may have an age of 700,000 years or more on these grounds. The mandible appears to be younger, and may be about 300,000 years old, but this shows an interesting absence of the third molar tooth, a trait which characterises about thirty percent of Mongoloids today[67].

The most famous *Homo erectus* (or *Sinanthropus*) population has been recovered since 1921 at the Lower Cave (locality 1) of Chou-k'ou-tien, 42 kilometres south-west of Peking. Most of these fossils were lost during the Second World War, but casts were very fortunately made before the event. The major finds consisted of 14 calvaria, 12 mandibles, with many loose teeth and a few post-cranial bones. The population is more advanced than the Javanese forms, with cranial capacities ranging from 850 to 1300 ccs., with a mean of 1075 ccs[68]. The skulls are still broad at the base, but are slightly higher and rounder than the Javanese specimens, and the brow ridges and teeth are also smaller (figure 2.12). Seven femora, two humeri, and a clavicle were found in the Chou-k'ou-tien deposits, and their closeness to modern forms indicates an almost completely erect posture[69]. The population therefore represents an advancement beyond the grade observed in the Javanese fossils, and faunal and palynological associations place Peking man in a temperate woodland environment which might possibly be correlated with the second interglacial in the Himalayas[70]. Dates for the latter are not secure, but estimates of age for Peking man place him between 300,000 and 200,000 years old[71].

With *Meganthropus* and *Homo erectus* we have scanned the evidence for human evolution in eastern Asia from perhaps 2 million years ago to about 200,000 years ago. In Java there is only one fossil population to fill the gap between *Homo erectus* and modern man, and this consists of 11 calvaria and 2 tibiae found between 1931 and 1933 on a supposedly Upper Pleistocene terrace of the Solo River at Ngandong in central Java. The fauna found with the remains consisted of some 25,000 mammalian bones, including panther, rhino, hippopotamus, pig, deer, cattle, and modern and primitive elephants, the whole suite suggesting a grassland environment[72]. There is no date for the site, and the suggestion that the fauna is Upper Pleistocene is of very little help in this respect, but T. Jacob has suggested an age of between 100,000 and 60,000 years[73]. The calvaria all lacked faces and bases, and some

have claimed that both Solo Man and also Peking Man were cannibals. Jacob has disputed this fairly convincingly for Solo Man by an examination of the features of truly cannibalised skulls from Papua, and von Koenigswald originally suggested that the Solo skulls might have been used as bowls[74].

Solo Man (figure 2–13) is regarded by most recent authors as an advanced *Homo erectus*, generally a little more archaic than the European Neanderthals. His intermediate position has led to terminological conflicts, and in recent years various authors have referred to him as *H. erectus soloensis*, *H. sapiens soloensis*, and *Pithecanthropus soloensis*. We seem to have a situation in which one may take one's pick. Coon[75] gives average male cranial capacity as 1150 ccs., and considers Solo Man to be *Homo erectus*, on the same evolutionary grade as Peking Man, although he is generally assumed to be later in time. His age is in fact the crux of a problem of particular importance.

Given the absence of any definite date, my own rather intuitive opinion would be to suggest that an age of 100,000 years is a likely minimum, and that Solo Man may be in fact older than this. However, since the problem is insoluble at the moment, we can only resort to hypotheses. For the sake of simplicity, there are two of these which merit consideration. Firstly, Solo Man may indeed be as recent as 60,000 years old. If so, he most probably represents an extinct and replaced line[76], since modern men were already present in Indonesia by 40,000 years ago, and 20,000 years seems too short a time for the necessary evolution to have taken place *in situ*. The same kind of replacement radiation could also apply to the earlier *erectus* line in Java, but in this case we have little idea of how this line compares with contemporary lines elsewhere. The other hypothesis, which seems a more likely one to me, is that Solo Man may be of a much greater age, and in the direct line of evolution of modern men, particularly the Australoids, in Southeast Asia. Of course, when Java was an island during the Pleistocene, it may be that its human inhabitants retained many archaic features in their isolation. But it is most unlikely that they ever diverged so far as to become extinct without some genetic transmission, and the modern Australoids of Southeast Asia are likely to have some degree of inheritance from an *erectus*-Solo line which has had sufficient gene flow from mainland populations to obviate speciation.

HOMO ERECTUS AND MODERN MAN IN EASTERN ASIA

Having reviewed the *Homo erectus* populations of east and Southeast Asia we turn to more modern men of the species *Homo sapiens*. Modern man is in fact classified as a subspecies *H. sapiens sapiens*, in order to differentiate him from more archaic members of the same species such as *H. sapiens neanderthalensis*, and *H. sapiens soloensis*, whom we have considered above. Modern man appears in the fossil record from about 60,000 years ago, and is found over most of the Old World by about 40,000 years ago. His origins are obscure, and the Neanderthal and Solo forms are not generally considered to be mainstream ancestors, although they have almost certainly passed on some of their genes. The original development of *H. sapiens* from *H. erectus* probably took place some 2–300,000 years ago, when brain capacity somewhere passed the arbitrary mean of 1300 ccs[77], but here our knowledge is almost non-existent.

We may now ask in more detail how, if at all, *H. erectus* relates to the modern Australoids and Mongoloids. In this section I adopt a hypothesis of partial continuity rather than replacement, partly on the grounds that partial continuity seems a more reasonable hypothesis than one which postulates complete extinction of earlier forms. And as we will see, there is some skeletal evidence in support. We commence with the Mongoloids.

The Mongoloids of eastern Asia and the Americas are a very widespread and varied group. Practically the only physical traits held in common by the majority of these peoples are dark eye pigmentation, generally straight dark hair, and wide, flat faces[78]. Acquisition of these features presumably resulted from the action of natural selection over a long period on a fairly varied population located somewhere in eastern Asia. It has been pointed out that the yellowish skins of Mongoloids contain little melanin and a dense outer *stratum corneum* packed with keratin. This type of skin reflects direct sunlight efficiently and resists the penetration of ultra-violet radiation to a greater extent than in Europeans[79]. Unfortunately, however, eastern Asia is not an area of high solar radiation, except in the south around the Gulf of Tonkin, so that resistance to ultraviolet light cannot have been the only selective factor in operation. Another possible

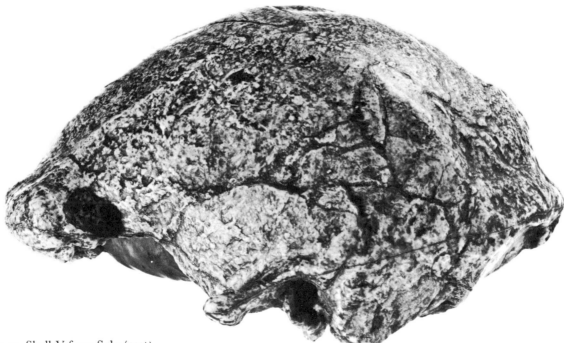

Fig. 2.13. Skull V from Solo (cast).

reason for the relative lightness of Mongoloid skins has been suggested by Brace, who feels it could be due to the use of clothing in northerly latitudes throughout the last glaciation, which would tend to remove some of the adaptive value of a dark skin[80]. The available fossil evidence suggests a possible origin for the Mongoloids around northern and central China, where one might expect the use of clothing to be of considerable antiquity.

The tracing of Mongoloid origins through skeletal remains is of course difficult, although there are a number of characteristic traits which are identifiable in the fossil record, such as shovelling of the upper incisor teeth, congenital absence of the third molar teeth, the mandibular torus, cranial keeling, the accessory Inca bone at the back of the skull, broad nasal bones, and platymeria (or relative antero-posterior flatness) of the femoral shafts[81]. By no means all Mongoloids have all these traits, and the traits themselves are by no means restricted to Mongoloids. The situation is therefore one of probability; Mongoloids tend to have more of these traits than do members of other populations.

From a long acquaintance with skeletal material, Franz Weidenreich originally suggested that at least certain groups of Mongoloids were in a direct line of inheritance from Peking Man, partially on the basis of the incidence of shovel-shaped incisors and mandibular tori[82]. In 1962 this suggestion was examined again by Carleton Coon[83], who was able to list 17 skeletal traits held in common between the two groups. He further claimed to be able to trace Mongoloid evolution from Peking Man through a series of Chinese Middle and Upper Pleistocene fossils, including the early *sapiens* forms of Mongoloid type represented by the Upper Pleistocene skulls from Tzu-yang, Szechwan, and Liu-chiang, Kwangsi[84]. Neither of these is well-dated, but David Hughes seems to be in agreement with Coon in suggesting that these two specimens represent the beginnings of Mongoloid subspeciation[85] at the *sapiens* level. Skeletal remains of later date from China, such as those from the Upper Cave at Chou-k'ou-tien, are considered Mongoloid by most present authors.

The evidence is of course weak in places, particularly in absolute dating, but perhaps we can hypothesise at present that the modern Mongoloids can trace at least some degree of descent from Peking Man. There is no evidence to suggest that he was exterminated and replaced by any immigrant *Homo sapiens* population, but we cannot on the other hand claim that Peking Man represents a hypothetical mainstream of Mongoloid evolution. The racial situation in eastern Asia in the Middle or Upper Pleistocene was perhaps as varied as it is now, and many heterogeneous breeding populations could have transmitted genes to what after all are a heterogeneous group of Mongoloid breeding populations today. A statement by Jean Hiernaux should give some idea of the complexity that one might expect:

> Even if we could reconstruct the intricate succession of mixtures that contributed to each living population, the final picture would look like a reticulum more than a tree[86].

If we now turn our attention to Southeastern Asia and Indonesia, the picture becomes even more involved than that in China, because this is an area where both Mongoloids and Australoids have been evolving and hybridising for a very long time. The east of Asia, from central China down to Southeast Asia, offers no major barriers to north-south movements of a local nature, and we may imagine that populations of *H. sapiens sapiens* evolved in a pre-existing situation of clinal variation. In the north one would expect an accumulation of characteristics of Mongoloid type, and in the south a similar accumulation of Australoid characteristics, but the two areas would be unlikely to be separated by a distinct line.

Looking at the distribution of phenotypes today in Southeast Asia, western Melanesia and Australia, the most likely explanation for the distribution would be that Mongoloids have moved southwards to replace an Australoid population, which originally inhabited the whole of Southeast Asia through to New Guinea and Australia, and which survives in Southeast Asia today as the isolated pockets of Negritos. But we should interpret the idea of replacement with care, by envisaging a complex situation with gene flow between two already highly varied human races, who may have been part of a single clinal distribution in the first place. It would be naive in the extreme to envisage mass migrations of identical Mongoloid populations swamping and exterminating their Australoid predecessors.

If we return again to Carleton Coon, his theory for Australoid descent, which is parallel to that for Mongoloid descent, and again foreshadowed by Weidenreich, is that the Australoids are

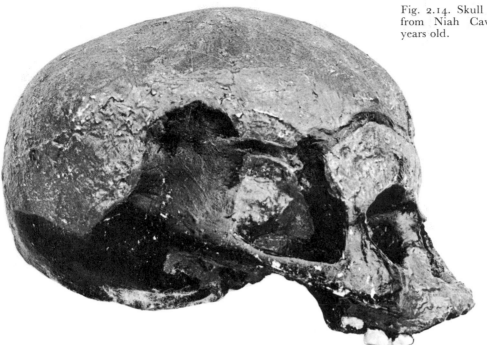

Fig. 2.14. Skull of *H. sapiens sapiens* from Niah Cave, possibly 40,000 years old.

lineal descendants in the Southeast Asian area of the *Homo erectus* population represented by the Javanese remains, through Solo Man, and through two poorly-documented sets of cranial remains recovered in 1890 by Dubois at Wajak in central Java. The latter are evidently of Upper Pleistocene or Holocene age[87], and are from a *Homo sapiens sapiens* population, although one skull retains fairly prominent brow ridges and a degree of cranial keeling. In addition, there is the well-known skull of *H. sapiens sapiens* from Niah Cave in Sarawak (figure 2.14), which has been likened to Tasmanian skulls by Brothwell[88]. An age of 40,000 years is reported for this, but there are certain grounds for caution in accepting this date. If it is correct, then the Niah skull is the earliest dated modern Australoid.

At present, the Weidenreich/Coon hypothesis of continuity in Southeast Asia seems to me to be the most acceptable for Australoid evolution. But recent evidence from Australia does raise the question of replacement radiation, if only on a local level. The earliest human remains from Australia are those of a cremated woman from the Mungo site in western New South Wales, which are about 25,000 years old[89]. The Mungo remains are of modern form, and there is no

reason to doubt that they are in the direct line ancestry of the modern Aborigines. However, the discovery of a number of burials of a very rugged and archaic population at Kow Swamp in northern Victoria[90] has raised problems. These date from about 10,000 years ago, and so must overlap chronologically with Australoids of the Mungo type, but they retain so many *erectus*-like characteristics that they can hardly be a sample of the same population. Some have mandibles more massive than *H. erectus* from Java, and the crania are up to 2 cm thick. On their overall features they seem to belong in the range of *H. sapiens*, but they certainly do not qualify to be grouped with the modern Australoids.

Although the Kow Swamp remains are remarkably late in time, they do raise the possibility of a very early settlement of a Solo-like population in Australia[91], which was replaced and partially absorbed by an incoming Australoid population, perhaps over a fairly long period. But it is rather hard to explain why the former should have survived for some 15,000 years, since the Mungo woman dates to 25,000 years ago, and the latest Kow Swamp burial may be as recent as 9000 years old. Fortunately, perhaps, Australia is outside the concern of this book, and it is sufficient here to indicate an Australoid settlement by at least 25,000 years ago, which may have involved a local population replacement. The theories concerning the settlement of Australia are a lively topic in their own right, and are particularly lively at the present time. The Kow Swamp evidence certainly suggests that Australia was settled more than once, although as far as the present Aborigines are concerned there is little agreement between scholars as to how many migrations into the continent are required to explain the level of variation[92].

Turning back to the Australoids in Southeast Asia in late Pleistocene and Holocene times, we find a situation marred by poor excavation and an absence of dates. The prevailing opinion seems to be that one major expansion of a Mongoloid phenotype, particularly into Indonesia and the Philippines, began in the Neolithic period[93], which on present evidence began before 3000 B.C. in most areas. The pre-Neolithic population of Indonesia and the Philippines appears to have been mainly Australoid, while the population of the pre-Neolithic Hoabinhian technocomplex on the Southeast Asian mainland appears to have combined both Australoid and Mongoloid traits. Such a simplification may be far from the real truth, but it is the best we can do at the moment, and it is clear at least that we are not dealing with a case of rapid 'swamping' of Australoids by Mongoloids.

Coon has suggested that a high degree of Mongoloid gene flow into Southeast Asia had already taken place by the beginning of the Neolithic, although he believes that the major period of Mongoloid expansion came about as a result of Han Chinese expansion at about the time of Christ[94]. If this is so, then one would expect basically Australoid populations to have survived widely in Mainland Southeast Asia until as recently as 2000 years ago, and this may indeed be the case. Even a Chinese text describing the people of the Indianized kingdom of Funan in Cambodia (*c.* A.D. 250) has an explicit reference to black skins and frizzy hair,[95] although the peoples of Cambodia today are almost totally of Mongoloid phenotype. The skeletal evidence for the above reconstruction is weak in detail, but it does present a coherent overall picture. A large number of skeletons from Hoabinhian sites on the Southeast Asian mainland in North Vietnam[96], Thailand[97] and Malaya[98] have been diagnosed as both Mongoloid and Australoid in henotype, and it appears that we have a clinal

population, with a possible predominance of Australoid traits in Malaya. But there is little skeletal evidence to throw light on Mongoloid expansion on the Mainland in the full Neolithic, apart from the appearance of a Mongoloid population in western Thailand by at least 2000 B.C.[99]. We are in fact thrown back mainly on the surmise of the previous paragraph.

In Indonesia and the Philippines, the situation appears to be a little clearer, with definite Mongoloid expansion into many previously Australoid areas. The Australoid skull from Niah Cave in Sarawak has been mentioned above, and in addition to this the cave has produced a series of pre-Neolithic burials which fall somewhere between 15,000 and 4000 B.C., and which are stated to have 'Melanesoid' dentitions[100]. Neolithic burials in the layers above, which date to between 1200 B.C. and 0, are stated to have Mongoloid dentitions.

A large number of prehistoric remains from Java, Sulawesi and Flores have been analysed in detail by T. Jacob[101], although very few of these were found in dateable archaeological contexts. Skeletons and other fragments from what would appear to be early Neolithic sites in eastern Java and Flores are diagnosed as Melanesian and Austromelanesian by Jacob, so they fall generally into the Australoid group. One of the sites on Flores has a carbon date of about 1600 B.C., but this is of no great assistance in tracing Mongoloid expansion, as Flores still has populations with some Australoid phenotypic traits today. The Javanese remains, which come from the Gua Lawa Cave near Sampung, have more potential significance as they are in an area which is predominantly Mongoloid now, but the absence of a date hampers interpretation. Nevertheless, we can fill out the picture with a collection of 2682 human teeth from a cave called Leang Cadang in southern Sulawesi, which Jacob identifies as fully Mongoloid. Leang Cadang has produced a Toalean flake and blade industry which could date back to about 5000 B.C. (see page 73), although the teeth seem more likely to belong to the period after 1000 B.C., according to parallels from other sites in the region. Perhaps we can interpret Jacob's results to suggest that Indonesian populations were basically Australoid until the beginning of the Neolithic, but that Mongoloid populations could have been expanding into the area earlier in the Holocene, probably through the Philippines.

If we turn now to the Philippines, we find that

the earliest evidence here is the frontal part of a skull from the Tabon Cave on Palawan, which dates to between 22,000 and 24,000 years ago[102]. No full report has yet appeared on this specimen, but a mandible, claimed to have Australoid affinities by Macintosh[103], has more recently been found in the same level. There is also a Neolithic burial from Duyong Cave on Palawan which dates to the early third millenium B.C.[104], but as with the Tabon skull there is no published information yet available. However, the remains from a series of jar burials from the Tabon Caves, which date to between 1500 B.C. and 0, have been described by Winters[105] as Mongoloids, with prominent cheek bones and shovel-shaped incisor teeth.

All this adds up to a situation in which the only prehistoric Mongoloid populations reported so far from Island Southeast Asia are from the Philippines, Sulawesi and Sarawak. This evidence may be heavily biased by the vagaries of discovery, but it does tie up with the linguistic and archaeological evidence which suggests that the ancestors of the Polynesians and Micronesians spread from somewhere in the Philippines or north-eastern Indonesia from about 2000 B.C. onwards. These ancestors were predominantly Mongoloid.

The evidence from Island Southeast Asia would therefore suggest widespread Australoid survival in the Sunda Islands until about 1000 B.C. or later, but with earlier Mongoloid gene flow, perhaps by 3000 B.C. or before, spreading through the Philippines and into northern Borneo and Sulawesi. The final major phase of Mongoloid expansion into western Indonesia could quite possibly fall within the past 2500 years. As for the reason behind Mongoloid expansion and success in Island Southeast Asia, we can only link it circumstantially with a general population increase in the Neolithic owing to the spread of horticulture and sedentism. The later economic success of the Indianised kingdoms doubtless accelerated the process.

THE RACIAL HISTORY OF OCEANIA

Although New Guinea has been settled for over 30,000 years, no human remains of Pleistocene age have been reported so far[106]. On genetic and phenotypic grounds the New Guineans have a fairly close phylogenetic relationship with the Australian Aborigines, but while the latter have developed in long-term isolation, the New Guineans have been exchanging genes with the more Mongoloid peoples who have settled Melanesia, Micronesia and Polynesia within the past 5000 years. The simplest explanation of Melanesian racial history would therefore stress two phases, the first being the long phase of Australoid settlement in New Guinea and neighbouring islands, under way by at least 30,000 years ago, the second being the expansion of the clinal groups with a more Mongoloid phenotype within the period of Austronesian language expansion generally within the last 5000 years. The later are not to be imagined as classic continental Mongoloids, but may have been more like some of the intermediate east Indonesian populations of today.

This interpretation follows basically that of Carleton Coon, as stated at the beginning of this chapter, but we may examine two rather different viewpoints from the past for good measure. W.W. Howells, in an article written in 1937[107], suggested four racial migrations to account for Melanesian diversity. First came Australian Aborigines, who settled New Guinea, the Bismarcks and New Caledonia, and these were followed by Negritos, then by Negroes, and finally by minor intrusions from Polynesia and Micronesia. Another quadrihybrid theory of the same type but different content was set out by Birdsell in 1949[108], and he suggested that the first to arrive was a Negrito population, which accounted for most aspects of the Highland New Guinea phenotype. This was followed by two other groups called Murrayians (archaic Caucasoids) and Carpentarians (Australoids). Neither of these groups had much impact in New Guinea, but the Murrayians achieved a greater importance in northern New Caledonia. The final group consisted of the later Mongoloids. For both Howells and Birdsell, the overall racial pattern in Melanesia reflected differential hybridisation of their four stocks.

The Howells and Birdsell theories both agreed in placing the Mongoloid expansion last, but their first three migrations were not in agreement, and neither of the alternatives are well supported today. Unless one wishes to separate a Negrito migration from the Australoids, there seems little reason now to look for more than two movements. Some anthropologists, perhaps a little hastily, have become so exasperated with racial migration theories that they have tended to the opposite extreme, which has been well expressed by D.R. Swindler[109]:

Melanesia's populations as seen today are the products of generations of racial churning, in which the evolutionary processes of mutation, migration, natural selection, genetic drift, and selective mating have effectively contributed to the racial diversity so demonstrable there today. . . The original ingredients which went to make up this mixture could have been represented by many polytypic populations slowly wandering out of Asia into Melanesia, populating the islands as they came, undoubtedly mixing with some neighbouring bands and at the same time establishing rules of endogamy with respect to others. Whether this exodus was represented by three or four separate migrations or simply was a slow gradual dribbling of small groups is not known. However, the latter assumption seems more plausible.

Swindler is quite right, but he has perhaps shelved the matter of separate migrations more than is necessary. We now know from archaeology and linguistics that there were two major periods of migration into Melanesia, even if there was a dribbling of small groups in between. These two groups, as stated at the beginning of this section, were firstly the Australoids, and then the more Mongoloid populations. The latter have been widely assimilated by the earlier Australoids in Melanesia, but come into their own in Polynesia and Micronesia. These latter two areas were settled solely by Austronesian speakers with a strong Mongoloid genetic heritage.

With Polynesia and Micronesia the question again arises of how many migrations are needed to account for the present racial pattern. For Polynesia, archaeology and linguistics make it very clear that we have only one major migration to deal with. For Micronesia we may have two; one from the west, and one from the south (see chapter 10), but these two do not seem to be separately visible in the physical anthropology of the area. There is in fact little more to be said about Micronesia in this chapter.

For the Polynesians, most earlier scholars tended to think in terms of migrations of two or more discrete groups into the area. For instance, L.R. Sullivan in 1924[110] suggested a quadrihybrid ancestry for Polynesians based on two sets of Caucasoid elements, a Negroid/Melanesian element, and a Negroid/Mongoloid element. These types had in the past combined in varying proportions in different islands. A slightly differing and more realistic view was expressed by H.

Shapiro in 1943[111], who suggested firstly a migration of an earlier dolichocephalic population, which still survived at European contact at marginal areas of Polynesia, and secondly a later migration of a brachycephalic population which became dominant in central Polynesia and the Hawaiian Islands. Shapiro's conclusions are well-worded, and still worthy of attention today:

> The Polynesian population possesses a fundamental unity in physical type which necessarily implies that the successive immigrants were derived from a common people. It is extremely doubtful that the various waves of invaders were profoundly different racially.

The view of fundamental unity still applies today, but we can now challenge the view that there was more than one major migration into Polynesia, although it cannot be disproved solely on the evidence of physical anthropology.

The most recent work in Polynesian physical anthropology is that by M. Pietrusewsky[112], who has analysed a number of Fijian and Polynesian crania with the aid of multivariate statistical techniques. His results (figure 2.15) suggest that three basic populations may be recognised. The first comprises crania from Fiji, Tonga and Samoa, which represent a population intermediate between Melanesian and Polynesian physical types. The second group comprises crania from the Society and Tuamotu Islands in central Polynesia, and possibly the Marquesas Islands. The third group comprises the marginal Polynesian populations of the Hawaiian Islands, New Zealand, the Chatham Islands, Easter Island, and perhaps the Marquesas Islands. The latter tend to change their affiliations according to the statistical technique used, but the groups otherwise seem to be fairly discrete. Recognition of two groups in central and marginal Polynesia of course takes us back to Shapiro's views, but the differences do not necessarily imply separate migrations from outside Polynesia, and local differentiation combined with small-scale population movement is a more likely conclusion.

Pietrusewsky's results do fit expectations, for Fijians, Tongans and Samoans have been intermarrying on a small scale for a long period, as have Society Islanders and Tuamotuans. The marginal Polynesian islands have been more isolated, and may have retained features of an early Polynesian phenotype in common. Concerning Polynesian origins generally, it is now clear from general linguistic and archaeological

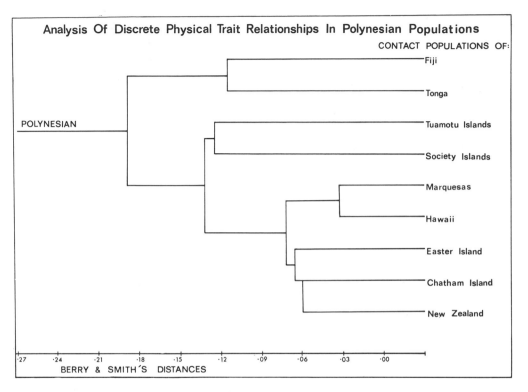

Fig. 2.15. Diagram of Polynesian skeletal relationships. From Green 1974, after Pietrusewsky.

evidence that the first settlers spread into the Polynesian triangle from one or more isolated communities located most probably in the area of Tonga or Futuna (Hoorn Islands), about 1000 B.C. or a little before. We will of course describe this evidence in due course, but the evidence from physical anthropology and genetics does not contradict Polynesian derivation from a single population of basically Mongoloid affinity which had had earlier contact with an Australoid gene pool in Melanesia. As Coon states, 'The Polynesians are just as clearly a part of the Mongoloid:Australoid clinal world as are the Formosans, the Filipinos or the Balinese, with more of the Australoid element in evidence than among some of the latter'[113]. The same applies equally to the Micronesians. The theory of a single basic migration into Polynesia does not rule out occasional gene flow from the Americas, but it is very hard to avoid the conclusion that Polynesia was basically settled once, and only once, and settled from the west.

At this point, a major question arises. How did the Polynesians, and for that matter the eastern Micronesians, reach their islands without having more impact on and receiving more influence from the western and central Melanesians? The answers to this extremely important question do not lie with physical anthropology alone, and different lines of evidence for an answer will be developed as this book proceeds. At this juncture I will merely hint that the Polynesians and eastern Micronesians may have spread through Melanesia as a series of non-exogamous, sea-borne colonising groups, and that they did not come into very intensive genetic contact with the Melanesian populations who, by the second millennium B.C. had already settled as far east as the New Hebrides and New Caledonia. The Austronesian-speaking groups who settled Polynesia and Micronesia retained much of their Mongoloid phenotype, while those who remained in Melanesia have become partially, but not entirely, absorbed into the surrounding Melanesian phenotype.

Footnotes

1. For a range of professional views concerning the concept of race, see Montagu, M. (ed.) 1964; Mead, M. *et al.* (eds.) 1968.

2. Biasutti 1959; vol. 1, Chapter 10. See also critical comments in Coon 1966: 211–2.

3. Coon 1962; Chapters 9, 10. Coon 1966; Chapter 6. Howells (1973a) has recently provided support for Coon's view, but uses the term 'Melanesian' rather than Australoid.

4. See also Garn 1961, Chapter 11. Acceptance of Coon's views may not please everyone, and I take full responsibility for my choice. I do not claim that Coon has had the last say, and I respect the rather divergent views expressed by Birdsell (1949, 1967, 1972). These views, however, mainly concern Australia, and are not incorporated in the text to avoid further confusion of an already tortuous topic.

5. Cole 1945; Chapter 4.

6. Coon 1966: 179; Reed 1904.

7. Bijlmer 1939; Graydon *et al.* 1958; Champness *et al.* 1960; Gates 1961; Howells 1973a: 173–4.

8. Battaglia in Biasutti 1959; vol. 4: 94.

9. Bijlmer in Graydon *et al.* 1958.

10. Brace in Montagu, M. (ed.) 1964: 142; Gajdusek 1970. Howells (1973a) is a strong supporter of the view of independence.

11. Gates 1961. Gates' hypothesis of a single gene for dwarfing is not generally accepted; see Birdsell 1967: 108.

12. Birdsell 1972: 498. Howells (1973b) has recently grouped the Andamanese with Africans rather than with Australoids.

13. e.g. very light in parts of the New Guinea Highlands (Macintosh 1960), very dark on Buka (Swindler 1962: 23).

14. Suzuki and Sakai 1964; Carbonell 1963; Riesenfeld 1956 (for shovel-shaped incisors). For the epicanthic fold see Biasutti 1959, vol. 1: fig. 171; Swindler 1962: 23 (absent amongst West Nakanai).

15. Coon 1966: 176. See also Littlewood 1972: 9.

16. Gill 1876: 230.

17. Recently demonstrated statistically by Howells (1970).

18. Howells 1933; 1970.

19. Gabel 1958.

20. Howells 1970; Swindler 1962: 39.

21. Coon 1966: 181; Keers 1948.

22. Keers 1948.

23. Howells 1933; Coon 1966: 182 and footnote 14.

24. For a Caucasoid element see also Heyerdahl 1952; Sullivan 1924; Linton 1956: 177; Suggs 1960: 32; Dodd 1972: 20. This is disputed by Coon (1966: 184).

25. Howells 1970; 1973a.

26. Simmons *et al.* 1961: 647.

27. Cavalli-Sforza, Barrai and Edwards 1964: 11; Cavalli-Sforza 1974.

28. Many geneticists and physical anthropologists today rule out any phylogenetic connections between African Negroes and Australoids; e.g. Simmons 1956: 506; Simmons *et al.* 1961: 662; Howells 1973a. But Birdsell (1972: 498) supports an ultimate African origin for both groups.

29. Kirk 1971: 336; Simmons *et al* 1964.

30. Kirk 1965: 212; Kariks and Walsh 1968.

31. Gc Aborigine and Transferrin D1 (Kirk 1971: 341). Lewis phenotype Le(a+) is also very low in Australia and New Guinea when compared to Indonesia, Polynesia and Micronesia (Simmons 1962: Table 5).

32. Kirk 1971.

33. Giles *et al.* 1965; 1970; Schanfield, Giles and Gerschowitz 1975.

34. Curtain *et al.* 1971; Curtain 1976.

35. Friedlaender 1970.

36. e.g. Baumgarten *et al.* 1968 for haptoglobins and transferrins. Howells (1973a: 73) has suggested that a higher percentage occurrence of wet ear wax could differentiate Papuan speakers from Austronesians in Melanesia.

37. Simmons 1962.

38. Gajdusek 1964.

39. Littlewood 1966.

40. Coon 1966: 229–35.

41. Loomis 1967.

42. Curtain *et al.* 1962; Kirk 1965; 1971. Hemoglobins bind incoming oxygen and outgoing CO_2 in the red blood cells.

43. Birdsell 1972: 436.

44. e.g. Macintosh *et al.* 1958; Nijenhuis *et al.* 1966.

45. Simmons and Gajdusek 1966: 170. Another complex cline running from Madang, through Manus and New Ireland, to New Britain has been reported by Booth and Vines (1968).

46. Garn 1961; Chapter 8.

47. Dobzhansky 1963: 71; Neel 1967: 5.

48. Chagnon *et al.* 1970.

49. Simmons *et al.* 1965–66.

50. Simmons *et al.* 1964–65; 1967; Giles *et al.* 1966; 1970; Dowell *et al.* 1967; Friedlaender 1971a; 1971b.

51. Oliver and Howells 1957; Simmons 1973.

52. Friedlaender *et al.* 1971a, See also Howells 1966.

53. Booth and Taylor 1974. For other New Guinea analyses see Livingstone 1963, Littlewood 1972.

54. Sinnett *et al.* 1970. The Murapin dwell to the west of Wabag.

55. e.g. Birdsell 1972.

56. Pilbeam 1966: Birdsell 1972: 209. There is a very extensive literature on human evolution; e.g. Le Gros Clark 1964; Campbell 1967; Pilbeam 1970; Tattersall 1970; Birdsell 1972. My latest information is from a paper given by P. Tobias at the IX Inqua Congress, Christchurch, December, 1973.

57. Wright 1972.

58. Von Koenigswald 1968a: Jacob 1972a.
59. Tobias and von Koenigswald 1964. See also Robinson 1964.
60. Lovejoy 1970.
61. See detailed descriptions of major finds in Day 1965; Brace, Nelson and Korn 1971. The first Javanese *Homo erectus* to be discovered was the Trinil calotte, found by the Dutchman Eugene Dubois in 1890. He regarded it at first as a form of chimpanzee, and then with the discovery of a femur at Trinil in 1892 he decided that the fossils belonged to a human ancestor, which he named *Pithecanthropus erectus*. For the most recent Javanese finds, see Jacob 1967a, 1967b; 1972c; Sartono 1972.
62. Bergman and Karsten 1962.
63. Day and Molleson 1973.
64. Simons and Ettel 1970.
65. Weidenreich 1946. Weidenreich wished to rename the fossil *Gigantanthropus*.
66. Woo 1966; Aigner and Laughlin 1973.
67. Hughes 1967.
68. From Le Gros Clark 1964: 105, but estimates of cranial capacity from skull fragments may vary markedly.
69. Although Coon (1962: 456) mentions several features of the Chou-k'ou-tien femora which are outside the modern range of variation.
70. Hsu 1966. See also Kurten and Vasari (1960), who placed the remains in the Mindel glaciation.
71. Oakley 1969: 301. Chang 1968: 50 (footnote 31) reports a Russian uranium—thorium date for Peking Man of 210,000–500,000+ years B.P.
72. Von Koenigswald in Weidenreich 1951 (Introduction).
73. Jacob 1967c: 39. However, Jacob (1974) has more recently classified Solo man as a *Pithecanthropus* on morphological grounds, and a much greater antiquity may be likely (as I suggest in the following text).
74. Von Koenigswald in Weidenreich 1975 (Introduction). See also Jacob 1972b.
75. Coon 1962: 390–99.
76. As suggested by Birdsell 1972: 319.
77. Birdsell 1972: 281.
78. Hughes 1967: 2.
79. Coon 1966: 234.
80. Coon 1966: 219; Brace 1964.
81. Hughes 1967: 3.
82. Weidenreich 1946: 84.
83. Coon 1962: Chapter 10.
84. Woo 1958. See also Chang 1962a: 752–4. There is a C14 date for the Tzu-yang site of 5500 B.C. (Barnard 1973: date ZK-19), but it is not known how this relates to the date of the skull. For a general description of South Chinese hominid material see Aigner 1973.
85. Hughes 1967: 7. Chang 1962 also gives mild support to this view.
86. Hiernaux in Montagu 1964: 42.
87. Jacob 1967c: 51.
88. Brothwell 1960.
89. Bowler *et al.* 1970; Bowler, Thorne and Polach 1972.
90. Thorne 1971b; Thorne and Macumber 1972.
91. A. Gallus (1970) has claimed a *Homo erectus* population in Australia at *c.* 100,000 years ago, which evolved into the earliest *Homo sapiens* population in the world, but this view has so far met with little acceptance.
92. Birdsell 1967; Thorne 1971a; Howells 1973a; Chapter 6.
93. e.g. Saurin 1951; von Koenigswald 1952. But see also Hooijer 1950b, 1952 for a different viewpoint. Barth (1952) postulated large-scale migrations of southern Mongoloids from China into Southeast Asia with wet rice cultivation, a little before 500 B.C. Present evidence does not support this, although the hypothesis has recently been stated in more detail by Marschall (1968; 1974).
94. Coon 1962: 416.
95. Pelliot 1903: 254.
96. Mansuy et Colani 1925; Mansuy 1931; Duy and Quyen 1966; Saurin 1971: 31; Patte 1965. A child's skull from a Neolithic site at Minh-Cam has been identified as Negrito by Patte (1925).
97. Sangvichien, Sirigaroon, Jorgensen and Jacob 1969.
98. Tweedie 1953: 16–18; Trevor and Brothwell 1962; Jacob 1967c.
99. Sangvichien, Sirigaroon, Jorgensen and Jacob 1969 (Ban Kao site).
100. Von Koenigswald 1958a; Harrisson 1959; 1976; B. Harrisson 1967.
101. Jacob 1967c.
102. Fox 1970: 40–1.
103. Macintosh 1972: L.
104. Fox 1970: 60.
105. Winters 1974. In addition to the material listed, the skeletal remains from the Neolithic urn cemetery at Melolo on Sumba Island are claimed to have both Australoid and Mongoloid characters (Snell 1948).
106. A braincase from Aitape, Sepik District of New Guinea, has a very archaic Solo-like appearance, but carbon dates suggest that it may be only 5000 years old (Hossfeld 1964).
107. Howells 1943. This is a historical reference and does not reflect Howells' present views, which are basically similar to my own (see Howells 1973a).
108. Birdsell 1949.
109. Swindler 1962: 48–9.
110. Sullivan 1924.
111. Shapiro 1943.
112. Pietrusewsky 1970; 1971.
113. Coon 1966: 184.

CHAPTER 3

Cultural Foundations

Recent discoveries on the African continent have revolutionised knowledge of human physical and cultural evolution, and Southeast Asia and China, which dominated the field of fossil man studies prior to the Second World War, have since tended to occupy a back-seat position. This may not mean, however, that the area was an isolated cul-de-sac throughout the Pleistocene period, and the slowing up of the rate of discovery may be more a reflection of present political situations in the area than of the absence of further potential. While fossil remains from Java and China have been found in considerable numbers, they are still rather poorly dated, and only rarely associated directly with stone-tool assemblages. As we have seen in chapter 2, hominids have probably inhabited Southeast Asia for at least 1.5 million years, and there are stone-tool industries there which date from at least 700,000 years ago. With future discoveries these dates might well be pushed back to relate more closely with those of Africa, where the genus *Homo* has been established on a tool-making evolutionary course for some 2 million years.

The stone-tool industries described in the first parts of this chapter belong to the Pleistocene epoch of geological time, while those which post-date 10,000 years before present (B.P.) belong in the Holocene epoch. These two terms defy rigorous stratigraphic or faunal definition in Southeast Asia, and my use of them is necessarily generalised, as I will explain.

The boundary between the Pleistocene and the preceding Pliocene epoch has not been defined and dated with any degree of finality, although there is now a tendency to place it at about 2–3 million years ago, when new cold-water molluscan faunas appear in the oceans[1]. The Pleistocene is no longer defined simply as a period of glaciation, because glaciations are known to have occurred for several million years before it. However, a quickening of the tempo of glacial advance and retreat does seem to have occurred within the past one million years[2]. As far as Southeast Asia is concerned, the Pleistocene is poorly defined in the absence of widespread glacial deposits, and from the point of view of the fossils and stone-tool industries found in the area, the most important method of relative dating involves analysis of mammalian faunas.

The faunas of the Eurasian Pleistocene develop from a suite known as the Villafranchian, which begins with the appearance of elephants, cattle and true one-toed horses before three million years ago[3]. The Villafranchian in fact spans the Upper Pliocene and Lower Pleistocene epochs, and lasts down to about one million years ago. In Northern Eurasia, the succeeding Middle Pleistocene faunas appear with extensive lowland glaciation from about one million years go, and many of the resulting arctic genera continue into the Upper Pleistocene, which may date from about 150,000 years ago until the extinctions at the end of the last glaciation, some 10,000 years ago. In Indonesia, faunal divisions which correspond to the Villafranchian, and the Middle and Upper Pleistocene are recognised, but here the dates are little removed from guesswork. Furthermore, Indonesia may have developed a fully modern fauna by at least 30,000 years ago, so that there are really no faunal criteria which can be used to pinpoint the Pleistocene-Holocene boundary. This is taken as 10,000 B.P. in this chapter, simply for convenience.

I will return to the Southeast Asian faunal divisions below, but this introductory section cannot close without reference to an important world-wide result of glaciation. Because glaciers trapped and immobilised such enormous amounts of water during their peaks of expansion, world sea-levels dropped and shallow coastal shelves, such as the great Sunda shelf of Southeast Asia (figure 2.9), were exposed as dry land. At glacial maxima the seas may have been between 100 and 140 metres below present level[4], and as there have been many such maxima over the past million years the opportunities for land-bridging are clearly very great. Such depths were probably reached at the last glacial peak about 16,000–18,000 years ago, and at this time the area of dry land on the Sunda shelf may have been more than doubled. Between 14,000 and 8000 years ago the seas rose gradually, and may have even exceeded the present level between 5000 and 8000 years ago[5], although the evidence for this is disputed. Nevertheless, marine shell middens which probably date to this period in North Vietnam and Sumatra are now well inland[6], and there is evidence for a warm spell which may possibly be correlated with higher mid-Holocene sea-levels from Taiwan[7].

THE PLEISTOCENE EPOCH IN SOUTHEAST ASIA

Because Southeast Asia lies within the tropics it was only subjected to glaciation in the high mountains of Borneo and New Guinea. However, the effects of continental glaciations far away are not to be minimised, for as well as the great fluctuations in sea-level, the average annual temperatures, even in tropical lowlands, may have dropped by up to 8°C below present averages. Because of this, archaeologists in the past have attempted to correlate the relatively well-known Pleistocene sequence of Java with the four glacial periods once recorded in the Himalayas[8], although recent re-analyses of the Pleistocene resulting from the introduction of radiometric dating reveal this approach as rather uncertain[9], and here we will be concerned chronologically with mainly the faunal sequence and the handful of potassium-argon dates. Glacial correlations for Malaya and central China seem to be more reliable, but Java itself is a geologically unstable island of late Pliocene and early Pleistocene origin, and its stratigraphy can best be correlated with mainland Asia by means of faunal links.

The history of man and other mammals in the Southeast Asian area is closely linked with the alternating submergence and emergence of the continental Sunda and Sahul shelves. In the case of the Sunda shelf, emergence meant that a vast area of Indonesia was physically attached to the mainland of Southeast Asia, and the area was probably laid open for human settlement several times during the Pleistocene. Between Borneo, Java and Sumatra the branching channels of two major river systems survive to depths of up to 130 metres below sea-level[10] – eloquent testimony of a vast drowned sub-continent which was once bigger then the sub-continent of India. In the case of the Sahul shelf, there is no sign of man until about 35–40,000 years ago, so here we are only concerned with emergence during the last Pleistocene glaciation.

The rich and varied mammalian faunas of Sundaland are related closely to those of the Southeast Asian mainland, although the recent millennia of separation have ensured that variations now occur from island to island. Bali and Palawan have the most impoverished faunas, as both lie at the eastern limit of Sundaland against the Wallace Line[11]. This line is one of the world's most famous biogeographical divides, which runs through the Straits of Lombok, north through the Straits of Makassar, on between Palawan and the central Philippines, and between Taiwan and Luzon (see figure 2.9). It is thought to have traced a continuous sea-gap throughout most of the Pleistocene, and if this is the case then it would have formed a considerable barrier to animals which were unable to swim even short distances, and also to man until the time that he first began to use rafts.

The Wallace Line forms the western boundary of the faunal zone of Wallacea, which comprises Sulawesi, Maluku and Nusatenggara. In this zone, the placental mammal fauna of Southeast Asia diminishes as one moves eastwards, while the marsupial fauna of Australasia comes into its own in New Guinea. Only one marsupial genus, *Phalanger* (the cuscus), reached beyond New Guinea to as far west as Sulawesi in pre-human times, and this may have been introduced into some islands, such as Timor, by man. Sulawesi had a highly endemic Pleistocene fauna which included small elephants, two genera of the elephant-like *Stegodon*, pigs and a small bovine, and most of these forms would appear to have reached the island from Sundaland during the Pliocene or Lower to Middle Pleistocene, possibly by land-bridges. The stegodonts are particularly interesting in this respect, since Flores and Timor also have two genera closely related to those on Sulawesi. Because of this, Audley-Charles and Hooijer[12] have recently suggested that Java, Sulawesi, Flores and Timor were linked by land-bridges in the Upper Pliocene or Lower Pleistocene, and if this is so then it naturally reduces the importance of the Wallace Line and makes the presence of *Homo erectus* in eastern Indonesia a distinct possibility.

As far as the islands of Maluku are concerned, the faunas here were probably derived by island hopping from Sulawesi and New Guinea. No land-bridge ever traversed the whole of Wallacea during the Cenozoic period, and the only placental mammals to reach Australia and New Guinea without the aid of man were the bats and the rodents.

To the north of Wallacea, the Philippine fauna combines a restricted range of species from both Borneo and southern China[13]. The Philippines (excluding Palawan) are surrounded by deep water channels which must have undergone tectonic subsidence if ever they were bridged, and it seems quite likely that they have been cut off through most of the Pleistocene, but not so cut off that large animals, such as elephants, rhinoceros and deer were unable to reach them. With both the Philippines and Sulawesi, there is no solid evidence that man arrived before 40,000 years ago, although future research may change this situation drastically. Another problem case is Taiwan, which was probably joined more than once to the Asian mainland during the Pleistocene, but from which there is so far no evidence of Pleistocene human settlement at all.

Having reviewed some of the biogeographical problems of Southeast Asia, we must now turn to Java for the first actual evidence of man. Central Java has a five stage faunal sequence[14] which runs from some point in the Pliocene right through the Pleistocene (figure 3.1), and the earliest *Homo erectus* fossils are found with the Jetis fauna, which contains some existing genera (20% or more of the total) such as orang-utan, gibbon, tiger, panther and water buffalo, as well as a majority of extinct genera (e.g. *Stegodon*). Since an intermediate stage of this fauna has recently been dated to almost two million years ago[15], it would appear to span the Upper Pliocene and Lower Pleistocene epochs[16], and may thus correlate with the later part of the Villafranchian fauna of Eurasia. No stone-tool industries have

been found with the Jetis fauna, but the associated human fossils are described in chapter 2.

INDUSTRIES OF THE MIDDLE PLEISTOCENE

The Trinil fauna, which succeeds the Jetis, is agreed by all authorities to be of Middle Pleistocene date, and it has yielded the majority of the Javanese *Homo erectus* fossils. The fauna itself contains a higher proportion (up to 50%) of modern forms than the Jetis, and both contain elements such as *Stegodon* and *Ailuropoda* (a giant panda) which link them closely with contem-

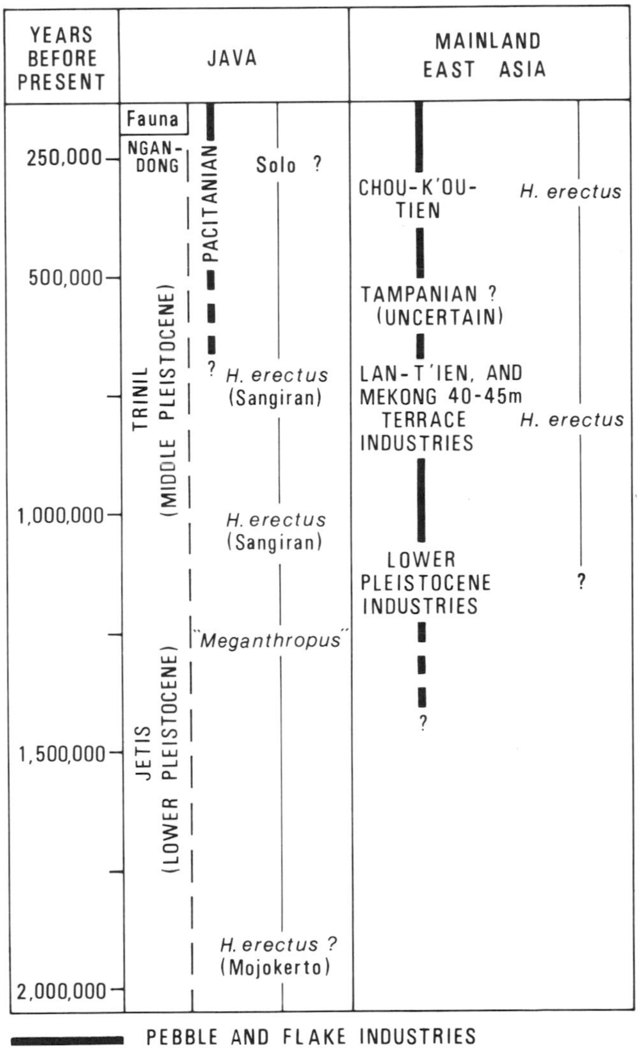

YEARS BEFORE PRESENT	JAVA		MAINLAND EAST ASIA	
250,000	Fauna NGAN-DONG	PACITANIAN — Solo ?	CHOU-K'OU-TIEN	H. erectus
500,000	TRINIL (MIDDLE PLEISTOCENE)	? H. erectus (Sangiran)	TAMPANIAN ? (UNCERTAIN) LAN-T'IEN, AND MEKONG 40-45m TERRACE INDUSTRIES	H. erectus
1,000,000		H. erectus (Sangiran)	LOWER PLEISTOCENE INDUSTRIES	?
1,500,000	JETIS (LOWER PLEISTOCENE)	"Meganthropus"	?	
2,000,000		H. erectus ? (Mojokerto)		

▬▬▬ PEBBLE AND FLAKE INDUSTRIES

Fig. 3.1. A tentative scheme for Pleistocene men and stone-tool industries in Southeast Asia.

porary faunas in southern China. Potassium argon dates would seem to place the Jetis-Trinil boundary at about one million years ago, and the Trinil fauna was still in occupation of Java at 500,000 years ago[17], although it is not clear at what date it gives way to the succeeding Upper Pleistocene Ngandong fauna.

None of the Javanese *Homo erectus* fossils have been found in direct association with stone tools, which is a little unfortunate as it makes it more difficult to date the latter. The earliest well-authenticated Pleistocene tools come from river gravels and terraces in the Baksoka, Serikan, Sunglon and Gedeh river systems of south-central Java, and belong to an industry termed the Pacitanian[18], which on faunal grounds may be referred to the late Middle and early Upper Pleistocene[19].

Unfortunately, neither the Pacitanian nor any of the other Palaeolithic industries to be described have been analysed by rigorous statistical methods, and the full assemblage has never been described in detail. The typology introduced by Movius in 1944 has not been satisfactorily replaced, even though Movius himself took care to point out its subjectivity. The major diagnostic tool types (see figure 3.2) are made on pebbles, more rarely on flakes, and may be described as follows:

Chopper – a large unifacially flaked pebble or flake tool, with a rounded or almost straight cutting edge.
Chopping tool – a bifacially flaked version of the chopper, usually made on a pebble.
Hand-adze – a tabular, unifacially flaked, adze-like tool.
Proto-hand-axe – a unifacially flaked oval or pointed tool, made on a pebble or flake.
Hand-axe – a more developed form of the proto-hand-axe with bifacial flaking.

In 1936, a total of 2,419 artefacts, mostly of silicified tuff, were collected from the gravels of the Baksoka River at Pacitan[20]. Over 50% of these were flakes, some of very large size, and some with the elongated proportions of blades. An unknown but quite large number of the flakes indicated preparation prior to removal from the core, although the technique is not as advanced as in the Levalloisian of Middle Pleistocene times in Europe and Africa. Of the remaining tools, mostly made on pebbles, all the above types described by Movius are present, with choppers being the most common at 18% of the total

assemblage. However, the hand-axes, at 6% of the total, are perhaps the most interesting tool type, and were thought originally by Movius to represent an independent and localised Javanese line of development on the basis of their manufacture by longitudinal flaking and because of their absence on the East Asian mainland. The hand-axes of the Chellean and Acheulean industries of Europe and Africa are mainly flaked transversely[21] to their long axes, and Movius attempted to separate the hand-axe industries of the West from the chopper-chopping tool industries of the East as two fundamental and separate Palaeolithic technological divisions. Although recent discoveries of hand-axes on the Southeast Asian mainland make any kind of permanent dividing line rather unlikely, Movius' concept of East-West relative isolation in the Middle Pleistocene still holds true today.

The Pacitanian is perhaps the best known member of a widespread East Asian pebble and flake tool technocomplex of Middle Pleistocene date, and it does have a crude appearance when compared with some of the hand-axe industries of the West. This crudity may be a little deceptive, for dwellers in the eastern tropics may of course have had a large and efficient wooden tool kit

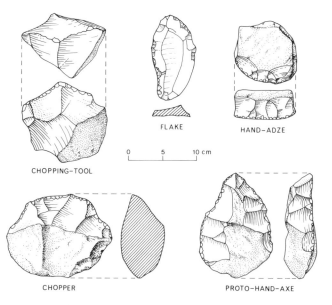

Fig. 3.2. Stone tools of Pacitanian type, after Movius 1944 (a,c,d,e), Glover and Glover 1970 (b).

which has not survived. It may therefore be unreasonable to suggest that *Homo erectus* in the East was at a more retarded stage of development than his western relatives, but since the archaeological record may never extend beyond stone tools, such problems may never be resolved.

Elsewhere in Southeast Asia the Middle Pleistocene stone-tool record is now quite extensive. Tools which belong typologically to the same tradition as the Pacitanian are reported across the Wallace line in Flores and Timor, in both cases in claimed association with the extinct small elephant genus *Stegodon*, which makes a Pleistocene date almost certain[22]. However, the finds are not closely dated, and *Stegodon* could have survived late in the isolation of eastern Nusatenggara, so that there is still no firm evidence that man crossed the Wallace line prior to about 40,000 years ago.

Problems similar to those of Flores and Timor are presented by the island of Luzon in the Philippines, where an industry of flake and pebble tools has been reported from sites in the Cagayan Valley in the north of the island[23]. The tools have been found eroding from the Awiden Mesa formation, which appears to be of Middle Pleistocene date, and they are associated with a fossil fauna which includes *Elephas* and *Stegodon*, together with rhinoceros, bovines, giant tortoise, crocodile, pig and deer. Ninety-three percent of the tools from surface collections are flakes, and high proportions of these – up to forty percent in one instance – are reported as retouched. The remaining tools are made on pebbles or larger cobbles, and are unifacially flaked. Pointed forms like the 'proto-hand-axes' of the Pacitanian are common, but there are also a number of the so-called 'horsehoof cores' which are so characteristic of the earliest industries of Australia, from about 40,000 years ago. Some restricted excavations have recently been carried out in the Cagayan Valley, and stone tools are claimed in association with a fossil elephant tusk at one site. There might in fact be a possibility that the Cagayan Valley contains big-game kill sites of at least Middle or Late Pleistocene date, although the work is still in progress, and from the preliminary reports at present available it would be unwise to be too optimistic. It would not cause great surprise to find man in the Philippines in Middle Pleistocene times, but evidence for a definite conclusion has not yet been published.

Passing on to mainland industries of Pacitanian type, we may begin with the now problematical Tampanian industry[24], which consists of tools recovered from a terrace of the Perak River in north-western Malaya. The excavator of this site uses a slightly different terminology from Movius, but again the industry is made mostly on pebbles and flakes, of quartzite in this instance. Secondary retouch along working edges is found on some of the smaller flake tools, and a few bifacial hand-axes are reported by Movius. The Tampanian industry may be slightly earlier than the Pacitanian on typological grounds, but Harrisson[25] has recently cast grave doubt on its attribution to the Middle Pleistocene, and suggests that it could in fact be less than 40,000 years old, and thus contemporary with the mainland Hoabinhian industries to be described below. Harrisson's evidence does indeed seem quite convincing in this regard, so the Tampanian could be holding a position of false importance.

Elsewhere on the mainland, the past decade has seen widespread and important discoveries. Recent discoveries in North and South Vietnam and Cambodia have filled in the gap in Middle Pleistocene industries which formerly existed between Malaya and northern China. From Nui-Do, near Thanh-Hoa in North Vietnam, an industry in basalt consisting almost entirely of flakes (95% of artefacts described) has been recovered from surface contexts, unfortunately not associated with faunal remains. Four percent of the flakes have secondary retouch, and hand-axes (2 only), choppers, chopping tools and cleavers total only about 30 of the 810 tools described so far[26]. Boriskovsky claims that the industry has Chellean affinities, and that it predates the Pacitanian on typological grounds, but my own feelings would suggest placing the Nui-Do material in the suspense account until further evidence is available.

In eastern Cambodia, along a stretch of the Mekong River north-east of Phnom Penh, Palaeolithic tools have been recovered from three successive Mekong terraces[27]. From the highest and earliest terrace at 40–45 metres above the present river level, tools of quartz, quartzite, rhyolite and silicified wood have been found, mostly made on pebbles and flakes and with unifacial cutting edges. Bifacially flaked cutting edges of the chopping tool type are very rare, and Saurin suggests similarities with the Tampanian of Malaya and with the African pebble tool industries such as the Oldowan. No faunal remains are reported from these terraces, but Saurin adopts a second glaciation (i.e. early

Middle Pleistocene) correlation for the 40–45 metre terrace, making the industry possibly earlier than the Pacitanian. The 40–45 metre terrace also contains tektites – small glass meteorites of deformed spherical shape, possibly of lunar origin – which appear to belong to a shower which struck Australia and Southeast Asia some 600,000 to 700,000 years ago, on the basis of potassium-argon and fission track age determinations[28]. Saurin thinks these Mekong tektite specimens are *in situ*, and if so, then the 40 metre terrace industry is the first Middle Pleistocene industry in Southeast Asia to be given an approximate absolute date[29]. Tektites also occur in the Trinil faunal zone of Java, approximately contemporary with the later fossils of *Homo erectus*, although the correlation here is not so clear.

A few tools have also been found in the lower and later Mekong terraces, at 20 and 25 metres, but these show little advancement over the earlier ones, despite a possible Upper Pleistocene date. On a 35–40 metre terrace at Nhan-Gia about 60 kilometres east-north-east of Saigon in South Vietnam, Saurin[30] has found a pebble-tool industry which is geologically contemporary with that of the 40–45 metre Mekong terrace. This industry is particularly interesting because it contains crude bifacial hand-axes which Saurin states to be connected with the Acheulean hand-axe industries of India. Since he also illustrates hand-axes from two other undated sites in South Vietnam and Laos[31], it is becoming clear that the old concepts of East Asian isolation may have to be modified a little, as noted above for the Pacitanian. Other scattered reports from the Southeast Asian mainland indicate the finding of a possible Middle Pleistocene bone industry in Cambodia[32], and many years ago a Pleistocene industry with remains of *Homo erectus* was reported from the Tam Hang caves in north-eastern Laos, although Movius disputes the authenticity of the latter[33].

Further indications of the achievements of *Homo erectus* in eastern Asia come from central China. A report of stone tools from Lower Pleistocene deposits at Hsi-hou-tu in southern Shansi suggests the existence of a site earlier than any other so far found in eastern Asia, and Middle Pleistocene industries are known from Lan-t'ien in east-central Shensi, from K'o-ho in south-western Shansi, and of course from the famous fissure deposits of Chou-k'ou-tien some 42 kilometres south-west of Peking[34]. At Chou-k'ou-tien locality 1 – a large collapsed cave with over 50 metres of deposits – enormous numbers of unutilized flakes have been recovered indicating that tool-making was carried out on the spot, commonly by means of the 'bipolar' technique, which involves striking a core with a hammerstone against a stone anvil, so that the resulting flake has a bulb of percussion at either end. The tools themselves are made on pebbles and flakes like those from Southeast Asia and Java, but bifacial hand-axes are not reported. Apart from the tools, however, Peking man was able to produce fire, and he seem to have been a very competent hunter. Some 70% of the animal bones recovered were of two species of deer – *Euryceros pachyostus* and *Pseudaxis grayi*, and, in addition, bones of leopard, cave bear, sabre-tooth, hyaena, elephant, rhinoceros, boar, horse, roebuck, antelope, sheep and musk-ox have been found in the deposits, although one cannot be certain that all these species were hunted by man, as some were clearly extremely dangerous. It is always possible that animals made lairs in the cave when man was not in occupance. Seeds of hackberry (*Celtis barbouri*) were eaten, and redbud (*Cercis blackii*) timber was used as firewood.

To summarise these east Asian industries, it is firstly very possible that those of genuinely Middle Pleistocene antiquity are the handiwork of *Homo erectus*, although only at Chou-k'ou-tien is the correlation conclusive. Otherwise, the Southeast Asian assemblages have particularly shaky contexts and some of them, especially the Tampanian (and perhaps the Pacitanian), now seem to be of Upper rather than Middle Pleistocene date, although I have retained them in this section in the absence of certainty. In general, the industries comprise pebbles and flakes for the most part, mostly flaked unifacially and only rarely showing signs of secondary retouch. The whole area east of the Himalayas was not closely connected with the Acheulean and Levalloisian developments of the west[35], but whether one can interpret this isolation to mean 'backwardness' is not at all clear. To date, the only evidence fuller than that from a collection of poorly stratified stone tools comes from Chou-k'ou-tien, and even here excavations were commenced at a time when archaeological techniques were not what they are today.

THE UPPER PLEISTOCENE PERIOD
  (*c.* 150,000 to 10,000 years ago)

During this period, a rather confused picture

extends down to *c.* 40,000 years ago, after which radiocarbon-dated sites provide a certain kind of clarity. In northern China and Japan stone-tool industries develop under the evident influence of the Mousterian and Aurignacian technocomplexes of northern Eurasia, but developments of this kind appear to be restricted to north of the Tsinling Mountains. In southern China, reference has been made (in chapter 2) to the Upper Pleistocene skull from Liu-chiang, Kwangsi, which may represent an early population of *Homo sapiens sapiens* with some Mongoloid characteristics. In addition, a skullcap found at Ma-pa in Kwangtung may be of late Middle Pleistocene date and of similar grade to Solo Man in Java. Several sites in southern China have flake industries of Upper Pleistocene date[36], and these seem to lack the heavy core-tool elements present in earlier sites in Southeast Asia, but otherwise on the Southeast Asian mainland the period appears to be very much a blank until evidence for the Hoabinhian technocomplex begins to appear after 12,000 B.C. This is described separately later in the chapter.

The most important Upper Pleistocene discoveries made to date come from Island Southeast Asia. The skulls of Solo Man found at Ngandong (page 42) were unfortunately not found in direct association with any artefacts, but nearby surface collections include stone flakes and two worked antlers of the extinct deer *Axis lydekkeri*[37].

Another possibly Upper Pleistocene industry has been found at Sangiran in central Java, and this consists of small flakes made of chalcedony and jasper. The forms are described as scrapers, points and borers[38], and there are also some fairly crude parallel-sided blades which may have been produced fortuitously, rather than by any specialised method of core preparation. Further to the east, similar industries have been found with bones of *Stegodon* at Mengeruda in western Flores[39], and from the 50 metre terrace of the Wallanae River at Cabenge in south-western Sulawesi[40]. The two latter sites have also produced pebble tools, and the whole group may represent an unbroken development from the Indonesian Middle Pleistocene industries. At present all are only weakly dated, but an Upper Pleistocene correlation seems to be generally agreed.

In the Philippines, flake tools like those from Cabenge and Sangiran have been found in what appear to be Late Pleistocene deposits in Rizal Province near Manila on Luzon, and also near Davao in Mindanao, while 'hand-axes' are reported from Batangas Province in south-central Luzon[41]. However, the vital dimension of time is on very weak ground in all these instances, and this is one reason why the recent discoveries in Tabon Cave on Palawan and in Niah Cave in Sarawak are of such fundamental importance, because both have carbon-dated sequences extending back for about 40,000 years.

The huge 10.5 hectare Great Cave at Niah is situated in a limestone hill about 16 km inland from the sea, and excavations were undertaken here between 1954 and 1967 under the direction of Tom Harrisson[42]. Stone tools have been recovered to a depth of about 3 metres, but bone and shell remains disappear below 2.5 metres owing to solution. The animal bones found with the tools belong to the lowland evergreen rainforest fauna of modern Southeast Asia, the only extinct member being a giant pangolin, *Manis palaeojavanica*, which was found only in the lower levels prior to *c.* 30,000 years ago[43]. Species present from the earliest levels include orang-utan, pangolin, porcupine, wild cat, tiger, tapir, pig, larger mouse deer, and cattle[44]. It has been estimated that the climate at Niah was cooler and seasonally drier during the last glacial maximum than at present[45], but it is by no means clear if such climatic fluctuations had great impact on the regional fauna. What is clear, and of extreme importance, is that a modern fauna was fully established at Niah by 30,000 years ago.

If we can assume that the animal remains left in the cave are representative of the meat diet of its inhabitants, then it seems that pigs, monkeys and orang-utan were the most popular prey. Cattle, deer and rhinoceros were less common, and even crocodiles added an additional spicy element to the diet. There is no evidence for the dog until the Neolithic period, approximately after 2500 B.C.[46], and the complete absence of this animal until Neolithic times in Southeast Asia suggests purposeful introduction by man. Apart from the mammals, the ancient Niah Cave dwellers also consumed fair quantities of fish, birds, reptiles and shellfish. The indication is that these early hunters caught and ate everything that they could lay their hands on, and this type of exploitation may characterise the whole span of pre-Neolithic cultural evolution in the eastern tropics. Why should man specialise amidst such variety?

The radiocarbon-dated sequence of industries for Niah is given in the following table, which is taken from one of Harrisson's recent reports[47].

Artefact categories	*Approximate date of first appearance*
Small waste flakes showing few signs of utilisation. Skull of modern form (see figure 2.14).	Prior to 40,000 B.C.
Unifacially flaked pebble choppers, with at least one bifacial chopping-tool, and large flakes without retouch. Bone points and 'spatulae' also reported.	*c.* 40,000 B.C.
Quartzite flakes without retouch, and large numbers of bone points, awls and spatulae present. Pebble choppers not reported.	*c.* 30,000 B.C.
Flexed, seated and fragmentary burials.	*c.* 15,000 B.C.
Edge-ground axes and adzes made on flattened pebbles, retouched flake tools.	*c.* 13,000 – 10,000 B.C.
Polished adzes of lenticular or rounded cross-section.	*c.* 6,000 – 4,000 B.C.[48]
Quadrangular adzes, pottery, mats, nets, 'Mongoloid' dentitions, and extended burials, some in wooden coffins.	*c.* 2,500 B.C.
Copper and bronze artefacts.	*c.* 250 B.C.
Iron artefacts, Chinese ceramics, glass beads.	*c.* A.D. 700

The absence of pebble tools after *c.* 30,000 years ago is of interest, because this trend is very different from that of contemporary Hoabinhian sites on the Southeast Asian mainland, where core and pebble tools continue in importance. An apparent dominance of flake tools is evident right through Indonesia and the Philippines after 30–40,000 years ago, and perhaps one can see the hand of the now present *Homo sapiens sapiens* behind these developments, although one would then have to explain why they are mainly restricted to island areas. Concerning the appearance of modern man, we may remember that Niah has the earliest modern skull found so far from Southeast Asia, with a suggested date of 40,000 years.

Apart from this isolated skull, an important sequence of human burials at Niah begins stratigraphically some time after 20,000 B.C., and consists of two main groups; flexed, seated, and some fragmentary burials without ceramic associations spanning the period *c.* 15,000 to 4,000 B.C.; and extended burials, cremations and 'burnt burials' spanning the full Neolithic period, mostly dating from *c.* 1200 B.C. to 0.[49] The Neolithic burials will be described later. The preceramic burials were in some cases sprinkled with haematite powder or partially burnt prior to burial, although there are no full cremations, and most skeletons remain articulated. No burial pits were observed in the stratification, but one burial had an associated edge-ground pebble, and another tightly-flexed example had a rhinoceros femur 'pillow' beneath its head. Twenty-two complete burials belong to the preceramic period, of which 18 were in flexed and four in seated positions with heels folded under buttocks. There is also a degree of circumstantial evidence for cannibalism and human sacrifice.

Finally, after about 13,000 B.C., we see the consecutive appearance of four types of artefact of considerable importance – the edge-ground pebble axe or adze, the fully polished axes and adzes of lenticular and quadrangular cross-section, and pottery. The significance of these innovations will later be evident.

The other cave with a sequence rivalling that of Niah is Tabon Cave, situated in a limestone massif on the western coast of Palawan Island in the Philippines. This cave is much smaller than Niah, and has a succession of stone-tool industries spanning the period from about 30,000 to 9000 years ago[50]. The cave today is close to the sea but during the whole period of occupation the sea was at lower levels, being perhaps as much as 35 kilometres away during glacial maxima. No shellfish or fish bones are reported from the excavations at all.

In the most recent report on the site, the chief excavator Robert Fox[51] refers to five successive flake assemblages which are separated stratigraphically but which nevertheless show definite similarities. Only one assemblage, of 337 pieces of chert dated to about 23,000 years ago (figure 3.3), has been described statistically, and Fox's table is reproduced below. The frontal portion of a human skull which is probably associated with the assemblage is described in chapter 2.

Artefact categories	*Percentages of total*
Unaltered lumps of chert	2
Cores – apparently unutilised	22
Waste flakes from manufacture	53
Primary flakes (defined as potential tools showing no signs of use)	6
Flake tools (without retouch but with edge-wear)	16
Flake tools with secondary retouch	1
	100%

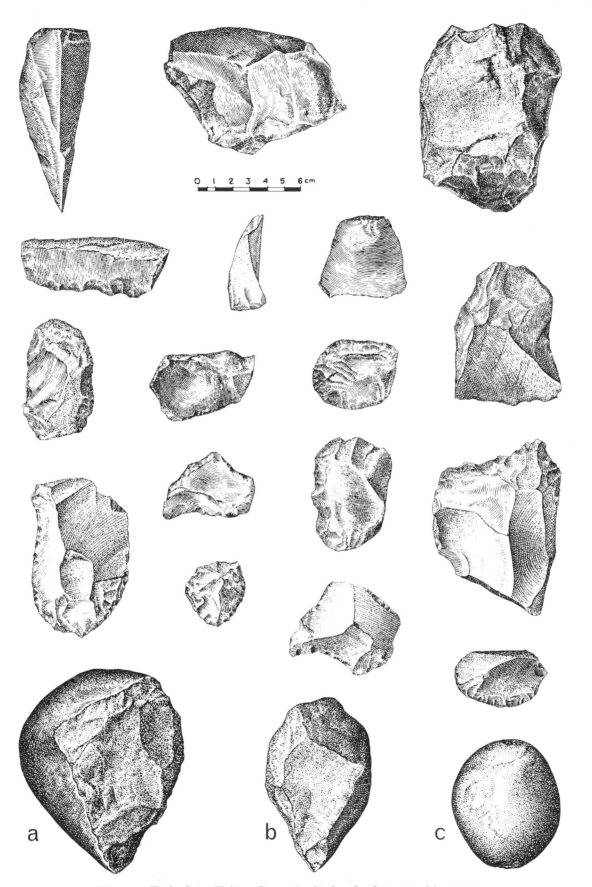

Fig. 3.3. Tools from Tabon Cave: (a, b) basalt choppers; (c) quartz hammerstone; *top and middle*, chert flakes from an assemblage dated to *c.* 23,000 B.P. From Fox 1970.

From the presence of cores and waste flakes it is clear that some manufacture took place in the cave. The cores, however, were not prepared according to a regular pattern prior to flake removal, and in this sense, together with the absence of true blades and the rarity of secondary retouch, the Tabon assemblages differ little in a basic technological sense from the other Upper Pleistocene assemblages of Island Southeast Asia. The proportions given are for chert tools only, and unifacial basalt choppers are illustrated in Fox's report, but are of very rare occurrence.

No bone tools were found at all in Tabon Cave, although animal bones occur at all levels, mainly of small game such as birds and bats, together with pig and a species of deer which is extinct on Palawan today. The large mammalian fauna described for Niah is absent, but may never have been present on Palawan to any degree in the Pleistocene owing to relative isolation.

The four main Upper Pleistocene assemblages from Island Southeast Asia examined so far – Sangiran, Cabenge, Niah and Tabon – appear to share a preference for the use of flakes, rather than cores or pebbles, for tools. The flakes are rarely removed from carefully prepared cores, and so only on rare occasions, and then perhaps fortuitously, do true parallel-sided blades occur. Secondary retouch is rare, partially because the flakes themselves tend to be much smaller than those, for example, from the Middle Pleistocene industries, and were perhaps designed for use immediately after removal from the core. At present, there is no outstanding evidence to suggest strong outside influences bringing technological innovations into the area of the Philippines or Indonesia generally,

at least not prior to *c.* 10,000 years ago. There is nothing inherently impossible about deriving these flake industries directly from earlier forms such as the Pacitanian, although this can only remain a hypothesis at the moment. Certainly, however, they share few resemblances with the contemporary blade and microlithic industries of northern China and Japan, although the possibility of southern Chinese parallels seems much stronger.

Before we examine the early Holocene developments of Mainland and Island Southeast Asia, two very important events placed firmly in the Upper Pleistocene must now be considered – the settlements of Australia and New Guinea.

AUSTRALIA

Australian prehistory is not a direct concern of this book, but certain aspects demand consideration because Australia and New Guinea were joined as a single land-mass several times during the late Pleistocene, until the shallow Torres Straits were finally drowned between possibly 6500 and 8000 years ago. Australia in fact has the earliest dated evidence for the human crossing of Wallacea. Exactly which route man followed to the new continent may never be known, but certainly at periods of low sea-level routes through either Sulawesi and Seram to New Guinea, or along the Nusatenggara chain to Timor and Australia would be feasible. The earliest dated site in Australia so far is the cremation deposit from Lake Mungo in New South Wales, which may be as early as 32,000 years old (see chapter 2), and the earliest stone tools from Mungo may

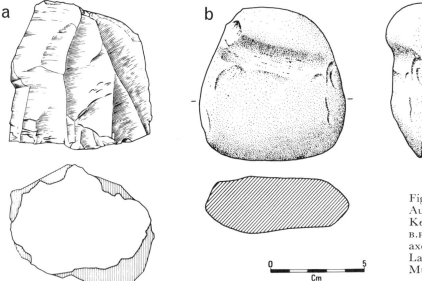

Fig. 3.4. Pleistocene tools from Australia: (a) horsehoof core from Kenniff Cave, Queensland, *c.* 10,000 B.P.; (b) grooved and edge-ground axe from Malangangerr, Arnhem Land, *c.* 23,000–19,000 B.P. From Mulvaney 1975.

be as much as 40,000 years old. There are now a number of sites in Australia which date from prior to 20,000 years ago[52], and, although there are regional variations, these sites have yielded industries for the most part based on unifacially or bifacially flaked pebbles, high-domed retouched cores with edge-angles approximating 90 degrees ('horsehoof' cores) which may have served as heavy scrapers, and a wide variety of flake tools, frequently retouched, and generally classified as 'scrapers'. Jones calls this industry, which dominated mainland Australia until some 5000 years ago and dominated Tasmania until European contact, the 'Australian core tool and scraper tradition'[53]. Australian prehistorians have not yet localised any point of origin for these industries in Southeast Asia, and perhaps they never will, for several migrating groups may have been involved from different areas. As we saw above, 'horsehoof' cores have been found in the Cagayan Valley on Luzon, and they are also reported from Tabon Cave and from scattered surface finds in eastern Indonesia. Although stone tools with Australian affinities have recently been found in southern Sulawesi (see page 73), these only date at present from the end of the Pleistocene, so we really cannot be too precise at the moment on the question of Australian origins[54].

One anomaly, however, is striking, and this involves the appearance of small edge-ground axes from about 22,000 years ago at three rock shelters near Oenpelli in Arnhem Land[55]. These axes were made either on unflaked pebbles or on bifacially flaked roughouts, and some have 'waists' or shallow grooves pecked around their butts, possibly to facilitate hafting (figure 3.4b). Edge-grinding in Arnhem Land predates by at least 7,000 years anything at present comparable from Niah or the New Guinea Highlands, although the technique may have an antiquity of up to 25,000 years in Japan[56]. Even in Australia the technique appears to be localised to Arnhem Land until it becomes much more widespread after 5000 B.C., and at present these tools are so uniquely early that one is tempted to view Arnhem Land as an original innovating centre, and not as a recipient of the technique from some outside area.

NEW GUINEA

So far, sites over 30,000 years old have not been found in New Guinea, and the earliest is from a locality called Kosipe in the Central Highlands of Papua, 2000 metres above sea-level[57]. Stone tools have been found here stratified between dated ash showers of between 19,000 and 26,000 years of age, and these are of two very important New Guinea types. One is the so-called 'waisted blade' – a hoe-like tool which is not strictly a blade at all, but usually made on a flake or a pebble (figure 3.5). The other is the flaked 'axe-adze' of lenticular cross-section, a remote forerunner of the polished Melanesian adzes of

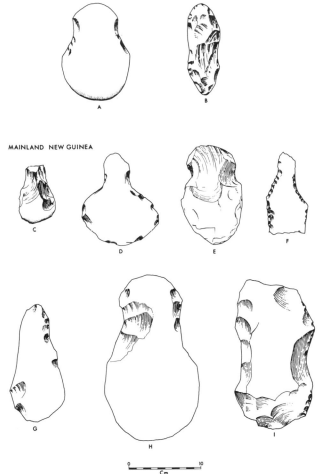

SOUTHEAST ASIA

MAINLAND NEW GUINEA

Fig. 3.5. Waisted tools from Southeast Asia (A, B) and the New Guinea Highlands (C–I). (A) Da-Phuc, North Vietnam (edge-ground); (B) Sai Yok, Thailand; (C) Niobe (edge-ground); (D, E) Kosipe; (F) Kiowa; (G, H, I) Yuku. From Golson 1972a.

Heine Geldern's Walzenbeil type, to which we will return in chapter 7. We have already noted the presence of contemporary ground and waisted axes in Arnhem Land, and in the case of this New Guinea assemblage we may be faced with the oldest assemblage of putative horticultural character anywhere in the world. Axe-adzes are not known from anywhere else at this date, but the waisted blades do turn up occasionally in Hoabinhian assemblages on the mainland of Southeast Asia. Perhaps, however, we would be unwise to suggest that horticulture was practised in New Guinea before 20,000 years ago on present evidence, for the Kosipe dates certainly need to be verified by more early sites, and of course the Arnhem Land axes were not used for horticulture if Australian ethnography is any guide.

If the New Guinea economy at 20,000 B.P. remains very much a matter of guesswork, so too does the actual extent of human settlement. When Kosipe was settled, the temperature seems to have been about 5°C below the present annual average, and the date is close to the peak of glaciation in higher latitudes. The main highland backbone of New Guinea did not escape glaciation, and at maximum extent the ice covered some 2000 square kilometres, compared to 10 square kilometres today[58]. There is no clear evidence yet that the main highlands were settled at all until about 15,000 years ago, when we have the first evidence for human activity from an open site called Wanlek in the Kairronk Valley, and by 11,000 years ago edge-ground axes were being used in the rock-shelter of Kafiavana in the Eastern Highlands[59]. It may be that the main highlands were first settled about this time by people with a tool kit adapted for forest clearance, if not for rudimentary horticulture, and the question arises of whether these people were speakers of ancestral languages within the Trans New Guinea Phylum (chapter 5). But here we must leave the problems of Pleistocene New Guinea for future researchers, and I must add, to qualify the above remarks about horticulture, that there is no direct evidence for it earlier than 4000 B.C. at present (see chapter 9).

THE HOABINHIAN TECHNOCOMPLEX[60] OF THE SOUTHEAST ASIAN MAINLAND

We now retrace our steps back to the Southeast Asian mainland, to begin again with the problem of the Upper Pleistocene 'gap'. What are generally termed Hoabinhian sites cover an immense area from southern China to northern Sumatra, and contain a developed pebble- and flake-tool industry which, when dated, falls into the period between approximately 13,000 and 4000 B.P. Yet there is a strong suspicion that the technocomplex goes back much earlier than has so far met the eye; an antiquity of at least 30,000 years may one day be demonstrated. It is certainly hard to imagine what else could fall into the Upper Pleistocene, and although all the sites have modern faunas, the faunal evidence from Niah Cave suggests that we can go back at least 30,000 years on this basis.

Apart from questions of antiquity, the Hoabinhian as known at present seems to hold the clues to a very early appearance of horticulture, pottery, and edge-grinding of stone tools. As is still common in Southeast Asian archaeology, the picture is hazy, despite half a century of sporadic research. In fact, the major burst of excavation activity took place in the 1920s and 1930s, when over 70 limestone rock-shelters were excavated in the regions of Tonkin (North Vietnam) and central and northern Malaya. From the first, excavation techniques were of mediocre standard, and matters were confused by use of a bewildering variety of subjective typological terms for stone tools[61]. In 1964 a degree of order was brought back into the subject in a Ph.D. thesis prepared by J. M. Matthews[62], and since then a number of scholars have attacked the problem with modern archaeological techniques.

To date, Hoabinhian sites are known almost entirely from limestone massif areas where caves and shelters are present. North Vietnam and Malaya contain several such massifs, and hence the great majority of sites. South China, Thailand and Cambodia are only gradually being placed on the Hoabinhian map, while South Vietnam and Laos are virtual blanks, and the islands have only one definite Hoabinhian outlier, in northeastern Sumatra. This distribution is almost certainly biased by the vagaries of preservation, because a large number of coastal shell middens may have been obliterated by the rise in sea-level after the last glaciation between 14,000 and 7000 years ago. It is clear, for instance in Sumatra, that coastal midden formation was a major by-product of Hoabinhian economy, and the absence of such sites in most gently shelving coastal areas suggests that the great bulk of the timespan of the Hoabinhian is older than 7000 years. Their absence might also suggest that shell-midden

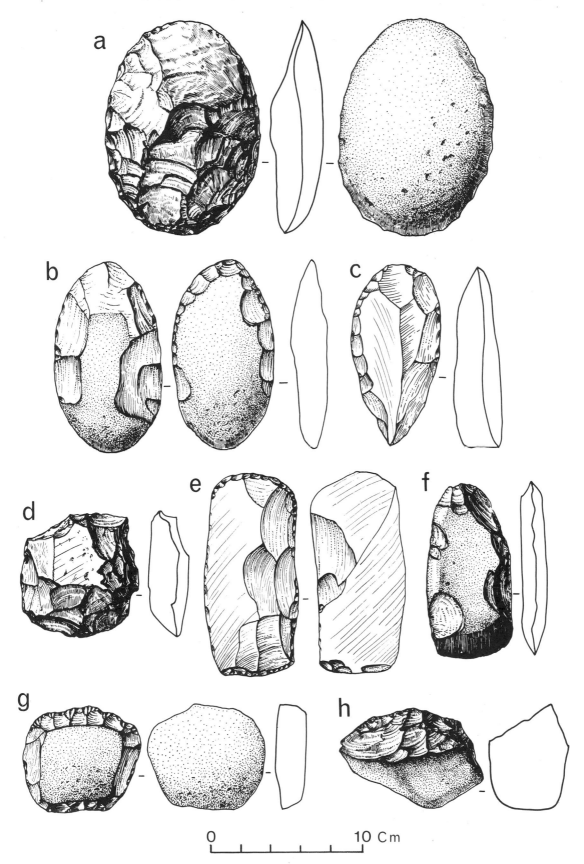

Fig. 3.6. Hoabinhian tool types from North Vietnam. (a) is the type often called a 'Sumatralith'; (d) is a short axe; (f) is an edge-ground axe of Bacsonian type.

formation was becoming less important after 7000 years ago, possibly because of competition from an incipient horticultural economy with tame pigs replacing shellfish as a source of protein.

The Hoabinhian technocomplex itself is defined purely with reference to tool categories, and comprises pebble tools, utilised flakes, and a small proportion of edge-ground tools and bone tools. The later mainland sites contain pottery and sometimes fully ground axes and adzes, and thus encompass the early Neolithic in a developmental sense. Blades are particularly rare (although not totally absent), and in this respect the technocomplex may be distinguished from its contemporary in Indonesia and the Philippines, where flakes and blades predominate.

Since no-one has yet been able to undertake a full statistical analysis of Hoabinhian tools from sites over the whole area of distribution, it is not possible to give a detailed break-down of tool types by area and through time. Discrete types do not seem to be characteristic anyway[63], and, as in the New Guinea Highlands in recent times[64], the tools were perhaps viewed more as vehicles for cutting edges than as blueprinted forms. As long as a tool will do its job its overall shape may not matter very much. In this regard, recent work on edge-wear on Hoabinhian tools[65] may hold promise, and one may expect to find evidence of the scraping of roots and tubers, and of the whittling of bamboo.

However, several attempts have been made recently to classify Hoabinhian tools, and most authors would recognise the following[66] (figure 3.6):

1. unifacially flaked pebble tools, retaining varying degrees of cortex. In this category there are almond-shaped, triangular and disc-shaped tools, together with oval pebbles flaked all over one surface which are often termed Sumatraliths.
2. bifacially flaked pebble tools of similar shape.
3. truncated pebble tools (short axes or *haches courts*), which are usually made on half of an oval pebble split transversely.
4. edge-ground axes.
5. a large category of other forms, including hammerstones and a few rare blades, together with cores and flakes which are frequently omitted from reports.

Since it is difficult to indulge in more generalisations about the Hoabinhian, we pass on to a brief regional survey.

North Vietnam In the year 1927, Madeleine Colani published a report[67] on nine rock-shelter excavations in the Province of Hoa-Binh, southwest of Hanoi, and the term *Hoabinhien* at this time with restricted areal connotations, was introduced into the archaeological literature. No stratification was reported for any site, but at Sao-Dong cave three phases were defined on tool typology. The lowest at about 2 metres depth contained large crudely flaked tools; the middle saw the appearance of some edge grinding, smaller and better made tools, and perhaps pottery (recorded as found *assez profondément*); and the upper phase above 80 cms was associated with more edge-grinding and further improvement in flaking technology. Colani's report is rather hard to evaluate, for her terminology is subjective and only selected tools are referred to and illustrated. Flake tools, which may have been as frequent as core and pebble tools, were almost totally ignored.

Between 1927 and 1930, Mlle. Colani excavated further caves and shelters in the neighbouring provinces of Ninh-Binh and Thanh-Hoa[68], and at the First Congress of Prehistorians of the Far East, held at Hanoi in 1932, a three phase division of the Hoabinhian was accepted[69]:

Hoabinhian I (i.e. the earliest): flaked implements only, rather large and crude.

Hoabinhian II: somewhat smaller implements of finer workmanship associated with protoneoliths (i.e. edge-ground tools).

Hoabinhian III (the latest): yet smaller implements, flakes with secondary working; with rare exceptions (such as Sao-Dong) no protoneoliths.

Matthews[70] has pointed out several weaknesses in this sequence, and it is of course most unlikely that the edge-ground tools should virtually disappear at the end of it, just prior to the full Neolithic. The three phase typological division seems in fact to have faded into oblivion, and the main markers in Hoabinhian evolution recognised generally in Southeast Asia now are the appearances of edge-grinding, pottery, and possibly incipient horticulture. The presence of the first two characterises the late Hoabinhian sites, while at present those which lack them can only be regarded as a rather loose category denoted early Hoabinhian.

The edge-grinding is rare in Colani's sites (normally about one or two percent of total tools), and is furthermore found only in the upper levels of most deposits. Pottery (usually not described) is restricted mainly to upper levels as well (it appears in the Hoabinhian II in the above classification), and was originally thought to have worked its way downwards, although it is now clear that pottery is directly associated with at least the later part of the Hoabinhian. In addition, Colani's sites produced bone points and spatulae, stone pestles and hollowed-out mortars, marine shells, and from the shelter of Trieng-Xen, stones with depressions carrying traces of haematite, as well as human bones stained with this substance[71].

More recently, further excavations in North Vietnamese Hoabinhian sites have been reported by Boriskovsky[72], but the results available so far do not really exceed those already known in 1932. No absolute dates are known at all for Hoabinhian sites in North Vietnam, so we do not know when the edge-grinding and pottery first appear, although edge-grinding has been found right from the base of some rock-shelter deposits. Neither do we have dates for the edge-ground and waisted tools from at least two sites[73] (see figure 3.5A), which are similar to those of late Pleistocene date from northern Australia. To make matters worse, the Hoabinhian seems to have a regional variant known as the Bacsonian, which was discovered in limestone caves in Bac-Son province by Henri Mansuy and Madeleine Colani[74]. In general, these Bacsonian sites are characterised on the one hand by a very small number of tools, and on the other hand by a very high proportion of edge-ground tools (figure 3.6f), some flaked prior to grinding, others made simply on unflaked pebbles. In addition, many pebbles have parallel longitudinal grooves (*marques bacsoniennes*) which indicate the sharpening of bone or bamboo chisels with curved bits[75]. Sherds of pottery bearing impressions made by cord- or basket-wrapped paddles were found in most sites, but the picture is complicated by the presence of fully ground Neolithic adzes in several sites in unknown stratigraphic contexts, so the Bacsonian may in fact overlap considerably with the full Neolithic. At Da-But, 30 km inland from the sea near Thanh-Hoa, Bacsonian edge-ground tools were found in a marine shell midden covering 50 by 32 metres by 5 metres deep, together with ochre-stained primary contracted and secondary burials,

pottery, and animal bones including those of dog[76]. Again, however, the presence of Neolithic adzes suggests that the site may be of relatively recent date.

At present the Bacsonian gives the impression, and little more, of being a late phase of the Hoabinhian in which for some reason the practice of edge-grinding was particularly emphasised. Absence of absolute dates is a problem, and because of this it is impossible to relate the Hoabinhian/Bacsonian to the interesting and recent discoveries made at Quynh-Van, a coastal shell midden covering an area of 7400 square metres, and like Da-But, containing layers of marine shell stratified to a depth of 5 metres[77]. The tool industry of Quynh-Van is of flaked basalt, and Hoabinhian pebble tools and edge-ground tools are in fact absent. Flake tools predominate, and pestles and mortars, sherds with cord or basketry impressions, and twelve contracted burials placed in seated positions were also found. Boriskovsky suggests that this site may be contemporary with the later Hoabinhian and Bacsonian, and if this is so then it represents a hitherto unreported culture lacking both the pebble tools and the edge-grinding.

The North Vietnamese Hoabinhian sequence is still therefore in an unsatisfactory state. The Bacsonian may be a late phase of the Hoabinhian, but Dani[78] has suggested that it is contemporary with the Hoabinhian for the most part, and that the technique of edge-grinding diffused from the Bac-Son area. With the reports available and the absence of absolute dates there is no way to resolve the situation. Faunal associations are all modern, but since a modern fauna has been dated from 30,000 years ago in Borneo, there seem to be few grounds for claiming that the Hoabinhian technocomplex in North Vietnam is entirely post-Pleistocene[79]. Another claim made for the Hoabinhian in the past has concerned the presence of engraved art on pebbles and cave walls, but the evidence is poor and it is not at all certain that the observed examples are man made.

Malaya At least sixteen sites in Malaya with Hoabinhian deposits have been investigated, mostly in limestone caves and shelters in the hills of the central and northern parts of the country, in particular in the provinces of Kedah, Perak, Kelantan and Pahang. Only two important sites would appear to have a near-coastal situation; a cave at Bukit Chuping in Perlis, and a shell midden at Gua Kepah in Province

Wellesley. To the great detriment of archaeology, many of the sites have now been damaged or destroyed by guano diggers, and the future for Hoabinhian archaeology in Malaya may be rather restricted[80].

Our knowledge of the Hoabinhian in Malaya is at present mainly concerned with the later phases, and, as in North Vietnam, there is good evidence for the appearance of edge-grinding and pottery, although again the dates are really a matter of guesswork. At the shelter of Kota Tongkat in Pahang, excavations in 1967[81] recovered Hoabinhian tools to the base of the deposit at 1.5 metres. Pottery, as usual cord-impressed, was restricted to the top 50 cm, where it was associated with a marked decline in the numbers of the Hoabinhian tools. Furthermore, the occurrences of shell, bone and stone flakes decreased upwards from levels even earlier than the first appearance of pottery, and it may be that the site documents an expansion in the use of open settlements at the expense of caves and rock-shelters, sometime before the general appearance of pottery in the area. This is a change which may well relate to the beginnings of horticulture.

Another recently excavated late Hoabinhian site, the cave of Gua Kechil in Pahang, provides more detailed information[82]. The deposits here were one metre deep, and the basal 25 cm contained bone and shell only, with no artefacts. Between 75 and 55 cm Hoabinhian pebble tools and flakes appeared, together with cord-impressed sherds with simple rims and a predominance of criss-cross over parallel line decoration. Between 55 and 35 cm the cord-impressed ware continues, but a plain burnished ware occasionally manufactured on a slow wheel appears, together with the first evidence for the use of polished adzes of Duff type 2 (described more fully in chapter 7). In the upper levels above 35 cm ring-footed open bowls of a red ware appear, polished stone tools predominate, and the Hoabinhian tools finally disappear. The beginning of this phase (Gua Kechil III) is associated with a radiocarbon date of 2850±800 B.C. (*c.* 3600 B.C. if calibrated) which is taken by the excavator to mark the end of the Hoabinhian and the appearance of the full Neolithic. Phase III also sees a marked drop in bone and shell counts, by this date almost certainly associated with the move away from caves to lowland horticultural settlements.

Another important Malayan site is the cave of Gua Cha, where well-made Hoabinhian tools and burials have been found in preceramic contexts stratified beneath extended Neolithic burials with pottery[83]. The Hoabinhian burials were in both contracted and extended postures, and some fragmentary ones showed signs of burning which might indicate cannibalism. In addition, no less than 25 heaps of pig bones, up to 1.3 metres in diameter, were found in the Hoabinhian levels, and most of the bones are reported as skulls and mandibles from immature individuals. Evidence of this nature could theoretically be taken to indicate pig domestication, although it has been pointed out that wild populations of bearded pigs migrate in herds at certain times of the year, and that massive kills can be made even today at river crossings[84].

The picture from the above sites is filled out a little by a number of earlier excavations. Two shelters in Perak, Gol Ba'it and Gua Kerbau[85], have both produced Hoabinhian tools, with gradually decreasing occurrences of pottery and edge-ground tools right down to near the bases of their deposits. The Gol Ba'it pottery is mostly impressed with a cord-bound paddle, and globular vessels and open bowls have been partially reconstructed[86]. Both sites also contained contracted or flexed burials, and these burial postures appear to be generally characteristic not only of the Hoabinhian, but also of the pre-Neolithic levels at Niah and Gua Lawa (described in the following section). On the other hand, a predominance of extended burial seems to be characteristic of the succeeding Neolithic cultures in Southeast Asia, although extended burial is occasionally reported for the Hoabinhian.

In general, the Malayan sites are characterised by tool forms similar to those of North Vietnam, although short axes are reported only rarely. Waste flakes are common at some sites, as one would expect in those cases where tools were made on the spot[87]. Some regional differences are apparent in the distribution of tool types – for instance the unifacial Sumatraliths form a notable component of the assemblages from Perak (geographically closest to the Sumatran sites themselves where the form is dominant), while in Pahang, Kelantan and Kedah, bifacially worked tools appear to be more important[88]. Whether this represents a chronological difference is not clear, although trends from unifacial to bifacial flaking are reported from a number of Malayan sites. Pounding and grinding stones, bone tools and red ochre are also of quite frequent occurrence. The Gua Kepah middens, now destroyed, are reported to have been massive shell heaps up to seven metres high, which contained Hoabinhian tools, cord-marked pottery, hollowed stone grindstones, a burial with red ochre on its face and jaw, and a large number of unique waisted and polished axes[89]. The latter resemble those from North Vietnam, Australia and New Guinea, but no stratigraphic information is recorded about them.

Thailand Thailand has produced two major reported Hoabinhian sites, of which the largest is a rock-shelter called Sai Yok, on the Kwai Noi River in Kanchanaburi Province. This site was excavated in 1960-2 by a Thai-Danish expedition, and the excellent report[90] is marred only by the total absence of dates, a circumstance which seems to have been beyond the excavators' control.

The Sai Yok tools are made from quartzite river pebbles, and numerous hammerstones and waste flakes indicate that tool-making was carried out in the shelter. The excavators have divided the deposits into three phases, and the lower phase, to the maximum depth of 4.75 metres, contained mainly large unifacially flaked choppers and core tools of horseshoe or flat-iron shape, together with a single waisted and bifacially flaked axe from the 3-3.9 metres level. The middle phase contained a higher proportion of the more typical Hoabinhian forms, such as Sumatraliths, short axes, and choppers, interstratified with four rough living floors made of lumps of stone. Near the top of the middle phase layers (between 1.4 and 1.7 metres) a number of crude blade tools made an appearance, together with bone tools and shell scrapers. A single flexed burial from this level was found with a mammalian long bone across its chest and two imported marine shells on its right arm. The soil near the burial was stained with red ochre, which may have been sprinkled over the body. The Hoabinhian tools continue right through the intensive middle occupation of the shelter, but finally disappear in the upper phase where they overlap with potsherds and adzes of the Neolithic Ban Kao Culture, which probably postdates 3000 B.C. (see chapter 7). At Sai Yok there is not quite the degree of continuity from Hoabinhian to Neolithic that one sees in the Malayan site of Gua Kechil, and it may be that the Neolithic remains here present a more marked cultural intrusion. Even the edge-ground pebble tools at Sai Yok are absent below the Neolithic levels. Despite the lack of absolute dates, Sai Yok is

of importance because it does seem to show evolution within the Hoabinhian. Stone tools show a definite size decrease over time, the tools at the base seem to be the largest and crudest. Should dates ever be acquired for this site, a time span of at least 40,000 years might be expected.

The other site to be discussed, called Spirit Cave, is in the north-west of Thailand[91]. The excavator, Chester Gorman, found the lower levels to contain a Hoabinhian assemblage together with some ochre-covered grinding stones, and, like Sai Yok, a few pressure-flaked calcite blades. Some of the edge-damage patterns on the stone tools suggest the working of small diameter wooden shafts, and the finding of quantities of bamboo charcoal suggests that a good part of the Hoabinhian tool-kit may have been of this very sharp and durable wood. The levels with this material are firmly dated to between c. 12,000 and 6800 B.C., and the top layer of the site, dated to c. 6000 B.C., sees the appearance of the earliest Neolithic assemblage so far discovered in Southeast Asia. This includes cord-marked and incised pottery, polished adzes, and slate knives, and the Hoabinhian tools continue with it until abandonment of the site at about 5700 B.C.

Spirit Cave therefore has the earliest dates both for Hoabinhian and for Neolithic assemblages in Southeast Asia reported so far[92]. Because the cave deposits are relatively shallow, the date of 12,000 B.C. is probably only the tip of an iceberg as far as the Hoabinhian is concerned.

Laos and Cambodia A number of scattered reports suggest that caves of great archaeological potential are present in a limestone area in the province of Luang Prabang, north-eastern Laos. Short reports are available on three of these caves – Tam Hang north, Tam Hang south, and Tam Pong[93]. The shelter of Tam Hang south contained Hoabinhian levels up to 3 metres thick, the tools being mostly unifacially flaked, and found together with a number of perforated pebbles[94]. Edge-ground pebble tools appeared at a relatively high level, and quadrangular-sectioned polished adzes at the top, in both cases with cord-marked or basket-impressed pottery. The cave of Tam Pong had Hoabinhian tools, a flexed burial, an edge-ground axe from an intermediate level, and round-based cord-marked pottery at the top. In view of the sequence represented, it is perhaps unfortunate that the sites were excavated prior to the development of modern techniques.

Rather more coherent results have come from recent excavations in the cave of Laang Spean in Battambang Province, western Cambodia[95]. Here, the lowest levels were found to contain only flakes of chert and hornfels, although there appears to be some doubt as to whether these were man-made. Above these levels Hoabinhian tools and cord-marked or incised sherds occur together, associated with several carbon dates between about 4300 B.C. (*c.* 5300 B.C. if calibrated) and A.D. 830, although the Hoabinhian tools become less frequent after *c.* 2000 B.C. A flake of a ground stone tool was also found around the 4–5000 B.C. level, so it appears that Laang Spean is another site which represents the late Hoabinhian when ceramics and edge-grinding had already made an appearance. So far this is the only Hoabinhian site to be excavated in Cambodia, and future discoveries both here and in Laos will one day, hopefully, be made.

Sumatra   In north-eastern Sumatra a rather distinctive aspect of the Hoabinhian has been known for many years, consisting of shell middens (many now destroyed) stretching along 130 km of the coast[96]. Many of these middens were of considerable size, one being reported as 30 metres in diameter and 4 metres high, and clearly they represent an economic mode similar to that of Gua Kepah and Quynh-Van. Today the middens are all about 10 to 15 km inland, and this suggests that they belong either to an early Holocene phase of high sea-level, or that the land has subsequently been uplifted or extended by coastal silting. The investigated sites consist of stratified layers of shell, ash and earth, with a tool kit comprising mostly unifacially flaked pebbles (up to 90% of all tools according to van Heekeren). Pestles, mortars and red ochre are found commonly, but pottery and edge-ground tools are absent. The term 'Sumatralith' does of course refer to the tools from these sites, but the term as used in a general Hoabinhian context is restricted specifically to oval-shaped forms. The Sumatran tools are in fact quite varied in shape, and discs, triangles and tabular forms occur together with the ovals.

South China and Taiwan   The northward limit of the Hoabinhian technocomplex is a matter which so far has received little attention in published reports. In Mongolia, northern China and Japan, the early Holocene is repre-sented by blade and microlithic industries, and at present it appears that Hoabinhian pebble tools are restricted to China south of the Tsinling mountains. In the middle Yangtze drainage system in Szechwan many surface finds of Hoabinhian-type tools, some showing distinctive techniques of waisting, mark the most northerly area of verified distribution[97]. The provinces of Yünnan, Kwangsi and Kwangtung also contain a large number of sites which appear to have Hoabinhian industries, in some cases associated with cord-marked pottery[98].

In eastern Taiwan, three caves in T'ai-tung county have recently produced stratified collections of unifacially flaked pebble choppers and flakes, dating from an unknown period down to about 3000 B.C.[99]. The excavators refer to this industry as 'Changpinian', and suggest that it may go back into Pleistocene times. No pottery was found, and the industry relates generally to the Hoabinhian as well as to the Tabon pebble and flake industry of Palawan. There is every reason to expect preceramic occupation in Taiwan, and these sites are the first of this kind to be excavated. They also suggest another major point of concern, which is that if earlier excava-tors of Hoabinhian sites in Southeast Asia had published full details of not simply the pebble tools, but also of all the flake material, then the apparent distinction between the Hoabinhian on the one hand, and the pebble and flake industries of the Niah, Tabon and Cabenge type on the other hand, might be reduced to something approaching a continuum rather than a sharp division.

The Hoabinhian Sequence – a summary   As we have seen, Hoabinhian sites have been found over a large area from southern China to Malaya and Sumatra. The technocomplex has no fixed date of commencement, and most probably merges back in time with the Middle Pleistocene pebble and flake technocomplex. Furthermore, Hoabinhian tools do not disappear at any fixed point in time, and it should be stressed that the Hoabinhian is not a time division at all but a tradition of stone-tool manufacture with succes-sive cultural accretions. By 6000 B.C. the manu-facture of pottery was probably widespread, and the edge-grinding techique almost certainly goes back into late Pleistocene times.

The Hoabinhian may therefore be viewed as a technocomplex with successive innovations, and its culmination, present by at least 6000 B.C.

in Thailand, is the Southeast Asian Neolithic which will be the subject of chapters 7 and 8.[100] With the Neolithic we reach a point where regional cultures can be observed beneath the generalised level of the technocomplex, and the tempo of culture change increases rapidly. One reason for this increase is the presence of horticulture and rice agriculture, and the roots of these may certainly be sought in the Hoabinhian. To avoid confusion, I have brought the evidence for Hoabinhian economy together in a separate section.

Hoabinhian Economy[101] The Hoabinhians certainly exploited a wide range of marine and terrestrial resources by hunting, gathering and fishing. The main question concerns their role in horticultural developments, and this unfortunately remains the most difficult question to answer. The only direct floral evidence available comes from the preceramic levels of Spirit Cave in Thailand, where Gorman recovered remains of almonds, betel nuts, peppers, gourds, Chinese water chestnuts, butternuts, candle nuts, beans, peas, and other edible plants. This is an impressive list, and we may guess that the betel chewing habit was already established. However, it is not known whether intentional planting was carried out, or if the plants show genetic changes away from the wild forms. Many of the plants are still of importance today, but it is unfortunate that there are no traces of any major cultigens such as rice, yam or taro. The only other indication we have that cultivation techniques may have developed by 9000 B.C. comes from central Taiwan, where a pollen sequence shows an increase in charcoal and second-growth species at about this time[102]. At present, however, we need more evidence before any conclusion can be drawn.

On a more generalised economic level, we have seen that most surviving Hoabinhian sites are in inland localities close to streams, although a marine component was certainly present once. A careful study by Gorman[103] has documented the fauna exploited at various sites, which includes large mammals such as rhinoceros and cattle, while pig and deer are particularly important. The heaps of juvenile pig bones at Gua Cha have been mentioned, and bones of bearded pig are also the most common at Gua Kechil[104]. Primates include pig-tailed macaque and langur monkeys, together with gibbons. Marine species, particularly shellfish, are naturally most common in the coastal sites, but also occur inland quite frequently. Some of the inland caves may have been seasonal camps, although Gorman has analysed the freshwater shellfish from Spirit Cave to show that the site was used for the whole year. At present we cannot say whether there were separate coastal and inland groups of Hoabinhians, or whether all groups exploited both environments.

THE EARLIER HOLOCENE IN ISLAND SOUTHEAST ASIA – THE FLAKE AND BLADE TECHNOCOMPLEX

From the mainland of Southeast Asia we turn to the islands of Indonesia and the Philippines, where developments in stone-tool technology took a different turn from those which characterised the Hoabinhian. We have already seen how flake tools dominate many of the island assemblages in the Upper Pleistocene, and this trend continues into the earlier Holocene with the important addition of a blade technology in certain areas. The flake and blade industries to be described are mainly of Holocene date, and in the case of Australia they continued in some areas until ethnographic times, while in the islands of Southeast Asia their production appears to have been phased out gradually throughout the Neolithic and Metal Ages. Hence the overall time span of production would seem to be between 6000 and 5000 B.C. until well into the first millennium A.D. At present it seems unlikely that they represent entirely an indigenous development, and possible sources of external influence will be examined later.

At the outset, we should perhaps consider the meaning of the sometimes misused term 'blade'. According to Valda J. Morlan, in a recent and excellent article on Japanese prehistory[105], blades are to be defined as 'elongate parallel-sided flakes with parallel arrises or parallel-sided facets on their dorsal faces. Blades are struck (by indirect percussion) from prepared, polyhedral cores which may or may not exhibit facetted platforms'. Tools of this kind are widespread in late Pleistocene industries in Europe, northern Asia, and northern Japan, where they form the bulk of excavated assemblages. The overall predominance of true blades within northern assemblages is highly important, because the flake and blade industries of Southeast Asia and Australia are in fact of a very different character. Here, blade tools form only minority components of the assemblages, which still consist mainly of flakes, and, furthermore, the true blades of the type made in northern areas are extremely rare. Many of the blades found in the southern area fall into Morlan's category of 'blade-like flakes', which are less symmetrical than true blades and which lack the parallel ridges. With these we cannot speak strictly of blade industries, for many of them were probably produced fortuitously from simple flake cores. Unfortunately, however, available reports on sites in the area rarely give details on blade production, and I use the term 'blade' in this section to encompass Morlan's categories of blades and blade-like flakes, since it is rather hard to differentiate between the two at present, particularly in Indonesia and the Philippines.

Another important point about some of these southern flake and blade industries is that the tools can sometimes be of very small sizes, and in southern Japan, southern Sulawesi and Australia, true microblades are of frequent occurrence[106].

Generally, one gains the impression that the blade technology has been introduced from one or more outside areas into an existing flake technology, and I will return to this interesting circumstance later.

We may commence a geographical survey with Palawan, where two caves continue the sequence after *c.* 7000 B.C., when the deposits of the main Tabon Cave came to an end. By this time, the sea-level was roughly at its present position, and both these caves contain shellfish; we may remember that during the late Pleistocene the Tabon Cave had in fact been some 35 km inland, and no shellfish were found in its layers at all. The first of the two caves is Guri Cave, in the same limestone massif as Tabon, and here the Tabonian flake tradition continues in developed form, with increasing retouch, down to about 2000 B.C.[107]. Blades are absent at Guri, but at Duyong Cave, 11 km north of Tabon, an industry of both flakes and blades was found to

0   4 Cm

Fig. 3.7. Blade tools (*top*) and two blade cores (*bottom*) from Leang Tuwo Mane'e Cave, Karakellang, Talaud Islands. *c.* 3000–1000 B.C.

date to between 5000 and 2000 B.C. The blades here are small and crude and seem to lack retouch, but some prepared blade-cores are reported by Fox. The Duyong flake and blade industry is contemporary with the late Tabonian flake industry at Guri Cave, but it is not clear whether this implies cultural or functional difference. Fox[108] thinks two separate cultures are involved, so we could be witnessing new arrivals in the Philippines at this period.

Elsewhere in the Philippines blade tools are widely reported, but generally undated. In the Rizal and Bulakan Provinces of Luzon, flakes and blades of obsidian (two percent are even made of tektites) have been found in large numbers in what appear to be late Pleistocene and early Holocene stratigraphic situations, and blade industries have recently been found on small islands in the Samar Sea[109]. In the Talaud Islands, just south of Mindanao (and politically a part of Indonesia), excavations undertaken in 1974 by a joint Australian and Indonesian expedition produced flake and blade tools of chert dating back to at least 3500 B.C., and possibly earlier (figure 3.7). All these flake and blade industries appear to lack the backed and microlithic forms, which seem generally to be absent from the Philippine region.

Moving southwards to Sulawesi, the above-mentioned Australian-Indonesian team (led by myself and Drs. I.M. Sutayasa) also located a large shell-midden on the shores of Lake Tondano, a volcanic crater lake in the centre of the Minahasa region near the northern tip of the island. The site, in the village of Paso, consists of lake and marine shells forming a stratified midden some 30 metres in diameter and about 1.5 metres deep, and the deposits contain many flakes (but no blades) of coarse vesicular obsidian, together with bone points (figure 3.8), hematite, and large numbers of animal bones (including many pigs). This material has not yet been analysed in detail, but the site is well dated to about 6000 B.C., and the absence of blades may reflect constraints imposed by the material used. As we saw in the previous section on the Hoabinhian, shell-middens of this age have rarely survived in Southeast Asia, and when the animal bones have been analysed in more detail this site could give many clues about early Holocene economy in the region.

Apart from this Minahasa discovery, it is from some twenty caves and rock-shelters in southwestern Sulawesi that perhaps the most interesting

Fig. 3.8. Bone points from the Paso shell-mound, northern Sulawesi, *c.* 6000–5000 B.C. The middle specimen is a bi-point.

of the Southeast Asian flake and blade industries has been recovered. This is the so-called Toalean industry[110], which contains some very specific tool forms such as backed blade-like flakes with blunting retouch, serrated and hollow-based triangular points (Maros points), crescentic and trapezoidal microliths[111], and bone points (figure 3.9). Part of the fascination of the Toalean lies in the resemblances of the blades and microliths with similar and contemporary forms in Australia, mainly from the southern part of the continent.

Working mainly from the findings of van Stein Callenfels at the cave of Panganreang Tudea, H.R. van Heekeren formulated a three phase sequence for the Toalean[112]. Crude flakes and plain blades, some shouldered, were thought to characterise the Lower Toalean, while microliths appeared in the Middle Toalean, and Maros points, two-ended bone points and pottery in the Upper. Although no subsequent investigators have found any evidence for the shouldered points, which could possibly be the result of fortuitous breakage, recent excavations by I.C. Glover in the cave of Ulu Leang[113] have tended to confirm parts of the sequence. For instance, plain unslipped potsherds, geometric microliths and Maros points are confined to the upper deposits which postdate 3000 B.C., while the middle levels, which may go back to *c.* 5000 B.C., contain higher percentages of backed blade-like flakes and flake scrapers. Bone points and stone tools with edge-gloss (see page 76) occur throughout the sequence. However, van Heekeren's concept of the Middle Toalean has received no real confirmation, and other excavations carried out by D. J. Mulvaney and R. P. Soejono in other Toalean sites[114] have also cast some doubt on the general sequence.

What we appear to have for the Toalean is an early phase with simple flakes and blades, followed by a later phase with the appearances of geometric microliths, Maros points and pottery after 3000 B.C. In the basal levels of Ulu Leang, Glover has also found an industry of thick and high-angled scrapers, similar to the earlier industries of Australia, and these tools have also

been found, together with a few blades, in a nearby cave called Leang Burung 2, where the deposits may extend back into the terminal Pleistocene. At present, the Toalean industry *per se* has rather unclear beginnings, but the earlier industries of Leang Burung 2 and basal Ulu Leang are clearly rather different from it, and a commencing date for the backed blades and the recognisable Toalean between 5000 and 4000 B.C. would seem reasonable. As for the earlier industries, these are the first ones with any real affinity to the Australian core tool and scraper tradition to be reported from eastern Indonesia (although the tools from the Paso shellmound are also similar), and much earlier assemblages of this type are to be expected from future research.

On the economic side, the faunas from Toalean sites are all reported as modern. Freshwater shellfish are common, and mammals include two species of the marsupial cuscus (*Phalanger* sp.), macaque monkey, civet cat, rats, bats, an endemic species of dwarf bovid (*Anoa*), and two species of pig (*Sus celebensis* and *Babyrousa* sp.). It may be significant that all of these species except *Sus celebensis* show a diminution in size from Toalean to present-day forms, while the latter get larger[115]. This may in fact be suggestive

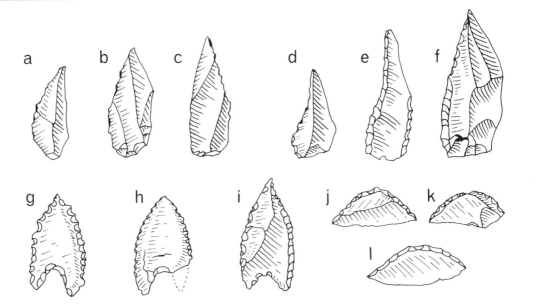

Fig. 3.9. Toalean tools from Leang Burung Cave, Maros, South Sulawesi: (a–f) backed blades; (g–i) Maros Points; (j–l) microliths.

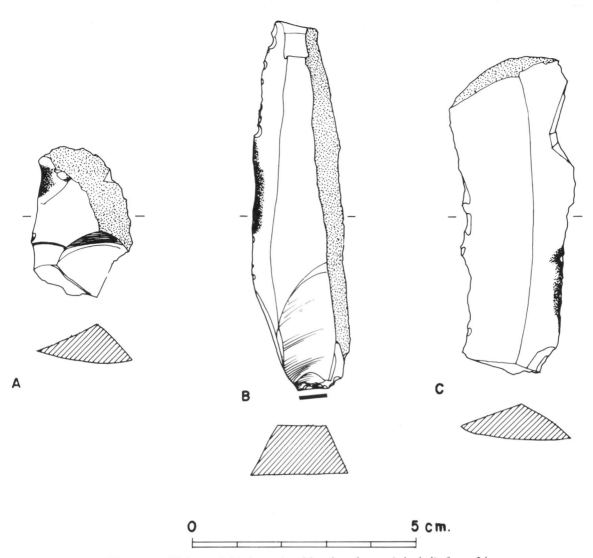

Fig. 3.10. Flake and blade tools with edge-glosses (stippled) from Lie Siri Cave, eastern Timor. *c.* 4000–1000 B.C.

evidence for pig domestication, which was almost certainly present in Southeast Asia and New Guinea by 3000 B.C., although *Sus celebensis* does not appear to be reported as a domesticated species from the ethnographic record.

The artistic side of Toalean life has survived through a small amount of cave art, which consists mainly of red hand stencils, made by blowing haematite powder over a hand, usually a left one, placed flat against the wall. This rather basic mode of self-expression is world-wide and of antiquity in excess of 30,000 years, and in our area of interest, hand stencils occur also in Timor, Seram, Kei, New Guinea and Australia. Apart from the hand stencils, three Toalean caves also have paintings of wild boar[116].

Because the Toalean industries do have parallels in Australia, we might move south briefly to take a closer look. Backed blades, microliths, and prepared blade-cores make an appearance within the Australian core-tool and scraper tradition, mainly in southern and eastern Australia (excluding Tasmania) from about 4000 B.C.[117]. The dingo seems to have been introduced at about the same time, either from Southeast Asia or from India. While the similarities between the Toalean and Australian industries are generally recognised by archaeologists[118], the rarity of the backed blades and microliths in northern Australia does pose something of a problem. Carefully finished spear points, sometimes made on blades, were produced in the north, but no single Australian assemblage, either in the north or the south, comes sufficiently close to the Toalean to make direct contact a certainty. Because of this, it is uncertain whether to look to Indonesia or India for the introduction of the blade technology and the dingo, although geographical considerations would naturally favour Indonesia.

Returning to Indonesia, another interesting sequence involving blade tools has recently been recovered by Ian Glover[119] from four caves in eastern (formerly Portuguese) Timor. The sequence goes back at least 10,000 years, and at one cave, Lie Siri, about 95% of the stone material recovered consisted of waste flakes, while the actual tools were made on both flakes and blades. The main forms were retouched scrapers, and sharp unretouched knives with an edge-gloss which may have resulted from the cutting and whittling of bamboo[120] (figure 3.10). A number of the retouched tools have very concave scraping edges, and this seems to be a distinctive feature of all the assemblages excavated by Glover. The tools are of flint or chert, and there are no prepared blade-cores present, although some of the cores recovered do have occasional scars left by the removal of blades. As noted above, blades of this kind are better described as blade-like flakes, and they comprise only around 2% of the total industry. Glover reports very few core and pebble tools, and the backed blades which characterise the Toalean and southeastern Australian industries are absent. This means that Timor is unlikely to be a source of direct contact with Australia in the Holocene.

The faunal remains found in the Timor caves prior to about 3000 B.C. consist only of bats and giant rats of extinct species. *Stegodon* had presumably become extinct by the end of the Pleistocene. Betel nut and *Canarium* nut were in use in the early Holocene as they were at Spirit Cave, but major changes are well documented in Timor from about 3000 B.C., particularly with the appearance of domesticated animals and pottery. We will come back to these in chapter 8.

To the west of the sites discussed so far, Borneo remains a blank apart from Niah, which does not seem to have shared at all in the spread of the blade technology. Java, on the other hand, does have a few poorly documented preceramic flake and blade industries. In eastern Java there are nineteen caves and shelters which appear to belong to a rather mysterious 'Sampung Bone Industry', first discovered in the Gua Lawa Cave near Sampung in 1926. The actual digging methods employed at Gua Lawa were rather crude, but van Stein Callenfels[121], the excavator, did adopt the commendable practice of making three-dimensional records of the find places of the more important artefacts. From this record, it seems that the lower occupation layer produced a preceramic assemblage of finely flaked and hollow-based stone arrowheads (figure 3.11), with a few round-based examples, and a number of hollowed stone grindstones with spherical rubbers and evidence for the use of red ochre. The top layer of the site produced a totally different assemblage of cord-marked potsherds, Duff type 2A adzes, grindstones and pestles, and right at the very top, a few pieces of metal.

The major problem with this site concerns interpretation of a large lens running between the lower and upper layers, which contained only bone and horn tools of unusual variety – spatulae (perhaps chisels or scrapers), points and awls. This is the so-called 'Sampung Bone Industry'. Bone fishhooks are also reported from the site, but not in definite association with this lens. As the lens contained no pottery or stone tools (apart from grindstones and pestles), it seems that it can only represent an intensive working area. Although Callenfels tended to think of it as a separate 'middle period' cultural layer, it seems to me that it is no more than a specialised facet of the upper layer in the cave. So perhaps we may accept a two-phase sequence[122]; the preceramic arrowheads at the base, and the Neolithic deposits above, with adzes, bone tools and pottery. Whether the cave produced flake tools is not clear, as these would probably not have been kept at the time of excavation.

Other shelters in eastern Java have produced similar bone implements, hollow or round-based arrowheads, shell scrapers, perforated pearl-shell discs, and crude flakes and blades. The perforated shell discs are of interest here, because they are common in Neolithic sites in Timor and Flores, so many of these Javanese sites may not be much older than 2000 B.C. Furthermore, the hollow-based arrowheads have been recovered from many surface sites around Pacitan and Punung in southern Java, oddly enough in apparent association with stone adzes, from which they are so markedly separated in the Gua Lawa deposits. The faunas of all these Javanese sites are modern, and the shelter of Gunung Cantalan to the south of Madiun contained such a preponderance of bones of crab-eating macaque monkey that Erdbrink[123] suggested that they reflected totemic practices. In addition, a number of flexed burials of generalised Australoid or Melanesian affinity have been found, including one of a child with a necklace of perforated shells

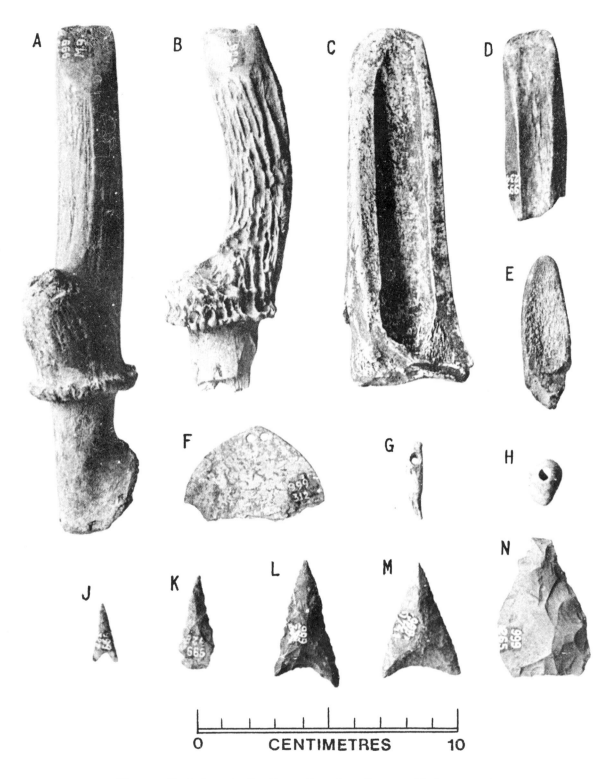

Fig. 3.11. Tools from the Gua Lawa Cave, Java (from van Heekeren 1972):
(A–E) antler tools; (F–H) perforated pendants of shell and tooth; (J–N)
projectile points.

from the middle level of the Gua Lawa cave[124]. Pottery is reported only from Gua Lawa, so some part of the 'Sampung Bone Industry' may be preceramic, but little more can be said. The whole complex still exists as a major problem in Javanese prehistory.

Seemingly unrelated to the above is an obsidian industry of flake and rare blade tools from surface sites on the Bandung Plateau in western Java[125]. This industry is generally regarded as preceramic, and it includes a few rare backed blades, triangular or leaf-shaped points, and burins, but the type of serrated retouch which is found in the Toalean is absent. In south-central Sumatra further obsidian industries, evidently of flake and blade type, are reported from the Lake Kerinci region, and from the caves of Ulu Tianko and Tianko Panjang near Jambi. In the latter case, excavations in 1974 under the direction of Bennett Bronson have shown that the obsidian industry is preceramic, although analysis is still in progress[126]. Cord-marked pottery appears in the upper layers of the Tianko Panjang cave, but no dates are yet available. The Sumatran obsidian industries are referred to again on page 220, as they do appear to continue on into the Neolithic. Further to the north-west of Sumatra, another flake and blade industry has been briefly described by Dutta[127] from the Andaman Islands, but he gives few details, apart from suggesting that it resembles the Toalean. The whole problem of these flake and blade industries in western Indonesia is obviously very important, and little progress can be made with the information that is at present available.

After the above survey, with all its limitations, we can at least see glimmerings of a few interesting conclusions. The Holocene flake and blade technocomplex is presently reported from the Philippines, parts of eastern and southern Indonesia, and from Australia. Microblades and geometric microliths are only found in southern Australia and south-western Sulawesi, although possible examples may be present in Java. The distribution of the technocomplex would suggest a degree of technological diffusion early in the Holocene epoch, and the spread of the domestic dog may in some way be connected with this. Of all the areas mentioned, Australia so far has the earliest evidence for the dog, at possibly 4000 B.C. or earlier[128].

If the origins of the technocomplex do involve diffusion, then we need to think in terms of a graft on to a basic flake technology which is undoubtedly indigenous to Island Southeast Asia. As we have seen, the blade technology was not generally adopted by the Hoabinhians of the Southeast Asian mainland, possibly because they were specialising in the production of heavier stone tools for the working of wooden tools. There are in fact a number of very significant differences between the Hoabinhian and flake-blade technocomplexes, not least being the absence of edge-ground axes in the latter, except in Australia. This does suggest that the Neolithic axes and adzes have a mainland rather than an island origin, and also that the Hoabinhians may have been more directly involved in horticultural clearance than their island contemporaries. In the islands, there is no good evidence for horticulture and animal domestication before 4000–3000 B.C., so the earlier part of the flake and blade technocomplex may have been prehorticultural.

As a final attempt to tie up a few loose ends, we may examine some of the external parallels for the blades and microliths. Industries with microliths which bear some similarity to the Toalean and Australian industries, and perhaps to the Javanese, are common over the whole of the Indian subcontinent, and it some cases date as early as 5000 B.C.[129]. Fairservis derives the Indian forms from Western Asia and Europe, and given the widespread Holocene appearance of small tools of this kind, some degree of Eurasian-wide diffusion is perhaps likely, unless one falls back on coincidence. Sea-borne movements from India to the Andamans and Sumatra were certainly possible, as they were of course in the opposite direction, but no definite statement of relationship can be made without further detailed study.

To the north, there are also many similarities to be noted with Japan. Blade-like flakes and bifacially flaked points (like some Australian examples) are known in southern and central Japan from possibly 30,000 B.C.; microblade industries appear after *c.* 15,000 B.C. in southern Japan[130]; and in the succeeding Jomon ceramic period there are hollow-based points like those of the Toalean and Java. Microliths are not apparently present, but this may not be very significant, and Japan generally has the closest relationships of any outside area with the flake and blade technocomplex of Island Southeast Asia. As with India, definite statements on the nature of the relationship cannot be made at present, but the possibility of contact would seem to merit a good deal of further research.

SUMMARY

We have seen that the record of stone-tool production in Southeast Asia goes back some 700,000 years, commencing with the pebble and flake industries of the Middle Pleistocene.

Unfortunately, these early industries have not yet been found in direct association with man outside China, but on circumstantial grounds they can almost certainly be attributed to *Homo erectus*. Industries of this type also occur to the east of the Wallace Line in the Philippines and Nusatenggara, but an antiquity in excess of 40,000 years for these areas cannot yet be proven.

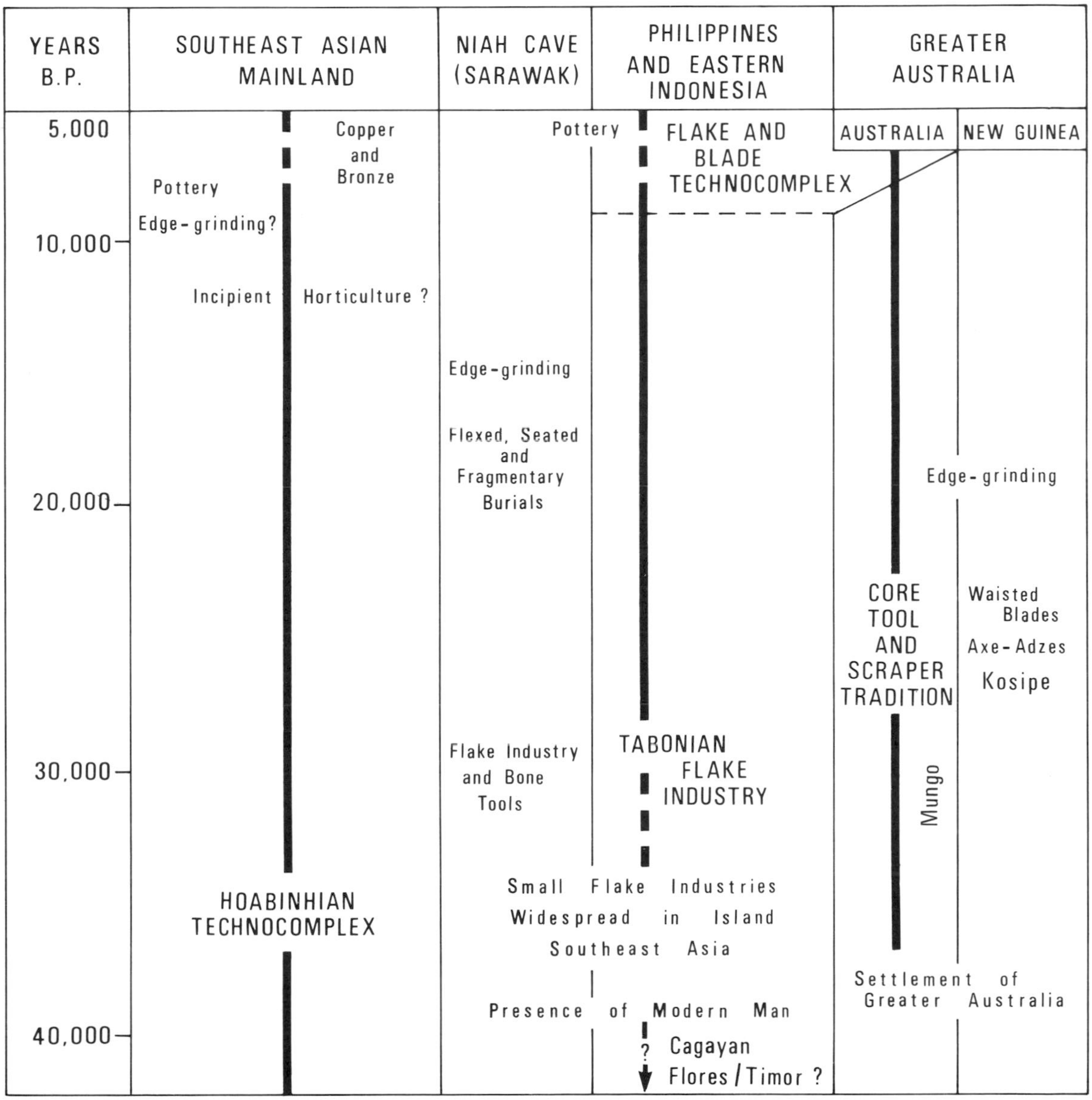

YEARS B.P.	SOUTHEAST ASIAN MAINLAND	NIAH CAVE (SARAWAK)	PHILIPPINES AND EASTERN INDONESIA	GREATER AUSTRALIA	
5,000	Copper and Bronze	Pottery	FLAKE AND BLADE TECHNOCOMPLEX	AUSTRALIA	NEW GUINEA
	Pottery Edge-grinding?				
10,000	Incipient Horticulture ?				
		Edge-grinding			
		Flexed, Seated and Fragmentary Burials			Edge-grinding
20,000					
				CORE TOOL AND SCRAPER TRADITION	Waisted Blades Axe-Adzes Kosipe
30,000		Flake Industry and Bone Tools	TABONIAN FLAKE INDUSTRY	Mungo	
	HOABINHIAN TECHNOCOMPLEX	Small Flake Industries Widespread in Island Southeast Asia			
		Presence of Modern Man		Settlement of Greater Australia	
40,000			? Cagayan Flores / Timor ?		

Fig. 3.12. Chart of Late Pleistocene and Early Holocene cultural developments in Southeast Asia.

On the Southeast Asian mainland, the Hoabinhian technocomplex with its important pebble-tool element seems to have developed without a break from the earlier pebble and flake industries, and this circumstance may help to explain the rather obscure nature of its commencement. Towards the end of the Pleistocene the innovation of edge-grinding of stone axes makes its appearance, and some developments in the direction of a horticultural economy have been postulated by some authors. Certainly, pottery was in production by 7000 B.C. in north-western Thailand, although, as in Japan, the presence of ceramics need not automatically imply horticulture. In fact, further knowledge of the Hoabinhian will probably depend on the application of modern excavation techniques to some of the coastal shell-middens, since these sites may contain evidence for a wider range of activities than the caves and rock shelters which have attracted most archaeological attention so far.

In Island Southeast Asia, the pebble and flake industries of the Middle Pleistocene give way in the Upper Pleistocene to industries concerned more with the production of smaller flakes, and pebble tools fade in importance after 40,000 years ago. During early Holocene times a more advanced flake and blade technocomplex spreads, possibly without major population change, through the Philippines and eastern Indonesia into Australia. The domestic dog may appear in these regions at the same time, but horticultural developments prior to the period of Austronesian expansion (5000–3000 B.C.) have not yet been demonstrated. The most likely point of origin for the blade technology is Japan, where an antiquity in excess of 15,000 years has been demonstrated.

The Hoabinhian and flake-blade technocomplexes are thus markedly different in technological terms, and edge-ground tools are so far unreported from the latter (except in Australia). Gradations from one to the other may one day be demonstrated for intermediate geographical regions such as Sumatra and Taiwan, and it is difficult at present to point to reasons, ecological or cultural, for the observed differences. Tropical forest environments may provide the milieu for the Hoabinhian, but the flake and blade industries are found through such a range of habitats – islands large and small, forests, savannas and deserts – that generalization is impossible. It may be that techniques of blade production spread with expanding Mongoloid populations in Island Southeast Asia, but this explanation would not of course apply to Australia. We still have a lot to learn.

So we have now examined the evidence for human activity in the Pleistocene and earlier Holocene epochs, bringing the record down to the later phases of the Hoabinhian and flake-blade technocomplexes. The human populations associated with these developments have been described in chapter 2, and a broader discussion was presented there of the present-day populations of the region and of their antecedents. The remaining chapters of this book are concerned mainly with the prehistory of the past 7000 years or so, and we are rapidly reaching a point where present distributions of ethnic groups, languages and economic systems are of direct relevance for archaeological interpretation. Accordingly, the following three chapters are devoted to these topics in turn, after which we take up the thread of archaeological prehistory again in chapter 7.

Footnotes

1. Flint 1971: 382.
2. Chappell 1968; Evans 1971.
3. Hooijer 1962; 1975.
4. Milliman and Emory 1969; Flint 1971: 318; Bloom 1971: 376; Emory, Niino and Sullivan 1971: 389; Chappell 1974.
5. Tjia 1973. See also Ashton 1972: 37 for high Holocene sea-levels in Malaya, and Fontaine and Delibrias (1973) for South Vietnam.
6. Colani 1927; Patte 1932. The inland situation could of course be caused by coastal silting or uplift, rather than by a higher sea-level.
7. Tsukada 1966; Chang 1970.
8. e.g. Movius 1944.
9. Evans 1971.
10. Kuenen 1950: fig. 203; Darlington 1957: 489.
11. Mayr 1945; Darlington 1957: 462–72. The Wallace Line as given here has been modified by Huxley.
12. Audley-Charles and Hooijer 1973. See also Hooijer 1958; 1967–8; 1969; 1975. Valuable comments on the Sulawesi faunas were provided by Dr Colin Groves (see Groves 1976).
13. Hooijer 1958; Darlington 1957: 504–5, 519. Lin (1963; fig. 4) shows Luzon joined to Taiwan during the second glaciation; von Koenigswald (1968a) also postulates second glaciation (Mindel) landbridges to take dwarf stegodonts to Flores, Taiwan and the Philippines. See also von Koenigswald 1956.

14. From Movius 1944: opposite p. 108; Hooijer 1962; Flint 1971: 674; Medway 1972.

15. Jacob 1972a.

16. Hooijer (1962; 1968) has suggested that the Jetis fauna could be Middle Pleistocene, but the early date makes this unlikely.

17. von Koenigswald 1968a.

18. On the Pacitanian and generally contemporary Southeast Asian industries see Movius 1944; 1948; 1949; 1955; van Heekeren 1972; Mulvaney 1970; Ghosh 1971; Bartstra 1976.

19. Movius 1944. In fact the dating of the Pacitanian is not as sound as might be wished; see Heine Geldern 1945: 155. Bartstra (1974) and von Koenigswald and Ghosh (1973) have recently supported an Upper Pleistocene date. Other small undated assemblages typologically similar to the Pacitanian are known from Sumatra, Java and Bali; Soejono 1961; C.R. Hooijer 1969.

20. Movius 1949: 355.

21. Soejono (communication at IXe Congres U.I.S.P.P., Nice 1976) states that hand-axes with transverse flaking have recently been found at Pacitan by G-J. Bartstra.

22. Glover and Glover 1970; Maringer and Verhoeven 1970a; 1970b; 1972.

23. Reports on Cagayan are not yet published, except for a preliminary notice by von Koenigswald (1958b). Papers presented at the Seminar on Southeast Asian Prehistory and Archaeology, Manila 1972 (Fox and Peralta), and at the IX International Congress of Anthropological and Ethnological Sciences, Chicago 1973 (Fox) are my main sources of information.

24. Walker and Sieveking 1962; Movius 1955: 531.

25. Harrisson 1975.

26. Boriskovsky 1967; 1968–71: part III.

27. Saurin 1966b.

28. Fleischer and Price 1964; Chapman 1964. On tektites generally see Beyer 1956.

29. Sørensen (communication at IXe Congres U.I.S.P.P., Nice, 1976) reports stone tools from the sites of Ban Dan Chumpol and Amphoe Mae Tha in northern Thailand which probably date between 0.5 and 1 million years on the basis of dated basalt flows.

30. Saurin 1971.

31. Saurin 1968b.

32. Carbonnel and Biberson 1968.

33. Fromaget 1940a; Movius 1955: 536.

34. Movius 1955; Chang 1968: 40–56.

35. Boriskovsky (1968–71: part II: 8–10) feels that the connections are stronger than most would admit.

36. Aigner 1973.

37. von Koenigswald, in Weidenreich 1951.

38. van Heekeren 1972: 49. See also von Koenigswald and Ghosh (1973) who suggest a Middle Pleistocene date for the Sangiran assemblage, although this is in turn disputed by Bartstra (1974), who prefers an Upper Pleistocene date.

39. Maringer and Verhoeven 1970a, b. See also Almeida and Zbyszewski 1967, for eastern Timor.

40. Movius 1955: 530; van Heekeren 1958a. van Heekeren (1972: 71) places the Cabenge industry in the late Middle Pleistocene, on faunal associations.

41. Beyer 1947: 246. The actual description is of 'Palaeolithic choppers or hand-axes'.

42. Harrisson 1957; 1958a; 1959b; 1963; 1967; 1970; Medway 1959; Harrisson and Medway 1962.

43. Harrisson, Hooijer and Medway 1961.

44. Hooijer 1963.

45. Petersen 1969.

46. Clutton Brock 1959.

47. Harrisson 1967.

48. Golson (1971a) has used a depositional rate of one inch every 400 ± 75 years (from Harrisson 1959; footnote 23) to calculate the higher dates of 13,000 and 6000 B.C. The lower dates are from Harrisson.

49. B. Harrisson 1967; T. Harrisson 1976: 17.

50. Fox 1967; 1970.

51. Fox 1970.

52. Mulvaney 1975; Jones 1973; Barbetti and Allen 1972.

53. Bowler, Jones, Allen and Thorne 1970.

54. See Glover 1973b. There are also similarities in the utilisation of food plants between Indonesia and Northern Australia (Golson 1971b).

55. C. White 1971.

56. Morlan 1967: 201; Blundell and Bleed 1974.

57. White, Crook and Buxton 1970.

58. Hope and Peterson 1975.

59. S. Bulmer: personal communication (Wañlek); White 1971; 1972a (Kafiavana). J. and G. Hope (1974) have suggested that the extensive high-level grasslands of late Pleistocene New Guinea could in theory have supported substantial human populations.

60. After Gorman 1971; Clarke 1968.

61. e.g. Colani 1927; Dani 1960.

62. Matthews 1964.

63. Gorman 1971: 312.

64. J.P. White 1967; 1969.

65. Boriskovsky 1968–71: part IV: 236–8; Gorman 1971.

66. From Matthews 1964, 1966; van Heekeren and Knuth 1967.

67. Colani 1927. For Vietnam generally see Bezacier 1972 (p. 25–53 on the Hoabinhian and the Bacsonian).

68. Colani 1930.

69. *Praehistorica Asiae Orientalis* 1932.

70. Matthews 1966.

71. Colani 1927: 25.

72. Boriskovsky 1968–71, part IV.

73. Da-Phuc, Thanh-Hoa Province; Colani 1929: fig. 24. Hang-Muoi, Hoa-Binh Province; Boriskovsky 1968–71, part IV.

74. Mansuy 1924; Mansuy et Colani 1925.

75. Boriskovsky 1971: 105.

76. Patte 1932; Boriskovsky 1968–71, part VI.

77. Boriskovsky 1968–71, part V, for Quynh-Van. Since this chapter was written a date of 8040±200 B.C. had been published for a Bacsonian site at Bo-Lum, but I know little of the context (Nguyen 1975: 36).

78. Dani 1960: 146.

79. As pointed out by Golson 1971a: 130.

80. Peacock 1965.

81. Peacock 1971.

82. Dunn 1964; 1966.

83. Sieveking 1954. Some of the Hoabinhian tools from Gua Cha are finely retouched, and thin bifacials of oval or square shape are frequent.

84. Medway 1969: 203.

85. Callenfels and Noone 1940; Callenfels and Evans 1928.

86. Collings 1940.

87. As at Gua Chawan: Peacock 1964c.

88. Tweedie 1953: 12, 74.

89. Tweedie 1953: 65–9.

90. Heekeren and Knuth 1967.

91. Gorman 1970; 1971.

92. Carbon dates between 7000 and 9500 B.C. are also reported for a Hoabinhian assemblage at Ongbah Cave in west-central Thailand. See Tauber 1973.

93. Fromaget 1940b: 68; Saurin 1966c.

94. Watson (1968) also mentions the presence of perforated pebbles in Hoabinhian deposits at Nguang Chang Cave in north-west Thailand.

95. Mourer C. and R. 1970.

96. van Heekeren 1972: 85–92. Similar shell-middens may also exist in the Andaman Islands. See Heine Geldern 1946: 164.

97. Cheng 1957; 1959: 47.

98. Cheng 1959: 47–51; 1966: 14–15; Chang 1968: 73–7.

99. Chang 1969b.

100. Further articles on the Hoabinhian generally are Callenfels 1936, Dunn 1970.

101. For general viewpoints see Chang 1970; Solheim 1972.

102. Tsukada 1966; Chang 1970.

103. Gorman 1971.

104. Medway 1969.

105. V. Morlan 1971: 143.

106. Defined as blades under 5 mm in width by Kobayashi 1970.

107. Fox 1970: chapter 3.

108. Fox 1970: 59.

109. Beyer 1947: figs 4, 5; 1948: 14, figs. 5a, 5b (for Luzon); Scheans et al. 1970 (for Samar).

110. van Heekeren 1949; 1950; 1972.

111. These microliths do not demonstrate the micro-burin technique of European microliths and are each apparently made as a separate blade or flake. In addition, it should be noted that the specific Toalean types mentioned are found with a much more numerous category of waste flakes.

112. Callenfels 1938; van Heekeren 1972: 113–4.

113. Glover 1975 and personal communication.

114. Mulvaney and Soejono 1970; 1971.

115. Hooijer 1950a.

116. van Heekeren 1950b; 1972.

117. Mulvaney 1975.

118. McCarthy 1940. van Heekeren (1972: 125) has suggested that geometric microliths and rock paintings may actually have spread to Indonesia from Australia.

119. Glover 1969; 1971; 1972a.

120. A similar edge-gloss on small blades has recently been reported from the east central Philippines (Scheans et al. 1970) and from northern Luzon (Peterson 1974).

121. Callenfels 1932. See also Heine Geldern 1945.

122. van Heekeren 1972: 94.

123. Erdbrink 1954. The Gua Lawa fauna included banteng cattle, pig, deer, monkey, rhinoceros and elephant.

124. Heine Geldern 1932: 554.

125. Bandi 1951; van Heekeren 1972: 133–7.

126. Dr B. Bronson: personal communication.

127. Dutta 1966: 183–4.

128. Mulvaney 1971: 10. But see also footnote 70 in chapter 6.

129. Fairservis 1971: chapter 3; Glover 1973a; Misra 1973. The Indian blade tools and microliths are more varied in form than those of Southeast Asia.

130. V. Morlan 1971.

CHAPTER 4

The Cultures of Southeast Asia and Oceania

Over the past four hundred and fifty years European explorers have contacted most, perhaps all, of the segments of a vast spread of ethnic complexity extending from Southeast Asia to Easter Island. If one is prepared to equate an ethnic group loosely with a linguistic group (see page 22), then there are possibly almost two thousand ethnic groups in the area, each with its own life style and idiosyncracies[1]. The literature on the ethnography of Oceania alone now comprises some twenty thousand books and articles, and at present over 300 pages of ethnographic information, including mimeographed reports, are produced in New Guinea alone every month[2]. It is not the aim of this chapter to synthesize this vast mass of material, and I am not qualified to attempt such a task. My intention is simply to bring some of the more salient facts of the subject before the reader, on the grounds that the prehistory of an area such as the Pacific would be rather meaningless if considered in isolation from the present ethnic situation. For if we exclude the cultures resulting from the historical civilisations of Southeast Asia and Indonesia, then it is true to say that Pacific Island ethnography is the direct end-product of prehistory, and conversely, Pacific Island prehistory is of course the story behind the formation of the present ethnic groups. One need hardly emphasise this point further.

I have therefore planned this chapter as a brief survey of some major aspects of Pacific cultures. These include systems of descent and local group membership and recruitment, together with systems of areal integration as expressed through concepts of rank and political organisation, and also through the workings of such phenomena as trade and tribute and the patterning of settlements. The archaeologist cannot of course reconstruct these features for prehistoric societies with equal degrees of confidence, but a comparative study of them in Pacific societies at European contact will certainly bring to light some very interesting questions concerning the general culture history of the area. Some of these questions will be considered in due course.

Unfortunately for the anthropologist, it is not always an easy matter to describe a society as it was at first European contact. European ships have roamed the Pacific for over four hundred years, and changes took place in local societies long before the period of intensive colonisation in the nineteenth and twentieth centuries. In Polynesia, for instance, many societies remained unrecorded until the Bishop Museum in Honolulu commenced a monumental campaign of research in the 1920s, and it is often a difficult matter to sort out those features of a society which are in fact indigenous and pre-European. These, of course, are the features which the archaeologist is most interested in. Unrecorded castaways from wrecked European ships[3] and the biases of early observers pose problems for the unwary, and it was often hard for early explorers to see Oceanic societies functioning in everyday manners – the mere presence of a shipload of Europeans in the eighteenth century was sufficient to impose on a Polynesian society a most unusual succession of activities. Captain Cook, perhaps the most observant of the eighteenth century explorers, noted for Tonga in 1777: 'it was always holyday with our visitors as well as with those we visited, so that we had but few opportunities of seeing into their domistick way of living'[4]. It need not be stressed that there is a great deal the ethnographer does not know, and never will know, about the domestic way of living in Tonga in 1777. On the other hand, recently contacted areas such as the New Guinea Highlands do not suffer from quite the same drawbacks, since anthropological studies can be made before too many changes take place.

Before turning to the societies themselves, a few points of terminology require clarification, particularly those pertaining to types of descent reckoning. A person's descent or parentage will determine to at least some extent where he makes his home, how he inherits or otherwise acquires land, property, and status, whom he marries, and many other events in his life trajectory. The majority of Oceanic societies have specific ideals determining descent, although these are more norms behind behaviour rather than rigid rules. From the viewpoint of terminology, societies may be of two kinds – unilineal and non-unilineal[5]. In the unilineal societies, which dominate most areas of Melanesia and Micronesia, a person of either sex will trace descent either in the male line (patrilineal) or in the female line (matrilineal). A group of unilineally related persons who can trace their relationship through specific genealogical links is referred to as a lineage, and a number of lineages may be linked by traditional bonds into a sib. By this definition, sibs acknowledge the bonding links of unilinear descent, but are unable to trace them specifically. Two or more sibs may be grouped into a higher order group known as a phratry, and if a society comprises two phratries, these groups are referred to as moieties. The lineage is a consanguineal kin group – all members being related by blood ties – and usually it is exogamous; i.e. no member may marry another member of the same group. The higher order groups are consanguineal to a lesser extent, but like the lineage are normally exogamous.

The factor of exogamy necessarily means that a local residential group must comprise more than a single lineage or sib, for spouses are always drawn from other lineages outside the range of exogamy. The ideal local group in a unilineal society is thus one which consists of lineage or sib members together with spouses and children, and such a group is referred to as a 'clan'. The clan is therefore a residential kin group, and should not be confused with the lineage, which is a consanguineal kin group. However, both

lineages and clans are really anthropological ideals, and as we will see in due course, societies in reality are made much more complex by allowable deviations from these norms.

The non-unilineal societies dominate Polynesia and Southeast Asia generally. In Polynesia and parts of Taiwan, descent may be classified as ambilineal, since a person has a choice of tracing descent, and therefore of acquiring land and group membership, either through his mother, or through his father, or perhaps through both. A child's affiliation will depend to some extent on the residence of his parents – for instance if they dwell with the mother's group, a child will affiliate with his mother's kinship group. The ideal local group in such societies is not of the clan type, but instead will comprise a group of cognatically related individuals (i.e. individuals related by blood, but not through one sex only) together with affines (persons related by marriage).

Another type of non-unilineal descent which is important in Indonesia and the Philippines is referred to as bilateral or bilineal (usually by the former term), in which both parents are equally recognised for purposes of filiation. Bilateral societies as defined by Murdock[6] have no functionally significant descent groups at all (on which point in particular they differ from ambilineal societies), no exogamous groups, and the nuclear family serves as a relatively independent unit which may retain a corporate function from generation to generation. If a person marries out or chooses to settle elsewhere, he simply becomes a member of the family with which he has taken up residence, or starts a new family by settling on a plot of freshly-cleared land. Such a system is of course fairly close to that characteristic of Western society today.

Systems of descent therefore vary considerably over the Pacific area, and the same may be said of systems of rank, which do not correlate in a one-to-one fashion with descent. Melanesian clans are frequently split into autonomous and virtually acephalous segments, while in areas of Micronesia the segments may be part of a complex ranking system culminating in a paramount clan chief. There are thus major differences between these two areas, even though both have the factor of unilineal descent in common. In Polynesia, the ambilineal descent groups are referred to as 'ramages', and within each ramage rank was determined partially by means of primogeniture and seniority of descent, the latter being remembered for twenty or more generations in the case of a high-ranking individual. Hence Polynesians developed aristocratic ranking of a kind which was uncommon in Melanesia, Indonesia or the Philippines, although similar concepts were more common in Micronesia.

In the remainder of this chapter various Pacific societies are described briefly. In the first two sections, on Mainland and Island Southeast Asia, the points made are fairly generalised because of the changes to indigenous societies wrought by Indian, Chinese, Islamic and European civilisations over the past 2000 years.

THE SOUTHEAST ASIAN MAINLAND

The area of Mainland Southeast Asia, here taken to include south China but not Burma, is the home of eight major ethnolinguistic groups (figure 4.1)[7]. Five of these will be described briefly in this section, while the last three will be described together with the peoples of Indonesia and the Philippines in the following section. The eight groups are as follows:

1. The Miao and Yao speaking peoples of south China, northern Laos and North Vietnam.
2. The Thai and Kadai speakers.
3. The Khmer speaking peoples.
4. The Vietnamese.
5. The Chams of South Vietnam and southern Cambodia.
6. The Malays.
7. The Semang of interior Malaya.
8. The Senoi of interior Malaya.

Crosscutting this ethnolinguistic classification is the important distinction between hill-peoples and plains-peoples[8], a distinction which has its origin both in the basic topographical character of the area as well as in its history. The flat coastal and riverine plains have for almost two thousand years been the backdrops for elaborate civilisations based economically on wet-rice cultivation. To these civilisations, India has contributed religion, royalty, the Sanscrit script, and a literary tradition. From China, on the other hand, the influence was more towards political and commercial intervention. By contrast, the hill peoples have remained generally isolated, heterogeneous, dependent upon shifting rice agriculture, and have retained small-scale political organisations without elaborate ranking

systems. Whether distinctions of a similar order between hill and plains cultures go back into prehistory is uncertain, but would seem to be rather likely.

The Indianized kingdoms of Southeast Asia of course brought prehistory to a close in many of the lowland areas, but since the activities of these kingdoms did not concern the Pacific Islands directly, they will only be mentioned in passing in this section. In the early years of the first millennium A.D. their influences did not spread far beyond Sulawesi, and the Philippines seem to have received little Chinese or Indonesian influence until after the seventh century. Concerning the lowland peoples of the Southeast Asian mainland on the eve of Indian contact, Burling[9] has suggested that wet-rice, buffalo, cattle and metals were part of the economy, and archaeology has recently thrown some very interesting light on the antiquity of these traits. On the other hand, there is as yet no firm evidence for urbanisation or writing prior to Indian contact.

We may commence our survey of the ethnolinguistic groups with the Miao and Yao speakers, who survive today as pockets of upland shifting agriculturalists scattered over a large area in south China, North Vietnam, northern Laos and northern Thailand. They share little cultural unity, although this situation may be a result of demographic fragmentation through Chinese and Thai expansion within the past two millennia. Before the Han period in China (202 B.C. to A.D. 220), the Miao and Yao are reported as dwelling along the lower middle Yangtze River, and their historical movements into northern Laos, Thailand and Hainan have all taken place within the past five hundred years. Today they contribute to an astonishing belt of ethnic diversity extending from south China into northern Laos and Thailand, in which cultures are far removed from undivided territorial entities, and villages of Thai, Han Chinese, Lolo or Miao affinity may exist side by side in a complex mosaic. The Miao and Yao speak languages which may be very remotely related to Chinese and some of the languages of Burma, and may have been an important ethnic element in south China during the period prior to Eastern Chou expansion in the first millennium B.C. On these grounds, they may prove to be of more than peripheral concern in Southeast Asian prehistory.

The Thai and Kadai speaking groups are of interest because of Benedict's inclusion of these

Fig. 4.1. Major ethnolinguistic groups of Southeast Asia.

languages, together with Austronesian, in an Austro-Thai family[10] . This will be discussed in more detail later, but the prehistoric implications of such a link, if ever fully vindicated, would be most interesting. The Thai speakers include the Shans of Burma, the Siamese of Thailand, the Lao of Laos, and several other groups extending up into south China. The history of the Thai speakers is not very clear, but a major period of Thai expansion southward into the area which is now Thailand may have taken place in the thirteenth century as a result of Mongol pressure from the North. However, the area of greatest linguistic and cultural diversity amongst the Thais lies in north Vietnam and in the Kwangsi and Kweichow provinces of south China, and prior to historical times this area may have been the centre of distribution of the group, to be followed much later by piecemeal migrations to the south within the past thousand years[11]. Such a distribution would bring the Thai into closer geographical relationship with their distant Kadai linguistic relatives, who include the Li of Hainan, and pockets of Keleo (or Keh Lao) who now survive some 800 kilometres away in Kweichow Province. Chinese records suggest that these Kadai speakers may be remnants of the Lao, a group recorded in Chinese records as inhabiting the areas of Kweichow, Hunan and Kwangsi by 110 B.C., with a culture characterised by pile dwellings, bronze drums and cave burial[12].

Within the Mon-Khmer linguistic group, the Mons today inhabit only a small area around the mouth of the Salween River in Burma, while the Khmers fall into two major groups – lowland and upland. The lowland Khmers of Cambodia are wet-rice cultivators who expanded widely after the fall of the ancient Indianised kingdom of Funan, which was probably established in the first century A.D. and survived until its incorporation into a succeeding Khmer kingdom in the early seventh century A.D.[13]. Funan achieved its maximum extent by A.D. 350, and extended from the border of Cham territory in South Vietnam right round the Gulf of Siam to include a number of subsidiary trading ports on the narrow neck of the Malayan Peninsula. Whether the language of Funan was related to Khmer is not known, but would appear likely. Surprisingly enough, from the viewpoint of physical anthropology (see page 46), Chinese records in one text describe the people of Funan at about A.D. 250 as having black skins and frizzly hair[14], and, in addition, they are reported as living in palisaded towns with pile dwellings, and as agriculturalists and metal workers in gold and silver.

The mountain Khmers are shifting agriculturalists who inhabit pockets of territory through Burma, northern Thailand, and Laos, and down into the extensive Annamite chain between the Mekong Valley and the coastal areas of South Vietnam. Many of these upland groups are described as darker skinned than the lowland Mongoloid peoples of Southeast Asia, although whether this is the result of environmental adaptation or assimilation of remnant Australoid groups cannot easily be determined.

The Vietnamese languages are related to Mon-Khmer, and both groups are widely agreed to belong to a widespread family called Austro-Asiatic, which also includes the Munda languages of eastern India, Nicobarese, and the languages spoken by the Semang and Senoi of Malaya. One estimate for the split between Vietnamese and Mon-Khmer would place it between 2000 and 1000 B.C.[15]. Originally, the Vietnamese were located in the area of the Red River Valley in North Vietnam, and were there under direct Chinese domination from 111 B.C. to A.D. 939. After this date they expanded to the south, and finally expelled the Austronesian Chamic speakers from the Mekong delta in the seventeenth century, after defeating the kingdom of Champa in 1471.

The Chams now occupy part of the Annamite chain in South Vietnam, together with isolated pockets of upland territory in southern Cambodia. Their languages belong to the great Austronesian family which today dominates the whole Pacific area apart from Australia and parts of western Melanesia, and linguistic evidence suggests that the Chamic languages broke away from related languages in Indonesia or Malaya prior to 1000 B.C.[16]. The Indianized Cham-speaking kingdom called Champa was established in South Vietnam in the second century A.D., and this kingdom survived until its above-mentioned defeat by the Vietnamese in 1471. A Chinese source of the late sixth century reports that the people of Champa lived in houses of fired bricks covered with a layer of lime, that they cremated their dead and deposited the ashes in the sea or a river, and that they were ruled by a king who travelled on an elephant and was surrounded, like the contemporary ruler of Funan to the west, by a great deal of ritual deference[17].

Apart from the lowland Chams, many Cham

groups such as the Churu, Jarai and Rhade, live in the hills of South Vietnam and southern Cambodia. Some of these people inhabit villages of longhouses built on piles, and cultivate rice by shifting cultivation. There is little political organisation above the village level, and political power is in many cases vested in an elected headman and a council of elders, as it still is in many of the remoter parts of Indonesia and the Philippines. The Chams have a matrilineal descent system, and represent an aspect of the rather astonishing diversity of social organisation amongst the Austronesian speakers.

On the linguistic history of Mainland Southeast Asia, present distributions and centres of diversity would suggest that prior to the period of Indian and Chinese expansion at or soon after the time of Christ, most of the area to the south of the Chinese border was inhabited by speakers of languages ancestral to the present Mon-Khmer and Vietnamese families[18]. The Semang Negritos of Malaya still retain an isolated language related to Mon-Khmer, although they are now geographically isolated owing to Thai and Malay expansion. Austronesian languages appear to have been established in Malaya and South Vietnam by perhaps 3000 years ago, and at a similar period languages related to the Thai-Kadai and Miao-Yao groups may have been dominant in southern China[19]. Paul Benedict has postulated ancient links between Thai-Kadai and Austronesian which some linguists do not accept, and no Austronesian languages are spoken in the area of south China today, nor do historical records clearly indicate that any ever were. However, languages remotely ancestral to Austronesian may have been spoken on the southern Chinese mainland prior to perhaps 7000 years ago (see page 123), and if these were obliterated by the expansion of Chinese and the Thai-Kadai languages then it is possible that no traces would remain. So Austronesian might have a very remote homeland in southern China beyond the range of linguistic reconstruction, but there is no definite proof. At present, the earliest reconstructible 'homeland' of Austronesian languages lies somewhere in Island Southeast Asia, as we will see in the chapter which follows.

ISLAND SOUTHEAST ASIA

The peoples of Indonesia, the Philippines and Taiwan are for the most part Austronesian-speaking Mongoloids, equipped with a sedentary agricultural or fishing economy. But before these people are surveyed, it is necessary to examine briefly three very different groups who, on convincing circumstantial grounds, represent the virtually direct descendants of an ancient and widespread Australoid population of hunters and gatherers. These groups comprise the Andamanese, the Semang of the lowland inland jungles of the Malay peninsula, and the Negritos of Luzon, Panay, Negros and north-eastern Mindanao in the Philippines[20]. The term 'Negrito' may be used legitimately to describe the whole group, and their physical characteristics are discussed in chapter 2.

The Negritos do not share any linguistic relationships, for the Andamanese have their own distinctive language which has no certain relatives, the Semang speak languages related to the Mon-Khmer family, and the Negritos of the Philippines speak Austronesian languages. Whether the Negritos ever once shared a common language is unknown, and far beyond the range of linguistic reconstruction.

The Negrito economy is based on hunting and gathering, with fishing being of importance in the Andamans. Local groups comprise exogamous bands of perhaps five to ten families, who inhabit groups of thatched lean-tos, usually around an oval or circular central open space. On Little Andaman Island, the lean-tos are linked into an annular construction. Camps are moved frequently, either for economic reasons or because of quarrels, deaths, feelings of ill luck, or even when a large animal has been killed and it requires less effort to move the camp to the animal than the animal to the camp[21].

Band leadership is normally by age or consensus, and the bands themselves are autonomous. Territories are normally exploited by the band in common, but concepts of private ownership may be applied to useful trees. All groups evidently hunted with bows and arrows in the past, but the Semang have recently adopted the blowgun. The Andamanese lack the dog, and are reputed to be unable to make fire, although they are the only group who make pottery. Today, several groups in Malaya and the Philippines are adopting a very rudimentary form of horticulture, in which clearings are planted but normally left untended until the harvest. Although horticultural techniques have evidently been borrowed from neighbouring peoples, these Negrito groups nevertheless represent an interesting transitional stage between gathering and serious horticulture.

Adjacent to the Semang, in the central mountains of Malaya, live the Senoi (or Sakai), a group who physically occupy a clinal position between the Semang Negritos and the Malays. Like the Semang, they speak a language related to the Mon-Khmer family. Where not in close contact with the Malays, the Senoi inhabit villages of pile-built longhouses, within which related groups of bilateral nuclear families dwell under the leadership of influential elders. Shifting agriculture is practised, usually of millet or rice[22].

Apart from the groups just mentioned, the whole area of Indonesia, the Philippines and coastal Malaya is occupied by Austronesian speakers, excluding of course the non-indigenous ethnic strains which have entered the area within the past two thousand years, and a few areas of Papuan speech in eastern Indonesia. In Malaya, the coastal Malays are now Islamicised, but the Jakun peoples of the southern interior of the Peninsula appear to have preserved more features of an indigenous way of life, and still practise shifting agriculture with rice and millet, inhabit villages of longhouses on piles, and evidently retain a fairly weak political structure.

The ethnic pattern in Indonesia is especially complex, with over three hundred ethnic groups and over two hundred and fifty languages according to Hildred Geertz[23]. Geertz distinguishes three broad types of society: the strongly Hinduised inland wet-rice cultivators; the Islamic coastal peoples; and the mainly pagan tribal groups of the mountainous interiors and eastern islands. Our main interest is with the latter group, which includes populations in central Sulawesi, Halmahera, interior Seram, parts of Nusatenggara, interior Borneo and parts of Sumatra. If we exclude the Islamic coastal peoples from consideration, then the division between Hinduised and pagan peoples corresponds roughly, but not exactly, with the division between 'Inner' and 'Outer' Indonesia, as defined by Clifford Geertz[24]. The former refers to the densely populated zones of wet-rice cultivation in Java, south Bali and west Lombok, the latter to the extensive band of territory with shifting agriculture stretching right across Indonesia. Rice irrigation was probably established on Java by at least the eighth century, and this fertile volcanic island today supports populations of astonishing density, in marked contrast to the much more sparsely settled outer islands where shifting agriculture is still practised.

The shifting agriculturalists with whom we are concerned, and who still occupy the greater part of Outer Indonesia, defy simple description in that they are broken into many small and culturally diverse populations[25]. However, prior to intensive contact with outsiders, it appears that an economy based on dry-land rice or tuber cultivation, and small and rather autonomous village settlements, was characteristic of much of the area. Until the early nineteenth century a hunting and gathering population (the Kubu) lived amongst the hills and swamps of southeastern Sumatra, and the Punans of interior Borneo still in many cases live on wild sago starch and other forest produce, in fairly mobile bands.

Throughout the non-Indianised and non-Islamicised areas of Indonesia, there is generally little emphasis on unilineality in descent group organisation. However, in eastern Nusatenggara and Maluku, close to Irian Jaya and Melanesia, patrilineal societies are widespread, and there are a few pockets of matrilineal descent in Timor and adjacent islands to the east. Elsewhere, bilateral societies predominate, with an organisation of fairly autonomous villages under headmen or hereditary petty chiefs. Murdock[26] characterises these societies as having a virtual absence of descent groups and extended families, a prevalence of monogamy, and ambilocal or neolocal post-marital residence (with ambilocal residence the couple may dwell with either the wife's or the husband's family, while with neolocal residence, a new household is established). Bilateral societies include the Iban, Land Dayaks and other peoples of Borneo, the majority of peoples in the Philippines (including the Negritos), the Andamanese and Nicobarese, and the Yami of Botel Tobago Island.

For an example of a bilateral society we may turn to the Ulu Ai Iban of Sarawak (East Malaysia), described by Derek Freeman[27]. The basic unit of social organisation here is the *bilek* family, which usually consists of a nuclear family together with a pair of grandparents – six or seven persons in all. The *bilek* family is a corporate land and property owning group, which survives from generation to generation as new members are born or join through marriage or other ties of relationship. It occupies an apartment in a longhouse (figure 4.2), and many Iban villages consist simply of one of these longhouses, which may be up to 200 metres long, raised on piles, and hold up to 50 families. The living apartments are in a line down one side of the building, and a

Fig. 4.2. Verandah of a Land Dayak longhouse at Mentu Tapuh, Sarawak.

thoroughfare and open verandah for everyday activities runs down the other side. The longhouse village is not strictly a corporate group – each family is independent, but many families are related through cognatic ties, and overall leadership is by an elected headman.

Longhouse villages of this type are common in Indonesia, but mainly occur with unilineal societies, where large extended families are more common. With the bilateral societies of Indonesia and the Philippines smaller nuclear or extended family houses are the dominant form, although longhouses are quite common amongst the bilateral societies of Borneo, as in the case of the Iban.

The non-Christian and non-Mohammedan peoples of the Philippines, like those of Outer Indonesia, are mostly shifting agriculturalists growing rice or tubers. Bilateral descent is predominant throughout the archipelago, and prior to Spanish contact, a hamlet or dispersed neighbourhood pattern of settlement predominated, as distinct from the longhouse village settlements of much of Outer Indonesia. To take one example, the Subanun of Mindanao have their houses scattered amongst swiddens, and move their locations frequently as new fields are cleared. Subanun nuclear families are bilateral, autonomous and impermanent, and there seem to be no concepts of a descent group of any kind. As another example, the Isneg of northern Luzon dwell in hamlets of between two and 25 pile-houses, each occupied by a bilateral nuclear family, and each hamlet forms a fairly autonomous unit led by influential headmen whose status is based mainly on wealth and (in the past) skill in headhunting. Hamlet membership is based on cognatic or affinal ties, and a person may normally dwell with any group where he has relations[28].

The pattern of small hamlet settlements and relatively open systems of group membership also characterises some of the wet rice cultivators of the Mountain Province of northern Luzon[29]. Of these, the best known are perhaps the Ifugao[30], who cultivate wet-rice in spectacular terraces covering large areas of hillside, with some terraces being up to 15 metres high (see figure 4.3). Population densities may extend up to 250 persons per square kilometre, but villages are usually small clusters of nuclear family houses built on piles, together with raised rice granaries, and there is only a weakly developed form of leadership dependent upon wealth and achievement.

Some difficulties arise when one tries to reconstruct the pattern of life in the Philippines at Spanish contact, now four hundred years ago, for many groups have evidently been deeply affected and most probably forced inland by Spanish expansion[31]. When Spaniards arrived on the west coast of northern Luzon in 1571 they encountered people growing wet-rice, living in large villages, and even using a script derived from Indianised sources in Indonesia. But Keesing has suggested that much of the inland settlement, of terracers and swiddeners alike, is a result of Spanish pressure on the coast, although there may have been inland groups mining copper for Chinese traders before 1571. Against Keesing's view are the results of recent excavations on house terraces in the Ifugao area, which do suggest at least some pre-Spanish antiquity for the rice terracing complex in inland northern

Luzon, and we may note here the older view of Otley Beyer that the terraces may have been present as early as the first millennium B.C.[32]. However, the question is still clearly open for debate.

In Taiwan[33], Austronesian-speaking aboriginal peoples today inhabit the central and eastern parts of the island, and the west coast has been predominantly Chinese since the seventeenth century. As in the Philippines and Indonesia, the Austronesians live mostly by shifting agriculture, growing foxtail millet, rice, and tubers. The Atayals of the north, and the Paiwan of the south east have ambilineal descent systems, and a child affiliates either with his father's or with his mother's cognatic descent group, although a person can change his natal affiliations later in life if he wishes. The Atayal live in villages of semi-subterranean houses, and authority is vested in the heads of patrilineal groups, of which there are several in each village. The Paiwan inhabit very large villages and have a highly developed

Fig. 4.3. Ifugao rice terraces at Banaue, northern Luzon.

form of genealogical ranking similar to that of some of the Polynesians. Elsewhere in Aboriginal Taiwan descent is reckoned unilineally; the Bunun and Tsou of the central highlands are patrilineal, while the Ami of the central part of the east coast are matrilineal. Social stratification is weakly developed in Taiwan generally, except amongst the Paiwan, where its development could possibly be recent.

Owing to the many changes which have taken place under the influence of different civilisations over the past 1500 years, it is very difficult now to reconstruct the 'original' characteristics of prehistoric Western Austronesian life. The American social anthropologist Fay Cooper-Cole[34] has listed a number of features which may once have characterised prehistoric Philippine cultures – these include belief in the active powers of spirits, importance of omens, human sacrifice usually following the death of an important person, the ceremonial eating of human victims in order to gain strength and valour, the tattooing of successful warriors, shamanism, and magic. In addition, the Austrian ethnographer Robert Heine Geldern[35] published in 1932 a reconstruction of early Austronesian culture in Southeast Asia and Indonesia derived from archaeological and ethnographic observations, which included pile-dwellings, rice, millet, cattle, megalithic monuments, headhunting, outrigger canoes, possibly bark cloth manufacture, and a number of archaeologically verifiable traits which must await later discussion. To these two lists one might add a cognatic form of kinship reckoning and an absence of rigidly inherited status (or aristocracy), but here one could be on very weak ground. Indeed, for all the traits listed a good deal of caution is needed, owing to the difficulty of determining whether a widespread trait has been distributed through common inheritance or later borrowing. As an example, only archaeology will tell us for certain whether pile-built dwellings really belong to an early phase of Western Austronesian culture, or whether they have been diffused at a much later date, and the evidence to make a decision is not yet forthcoming. For more ethereal traits such as belief in omens, direct evidence may never be forthcoming. However, the matter of historical reconstruction from comparative surveys will be raised again later in connection with the whole Austronesian speaking world.

THE PEOPLES OF OCEANIA

Within Oceania, the prehistorian who wishes to make inference from present cultures is on firmer ground, for here prehistory ended in a piecemeal fashion between Magellan's discovery of Guam in 1521 and the last minor discoveries of the early nineteenth century. The difficulties of reconstructing the forms of societies at contact is sometimes great, however, particularly in the case of parts of Polynesia and western Micronesia, where Europeans were not slow to take advantage of the possibilities of exploitation.

MELANESIA

Melanesia has by far the greatest degree of ethnic diversity of any area in the Pacific. In the following pages it will be described in two sections – the New Guinea Highlands, and Island Melanesia (which also includes coastal New Guinea). This division is basically geographic and ecological, and does not coincide with any rigid and clearly-defined cultural boundaries, although it is true to say that Highland cultures do have many distinctive traits which mark them as a related group. These traits are in large part due to the unique ecological conditions of the area, and in part due to the lack of Austronesian influence – in other words, the present New Guinea Highland cultures would appear to be the descendants of a long-established Papuan-speaking culture group. The question of whether Austronesian and Papuan speakers in Melanesia can be differentiated as a whole with respect to culture is of course an important one, but one to which no clear answer is available. In some places there are a few distinct differences, as along the southern coast of Papua, where early European visitors noted that some of the Austronesian speakers were lighter skinned than their Papuan neighbours (see page 29), and also that they had more respect for their women[36]. On the other hand, such distinctions are not common elsewhere in Melanesia, where Austronesians and Papuans may have existed side by side for several thousand years, and cultures belonging to both language families are intricately intermixed in the Bismarcks and Solomons, where they are no obvious lines of demarcation. On Bougainville, for instance, societies belonging to the two linguistic categories cannot be well differentiated either physically or culturally[37].

The majority of the societies of western Melanesia, whether Austronesian or Papuan, do have in common a basic egalitarianism. Forge[38] has noted that local group sizes in western Melanesia fall around an average figure of 250 persons; beyond this figure it is assumed that face to face relationships would become attenuated, and ascriptive hierarchies would, in theory, evolve. Some villages in coastal riverine areas of New Guinea are in fact much larger than this, but are internally segmented into two or more clan or sub-clan groups who each retain their independence. Settlements of over 1000 people can occur in some favourable riverine areas, for instance on the Sepik River and in the swampy areas of southern New Guinea, but here the large settlement size may be directly related to a need for defence in numbers.

THE NEW GUINEA HIGHLANDS

The majority of the population within the 1000 kilometre long highland area between Lake Paniai and Kainantu inhabit broad valleys or sloping uplands between elevations of 1300 and 2300 metres[39]. Prior to the 1930s their existence was for the most part unknown, although the area contains the greater part of New Guinea's population and also perhaps the most favourable

ecological situations. Indeed, the area is the scene of some of the most intensive agricultural practices and highest population densities in Oceania, and this fact underlies a rather paradoxical situation in which high population density is combined with generally acephalous political groupings which are of a comparatively small scale.

New Guinea Highland societies are characterised generally by 'a commitment to agnation as a recruitment principle, preferential patrivirilocal residence, and the general existence of named patrilineal descent groups'[40]. But as the author of this statement and many other anthropologists have pointed out, local social systems incorporate a high degree of flexibility, and the individual often has a great deal of choice concerning affiliation to a group[41]. The basic ideal of a Highland residential and corporate group is the clan, which consists of a core of male agnates, unmarried female agnates who will leave the group at marriage, and the wives of the male agnates (who belong to other exogamous lineages). However, many of these clans contain in some cases as many as 50% of male members who are not *bona fide* agnates at all, but who

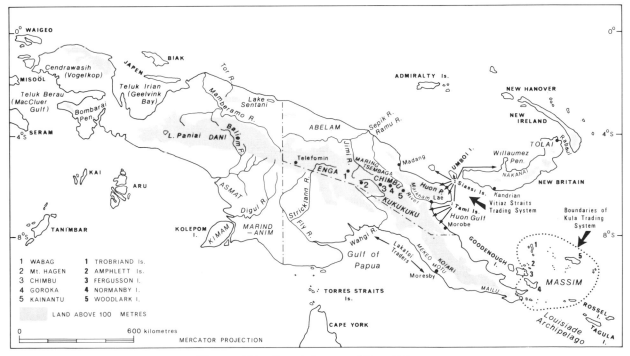

Fig. 4.4. Ethnolinguistic map of New Guinea.

have become affiliated through affinal ties or a number of different avenues[42]. The result, as described by De Lepervanche, is frequently that 'common residence and working together rather than descent group membership ascribed at birth are the bases of group solidarity'[43].

The Highland clans are normally described as segmentary groups, and in most societies are divided into a number of subclans and subclan sections, whose members may be either localised or scattered throughout clan territory. In turn, the patrilineal sibs on which the clans are centred may be grouped into moieties or phratries, and in the case of the Chimbu of the Eastern Highlands a number of phratries may be grouped together in territorial and military alliances which are referred to by Paula Brown as 'tribes'[44]. although examples of such a high degree of areal integration are rare. Residential segmentation within clans is rarely along purely agnatic lines[45] and may be due more to the movement of 'Big Men' and their followers. The segmentary hierarchy is therefore not based on genealogical criteria, and although the sibs of a phratry may have a common mythological origin, the sib sections themselves (with some exceptions) rarely retain genealogical links for more than five generations.

Local residential groups in the Highlands, and indeed in many other parts of Melanesia, are often centred on individual entrepreneurs who are usually referred to as 'Big Men'. The Big Man is neither an elected headman nor a hereditary chief, but is a man who has utilised his kin and non-kin ties to build up wealth and a following of supporters. He can initiate large pig feasts, advance loans of bridewealth to impoverished young men, and afford in some cases several wives, who in turn can raise pigs, till fields, and generally increase his standing[46]. On the other hand, he cannot afford to alienate by overexploitation, and should he indulge in oppression of his followers he could be murdered or deposed in extreme cases. His main interest is in prestige rather than in cumulative wealth, and Highland societies are only prepared to tolerate a certain amount of deviation from egalitarianism. Some societies, such as the Maring of the Bismarck Ranges, do not have leaders of this kind at all and rely upon a general consensus of opinion in decision-making[47].

In terms of social structure the New Guinea Highland societies do seem to fit a general model, although in an area so ecologically varied, it is not surprising to find many differences in specific aspects of culture. For instance, in the area east of Chimbu, hamlets or villages predominate, but from Chimbu west to the Strickland Gorge, settlements are dispersed[48]. Men's club houses are found very widely, however, and function as sleeping houses for married men, while women, children, and often pigs, occupy separate dwellings. Two interesting examples of differing settlement type, but both incorporating the widespread Highland concept of separation between sleeping accommodation for men and women, may be illustrated from the Wabag area of the Western Highlands of Papua New Guinea and the Gahuku-Gama of the Eastern Highlands near Goroka[49]. In the Gahuku-Gama case, the village males belong to two related patrilineal subclans, and the wives and children of each occupy one half of the rectangular fenced village. The men, married and single, sleep in a single house which is fenced off from the rest of the compound and from which women and children are excluded, while each wife and family has a separate house, which the men may sleep in when they wish (figure 4.5).

The Wabag example illustrates a scattered settlement pattern, in which four subclans occupy the territory shown in figure 4.5, and the houses of each subclan are spread amongst each other around the gardens and the ceremonial ground. The women's houses are more scattered than those of the men, both for safety and easier access to pig food, since pigs are cared for by the women[50]. In many Highland areas there is also a fear amongst males of pollution from constant contact with women, and this factor may also serve to keep the sexes apart residentially. These two examples described do not of course cover the whole range of residential patterning in the New Guinea Highlands, but they are at least focussed towards two opposite poles of variation.

One very widespread characteristic in the Highlands, and in much of Island Melanesia too, is the presence of infrequent but massive pig festivals. In the Highlands in particular, pigs are the main source of protein, but their killing is not so much a matter of convenience as of complex ritual requirements. For instance, the Tsembaga – a group of the Maring people of the Bismarck Mountains – utilise up to 40% of their root crop produce for the feeding of pigs, and yet normally only kill them in massive ceremonies held every eight to twelve years to honour and pay the ancestors for favours received. Tsembaga pig populations therefore go through long cycles of gradual increase followed by sudden decimation, and the main kill usually comes at the end of a year-long 'Kaiko' festival (see page 151) at which up to 1000 people may be assembled[51].

The pocket-like isolation of many Highland societies means that contacts with coastal peoples were dependent in the past upon a very small number of routes, amongst which one of the most important seems to have been the Markham Valley. While trade contacts, usually involving many links, did bring coastal goods to the interior and vice versa, the Highlands were clearly not heavily influenced by incoming Austronesian settlers to any great extent. Pottery, except on the eastern fringes, is not made, and art is mainly restricted to bodily decoration, in contrast to the great wood-carving and mask-producing societies of the Sepik River, coastal Papua and Massim areas.

Before leaving the Highlands, one more topic requires discussion. Except in some remote areas around the border with Irian Jaya, where taro dominates, the sweet potato is by far the major crop of the area. J.B. Watson[52], taking the traditional view that the sweet potato was not introduced into this part of the world until the Spanish and Portuguese took it to Indonesia and the Philippines in the sixteenth and seventeenth centuries, has suggested that prior to this time the Highlands were occupied by patrilocal hunting bands, perhaps with some supplementary shifting cultivation of taro and other crops of restricted importance. The sweet potato, because of its high yields at altitudes above the limits of malaria and taro cultivation (1500–2000 metres), led to an unprecedented population explosion, according to Watson, which he has termed the 'Ipomoean Revolution'. The present patrilineal bias and rather unstable nature of Highland social organisation may thus result from the short time available for adaptation since the Revolution took place. Watson's hypothesis is convincing enough, but it has been attacked on equally convincing grounds by Brookfield and White[53]. The sweet potato has certainly had an effect in allowing a move from malarial areas, and a population increase may well have resulted, but since Watson published his theory, archaeologists have uncovered evidence of intensive cultivation systems dating from around 4000 B.C., probably for taro, in the Wahgi Valley near Mt Hagen. We will be examining these in more detail later

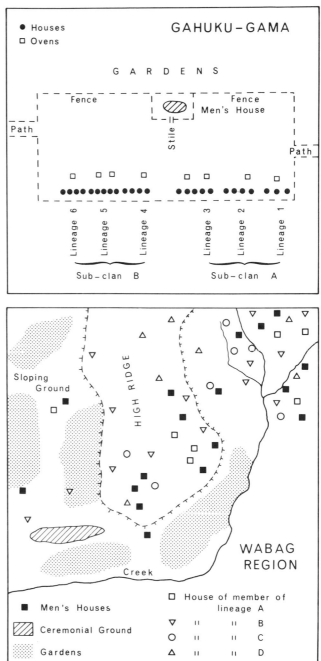

Fig. 4.5. Contrasting settlement patterns in the New Guinea Highlands. After Read 1954.

(chapters 6 and 9), for the sweet potatoes, intensive cultivation systems, and possibly the high population densities appear not to be as recent as once thought.

From an archaeological viewpoint, the Highlands bring up several points which may be worthy of consideration. In such an area, archaeological recovery and definition of meaningful units which might correspond to ethnic entities will almost certainly be extremely difficult[54]. Local groups may be assimilated and change their language and culture, and territorial shifts and expansions appear to be very numerous and almost impossible to unravel even in very recent cases. Political relationships do not necessarily follow close cultural or linguistic relationships, and while archaeologists may be able to reconstruct trade patterns quite competently, these may not correspond at all with cultural patterns. Furthermore, a Highland ethnic group is particularly difficult to define, even at the present day. In the case of the Gahuku-Gama, as discussed by Read[55], there is no distinct linguistic or social group at all, and there is no political unity. The Gahuku-Gama are only a distinct group – and they do indeed view themselves as a group – in the sense that a few conspicuous differences with surrounding peoples are emphasised, but similar differences within the group are subordinated. The boundaries of the group are extremely loose, and depend very much on ego position. As Read states:

> We may say that the unity which characterises the tribes of the Gahuku-Gama is that of a socio-geographic region which contains an aggregate of people who have more essential features in common and closer ties *inter se* than they have with groups in similar surrounding regions. The group thus defined is not absolute or static, but relative and dynamic[56].

ISLAND MELANESIA

The societies of Island Melanesia are rather more varied than those of the New Guinea Highlands. In the west, ethnic diversity is very marked, and here we see the presence of mainly small-scale political groupings centred on Big Men, or more occasionally on hereditary petty chiefs[57], together with widespread trade networks which link many of these communities through ceremonial and economic exchanges. Matrilineal, patrilineal and cognatic societies exist side by side in many areas of the New Hebrides, Banks, Santa Cruz, Solomon

and Bismarck island groups, and around coastal New Guinea, and the actual patterns of variation may be of surprising complexity. On the other hand, in New Caledonia and Fiji patrilineal descent is the almost invariable norm, and systems of political integration were generally more extensive and more highly developed on a basis of hereditary ranking.

The degree of cultural complexity in Island Melanesia would appear to reflect the prevailing situation of small isolated social groups, as well as the long period – perhaps 5000 years – of interaction between peoples of Austronesian and Papuan linguistic affinity. An attempt to reduce this heterogeneity to the level of generalisations would be rather futile, so that the approach I have adopted here is to select a small number of societies and areas, for which there are published descriptions, to illustrate the range of diversity and indicate some regularities. The geographical progression is roughly from west to east.

The vast swamplands of the south coast of Irian Jaya form one of the strangest and most watery environments for human occupation in Melanesia. Here dwell the individualist woodcarvers of the Asmat, recently made known through a study published by the Dutch anthropologist Adrian Gerbrands[58], and on swampy Kolepom Island dwell the Kimam people[59], whose remarkable techniques of cultivation will be described in chapter 6. This low-lying island is flooded for a large part of the year by heavy rains, and the villages of the Kimam, of up to seven hundred people living in open-sided day houses and closed-in mosquito-proof night houses, are constructed on artificial mounds built up out of the swamp. Each village has two ceremonially opposed residential sectors, each sector being occupied by two exogamous clan-like units called *kwanda*. To each *kwanda* belong a number of agnatically related family groups, each with its own separate dwelling island. Leadership is focussed on Big Men, who attain and retain prestige by giving periodic competitive feasts for their followers. Kimam society in fact resembles New Guinea Highland society in a general way, and its members are Papuan speakers. The type of village division into opposed sections has already been described for the Gahuku-Gama of the Highlands, and more examples will be given below, for it is particularly common throughout western Melanesian societies where villages are present. To give another example, the splendid villages of the Sepik coast may contain up to one thousand people dwelling in two lines of long extended family houses, each belonging to a patrilineal moiety[60]. Here the houses are built up on piles, as in parts of Indonesia, and face on to a dancing ground with one or more high-gabled men's club houses, which are artistically amongst the most remarkable in the Pacific (figure 4.6).

The phenomenon of village division is of considerable theoretical interest for the archaeologist, and hopefully one day large-scale excavations may be able to trace it back into the past. Also of interest is the variety in village function in some areas of western Melanesia. For instance, the people of the Tor Valley, west of the Sepik, construct not only residential villages, but also temporary hamlets by sago plots, special 'hotel' villages on tribal boundaries for visitors, and refuge villages hidden away from the influences of sorcery[61]. Many of the peoples of the New Guinea Highlands also construct special villages for their periodic pig-killing festivals.

The New Guinea peoples described so far are all Papuan speakers. The pockets of Austronesian speakers around coastal New Guinea do not clearly stand apart as a group with respect to social organisation, and in fact are not readily differentiable at all apart from the factor of language. For the Papuan coast, I have referred above (page 92) to the observations of the Rev. W.W. Gill, and these are of course meaningful, but the fact remains that such distinctions are not wide-spread. To illustrate the forms of Austronesian social organisation in New Guinea I have chosen two groups, one patrilineal and one matrilineal, both in the southern part of Papua New Guinea.

Along the south-eastern coastline of Papua, the Austronesians are generally patrilineal in the west, and matrilineal in the east from the south-eastern tip of the mainland into the Massim archipelago[62]. In the west, the Motu of the Port Moresby area are perhaps the best-known patrilineal group, and these people occupy villages of pile-built houses constructed out into the sea below high-tide level. Each village comprises a number of wards or sections, and each section is occupied by a patrilineal clan known as an *iduhu*. These localised *iduhu* are grouped into larger non-localised entities, also called *iduhu*, which are distributed through several

Fig. 4.6. A northern Abelam ceremonial house, Sepik District. For a discussion of the painted designs see Forge 1973. (See also colour plate.)

villages and do not retain any genealogical coherence, but which are said to derive from the sections of an original Motu ancestral village. The localised village *iduhu* have hereditary headmen, although at the level of the whole village leadership tends to be achieved on the basis of personal qualities rather than ascribed by birth[63].

Agnatic units of the *iduhu* type are found amongst several of the Austronesian speaking groups of central Papua[64], and correspond structurally to the patrilineal clans of the Highlands and other parts of New Guinea. As in the Highlands also, the rules of agnation are not adhered to as laws, and amongst the Motu land may frequently be inherited through cognatic ties, although a strict ideal of agnation may be applied in the case of inheritance of scarce resources. Such situations seem to be universal in Melanesia despite the prevalence of unilineal ideology, and this of course reflects a pragmatism which involves recognition of human needs in specific cases.

Eastwards in the matrilineal area of the Massim Archipelago lie the Trobriand Islands[65], scene during the First World War of the now classic researches of Bronislaw Malinowski. These islands are famous for their part in a trade cycle which we will examine at a later point, and today still retain, visually at least, a kind of timelessness which cannot fail to impress itself upon the casual visitor.

Trobriand villages consist of circles of rectangular nuclear family houses grouped around a central ring of splendid yam storage houses (figure 4.7), and each village comprises a number of sections, each section containing the houses of a number of matrilineally related males and their families. These localised matrilineal lineages belong in turn to four dispersed exogamous phratries. It should be pointed out, however, for all of Melanesia as well as for the Trobriands alone, that while the lineages and higher order unilineal descent groups are exogamous, the villages themselves of course may not be, for each village usually comprises two or more unrelated lineages who may intermarry. Therefore Melanesian society is characterised by descent group exogamy, but frequently also by settlement endogamy, a factor which serves to reinforce isolation of communities, unless the communities are so small that a high proportion of spouses must necessarily come from elsewhere. The genetic isolation which accrues from such a situation has already been described in chapter 2.

The Trobriands are also of interest because of the presence of avunculocal post-marital residence, which means that a boy will not belong to the village in which he is born, but on maturity will have to move to the village of his mother's matrilineal kin, to which he in turn will take his wife. Leadership in a Trobriand village is usually hereditary in the senior village lineage, and the village headman can usually increase his wealth and status by polygyny, for each wife is allotted a share of the produce of her own kin land around her natal village, and this situation naturally accrues to the advantage of a man who can afford several wives. On the other hand, a headman's authority does not really extend beyond his own village, even though the villages themselves may be loosely ranked on a basis of wealth and status in the trade cycle. This localisation of authority within homologous social units is characteristic of virtually all of Melanesia apart from New Caledonia and Fiji, and as we will see is in contrast to some of the hierarchical societies of Micronesia and Polynesia.

In central Melanesia – that is, the Solomon, Santa Cruz, Banks and New Hebrides Island groups – the degree of diversity in social organisation which characterises the New Guinea area is continued. Most of the central Melanesians are Austronesian speaking, although extensive pockets of Papuan speech are found in the Solomon and Santa Cruz groups. A basic anthropological treatise on this area was published as early as 1891 by the missionary R.H. Codrington[66], in which he recorded the presence, in terms of ideology, of matrilineal societies in the northern and southern New Hebrides, Banks and Santa Cruz Islands, and parts of the southern Solomons, while patrilineal societies are found in the central New Hebrides and on the islands of Malaita, Guadalcanal, San Cristobal, Ugi and Ulawa in the southern Solomons. Most of these societies are of the generally small-scale and relatively acephalous type characteristic of western Melanesia, although some groups, such as the Lau of north-eastern Malaita, are reported as having hereditary petty chiefs drawn from high-ranking patrilineal lineages[67]. The Lau are also of interest because they inhabit villages constructed on artificial islets which are built offshore in an extensive lagoon, and these artificial islets; together with others which more rarely occur in other parts of central Melanesia, have led Parsonson to suggest that they were constructed by Polynesian and Micronesian immigrants in an attempt to escape malarial mosquitoes. This theory may have certain merit, but it has been attacked strongly by Chowning, on rather convincing grounds[68].

Of the matrilineal societies, the best description is perhaps that by Oliver[69] for the Siuai of south-eastern Bougainville. These people dwell in villages centering on men's club houses, and have a system of Big Man leadership involving a considerable degree of status rivalry. With the Siuai, however, as with many other matrilineal peoples in Melanesia, virilocal post-marital residence happens to be of considerable importance. This means that the matrilines are rarely localised, and instead of controlling residence, as in the Trobriands, matriline membership involves such matters as taboos, shrine membership, rituals, totemic relationships, and of course controls to some extent a person's choice of a marriage partner. Codrington had already pointed out the frequency of this type of situation in central Melanesia in 1891, and clearly one would not expect local corporate groups in these societies to correspond to clans as defined earlier in this chapter. Local group composition, on the other hand, would simply be cognatic, and

transmission of property and land from father to son (who belong to different lineages) is quite common.

The societies with patrilineal ideologies may suffer from similar complications, as shown by Scheffler in his analysis of Choiseul Island social structure[70]. The Choiseulese occupy hamlets which were originally often trenched and stockaded against enemies. Each hamlet contains a core of agnatically related males, and post-marital residence is normally patri-virilocal (i.e. with the husband's agnates). But because many men acquire land through their wives, and because their children may eventually be incorporated as full members of their mother's descent groups, Scheffler specifically classifies Choiseul society as ambilineal – in the sense that a child may affiliate with the descent group of either parent, but not with both (although in most cases a child will tend to reside with his father's group). It is clear that many of the so-called unilineal societies of Melanesia may well be of this kind,[71] although anthropologists hitherto have not always made the real situation very clear. The Choiseulese are also quite explicit about their attitudes to ideology, and told Scheffler, 'Our customs are not firm. We look

Fig. 4.7. A village on Kiriwina, Trobriand Islands. The tall structure at centre left is a yam-storage house (see also figure 6.4). (See also colour plate.)

only for that which will help us live well, and the rest is just talk'[72]. Scheffler goes on from this to view behavioural norms as rhetorical elements with which persons defend their own actions and support or condemn the actions of others[73], and in view of this, one wonders how the old concepts of matrilineal versus patrilineal society will survive in the future.

Between the Solomons and the New Hebrides lie the Santa Cruz Islands, which are linked together by a most interesting and elaborate trade network which involves Polynesians from the island of Taumako (Duff Islands), as well as the Melanesians of the Reef Islands, Utupua, and Vanikoro[74]. On Santa Cruz Island itself most societies are matrilineal, but both patrilineal and truly cognatic societies coexist with them. In the matrilineal societies post-marital residence is virilocal, as amongst the Siuai, and the villages are divided into sections, each occupied by a group of agnatically related males with its own men's house and system of achieved and competitive leadership. Marital patterns are governed by the non-localised exogamous matrilineal descent groups (moieties or phratries), and local group leaders succeed by the type of entrepreneurial activity so common in Melanesia, the use of red feather currency belts being associated with a marked profit motive. A Big Man also once acquired status from the number of concubines, usually traded from the Reef Islands in return for red feather currency belts, which he was able to install in the men's house over which he had authority.

The societies of the Banks Islands and New Hebrides are very similar in general type to those of the Solomon and Santa Cruz Islands. In the northern area, the institution of the men's house receives an interesting form of elaboration, to give rise to the graded men's societies such as the Suqe society of the Banks Islands[75]. In the Suqe and similar societies a man rises in prestige by progression through successive grades, and he is able to do this by presenting gifts and currency, often in the form of highly-curved pig tusks, to society members in and above the grade to which he aspires. Powerful men thus rise high in the hierarchy, and increase their wealth at the expense of lesser members who are rising in the ranks below them. The Suqe houses (*gamal*) of the Banks Islands are built on stone-faced platforms, and are subdivided internally into separate segments for each grade, from which women and uninitiated children are rigidly

excluded. In the graded society of Matanavat in northern Malekula, up to 1000 pigs may be sacrificed when a man moves to a higher grade, and the most valuable pigs have their top canine teeth removed so that the lower tusks may grow in up to three complete circles, often growing directly through the lower jaw of the pig in the process. When a Matanavat man reached the highest grade, the ceremony was often accompanied in the past by the sacrifice of a bastard boy[76]. These strongly institutionalised grades, with their elaborate rituals of entrance, represent a more conscious regulation of the means by which Big Men rise to power in other societies, and wealth and skill are still the basic keys to success.

In New Britain, the Banks Islands, the northern New Hebrides, and parts of New Caledonia, there were until the coming of Christianity so-called 'secret societies', which involved gatherings of initiated men in secluded places from which all women were excluded, and rituals in which members wore elaborate headdresses and, by pretending to be reincarnated ghosts, terrified the women and children by the use of eerie noises and physical force. Initiation often involved considerable cruelty, and if a woman had the misfortune to observe initiation rites, in some areas she could be buried alive. Such secret societies (which were really only secret to women and children) are a little hard to interpret, since they appear to have had little religious motivation, and indeed may be seen as deliberately organised institutions designed to keep social order and to enhance the status of males in the society. In such societies as the *Tamate* or the *Qat* of the Banks and northern New Hebrides, members could rise through a hierarchy of grades if they had sufficient wealth, so that high status in a secret society normally correlated with high status within the society as a whole.

In New Caledonia and Fiji descent is almost universally reckoned patrilineally, and New Caledonia in particular would seem to represent a large land mass which has never had a great deal of contact with other areas. Some features of the New Caledonian physical type are frequently referred towards an Australian Aboriginal pole of variation, and while the island was certainly in contact with the New Hebrides and Fiji some 2 or 3000 years ago, as we will see, the puzzling absence of both pig and dog at European discovery would suggest long isolation. Apart from the Polynesian outlier of Uvea in the

Loyalty Islands, the languages of New Caledonia and the Loyalties do not relate clearly to any particular outside area, although they are certainly Austronesian.

The New Caledonian hamlet or village of the earlier part of this century, as described by Leenhardt[77] for the central part of the east coast, consisted of a circular men's house for male lineage members, with an adjacent chief's house and rectangular working houses. Around this central complex were arranged the smaller circular family houses. The central part of the village consisted of a rectangular cleared ceremonial area, lined with coconut and other ornamental trees, and the central strip of this area was for the activities of the patrilineal lineage or sib of the village, while peripheral areas were reserved for the activities of groups related matrilineally to the patrilineal land-holding groups.

The patrilineal descent groups were exogamous, and internally ranked on a basis of seniority, although not always by genealogical seniority as unrelated lines were able to affiliate themselves in some instances. Expanding clans segmented, and new lines in some cases expanded over large areas, retaining their original consanguineal kin affiliation by means of widespread moiety or phratry organisations. The clan chief was usually the senior male, by age rather than primogeniture, of the senior line of descent, and a hierarchy of political powers was developed in some areas, particularly in the Loyalty Islands. Usually, however, the powers of the chief were mediated by the presence of a council of elders, and many of the chief's duties concerned ritual matters connected with the well-being of the clan[78]. Matters concerning land tenure were under the jurisdiction of a separate 'Maître de la terre', and warfare was conducted under the auspices of priests and separate warchiefs. But chiefs in many areas could receive considerable deference. For instance, in 1842, Chief Touru of the Ile des Pins had extended his control over the south-eastern part of the New Caledonian mainland, and was able to exact tribute from the inhabitants. His subjects approached him on hands and knees – a form of deference which resembles that paid to the ruling chiefs of Tonga and some of the other highly ranked societies of Polynesia[79]. Thus in some areas of New Caledonia were developed systems of political integration which, like those of Fiji, tend to fall in an intermediate position between those of western Melanesia and those of parts of Polynesia.

In Fiji, as in New Caledonia, a nucleated village settlement pattern was and still is prevalent, and each village comprises one or more pro-patrilineal *yavusa*, or maximal lineages, which normally contain about 100 persons under a hereditary leader from the senior descent line. The *yavusa* is a land-owning group, and comprises several *mataqali*, which also are normally ranked by seniority of descent in the male line, and each *mataqali* in turn consists of a number of ranked *tokatoka*, or groups of patrilineally related extended families[80].

The most detailed account of a Fijian social system is that provided by Marshall Sahlins in his study on the island of Moala, between Viti Levu and the Lau group[81]. Originally, Moala was divided into three territorial chiefdoms, each of which comprised a number of villages with patrilineally related families grouped in sections around a ceremonial ground with a men's house and a chief's house. A single extended family would occupy several nuclear family houses around a communal cookhouse, and several extended families comprised a localised landowning *tokatoka*. The *tokatoka* were in turn ranked within larger *mataqali*, and the latter into local *yavusa*, one of which might comprise all the agnatically related males in a village, although genealogical links were not always kept accurately, and unrelated kinship groups could, if necessary, combine in a residential arrangement which would also be regarded as a *yavusa*. Each local *yavusa* was focussed on a chiefly lineage, and the local *yavusa* were in turn grouped into four island-wide non-localised *yavusa*, grouped into two exogamous moieties. As with Polynesian systems the Fijian system of genealogical ranking lent itself to the formation of centralised chiefly courts in the nineteenth century, and a degree of political integration never achieved by the societies of western Melanesia.

The *yavusa* organisation is surprisingly homogeneous in Fiji, at least when one compares it with the situation in the Melanesian islands to the west. Viti Levu has over 600 *yavusa*, some having a mythical origin place in the Kauvadra Mountains of north eastern Viti Levu, while others have no origin traditions at all. Gifford[82] thinks that those without origin traditions descend from early arrivals on the island, while those with Kauvadra origins entered the island about A.D. 1600. So far, there is little evidence to evaluate this view, apart from that described on pages 264–265.

If we exclude Fiji and New Caledonia from consideration, it is clear that Melanesian society is characterised by high diversity within small areas, together with very restricted systems of political integration beyond the local group level. Melanesian local groups are structurally homologous and relatively independent, and residential and spatial organisation differs markedly from place to place[83]. On the subject of leadership, it is clear that the 'Big Man' entrepreneur is to some extent dominant in Melanesia[84], apart from New Caledonia and Fiji, but hereditary leadership is scattered throughout the area, and a system of quite elaborate petty chieftainship at the village level has recently been described for the Mekeo of central Papua[85]. On the other hand, no western Melanesian chief was ever placed at the head of a large areally-integrated network of kin and subjects, as were his counterparts in some parts of Polynesia or Micronesia. However, this does not mean that Big Men or petty chieftains all conform to a single type, and indeed the highly competitive Big Man system of the Siuai of Bougainville can hardly be ranked with the egalitarianism of parts of the New Guinea Highlands.

TRADE NETWORKS IN MELANESIA[86]

Melanesian trade is a distinctive phenomenon for a number of reasons. Firstly, Melanesian societies are often specialised in terms of production – some depend on fishing, others on pottery production, others on taro growing, and so forth. For one local group to acquire all its necessities, it will frequently have to engage in trade with another, often totally unrelated group. Secondly, Melanesian trade is in many ways a very individual activity, and frequently takes the form of immediate or delayed exchange between two trade partners from different localities, who may or may not be related to each other. This does not mean that all trading expeditions are undertaken by individuals, for large expeditions may indeed be mounted, but the prevailing Melanesian system, at least in the west, does differ somewhat from that in Polynesia. In Polynesian islands, which are small and ethnically homogeneous, each tribe generally has access to the majority of required resources through its own members, and the equivalent of trade within the tribe takes place through periodic collection and distribution, often centred on a chiefly personage. New Zealand appears to have been the only Polynesian locality with the long distance type of trade with many intermediate links which characterises Melanesia. In Polynesia, therefore, the emphasis is on redistribution, with a tendency towards tribute and chiefly advantage in the more highly stratified societies of Hawaii and perhaps Tahiti. In Melanesia, redistribution in the sense of inflow and outflow from a central position is not much developed beyond the spheres of influence of Big Men, and the general trade situation in the west is based on a 'particularistic, entrepreneur-centred, dispersed network'[87]. The profit motive is by no means lacking in Melanesia, and lies behind the Big Man concept as well as behind the monetary systems which are particularly controlled by the Big Men.

The most famous trade cycle in Melanesia is the *Kula* cycle of the Massim District (see figure 4.4), which has been so well described by other authors[88] that only a brief summary is required here. The Kula cycle is based on a partner system, and on group voyages between neighbouring islands (never around the whole system at once) when trade partners engage in exchange, both of utilitarian goods and also of the non-utilitarian armshells and necklaces which travel in fixed directions around the islands and integrate the whole system. The Big Men are those who can usually attract many partnerships, and acquire temporary ownership of the most valuable status objects. Many of the islands in the cycle are ecologically poor and highly specialised – the Amphlett Islands, for instance, are poorly supplied with food, and can obtain this by trading the pots which they make from clay brought from Fergusson Island. The Kula cycle may be seen in fact as a highly elaborate ritual, closely bound up with magic and considerations of personal status, which at base circulates needed goods to needy localities, but in more general terms serves a fundamental social function of high complexity.

Another famous example of Melanesian trade concerns the great *lakatoi* expeditions of the Western Motu[89]. The Motu, as described in the above section, are coastal-dwelling fishermen and potters of the Port Moresby area, who undertook in the past yearly voyages to the head of the Papuan Gulf, normally initiated by individuals rather than persons of any official status, in order to exchange pottery for sago, and for new hulls for their *lakatoi*. Every year, towards the end of the south-east trade-wind season in

September or October, the Motu would fit out several *lakatoi* – giant canoes up to 20 metres long by 16 broad with covered superstructures and several parallel hulls, capable of carrying in some cases over 1600 pots or 30 tonnes of sago – and head along the coast to the north-west to carry out exchanges along the normal partnership pattern. They would then return with the sago on the north-west monsoon after about three months. Because the trade system includes several linguistically diverse groups, a special trading *lingua franca* was in use. Furthermore, the *lakatoi* expeditions were not the only kind of trade carried out by the Motu, for like many coastal groups in Melanesia they traded widely with their interior Papuan speaking neighbours, the Koita and Koiari, and indeed many of the former moved into Motu villages to settle[90].

A further trade system, which in some ways combines the long distance transfer of the Motu type with a short transfer characteristic of the Kula, is that which integrates hundreds of local communities over an enormous area stretching from the western end of New Britain, through the islands of the Vitiaz Straits, to the long coastline of north-eastern New Guinea between Madang and Morobe[91] (figure 4.4). The trade networks involved in this system are very complex and transcend any form of local identity. Hundreds of ecologically and culturally specialised communities are involved, exchanging inland root crops for coastal fish, coconuts, and pottery, and three groups of sea-borne middlemen, based on Bilibili Island in Astrolabe Bay, the Siassi Islands to the south of the island of Umboi in the Vitiaz Straits, and the Tami Islands in the northern Huon Gulf, articulate the flow of commodities with three overlapping trading spheres. The Siassi and Tami dialects once served as *lingua franca* amongst the many linguistic groups involved, and while no one group ever had access to all the trade networks involved, it was possible, for instance, for obsidian from the base of the Willaumez peninsula in New Britain to move, step by step and increasing in value all the time, right through the system and along the New Guinea coast. Obsidian was only one of many items traded, and Harding lists live pigs, dogs' teeth, bows and arrows, net bags, pottery, and taro amongst present-day mainland New Guinea exports – while from the islands of the Straits boars' tusks, live dogs, mats, disc beads, betel nut, red ochre and sago move in return to the mainland. The trade operates through the general

Melanesian system of trade partnership with delayed exchange, and each group involved gains access to goods otherwise not available.

Before leaving the Vitiaz Straits system, some points of interest concerning overall function may be mentioned. As with the Kula cycle, the Vitiaz Straits trade serves to distribute more evenly highly localised resources, but beyond this, many factors of social organisation have become involved. For instance, Siassi Big Men gain prestige by giving competitive feasts, but since their islands are rather barren, they depend on the trade system to acquire the necessary pigs and taro for these feasts. In fact, given the central position of the Siassi middlemen, perhaps it was they who first initiated their own sector of the system, for certainly they are more dependent upon and derive more from trade than do the majority of the mainland communities, and they also, with the Tami Islanders, make by far the best canoes. So by European contact the system had grown far beyond being a mere ecological leveller to satisfy subsistence needs, and the movements of the commodities themselves cannot always be easily related to ecological criteria. As an example, the localisation of pottery manufacture is by no means governed by a restricted occurrence of clay, and given dire necessity, no doubt many communities could make pots. They evidently do not need to because of the ease of importing, and also because certain communities now dependent on potting have acquired the necessary prestige and magic to defend their interests. They may forbid out-marrying women to practise the craft in other settlements, and the other settlements know that if they try to break the monopoly unpleasantness would ensue, perhaps with hostilities and general hardship for all involved.

Trade systems of this kind, which integrate large numbers of acephalous communities, many of whom are unaware of the size of the structure in which they participate, are one of Melanesia's most distinctive features. There are many others apart from those mentioned – for instance, in parts of the Solomon and Santa Cruz Islands[92], along the Sepik Coast[93], and in the northern New Hebrides[94]. In the Admiralty Islands there is a complex system of exchange involving three separate ethnic groups in interior, coastal and offshore island ecological situations[95]. In the New Guinea Highlands, widespread trade networks involve movement of axes from quarries in the Wahgi and Jimi areas, together with pigs, salt, shells, feathers, and even women[96]. Amongst the Tsembaga, for instance, marriages with outside groups can be used to enhance affinal and trade relationships, through which Tsembaga salt could be exchanged for pigs, shells, and working and bridal stone axes[97].

A description of trade leads to a brief description of currencies, for throughout Melanesia generally, and also in western Micronesia, goods and services could be exchanged for various kinds of money. These currencies were normally specially manufactured and always had some kind of scarcity value, in the sense that they could not be mass-produced indiscriminately. They were not used of course simply for trade, but also enabled a man to pay bride-price, to recompense injury or murder and to pay other unilateral payments, and also to give loans with interest in order to accumulate the wealth necessary to become a Big Man.

The currencies were of many forms: shell discs on strings kept in coils amongst the Tolai of New Britain[98], belts of scarlet feathers in the Santa Cruz group[99], or cowrie shells in parts of the New Guinea Highlands. In the New Hebrides pigs acted as a kind of currency, their value depending upon the degree of tusk curvature, and on the island of Maewo soot-encrusted mats were stored in special smoky huts, and accrued value according to their ages and thicknesses of sooty covering. The mats were not moved but remained *in situ* while exchanging ownership. Many of the Melanesian currency systems involved very complex concepts of value and rates of interest, as a number of detailed accounts will indicate[100].

MELANESIAN MATERIAL CULTURE

Looking generally at the distribution pattern for some aspects of material culture in Melanesia[101] one can detect the outlines of three main provinces – namely the New Guinea Highlands, coastal New Guinea and Island Melanesia as far east as the New Hebrides and New Caledonia, and finally Fiji, which shares a good deal of its material culture with western Polynesia. These three provinces cannot be rigidly defined, since they are little more than vague nodes in a continuum. However, a number of quite distinctive culture traits are restricted in distribution to parts of coastal New Guinea and Island Melanesia (excluding Fiji). These include headhunting and its associated paraphernalia, the manu-

facture and use of currencies, the making of composite and elaborate face masks, head deformation (southern New Britain and southern Malekula), the use of bull roarers and skin drums, the use of shields, and chewing of betel pepper and the areca nut as stimulants. Many of these traits are of fairly restricted distribution within this general area, and there are a very large number of quite local idiosyncracies, such as the use of blow-guns in south-western New Britain, or the use of a simple tension loom of Southeast Asian type in the Santa Cruz and Banks Islands, and in a number of the adjacent Caroline Islands of Micronesia[102]. Pottery production is extremely localised, and house shapes may vary from circular in parts of the New Guinea Highlands and New Caledonia, through the more common and widespread rectangular type, to the longhouses of the Fly Delta area of New Guinea, which may be up to 50 metres long. Attempts have been made to explain these variations in material culture distribution and art styles in terms of different population movements through the area, and we will have occasion to examine some of these aspects of historical ethnology in the later chapter on Melanesian prehistory.

Fiji, in terms of material culture, has as much in common with Polynesia as it does with Melanesia. For instance, Fijian wood sculpture stresses shallow surface carving rather than painting as the chief medium of decoration, and the Fijian forms of human figures, bowls and clubs have more in common with Polynesia. The melodramatic and brilliantly coloured wood carvings and composite masks of western Melanesia are rarely paralleled east of New Caledonia and the New Hebrides, and Fijian and Polynesian art is characterised by a lesser degree of extroversion and ebullience.

To say more about material culture at this stage is unnecessary. Trait distributions are difficult to interpret in the absence of a full archaeological background, for the complexities of borrowing, common retention and common loss make it almost impossible to reconstruct a diachronic frame-work of migration and influence. Furthermore, the facts of distribution of material culture in Melanesia are by no means well plotted, and it is not my purpose here to give anything but the barest outline.

MICRONESIA[103]

Micronesia (figure 4.8) consists of 2500 individual

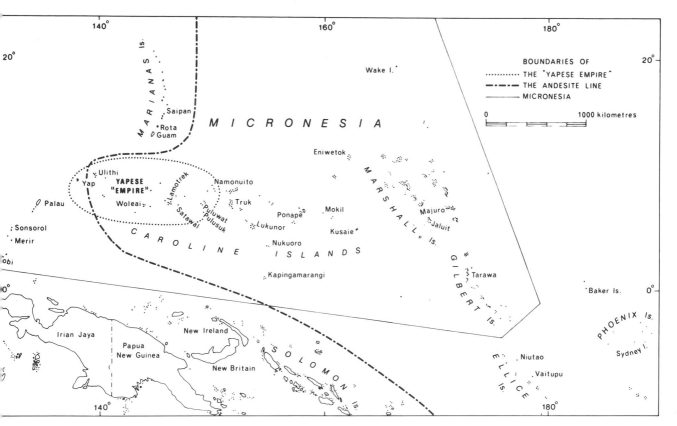

Fig. 4.8. Map of Micronesia.

islands, which together total only 2000 square kilometres of land. It is possible to recognise eight intergrading ethnolinguistic groups in the area, which are as follows:

1. the Chamorros of the Marianas Islands
2. the Palauans
3. the Yapese
4. the peoples of the eastern Carolines (Ponape, Kusaie and neighbouring islands)
5. the peoples of the western Carolines (Ulithi to Truk)
6. the peoples of the south-western Micronesian Islands – Tobi, Sonsorol, Pulo Anna and Merir.
7. the Marshallese
8. the Gilbertese.

Of the islands inhabited by these ethnic groups, nearly all are atolls apart from the Marianas and Palau Islands, and Yap, Truk, Ponape and Kusaie in the Carolines. A few of the Marshalls and Gilberts are of raised coral.

Micronesian social organisation is predominantly matrilineal, although there are patrilineal societies on Yap and in the south-western Carolines, and the Gilbertese have a cognatic form of social organisation similar to that of Polynesia[104]. A good example of a matrilineal type of organisation is described for Truk[105] in the central Carolines, where 16 separate volcanic islands cluster in a lagoon some 65 kilometres in diameter. There are about 40 exogamous matrilineal sibs on Truk, which are not localised and which are also represented on other islands in the area to as far as Lukunor in the east and Puluwat in the west. Trukese hamlets are centred around localised matrilineal and uxorilocal lineages, and these hamlets are grouped into districts which are under the jurisdiction of chiefs drawn from the highest ranking lineages (usually those lineages which hold the most land). Similar matrilineal organisations exist in the Palau Islands[106] and in most of the Carolines, although post-marital residence patterns vary considerably, and are not always uxorilocal. The degree of power held by chiefs in Micronesia also varied considerably in the past, and ranked chiefdoms akin to those of Polynesia were established on many islands right through the region[107].

The island of Yap was, and to an extent still is, the focus of perhaps the most distinctive form of social and political organisation in Micronesia. The villages of Yap are grouped into eight districts, and each district comprises several unrelated and virtually autonomous patrilineal lineages. These lineages are ranked, and the district chiefs are drawn from those of highest rank. However, what makes Yap unique is that the lineages and villages are sharply differentiated into two major caste groups with fairly rigid controls against intermarriage[108]. The low caste villages are located inland, and their inhabitants provide manufactured goods and labour for the high caste villages, which are located in coastal areas. The high caste villages own all the land, and have the lesser degree of social and religious restriction. So we have a situation in which the patrilineal lineages are not only ranked, but ranked on a strongly bipolar basis and geographically separated.

Cross-cutting the Yapese patrilineal organisation are a number of matrilineal sibs, which do not appear to be restricted to either high or low caste groups, and which have little political function apart from some control over the succession to the district chieftainship[109]. The distribution of these matrilineal sibs tends to argue against a separate outside origin for the populations of the two castes, although this problem cannot be satisfactorily resolved at present.

Yap, and the string of western Caroline Islands (all with matrilineal societies) running for 1100 kilometres east to Namonuito, were, and again still are to an extent, combined into one of the most wide-ranging systems of areal integration reported for the whole of Oceania. The system was dependent upon orders which were transmitted from the paramount chief of the Gagil District on Yap, which led to a complex chain of tribute and gifts flowing at intervals of two or three years right from Namonuito, Pulusuk, and many other atolls, through Woleai and Ulithi, and finally to the Gagil District. In return, Gagil sent gifts of high island produce to the atolls, and in this sense the system was reciprocal, although the movement of goods was at the command of the Gagil paramount, and several writers have spoken of a 'Yapese Empire' (figure 4.8). The system was in fact particularly complicated, with each matrilineal lineage on Ulithi being subordinate to a patrilineal lineage in the Gagil District, each matrilineal lineage on Woleai being subordinate to a matrilineal lineage on Ulithi, and so on in progression right down the line of islands to Pulusuk and Namonuito. The orders from Yap were transmitted from island to island down the chain, and the tribute flowed in

the reverse direction, finally to pass through Woleai, then Ulithi, and on to Yap (figure 4.9). The tribute was in the form of coconut oil, sennit, and pandanus sails and mats, and a variety of other goods were sent as gifts and religious offerings, as shown in figure 4.9. All the islands may be seen as continuously ranked from east to west, with Yap at the peak, and rigid bars against intermarriage between members of the higher Yap caste and outer islanders were enforced. The outer islanders, when on Yap, were considered to belong to the lower caste, although an endogamous caste system of the Yapese type was not present on the outer islands themselves.

Why Yap achieved this type of dominance is a mystery, for the Carolinean atolls are in fact closer culturally to Truk, and it is from this direction that initial settlement appears to have been initiated. The system was reinforced by religious considerations and fear of sorcery, and it is evident that Yap was fully able to enforce the chain of command.

Like the Kula cycle, the system may have been developed originally to ensure a circulation of needed goods round ecologically poor islands, and this economic function is certainly served, so that the pattern of ranking may be an expression of economic dependency[110]. Like the Kula cycle, however, the origin of the 'Yapese Empire' remains problematical.

It is possibly not without significance that Nuclear Micronesia (the Marshalls, Gilberts, and the Carolines east of Yap) should have its closest linguistic relationships with the New Hebrides (see page 126), which form the eastern outpost of matrilineal organisation in Melanesia. The Micronesian ranking system is generally more complex than that of the New Hebrides, as we have seen, but there may be a historical tie. The Gilberts have closer relationships in social organisation with Polynesia, while the Palaus and Marianas are, linguistically at least, closer to Indonesia and the Philippines. In the Palaus a monetary system of glass beads and sections of glass rings was in use[111] (figure 10.4), the glass itself possibly being of Philippine or Indonesian origin. Similar glass money was in use on Yap, and here also there was a unique type of currency in the form of large perforated discs of aragonite (figure 4.10), up to 4 metres in diameter, quarried in and transported from the Palau Islands over 250 miles away by canoe[112].

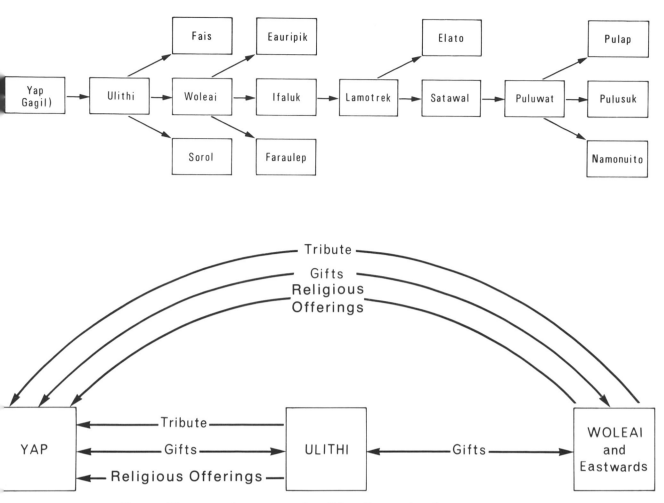

Fig. 4.9. Diagrammatic representation of the tribute and exchange system focussed on Yap. After Lessa 1966.

POLYNESIA

Polynesia is usually considered to be the most homogeneous culture area in Oceania. This is true, but with reservations, for the majority of Polynesian islands are small and isolated, and provide ideal environments for local idiosyncracies to develop. The Polynesian societies which have been described by anthropologists do not adopt strict unilineality as a norm for descent reckoning, although there is a strong patrilineal bias which appears to be most marked in Tikopia. Whereas in many western Melanesian societies the localised clan or clan segment is ideally an exogamous group composed of a lineage together with affines, the Polynesian ramage or ramage segment is non-exogamous, and local groups are centred on a core of cognatically related individuals of both sexes. It has been pointed out previously that local groups in many parts of Melanesia may also have a cognatic composition in reality,

Fig. 4.10. A *bai* or lodge on Yap, with rows of stone money. From Christian 1899.

but this circumstance does not invalidate the ideological differences between the two areas.

The ramage[113] is present in its most ideal form in New Zealand, and variant forms are found in all the high islands, although social evolution has reduced them to remnants in some island groups such as the Hawaiian Islands or Samoa. The ideal is described by Sahlins[114] as a non-exogamous, internally stratified patrilineal descent group, with succession to statuses by primogeniture, and a ranking of local segments according to the genealogical position of their founder (see figure 4.11). Genealogies in Polynesia may go back with fair accuracy for 25 generations, or many more in some cases, and the

preservation of genealogical knowledge is clearly essential in order to validate rights and rank in the face of competing interests.

Characterisation of the ramage as patrilineal is only partially true, however, and this is pointed out by both Sahlins and Firth[115]. For Firth, Polynesian descent is optative (excluding Tikopia and Pukapuka), so that, for instance, a person may acquire title to land through either his father or his mother, or very rarely through both. Firth uses the term ambilineal (see page 84) to describe this kind of descent, which distinguishes it from bilateral descent in which a person inherits through both parental lines, and it would in fact be more correct to define the

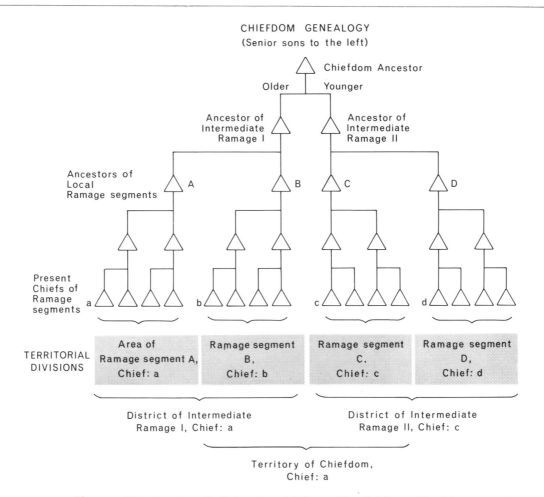

Fig. 4.11. The structure of a Polynesian chiefdom. After Sahlins 1968, with minor modifications.

ramage as an ambilineal non-exogamous internally ranked descent group. In addition, while seniority of descent as expressed through primogeniture is a major validator of rank, the factors of skill and prowess were always considered in the matter of election to a rank, and an eldest son would by no means always succeed his father.

The ranking system in Polynesia is loosely pyramidical, and the *ariki*, or paramount chief, would normally be elected from the line closest to the ideal of first-born male descent leading back to an apical ramage ancestor. The Polynesian chief of the past was generally a more awe-inspiring fellow than his western Melanesian counterpart, and was regarded by his people as a source of great *mana*, which was protected by a variety of *tapu* institutions and deferences. Primogeniture and senior line in inheritance are of most importance in Tikopia[116] and New Zealand, while elsewhere the system has tended to become more flexible. In New Zealand, to use an example of a fairly traditional Polynesian system, the next status below that of *ariki* would be that of *rangatira*, and this status would be inherited in more junior lines and would involve leadership of a ramage segment (*hapu*). However, in parts of tropical Polynesia, for instance Rarotonga and especially Samoa, the ranking system has become partially transferred away from individuals and their personal genealogies to a relatively fixed hierarchy of titles. For instance, on Rarotonga the *ariki* titles of Makea, Pa, Kainuku and Tinomana have been perpetuated from generation to generation, and persons with a suitable genealogical background are elected to them by the other chiefs. There is a subtle change of emphasis here away from the New Zealand traditional system where each chief is a named individual who rules as an individual – for instance, as Hongi Hika of the Ngapuhi or Te Rauparaha of the Ngatitoa. As we will see, in the case of Samoa the change to a title system is complete, and as Margaret Mead has concisely expressed the situation for these islands: 'Names and their rank, not individuals, are the units of construction'[117].

Let us look in more detail at the New Zealand case to broaden our description of a basic kind of ramage organisation. In New Zealand the tribe or ramage (*iwi*) is ideally a territorial unit (that is, if not dispersed by war or migration) under the leadership of an *ariki*, and its territory contains sub-territories each occupied by ranked lesser order *hapu*. Each *hapu* is basically a patrili-

neal and virilocal group, with relationships reckoned back about ten generations, but any child has a choice of taking up rights in land in either his father's territory or his mother's, even if the latter comes from a different and distant *hapu*[118]. The *hapu* normally owns lands which cover a range of ecological zones so that it may be self-supporting, and in tropical Polynesian islands such as Tahiti, Rarotonga or Hawaii, the land is divided like a pie from seashore to mountain peak[119], although such regularity was not attained in the much larger land mass of New Zealand. Within the *hapu* territory (or *ngati* territory in parts of central Polynesia) land is apportioned amongst the constituent families, and any necessary redistribution comes under the general jurisdiction of the chief, who in this respect and many others acts as steward over common tribal property.

The ramage is therefore a useful ideal model, which may have characterised Proto-Polynesian society and which has survived most clearly in spacious New Zealand, where ramages in theory can segment into unoccupied neighbouring territory and retain genealogical ties. In other high islands successful warriors achieved power in the past which was not theirs by genealogical ascription, and territorial wars were a common theme. This was also of course the case in New Zealand, and many groups were reduced to slavery by conquerors, but New Zealand was large enough to absorb local changes so that the breakdown of an integrated ramified system, while undoubtedly taking place through dispossession and resettlement, was nevertheless taking place more slowly than in some of the tiny tropical islands to the north.

Some of the atolls, in particular Pukapuka, Luangiua (Ontong Java) and the Tokelaus present a rather different picture from that described above. In the Tokelaus, for instance, status and authority are ideally inherited patrilineally, but house sites are inherited matrilineally, and post-marital residence is uxorilocal[120]. Pukapuka recognises both lines of descent, as does Ontong Java. Atolls usually lack strong paramount chiefs, and leadership is frequently through a council of elders. Sahlins has suggested that atolls, with markedly fluctuating yields from resources, cannot afford to have all resource distribution channelled through a limited number of nodes, and the result is that every person is able to draw on a very wide range of consanguineal, affinal and age-grade ties to ease the labour of survival. This explanation has also been suggested for the Yapese Empire (above), and has recently been given support for the Tokelaus by Hooper[121]. On the other hand, Manihiki, Rakahanga and Tongareva are atolls in the northern Cook group which had apparently normal ramage systems at European contact[122], so it is not really possible to make overall generalisations about islands of this type.

In recent years two theoretical works on the evolution of the varying forms of Polynesian society have appeared in print. In the earlier one, Marshall D. Sahlins[123] has attempted to demonstrate evolutionary relationships between the varying degrees of social stratification shown in Polynesian societies and ecological factors and resulting chiefly roles in food and resource redistribution. Basically, he has suggested that the larger and more frequent the redistributions, the more developed the social stratification. Furthermore, he has scaled the Polynesian societies which he studied with respect to degree of stratification as follows:

Group I (highly stratified): Tonga, Hawaii' Samoa, Tahiti.
Group IIa: Mangareva, Mangaia, Easter Island, Uvea (Wallis Island).
Group IIb: Marquesas, Tikopia, Futuna (Hoorn Is.).
Group III (least stratified): Pukapuka, Ontong Java, Tokelau.

While Sahlins has been heavily criticised owing to the difficulty of measuring social stratification objectively[124], it might be reasonable in theory to expect such a correlation. On the other hand, another suggestion by Sahlins, that ramages tend to occur in areas where resources are dispersed, and hence ensure distribution of localised resources to a large number of people through kinship lines, has not met with validation. At first view the argument is reasonable, but it does not stand up to detailed testing, since resources may, as in Mangaia or the Marquesas, be quite localised in the sense of allowing the inhabitants of a small area to be self-supporting, and yet still be associated with ramified systems of social organisation[125].

A more recent and detailed analysis of Polynesian society has been published by Irving Goldman[126], who has examined the theme of aristocracy in Polynesia, and the ways in which the ideal of the genealogical elite has been transformed by the complexities of status rivalry.

For Goldman, status rivalry rather than ecological variation lies behind the course of social evolution in Polynesia.

Goldman analyses the societies of Polynesia into three categories, based on the degree to which ascribed status rates against achieved status and on the degree of class stratification. In societies of his Traditional class, rank is based to a large extent on ascribed genealogical status through primogeniture in the male line, and these Traditional societies, such as New Zealand, Tikopia, Manihiki and Rakahanga, correspond most closely to the ramage ideal. Statuses are gently graded by genealogical continua, marked class divisions are absent, and ramage territories are relatively unified[127].

Goldman's second class, of Open societies, is characterised by the rise of achievement as a way to political power. In Mangaia, Easter Island and Niue, religious status remained with the traditional hereditary chiefs, but political power and the power to dispossess from and reward with land was frequently held by successful warriors, amongst whom the temporal power fluctuated with high frequency. On Mangaia a successful warrior could be made Temporal Lord through a ceremony depending upon an influential priesthood, and would be able to redistribute land amongst kin or followers. The result of such activities was that ramages lost their discrete territoriality and became scattered widely over the island as a result of political fortunes[128]. In the Open societies of the Marquesas Islands, where tribes were localised by the rugged nature of the terrain, the status system was more stable, and the American naval captain Porter was rather unimpressed by chiefly power when he visited Nuku Hiva in 1813[129]. The Marquesans also practised an unusual form (for Polynesia) of polyandrous marriage[130], and the status of women in this group seems to have been very high. Despite local variations, however, the Open societies do have one important factor in common, which is that they are found on islands which are ecologically rather unfavourable, and on which resources tend to be highly localised and therefore worth fighting over. This is unlikely to be coincidental, and seems to be a major factor behind the dominance of warfare in these societies.

Goldman's Stratified societies, which form the third and most highly developed class, were characterised by strong central authorities, which sometimes enveloped whole islands rather than single ramages, and the classes – aristocracy, common landholders, landless, and frequently slaves – were quite rigidly defined. However, Polynesian class systems were not to be equated with caste systems with enforced endogamy, and class mobility could be indulged in by anyone with the necessary skills to succeed. The ramage ties which linked commoners to chiefs in the Traditional societies were in most cases severed in the Stratified societies, resulting in a super-ordinate ruling ramage ranked over localised cognatic groups of commoners. This type of class stratification was characteristic of Tahiti, Mangareva, and Tonga, and in the Hawaiian Islands the expansion of quite elaborate bureaucracies around the chiefly courts, together with the growth of mobile cognatically related groups of commoners with land rights dependent upon the goodwill of the ruler, had produced a type of organisation at European contact which may be described as that of a number of incipient states. If a state be defined as a politically centralised and territorial entity, with a class structure characterised by kinship heterogeneity at and between the various levels, then the Hawaiian Islands may indeed provide the best examples, perhaps the only examples, of incipient state organisations in prehistoric Oceania.

Whether Goldman's analysis will be accepted as valid is for the future to decide, as anthropology is notorious in providing scope for disagreement. Sahlins has seen ecology as the fundamental factor behind Polynesian social evolution, Goldman sees status rivalry. Perhaps a future scholar will combine the two approaches.

One society remains to be described in more detail, namely Samoa, which has a number of unusual features which serve to set it apart from most other areas of Polynesia. At present, the majority of Samoans dwell in large villages (figure 4.12), which are comprised of a number of relatively autonomous cognatic land-holding groups called *aiga*. Certain high-ranking men (usually heads of families) in each *aiga* are elected to titles which they generally hold for life, and these title-holders (*matai*) are entitled to certain seating positions in the circular council houses (*fale tele*), where meet the village or district councils (*fono*) which govern local affairs. Specific titles are transmitted normally through specific *aiga*, and they are ranked into a definite hierarchy, although a powerful and influential *aiga* can advance the status of its title by a variety of means.

The *matai* titles are also divided into two interdependent functional categories, *ali'i* and *tulafale*. The former were regarded originally as having the highest degree of sanctity, while the latter served as the spokesmen for *ali'i* and carried out various ceremonial functions, although

Fig. 4.12. Circular houses in a Samoan village at Matautu, Upolu. (See also colour plate.)

both groups participated in *fono* discussions[131].

Since ethnographic records have been kept, the villages have been organised into districts, and 'the particular communities and localities with which the higher seniority descent lines and higher elite titles were associated residentially tended to become most important. Out of this emerged a recognised series of district and subdistrict alignments in a complex hierarchy of power, ceremonial and other relationships'[132]. While the villages and local councils functioned with a high degree of autonomy, a number of the highest *ali'i* titles did confer authority over very large districts, and their transmission was often accompanied by warfare.

What may once have been a traditional ramage organisation such as that in New Zealand has been greatly transformed in Samoa, although descent and primogeniture are not always negligible factors in enabling a man to acquire a title. The *fono* itself is duplicated in councils of the wives of the *matai*s, and of unmarried men, and the whole system is one of intricate checks and balances based partially on the oppositions between chiefs and talking-chiefs, between patrilineal and matrilineal kin alignments, and between the parallel *fono* councils[133]. The nature of the *aiga* themselves, and of the political relationships and degrees of authority between them, have caused some argument amongst anthropologists, and additional complications arise if one tries to reconstruct the nature of Samoan society at European contact. The large villages, for instance, may have developed from a base of dispersed settlement, similar to that in most other Polynesian islands, since European contact[134]. The existence of a chiefly hierarchy has been disputed for the present day[135], but there are strong indications that a ramage type of hierarchy was important in the past, especially that which culminated in the person of the paramount Tui Manu'a[136].

In general, the Polynesian ramified chiefdoms represent a type of society which was rarely developed elsewhere in Oceania, and it is reasonable to assume that the basic form was developed prior to the effective settlement of most of Polynesia. Its earlier history can only be conjectured, since today the basic form has no really close parallels elsewhere in Melanesia or in Indonesia, and it is not possible with certainty to decide whether its origins lie within or beyond eastern Oceania.

THE ETHNOHISTORY OF ISLAND SOUTHEAST ASIA AND OCEANIA

We must now turn to an overview of Pacific societies, and consider first the trends visible from western Melanesia, through Micronesia and Fiji, and into Polynesia. Geographically, the trend is from large close-set islands to small isolated ones, and from ethnic groups which exploit extensive homogeneous resource zones in specialised fashion and trade their produce, to ethnic groups which exploit ecologically more heterogeneous zones and need only engage in localised resource distribution. The distinction here is between Melanesian trade networks, and the corresponding absence of trade, as opposed to redistribution, in tropical Polynesia. Politically, there is a trend from west to east, towards greater political integration, from Big Man to chief, from unilineal segmentary clans to ramified ambilineal chiefdoms, and towards greater emphasis on genealogical rank. The competitive feasts and currency systems which bolster western Melanesian prestige fade away with the development of inherited rank which does not require such secular validation – the Polynesian chief inherits, as well as achieves his *mana*.

Historical explanation of these observed variations is naturally not an easy problem. On one matter there might be a fair degree of agreement, which is that Australian Aboriginal and New Guinea Highland societies are without exception unilineal and patrilineal, so that this type of social organisation is by far the most likely reconstruction for the original non-Austronesian settlers of the western Pacific. Many more complications arise with the Austronesians, however, for here we have to deal with bilateral Indonesians, unilineal Melanesians and Micronesians, and ambilineal Taiwanese and Polynesians. Perhaps the best way to start looking for an explanation is to see what can be reconstructed for Proto-Austronesian society from comparative studies on modern societies.

In an earlier part of this chapter we have already discussed some reconstructed traits for early Western Austronesian society, although these cannot be accepted as possibly Proto-Austronesian without more evidence, for quite clearly they might have developed in western Austronesia after the initial dispersal of settlers into Oceania. On the other hand, we do have a fair list of reconstructions for Proto-Austronesian based on linguistic evidence – these are discussed in chapter 5, and include taro, yam, rice, bread-fruit, banana, coconut, pigs, outrigger canoes, and pottery, but not metals. To this list we may add, from comparative ethnography[137], the spear, sling and club, a religion based on ancestor worship, nature deities and local spirits, and possibly – but by no means certainly – a concept of *tapu*. Goodenough[138] has suggested that society may have been characterised by an absence of unilineal kin groups, with cognatic (bilateral) residential groups predominating. Murdock[139] has reconstructed a Hawaiian-type kinship terminology, within which most relations of the same generation and sex are called by a single term regardless of matrilineal or patrilineal considerations, and this type of terminology is generally characteristic of bilateral descent. Finally, Frake[140] has suggested that land was a free-good, rather than being vested permanently in territorial land-holding groups as it is today in many parts of Oceania.

The problem arises, if Proto-Austronesian society was in fact bilateral, of why unilineal societies should have come to dominate Melanesia and Micronesia. One important factor here is almost certainly the presence of long-term contact and inter-marriage with the non-Austronesian (Papuan) unilineal societies. This does not of course explain why so many societies in Melanesia and Micronesia should be matrilineal rather than patrilineal, and quite frankly no anthropologist has yet suggested a really satisfactory explanation for this. It might also be possible to explain unilineality as a response to population pressure on small islands and a need to keep the rights to land within the jurisdiction of a descent group, the membership of which might be strictly regulated through adhesion to unilineal norms[141]. In this respect, it might be noted that while Polynesian societies have an ambilineal form of cognatic descent, descent in the male line is often heavily stressed. Whether this really does relate to population density is not clear, however, for in some islands, such as the Tokelaus, land shortage is correlated with increasing emphasis on cognatic ties.

The questions discussed above may never of course be given firm answers. Perhaps as a working hypothesis we may suggest the following sequence of events, and then leave the matter to rest.

1. Firstly, the settlement of island Southeast Asia, Australia, and western Melanesia by non-Austronesian speakers with a patrilineal form of social structure. This settlement was evidently well under way by 30,000 years ago.
2. Secondly, a presence of Austronesian speakers with a bilateral form of social structure in Island Southeast Asia by about 5000 years ago.
3. Thirdly, an expansion of Austronesian speakers into Oceania, where a variety of unilineal and ambilineal forms of social structure were developed, possibly as a result of contact with non-Austronesian societies, and possibly owing to ecological factors and their effects on land inheritance and the distribution and availability of resources. Whether Polynesians inherited their forms of ambilineal kinship reckoning and genealogical ranking from an earlier pre-Polynesian period of Austronesian society, or whether they developed them independently immediately prior to dispersal, is an intriguing question which cannot yet be answered.

Footnotes

1. See summary in Murdock 1967.
2. Bulmer 1971: 37.
3. e.g. Langdon 1975.
4. Beaglehole 1967: 166.
5. For definition see Murdock 1960a. These definitions differ from those sometimes used by British social anthropologists.
6. Murdock 1960b: Chapter 1.
7. Much of this section is summarised from LeBar, Hickey and Musgrave 1964.
8. Burling 1965.
9. Burling 1965: 64.
10. Benedict 1942.
11. Coedes 1967: part 4. Haudricourt (1970) has suggested that the Thais may have spread from Kwangtung following Sinicisation, and that they moved south into Thailand after adopting a Khmer script. For a number of views on the importance of the Thais in pre-Han China, see Lamberg-Karlovsky 1967.
12. de Beauclair 1946.
13. For summaries of the Indianised kingdoms see Wheatley 1964; Coedes 1967; 1968; Giteau 1958.
14. Pelliot 1903: 254.
15. Diffloth 1974.
16. Thomas and Healey 1962. This does not necessarily mean that the Chamic languages were actually established in South Vietnam by this date.
17. Burling 1965: 73–4.

18. The view of the Mon-Khmers as the main autochthonous ethnolinguistic group of Mainland Southeast Asia is supported by the unusually high frequency of the abnormal haemoglobin E amongst them. This suggests the operation of long term natural selection within malarial environments in Southeast Asia (Flatz 1965).

19. Eberhard 1968.

20. Data on Negritos from Cole 1945; LeBar, Hickey and Musgrave 1964; Garvan 1963; Wallace 1971.

21. Garvan 1963: 28.

22. Dentan 1968.

23. H. Geertz 1963: 24. For detailed surveys of Indonesian ethnic groups see LeBar 1972.

24. C. Geertz 1963: 14.

25. Summary taken from Cole 1945; Loeb and Broek 1947; Harrisson 1959a; Kroeber 1928; Robequain 1954; Wallace 1971.

26. Murdock 1960b: Chapter 1.

27. Freeman, D. in Murdock 1960b: Chapter 5.

28. Keesing 1962b.

29. Eggan 1967.

30. Cole 1945; Wallace 1971.

31. Keesing 1962a.

32. Beyer 1955. For the Ifugao excavations see Maher 1973.

33. Mabuchi in Murdock 1960b: Chapter 8; Ferrell 1969.

34. Cole 1945: 291. See also Kroeber 1928: 227.

35. Heine Geldern 1932.

36. Gill 1876: 242; Moresby 1876: 177. Gill even referred to the Austronesian speakers as 'Malays'. See also Seligmann 1910.

37. Oliver 1961: 42–3.

38. Forge 1972.

39. Brookfield 1964.

40. Nelson 1971: 204.

41. Nelson 1971; Barnes 1962; Brookfield and Hart 1971: Chapter 9. It is possible that local land shortage can cause emphasis on agnatic principles for recruitment; see Waddell 1972: 192, and also footnote 141.

42. Kelly (1968) relates the proportions of non-agnates in the Enga and Chimbu cases to ecological and demographic factors.

43. De Lepervanche 1968.

44. Brown 1960; Brookfield and Brown 1963. The term 'tribe' is difficult to define, and G.P. Murdock, in his work on social structure (1960a), avoids its use altogether. The word is often used in a Polynesian context, where territorial kinship groups may be quite large-scale, but some authors (e.g. Codrington 1891: 21) contend that 'tribes' are absent in Melanesia. The use of the term for the Chimbu is therefore specialised and refers to the larger political rather than kinship groupings which are found amongst the Chimbu, but which are evidently not common elsewhere in western Melanesia.

45. Barnes 1962.

46. Sahlins 1963.

47. Rappaport 1967: 28.

48. Waddell (1972) has suggested that dispersed settlements in the New Guinea Highlands are found with highly intensive cultivation systems, where individual families tend to dwell close to their fields.

49. Read 1954.

50. Brown and Brookfield 1967.

51. Rappaport 1967.

52. Watson 1965a; 1965b. Support for Watson's view has recently been supplied by Nelson (1971) and Heider (1967a).

53. Brookfield and White 1968.

54. Heider 1967b.

55. Read 1954.

56. Read 1954: 42.

57. The term 'petty chief' is used after Sahlins 1968: 21, to denote a position of hereditary or otherwise ascribed leadership within a segmentary social grouping.

58. Gerbrands 1967.

59. Serpenti 1965.

60. Oliver 1961: 52–6.

61. Oosterwal 1961: 18.

62. Seligmann 1910.

63. Groves 1963.

64. Hau'ofa 1971.

65. Summarised from Malinowski by Uberoi 1971.

66. Codrington 1891.

67. Ivens 1930. Codrington 1891: 47 also records hereditary chieftainship amongst the Sa'a of Malaita.

68. Parsonson 1965, 1968; Chowning 1968.

69. Oliver 1955.

70. Scheffler 1965a.

71. As pointed out by Chowning (1973: 26–7).

72. Scheffler 1965a: 112.

73. Scheffler 1965a: 299.

74. Davenport 1964.

75. Williamson 1939. M. Allen (1972) gives a good account of a similar society in the New Hebrides.

76. Harrisson 1937; Chapter 1.

77. Leenhardt 1930: Chapter 1. See also Guiart 1956: 20.

78. Guiart 1963. Reviewed by H. Scheffler 1965b.

79. Crocombe and Crocombe 1968: 27.

80. Nayacakalou 1955; 1957; Capell and Lester 1940–2. There are apparently some traces of matrilineal organisation in inland Vanua Levu: Hocart 1915.

81. Sahlins 1962.

82. Gifford 1952.

83. See Hogbin and Wedgwood 1953.

84. Sahlins 1963.

85. Hau'ofa 1971.

86. Melanesian trade is discussed fully by Brookfield and Hart 1971: Chapter 13.

87. Schwartz 1963: 68, 89.

88. Malinowski 1961: chapter 3; Uberoi 1971; Lauer 1970a.

89. Barton in Seligmann 1910: Chapter 8.

90. Groves *et al.* 1958.

91. Hogbin 1947; Harding 1967.

92. Specht 1974a (Buka); Mead 1973 (south-east Solomons); Davenport 1964 (Santa Cruz Islands).

93. Hogbin 1935.

94. Harrisson 1937.

95. Schwartz 1963.

96. Strathern, M. 1965; Chappell 1966; Hughes 1971.

97. Rappaport 1967: 105.

98. Epstein 1968.

99. Davenport 1962; 1964.

100. Armstrong 1928; Epstein 1968; Einzig 1966.

101. e.g. Krieger 1943; Lewis 1951; Cranstone 1961; Guiart 1963; Wingert 1965; Schmitz 1971.

102. Riesenberg and Gayton 1952.

103. General accounts in Mason 1968; Oliver 1961; Alkire 1960; 1972.

104. Goodenough 1955.

105. Murdock and Goodenough 1947.

106. Mason 1968; Barnett 1960.

107. Mason 1959; Lessa 1962: 350–2.

108. Beauclair 1968.

109. Mason 1968; Lessa 1950.

110. Alkire 1965; Lessa 1950; 1966.

111. Osborne 1966.

112. Beauclair 1963.

113. After Firth 1957.

114. Sahlins 1958.

115. Sahlins 1958: 146; Firth 1957. See also Hanson (1970) for Rapa, and Scheffler (1963) for Mangaia.

116. Firth 1960.

117. Mead 1969: 11.

118. For New Zealand generally see Winiata 1956; Firth 1959; 1963; White 1885: Lecture II, part I.

119. Bellwood 1971a.

120. Hooper 1968.

121. Sahlins 1958: 245–6; Hooper 1968.

122. Buck 1932a; 1932b.

123. Sahlins 1958.

124. e.g. Freeman 1961.

125. Bellwood 1971a.

126. Goldman 1970.

127. Burrows 1939.

128. Buck 1934.

129. Porter 1823: 98.

130. Linton 1939.

131. Gilson 1970: Chapter 1; Holmes 1974: chapter 2.

132. Keesing and Keesing 1956: 18–21.

133. Mead 1969.

134. Davidson 1969.

135. Ember 1962.

136. Freeman 1964. See also Turner 1884: chapter 16; Williamson 1924, vol. 1: chapters 2 and 3.

137. Linton 1956: 174.

138. Goodenough 1955.

139. Murdock 1960a: 230–1.

140. Frake 1956.

141. Bulmer (1971: 38) has suggested that if women were under-represented on colonising expeditions, and if they had economic roles in horticulture and pottery manufacture, then uxorilocal residence may have been at a premium, resulting in an eventual tendency towards matrilineality. This explanation would not account for a patrilineal bias, which may have been due to land shortage if males were responsible for land allocation (see footnote 41).

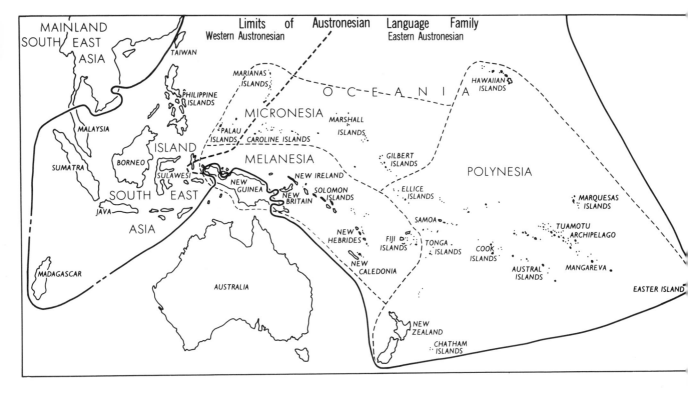

Fig. 5.1. The distribution of the Austronesian languages.

CHAPTER 5

The Linguistic History of the Pacific Area

For a number of reasons, including a desire to keep the topic within manageable limits, I will consider in detail in this chapter only the Austronesian languages of Oceania and Island Southeast Asia, together with the Papuan (or non-Austronesian) languages of Melanesia. A few aspects of the possible linguistic prehistory of the mainland of Southeast Asia have been discussed in chapter 4, but any attempt to expand on these aspects would lead us into specialist fields which are not a direct concern of this book.

At the present day some 1400 indigenous languages, perhaps over one quarter of the world's total, are spoken in Oceania and Island Southeast Asia. One reason for this large number is almost certainly the highly fragmented geographical nature of the area, and the correspondingly infrequent nature of communication between many islands or island districts, especially in Oceania. The total number of indigenous language speakers in the whole area is over 150 million, which is of course a much smaller proportion of the world total than is the number of languages, and the vast majority of this population which inhabits the larger islands of western Indonesia speak only a small number of languages. Over many areas of eastern Indonesia and Melanesia it is quite a common situation to find that neighbouring villages, or small groups of villages, speak totally different and mutually unintelligible languages.

This chapter attempts to survey some of the most recent views on the linguistic history of the Pacific area. Some of these views differ, especially those dealing with the complex linguistic area of Melanesia, but these differences should not be allowed to obscure the fact that linguists are in a position to raise hypotheses concerning almost 10,000 years or more of Pacific prehistory. How one relates linguistic history to the findings of archaeology and physical anthropology is not of course a simple matter, but it is one with which we will continually be concerned throughout this book.

The majority of inferences concerning the linguistic history of the Pacific are derived from the comparative study of the languages of the area as spoken at present or as recorded at European contact. Pre-European indigenous writing systems are not known from anywhere in Oceania, unless it can one day be shown that the script of Easter Island predates 1722, when Jacob Roggeveen brought the island's pre-history to a close. The Indianised kingdoms of Southeast Asia were literate from the mid-first millennium A.D., but the rather meagre epigraphic remains do not provide information that is of direct concern here.

Let us turn now to some theoretical matters, particularly those concerning the identification and grouping of languages[1]. In an area such as Oceania, where small-scale social groups existed right up to the period of European contact, it is frequently not possible to separate languages as neatly as one would separate English from French. Of course, homogeneous populations on isolated islands often did develop their own distinctive languages which stand out in clear-cut fashion. A lot of the Polynesian languages have developed in this way, but in the larger islands of western Melanesia and Indonesia, where communication between different villages may be restricted but not completely cut off, the situation is generally much more complicated.

The result of such a situation may be what is termed a dialect chain[2].

Let us consider a string of villages A to Z, each member of which has fairly regular contacts with its nearest neighbours, but not with villages large distances away. In such a situation villages A and B may develop slightly different dialects (or communalects[3]), but members will still be able to communicate freely. People from A will be able to communicate with people from C and D less freely, and, owing to the compounding of slight differences all along the line, would be totally unable to understand anyone from village Z. In such a situation there may be no distinct breaks in mutual intelligibility between neighbouring settlements, and it is not always possible to isolate different languages and draw geographical boundary lines around them. Linguists have attempted to allow for such situations, and there are statistical ways by which to quantify these complex speech systems[4], but as might be expected different linguists use different methods and often come up with different conclusions. So the figure of 1400 languages for Indonesia and Oceania will always be an approximation, depending upon where one wishes to draw the classificatory dividing line between dialects and different languages.

Moving on from problems of identifying languages to problems of grouping them genetically for historical inferences, we may first of all examine some of the basic concepts behind linguistic differentiation. Languages, like races and cultures, change constantly and inexorably through time – in grammar, phonology and lexicon. They innovate, abandon, and borrow features, and any two communities with a common language in very close contact will tend to share the same innovations and losses. As the degree of communication becomes less and the amount of time increases, so dissimilarities compound. Thus, if some inhabitants of a settlement denoted A move away and found two daughter settlements B and C, and if communication between the resulting three settlements is restricted, as it would be in many cases in Oceania, then the dialects of B and C will gradually diverge from A and from each other, so that after a long period of time the result may be three mutually unintelligible languages, similar to the divergence of the Romance languages from a Latin forbear. The rate of divergence of a group of dialects sharing a common parent will of course depend upon the degree of continuing intercommunication between them, and the number of situations which may occur in reality is immense. Linguistic divergence is a very complex phenomenon, as too is linguistic convergence, for genetically unrelated languages may borrow specific items from each other and so make relationships look closer than they really are. Despite difficulties, however, it is now possible for linguists to provide a 'family-tree' for most of the well-studied language groups of the Pacific, although the real situation is complicated by inter-language borrowing and influence and really resembles the reticulate model of physical evolution.

Genetic grouping or classification of languages into subgroups and families[5] proceeds basically by a process of comparison. Comparisons of grammar, phonology and lexicon between related languages allow reconstruction of aspects of the ancestral language from which they were ultimately derived. Such an ancestral language is called a 'proto-language'. Often, as in the case of the Austronesian family, proto-languages for subgroups of increasing time depth and geographical area can be reconstructed until one gets back to what would appear to be the original proto-language for the whole family, in this case Proto-Austronesian. However, the term 'proto-language' in the singular may be a little misleading, despite its universal use, for it would be most unrealistic to assume that a large family such as Austronesian can be traced back to a single point on a map. Languages at 5000 or 10,000 years ago were probably as varied as they are today, and what linguists term a proto-language could in fact have been a very extensive chain of dialects.

Words which are shared by two or more languages, both in sound and in meaning, and which have been inherited from an ancestral language rather than borrowed, are termed 'cognates'. The words reconstructed for a proto-language are cognates which have survived in two or more daughter languages within the subgroup; the age with which such a cognate can be attributed will depend on the diversity between the languages in which it occurs. Thus, for Proto-Austronesian, cognates which are found in Philippine, Indonesian and Polynesian languages are potentially valid reconstructions, so long as the possibility of borrowing can be discounted.

The principles of comparative linguistics are too complex for further description here, but one technique which has been used widely for subgrouping in the Pacific, and which has a fairly simple theoretical basis, is lexicostatistics[6]. This technique is concerned solely with lexical items, and operates on the basic premise that the more cognates two languages have in common, the more closely related they are likely to be. In any group of languages under investigation, each member language is compared with every other member language, and a tally is kept of the number of cognates all pairs of languages share from a list of one or two hundred meanings, or some intermediate number. The lists are of what are termed non-cultural, basic or universal meanings, such as 'man', 'woman', 'sun', 'sky', which are not restricted to particular types of culture or environment. The number of shared cognates between each pair of languages is expressed as a percentage of the one or two hundred word list, and the percentage figures can then be used to construct a family tree.

Lexicostatistics also has a related technique known as glottochronology, which, as the name suggests, is concerned with the allocation of a chronology to linguistic history. One basic assumption of glottochronology is that words in the list of basic meanings are replaced at a constant rate for all languages, and this constant rate can be calculated and applied mathematically to any given case. Unfortunately, most linguists now recognise that the rate of replacement of basic words is not a constant, either for all languages or for all words, and some have grave doubts about the accuracy of the technique[7]. However, it does seem that it can have a rough validity, and we will see that in Polynesia the time depths calculated from glottochronology are remarkably similar to those from radio-carbon-dated archaeology.

Linguists generally make the logical assumption that the origin area, or homeland, of a language family is most likely to be located in one of the areas of highest linguistic diversity at the present day. In other words, an area with a few closely related languages (such as Polynesia) has been settled for a shorter time than an area with a large number of diverse languages which are only related at a very distant level (such as Melanesia). Isidore Dyen has perhaps been the clearest exponent of this view[8], and he adds that determinable positive migrations should be from linguistically complex to linguistically simple areas. This concept of the meaning of diversity is very important, as we will see throughout this chapter.

THE LANGUAGE FAMILIES OF THE PACIFIC

There are two main groups of languages in Island Southeast Asia and Oceania: Austronesian (once called Malayo-Polynesian) and Papuan (sometimes called non-Austronesian in New Guinea and adjacent areas). The Austronesian languages constitute a single family, and are descended from a proto-language which existed some 5–7000 years ago; the Papuan languages are much more diversified and comprise a large number of separate but distantly related families.

THE PAPUAN LANGUAGES

The Papuan languages are spoken by about 2.7 million people, mostly in New Guinea, and they number between seven and eight hundred, depending upon how one wishes to differentiate between dialects of languages and separate languages[9]. The vast majority of these languages occupy the greater part of New Guinea, but outliers occur on northern Halmahera, inland Timor, Alor and Pantar in eastern Indonesia, and scattered outliers to the east of New Guinea are to be found on New Britain, New Ireland, Bougainville, on Rossell Island in the Louisiade Archipelago, and on Vella Lavella, Rendova, New Georgia, Savo and Santa Cruz in the British Solomon Islands[10].

Because of the diversity of these Papuan languages, it is logical to conclude that some of them may have descended from the original languages established by the Australoid settlers of western Melanesia some 30,000 or more years ago. However, the diversification has not been proceeding in small isolated pockets all over the area for this length of time; had it done so, then the degree of observable linguistic relationship across New Guinea would be virtually nil. As it happens, widespread relationships are now well plotted, and they show that a lot of inter-linked population expansion has taken place within the past 10,000 years.

Before we look at this further, let us go back to some more definitions. Over the past fifteen years or so, a great deal of linguistic comparative work has been done in New Guinea, mostly using lexicostatistics, although the technique is regarded by New Guinea linguists as insufficient alone for a reliable classification, and it often needs to be bolstered by more detailed analyses. New Guinea classifications do not normally use the family and subgroup terminology in the sense that it is applied to the Austronesian languages, but resort instead to terms based more on lexicostatistical criteria. The highest-order group recognised is called a *phylum*, the members of which share at least 5–12 percent of basic vocabulary. Next to the phylum is the *stock*, with more than 12–28 percent of shared vocabulary, and next again is the *family*, with more than 28–45 percent of shared vocabulary. None of these percentage boundaries are rigidly defined, as grouping is not done entirely on the basis of word sharing alone.

The phylum is our most important concept, and it is interesting to note that the Austronesian languages would probably fall mainly into one phylum only. New Guinea has several phyla, and it is possible to trace linguistic relationships here back to about 10,000 years ago, although before that time they become increasingly hypothetical.

Concerning New Guinea relationships, the major result of recent work has been to classify the vast majority of all Papuan languages into some eighteen groups, comprising six phyla and twelve isolated stocks and families. The ten most important of these groups are labelled on figure 5.2. Of the other eight, each of very restricted distribution, six are located between the Geelvink Bay and Sepik-Ramu phyla, while the other two are in Papua. The Trans

New Guinea phylum[11] is by far the most widespread, and accounts for about 84% of Papuan speakers, and 67% of Papuan languages. It also has outliers in Timor, Alor and Pantar in eastern Indonesia. Other large phyla include the West Papuan, Geelvink Bay, Sepik-Ramu[12], and East Papuan, the latter including all the Papuan languages of the islands east of New Guinea.

According to Wurm[13], the most deeply rooted groups are the Torricelli, Sko, Kwomtari, Left May, Geelvink Bay and East Vogelkop, and it may be that these have been developing *in situ* since the early days of New Guinea settlement. The West Papuan phylum seems to have developed a little later, while the Trans New Guinea phylum represents a sweep of more recent movements, presumably from west to east, in perhaps three stages beginning about 10,000 years ago. These movements were followed by a back-movement from the Markham Valley region into the Highlands, which Wurm suggests spread Austronesian loan-words quite widely after about 3000 B.C. The East Papuan phylum may have spread from south-eastern New Guinea owing to the expansion of Trans New Guinea speakers, and the Sepik-Ramu phylum may approximate the Trans New Guinea in date of origin.

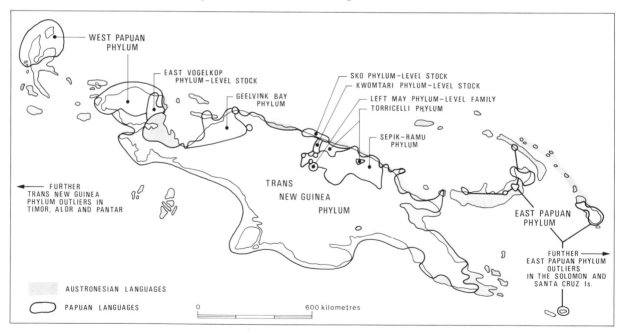

Fig. 5.2. The distribution of the Papuan languages.

Nevertheless, from a reading of Wurm's recent surveys of New Guinea linguistic prehistory it is clear that ideas are still in flux, and it might be rash to draw final conclusions at the present time. Wurm visualises a complex mixing process for the Papuan languages in general, but it is not clear whether all the postulated movements originate from within the New Guinea area, or whether some come from further west in Indonesia. Unfortunately, as far as the Papuan languages are concerned, there is little archaeological evidence which could help to resolve these problems.

Furthermore, it is not yet clear how one can explain the rather surprising expansion of the Trans New Guinea phylum, unless it has some connection with the horticultural developments now known to be present in the Highlands from at least 4000 B.C. (see page 238). We do know that only a few coastal pockets escaped the expansion, and Highland populations after the end of the Pleistocene may have been too sparse to offer much linguistic resistance.

The other languages of the Pacific area which are not Austronesian are those of Australia, Tasmania and the Andaman Islands. We do not need to consider these, but we may note a rather daring hypothesis by Greenberg[14] that the Andamanese, Tasmanian and Papuan languages are ultimately related. However, it is not at all clear how this view can be interpreted by a prehistorian, as Greenberg does not include the Australian languages in the relationship. We might also note that most of the Australian languages, except for those in the northern regions west of the Gulf of Carpentaria, have a glottochronological time depth of only around 5000 years[15]. This is possible evidence for population movement at about the time when blade industries and the dog make their first appearance on the continent (see chapter 3).

THE AUSTRONESIAN LANGUAGES

The Austronesian languages sweep in a great arc around the resistant core of Papuan languages in western Melanesia, and their spread seems to have taken place entirely within the past 5000 to 7000 years. There are between 700 and 800 of them today, spoken by about 150 million people, and some 300 of these languages occupy most of Indonesia, the Philippines, parts of Taiwan, Malaya and South Vietnam, and Madagascar. The vast bulk of the population inhabits this western region, while the remaining 400–500 languages of geographically and culturally fragmented Oceania are spoken by only about one million people. The east-west geographical spread of the family, from Easter Island to Madagascar, covers 210 degrees of longitude, or well over half of the earth's circumference in the tropics.

THE MAJOR AUSTRONESIAN SUBGROUPS

At the present time it is not possible to present a detailed family tree for the Austronesian languages as a whole, although genetic relationships between languages in some areas are now well established. There seem to be some grounds for recognising at least three major divisions within the family, and one includes some of the languages of Taiwan, while another has recently been defined as Eastern Austronesian[16], which includes the languages of southern Halmahera and Oceania (excluding parts of western Micronesia). The third division, generally known as Western Austronesian, includes the languages of the Philippines, most of Indonesia, South Vietnam, Malaya, Madagascar, and the Palau and Marianas Islands of western Micronesia. Western Austronesian is not at present recognised as a true subgroup with a reconstructed proto-language[17], and I am simply using the term geographically in the present context. However, the majority of the languages defined as Western Austronesian are clearly closely related, and a limited outline of their historical development can be given.

Eastern Austronesian, as a well-defined linguistic subgroup, is composed mainly of the large grouping known as Oceanic[18], which includes all the languages of Oceania to the east of the Mamberamo River region of Irian Jaya. The other members of Eastern Austronesian are located in southern Halmahera and western Irian Jaya, and it is possible that some other Maluku languages could belong as well. The greatest diversity within the subgroup lies in eastern Indonesia and western Melanesia, and the latter area is particularly complex from a linguistic viewpoint. A tentative family tree for Austronesian is shown in figure 5.3, although it should be remembered that a tree model may be rather simplistic, and the true model would be more like a reticulum[19], as pointed out above.

The entity denoted 'Proto-Austronesian', whether it be one language or several related ones, was probably in existence between five and

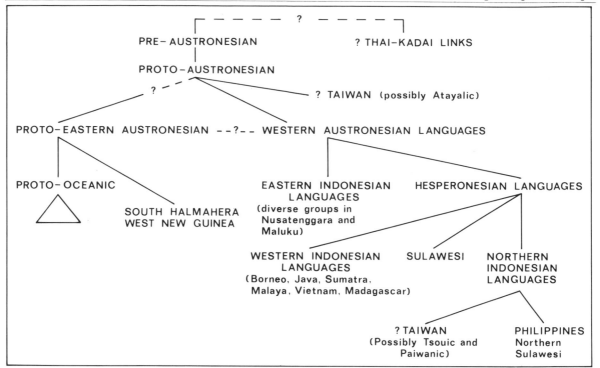

Fig. 5.3. A tentative family tree for Austronesian.

seven thousand years ago on glottochronological grounds[20], somewhere in the large area extending from Taiwan, through the Philippines, eastern Indonesia, New Guinea, and to the Bismarck and Solomon Islands. Proto-Austronesian is probably not to be located anywhere on the Southeast Asian mainland, as there are no Austronesian languages ever recorded with certainty from southern China, and the Austronesian languages of Malaya and South Vietnam have island origins. Different scholars incline to different homeland areas within the great sweep of possible islands, and perhaps the most controversial view is that of Isidore Dyen[21], who has suggested on lexico-statistical grounds that the Austronesian homeland is to be found in western Melanesia. This view is not accepted in this chapter, although Dyen's results are given consideration later on. General comparative linguistics suggest an origin to the west of Melanesia[22], and there is of course a fundamental racial consideration which cannot be ignored; the majority of the Austronesian speakers are mainly of Mongoloid derivation, so that an origin area amongst the Australoid populations of Melanesia would be very difficult to uphold. The matter is far from resolved at the

present, but there are good linguistic grounds for regarding Taiwan as the location of Proto-Austronesian, as we will see below. However, the location of a proto-language is not necessarily the most significant area with respect to subsequent population expansion, and the major expansion of Austronesian speakers through Indonesia and Oceania may well have taken place from areas to the south of Taiwan, particularly the Philippines and eastern Indonesia.

The reconstruction of the lexicon of Proto-Austronesian is of considerable importance for prehistory. Its speakers undoubtedly lived in a tropical area, and, according to Pawley and Green[23], had a way of life with the following characteristics:

They had a mixed economy, based on agriculture and fishing, but supplemented by hunting and arboriculture. Cultivated crops included taro, yams, banana, sugar cane, breadfruit, coconut, the aroids *Cyrtosperma* and *Alocasia*, sago, and (probably) rice. They kept pigs, and probably dogs and chickens, and made pottery. They exploited a maritime environment, gathering shellfish and using a variety of fishing techniques and gear including nets, basket traps, hooks, and *Derris* poison. They sailed outrigger canoes. Their tools were of stone, wood and shell; terms for metallurgy are not sufficiently widespread to be attributed with any confidence to Proto-Austronesian.

The significance of this reconstruction for a population living somewhere in Island Southeast Asia about 5000 years ago or more is quite obvious. But one problem still remains. If Proto-Austronesian was spoken somewhere in Island Southeast Asia, then what about its direct ancestors, which are virtually beyond the range of linguistic reconstruction, but which certainly did once exist and which may be called 'Pre-Austronesian'? We may note here that we have two obvious and simple possibilities: Pre-Austronesian may be indigenous to Island Southeast Asia, or it may not. Quite frankly, this problem has no answer yet, but there are possibilities that Pre-Austronesian speakers may have moved into the area from mainland southern Chinese or perhaps even Japanese source regions, and these possibilities are certainly worthy of brief attention.

The evidence in favour of southern China comes from linguistic work carried out by Paul Benedict, who suggested in 1942[24] that the Indonesian languages were remotely related to Thai, and to a group of minority languages spoken in southern China and North Vietnam which he called Kadai. He went on to propose that Thai, Kadai and Austronesian formed an Austro-Thai family[25], although he does not appear to have received a great deal of support for his view, and one problem is that the Thai and Kadai languages are now monosyllabic and tonal, while the Austronesian languages are polysyllabic and do not have a tonal system. The existence of an Austro-Thai family is still really unproven, but if Benedict is correct, then the common ancestral languages would have been spoken well in excess of 5000 years ago.

The same kind of possibility also applies to Japan, but here the evidence is purely archaeological and not linguistic. It revolves around the Japanese parallels for the Philippine and Indonesian flake and blade industries of the early Holocene, as discussed on page 78. And although the modern Japanese language does not have any known genetic relationship with Austronesian, we cannot entirely rule out the possibility that other languages were spoken in

the archipelago in earlier times.

THE WESTERN AUSTRONESIAN LANGUAGES

From figure 5.3, it can be seen that the most extensive subgroup of Western Austronesian, in geographical terms, is Hesperonesian. The contents of the Hesperonesian subgroup do not seem to be in major dispute, apart from the languages of Taiwan, where we seem to have a notably complex situation. Although Chinese is now the major language of Taiwan, particularly in the west, it has only really become established there since the early seventeenth century. Indigenous Austronesian languages consist of three subgroups, namely Atayalic (Atayal and Seedik of north Taiwan), Tsouic (several languages of central Taiwan), and Paiwanic (several languages in eastern and southern Taiwan)[26]. Many authors[27] have pointed out the aberrant nature of the Taiwanese languages within the Austronesian family, and this applies particularly to Atayalic. There is in fact phonological and lexicostatistical evidence which could point to Taiwan as the location of Proto-Austronesian[28], and if this is indeed the case, then the Atayalic languages, which occupy a rather isolated classificatory position, may well represent the first split in the family tree. The Tsouic and Paiwanic languages could also result from this split, or they could represent later migrations to the island from a Hesperonesian source. Hence the rather tentative placing of the Taiwanese languages on figure 5.3. The problem of Taiwan is discussed again in chapter 8, together with the archaeological evidence, since it is clear that the island is a major but poorly understood keystone in the culture history of Island Southeast Asia.

The eastern Indonesian languages of Nusatenggara, Maluku, and Sulawesi are also very diverse, and this area could well be an important centre for Austronesian dispersal. Internal relationships are still uncertain, and Sulawesi alone contains about 40 languages, although some of those on the Minahasa arm in the north seem to have their closest relationships with the Philippines[29]. The Sulawesi languages outside the northern arm also have strong Hesperonesian affiliations, and are so classified on the family tree shown in figure 5.3. However, the diversity and importance of the whole of eastern Indonesia is now well supported by archaeological evidence, which shows that peoples with pottery and horticulture were in the area by as early as 3000 B.C.

To the north, the Philippines contain some 70 languages, which have been subgrouped lexicostatistically by Thomas and Healey[30]. The time depths which they give, from glottochronology, suggest that Austronesian languages are fairly recent in the area, and they do seem to be less diverse than those of Taiwan or eastern Indonesia. But it would be rather unreasonable to suggest that the Philippines were really settled by Austronesians one thousand years later than the islands to the immediate north and south, so we may have a situation where linguistic movements within the past 3000 years have obliterated earlier diversity. This has been suggested by Grace[31], and it does of course raise the important point that diversity can only be recognised by linguists when historical factors have allowed it to survive. This makes it difficult to locate a homeland for Proto-Austronesian with any degree of certainty, and the claims for Taiwan could, in this respect, only stand out by default.

From figure 5.3, it will be seen that the Philippine languages belong to the Hesperonesian subgroup, as do those of western Indonesia – Sumatra, Java, Madura, Bali, Lombok, and southern Borneo. Closely related languages, within the western Indonesian subgroup, are found in Malaya (excluding the interior Semang and Senoi languages which are distantly related to the Mon-Khmer family), in South Vietnam and eastern Cambodia (the Chamic family), and on Madagascar. These Hesperonesian languages do not reveal great diversity, and indications are that they have spread within the past 3–5000 years. Malay is closely related to the languages of southern Sumatra and western Borneo, and it may have replaced older Mon-Khmer languages after establishment on the mainland. Chamic seems to be related to Malay and south-west Bornean languages, and its proto-language may have separated about 1300 B.C., according to Thomas and Healey. Archaeological evidence (chapter 7) suggests that the Chams may have settled South Vietnam by at least 600 B.C., and possibly several centuries before.

From southern Borneo, speakers of the Maanyan language were evidently responsible for the first settlement of distant Madagascar in the early first millennium A.D. By this time Indonesia was drawing increasing numbers of Indian merchants, and Malagasy does contain a number of Sanscrit loan words which it seems to have acquired from its Indonesian source, rather than directly from India. Because of this Dahl[32] has suggested

a date between 0 and A.D. 400 for initial Austronesian settlement.

One western Indonesian language remains as something of a misfit, and this is Engganese, spoken on a small island off the southern end of Sumatra. Dyen's study (see below) showed that Engganese does not relate closely to any other language, and if this is correct, then it may be a survival of earlier diversity in western Indonesia which has been wiped out by the expansion of the Hesperonesian subgroup within the past 3000 years or so. This again brings up the problem that we noted for the Philippines, and it does seem that western Indonesia cannot be ruled out entirely as a possible (but unlikely) location for Proto-Austronesian.

Two other Western Austronesian languages might finally be noted, namely the Palauan and Chamorro (Marianas Islands) languages of western Micronesia. These retain remote relationships with the Philippines and north-eastern Indonesia, but they seem to have diverged considerably owing to several millennia of relative isolation.

THE EASTERN AUSTRONESIAN AND OCEANIC SUBGROUPS

The Oceanic subgroup includes the languages of Melanesia, Polynesia and Micronesia (excluding Palauan, Chamorro, and possibly Yapese). The languages of western Irian Jaya have tended to resist classification in the past[33], but are now placed by Blust in the larger Eastern Austronesian subgroup[34].

The Melanesian area contains more than 300 of the total of 4–500 Oceanic languages, and is an area of extreme linguistic diversity around which there appears to be some scholastic disagreement. Melanesian islands tend to have dialect chains or networks rather than discrete languages, and their high degree of diversity may reflect not only a considerable time depth, but also the presence of long-term borrowing from Papuan languages, the high degree of social and political fragmentation which has given rise to highly localised communication networks, and also the presence of bilingualism between members of different ethnic groups[35]. As we will see later, Isidore Dyen has taken the degree of Melanesian lexicostatistical diversity at its face value to suggest that Proto-Austronesian was located in Melanesia, but it seems more likely that the rate of diversification has been unusually speeded up in this region.

Because the Oceanic subgroup is phonologically and grammatically well established, it may be accepted that the mainstream of development of the Melanesian languages goes back to a forbear called Proto-Oceanic, which was spoken in the New Guinea area about 3000 B.C.[36]. According to Milke[37], the speakers of Proto-Oceanic prior to dispersal retained contact for an extended period with speakers of earlier stages of Philippine, Sulawesi and eastern Indonesian languages, a point of some historical significance. But the Melanesian languages are unlikely to have evolved in total isolation subsequent to the break-up of Proto-Oceanic, and in 1943 Arthur Capell[38] claimed later successive movements into western Melanesia (particularly south-east Papua) from Borneo, central Sulawesi, and Java or Sumatra. These three movements took place, according to Capell, between A.D. 400 and 1200. Milke[39] has refuted the views of Capell, and Chretien[40] has suggested that there may only have been one movement. But regardless of who is right, there is good archaeological evidence for late movements from Indonesia into Melanesia, and it is likely that these have contributed at least something to Melanesian linguistic diversity.

Furthermore, a number of linguists have suggested that the Papuan languages of Melanesia have influenced and diversified the later Austronesian languages[41]. Although this so-called 'pidginisation' theory has numerous opponents, Capell[42] has shown quite convincingly that the Austronesian languages of the eastern half of New Guinea and the islands of the Milne Bay District have adopted a Papuan grammatical word order, and often have a predominantly Papuan lexicon, while those of the Bismarcks and eastern Melanesia, where the expected influence from Papuan languages is much less, have retained the more usual Austronesian word order. Therefore, it does seem likely that the observed diversity in Melanesian languages may partially reflect the influences of a varied Papuan substratum as well as successive movements of Austronesian speakers from Island Southeast Asia. Although linguists tend either to support these views or vehemently to oppose them, it nevertheless seems to me that the real answers may come with compromise, as in so many aspects of Pacific prehistory.

On New Guinea, Austronesian languages are restricted to pockets along the northern and south-eastern coastal areas, and their absence in the south-west and on the Torres Straits Islands suggests very strongly that Austronesian penetration into Melanesia was along the north coast of New Guinea. The languages of the greater part of Melanesia, apart from those in the Eastern Oceanic subgroup to be described below, have generally resisted attempts at genetic classification and so provide a rather uninteresting family tree (figure 5.4)[43]. Glottochronological reckoning suggests a date of about 3000 B.C. for the break-up of Proto-Oceanic, and of about 2000 B.C. for the break-up of Proto-Eastern Oceanic[44]. The small cluster of related languages in Papua may have a similar time depth to Eastern Oceanic, although these two subgroups do not seem to be closely related.

Evidence for the very important Eastern Oceanic subgroup results from the work of Grace, Biggs, Dyen and Pawley[45]. Pawley lists 30 languages (taking Polynesian as one unit) as belonging to the subgroup, which includes the following (figures 5.4, 5.5):

1. Several languages on the islands of Isabel, Florida, Guadalcanal, San Cristobal and Malaita in the south-eastern Solomons.

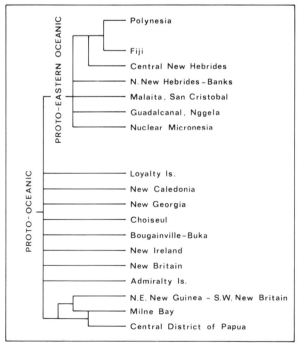

Fig. 5.4. A tentative family tree for the Oceanic languages.

2. The languages of the Banks Islands.
3. Several languages in the central and northern New Hebrides.
4. Fijian, consisting of two major dialect chains.
5. Polynesian, a closed and homogeneous sub-group which shares closest relationship with Fijian.

The initial break-up of Proto-Eastern Oceanic probably took place somewhere in the south-east Solomons-New Hebrides-Banks area at about 2000 B.C., with no particular area at present having chronological priority. Fijian and Tongan probably separated about 1500 B.C., and these dates are well supported by archaeology as we will see in chapter 9. One other isolated Melanesian language which may belong in the Eastern Oceanic subgroup is Rotuman, spoken on a small island to the north of Fiji[46], but attempts to add other Melanesian languages to the list given above have not so far been successful[47]. However, Grace[48] feels that the languages of Nuclear Micronesia (Carolines, Marshalls and Gilberts) have their closest relationships with the languages of the New Hebrides, although Pawley[49] is hesitant about grouping them with Eastern Oceanic.

The two dialect chains of Fiji comprise the closest relatives in Melanesia to the languages of Polynesia. At approximately 1500 B.C., the Proto-Fijian-Polynesian language (or dialect chain) was located somewhere in the Fijian Islands, and the first movement into Polynesia, probably to the Tongan Islands, took place from here soon afterwards. By a little before the time of Christ it appears that two separate dialect chains – Western Fijian and Eastern Fijian – were in the process of development in Fiji, and today about 58 to 68 percent of basic vocabulary is usually shared between dialects of one chain and those of the other[50]. Even within one of the chains, dialects will be found to be mutually unintelligible if they are not geographically close, and this situation is like that characteristic of most of the large islands of Melanesia. In the Fijian case the range of high mountains running from north to south through the main island of Viti Levu has been an important barrier to communication, and it is the degree of communication, or the lack of it, which has almost certainly been a major factor behind chain formation. The Western Fijian chain includes the dialects of the Yasawa Islands, western Viti Levu, and possibly also western Kadavu, while the Eastern Fijian chain includes eastern Kadavu, eastern Viti Levu, Vanua Levu and the Lau Islands. Around the coast of Viti Levu the division between the two chains is quite well marked, but there is a degree of intergradation which suggests that they are more polarities in a continuum than distinct entities.

THE LANGUAGES OF POLYNESIA

The Polynesian islands are small, and have been settled for a shorter time than most of those in Melanesia. Hence well developed dialect chains are absent, and Polynesia present a fairly homogeneous series of well defined languages which are eminently suited to genetic analysis. The basic classification has been established from the work of Elbert, Emory, Dyen, Pawley and Green[51], and is shown in figure 5.5.

We have seen above that the Proto-Fijian-Polynesian language was spoken in the Fijian islands about 1500 B.C. Probably by 1300 B.C. a single language which is strictly termed Pre-Polynesian was established within Polynesia, on all available evidence in the Tongan Islands[52]. By 1000 B.C. speakers of Pre-Polynesian may well have spread through the northern islands of the Tongan group to Samoa (see page 253), and then for some centuries these earliest colonies may have remained in contact, but isolated from Fiji and Melanesia. This period of isolation, before further settlements were made to the east, could well have been 500–1000 years long[53], and it is during this time that the early Polynesian languages developed a number of innovations which now characterise the descendant Polynesian languages as a whole and serve to set them clearly apart as a closed subgroup. The present members of this subgroup comprise the 16 languages of Triangle Polynesia, and the 14 languages of Outlier Polynesia.

Before examining the Polynesian family tree in more detail, it is first necessary to look at some of the Proto-Polynesian vocabulary reconstructions, since these enable us to make many inferences about the early Polynesian way of life. Proto-Polynesian is defined as the language spoken at the time of initial dispersal from the location of Pre-Polynesian, and as we will see later it is possibly to be located at around 1000 B.C. in Tonga, just prior to the initial settlement of Samoa. To date, some two thousand words have been reconstructed for Proto-Polynesian[54], and it is fairly certain that it was spoken on a volcanic island with a barrier reef. The speakers had domestic dogs, pigs and fowls, grew bread-fruit, bananas, coconuts, taro, and the paper mulberry tree (*Broussonetia papyrifera*), the inner bark of which was used for the production of bark-cloth. They were adept fishermen and voyaged in canoes with outriggers, and fought with bows, arrows, slings and spears. They probably had fortifications of some kind, built their houses and religious structures on raised platforms of earth or stone, but evidently did not live in villages. These are just a few of the facts which one can glean from the Proto-Polynesian word list, and there are of course many more relating to environment, horticulture, sea life, navigation, cooking and food preparation, clothing and other subjects.

The family tree for Polynesian (figure 5.5) shows that Tonga was settled at a very early date, although Tonga itself has only been responsible for the colonisation of Samoa, and of the isolated island of Niue, which was probably settled in the early first millennium A.D. on glottochronological reckoning. By the beginning of the first millennium B.C., Proto-Polynesian had split into its Tongic and Nuclear Polynesian descendant branches, the latter almost certainly being established on Samoa, which was settled at about this time. Later settlements from Samoa have given rise to the Samoic-Outlier subgroup, which contains the languages of probably all of the Polynesian Outliers in Micronesia and Melanesia, and these are discussed in more detail below.

The first settlement of eastern Polynesia (defined on page 308) took place in the early first millennium A.D., and was followed by a period of isolation in one locality of perhaps several centuries during which a number of innovations restricted to the Eastern Polynesian subgroup took place. The location of Proto-Eastern Polynesian is not certain, but may have been either in the Marquesas or Society Islands, perhaps the former. Pawley[55] has pointed out that the presence of two fairly well-separated dialects in the Marquesas might indicate long settlement, and archaeological evidence suggests that the group

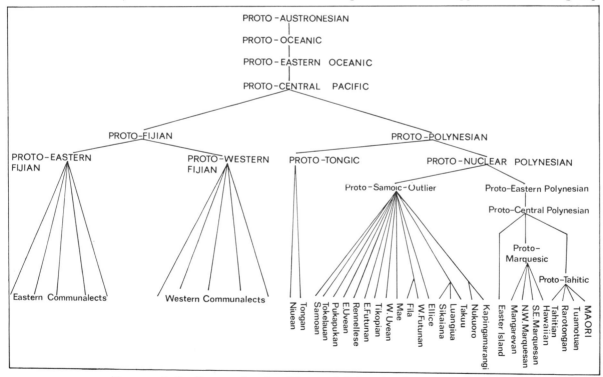

Fig. 5.5. A family tree for the Fijian and Polynesian languages. From Green 1974.

might have been peopled for about 2000 years. On the other hand, Biggs[53] feels that the Marquesas are geographically too isolated to be the location of Proto-Eastern Polynesian. Another problem arises in connection with the shell of pearl-oyster (*Pinctada margaretifera*), for Pawley and Green[57] point out that a term for this cannot be reconstructed for Proto-Eastern Polynesian, while one can be for Proto-Polynesian. This may mean that the first settlers of eastern Polynesia lived on an island with no pearl-oysters, and this would rule out the Society or Marquesas islands, and make remote Easter Island, where the pearl-shell does not occur, an interesting possibility. But it seems most unlikely that Easter Island was the location of Proto-Eastern Polynesian for geographical reasons, and it is more likely that an original Proto-Eastern Polynesian word for pearl-oyster was abandoned and replaced at a fairly early date.

Despite these problems of locating the first eastern Polynesian settlement, the Marquesas remain the most likely candidate, and it is generally agreed that the first settlement which took place from here may well have been to Easter Island. On both glottochronological and archaeological grounds Easter Island was settled before A.D. 500, which is surprisingly early considering its extreme isolation. By about A.D. 700 or perhaps a little earlier, the Eastern Polynesian subgroup had divided into two lower order subgroups – Marquesic and Tahitic, and the Society Islands were almost certainly settled by this time. Speakers of Marquesic dialects may have been responsible for the settlements of Mangareva and the Hawaiian Islands, according to Green[58], but there is some uncertainty about this[59]. The Tahitic subgroup is founded on stronger evidence than the Marquesic, and this includes the languages of the Society Islands, the Cook Islands (excluding Pukapuka), the Australs, the Tuamotus, and New Zealand Maori. These areas were all settled by the end of the first millennium A.D. Green[60] has also suggested that the Hawaiian Islands were settled a second time after initial Marquesan settlement from the Society Islands, and in addition, he points out that New Zealand Maori and the Moriori language of the Chatham Islands may reflect some linguistic influence from the Marquesas, despite their overall Tahitic affiliations.

The linguistic evidence pertaining to Polynesia indicates very strongly that the Polynesian languages have one single ancestor, i.e. Proto-Polynesian, and that they have received probably no influence at all from any other Oceanic or American linguistic areas. The significance of this 'bottleneck' situation needs no emphasis. It is also of interest to note that the technique of glottochronological dating gives results in Polynesia which are well supported by archaeology. In this sense Polynesia is a useful laboratory for the testing of techniques, for in linguistically more complex areas linguists have tended to mistrust results derived from glottochronology. That the technique seems to work for Polynesia does not however mean that it will prove as useful in other areas where heavy borrowing may be expected and different retention rates may apply. Even in Polynesia, some of the smaller islands may have undergone rather rapid linguistic change according to Pawley[61], although this does not appear to have affected the overall degree of correlation between linguistics and archaeology to any great extent.

THE POLYNESIAN OUTLIERS[62]

Some fourteen Polynesian languages are spoken on nineteen separate islands in the region of Outlier Polynesia (figure 5.6). The majority of these islands are small, and lie to the east (windward) of the series of large islands forming the Solomon and New Hebrides chains, as well as New Caledonia. In general, these Polynesian languages seem to have had few effects on the Melanesian languages of the larger islands, although some evidence for pre-European borrowing, probably from West Uvea in the Loyalty Islands, has been detected for New Caledonia[63]. All the Outlier languages are now classified within the Samoic-Outlier subgroup of Nuclear Polynesian, and this subgroup also includes the languages of a number of western Polynesian islands; the Samoan group itself, the Ellice and Tokelau Islands, East Uvea and East Futuna (Hoorn Islands) to the north-east of Fiji, and Pukapuka in the northern Cook Islands.

Inclusion of the Outlier languages in the Samoic-Outlier subgroup necessarily implies that the languages have reached their present locations by back-migrations from western Polynesia. In earlier years, many scholars thought that they represented Polynesian settlements left behind in the wake of the main eastward Polynesian movement[64], but support for this view has dwindled with recent linguistic research. Purely on the linguistic evidence, Pawley[65] has recognised three

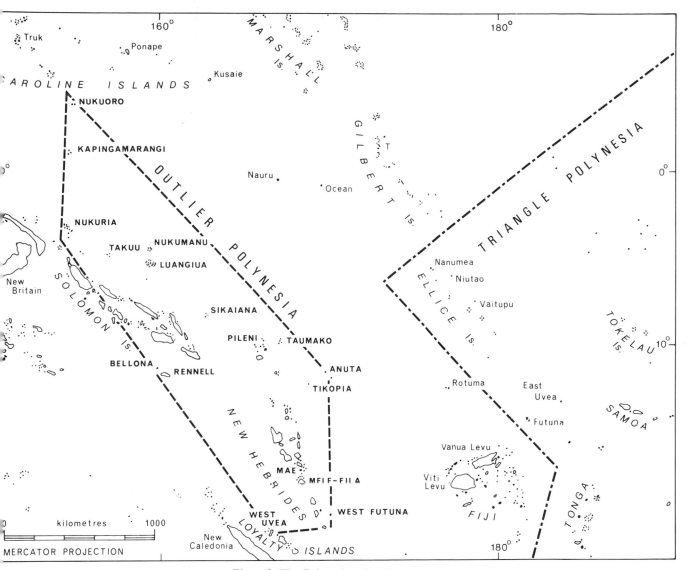

Fig. 5.6. The Polynesian Outliers.

Outlier subgroups – one consisting of Nukuoro and Kapingamarangi in the north; a second consisting of Sikaiana, Takuu and Luangiua (Ontong Java) to the north of the Solomons; and a third comprising Mele, Fila, West Futuna and Aniwa in the New Hebrides. More recently[66] Pawley has tentatively combined the first two subgroups as one, together with Nanumea and Vaitupu in the Ellice Islands, although he does not commit himself with respect to the remaining Outliers. Green[67] has since expanded the third subgroup to include all the southern Outliers, i.e. Anuta, Tikopia, West Futuna, West Uvea, Mae, Mele-Fila, Rennell and Bellona.

In another very important work on the Polynesian Outliers, D. Bayard[68] has made comparisons between the islands on the basis of a 200-word basic vocabulary list, 22 kinship terms, and 58 technological items. His results are not therefore based entirely on linguistics, but his main conclusions, apart from a few now rendered unlikely by the more recent work of Pawley and Green, are as follows:

1. Many of the islands have had primary and secondary settlements, and in some cases have been in continued contact with other Outliers.

2. In chronological order, the following settlements may have taken place:

   a) East Futuna (Hoorn Islands) settled from Samoa, and the Ellice Islands settled from both.

   b) Tikopia settled from East Futuna and/or the Ellice Islands, Nukuoro settled from an unknown source.

   c) The settlement of the Outliers in the

northern Solomons, probably from the Ellice Islands.

d) The settlement of most of the southern Outliers, in most cases ultimately, but not in all cases directly, from East Futuna.

Bayard's conclusions point to the importance of East Futuna in the settlement of the southern Outliers, and Elbert[69] draws similar conclusions for Rennell and Bellona. Bayard also suggests that East Futuna was settled about 2000 years ago, and that most of the Outliers were settled during the first millennium A.D., especially in the later part. The results of all these investigations suggest that we might at present derive the settlement of the northern atoll Outliers from the Ellice Islands, and of the southern high island Outliers from East Futuna, with Pileni and Taumako in the centre remaining unplaced. But it is quite clear that much more study is needed on Outlier languages, and at present it is only possible to emphasise East Futuna and the Ellice Islands as sources, and at the same time to suggest that direct settlement of any Outliers from the Samoan Islands seems unlikely.

THE LANGUAGES OF NUCLEAR MICRONESIA

The Nuclear Micronesian area (that is Micronesia excluding the Palau and Marianas Islands) contains Oceanic languages which are rather more diverse than those of Polynesia, and grammatically closer to the languages of Melanesia. As noted above, Grace[70] has indicated that their closest relationships are with the New Hebrides and Banks Islands, and they may possibly be closely related to the Eastern Oceanic subgroup, although the exact nature of the relationship is not clear. Bender[71] lists 13 languages for Micronesia, of which 8 are in the Nuclear subgroup:

Non-Nuclear

Chamorro (Marianas) ⎫
Palauan ⎬ Western Austronesian

Yapese

Nukuoro ⎫
Kapingamarangi ⎬ Polynesian

Nuclear

Nauruan[72]

Ulithian ⎫
Carolinean ⎬ Trukic Continuum
Trukese ⎭
Ponapean

Kusaiean
Marshallese
Gilbertese

Although Bender excludes Yapese from the Nuclear subgroup, its external affinities remain unknown[73]. Within Nuclear Micronesian, the Trukic Continuum covers a remarkable 2500 km span from Tobi Island south of the Palaus, right through the Caroline chain to as far as Truk. No two dialects along this chain share much below 70 percent basic vocabulary, and Bender divides the dialects into a Ulithian group in the west, a Carolinean group in the centre, and an eastern group (the most diverse) centred on Truk. East of the Trukic Continuum are five dialect groups of higher diversity, namely Ponapean, Kusaiean, Marshallese, Gilbertese, and Nauruan (an isolated language). Gilbertese has evidently borrowed considerably from Polynesian languages, perhaps through the Ellice Islands. Lexicostatistical considerations would suggest that the Proto-Nuclear Micronesian language was spoken somewhere in the area east of the Carolines, and glottochronology could suggest a date of 1000 B.C. or earlier. But the almost complete lack of archaeological research in the area does not allow the type of chronological checking that is available for Polynesia.

A PROBLEM OF CORRELATION

Having reviewed the linguistic prehistory of the whole Pacific area, we may turn briefly to a problem of correlation within Oceania which will be of frequent concern in later chapters. Linguists subgroup the Austronesian languages of Melanesia, Polynesia and Nuclear Micronesia together as one entity (the Oceanic subgroup) with a single major origin, while physical anthropologists are generally agreed that the people who speak these languages are certainly not of one common origin. In other words, the Polynesians and Micronesians have most certainly not originated in Melanesia, even if their languages did originate there in their proto-forms.

One linguist has attempted to solve the problem, namely S.A. Wurm[74], who suggested that the first Austronesian speakers in Melanesia were relatively light-skinned, as the Polynesians and Micronesians of today, while the darker Melanesians spread eastward to Fiji later, perhaps after adopting voyaging techniques from the initial Polynesian-like settlers in western Melanesia. Recent archaeological research suggests very strongly that Wurm could be wrong, and that Melanesians had already settled to as far east as the New Hebrides when ancestral Polynesian and Nuclear Micronesian peoples entered the area. We will return to this again in more detail in chapter 9, but there is one linguistic matter of some importance which remains.

By classifying Polynesian and Nuclear Micronesian languages as Oceanic, linguists necessarily make the assumption that they are to be derived entirely from within Oceania. But some linguists have noted that these languages do have relationships with languages in Island Southeast Asia, separate from those which they have with the Melanesian languages[75]. It may be that the Polynesian and Nuclear Micronesian languages were strongly influenced from Western Austronesian as well as Oceanic sources in the early stages of their history within Melanesia, although the Oceanic characteristics may seem most evident today. The importance of this observation is clear, for it does enable us to reconcile so much more easily the evidence from linguistics and physical anthropology; both the languages and the physical types of Polynesia and Nuclear Micronesia do have definite if linguistically remote Island Southeast Asian ancestries.

DYEN'S LEXICOSTATISTICAL CLASSIFICATION OF THE AUSTRONESIAN LANGUAGES

The monumental lexicostatistical classification of the Austronesian languages by Isidore Dyen was published in 1965[76], and discussion of it has been left until this point because many of the conclusions are at variance with the findings of other linguists. The work is based on paired comparisons of 245 languages by means of a 196-word basic vocabulary list, and the seven million individual word comparisons were processed by computer. Dyen's main conclusions suggest that Proto-Austronesian was located in the area including New Guinea, the Bismarck and Solomon Islands (i.e. western Melanesia), they do not support the splitting of Austronesian into the Western and Eastern Austronesian divisions, and they militate strongly against a location for Proto-Austronesian anywhere on the Southeast Asian mainland, or anywhere in Island Southeast Asia except perhaps Taiwan or Maluku.

According to Dyen's classification (figure 5.7), Austronesian has 40 branches, of which 34 are restricted to Melanesia – the outstanding centre of diversity. Another four branches consist of

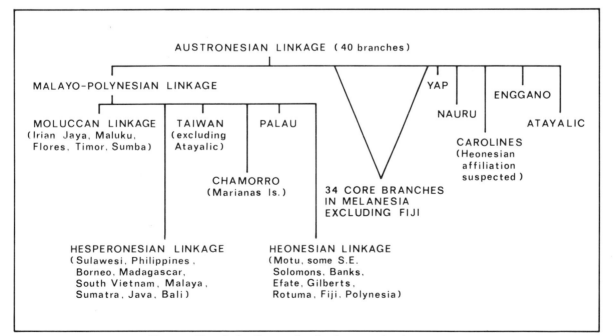

Fig. 5.7. Dyen's family tree for the Austronesian languages.

the isolated Yapese, Nauruan, Engganese and Atayalic languages, but while Carolinean is shown as another separate branch there do seem to be good grounds for placing it in the Heonesian linkage (below). The final branch of Austronesian is what Dyen terms the 'Malayo-Polynesian linkage', which consists of one hundred and twenty-nine languages surrounding Melanesia in a giant arc from Island Southeast Asia, through Micronesia, to Polynesia. Malayo-Polynesian comprises six major linkages, namely Heonesian (virtually the same as Eastern Oceanic, but with minor differences), Palauan, Chamorro (Marianas Islands), Taiwanese excluding Atayalic, Moluccan, and Hesperonesian (Sulawesi, Philippines, western Indonesia, Madagascar).

Dyen takes note of the diversity shown by Atayalic and the languages of eastern Indonesia and Irian Jaya, but in accord with his hypothesis that the area of greatest lexicostatistical diversity is the area of origin of a language family, his conclusions can only point at face value to a Melanesian homeland. As I have discussed in some detail above, the Melanesian languages have probably been subjected to unusually rapid change, and there are very strong archaeological and physical reasons for excluding Melanesia as a possible Austronesian homeland.

Despite this, Dyen's historical conclusions are of some interest, and are given as follows:

1. The Austronesian languages have their origin in western Melanesia, in an area centred on the Bismarck Archipelago.
2. Initial Austronesian expansion was to northern and eastern New Guinea, New Caledonia and the Loyalty Islands, and the New Hebrides.
3. A proto-language for the vast Malayo-Polynesian linkage was probably spoken in the New Hebrides or New Britain. The New Hebrides are the most likely origin for the Heonesian linkage.
4. The Malayo-Polynesians probably made two separate migrations from Melanesia into Indonesia; (a) through eastern Indonesia to as far as Flores, (b) through Palau and/or Guam to northern Sulawesi, Borneo and

southern Mindanao. Taiwan was probably settled via the Philippines, and the western Indonesian and Chamic regions probably through Borneo.

Dyen's conclusions are of interest, even if they do now appear to be erroneous. In 1964, George Murdock[77] attempted to expand them into an extremely unlikely hypothesis for Austronesian culture history, which ran as follows:

1. Before the Austronesians arrived in Indonesia from Melanesia, the area was peopled by non-agricultural Negritos and Veddoids speaking languages related to the Mon-Khmer family.
2. The first Austronesians to move westwards from Melanesia were sea-borne traders who did not practise agriculture.
3. After Austronesian dispersal into Indonesia, agriculture was introduced by immigrating Asian Mongoloids, who adopted the Malayo-Polynesian languages and substantially altered the Island Southeast Asian phenotype.

The sheer impracticability of Murdock's argument is clearly evident, and this alone is probably sufficient to place it in grave doubt.

THE PROBLEM OF AUSTRONESIAN DOMINANCE IN INDONESIA

One niggling problem remains. We have seen how Austronesians have attained little but a meagre toehold around the coasts of New Guinea, and their main successes in Melanesian colonisation have been on islands where there probably were no previous inhabitants. Yet when we look at Indonesia, we see that Austronesian languages with a time depth of perhaps three to five thousand years in different areas are absolutely universal, except in the far eastern islands which adjoin Melanesia. Even the Negrito peoples in the Philippines speak Austronesian languages, and it is true to say that the Austronesian takeover of Island Southeast Asia has been complete. I will not anticipate possible answers to this problem at this point, but the matter will be raised later.

Footnotes

1. A good definition of a language is given by Wurm and Laycock (1961: 128) as 'a system of vocal sounds with conventionalised references accepted by a community or group and understood within it, and having the social function of carrying information from speaker to hearer.'

2. For discussions of dialect chains see Swadesh 1964a: 581; Wurm and Laycock 1961; McElhanon 1971. Good illustrative examples from Papua are given by Dutton (1969).

3. The term 'communalect' is often used for a homogeneous dialect spoken in one or a few villages or communities.

4. As illustrated by Dutton 1969; McElhanon 1971.

5. These two terms 'family' and 'subgroup' are widely used by linguists, and have no strict statistical definition. Subgroups are ranked hierarchically as in a family tree, and the term 'family' is used for major groupings such as Austronesian or Indo-European. On the concept of the subgroup, Grace (1959:11) states, 'In a strict sense any group of languages which have passed through a period of common development exclusive of the other languages of the same family, and during which period some linguistic change has occurred, constitute a subgroup.' However, for statistically defined terminologies in use by Oceanic linguists see Wurm 1964 (for New Guinea); Dyen 1965a (for the whole Austronesian family).

6. On the basic concept of lexicostatistics see Gudschinsky 1964; Swadesh 1964b.

7. For general drawbacks to lexicostatistics and glottochronology, see Teeter 1963. For specific problems concerned with uses of these techniques in the Pacific, see McElhanon 1971; Grace 1967.

8. Dyen 1956.

9. Wurm and Laycock 1961. Wurm (personal communication 1975) now estimates the total as 760.

10. Grace 1968: 63–4.

11. McElhanon and Voorhoeve 1970; Wurm 1972a; 1972b. Wurm (1971) gives a detailed list of these languages, but calls them the Central New Guinea Macro-Phylum. For the latest picture (1975) as shown in figure 5.2, I must acknowledge Professor Wurm's assistance.

12. Laycock 1973.

13. Wurm 1972a; 1972b; and personal communication 1975.

14. Greenberg 1971.

15. Wurm 1972a; Tryon 1971.

16. Robert Blust: personal communication; Blust 1974.

17. Shutler and Marck 1975.

18. e.g. Milke 1961; Grace 1968; 1971; Pawley 1974.

19. See Swadesh 1964a:582.

20. A date much in excess of this may be indicated by recent lexicostatistical analyses. See Kruskal, Dyen and Black 1971.

21. Dyen 1962; 1965a. Dahl (1973:123) feels that the homeland cannot be located from linguistic data alone.

22. Grace 1964:366; Wurm 1967:30–1.

23. Pawley and Green 1975:36. See also Chowning in Barrau ed. 1963. Blust (1976) adds millet, and suggests the use of iron, although the latter is much more problematical.

24. Benedict 1942.

25. Benedict 1966; 1967.

26. Dyen 1965b; 1971b; Ferrell 1969.

27. e.g. Haudricourt 1965; Benedict 1966; Dyen 1965a.

28. Dyen 1971a; 1971b. Dahl (1973: 125) considers the Formosan subgroup to represent the first offshoot from the main Austronesian family, and Shutler and Marck (1975) have recently attempted to locate the Proto-Austronesian homeland in Taiwan (see also chapter 8).

29. Pawley 1974.

30. Thomas and Healey 1962.

31. Grace 1964: 367.

32. Dahl 1951. See also Dyen's review (1953).

33. e.g. Milke 1965; Grace 1968:72.

34. Blust 1974.

35. Bulmer 1971: 42. Institutions involving word taboos might also have speeded linguistic change in Melanesia.

36. Pawley and Green 1975.

37. Milke 1961. Shutler and Marck (1975) have suggested that Proto-Oceanic was most closely related to languages of the Minahasa region (north Sulawesi), although this view is not in accord with the existence of an Eastern Austronesian subgroup as defined by Blust (1974).

38. Capell 1943. See also Capell 1964; Kahler 1962.

39. Milke 1961. Also Pawley 1972: 3; Grace 1968 for contrary views.

40. Chretien 1956.

41. Capell 1962; Cowan 1965; Capell 1969.

42. Capell 1969; 1971.

43. From Pawley 1974. See also Grace 1955; 1971; Dyen 1965a.

44. Pawley and Green 1975.

45. Grace 1959; Biggs 1965; Dyen 1965a (Heonesian linkage); Pawley 1972.

46. Grace 1959; Biggs 1965. Rotuman has borrowed heavily from western Polynesian languages.

47. Goodenough (1961) has attempted to relate Nakanai of New Britain to the New Hebridean and Fijian languages, but Capell (1971:266, 317–8) rejects the theory.

48. Grace 1964: 367.

49. Pawley 1972:135.

50. Pawley 1970:313; Pawley and Sayaba 1971. Schütz (1972: chapter 9) warns that the view of two dialect chains for Fiji may be rather simplified.

51. Elbert 1953; Emory 1963a; Dyen 1965a; Pawley 1966; Green 1966. General surveys of Polynesian linguistics are given by Biggs 1967; 1971; and Krupa 1973.

52. Pawley and Green 1971. King and Epling (1972) have challenged Tongan primacy on the basis of a computer analysis, but seem unable to present any definite conclusions. See also Groube 1973.

53. Pawley 1970:313; Pawley and Green 1971:24.

54. Walsh and Biggs 1966; Pawley and Green 1971.

55. Pawley 1970:311.

56. Biggs 1972.

57. Pawley and Green 1971:22–3.

58. Green 1966.

59. Pawley (1970:311) has pointed out there is little lexicostatistical evidence for the Marquesic subgroup.

60. Green 1966:24.

61. Pawley 1970:354.

62. Polynesian Outlier languages are spoken on the following islands: Nukuoro and Kapingamarangi (southern Carolines) – both atolls. Nukuria, Takuu, Nukumanu, Luangiua (Ontong Java) and Sikaiana (Solomon Islands) – all atolls. Pileni (a raised coral island) and Taumako (a partially artificial island) in the Santa Cruz group. Tikopia (volcanic) and Anuta (raised coral) to the east of the Santa Cruz group. Mae, Aniwa and Futuna, together with two small islands called Mele and Fila off southern Efate (New Hebrides) – all volcanic. Uvea (Loyalty Islands) – raised coral. Bellona and Rennell (Solomon Islands) – both raised coral. The above list will show that the northern seven islands are atolls, the southern eleven are raised coral or volcanic, while Taumako is partially artificial. For a general survey of Outlier culture history, see Davidson 1970c.

63. Hollyman 1959.

64. e.g. Churchill 1911; Capell 1962.

65. Pawley 1967.

66. Pawley 1970:306.

67. Green 1971c.

68. Bayard 1966.

69. Elbert 1967.

70. Grace 1955; 1964. Grace's view has recently been supported by Shutler and Marck (1975).

71. Bender 1971.

72. Bender grouped Nauruan as non-Nuclear in his 1971 paper, but since appears to have changed his mind (see Pawley 1972:133).

73. Dyen (1965a) places Yapese as a separate branch within the whole Austronesian family, thus placing it on a par with other extremely divergent languages such as Atayalic and Engganese.

74. Wurm 1967.

75. e.g. Kahler 1964; Dyen 1965a.

76. Dyen 1965a; 1962 (preliminary report). Reviewed by Grace 1966.

77. Murdock 1964.

CHAPTER 6

Subsistence Patterns and their Prehistoric Implications

The early inhabitants of the western Pacific who undertook the settlements of Australia and New Guinea before 30,000 years ago were in all probability hunters and collectors. For these peoples, the dietary significance of available terrestrial or marine resources would naturally depend very much on location, as well as on cultural preference and technology. As far as one can tell, population densities in the humid tropics were probably quite low, with small isolated bands roaming quite large territories of coastline and rainforest. Perhaps the Negritos of Southeast Asia have preserved some aspects of this way of life, while the Australian Aborigines have clearly adapted for the most part to a different and much drier environment.

My main concern in this chapter is not with ancient hunting and collecting patterns of Southeast Asia and Oceania, but rather with the almost completely dominant present-day patterns of plant cultivation and animal husbandry. These evolving patterns have provided greater resources for Pacific man in the past, and have allowed population increases of a major order. On these grounds, I feel that it is no coincidence that the settlement of most of the vast area of Oceania, excluding western Melanesia, began soon after the time (*circa* 3000 B.C.) that the first definite evidence appears for developing plant and animal domestication in Southeast Asia. Accordingly, this chapter will examine the major Indo-Pacific food plants and their origins, the systems of cultivation and their origins, and the domesticated animals[1].

In an area as large as Southeast Asia and Oceania, it is to be expected that the patterns of animal and plant exploitation will be varied, both for historical and for environmental reasons. At the present time, the most important and widespread subsistence activities of pre-European origin are rice or tuber cultivation by swidden or irrigation techniques, tree-crop exploitation, pig husbandry, and hunting, gathering and fishing. In Southeast Asia, wet-rice cultivation is dominant on the more densely settled alluvial and volcanic soils, while dry-rice or millet cultivation dominates the remoter and less fertile areas. In Melanesia, tuber cultivation is dominant, while the Polynesians and Micronesians depend more on both tuber and tree-crop exploitation.

Amongst the domesticated animals, the pig was by far the most important and widespread prior to European contact, with dog and fowl occupying lesser positions. In Southeast Asia, goats, cattle and water buffalo were domesticated in prehistoric times, but none of these herbivores, or cereal crops, were introduced into Oceania. Terrestrial hunting and gathering on a small scale was undoubtedly universal in the pre-urban past, but only in southern New Zealand, the Chatham Islands, parts of inland Sumatra and Borneo, and amongst the Negritos of Malaya, the Philippines and the Andaman Islands does it appear that plant cultivation was entirely absent. Many peoples of coastal New Guinea depend to a large extent upon wild sago palm exploitation, but in most reported cases there is always at least a small amount of subsidiary cultivation. Indeed, there is an observable gradation in economies within the area from non-cultivation right through to intensive cultivation, and, if we perhaps exclude wet-rice, at no point is there any marked break in this gradation.

THE ORIGINS OF CULTIVATION

One of the most intensely researched fields of modern archaeology concerns the origins of plant domestication. In western Asia, it is becoming evident that the wild ancestors of wheat and barley were enjoying an active period of colonisation in certain ecological zones at the end of the last glaciation, and that man had selected strains which diverged morphologically from these wild ancestors by the eighth millennium B.C. Within what is generally taken to be an economic background of conscious domestication, involving field preparation, planting and harvesting, a substantial and fairly reliable food supply was ensured which by 7000 B.C. allowed permanent nucleated settlements to develop, and by 3000 B.C. provided the economic roots of the world's first civilisations in Egypt, Mesopotamia, and the Indus Valley. In the Huangho Valley of north-central China a further centre of civilisation developed on an economic basis of millet cultivation, which most probably originated prior to 6000 B.C., and in southern China and Thailand there is now evidence that rice cultivation and large villages appear sometime during the fourth millennium B.C. (see chapter 7). Across the Pacific, domestication of native cultigens in Mexico appears from the eighth millennium B.C., and soon after this in Peru, although the American developments seem to be unconnected with those of the Old World.

Plant cultivation and permanent settlements are primarily post-Pleistocene phenomena. Why this should be so is a matter of obscurity, although in western Asia climatic trends at the end of the Pleistocene may have favoured cereal expansion to man's advantage. For the other areas there is as yet no explanation of world-wide validity, and final answers may lie in a combination of changing ecological and demographic factors. Certainly, it seems unlikely that the idea of cultivation was ever 'invented', and the principles of plant propagation were undoubtedly known to hunters and collectors for many millennia before evidence for cultivation appears in the archaeological record.

As far as Southeast Asia is concerned, there is quite good evidence that tuber, fruit and cereal cultivation methods were in existence prior to 3000 B.C., and these could of course extend back in incipient form towards the end of the last glaciation. There is no particular reason to invoke major diffusion from without, for the crops and techniques of cultivation (i.e. vegetative rather than seed reproduction) are in large part indigenous and specific to the area. More than twenty years ago, the American geographer Carl Sauer[2] suggested that Southeast Asia could have been the earliest centre of plant domestication in the world, partially on the grounds of its great vegetational and climatic diversity. The area contains a tremendous number of plants useful to man, and many produce useful fibres and leaves as well as food. Fishing and gathering communities based on rivers and coastlines would therefore be in an ideal theoretical position to engage in the vegetative reproduction of these plants, particularly those with multiple uses. Forest clearings and enriched soils around settlements would also encourage growth of the many useful light-loving plants, and thus bring them to the attention of man. As it happens, Sauer's theory was based on ideas rather than facts, but it has nevertheless remained convincing to a number of scholars up to the present[3]. Whether Southeast Asia did develop the earliest cultivation in the world is a question to which we will return later.

INDIGENOUS MAJOR FOOD PLANTS OF SOUTHEAST ASIA AND OCEANIA[4]

As with the majority of cultigens of importance, those of Southeast Asia and the Pacific are now in many cases far removed morphologically from their wild progenitors, owing to several millennia of selection by man. Fruits and tubers have been selected for increasing size, and some species, particularly breadfruit and bananas, have lost the capacity to produce seed, and can thus only be propagated by vegetative means. These observations indicate that plant cultivation is of considerable antiquity in the area, and this circumstance is well supported by linguistic evidence. Words for taro, yam, breadfruit, banana, coconut, and probably rice are all present in the Proto-Austronesian vocabulary (see page 122), and this makes it highly likely that each of these vitally important plants was present in Island Southeast Asia by some 5000 years ago, possibly in domesticated form. Let us look at these and others in turn, progressing from tree crops to tubers and finally, cereals.

The coconut palm (*Cocos nucifera*) is a pantropical cultigen throughout Southeast Asia and the Pacific, and it has an astounding range of uses. Prior to European contact it appears to have had a restricted distribution on the Pacific coast of central America, from Panama to the Gulf of Guayaquil, and Heyerdahl[5] has assembled a degree of botanical support for an American origin of the domesticated species. The question is an open one, because the coconut has no known ancestors. On the other hand, fossil members of the genus *Cocos* are known from New Zealand, fragments of charred coconut shell from Aitape in northern New Guinea are reliably carbon-dated to within the third millennium B.C.[6], and the Indo-Oceanic area supports a majority of insects specific on *Cocos*, together with the coconut crab[7]. Interestingly enough, the evidence from insects might well suggest a Melanesian origin,

and an origin within the Indo-Pacific area generally seems more likely than an origin in the Americas[8]. The ability of the coconut to remain viable at sea for long periods might also have assisted its dispersal, although there is in fact no need to invoke this mechanism to explain its prehistoric distribution.

The breadfruit tree (*Artocarpus altilis*), ultimate source of the mutiny on H.M.S. *Bounty*, occurs across the Pacific but not in the Americas. Wild relatives of the tree are found in Indonesia, the Philippines, New Guinea and the Marianas Islands[9] (see figure 6.1), and it attains great importance as a cultigen in parts of Micronesia and Polynesia. As well as producing a large edible

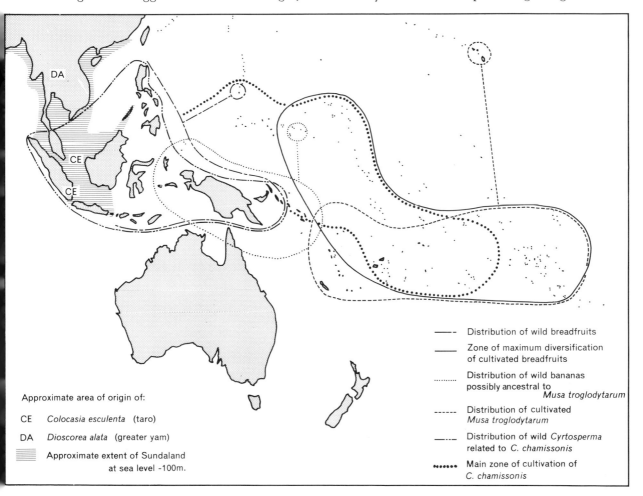

Approximate area of origin of:

CE   *Colocasia esculenta* (taro)

DA   *Dioscorea alata* (greater yam)

≡≡≡   Approximate extent of Sundaland
        at sea level -100m.

——-   Distribution of wild breadfruits

———   Zone of maximum diversification
         of cultivated breadfruits

·········   Distribution of wild bananas
         possibly ancestral to
                              Musa troglodytarum

------   Distribution of cultivated
         Musa troglodytarum

—··—   Distribution of wild *Cyrtosperma*
         related to *C. chamissonis*

••••••   Main zone of cultivation of
         C. chamissonis

Fig. 6.1. The origins and distributions of some major Pacific food plants. After Barrau 1965; Spencer 1966, fig. 4.

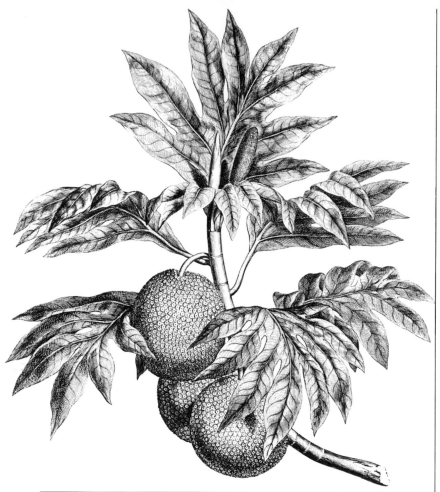

Fig. 6.2. The breadfruit.

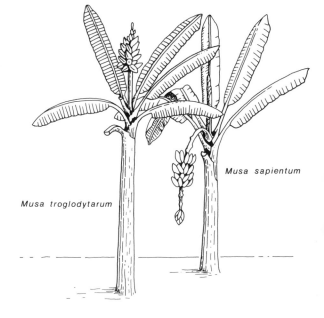

Fig. 6.3. The Pacific bananas, from a drawing by Jacques Barrau.

Musa troglodytarum

Musa sapientum

fruit (figure 6.2), the breadfruit also has a fibrous inner bark which can be used for making bark-cloth.

The indigenous cultivated bananas of the Pacific area belong to two major species (figure 6.3): *Musa troglodytarum*, with a vertical fruit stalk, and the more familiar looking *Musa sapientum*. The distribution of the former is shown in figure 6.1, while the latter appears to be a hybrid cultigen of Indian or Southeast Asian origin. There is some evidence for cultivation of bananas in pre-Columbian South America, and prehistoric transportation from Polynesia is a possibility[10].

A tree of great importance in the swampy areas of coastal New Guinea and eastern Indonesia is the sago palm (*Metroxylon* sp.), which may once have been utilised to as far east as Fiji. It is not a true cultigen and is generally exploited from wild stands, although some planting may be carried out. Between approximately the eighth and fifteenth years of life the tree flowers and dies, exhausting in the process a reserve of starch contained within its trunk. Therefore, the palms are felled before they flower, and the starch is washed out from the grated pith which is chopped out from the trunk. In some cases sterile palms may produce up to 400 kilograms of starch, but the normal yield is between 100 and 160 kilograms[11]. The starch may be made into porridge or cakes, and was at one time traded for long distances by sea along the Papuan coast of New Guinea (see page 102). The sago palm is native to New Guinea and Indonesia, as possibly is the sugar cane (*Saccharum officinarum*)[12], although this plant does not appear to have had a great economic importance in prehistoric times.

Two other cultivated trees merit mention, the first being the paper mulberry tree (*Broussonetia papyrifera*), the inner bark of which was at one time beaten into a felt used for clothing throughout the Pacific. Secondly, the betel-nut palm, *Areca catechu*, provides a nut which is chewed as a stimulant together with a pepper (*Piper betle*) and crushed lime. This is grown from India, through Southeast Asia, to as far east as western Micronesia and the Santa Cruz Islands. East of the betel zone a different stimulant was prepared from the root of the shrub *Piper methysticum*, which was chewed and mixed with water to provide the Fijian *yaqona* and Polynesian *kava*. In Fiji, Tonga and Samoa, *kava* drinking was elevated into a ritual which accompanied many important events involving high ranking personages[13]. The *kava* and betel zones are approximately exclusive, although *kava* is used in parts of coastal Irian Jaya. The paper mulberry tree, the betel complex and *kava* are each almost certainly of Indo-Pacific origin, and there is evidence for the use of betelnuts in the lower layers of Spirit Cave in Thailand, between 10,000 and 6000 B.C. (see page 71).

The list of other useful Indo-Pacific plants in the tree or shrub class is rather lengthy, and only a few can be mentioned. The ubiquitous *Hibiscus tiliaceus*, a pan-tropical plant whose distribution may bear little relationship to the activities of man[14], produces edible shoots and a most useful fibre. Other semi-cultigens, which were tended rather than planted and quite possibly transported by man in some cases, include *Inocarpus edulis* (Tahitian chestnut, utilised from the Philippines to eastern Polynesia); several species of *Pandanus*, a very widespread plant with useful leaves and edible fruits which can be stored after cooking – a factor of considerable importance on some of the less fertile atolls[15]; and the fruits of the giant *Barringtonia asiatica*, which provide a fish poison throughout the Pacific.

Before passing to the tubers, one rather enigmatic plant requires consideration, namely the gourd (*Siceraria lagenaria*). This was the only true cultigen to be widespread in Asia, the Pacific and the Americas in prehistoric times, probably prior to 7000 B.C. It is also the only important Oceanic cultigen which requires seed propagation, and is a monotypic species evidently of African origin, which may have spread naturally by sea[16]. In Oceania it was used mainly for containers, but young gourds could also be eaten.

With the exception of the coconut and breadfruit in localised areas, none of the tree crops listed could rank in importance with the two groups of edible tubers – the yams and the taro-like plants (aroids). The yams and the aroids are both Indo-Pacific cultigens of high antiquity, although both groups have largely given way to rice and recently introduced crops in Island Southeast Asia.

The yams (*Dioscorea* sp.), of which there are five main species in Southeast Asia and Oceania, were probably first brought into cultivation in the areas of seasonal monsoon rainfall in northern Southeast Asia, and secondarily perhaps in the Philippines and Sulawesi[17]. Today, yams have retained their importance mainly in Melanesia, and never seem to have attained much importance in comparison with the aroids in most parts of Micronesia and Polynesia. They do not thrive in areas of high all year round rainfall, and where necessary are grown on ridges of friable drained soil.

The aroids belong to the family Araceae, and the most important species, *Colocasia esculenta* (taro), is grown throughout the Pacific and may have originated as a cultigen in equatorial Indonesia. It thrives in conditions of constant dampness, and requires irrigation in many areas of Oceania where rainfall has a seasonal occurrence, for instance in New Caledonia, Fiji, and the Cook, Hawaiian and Society Islands of Polynesia. Another aroid, *Cyrtosperma chamissonis*, is a major cultigen of the atolls of Micronesia and Polynesia to as far east as the southern Cook Islands, and is normally grown in deep pits excavated through the coral to the water table and filled partially with decomposed organic materials[18]. The labour involved in the construction of such pits was often immense. On the island of Pukapuka in the northern Cooks the taro excavations cover several hectares, and the amount of soil moved may probably be measured in thousands of tons. *Cyrtosperma* has wild relatives in Indonesia and

New Guinea, but is mainly cultivated outside this zone (figure 6.1). As pointed out by Barrau[19], a distinction between area of natural occurrence and area of cultivation applies to a number of Oceanic crops, including breadfruit and the banana *Musa troglodytarum*, and the importance of such a distinction in crop plant evolution is now well known to botanists and archaeologists alike. In these cases the domesticated forms probably arose owing to the removal of plants from the natural habitat into areas where new selective factors gave rise to different varieties, which are now used as cultigens.

Another plant which produces an edible tuber, *Pueraria lobata*, is cultivated in localised areas of eastern Indonesia, the New Guinea highlands, and New Caledonia, and may once have been cultivated to as far east as Samoa[20]. The plant is of interest because of suggestions that it represents a survival from a very ancient stage of Melanesian cultivation – an argument which has been also used for other crops of present marginal importance, such as *Cordyline fruticosa* and the yam *Dioscorea nummularia*. However, these inferences are based mainly on widespread occurrence and apparent obsolescence, and the idea that these crops represent a stage of cultivation prior to the introduction of the major yams and the Araceae should be accepted with reserve – there is no *a priori* reason why this should be the case.

Amongst the other plants with edible tubers, the most controversial is undoubtedly the sweet potato, *Ipomoea batatas*. Botanists now seem to agree that the plant is American, with a possible ancestry in tropical Central and South America[21]. It has been recovered from eighth millenium B.C. archaeological contexts in Peru, and was certainly cultivated by the second millenium B.C.[22]. It is possible that it could only have reached Polynesia with the aid of man, and Merrill[23] suggested that it must have been transported as a living plant in a bed of soil, although the possibility of transporting seeds would seem to merit more attention[24]. The Polynesian word *kumara* (or close cognate) is paralleled by the word *cumar*, which is used for sweet potato in the highlands north-west of Cuzco by speakers of the Chinchasuyo dialect of Quechua[25]. The word is not in use on the coast of Peru, perhaps because of linguistic changes in this area during the past

Fig. 6.4. A yam store-house on Kiriwina, Trobriand Islands. (See also colour plate and Fig. 4.7.)

2000 years, and despite recent claims to the contrary, it would seem to me that the two words could indicate a prehistoric link.

In Polynesia, the sweet potato was probably introduced to an eastern island group, perhaps the Marquesas, before 1500 years ago. From there it was carried by Polynesians to the Hawaiian Islands, Easter Island and New Zealand, and it also attained minor importance in the Society Islands[26]. It was not certainly present anywhere else in Oceania, although it has recently been suggested that it may have reached New Guinea in prehistoric times[27], and this certainly stands as an interesting possibility. However, the various claims for Spanish or Portuguese introduction into Polynesia after A.D. 1500 remain unconvincing.

There is also a small amount of archaeological evidence which bears on the antiquity of the sweet potato in Polynesia. Field boundary walls and underground storage pits are known to date from the thirteenth century A.D. onwards in New Zealand, and there is strong evidence for associating these with sweet potato cultivation. Actual remains of tubers are reported from archaeological sites in New Zealand, Easter Island, and the Hawaiian Islands, but unfortunately the radiocarbon dates applicable to these situations do not make a date prior to A.D. 1500 for the plant a certainty[28]. Because sweet potato so rarely flowers in Polynesia, future assistance from pollen analysis is not very likely. However, my own view, as noted above, is that the plant is a prehistoric introduction from America into central Polynesia, possibly about 1500 years ago when the Polynesian peripheries were about to be settled[29]. Its later importance in New Zealand and Easter Island almost certainly arose because it was one of the few Polynesian crops which would thrive outside the tropics.

As for other possible American introductions into Polynesia, a lot of literature has given very few conclusive results which do not require detailed consideration here (but see page 362). Heyerdahl[30] has culled evidence from the botanical literature for several American plants on Easter Island, and there is also the problem of a wild cotton of American origin in Hawaii[31]. Nevertheless, the prehistoric cultivation systems of the Pacific were based on vegetative propagation of a range of Southeast Asian and Melanesian fruits and tubers, and they have been under development within the area for at least 5000

years. Seen in perspective, the sweet potato and cotton are rather insignificant intruders from the east, whether brought by man or spread naturally.

Of cereals grown in Southeast Asia, only two appear to have achieved prehistoric significance, namely millet and rice. The foxtail millet (*Setaria italica*) was certainly domesticated by Yang-shao times in fifth millennium B.C. central China, and was cultivated in prehistoric times in Southeast Asia, possibly to as far east as New Guinea. It retains economic importance today amongst some of the Austronesian peoples of Taiwan, and a probable seed of *Setaria* has been recovered archaeologically in eastern Timor in a context which may be as early as 1000 B.C.[32]. However, whatever its prehistoric importance, it has now given way largely to rice cultivation in Southeast Asia, and there is in fact little which may be said about prehistoric millet cultivation from present knowledge.

The cultivation of rice (*Oryza sativa*) was restricted to Southeast Asia in prehistoric times. The plant was absent in Oceania, except for the Marianas Islands of western Micronesia[33], and even in eastern Indonesia and the Philippines it may have attained much of its importance since European contact. Rice was perhaps first domesticated in the monsoonal areas stretching from north-eastern India through northern Indochina into southern China[34], and the earliest archaeological evidence for the plant comes from sites in Kiangsu and Chekiang Provinces in China (c. 3300–4000 B.C., see page 158), and from the sites of Non Nok Tha and Ban Chiang in north-eastern Thailand, where rice husks were used for tempering pottery from about 3500 B.C. (see page 162). Because rice is absent in Oceania it is generally accepted that it was domesticated in Southeast Asia later than the fruits and tubers, but there is no strong archaeological evidence to support this view. In addition, the plant is particularly sensitive to temperature, length of daylight, cloud cover and light intensity, and seems to prefer a monsoonal to an equatorial climate. Spencer[35] has suggested that rice did not enter Oceania because of its slow rate of adaptation and its vulnerability, and that it was not able to compete with the dominant crops of the area. Therefore, environmental factors rather than a late date for domestication may perhaps more legitimately explain its distribution. The question of whether the first rice was cultivated in wet or dry fields is discussed on pages 148–149.

CULTIVATION SYSTEMS AND THEIR DEVELOPMENT

The prehistoric cultivation systems of Southeast Asia and Oceania ranged from the most simple forms of swidden (or shifting) cultivation to intensive monocropping of irrigated fields. Between these extremes there is an even continuum, and many societies practice both swidden and irrigation in combination at the present time. In this section I propose to describe various economies along this continuum, beginning with incipient cultivation practices amongst hunter-gatherers, and proceeding through swidden gardeners to irrigation farmers. The culmination will be a brief discussion of wet (as opposed to swidden) rice agriculture, which on present evidence may well be of relatively recent development in Southeast Asia and certainly not connected with the early expansion of the Austronesians into the Pacific. To ease presentation this section is in the present tense, although I am aware that some of the systems described are undergoing rapid transformation, and some are of course extinct.

To begin at the simplest end of the scale, the Senoi Semai of interior Malaya still tend patches of giant wild yams, the tubers of which may grow to a length of two metres. The tubers, fruits and seeds are harvested, and some seeds dropped or excreted around settlements, after which they germinate and grow[36]. The Semai periodically move their settlement sites, but often find a supply of yams when they return to a previously settled locality. Although these people are now cultivators of rice and millet, it is possible that their use of yams reflects an aspect of their hunting and gathering past. The Andamanese hunter-gatherers also harvest wild yams, and even provide them with ritual protection during the growing season; the theoretical implication of this was pointed out over twenty years ago by the botanist I.H. Burkill[37]. In addition, wild yams are widely exploited in northern Australia, and artefacts identified as seed grinders are possibly up to 10,000 years old in the Western Desert of Australia[38]. In theory, such instances could indicate a context for early cultivation, although the mere fact that it never did begin with these peoples certainly weakens any analogy.

The most widespread form of crop production in Southeast Asia and Oceania is swidden or shifting cultivation[39], which has long been regarded as the original and once-universal system prior to the development of wet-rice cultivation.

This view may well be correct on distributional grounds, and it acknowledges the fact that swidden in its simplest form can operate quite closely within the natural forest cycle[40]. The natural climax forest of the tropics forms a self-perpetuating and closed system, in the sense that nutrients are not lost in large quantities because the forest itself serves to reduce leaching and erosion. The plants extract nutrients from the soil, flourish, die, and thus return what they have extracted. While this cycle is not of course totally watertight, deep-rooted trees can tap food resources at deep levels, and thus assist in the maintenance of an overall equilibrium.

When man enters this system as a cultivator, his first requirement is to clear a space and burn the vegetation, since most cultigens demand light and would not survive forest floor competition. The burning process releases nitrogen and sulphur in the form of smoke, while other nutrients, particularly calcium, fall to the surface as ash, within which the crops can be planted. In the simplest systems, crops are merely pushed into the ash and topsoil and allowed to grow, and the ground need not even be dug over.

These processes of course break the natural cycle, as nutrients go up in smoke, away with rainwash, or eventually into human stomachs. Without use of fertilisers yields decline after a few years, and the plot has to be abandoned so that secondary growth can establish itself and re-establish the nutrient cycle; a process which can take many years. In time the climax forest may become re-established, but if the plot is recleared too frequently then grasses may colonise the area at the expense of forest, and the land may become useless. Freeman's analysis[41] of shifting cultivation amongst the Iban of East Malaysia shows the danger of overexploitation very clearly. In Iban country the land is best used for a single rice crop and then left to a fallow period of about fifteen years. The Iban themselves, an expansive and warlike people, have in many cases cropped land too heavily, with resulting poor grasslands and food shortages. In the Eastern Highlands of Papua New Guinea there are large areas of grassland which may represent a similar degradation owing to long occupation and perhaps burning during warfare[42].

However, the system of shifting cultivation, with small population and adequate fallow periods, need not destroy the natural forest cycle on a long term basis. As seen by Clifford Geertz[43]:

Fig. 6.5. A fenced swidden plot in New Ireland.

In ecological terms, the most distinctive positive characteristic of swidden agriculture (and the characteristic most in contrast to wet-rice agriculture) is that it is integrated into and, when genuinely adaptive, maintains the general structure of the pre-existing natural ecosystem into which it is projected, rather than creating and sustaining one organised along novel lines and displaying novel dynamics.

Geertz also makes the point that shifting cultivation, by depending on the ash from burnt vegetation for nutrients, is not heavily dependent on soil fertility. However, topography does appear to be of some importance, for mature soils on flat land in the tropics are physically stable, and their mineral contents tend to be leached to form clay. Immature soils on slopes are more suitable for swidden because the constant but slow downslope erosion does result in constant replacement of minerals in the topsoil[44]. Hence the fallow cycle on sloping lands may be shorter than on flat lands, and in addition the latter often suffer from drainage problems in riverine situations. Many of the great river valleys of Southeast Asia were probably only thinly settled until flood-control

systems were established for wet-rice cultivation[45].

Some of the characteristics of shifting cultivation can be illustrated from a number of examples. Amongst the Hanunoo of Mindoro Island in the central Philippines[46], shifting cultivation supports between 25 and 35 persons per square kilometre in settled areas. At the end of the winter dry season, which is well marked in this area, gardens are selected, averaging about two-fifths of a hectare in size, sufficient for about three people. The big trees, in the case of virgin forest, are pollarded, fences built, and the brush burnt. In May a crop of maize (a recent introduction) is planted, to be followed by the main rice crop in June, which is in turn harvested in October or November with a yield of thirty or forty times the amount of seed planted. In September or October subsidiary swiddens in second-growth bush are cleared for crops of maize and sweet potato, which ripen during the dry season. Many other lesser crops, up to forty varieties, are planted in and around the main crops, including legumes which help to return nitrogen to the soil. The cropping cycle continues

Fig. 6.6. Gridiron ditching for sweet potato cultivation in the Chimbu District, New Guinea Highlands.

for five or six years to finish often with bananas, and then the swidden goes into fallow, in which bamboo is encouraged, for a period generally over ten years.

The Hanunoo Case is given as an example of the type of swidden agriculture involving little or no modification of the surface of the land, which is still common throughout large areas of upland Southeast Asia, Indonesia and the Philippines. Similar systems (but without rice) are present through many areas of Melanesia, for instance amongst the Siuai of Bougainville[47]. Taro forms about 80% of Siuai diet, and is planted in swiddens cut from second-growth bush of up to half a hectare in size. These swiddens are cleared in linear succession up ridges, or in cyclical succession in lowlands, and taro is harvested continuously until the plot is exhausted. Breadfruit trees are also planted, which of course outlive the swiddens, and pigs are kept away by fences. Fallow periods last for about six years, after which the plot is recleared in another cycle.

Such basic swidden systems as the ones described were widespread but certainly not universal in Southeast Asia and Oceania. In New Guinea, New Caledonia, Fiji, Polynesia and Micronesia, some highly intensive land-use systems have been established which have achieved long-term field use with short fallows, and consequent high populations. In the New Guinea Highlands there

is a very interesting continuum from simple swidden systems, such as those of the Bismarck ranges described recently by Clarke[48], through increasing levels of intensity and efficiency, achieved by means of such techniques as drainage, tillage (especially in grasslands), mounding, and terracing[49]. With the most complex systems, the intervals of cropping and fallow may be almost equal, and such systems in the New Guinea Highlands are interestingly confined to two distinct areas of high population density – the Lake Paniai and Baliem Valley areas of Irian Jaya, and the Chimbu and Wahgi Valley areas of Papua New Guinea. In these areas sweet potatoes are grown on beds which are divided by drainage ditches of gridiron pattern in the Lake Paniai, Chimbu and Wahgi areas (figure 6.6), and of parallel pattern in the Baliem Valley. The soil from the ditches is thrown on top of the beds together with cleared grasses, and nutrients can be added at intervals by cleaning out the ditches and adding to the beds. This kind of system provides well-drained plots for sweet potato, while taro can be grown in the wet ditches. Plots in the Chimbu District, which average about three or four metres square, can be used for several years with secondary fallows before full fallow abandonment is necessary, and for the latter, casuarina trees are commonly planted to provide humus and fix nitrogen[50].

The Enga of the Western Highlands of Papua New Guinea have adopted another form of intensification for sweet potato cultivation, and this involves tilling the soil and piling it into circular mounds about 4 metres in diameter and 60 centimetres high. Waddell's[51] recent work on the Raiapu Enga of the Lai Valley indicates that these mounds can attain densities of 840 per hectare, and they are in continuous cultivation, being opened and filled with vegetable matter after every harvest. Accordingly, this is perhaps the most intensive system reported from New Guinea, and supports population densities of up to 100 per square kilometre. It appears that the mounds also protect the plants from night frosts, by allowing the cold air to drain downwards.

From the work of Golson and his colleagues in the Mt. Hagen region (described on pages 238–240), we now know that some form of intensive cultivation with drainage goes back to at least 4000 B.C. in the New Guinea Highlands. So these intensive systems have not simply developed with sweet potato cultivation, and may well have begun with a crop such as taro. Why they developed in localised Highland areas is an intriguing question, and most authorities directly concerned with providing an answer seem to favour a hypothesis presented with considerable clarity by the economist Ester Boserup in 1965[52].

Boserup's hypothesis is that societies will only intensify their cultivation methods if they are forced to do so by increasing population pressure on land. When people intensify cultivation, for instance from long to short fallow, or from short fallow to irrigation, they are obliged initially to increase labour input to such an extent that the actual output of food per man hour invested drops. For obvious reasons, a change of this nature will be unpopular unless really necessary, and this may indicate why simple shifting cultivation, with high output per man hour invested, appears to be so stable and long-lived in the tropics. Technological developments, such as the plough, can eventually cause a reversal in this adverse trend, but in the cases of the societies of main concern in this book such major developments would not in general have been available. Hence, according to Boserup, population density is the key independent variable, and its increase may necessitate eventual intensification of cultivation if a population is to maintain its food supply without geographical expansion or migration. If a population can expand, as have many populations in Borneo, then intensification may

not, of course, be necessary.

From the viewpoint of the New Guinea Highlands, this hypothesis seems acceptable, and quite clearly the intensive cultivators do have dense populations. Boserup argues strongly against the opposed view, which is that intensive cultivation develops due to different environmental conditions regardless of population density, although individual cases can quite naturally be expected to differ in precise causality. And while she does not attempt to give a general explanation as to why population density should increase in the first place, one can of course point to specific factors such as immigration, warfare, increasing environmental limitation, or even lack of adequate birth control. Just which factors operated in particular cases of prehistoric intensification we may never know.

Apart from the Highland areas of intensive cultivation, there are also local pockets of intensification in coastal New Guinea. For instance, the Kimam of Kolepom Island in south-western Irian Jaya cultivate a swampy and difficult environment by building up artificial gardens above water level with alternate levels of reeds, clay and grass. The beds for yams and sweet potatoes are raised higher above water level than those for taro, and the beds themselves are revitalised by frequent applications of rotting vegetation as manure. Coconuts, sago and bananas are usually planted on the separate mounds which support the dwelling houses, and the system as a whole is capable of supporting villages of up to 700 persons, although it is very vulnerable to high tide inundation every seven years or so[53]. The Marind-Anim of southern Irian Jaya also construct raised beds with surrounding drainage ditches in coastal swamps, and plant yam and taro for one season, after which banana, areca and sago palms are planted. The Marind-Anim, however, are not full-time gardeners, and move to inland camps in savannah areas during the dry season to hunt wallabies, deer, cassowaries and other game[54]. The Abelam of the Sepik District adopt a different method for yam cultivation, by digging holes up to three metres deep for each tuber, and filling them with topsoil. The diversity of economic techniques in New Guinea is in fact outstanding, and needs little further emphasis.

In the Oceanic islands beyond New Guinea, agricultural intensification usually takes the form of wet-field cultivation of taro, which is found in the Palau and Marianas Islands, localised areas

Fig. 6.7. Swamp cultivation of taro on Mangaia, Cook Islands. (See also colour plate.)

Fig. 6.8. 'Staircase' terracing for taro cultivation on Rarotonga, Cook Islands. (See also colour plate.)

of eastern Melanesia, and on many of the Polynesian high islands[55]. The related technique of pit cultivation, already referred to above, is found on many atolls, particularly in Micronesia. In general, the importance of shifting cultivation fades from west to east, and the islands themselves decrease in size in an irregular fashion in the same direction. For reasons which may in some way be related to this factor, the islands of eastern Polynesia supported dense prehistoric populations who depended to a great extent on intensive taro cultivation and utilisation of tree crops, particularly coconuts, breadfruit, bananas and pandanus. Shifting cultivation did remain important in some of the volcanic islands of Micronesia and Polynesia, but was totally unsuited to atoll conditions.

The most remarkable evidence for prehistoric wet-field taro cultivation in Melanesia comes from New Caledonia, where contour terraces were constructed along the sides of steep slopes, staircase terraces alongside stream beds, and raised beds built up in swamps in which the plants were grown in holes sunk to the water table[56]. Yam cultivation was carried out on drained crescentic mounds up to 1.5 metres high, sometimes stone faced. Wet-field cultivation of taro was also present in the Solomons, New Hebrides and Fiji, and recent work by Groube[57] on Aneityum in the southern New Hebrides has shown that quite large-scale irrigation systems there may date back for at least 2000 years. In the Hawaiian Islands of Polynesia, recent excavations in the Makaha Valley on Oahu have indicated the presence of wet-field terracing from the fourteenth century A.D. (see page 360), and wet taro seems to have been the mainstay of the powerful chiefdoms which developed in Hawaii prior to European discovery.

In the southern Cook Islands, the wet-field two terraces of Mangaia (figure 6.7) have been described by Allen, and I have recently surveyed staircase terraces on Rorotonga[58] (figure 6.8).

It seems from a fairly superficial examination that the wet-field terracing (as opposed to simple planting in swamps) is confined mainly to areas with seasonal variation in rainfall, as is the case for New Caledonia and many of the Polynesian islands. In areas of high all year round rainfall, such as Samoa, and the Bismarck and northern Solomon Islands, this form of cultivation appears to be absent, and there is sufficient rain for dryland cultivation of taro. Whether wet-field taro cultivation was practised by the earliest settlers of eastern Melanesia and Polynesia is not clear, but the widespread distribution of the technique seems to suggest a high antiquity.

In Polynesia, with its limited native flora and fauna, prehistoric societies were particularly dependent on marine resources and the introduced cultigens for survival[59]. The distributions of the latter are in many cases irregular; for instance, coconuts were apparently absent on Mangareva at European contact, Rapa lacked breadfruit and coconuts did not flourish, Easter Island lacked breadfruit and coconut entirely, and New Zealand had an even narrower range owing to its temperate climate. Compared to Melanesia, yams tend to fall behind taro in importance, while breadfruit became a very important staple in the Marquesas and Society Islands. On some of the atolls the only cultigens recorded with certainty are coconut and pandanus, and these islands obviously present marked contrasts to the luxuriance of a high volcanic island such as Tahiti.

It is from early descriptions of the more fertile islands of Polynesia that the modern reader can extract those visions of benevolent plenty so beloved to the modern tourist industry. As an example, we have the description made in the 1820s by the missionary John Williams of the island of Rarotonga in the southern Cook Islands. Rarotonga, like Tahiti, has high interior mountains surrounded by a narrow but fertile coastal plain. Williams describes a section of this plain as follows[60]:

> In the first place there are rows of superb chestnut trees, *inocarpus*, planted at equal distances, and stretching from the mountain's base to the sea, with a space between each row of about half-a-mile wide. This space is divided into small *taro* beds, which are dug four feet deep, and can be irrigated at pleasure. These average about half an acre each. The embankments around each bed are thrown up with a slope, leaving a flat surface on the top of six or eight feet in width. The lowest parts are planted with *taro*, and the sides of the embankment with *kape* or gigantic *taro**, while on the top are placed, at regular intervals, small beautifully shaped breadfruit trees. . . There is a good road round the island which the natives call *ara medua*, or the parent path, both sides of which are lined with bananas and mountain plantains.

* *Alocasia macrorrhiza*

Such small but fertile Polynesian islands seem to be further cases where increasing population densities have stimulated intensification of cultivation, but it is quite clear that both the crops and the techniques vary from place to place, for both cultural and ecological reasons.

CULTIVATION IN NEW ZEALAND

New Zealand stretches over 12 degrees of latitude entirely within the temperate zone, and is therefore an area of unique interest in Oceania. The adaptations which Polynesian settlers were forced to make were unparalleled elsewhere, and from the outset they found themselves in a land in which breadfruit, coconut and banana would not grow at all, while the root crops which they brought with them were greatly restricted. In the north and sheltered parts of the east coast of the North Island the yam and taro would grow, but the latter evidently took one year or more to reach a fair size, and growth could be seriously set back by frost. There is no definite evidence that taro was irrigated artificially, and it seems generally to have been planted in holes about 60 centimetres wide by 20 centimetres deep in coastal swamps or swiddens to as far south as the Queen Charlotte Sounds. Gourds and the paper mulberry were also grown on a limited scale in the North Island, but the latter seems to have been almost extinct by the time of European contact.

Of the introduced cultigens, it is interesting that the sweet potato, of marginal importance in tropical Polynesia, should have become dominant in New Zealand. Its cultivation was strictly seasonal, involving spring planting and autumn harvest, as the tubers are highly vulnerable to frost. Through the winter these tubers were stored in sealed semi-subterranean storehouses (see figure 13.26), in which the temperature needed to be kept above a minimum of 5°C. The plant was restricted to coastal areas of the North Island, and to the northern and eastern parts of the South Island to as far south as the vicinity of Banks Peninsula, and it flourished particularly on the fertile volcanic or well-drained alluvial soils of the warmer north. Shifting cultivation was universal, and generally on sloping land, but in cases where soil was fertile but heavy, poorly drained and subject to heat loss, gravel might be added to improve the structure. After a plot was cleared and the vegetation burnt, the propagated shoots were placed in small mounds loosened with digging sticks, the planting operation being attended with a great degree of ritual and the active participation of one or more priests. Breakwinds and drainage ditches were constructed where necessary, and after the harvest the tubers were carefully sorted into batches for food and seed, and gently stacked in the storehouses. The sweet potato is of great importance archaeologically, because of the wealth of structures associated with its cultivation which still survive. The evidence for prehistoric cultivation in New Zealand is discussed more fully in chapter 13, so no further comment is necessary at this stage. However, it may be noted that perhaps the most important plant food in New Zealand was the rhizome of the native fern, *Pteridium esculentum*[61], and this almost certainly provided more food by weight than all the introduced cultigens put together. Furthermore, the inhabitants of the southern part of the South Island and the Chatham Islands were unable to practice any cultivation at all, owing to climatic conditions.

THE WET-FIELD CULTIVATION OF RICE

Having reviewed some of the evidence for diversification and intensification of cultivation in Oceania, we may now turn for a brief look at the most important form of intensification in Southeast Asia: wet-field rice cultivation. Prior to A.D. 1500, rice was the major crop (as it still is) of the Southeast Asian mainland and western Indonesia. However, in Sulawesi and the Philippines both yam and taro retained considerable importance at this time, and rice faded rapidly in importance before reaching the area of Maluku. Cultivation was most widely of swidden type, wherein the seed grains were simply planted in small prepared holes. But in the large mainland river valleys, on the fertile islands of Java and Bali, and in northern Luzon in the Philippines, the plant was grown in irrigated fields.

For wet-field cultivation, rice grains are usually propagated into shoots in special seed beds, and then transplanted into the wet terrace soil. Water is led in gradually and increased to a depth of about 30 centimetres, and then slowly drained for the harvest. The water is not allowed to stagnate, and may come from stream or rainfall sources. The terraces themselves may be on slopes, like those of northern Luzon, or on flat land where the water is controlled by a dyke system. There is a continuous replacement of fertility by fresh silt, organic matter, and by the nitrogen fixing properties of certain algae which inhabit the fields, and this means that the system is in fact self-perpetuating. In this regard, Clifford Geertz[62] has described the Javanese fields as 'artificial, maximally self-perpetuating, continuous-cultivation, open-field structures'. Harvests are yielded once or even twice every year from the terraces, and in Java the system supports populations of up to 2000 persons per square kilometre in rural areas.

Needless to say, the amount of labour required to produce such yields is great. A family can guarantee itself subsistence, barring natural calamities, if it is prepared to keep the terraces in order, and of course to indulge in the labour of construction in the first place. We are in fact back with the Boserup hypothesis again. In Java the system is now indispensable, and the huge population has risen hand in hand with its expansion. But in sparsely populated areas of Outer Indonesia or Melanesia, even where the specific conditions of topography, water and soluble nutrient availability are met, it is not surprising that there has been no widespread adoption of the system under European persuasion[63].

Rather surprisingly, wet-field rice cultivation in Southeast Asia is totally without direct archaeological documentation at the moment. One problem is that botanists are not yet sure whether cultivated rice originated as a wet or a dry crop, and without this crucial information too much surmise would be pointless. While the prevailing view in recent years has been that dry rice preceded wet, Ho[64] has recently suggested that the earliest rice grown in southern China was grown in swamps or simple man-made wet fields, and archaeologists working in Thailand have recently suggested on ecological grounds that wet-rice was cultivated in the fourth millennium B.C. at Ban Chiang and Non Nok Tha[65]. On the other hand, Whyte[66] has argued that wet-field cultivation of rice would not have been possible until iron was in common use, and iron, together with the water buffalo, does not appear in Thailand until about 1500 B.C. or later. Chinese written records only mention wet-rice in northern Indochina after 200 B.C., and we really know nothing conclusive about the antiquity of the systems in northern Luzon (see page 91). The history of wet-rice cultivation is thus a vital topic which must be tackled very soon. Despite recent claims for a high antiquity, it does appear to me that he huge and complex terrace systems which one can see in parts of Southeast Asia today may have developed since the commencement of Indianisation some 2000 years ago; if wet-rice were indeed cultivated as early as 3000 B.C., one would expect it to be relatively localised, and perhaps confined to the vicinity of natural swamps and streams.

DOMESTICATED ANIMALS

Only three domesticated animals were taken by man right across Oceania and these are the pig, dog and fowl. The rat was also transported, probably accidentally, to most island groups, and was frequently eaten. However, it was never to my knowledge kept in captivity, and as an extraordinarily aggressive and adaptable animal it may well have spread partly by natural means; rats were the only placental land mammals to reach Australia and New Guinea across the sea lanes of Wallacea in pre-human times[67].

The pig, dog and fowl have no wild ancestors in Oceania, and this is of course a matter of great significance; wherever and whenever they are found in archaeological deposits beyond their wild habitats, the hand of man may be inferred. Of the three, the least is known about the fowl (*Gallus gallus*), which is a descendant of the wild jungle fowls of Mainland Southeast Asia, Sumatra and Java[68]. Domesticated fowls provided meat and feathers, but the eggs seem rarely to have been eaten. In addition, cockfighting is well recorded from Indonesia, Tahiti and Hawaii, and may have been a very widespread sport in prehistoric times. Generally, fowls are allowed to scavenge freely, and many feral populations exist in the interior forests of many Pacific islands. Archaeologically, there are few observations to make, except to note the occurrence of fowl bones in Chinese prehistoric sites before 1700 B.C. and in Melanesia by 500 B.C., and to note also that the fowl was the only domesticated species to reach Easter Island, the easterly limit of Austronesian settlement in the Pacific.

The evidence for the dog in prehistory is only slightly better than that for the fowl[69]. No dogs of the *Canis* genus are reported from the Pleistocene deposits of Java, although they were present in the Upper Pleistocene of China. In China and Thailand dogs seem to have been domesticated by at least the fourth millennium B.C., although their presence in Southeast Asia before this time is uncertain. In Island Southeast Asia we have little evidence for them before 2000 B.C., but dingoes were possibly taken to Australia by about

6000 B.C.[70]. In this case they were undoubtedly brought by man, and the logical route is through Indonesia.

The role of the dog in prehistory is now uncertain, but it was clearly more than a hunting companion in many areas. In the Hawaiian Islands, for instance, dogs were bred on a vegetable diet for meat, and up to 200 were killed for recorded feasts[71]. Others were kept as pets, and puppies occasionally suckled by women. The eating of dog meat is widely recorded throughout the Pacific, and the industrial uses of a dog carcass were quite numerous, particularly in New Zealand, where it was the only introduced domesticated animal.

The most important animal of the triad, and the one about which there is a wealth of archaeological and ethnographic information, is the pig. The domesticated pigs are of the species *Sus scrofa*, and the native distribution of this animal in prehistoric times was probably restricted to Mainland South-east Asia, Sumatra and Java. Other endemic pig species on Borneo, Sulawesi, and in Maluku and the Philippines appear never to have been domesticated. Pig bones (*Sus scrofa*) in archaeological sites beyond Java not only strongly indicate transport by man, but if there are grounds for considering them domesticated (and transport of wild pigs is always a possibility), then they may also indicate the existence of plant cultivation. Pigs in captivity need to be fed to some extent on food which is actually produced by man, and therefore would be a most uneconomic proposition for a society dependent upon hunting and gathering.

The archaeological evidence for pig domestication in Southeast Asia is extensive, but all unfortunately of a partly circumstantial nature. I have reviewed some of the problems connected with this elsewhere[72], and it is only necessary here to note that domesticated pigs were probably present throughout Southeast Asia to as far east

Fig. 6.9. Feeding domestic pigs on coconuts in New Ireland.

as New Guinea by at least 3000 B.C. Neither pigs nor fowls were ever introduced into Australia, and beyond New Guinea their transmission probably took place from about 1500 B.C. onwards.

It is of course necessary to keep Pacific animal domestication in some perspective, for the above triad can hardly be considered in the same category as the herd grazing animals of Eurasia. They provided an occasional and often ceremonial meat supply, rather than a daily dinner, which in coastal areas more often took the form of fish. However, in inland areas pigs might be the major meat supply, and their role in subsistence is best recorded in the New Guinea Highlands. Rappaport's unique survey[73] of the socio-economic functions of pigs amongst the Tsembaga of the Bismarck Ranges, Papua New Guinea, presents some extremely interesting if localised information. Ninety-nine percent of Tsembaga diet by weight comes from plant foods, cultivated and gathered, while the other one percent is mostly from pork. Yet pigs are obviously a very major fact of life amongst the Tsembaga; they are cared for individually by the women, and may consume up to forty percent of Tsembaga cultivated foods. They are killed occasionally to provide food for the sick, for birth and marriage ceremonies, but the majority are killed in a veritable bonanza every eight to twelve years, when special ritual cycles of great social importance take place. The Tsembaga case may be rather extreme, and many peoples probably ate pork more frequently than this in prehistoric times in Oceania[74]. Furthermore, the roles of the domesticated animals in the Pacific may have been very varied, and it is of interest in this respect to note the very spotty distribution of the three members of the triad amongst the scattered islands of Oceania[75].

The fowl, pig and dog were of course not the only domesticated animals present in prehistoric times in Southeast Asia, and Indonesia at least seems to have received cattle and caprovines (probably goats) prior to Indianisation. So far the only reliable evidence comes from Glover's excavations in eastern Timor (see page 217), where it appears that caprovines and bovids of undetermined species were introduced around, perhaps before, 1000 B.C. The presence of bovids so far east by this date may be surprising, but domesticated cattle (probably *Bos indicus*) are reported from Thailand at or before 3000 B.C.[76] Caprovines are not reported archaeologically anywhere in Southeast Asia, but were of course present in India and China by this time. The history of the domesticated water buffalo is an open question, but recent evidence from Thailand suggests that here it makes an appearance together with iron and wet-rice cultivation about 1000–500 B.C.[77]

Having reviewed the information about plant cultivation and animal husbandry in Southeast Asia and Oceania, we are now in a better position to move straight into the archaeology. However, two questions of an economic nature which have been touched upon in this and the previous chapter will require further comment in due course. When and why did plant cultivation develop in Southeast Asia, and why (as asked at the end of chapter 5) have the Austronesians been so successful in the colonisation of Island Southeast Asia?

Footnotes

1. For a similar review of this topic, see Bellwood 1976a.

2. Sauer 1952.

3. However, Sauer's botanical data have been severely criticised by Merrill (1954:271–87), and his general conclusions involve a degree of diffusion which would be unacceptable to most scholars today, although this does not detract from the general merits of the book.

4. For detailed descriptions of cultigens and data on yields, see Massal and Barrau 1956. Barrau (1965a) gives a good general discussion on the origins of the Pacific cultigens.

5. Heyerdahl 1968b: chapter 7.

6. Hossfeld 1964.

7. Child 1964: chapter 1.

8. Merrill 1954:241; Barrau 1965a:70; Sauer in Riley *et al.* 1971: 309–19.

9. Barrau ed. 1963:4; 1965a:67–8.

10. Heyerdahl 1968b:67–8; Merrill 1954:272–9.

11. Barrau 1958:38–9.

12. Barrau 1965a:71.

13. Williamson 1939: chapters 2 and 3.

14. Merrill 1954:222. See also Carter 1950:164–5.

15. Stone, in Barrau ed. 1963:61–74.

16. Whitaker, in Riley *et al.* 1971:320–7; Merrill 1954:223, 257–8; Gorman 1971:311. Childe (1957:108) pointed out that 5th millenium B.C. Danubian pottery from central Europe could also have taken its shape from gourds.

17. Barrau 1965a:65–6; Alexander and Coursey 1969; Coursey 1972. As Harris (1973) points out, a seasonal

climatic regime would tend to increase tuber size, owing to the need for the plant to survive a dormant season.

18. Barrau 1968: 121.

19. Barrau 1965a:68, 1970:498–9.

20. Watson 1964; Barrau 1965b.

21. Nishiyama in Barrau ed. 1963:119–28; Brand in Riley *et al.* 1971:343–65; Yen in Riley *et al.* 1971:328–342; O'Brien 1972. For a thorough review of all matters concerning the sweet potato in the Pacific, see Yen 1974.

22. Yen 1971:12; O'Brien 1972.

23. Merrill 1954:212.

24. Yen 1960; Baker in Riley *et al.* 1971:433–5. Purseglove 1968, I:80, states that seeds of sweet potato can survive for long periods in sea water.

25. Brand in Riley *et al.* 1971:359–63.

26. Dixon 1932. Barrau (1965a:66) has suggested that early reporters of sweet potatoes in New Caledonia and Tonga may have confused them with a species of yam, *Dioscorea nummularia.*

27. O'Brien 1972: Professor J. Golson, personal communication.

28. Rosendahl and Yen 1971.

29. See Yen 1971:12 for a more detailed statement of this view. See also Hornell 1946.

30. Heyerdahl in Barrau ed. 1963:23–35; Heyerdahl 1968b:51–74.

31. Cotton seeds can also survive for long periods in sea water (Purseglove 1968, I:80). Furthermore the Hawaiian cotton is endemic and may be of pre-human origin (Mangelsdorf, McNeish and Willey 1964). See also Pickersgill and Bunting 1969.

32. Glover 1972, vol. I:320.

33. Yawata in Barrau ed. 1963:91–2.

34. Spencer in Barrau 1963:83–90; Bartlett 1962; Whyte 1972; Ho 1975.

35. Spencer in Barrau 1963:83–90. Gorman (1974) has recently suggested that rice could have been one of the earliest domesticated plants in Southeast Asia.

36. Dentan 1968:47. See also Coursey (1967:12) on wild yam harvesting in Africa.

37. Burkill 1953:12.

38. Gould 1971:171.

39. For the general characteristics of shifting cultivation, see Freeman 1955; Barrau 1958; Watters 1960; Conklin 1961; Geertz 1963; Spencer 1966; Boserup 1965; Grigg 1974.

40. Harris 1972; 1973. Harris has suggested that the maintenance of small gardens around houses may have been the very first stage in horticultural evolution.

41. Freeman 1955.

42. Robbins in Barrau ed. 1963:45–60; Brookfield 1964:33.

43. C. Geertz 1963:16.

44. Watters 1960:79–80, 86; Wright 1962.

45. Spencer 1966–27.

46. Conklin 1954.

47. Oliver 1955.

48. Clarke 1971.

49. Clarke 1966; Brookfield and Hart 1971: chapters 3 and 4; Brookfield 1962.

50. Brookfield and Brown 1963.

51. Waddell 1972.

52. Boserup 1965. For generalised application to the New Guinea Highlands see Brookfield and Hart 1971:92; Waddell 1972. However, the validity of Boserup's hypothesis has recently been questioned by Cowgill (1975).

53. Serpenti 1965.

54. Barrau 1958: 16–17.

55. Damm 1951.

56. Barrau 1956.

57. Groube 1975.

58. Allen 1971; Bellwood 1977a.

59. On Polynesia generally, see Barrau 1961.

60. Williams 1838:206–7; see also Lewthwaite 1964 for Tahiti.

61. K. Shawcross 1967.

62. C. Geertz 1963:28. For a general survey of wet-rice cultivation see Grigg 1974: chapter 6.

63. Barrau 1958:87.

64. Ho 1975.

65. Gorman 1974; Higham 1975. For the antiquity of rice terracing see also Spencer and Hale 1961; Wheatley 1965.

66. Whyte 1972: 144.

67. Darlington 1957:388–9, 573.

68. Ball 1933; Carter in Riley *et al.* 1971:181–3; Darlington 1957:294.

69. Bellwood 1976a.

70. Mulvaney 1975:138. However, Mulvaney (personal communication) cautions that the earliest really reliable date for the dingo in Australia is only 1000 B.C.

71. Titcomb 1969:8.

72. Bellwood 1976a.

73. Rappaport 1967. See also Waddell 1972 for pig husbandry amongst the Raiapu Enga.

74. Vayda, Leeds and Smith 1961.

75. Urban 1961: map 1.

76. Higham and Leach 1972; Higham 1972; 1975.

77. Higham 1972 and personal communication.

CHAPTER 7

Neolithic and Early Metal Age Cultures
on the Southeast Asian Mainland

The terms 'Neolithic' and 'Metal Age' are used to refer to two rather vague pigeon-holes for Southeast Asian archaeological material. They are of course somewhat old-fashioned terms, and their use is full of pitfalls. Some attempts have even been made to replace them[1], but owing to the present rudimentary state of archaeology in this area I prefer to err on the side of conservatism. Hence I retain them, and use the term Neolithic to refer to those cultures which do not have metal artefacts, and which demonstrate two of the following three traits: pecked or ground stone adzes, pottery, and horticulture. Since evidence for the latter is often elusive, stone tools and pottery will take up a good deal of space in the following pages.

As defined, the Neolithic period begins at different times in different areas of southeast Asia, but it is generally superseded by bronze using cultures soon after 1000 B.C., and perhaps by as early as 3500 B.C. in Thailand. It is in fact difficult to generalise. However, the material to be covered in this chapter does have a quite well defined termination at about the time of Christ, after which the historical civilisations develop under the influences of India and China.

As with all prehistoric cultures, those of Southeast Asia gain by being considered in a wider context. Hence we spend some time with China – the home of an ancient civilisation, and also a country once considered to be the home of almost all developments in prehistoric Southeast Asia. This view is erroneous and has not stood up to research, although contacts throughout eastern Asia generally were undoubtedly widespread, and a cursory glance at Chinese and Southeast Asian Neolithic cultures will show that they do share many elements. These include specific types of stone adzes and knives; pottery types with such distinctive features as ring feet, tripod legs, and cord-marked, stamped and incised decoration; rings and discs of stone, pottery and shell; extended burials; timber architecture; the use of spindle whorls; and the domesticated dog and pig. Let us begin at the beginning, at least as far as the pottery is concerned.

THE EARLIEST POTTERY IN SOUTHEAST ASIA

Throughout eastern Asia, from Japan right down to Malaya, the earliest pottery is almost always associated with a high degree of cord- or basket-marking. This is produced by beating the outside of the pot with a wooden paddle wrapped in cordage or basketry before firing, and the result is a roughened surface which can be both decorative and functional (it makes the pot easier to hold). Such marking is so wide-spread, not only in early sites but right through the prehistoric period, that it is almost a hallmark of prehistoric east Asian mainland pottery. In this section we look at some of the rather disjointed first appearances of cord- and basket-marked pottery, before we proceed to the more 'classic' Neolithic sites.

The earliest pottery in eastern Asia, and indeed in the world, comes from Japan. In the Fukui Cave site on the southern Japanese island of Kyushu, sherds of pottery decorated with applied strips or dots have been found to date back to the eleventh millennium B.C., and pottery with actual cord-marking seems to be quite wide-spread on Honshu by 7000–6000 B.C.[2]. Whether pottery was actually invented in Japan cannot be known until we have a fuller knowledge of

Fig. 7.1. Neolithic and Metal Age sites in Mainland Southeast Asia.

adjacent mainland areas, and there is as yet no good evidence to postulate contact between this area and Southeast Asia. The Ryukyu Islands, which from a geographical standpoint might serve to link Japan and Southeast Asia, have as yet produced no evidence for Neolithic contact between the two areas[3].

The nearest relative of the earliest Japanese pottery may one day be found in China. Chang has suggested that a cord-marked ceramic horizon may predate the early Neolithic cultures of the fifth millennium B.C. in the Huangho loesslands[4], and there are sites which apparently support his view. But there is little evidence yet to match that from Japan. In southern China there is further evidence for cord-marked pottery cultures at the base of the ceramic Neolithic, with sites in Kiangsi and Kwangtung, but as Chang[5] points out, the data on these sites are scarce. Generally, the southern Chinese corded ware sites appear to

be associated both with stone tools of Hoabinhian type, as well as with polished stone tools of Neolithic type, and in some cases skeletons with Mongoloid dental features have been reported.

Clearer contexts for the southern Chinese corded pottery have recently been provided by excavations in Hong Kong and Taiwan. At a site called Sham Wan, on Lamma Island, Hong Kong, several successive pottery styles have been found in a deep but homogeneous raised beach deposit. The earliest pottery was coarse and cord-marked, and the excavators suggest that it may date back to about 5000 B.C.[6]. Clearer information comes from Taiwan, where an excavation team led by K.C. Chang in 1964–5 recovered cord-marked ceramics from occupation levels at the sites of Feng-pi-t'ou and Ta-p'en-k'eng, in both cases predating 2500 B.C. by an unknown margin of time[7]. The pottery has all-over cord-marking, with incised designs on rims and

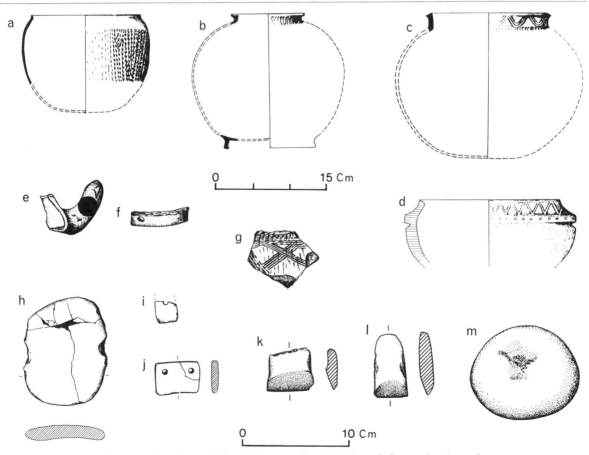

Fig. 7.2. Artefacts of the Taiwanese Corded Ware Culture: (a–g) cord-marked and incised pottery, including a lug (e) and a perforated ring-foot (f) – all from Feng-pi-t'ou, except (d) which is from Ta-p'en-k'eng; (h) waisted 'net sinker' from Feng-pi-t'ou; (i) perforated slate projectile point from Feng-pi-t'ou; (j) perforated clay object from Feng-pi-t'ou; (k–m) stone adzes and pitted pebble from Ta-p'en-k'eng. From Chang 1969a.

upper surfaces, and common forms are bowls and globular jars, some with ring feet with cut-out designs. Some of the pots also have lug handles for suspension. The material culture found with these sherds is of great importance, for it includes polished adzes with rectangular cross-sections, and sometimes with stepped butts, together with perforated slate projectile points (figure 7.2). Chang tentatively associates the Taiwanese Corded Ware Culture with horticulture on the evidence from pollen diagrams for forest clearance in central Taiwan from about 9000 B.C., although the two sites excavated are unlikely to be earlier than 5000–4000 B.C., if carbon-dated sites on the Chinese mainland are any guide. At present there is no clear source for this culture, however, although the pottery does have generic parallels in southern China and northern Indochina.

On the Southeast Asian mainland, corded pottery makes its first definite appearance in a late Hoabinhian context at Spirit Cave in northwest Thailand soon after 7000 B.C.[8]. The sherds found in level II of the site (*c.* 6800 to 5700 B.C. from carbon-14 dates) have cord or net-impression, and some of the net-impressed sherds have applied strips, and an organic resin coat added after firing. The associated material culture is again of great interest, and includes two polished rectangular cross-sectioned adzes (figure 7.3) and two polished slate knives. Both the date for this site, and the simple rim shapes of the pottery, suggest that it may be considerably earlier than the Corded Ware Culture sites on Taiwan, and Spirit Cave is in fact the earliest dated Neolithic site presently known in Southeast Asia.

Elsewhere on the mainland, a number of late Hoabinhian sites have cord-marked pottery, as we have seen in chapter 3. But good dated sites are few and far between. At Gua Kechil in

Malaya, corded and plain burnished sherds from round or flat-bottomed vessels appear in late Hoabinhian contexts prior to 3000 B.C.[9], and ring feet make their first appearance with the Neolithic red ware from the site which postdates 3000 B.C. At present, it appears that the idea of a ring foot on a pot first developed in China, and spread from there to Taiwan and Southeast Asia; this is not a certain conclusion, but at least the form cannot at present be traced to the Hoabinhian, or for that matter to Japan.

Enough has now been said to indicate that corded pottery makes an appearance over most of the Southeast Asian mainland by at least 5000–3000 B.C., and this date may well be pushed back two thousand years by further research. The general cultural context for its first appearance is late Hoabinhian or Bacsonian, and what may be early corded pottery is in fact present over a much wider area than indicated above, particularly in Szechwan[10], an area which is intermediate between northern Southeast Asia and the Weishui-Huangho region of central China. On the other hand, as we will see in the next chapter, there are plain ceramics in parts of eastern Indonesia and the Philippines by 3000 B.C., but since these are not cord- or basket-marked[11] they raise interesting questions concerning their relationships with the ceramics of the Southeast Asian mainland. We will return to them later.

THE PREHISTORY OF CHINA

It is impossible to evaluate the significance of the Southeast Asian Neolithic without at least some knowledge of the Neolithic and early historic cultures of China – the forerunners of one of the greatest civilisations of the ancient world. This is not to say that Southeast Asia may be viewed

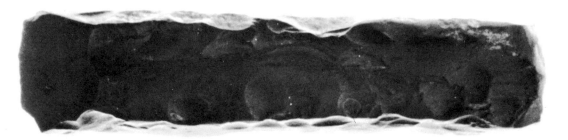

Fig. 7.3. Stone adze of rectangular cross-section from Spirit Cave, *c.* 7th millennium B.C. Length 11 cm. From Gorman 1970.

as a mere cultural province of China, for this view would be loudly contested today. On the other hand, I have already pointed out the basic similarities between Chinese and Southeast Asian Neolithic cultures, and it is clear that many innovations spread rapidly between the two areas.

At present, the earliest fully-fledged Chinese Neolithic culture[12] is the Yang-shao Culture of the primary loesslands in the Weishui and Middle Huangho River systems (central Shensi, southern Shansi, and western Honan provinces). Sites of this culture flourished in a climate perhaps 2°C higher than present, and appear to represent a well-developed dry-farming economy based on the cultivation of foxtail millet (*Setaria italica*) and broomcorn millet (*Panicum miliaceum*), both being cereals which are probably native to China. There is as yet no evidence for irrigation, or rice or wheat cultivation in the Yang-shao, and the development of agriculture and sedentary villages on the semi-arid loesslands appears to be almost entirely a result of local enterprise. The most important Yang-shao settlement excavated to date, at Pan-p'o-ts'un in Shensi, consisted of a circle of houses and storage pits around a central communal hall, the whole being enclosed within a deep defensive ditch. While the whole village has not yet been excavated, it would appear to have had about 200 houses at any one time, and a population of perhaps 5–600 people. Outside the dwelling area lay pottery kilns, and a cemetery of extended adult burials, children being buried in pots between the houses.

The Yang-shao Culture as represented at Pan-p'o-ts'un is unlikely to be the earliest Neolithic culture of central China, and its roots may well in future years be found to lie in the cord-marked ceramic horizon of the area (see above). Radiocarbon dates place its beginning at about 5000 B.C., and parallels in painted pottery between this area and the Near East also indicate a commencement from at least the end of the sixth millennium B.C.[13].

The intricate details of Yang-shao material culture are of little concern here, but the general range of artefact types is highly relevant. Much of the pottery is cord-marked, and there are also incised, applied and painted designs, the latter having a deserved fame amongst art historians. Possible incised numerals are also found on some Pan-p'o-ts'un sherds, perhaps heralding the origins of the Chinese writing system. Pot shapes are very varied, but the presence of ring feet and tripod legs is significant for subsequent Chinese developments. Pig and dog were domesticated, together with the silkworm, and there is evidence that hemp was woven into textiles. Bone artefacts include tanged projectile points, fishhooks, needles, and rings of various forms and sizes. Stone artefacts include net sinkers, spindle whorls, adzes with rectangular and oval cross-sections, and rectangular or crescentic perforated slate knives. The burials from Pan-p'o-ts'un are reported to have Mongoloid characteristics which relate them most closely to past and present Southeast Asian populations[14], an observation of more than passing interest.

However, the significance of the Yang-shao for our purposes lies not so much in its generalised parallels with Southeast Asian Neolithic cultures as in the likelihood that it represents the source of the next major phase of the Chinese Neolithic, called the Lungshanoid by Chang[15]. The Lung-shanoid cultures represent, according to Chang, a development from the Yang-shao Culture, and they spread most probably as a result of actual migration through vast areas of central and coastal China right down to Kwangtung and Taiwan. In central China they date to between perhaps 4000 B.C. and the beginning of the Shang Bronze Age, the latter event falling somewhere between 1722 and 1514 B.C. according to historical records.

As a result of its vast distribution, the Lung-shanoid is much more than an archaeological culture, and is better described as a culture group with varied components. Technological features which may be used to differentiate the Lung-shanoid from the preceeding Yang-shao include a dominance of rectangular cross-sectioned adzes and rectangular stone knives, and the presence of wheel-made or wheel-finished pottery in a great variety of shapes. In the Huangho Valley, the appearance of earthen fortification walls, animal bone divination (or scapulimancy) and a complex of phenomena indicating increasing social stratification gradually develop to herald the Shang Dynasty. These developments are beyond our interests at the moment, since they do represent a localised aspect of cultural evolution. On the other hand, the Lungshanoid cultures of the Lower Yangtze region, southern coastal China, and Taiwan, are of more than passing significance for Southeast Asian prehistory.

The mainland southern Chinese Lungshanoid cultures include the Ch'ü-chia-ling of the lower

Hanshui Valley[16], the Ch'ing-lien-kang of Kiangsu[17], the T'an-shih-shan of Fukien[18], and probably some of the sites excavated many years ago by Fr. Maglioni at Hai-feng, in Kwangtung Province[19]. In addition, the Sham Wan site in Hong Kong (see above) has hand-made incised pottery with possible Lungshanoid affinities appearing in levels above the first appearance of the corded ware, although the corded ware continues in production with it. While the reports on these Chinese sites vary in detail, it would appear that they share a polythetic assemblage with a fair degree of homogeneity dating generally within a time span of *c.* 4000 to 1000 B.C.[20]. This includes mostly hand-made and corded, stamped, or painted pottery of a wide variety of shapes and pastes, some with ring feet or tripod legs. In northern sites a greater proportion of the pottery is reported as wheel-made, while more incised decoration seems to be reported from Hong Kong and Taiwan, perhaps in line with the general importance of this decorative technique in Southeast Asia. Adzes generally have rectangular cross-sections, and may be shouldered or stepped, the latter form being restricted to the coastal areas. Plain or perforated stone knives of rectangular or crescentic shape, together with leaf-shaped or perforated projectile points are also present. Burials are generally of the extended

inhumation type, and fragmentary cremations are reported from Sham Wan. In the lower Hanshui Valley pottery rings, bracelets and spindle whorls have been recovered, and spindle whorls are also known from T'an-shih-shan, although it is not clear just how widespread all these items are.

Of particular importance is the presence of rice from about 4000–3300 B.C. in the lower Yangtze region (Kiangsu and Chekiang Provinces). The first evidence for irrigation in China comes from historical records for about 600 B.C. in the Huangho Valley, and there is no direct evidence for it before this date anywhere in eastern Asia. This does not of course mean that there was no irrigation in southern China before this, and the history of rice irrigation is still very much an open question (see pages 148–149). Cattle, sheep, goat and chicken may also have been domesticated during the Lungshanoid in China, and there is no evidence for their domestication during the earlier Yangshao.

The most important results to date on the Lungshanoid in southern China come from Taiwan[21]. Strictly speaking, this island should and will be dealt with in the next chapter, but I have described its Corded Ware Culture above, and its Lungshanoid sites are of direct relevance

Fig. 7.6. Fine red ware of Lungshanoid type from Feng-pi-t'ou, *c.* 2000 B.C. From Chang 1969a.

here. The main one is at Feng-pi-t'ou on the south-western coast. The lower levels of this site belong to the Corded Ware Culture, and these were succeeded, after a gap of unknown duration during which the site was unoccupied, by a Lungshanoid settlement. This had four successive but continuous phases, which seem to have covered varying areas of between 20,000 and 50,000 square metres. The chronological subdivisions are given by Chang as follows:

Phase 1 – a settlement characterised by fine red pottery, with estimated dates of 2400–1900 B.C.

Phase 2 – a settlement characterised by sandy red pottery, with estimated dates of 1900–1400 B.C.

Phase 3 – a settlement characterised by sandy grey pottery and shellfish dumping, well fixed by radiocarbon dates to *c*. 1600–800 B.C.

Phase 4 – a final settlement characterised by sandy red pottery and further shellfish dumping, with a single radiocarbon date of *c*. 500 B.C.

The pottery from these settlements is well within the range of the Chinese Lungshanoid, and is made by coiling (a common technique in the mainland Lungshanoid), and finished by paddle and anvil. Some of the pots were also finished on a turntable of some kind. Forms include many of the basic Chinese Neolithic types, such as globular jars and bottles, dishes with ring feet with cut-out designs, or with three tripod legs, and round or flat bottomed bowls (figure 7.6). Some of the vessels were provided with lids. Decoration includes cord marking, basket impression, and a variety of incision, sometimes with a multi-pronged tool. The painted designs in red or brown include hooks, scrolls, and simple geometric designs.

The material culture of Feng-pi-t'ou (figures 7.4, 7.5) includes part of a rectangular timber house; perforated slate knives of both rectangular and crescentic shapes; perforated, triangular or tanged projectile points of slate or bone; bone harpoons; a notched stone net sinker; rings, bracelets, buttons and spindle whorls of clay; and buttons and rings of serpentine, which was imported from the Pescadores Islands to the west of Taiwan. The adze kit is particularly interesting, and includes a number of thin-sectioned tools which may be hoes, some of which are waisted or perforated. Items clearly recognisable as adzes

are of quadrangular cross-section, and without shoulders or stepped grips, although one has a grooved grip. One extended burial, without goods, is identified as Mongoloid.

Elsewhere in Taiwan, a late Lungshanoid site has been identified at Ying-p'u on the central western coast, and it does appear that the Lungshanoid is generally restricted to the west coast of the island. Pollen evidence from central Taiwan indicates a marked increase in grass pollen from about 2500 B.C., and this may indicate the spread of cereal agriculture, presumably of rice and millet. Rice impressions in pottery are known from Ying-p'u, which is of first millennium B.C. date, and rice may well have been cultivated in the earlier Lungshanoid phases at Feng-pi-t'ou, as it certainly was in the mainland Lungshanoid.

The dates for the Taiwanese Lungshanoid do seem to be a little later than those on the mainland of China, and this reinforces Chang's view that the Lungshanoid Culture Group is a result of

Fig. 7.4. Bone points from Feng-pi-t'ou. From Chang 1969a.

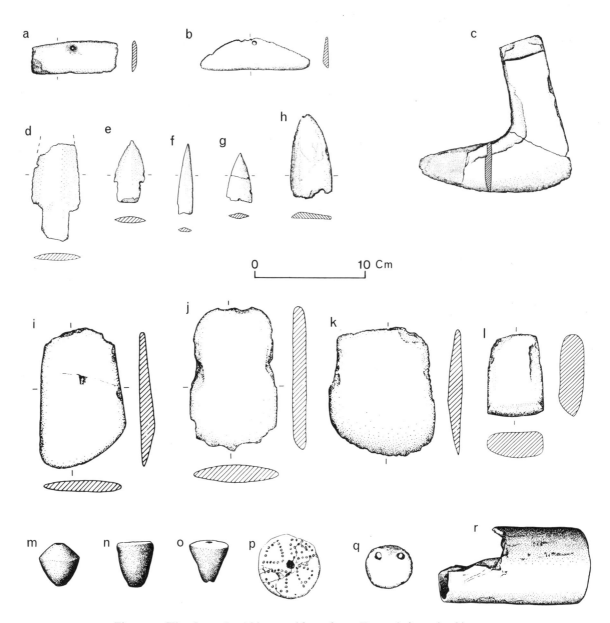

Fig. 7.5. The Lungshanoid assemblage from Feng-pi-t'ou: (a, b) stone knives; (c) stone boot-shaped knife; (d–h) stone projectile points; (i–k) stone hoe-axes; (l) stone adze; (m–o) clay spindle whorls; (p–r) clay discs and possible bracelet. From Chang 1969a.

expansion from central China. Chang in fact links the Feng-pi-t'ou Lungshanoid with the mainland Ch'ing-lien-kang and T'an-shih-shan Cultures, which have already been referred to above, and the Feng-pi-t'ou ceramics, quadrangular adzes, stone projectile points and knives are all paralleled in stratified assemblages from Sham Wan in Hong Kong, where they possibly postdate 2000 B.C. However, the question of Lungshanoid ex-

pansion into Southeast Asia proper, beyond Taiwan, is an important question which will require further consideration later on.

At this point enough has been sketched in of the Chinese Neolithic achievement to provide a background for the remainder of this chapter and the next. We must now move down into the Southeast Asian mainland to follow progress in the tropics, but it will be necessary at several points to return to China to assess its relationships with the developing Southeast Asian and Austronesian cultures.

THAILAND – AN INDEPENDENT FOCUS OF INNOVATION?

In the light of the example set by China, how does the mainland of Southeast Asia fare as a centre of Neolithic innovation? On present evidence it does not fare too badly, in both the Neolithic and the Metal Ages. The best evidence comes from Thailand, which has been stable enough politically in past years to receive a good deal of modern archaeological attention.

The Thai discoveries have the potential to cause a major revolution in Asian prehistory, and throw considerable doubt on the long established view of a backward Southeast Asian

Neolithic followed, about 500 B.C., by a Metal Age culture (Dong-Son) heavily influenced from China. Three sites provide the key to this revolution: Spirit Cave is one, and this has already been described; the second is a habitation and burial site called Non Nok Tha in the Phu Wiang region in the central piedmont area of northern Thailand, and the third is a habitation and burial mound called Ban Chiang, recently excavated, and situated about 120 kilometres north-east of Non Nok Tha.

Non Nok Tha consists of a low mound, with cultural deposits about 1.4 metres deep over an area of 100 by 150 metres. It was excavated in 1966 and 1968 by archaeologists from the Universities of Hawaii and Otago (Dunedin, New Zealand) under the general direction of W.G. Solheim[22]. The deposits, which contain a large number of inhumation and cremation burials,

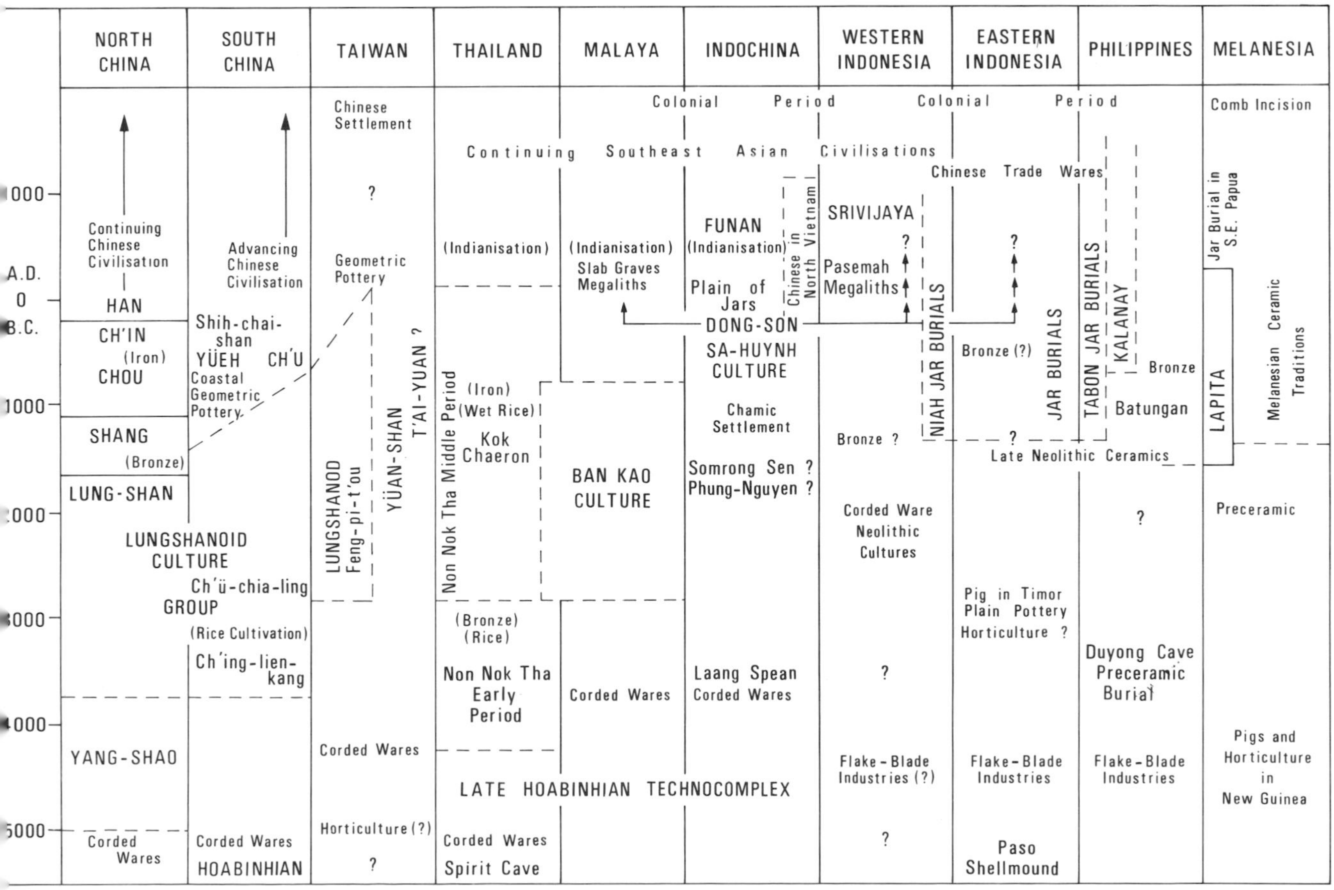

	NORTH CHINA	SOUTH CHINA	TAIWAN	THAILAND	MALAYA	INDOCHINA	WESTERN INDONESIA	EASTERN INDONESIA	PHILIPPINES	MELANESIA
			Chinese Settlement	Colonial Period			Colonial Period			Comb Incision
				Continuing Southeast Asian Civilisations						
1000 A.D.	Continuing Chinese Civilisation	Advancing Chinese Civilisation	?	(Indianisation)	(Indianisation)	FUNAN (Indianisation)	SRIVIJAYA ? Pasemah Megaliths	Chinese Trade Wares ?	Jar Burial in S.E. Papua	
0 B.C.	HAN CH'IN (Iron) CHOU	Shih-chai-shan YÜEH CH'U Coastal Geometric Pottery	Geometric Pottery	(Iron) (Wet Rice)	Slab Graves Megaliths	Plain of Jars DONG-SON SA-HUYNH CULTURE	Bronze (?)	Bronze	LAPITA	Melanesian Ceramic Traditions
1000	SHANG (Bronze) LUNG-SHAN			Kok Chaeron		Chamic Settlement	Bronze ?	Batungan	Bronze	
2000	LUNGSHANOID CULTURE Ch'ü-chia-ling GROUP	LUNGSHANOID Feng-pi-t'ou YÜAN-SHAN T'AI-YÜAN? Non Nok Tha Middle Period		BAN KAO CULTURE	Somrong Sen ? Phung-Nguyen ?	Corded Ware Neolithic Cultures	Late Neolithic Ceramics ?		Preceramic	
3000	(Rice Cultivation) Ch'ing-lien-kang		(Bronze) (Rice) Non Nok Tha Early Period		Laang Spean Corded Wares	?	Pig in Timor Plain Pottery Horticulture ?	Duyong Cave Preceramic Burial		
4000	YANG-SHAO	Corded Wares		Corded Wares		Flake-Blade Industries (?)	Flake-Blade Industries	Flake-Blade Industries	Pigs and Horticulture in New Guinea	
			LATE HOABINHIAN TECHNOCOMPLEX							
5000	Corded Wares	Corded Wares HOABINHIAN	Horticulture (?) ?	Corded Wares Spirit Cave		?	Paso Shellmound			

Fig. 7.7. Cultural developments in Mainland and Island Southeast Asia since 5000 B.C.

Fig. 7.8. Non Nok Tha Early Period burial with socketed copper tool on chest, offering vessels, and cover of sherds over lower legs.

appear to span the period between 4000 B.C. to a few hundred years ago, with the exception of a gap throughout the first millennium A.D. The following account incorporates the chronology favoured by the excavators, although this has not yet been fully accepted by all archaeologists working in the region.

The Early Period at Non Nok Tha is dated to between about 4000 and 3000 B.C., and contains a large number of extended inhumation burials (figure 7.8), some covered by low mounds. A number of the burials were headless, and this may suggest the practice of head-hunting. The grave-goods include thin rectangular-sectioned adzes without shoulders or stepped butts, strings of small shell beads, and round-based pots which

are mainly cord-marked below the necks. A small number of pots have ring feet, and some have curvilinear incised or painted decoration (figure 7.9). The pottery therefore appears to represent a local variant of the earliest cord-marked pottery of Southeast Asia, with some local innovation represented by the few painted sherds.

Amongst the animal bones placed with the burials are those of dog, pig, cattle and deer. The cattle almost certainly belonged to a domesticated species, perhaps *Bos indicus*[23], and the presence of a high proportion of juvenile female cattle bones with the burials may suggest ritual practices. The pigs and dogs were presumably, but not certainly, domesticated as well. Rice chaff is present in some of the earliest potsherds, indicating cultivation of this cereal at the site. Last, but certainly not least, a burial from the end of the Early Period produced a socketed copper object, perhaps a digging tool, together with some other fragments of bronze (figure 7.8). These objects are of smelted metal, and have pushed back the beginnings of the Southeast Asian Metal Age by almost 2000 years to a possible date of 3000 B.C.

These important discoveries at Non Nok Tha have recently been paralleled in the excavations by Gorman and Charoenwongsa[24] at the Ban Chiang site; a mound with a depth of 4.5 metres and thus much larger than Non Nok Tha. Although Ban Chiang is not yet fully published, enough is reported for a brief summary, and seven phases have been recognised spanning the period between 3600 B.C. and A.D. 1800, again with a gap in the first millennium A.D. like Non Nok Tha. Of these seven phases, the first two are contemporary with the Early Period at Non Nok Tha, and they have produced burials, some crouched in the Hoabinhian fashion, with burnished, cord-marked and incised pottery, a

socketed copper or bronze spearhead, and a bracelet of elephant ivory. The curvilinear incision found at Non Nok Tha is not paralleled until about 2000 B.C. at Ban Chiang, but the significance of this observation remains uncertain for the time being. The rice chaff temper is also present at Ban Chiang.

At Non Nok Tha, the Middle Period runs from approximately 3000 B.C. to A.D. 200, and the burials and basic pot forms continue right through. New pot forms appear, such as footed globular bowls and pedestalled shallow bowls like some of the Lungshanoid forms, but the cord-marking continues to dominate, and indeed the curvilinear incised and painted designs of the Early Period now disappear. The shell beads and stone adzes also continue, baked clay spindle whorls make an appearance, and the bronze finds become more frequent. Socketed bronze axes, bronze bracelets (17 on one burial alone), and a socketed bronze halberd have been found, together with the two-piece sandstone moulds for casting the axes (figure 7.10), and small pottery crucibles. The copper seems to have been smelted elsewhere to judge from the absence of slag in

Fig. 7.9. Non Nok Tha Pottery – Early Period: *left*, red-painted and footed vessel 23 cm high; *right*, cord-marked jar 15 cm high. From Solheim 1970.

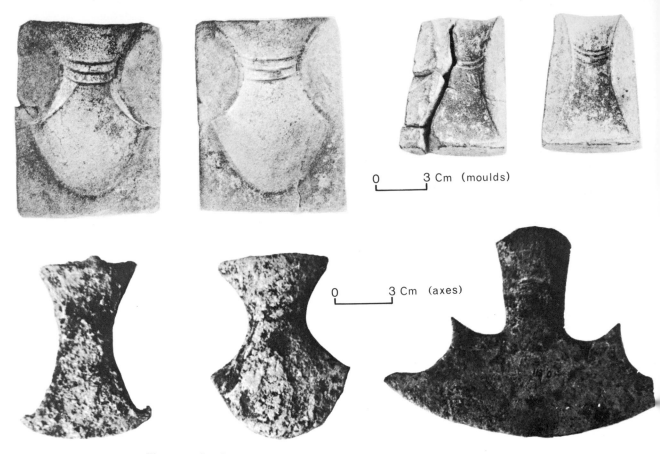

Fig. 7.10. Sandstone bivalve moulds and bronze axes from Non Nok Tha, Middle Period.

the site, and copper may have been traded in from sources 130 kilometres west or 100 kilometres north-west. Lead and tin were added in equal proportions to make the bronze, and the tin may have come from 300 kilometres to the north-east in Laos.

This period at Non Nok Tha is paralleled by Phases III-V at Ban Chiang, which run from 2000 to about 250 B.C. After 1600 B.C. red-on-buff incised and painted ware is common at Ban Chiang, and this develops between 1200 and 250 B.C. into the curvilinear painted pottery for which the site has recently become rather famous[25] (see figure 7.11). The well-known rollers with carved designs, perhaps for rolling motifs in pigment on cloth, also appear at this time. The most important discovery, however, is that iron was perhaps in use at the site between 1600 and 1200 B.C., in the form of an iron spearhead with a cast-on bronze socket, and a bronze bracelet with decorative strands of iron wire wound around the outside. Unfortunately, the painted pottery and iron does not seem to have been found at Non Nok Tha, and these dates for iron

are similar to those for the first use of the metal in Turkey and Western Asia. Clearly, a full report on the excavations will be required before these dates can be established as certain, but the Ban Chiang site may turn out to be the most remarkable ever excavated on the mainland of Southeast Asia.

As far as the bronzes are concerned, it is apparent that the techniques of casting, cold-working and annealing were in use at Ban Chiang from a very early date[26]. Furthermore, Bayard has recently suggested that the Non Nok Tha bronze industry most probably represents an indigenous and independent Southeast Asian innovation[27]. If the dates are correct, thus indicating bronze production from before 3000 B.C., then these Thai industries predate the earliest evidence for bronze in the Indus Valley Civilisation (c. 2500 B.C.), and in China (c. 2000 B.C.). But in Mesopotamia, bronze is found from the Uruk period (c. 3500 B.C.), and objects of hammered copper are known from Turkey prior to 7000 B.C.[28], so diffusion from this area cannot be ruled out. On the other hand, the Non Nok

Tha round-edged and socketed axes are clearly a local and long-lasting Southeast Asian form which has no precedent elsewhere. The socketed axes of central and northern China[29], Siberia and Europe have straight cutting edges, and do not commence much before the mid-second millennium B.C. In the Indus Valley and Mesopotamia, simple flat axes or shaft-hole forms are dominant, and these belong to a casting tradition which is not obviously related to that of Southeast Asia. Perhaps Thailand did witness an independent invention of copper and bronze metallurgy, although it would be premature to draw definite conclusions at the moment.

The Late Period at Non Nok Tha commences about A.D. 1000, after a gap in occupation which lasts through most of the first millennium A.D. Details of this period are not so significant for our purposes, but they include cremation burials in pots which are in the same ceramic tradition as those of the earlier periods, together with indications of an iron-using economy with wet-rice agriculture and water buffalo plough traction. Archaeologists working in Thailand seem to be in reasonable agreement that the iron, wet-rice and water buffalo complex appears widely from about 500 B.C.[30], and the iron may well be much earlier as we have seen. This complex then becomes a part of the development of the Indianized

kingdoms of the early first millennium A.D.

So far, the sites of Non Nok Tha and Ban Chiang are unique in Thailand and in the whole of Southeast Asia. Test excavations at another site called Non Nong Chik, near Non Nok Tha, have produced a sequence overlapping with the later part of the Middle Period[31], and another site called Kok Charoen in Lopburi Province (central Thailand) has produced extended burials with cord-marked pottery, stone adzes and some pieces of bronze; thermoluminescence dates place this site rather uncertainly between 1500 and 700 B.C.[32].

On a more general level of interpretation, D. Bayard[33] has presented a complex hypothesis which, amongst other proposals, has a spread of metallurgy by Thai-Kadai speaking peoples from northern Southeast Asia into the Huangho area of central China. This is a very risky hypothesis, but it is supported by Benedict's linguistic evidence that various terms for metals, domesticated animals, and rice were borrowed into Chinese before 1200 B.C. from an extinct Austro-Thai language, related to but not ancestral to present-day Thai, Kadai and Austronesian[34]. Whether one accepts Benedict's theories plus the early dates and their consequences or not, the present state of Thai archaeology is a rather exciting one.

Fig. 7.11. Red-painted pottery from Ban Chiang, north-eastern Thailand. Approximate heights (*left to right*) 23 cm, 36 cm, 23 cm. From van Esterik 1973.

LUNGSHANOID INFLUENCES IN THAILAND AND
MALAYA? THE BAN KAO CULTURE

Our interest in Thailand continues further, for
we still have some hitherto undiscussed sites which
provide rather different problems. These sites lie
in western and southern Thailand and northern
Malaya; they lack metals, their pottery is a little
different from that at Non Nok Tha and the
northern Thai sites, and their dates seem to be
later than those of Non Nok Tha. The Danish
archaeologist Per Sørensen has grouped these
sites together as the Ban Kao Culture[35], to which
he ascribes a Chinese Lungshanoid origin. Hence
we appear to have developing a confusing situation, with an indigenous and early bronze-using
culture in northern Thailand, and a slightly
later Neolithic culture to the south, of possible
Chinese origin. This is a little hard to accept,
but all we can do at present is to examine the
evidence and avoid drawing firm conclusions. As
we will see in due course, the evidence from
Indochina is not rigorous enough to be of much
assistance in sorting out the situation.

The key site of the Ban Kao Culture is a habitation site with extended inhumation burials at
Ban Kao, in Kanchanaburi Province to the west
of Bangkok. So far, only the burials have been
published[36]. There are 44 of them, all extended,
and because none overlap they appear to have
been laid to rest within a fairly short time, during
which the positions of existing burials were either
remembered or marked in some way. Radiocarbon dates suggest that the majority date to
between 2000 and 1300 B.C. The grave goods
include lenticular and rectangular-sectioned ungripped adzes, a small number of barbed or
knobbed projectile points, and bracelets and
necklaces of small perforated shell discs (figure
7.12). Pots were placed in large numbers at
heads and feet, and some of the bodies were
covered by pig skins. One burial contained a stone
phallus, and another, of an old man, contained
a perforated stone disc, and an antler with
sawn-off tines which Sørensen believes may
represent part of a shaman's headdress[37]. In
addition, the habitation levels of the site con-

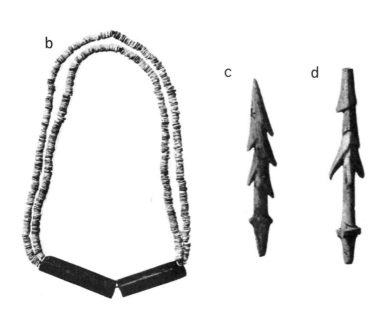

Fig. 7.12. Ban Kao grave-goods: (a)
worked antler, thought to be part of a
shaman's headdress, length 52 cm; (b)
necklace of shell discs and two jade or
nephrite tubes; (c, d) barbed bone
points, 10.5 and 13 cm long. From
Sørensen and Hatting 1967.

Fig. 7.13. Ban Kao vessels: upper five are described as early sub-phase, the lower five as late sub-phase. From Sørensen and Hatting 1967.

tained stone bracelets, stone net-sinkers, bone one-piece fishhooks, bone combs, clay bark-cloth beaters, clay spindle whorls, and crescentic stone knives.

The pottery has been divided by Sørensen into an early and a late group, the early having many footed, pedestalled and tripod-legged forms, the later having mostly round or flat-based vessels without feet of any kind (figure 7.13). Much of the pottery is cord-marked, and a few rare examples of incision are recorded, but there is no painting. The degree of variation in form is remarkable, and the excellent finish of most pots would suggest the use of a slow wheel. The tripods in particular serve to differentiate this site from Non Nok Tha and related sites to the north.

A number of reviewers have challenged Sørensen's conclusions about the date of the site, in particular the New Zealand archaeologist R.H. Parker[38], who feels that all the burials date to between 500 B.C. and A.D. 500. Two of the latest burials may be as late as this, because they contain iron tools, but the total absence of bronze would suggest that the majority are earlier, as Sørensen claims. Other extended burials with similar pottery are known from near to Ban Kao in the upper levels of Sai Yok Cave, and from an open site at Nong Chae Sao, where they were buried under the floor of a small house raised on piles. Sherds of the same type of pottery, including the tripods, have also been found in a cave at Buang Bep in peninsular Thailand. The whole Ban Kao Culture as known at present is predominantly a burial complex, and this restriction also applies to the related sites in Malaya.

The Malayan sites are all burial caves, the most important being Gua Cha in Kelantan Province, excavated by the British archaeologist Gale Sieveking in 1954[39]. The lower levels of this cave contained Hoabinhian tools and contracted and extended burials (see page 68), which were succeeded by Neolithic burials after a period of abandonment. The earliest of these retain the varied Hoabinhian postures, but contain handmade and cord-marked vessels with round or flat bases which, like the early ceramics at Spirit Cave and Gua Kechil, seem to be a late Hoabinhian development. However, the later Neolithic burials at Gua Cha belong to the Ban Kao Culture, and are all fully extended. The pottery (figure 7.14) is now made on a slow wheel, and is predominantly cord-marked, but there is some

rare curvilinear incision which resembles that from the Early Period at Non Nok Tha[40], and also the Neolithic pottery of Indochina. The Gua Cha pots lack tripods, and in this respect equate with the late Ban Kao pottery as defined by Sørensen. Some of the burials were found with ungripped adzes with lenticular or rectangular cross-sections, shell bead necklaces, shell spoons, and one had a cylindrical barkcloth beater of stone. Several bracelets of nephrite and marble were found in position on arms, and these had D- or T-shaped cross-sections. The latter are of particular interest, and as we will see later, are paralleled in second and first millennium B.C. contexts in Hong Kong and North Vietnam. Other unusual features at Gua Cha include votive groups and alignments of potsherds (without burials), and these are also reported from Non Nok Tha.

Elsewhere in northern Malaya, pottery of Ban Kao style has been found in a number of caves. These include Bukit Tengku Lembu in Perlis[41]; Gua Berhala in Kedah, which has produced some 30 perforated tripod legs[42]; and Gua Musang in Kelantan[43]. Like Gua Cha, none of these sites have absolute dates, but this situation may be partially remedied by Dunn's excavations at Gua Kechil in Pahang[44], where red-slipped pottery which appears to be in the Ban Kao tradition intrudes into the earlier traditions of corded and plain ware at around 3000 B.C. Some of these red-slipped sherds come from ring footed bowls made on a slow wheel, and there are also two bone projectile points, similar to but not identical to those from Ban Kao. Given the dates from Gua Kechil, and Ban Kao itself, we may say that the Ban Kao Culture spans the period roughly between 3000 and 1000 B.C.

The economy of the Ban Kan Culture is known only sketchily, but, as we have seen above, the site of Ban Kao has produced objects identified as barkcloth beaters, spindle whorls, and fishing equipment. The beating of barkcloth is evidently an Austronesian innovation, and prehistoric beaters on the mainland are only reported otherwise from South Vietnam and Malaya, both areas of Austronesian settlement. Furthermore, these beaters are all reported to be of stone (see figure 7.16), while the Ban Kao examples are rather strangely made of pottery. The spindle whorls suggest the spinning and weaving of vegetable fibres or cotton, and while the antiquity of the latter is unknown in Southeast Asia, cotton textiles are known from Mohenjo Daro in

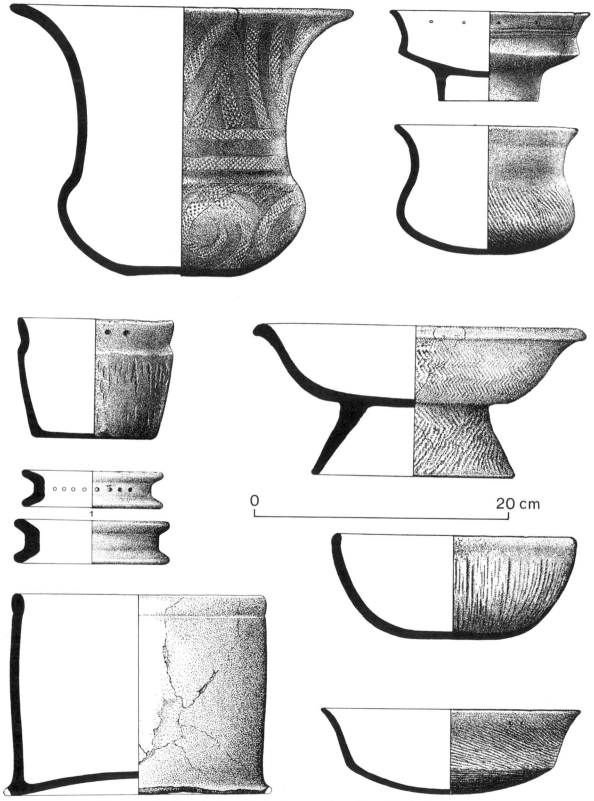

Fig. 7.14. Cord-marked and incised pottery from Gua Cha, including two
pot-stands at centre left. From Sieveking 1954.

Pakistan at about 2000 B.C. However, the absence of certainly identified sheep in the Southeast Asian Neolithic would seem to rule out wool. Dogs and bovids were present at Ban Kao, most probably domesticated on analogy with Non Nok Tha, and it would not be exceeding the bounds of probability to assume that rice agriculture was present. The nature of settlement is generally unknown, apart from the possible pile-dwelling at Nong Chae Sao mentioned above.

The external affinities of the Ban Kao Culture are a matter of some dispute at present. Sørensen has presented detailed arguments for a Lungshanoid derivation[45], specifically from the Yangtze Valley by a migration route up the Yangtze and possibly down the Salween River into Thailand. His arguments are too detailed to be examined closely here, but are concerned particularly with pottery types and the artefacts found in the 'shaman's grave' which was mentioned above. He also points out that the Ban Kao ceramics are not related to the Neolithic pottery of Indochina, which has much more incised decoration and different forms, including an absence of tripods. On the other hand, Ban Kao ceramics lack the cut-out ring feet which are common in the Lungshanoid, so the correspondences with China are by no means complete.

A major archaeological problem arises with the Ban Kao Culture, and this concerns the recognition of migrations from archaeological data. This problem is of course logically soluble, until one comes to examine actual evidence, at which point the logic often turns into a pipe-dream. The point about the Ban Kao Culture is that it may indeed resemble the Lungshanoid, but its non-ceramic artefacts are not out of place in the Southeast Asian Neolithic, and its pottery is in fact quite close to that of Non Nok Tha, particularly in the predominance of cord marking. My own view would be that the Ban Kao Culture is indigenous to Southeast Asia, and that it represents another aspect of the Thai-Malayan Neolithic as represented by the early levels at Non Nok Tha, with possible trade influences bringing tripods from the Yangtze, but perhaps little else. The sequences at Gua Cha and Gua Kechil, with their apparent Corded Ware to Ban Kao cultural continuity, would seem to support this view. Riverine trade along the major waterways of Southeast Asia is certainly very probable, and the degree of similarity shown by all Southeast Asian Neolithic cultures would argue for its operation. But in the Ban Kao case, the evidence is not sufficient to prove migration and colonisation from China.

The arguments for a high degree of indigenous development can be supported from physical anthropology. For instance, the Gua Cha burials do not suggest any degree of population replacement between the Hoabinhian and the Neolithic[46]. The Ban Kao skeletons appear to be similar to those of modern Thais[47], and some belonged to individuals who had probably suffered from beta-thalassemia – Hemoglobin E disease, which is wide-spread in Southeast Asia today, particularly amongst the indigenous Mon-Khmer speaking populations[48], but absent in China. Hence the bearers of the Ban Kao culture were most probably Southeast Asian indigenes, and may have had a fair degree of Australoid affinity in the case of Gua Cha. It is in fact conceivable that the Malayan sites may be associated with the local expansion of rice-growing populations into the rather peripheral peninsula formed by Malaya, which until the arrival of the Ban Kao Culture was occupied mainly by late Hoabinhian populations.

We may at this point note the general Neolithic isolation of Malaya and its apparent lack of connection with the early Austronesian cultures of eastern Indonesia and the Philippines. Southern Malaya is almost unknown archaeologically, apart from a few lenticular and quadrangular cross-sectioned adzes found at Tanjong Bunga in Johore[49], and Sumatra is almost a total blank for prehistory. While it may be premature to suggest that southern Malaya was a backwater in the Neolithic, this is what the evidence suggests at present, despite earlier opinions about its importance as an Austronesian migration route[50].

In conclusion, the Thai-Malayan Neolithic suggests the presence of a Corded Ware Culture Group from perhaps 6000 to 3000 B.C., represented by the late Hoabinhian levels at Spirit Cave, Gua Cha and Gua Kechil, with localised descendants represented by Non Nok Tha and its contemporaries in northern Thailand, and the Ban Kao Culture to the south. Hopefully, we should be able to see evidence of similar developments in Indochina, but before we turn to this area, it would be apposite to look briefly at that black sheep of Southeast Asian archaeology – the stone adze.

THE ADZE TYPES OF SOUTHEAST ASIA

Apart from potsherds, the most obvious feature

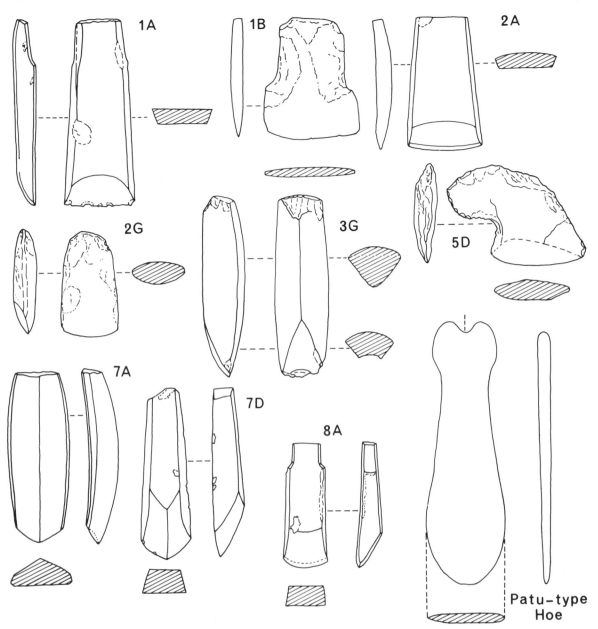

Fig. 7.15. Southeast Asian stone adzes, with Duff terminology. Provenances as follows: (1A) Luzon; (1B) Central Sulawesi; (2A) Java; (2G) North Vietnam; (3G) Luzon; (5D) Malaya; (7A) Sumatra; (7D) Malaya; (8A) Indochina; Patu-type hoe, Taiwan. After Duff 1970.

of museum collections of the Southeast Asian Neolithic is the stone adze. Unfortunately, the vast majority are undated and weakly provenanced, but this has not prevented adzes from being used as the bases of the most far-reaching syntheses on the area, particularly those of Robert Heine Geldern and Otley Beyer. Recent research has shown that these older syntheses are no longer fully tenable, although they still contain much

valuable and valid information. We will consider them in due course, after a brief excursion into adze typology and distribution, both of which have been exhaustively surveyed in a recent monograph by New Zealand archaeologist Roger Duff[51].

Duff's typology depends upon cross-section, and the presence or absence of a hafting device on the butt. The particular forms which are of significance in Southeast Asia (figure 7.15) are type 1A, with a rectangular section and stepped butt; type 1B, with a rectangular section and shouldered butt; type 2A, with a rectangular section and unmodified butt; and type 8, with a rectangular section and markedly shouldered butt. There are many sub-types within these groups, but these need not be discussed in detail. It is important to note that most of the tools are uni-bevelled adzes, as opposed to bi-bevelled axes, although the latter are found quite frequently, particularly with an oval or lenticular cross-section.

The basic adze form, which is common in most areas and phases of the Southeast Asian Neolithic, is the Duff type 2A – the simple quadrangular adze. This seems to be the ancestor for most of the later forms, and we have already noted its presence with early corded pottery in Spirit Cave (figure 7.3) and in Taiwan. The Spirit Cave dates place it as early as 6000 B.C., and this is the first clearly defined adze form to appear out of the milieu of Hoabinhian edge-grinding. These adzes are generally flaked to shape from a large core, and then ground and polished over much or all of their surfaces. Duff sees an Arctic origin for the type 2A adze, but the Spirit Cave dates must make a local development a strong possibility.

The type 2A quadrangular adze has a counterpart in another simple adze or axe with an oval or lenticular cross-section. This type would be 2F or 2G in the Duff classification, and as we will see, it has been a source of much confusion, because several authors have equated it with a culture and migration separate from that which produced the quadrangular adze. These attempts to read cultures and migrations from adzes alone are now almost completely rejected by prehistorians, and the oval forms turn up sporadically with or without the other Duff types in many areas. They are dominant forms in Melanesia and Australia, and the case of Melanesia is an important one which we will later consider. But otherwise, in a Southeast Asian context they appear to be the result of shaping hard rocks by hammer-dressing, which tends to give a rounded section[52], while the quadrangular forms are flaked from more tractable rocks such as basalts. A similar differentiation can be observed in Polynesia. Sometimes the oval forms have waisted or necked hafting devices which again appear to be closely related to the hammer-dressing technique, and these types are found in Australia,

eastern Indonesia and Melanesia, as well as in Japan and north-eastern Asia. Whether these occurrences are connected by diffusion is unknown.

The later developments from the type 2A adze are centred, according to Duff, on three focal areas. The first is southern China, which spreads influences through the southern Ryukyus, Taiwan and the Philippines. The second is northern Indochina, which influences Indochina itself, together with Thailand and northern Malaya. The third is placed by Duff around Singapore, and this influences most of southern and eastern Indonesia. The foci of Duff are based entirely on adze distribution, and are therefore schematic and not intended to imply small localised innovating centres.

The southern Chinese focus is characterised by the type 2A adze (which is found everywhere), the stepped 1A, and the slightly shouldered type 1B. The stepped 1A and shouldered 1B forms occur in the southern Lungshanoid cultures to as far north as the Yangtze, but in central China the simpler untanged 2A varieties are characteristic of both the Yang-shao and the Lungshanoid cultures, although quite a number in the latter are perforated. On Taiwan, the stepped 1A is mysteriously absent in the Lungshanoid, but it is present, together with a shouldered form like the 1B, in the Yüan-shan Culture which will be described in the next chapter. The type 1B also spread into the southern Ryukyu Islands, but is here undated[53]. Taiwan also has a peculiar 'boot-shaped axe' (compare figure 7.5 [c]) with mainland Chinese parallels[54], as well as shouldered hoes and 'patu-shaped' hoes which may be of quite recent date. The term 'patu' refers to a well-known New Zealand Maori weapon, which in reality is probably unconnected with the Taiwanese hoes. In the Philippines, adze forms 1A, 1B and 2A are common, and in addition there are forms with triangular cross-sections, and round-sectioned chisels and gouges, which overlap considerably with the Polynesian adze forms. Of all the Southeast Asian areas, the Philippines are the closest to Polynesia, despite the absence of the majority of the shared forms in the intervening areas of Melanesia and Micronesia.

The northern Indochinese focus is characterised by the absence of the stepped type 1A, and the development of the markedly shouldered type 8. The simple type 2 adzes are common, as indeed they are in all areas, and the forms with oval or lenticular cross-sections are quite frequent. At

Sai Yok and Ban Kao, for instance, all three forms occur together – types 2A, 2G and 8. To the west, type 2 and type 8 adzes extend as far as Assam and Yünnan, and on into north-eastern India[55], but the whole question of Indian links with Southeast Asia in prehistoric times is hampered at present by an almost total lack of archaeological information from Burma.

The third focus has its main expression in Malaya and western Indonesia. The basic type 2 is again widespread, but the lenticular sectioned and hammer-dressed forms have only been found to date in Malaya and Sulawesi. Northern Sulawesi has a few stepped 1A adzes which clearly link it with the Philippines. However, two distinct adze forms were developed in the Malayan-Indonesian area – the pick adze of western Indonesia (Duff types 7A, B, C), and the beaked adze of Malaya (types 7D, E). One of the Gua Cha burials was provided with a beaked adze, and most of the archaeological assemblages of Malaya and western Indonesia appear to be restricted to types 2 and 7[56].

Duff's recognition of three foci is fairly sound on distributional grounds, although the differences between his types 1B and 8 (i.e. the shouldered forms) appear to be rather insignificant. For this reason his southern Chinese and northern Indochinese foci can only really be distinguished by the absence of the stepped type 1A in the latter. The stepped 1A adzes had certainly developed by 2000 B.C. in Taiwan, while the shouldered and beaked or pick forms may have developed slightly later in their areas of distribution. As we will see, stone adzes continue in use well on into the Metal Age, and almost to the present in some areas. There are also a number of highly idiosyncratic tool types which appear to represent localised developments. These include the 'Tembeling Knives' of northern Malaya[57], and the waisted *chichivchiv* axes of Botel Tobago and southern Taiwan[58], but in both cases dates are unknown.

Another stone artefact type of some importance in Southeast Asia is the barkcloth beater. These are of various forms (figure 7.16), such as the horned types of Taiwan and the Philippines, the cylindrical types of Malaya (like the example from Gua Cha), and the straight-backed beaters of the Philippines and Vietnam. Sulawesi, the Philippines and Malaya have an unusual form hafted in a rattan handle, which is paralleled, perhaps through prehistoric contact, in Mexico[59]. One of the most significant points about these barkcloth beaters is that they are generally found only in Island Southeast Asia and its closest mainland fringes, particularly in Austronesian speaking areas, while most of the mainland sites produce spindle whorls instead. This may be an early reflection of a strong Austronesian tradition of barkcloth rather than woven clothing, a tradition which is still of course of paramount importance in Oceania.

AN ADZE-BASED MIGRATION THEORY

In the year 1932 a whole new perspective was given to Southeast Asian prehistory by the publication of an article entitled 'Urheimat und früheste Wanderungen der Austronesier'[60], by the Austrian prehistorian Robert Heine Geldern. What had previously been a rather hopeless obscurity was suddenly brought to clarity, and this work was to dominate Southeast Asian prehistory for thirty years or more. From our present vantage point, we can now see that his overall interpretations were incorrect, although with the evidence to hand in 1932 he can hardly be criticised because of this. In company with many other scholars of his day, his interpretation was necessarily based on a view of rather simplistic diffusionism.

Heine Geldern began his reconstruction with the simple oval or lenticular-sectioned adze – the 'Walzenbeil' – which he felt to be a type fossil of the earliest Eurasian Neolithic. Partly because of the rarity of this form in western Indonesia and on the Southeast Asian Mainland, the spread of the Walzenbeilkultur was seen as the result of a migration from northern China or Japan, through Taiwan and the Philippines, and into eastern Indonesia and Melanesia. The original inhabitants of western Melanesia adopted this culture, together with the Papuan (non-Austronesian) languages, which Heine Geldern thought were introduced by Mongoloids owing to their present existence amongst Mongoloid populations in northern Halmahera. This migration also brought coiled pottery, perhaps secret societies and dancing masks, and Heine Geldern attributed the 'partial Neolithicisation' of Australia to it.

In the light of present knowledge, it can be stated firmly that the Walzenbeilkultur as envisaged by Heine Geldern has not stood the test of time. Certainly, the Walzenbeil adzes (Duff types 2F and G) are an early form; they appear in the mainland Bacsonian, predate the type 2A adzes at Niah Cave, and appear to have a continuous ancestry going back over 20,000 years in northern Australia and New Guinea. The form is in fact indigenous to Southeast Asia, and does not appear to be associated with any kind of migrating culture. Furthermore, the Papuan languages of New Guinea seem to be the original indigenous stock, and the only possibility remaining in favour of Heine Geldern's original reconstruction is a possible spread of coiled pottery from Japan or China. As we will see, even this is still a weak hypothesis.

The next migration according to Heine Geldern was marked by the spread of the Schulterbeil (shouldered adze, Duff types 1B and 8) from north-eastern India into Southeast Asia. The Schulterbeilkultur was associated with people of Austroasiatic speech, a language group which today includes the Mon and Khmer languages, Semang and Senoi of Malaya, Vietnamese, and some of the languages of Burma and Assam. These people appear to have been Mongoloids of unknown origin, and they penetrated to Taiwan, the Philippines and Japan. But again, the Schulterbeilkultur has dissolved with the passage of time, and the shouldered adzes are probably the result of late Neolithic local elaboration within Southeast Asia. Recent excavations at the site of Sham Wan on Lamma Island, Hong Kong, have shown that here the shouldered adzes appear within the first millennium B.C. in a stratigraphic context well above the first simple 2A adzes[61].

Heine Geldern's third migration is still by far the most important. This involved the Vierkant-beilkultur, characterised by the quadrangular

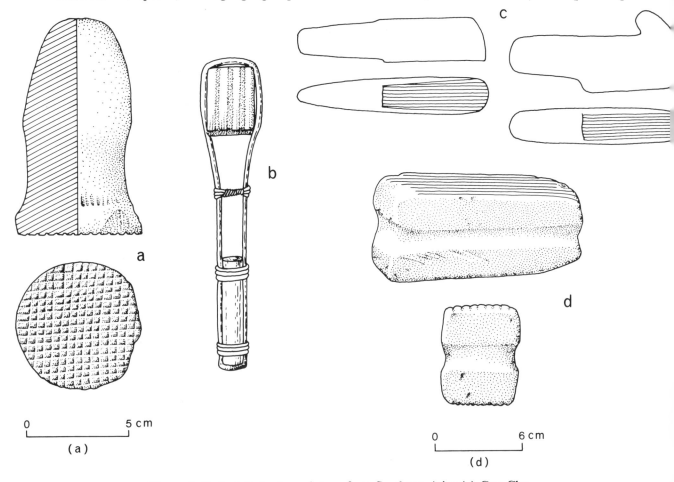

Fig. 7.16. Bark-cloth beaters of stone from Southeast Asia: (a) Gua Cha, Malaya (after Sieveking 1956); (b) Sulawesi, with rattan handle (after Ling 1962); (c) straight-backed and horned Philippine types (after Beyer 1948); (d) Cebu, Philippines (after Beyer 1948). (b) and (c) are not to scale.

type 2A adze, which was carried by early Austronesians (the Uraustronesier) from China into Southeast Asia in the first half of the second millennium B.C. Heine Geldern traced the Vierkantbeilkultur back to the Danubian Neolithic cultures of Europe, and stressed its close relationship to the Yang-shao Culture. It was, he thought, associated with stone sawing techniques, cord- and basket-impressed pottery made with paddle and anvil, lanceheads of slate, bone arrowheads, stone and shell rings and beads, pile-dwellings, rice and millet agriculture, domesticated pigs and cattle, megalithic monuments, headhunting, outrigger canoes, and possibly barkcloth manufacture. The Vierkantbeilkultur mixed with the Schulterbeilkultur (according to Heine Geldern) in the areas where the latter was found, but a fairly pure group of the former (i.e. the Uraustronesians) managed to get through very rapidly into southern Malaya, at this time still a Palaeolithic backwater, where they developed ocean-going outrigger canoes, and began the first Austronesian migrations eastward through Indonesia. These migrations followed two major routes – one along the southern Indonesian Islands to New Guinea, the other through Borneo, the Philippines, Taiwan, and on to Japan. At this point Heine Geldern went on to consider Polynesian and Melanesian origins, but we will leave this particular set of problems until later.

We may now ask how such a remarkable reconstruction has stood the test of forty years of research. The basic three stage migration theory quite clearly has not. The Walzenbeilkultur does not exist, and there is no stratigraphic evidence whatsoever for the Schulterbeilkultur. Strangely enough, Heine Geldern based a good deal of his reconstruction on an assumed sequence for the Japanese Neolithic, a rather unsound crutch at that time, and also of course he grossly overemphasised the evidence from stone adzes. On the other hand, his Vierkantbeilkultur is quite an accurate distillation of the broad polythetic assemblage represented by the Southeast Asian Neolithic, within which the Walzenbeile and Schulterbeile are rather insignificant localised variants. But there is in fact no such thing as a migrating Vierkantbeilkultur at about 1750 B.C. from which came the Austronesians, for the Vierkantbeile themselves go back to at least 6000 B.C., and the early Austronesians have had little traceable contact with the mainland, least of all with Malaya.

Heine Geldern's theory therefore passes into limbo, but not without its deserved quota of praise. Some of its more stultifying aspects w ll be examined in due course, particularly in the Philippines. But it is interesting to observe how migration loses its credibility as an all-embracing form of explanation as the amount of reliable archaeological data increases. While still a vital and valid concept, its real heyday in Southeast Asia is past.

THE NEOLITHIC SITES AND CULTURES OF INDOCHINA

Now that we have surveyed the Neolithic cultures of China, Thailand and Malaya, together with some aspects of Neolithic adze typology, we can turn to the last but not the least of the mainland regions. Indochina comprises the modern states of Cambodia, Laos, and North and South Vietnam, and remains in a rather confused archaeological state despite a century of sporadic research[62]. This of course means that it is not yet possible to see in full perspective the dated sequences recovered from territories on either side, in particular those from Thailand and Taiwan. But because Indochina is undoubtedly an area of importance for both Indonesian and Austronesian prehistory, some attempt at a synthesis is required, and at this point I propose to examine some of the Neolithic sites, leaving those sites with a metal component for a later section.

Despite the potential barrier to communication offered by the Annamite Mountain chain, the Neolithic sites of Indochina reveal a high degree of homogeneity. For several millennia, there appears to have been considerable contact between settled areas, undisturbed by any major influx of new styles or ideas. The basic assemblage shows little variation: adze of Duff types 2A and 8, stone and shell bracelets and earrings, spindle whorls, corded and especially incised pottery in a restricted range of shapes, and a small range of pendants and other ornaments. Economic evidence is rather restricted at present, but it seems that some circular earthwork enclosures in Cambodia could be Neolithic, and thus suggestive evidence for a degree of settled village life[63].

Cambodia Cambodia does at least have the benefit of a single dated site, in the cave of Laang Spean, Battambang Province[64]. We have already considered this site with the Hoabinhian, and it is of interest because it has pottery and Hoabinhian stone tools co-existing from about 4000 B.C., perhaps into the first millennium A.D. The ceramic assemblage is very limited, and comprises sherds of pottery with horizontal bands of incised or pointillée decoration (figure 7.17 [o]), arranged in very simple motifs which would not be out of place anywhere in the Indochinese Neolithic. One unusual piece is a pedestal pot with pointillée decoration, which probably dates from about 500 B.C. Unfortunately, adzes and ornaments are absent from the assemblage.

Moving eastward, to a point about 30 kilometres south-east of Cambodia's great inland lake, we come to one of the most intriguing and mysterious sites ever reported in Southeast Asia. The site, called Somrong Sen, consists of a mound, about 350 metres long by 200 wide, and up to 5.5 metres deep. Its archaeological importance was noted as early as 1876, and sporadic trenches have since been dug into it at various times. Two important investigations were published by Henri Mansuy in 1902 and 1923[65], and these form the basis of our present knowledge.

The Somrong Sen mound was built up partly as a result of the dumping of freshwater shells, and partly by flood silt deposited by a neighbouring stream. The stratigraphy comprises an upper layer one metre thick with debris from modern settlements, and below this comes the archaeological layer which is 4.5 metres thick, and built of silt, localised shell middens, and scattered charcoal. A recent French report announces a carbon date from shell of 1280±120 B.C. (c. 1500 B.C. if calibrated) from only 1.5 metres down inside the archaeological layer[66]. If the date is correct, then Somrong Sen should span a very long prehistory.

Unfortunately, as one might expect, we have no stratigraphic information about the objects recovered. Some items of bronze have been recovered in very suspicious circumstances, and we will leave discussions of these until later. The Neolithic assemblage (figure 7.17) appears to be homogeneous, and it is outstandingly rich. Amongst the diagnostic items are adzes of Duff types 2 (rectangular and lenticular cross-sections) and 8, bracelets and rings of *Tridacna* and *Hippopus* shell or stone, perforated shell plaques, grooved pottery net sinkers and pottery spindle whorls, bone fishhooks and points, and a number of other unusual bone and shell ornaments. Of particular interest are penannular rings of limestone, of a type present in many other prehistoric Indochinese sites, which appear to be earrings. Other important items are beads of shell or limestone, unusual pottery anvils (for potting?) and pounders, and pulley-shaped pot-

tery earplugs with incised cross designs (figure 7.18), which resemble similar objects in schist from megalithic sites in north-eastern Laos (see below). Apart from an absence of stone knives or points, this assemblage represents the greater part of the known Neolithic artefact range from Southeast Asia.

Somrong Sen pottery is all hand-made, and apart from one round-based cord-marked jar, is entirely decorated by incision and pointillée. The forms and decorative motifs are particularly varied, as may be seen from figure 7.18, and far exceed those of any other Southeast Asian Neolithic site. Many of the Somrong Sen artefacts are probably funerary, for scattered and fragmentary human bones were found in the site, perhaps from burials damaged by flooding, One is left with the nagging suspicion that one of the most flamboyant and innovative Neolithic settlements in Indochina requires further investigation before it is too late. And could complete burials be found, they might add authenticity to our image of the well-dressed Neolithic villager of Cambodia, with his shining panoply of necklaces, bracelets, anklets and ear ornaments.

Vietnam Most of the evidence for the Indochinese Neolithic comes from North Vietnam, and only a few scattered and rather minor finds are known from South Vietnam and Laos[67]. Therefore I propose to deal first with North Vietnam, even though the scattered nature of the material recovered so far does not allow a neat presentation.

According to the Russian archaeologist P. I. Boriskovsky and the Vietnamese archaeologist Nguyen Phuc Long[68], the North Vietnamese Neolithic may be divided into Early, Middle and Late phases. The Early Neolithic corresponds to the Bacsonian, while the Middle Neolithic, with estimated dates between 6000 and 4000 B.C., has two major sites – the shell mound at Da-But, described in chapter 3 as basically a Hoabinhian site after Patte's original report, and a flaking area for Duff type 2 adzes at Dong-Khoi, near the city of Thanh-Hoa. Waste flakes of basalt apparently cover an area of 1.5 kilometres in diameter at Dong-Khoi, and a few roughed-out or finished adzes were found, none of which were shouldered.

Boriskovsky and Nguyen group the great majority of the Neolithic sites of North Vietnam as Late Neolithic, with estimated dates between 4000 and 2000 B.C. These dates may be a little

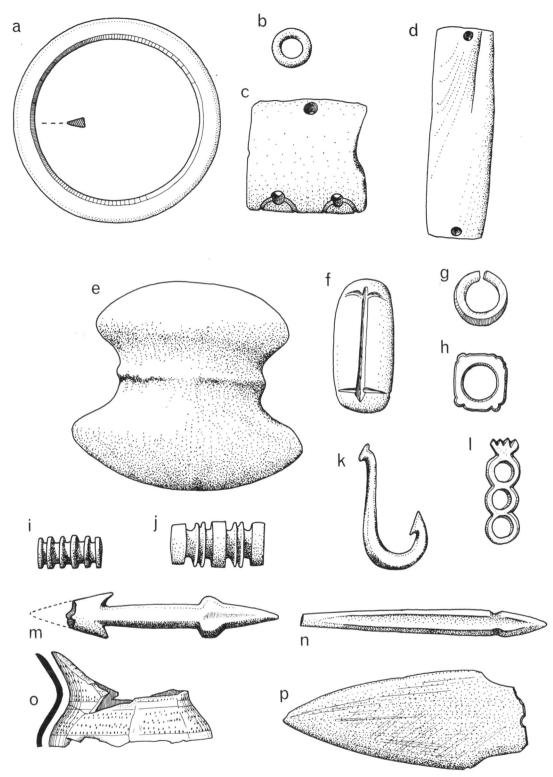

Fig. 7.17. Artefacts of the Indochinese Neolithic, mainly from Somrong Sen (after Mansuy 1902, 1923) unless otherwise stated:

(a) stone bracelet, diameter 78 mm; (b) stone ring, diameter 15 mm; (c) perforated shell, possibly a bracelet fragment, 45 by 43 mm; (d) shell pendant, length 80 mm; (e) ceramic potter's anvil, max. diameter 87 mm; (f) pottery net sinker, length 50 mm; (g) limestone earring, diameter 19 mm; (h) shell or limestone ring, 20 mm square; (i) pottery roller, perhaps for printing designs on cloth, length 30 mm; (j) pottery roller from Ban Chiang, Thailand, length unknown (after Griffin 1973); (k) bone fishhook, length 7 mm; (l) shell (?) pendant, size unknown; (m) bone point, length 80 mm; (n) bone point, length 93 mm; (o) pot with incised and pointillée decoration, diameter 120 mm, from Laang Spean (after Mourer and Mourer 1970); (p) polished schist point with basal perforation from Binh Ca, length 90 mm (after Mansuy 1920).

Fig. 7.18. Somrong Sen: pots (1–4); incised ceramic decoration (5–21); incised pottery earplugs (22–29). Not to scale. From Boriskovsky 1968–71.

early, and so far there are no published carbon dates for the phase. The diagnostic artefacts of the Late Neolithic appear to be wheel-made pottery and the shouldered Duff type 8 adze, although the latter are almost unknown in the Red River basin. Major expansion into the Red River Delta probably began in this phase, and it is here that the most spectacular recent discoveries have been made. The following paragraphs list some finds which may belong to the Late Neolithic – it is impossible to be certain in many cases – proceeding from south to north.

In the southern part of North Vietnam, many sites were investigated by French archaeologists in the 1920s and 1930s, and while the artefacts are often well described, there is very little stratigraphic information. At Bau-Tro, in Quang-Binh province, an occupation level in a sand dune[69] has yielded adzes of Duff types 2 and 8, flint blades, a number of grooved polishing stones, perhaps for sharpening adzes or points, and corded and incised potsherds which may have belonged to round bottomed vessels. Some sherds have ochre painted designs, but they were too small for the motifs to be preserved. Similar assemblages are known from other sites in the area, and more fragments of red painted pottery have been recovered from a cave at Minh-Cam, close to Bau-Tro. Colani[70] reports sherds of incised and pointillée pottery, similar to those from Laang Spean in Cambodia, from other caves in Quang-Binh province, and this type of decoration seems to be the most common in Indochina. The painted sherds at Minh-Cam and Bau-Tro are apparently quite unique.

From the provinces of Nghe-An and Thanh-Hoa in central North Vietnam, other Neolithic cave sites are reported by Saurin[71]. Again the adzes are of types 2 and 8, and there are also stone bracelets, and pulley-shaped pottery ear-plugs like those from Somrong Sen. At a rock-shelter called Cho-Ganh in Ninh-Binh province, a manufacturing area for limestone and jade bracelets was discovered by Colani[72]. In most of these sites the usual incised pottery is found, sometimes with comb-incision like that from the Plain of Jars in Laos, and sometimes with stamped circles, these being a common motif in the Taiwanese Yüan-shan and Philippine Neolithic cultures. Whether these parallels are of significance remains to be seen, and the literature holds many more of a similarly imprecise nature.

In the northern part of the country, a number of Neolithic settlements have been excavated by North Vietnamese archaeologists in recent years, evidently with outstanding results[73]. At present, it is a little difficult to assess these findings, particularly as I have no detailed reports available to me. The richest site appears to be Phung-Nguyen, in the Red River Delta area a little north of Hanoi. This site is a low mound, covering 150 by 50 metres, with a cultural stratum about 80 cm thick. Over 3800 square metres have been excavated by Vietnamese archaeologists, and the assemblage includes Duff type 2 adzes, axes and hoes (shouldered forms, generally rare in the Red River region, are absent); stone bracelet fragments, some having flanges like those from Gua Cha in Malaya and Hong Kong; grooved polishing stones of the very common Indochinese type; and wheel-made kiln-fired pottery. Ring feet, and cord-marked and comb-incised decoration are common ceramic features, but many pots were decorated with impressions from carved stone dies or paddles. One problem is that wheel-made and carved-paddle-impressed pottery belongs to the late second and first millennia B.C. in southern China, yet Vietnamese archaeologists date Phung-Nguyen to *c.* 3000 B.C., which on these grounds seems very early, but certainly possible. Also from this site and other contemporary ones have been recovered rice grains, and bones of pig, cattle and chicken. From the Thai evidence related above it is very likely that these were domesticated, and baked clay figurines of cattle, dogs, pigs and chickens have also been found.

A little south of Hanoi lies a similar site at Van-Dien, where over 275 hoes, axes and adzes of type 2 have been found, together with so many bracelet fragments that it has been suggested[74] they may have formed some kind of exchange medium. On the basis of parallels in Melanesia and Micronesia, this is in fact a very attractive hypothesis, and would explain why stone rings, many too small to be bracelets and too large to be finger rings, should be so common in Indochinese Neolithic sites. Many of these items have of course been found round wrists and ankles in the Thai and Malayan sites, but a combined function of ornament and money is still not unlikely. The same might well apply to the common stone and shell beads.

Elsewhere in the northern part of North Vietnam, a number of sites have yielded the basic assemblage of shouldered and untanged adzes, corded pottery, and stone and shell rings[75]. Additional unusual items include three slate points like those of the Taiwanese Neolithic, one with a tang, from an unknown locality at Binh-Ca in Tuyen-Quang province (figure 7.17 [p])[76], and fragments of perforated and incised pots from a rock-shelter at Mai-Pha, near Lang-Son, which Mansuy has interpreted as burners for making vegetable perfumes[77]. We might finally mention some of the most remarkable objects of all, which are the flaked musical stone bars which appear to have belonged to lithophones; a lithophone being a kind of stone-keyed xylophone which may have produced music on a scale similar to that of the Indonesian gamelan. Finely flaked stone bars of this type have been found mainly in South Vietnam, especially at a locality called Ndut-Lieng-Krak, Darlac province, but unfortunately it is really only by guesswork that they can be called Neolithic. Condominas has even suggested that they have Bacsonian affinities, but this seems rather unlikely given the excellence of their flaking[78].

The Indochinese Neolithic as a whole does seem to present a fair degree of homogeneity, with some local variation represented by the Red River sites. As far as we can see, the other sites share a basic polythetic assemblage which differs from that in the other Southeast Asian Neolithic areas mainly in the high frequency of incised pottery and shouldered adzes. The penannular earrings and the pulley-shaped earplugs are also quite distinctive, but the former are present outside Indochina in Hong Kong. Generally, we see a gradation into the Neolithic cultures of Thailand and Malaya, and a similar gradation into those of southern China and Taiwan. But there are no very close links with the developing Austronesian cultures of Indonesia and the Philippines, as we will see in due course. Of the tempo of development in Indochina we know little, because of the absence of dates. There is obviously a good deal of continuity from the Hoabinhian, and the homogeneity of the Neolithic sites would suggest that new innovations spread widely. But fundamental conclusions escape us for the time being, and we pass on to consider the developing bronze and iron using cultures of the first millennium B.C.

METAL AGE CULTURES IN SOUTHEAST ASIA

In the earlier part of this chapter evidence was presented which suggested that the Metal Age may have begun in Thailand by or before 3000 B.C. At present this evidence is rather isolated,

and otherwise we can only recognise a definite and wide-spread use of metal in Southeast Asia from about 1500 B.C. Because bronze and iron are in use together in most sites, I use the term 'Metal Age' rather than try to separate a bronze from an iron age. Non Nok Tha might of course represent a 'Bronze Age' if we choose to use European archaeological terminology, but this term is a little too specific for application to Southeast Asia at the present time.

In the mid and later first millennium B.C., the Southeast Asian mainland and Indochina come under the influence of the distinctive Dong-Son style of bronze metallurgy, which appears to be centred on North Vietnam and the southern fringe of China. Prior to the discoveries at Non Nok Tha, virtually all pre-Han bronzes in the area were attributed to this style, which is characteristically represented on a variety of bronze objects such as drums, situlae and ceremonial axes. However, before describing these developments, it is necessary to bring the area into perspective with a rather rapid review of Bronze and Iron Age developments in China.

In central China, the developed Lung-shan Culture Group, which follows Chang's Lung-shanoid, is succeeded by a literate bronze-using civilisation, historically associated with the Shang Dynasty (traditionally dated to c. 1600 to 1027 B.C.). The essential details of this civilisation need only concern us briefly, and they include elaborate piece-mould bronze casting, the earliest known examples of the Chinese script, and a centralised aristocratic form of government associated with royal burials of a most spectacular kind, reminiscent of the Royal Tombs of Ur in Mesopotamia. This is the first of the great Chinese civilisations, and it may have reached a level of considerable urbanisation, demonstrated perhaps by the great unexcavated earthen walled enclosure of 3.4 square kilometres at Cheng-chou in Honan Province. Shang civilisation was clearly in contact with steppe societies to the west, but seems to have had relatively little impact on the Neolithic societies of southern China.

The Western Chou period, which succeeds the Shang, dates from about 1027 to 771 B.C. In style of civilisation, this represents a continuation of the Shang, but during this period bronze metallurgy spreads to as far south as Chekiang Province, where it is associated with an important kind of geometrically stamped pottery. In the following Eastern Chou period (770 to 222 B.C.) there comes the first definite evidence for irrigation in China together with the introduction of cast iron metallurgy at about 600 B.C. or a little later. Urbanisation develops further in the form of regularly laid-out earthen walled cities, and now we see the archaeological appearance, between 600 and 200 B.C., of a powerful state known as Ch'u[79] in the Middle Yangtze region to as far south as Hunan Province. As a centre of superb bronzeworking, Ch'u has an undoubted importance in any consideration of the Dong-Son Style.

The Chou dynasty closes with the eventual unification of China in 221 B.C. by the emperor Ch'in Shih Huang Ti, and with the later establishment of the Han dynasty in 206 B.C. In 111 B.C. North Vietnam was conquered by a Han army, and organised as a province of the Chinese Empire, although fairly direct Chinese interference in the affairs of North Vietnam seems to have commenced as early as 256 B.C.[80]. In fact a good part of the time-span of the Dong-Son Culture in North Vietnam may fall into this early period of Chinese influence.

Before we close this potted version of Chinese early civilisation and move on to Dong-Son, we should perhaps return briefly to the geometrically stamped pottery mentioned above, which Chang[81] sees as a marker of a 'Geometric horizon', comparable to his preceding Lungshanoid horizon. The Geometric pottery is spread very widely in south-eastern China south of the Yangtze (but not in the Ch'u province) through the first millennium B.C., and its influence eventually reaches Taiwan, and perhaps the Philippines and Indonesia, although the latter spread is too late to concern us[82]. Chang believes the development to be a product of Shang and Western Chou influences in otherwise Neolithic areas, and a very large number of sites are known to belong to the horizon. The pottery is often hand-made, and round-bottomed short-necked vessels are very common. The elegant forms and painted styles of some of the Lungshanoid cultures fade out of fashion, and the geometric pottery is simply stamped over most of its surface, with a carved wooden or stone die of some type, in patterns composed of regularly repeated geometric forms (figure 7.19). This kind of geometric stamping is quite clearly paralleled in Shang ceramics in the Huangho region. The Geometric material

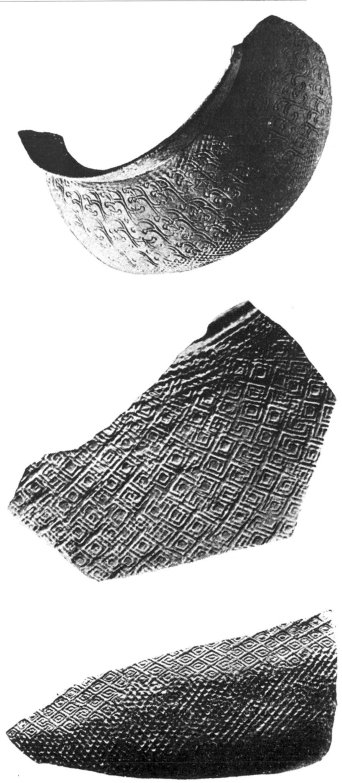

Fig. 7.19. Geometric pottery from Lamma Island, Hong Kong. The top piece shows the double-F pattern. From Finn 1958.

culture is basically that of the earlier Neolithic cultures of the area, but during this period of Eastern Chou and Ch'u expansion after 600 B.C., bronze and iron tools make their appearance in the south-eastern coastal regions of China.

The bronze objects found with the later Geometric sites in the south-east include socketed axes with splayed, fan-shaped or lunate cutting edges, tanged or socketed arrowheads or spearheads, and halberds and daggers, together with occasional rarer forms such as fishhooks. Other cultural materials associated with these bronzes are well represented in Kwangtung and Hong Kong, and in the latter area there are well-reported assemblages from sites on Lamma Island[83] (figure 7.20) and Lantau Island[84]. The non-metallic artefacts include the stepped and untanged stone adzes (types 1A, 1B and 2A); stone rings and bracelets, some having T-shaped cross-sections similar to the examples from North Vietnam, Gua Cha and Shang China; smaller penannular 'earrings'; and lancet or triangular shaped ground stone points, many with grooved bases. The Hong Kong sites as well as some of the sites in the Hai-feng district of Kwangtung examined by Maglioni[85], have yielded quite a lot of

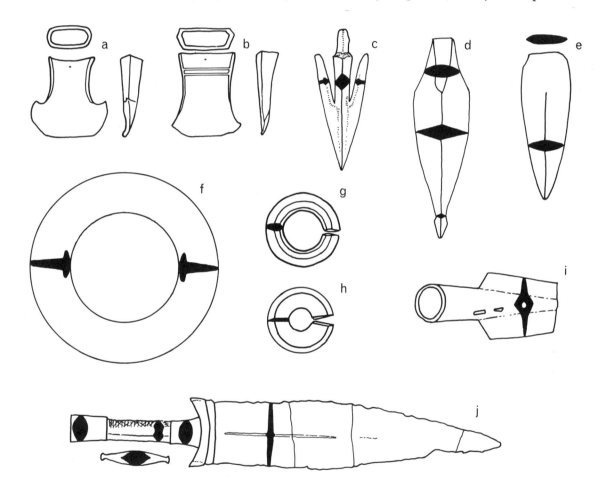

Fig. 7.20. Artefacts from the Geometric horizon on Lamma Island, Hong Kong: (a, b) socketed bronze axes(x 0.4); (c) barbed bronze arrowhead (x 0.4); (d, e) polished stone projectile points(x 0.4); (f) T-sectioned stone ring(x 0.6); (g, h) penannular jade earrings(x 0.75); (i) socketed bronze spearhead(x 0.4); (j) bronze dagger(x 0.4). After Finn 1958.

Fig. 7.21. Bronze drum of Heger type I in the Musée National, Phnom Penh. Tympanum approximately 65 cm diameter.

pottery stamped with a double F pattern, which appears to be derived from Chinese bronze motifs. Although there is not total agreement on the date of this ware, it is generally taken to indicate a date within the Eastern Chou period, and Finn places it between 500 and 250 B.C. This means that these bronze-bearing sites of mid or late Geometric aspect are contemporary with the Dong-Son sites to the immediate south-west.

THE DONG-SON STYLE OF BRONZE METALLURGY

The Dong-Son Style is the classic expression of prehistoric and protohistoric bronze metallurgy in Southeast Asia, and objects in the style occur in Thailand, Malaya, Indochina, and on through Indonesia to as far as the western tip of Irian Jaya. The Indonesian group will be examined in the next chapter. I should mention here that I use the term 'Dong-Son Style' to refer to the related assemblages found over the whole area, while the term 'Dong-Son Culture' refers to the focal North Vietnamese area, with its dense concentration of find spots and sites in the Red River Valley and Thanh-Hoa regions[86]. Due to

the relative lack of knowledge about the areas outside North Vietnam, it is not clear whether one can talk of a Dong-Son Culture Group at the present time, and use of the term 'style' does not therefore imply a basic commonality of culture through the whole area. Many of the objects were probably imports rather than indigenous products in the outer areas of distribution.

The Dong-Son Style is known mainly from bronze objects, and iron, while present in the more important mainland sites, was used mainly for utilitarian tools and weapons without decoration. The most famous Dong-Son artefact is the drum of bronze with a flat top, bulbous rim, straight sides and splayed foot (figure 7.21), which has been found throughout the whole area of distribution. Technically, these drums are referred to as Heger type I, and they have been found with rich and important burial assemblages at the eponymous site of Dong-Son near Thanh-Hoa, at Viet-Khe near Haiphong, and also at Shih-chai-shan near Lake Tien in Yünnan. Bronze drums have been used widely in Southeast Asia over the past 2000 years; there are

Fig. 7.22. Rubbing of the tympanum of a Heger type I drum from Yünnan, 70.5 cm diameter. The main frieze shows saddle-roofed houses with peacocks above, persons beating drums, and dancers with headdresses. The four-footed structures are possibly altars. From Bernatzik 1947.

records of them in use by the Lao of Kweichow in Han times, and they are still in use in parts of Laos, where they serve as symbols of status and as instruments for calling on ancestral spirits. However, the specific Dong-Son type (Heger I) is distinctive in shape and decoration, and seems to represent the indigenous basic form to which the later types trace their origins. From a consideration of stylistic connections, Chinese imports, and a few radiocarbon dates, the Dong-Son Style spans a period from 800 B.C. to A.D. 400 at outside limits, and more probably the period between 500 B.C. and A.D. 100. North Vietnamese archaeologists have recently found antecedent sites with bronze going back to 1500 B.C., but I will describe these later.

In decoration, the Dong-Son drums offer both amazing expertise and a high degree of social and ritual documentation for an otherwise mainly prehistoric period. On the earliest drums, reviewed in detail by Goloubew and Karlgren[87], the tympani have circular zones of decoration focussed on a central star, and these zones contain bands of incised geometric ornamentation, or sometimes remarkable incised friezes which may illustrate armed humans with bird-feather headdresses, flying birds, deer, lizards, fish, drums, and what appear to be houses with floors raised on piles (figure 7.22). Karlgren discusses a number of motifs which are closely paralleled on Ch'u bronzes in Hunan and the middle Yangtze region, and these include the central star, plaits, zig-zags, spiral motifs, and the very characteristic Dong-Son trademark of circles linked by tangential lines. The bird and deer symbolism is also paralleled in southern China, and perhaps also in prehistoric Thailand, if we accept Sørensen's identification of a shaman's deer antler headdress at Ban Kao[88]. As a result of these Ch'u parallels, Karlgren thinks the Dong-Son Style commences about 400 B.C.

The sides of some of the finest drums are decorated with friezes of boats, with bird-head prows and tail-feather sterns, and in the case of the Ngoc-Lu and Hoang-Ha drums (North Vietnam), the boats contain a cabin with a drum inside, and armed men in bird-feather headdresses (figure 7.23). Goloubew regards these as soul boats to take the dead to Paradise, and the concentric processions on the tops of the drums as representing festivals for the dead. To support his interpretation he refers to similar soul-boat symbolism, festivals for the dead, and associated Dong-Son art motifs which survive today amongst the Ngaju peoples of Borneo[89], and if he is right, then the drums probably had mainly a funerary purpose. Goloubew has certainly emphasised an important point about the widespread survival of Dong-Son-like motifs and symbolism in modern Indonesia and Melanesia, but this does not mean that the boats and processions are the only indicators of function for the drums. It is not of course certain that the decoration on the drums will reflect their functions anyway, and Bezacier[90] has reviewed some of the opinions about functions given by various authors. These include associations with shamanism, a sun-cult, the struggle between the powers of humidity and dryness, and the summoning of spirits to cure sickness. As far as we may ever know, the drums could have had all these associations and more.

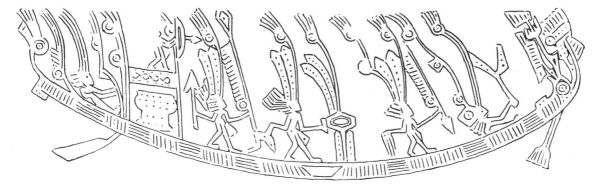

Fig. 7.23. Boat with warriors, and cabin with drum, from the side of the Ngoc-Lu drum, North Vietnam. From Goloubew 1929.

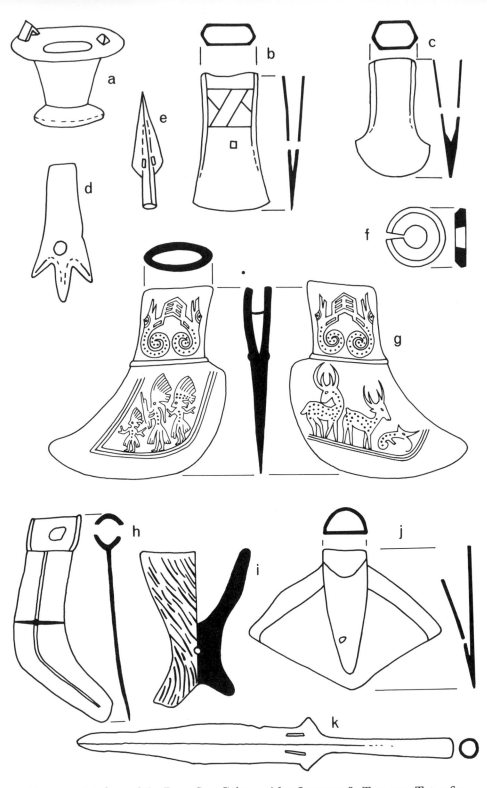

Fig. 7.24. Artefacts of the Dong-Son Culture. After Janse 1958; Tran van Tot 1969;

(a) 'miniature spittoon' of bronze (no scale);
(b, c) socketed bronze axes (x 0.36);
(d) tanged and perforated bronze arrowhead (x 0.6);
(e) socketed bronze arrowhead (x 0.8);
(f) penannular earring of stone (x 0.6);
(g) socketed boot-shaped axe of bronze from Dong-Son (x 0.36) – the central human plays

a khène, while the animal scene may illustrate two deer and a fox;
(h) socketed bronze sickle (x 0.4);
(i) pediform pottery vessel of unknown use (x 0.36);
(j) socketed spade or hoe of bronze (x 0.36);
(k) socketed spearhead of bronze (x 0.4).

Chinese parallels are of no help, because the bronze drums had no place in Chinese metallurgy, and the Heger type I is not found north of Yünnan.

The major habitation and burial site of Dong-Son itself, on the banks of the Song-Ma River in Thanh-Hoa Province, is known through excavations by M. Pajot in 1924–8, O. Janse in 1935–7, and North Vietnamese archaeologists in 1961–2[91]. In A.D. 43 the site may have been sacked by the Chinese general Ma-Yüan, during the suppression of a native rebellion, and the majority of the artefacts recovered probably predate this event. Janse's excavations revealed remains of pile houses, and a black occupation layer about 60 cm thick with many artefacts and two rich burial trenches. Although no bones survived in the two trenches, they each contained a bronze drum, bronze vessels and pottery, together with an assortment of minor goods, and they suggest, as we might expect, that Dong-Son society was stratified to some degree. While the Dong-Son Culture cannot be definitely called an urbanised civilisation in an overall sense, we are at least entitled to describe it as a stratified village farming society[92].

The material culture of the Dong-Son site, apart from the two drums which are of the normal decorated Heger I form, and a few Chinese imports including a footed situla and a sword, presents a combination of bronze and iron forms together with a traditional Neolithic assemblage (figure 7.24). Bronze artefacts include situlae with bands of Dong-Son motifs, miniature situlae, miniature drums, miniature bells, and miniature spool-shaped artefacts which Janse refers to as spittoons for betel chewers[93]. Tools and weapons include socketed axes with splayed or lunate cutting edges, 'boot-shaped' axes with boat and bird-human decorations[94] which seem to relate to earlier Lungshanoid boot-shaped axes[95], socketed spearheads and arrowheads with two slots alongside the midrib, socketed spades or hoes, tanged arrowheads, and daggers of several types. The most interesting dagger is one with a handle formed by a man standing arms akimbo, wearing a loincloth, bracelets, earrings, and with hair coiled around the top of his head, with a plait running down the back (figure 7.25). This of course gives a first hand observation of personal ornamentation in this period, and supports the impression which we have already derived above from Neolithic assemblages. An anthropomorphic dagger almost identical to the

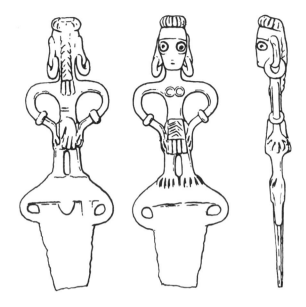

Fig. 7.25. Bronze dagger handle from Dong-Son, 11 cm long. From Goloubew 1929.

one from Dong-Son is known from Ha-Dong province[96], and another remarkable example comes from Nui-Nua, near Thanh-Hoa, which has a handle in the form of a woman with a high headdress, large earrings, and tightly fitted jacket and long skirt[97]. Another anthropomorphic figurine (not necessarily from a dagger) comes from the site of Thao Kham in Laos, of which more in due course, and an anthropomorphic dagger is reported from the Geometric site of Ch'ing-yüan in Kwangtung[98]. Clearly the form was an important one in the Dong-Son and related southern Chinese repertoires, but it has not been conclusively established whether there is any connection with the anthropomorphic daggers of Iron Age Europe.

Other bronze objects from the Dong-Son site include bracelets, belt hooks and buckles, and ornamental square and rectangular plaques which may have been sewn on to clothing. These plaques often have zones of ornament in the Dong-Son style. Swords and halberds, although recovered, are more likely to be imports from China than products of Dong-Son workshops. Finally, several spearheads were made of iron, and there is a single silver ring.

The stone assemblage includes penannular earrings of the wide-spread southern Chinese and

Indochinese type, a few axes, and beads. Beads
of glass, stone and gold have been found in the
site, and glass beads seem generally to be of
Metal Age context in eastern Asia, perhaps
introduced from Western sources[99]. The pottery
from Dong-Son is most unimpressive, and comprises a number of globular footed or flat-based
forms with crude corded or incised decoration
(figure 7.26), directly in the North Vietnamese
Neolithic tradition. A number of Geometric
pots, probably made by resident Chinese artisans,
are also present. In addition, there are pottery
spindle whorls and grooved net sinkers, almost
identical to the sinkers from Somrong Sen in
Cambodia.

The total corpus of material from the Dong-Son
site clearly provides a fairly full definition of the
Dong-Son Culture, and the site does still seem to
be the richest reported for its period in North
Vietnam. The country has of course produced

Fig. 7.26. Cord-marked pot from Dong-Son. From
Bezacier 1972.

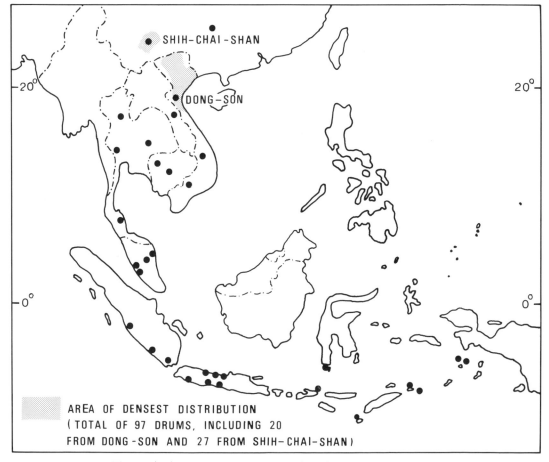

Fig. 7.27. The distribution of Dong-Son drums of Heger type I.

many hundreds of other Dong-Son finds, and a few of the more recent ones are illustrated and described by Tran van Tot[100]. Of perhaps 150 drums of Heger type I known, over seventy are from North Vietnam[101], and this is obviously a very strong argument for regarding the Dong-Son Culture as an early Vietnamese enterprise. On the Southeast Asian mainland outside Vietnam, a few Heger I drums are known from Thailand, Laos, Cambodia and Malaya[102], and at Kampong Sungai Lang in the state of Selangor (Malaya) two drums were found under a clay mound, resting on a plank which has been radiocarbon-dated to *c.* 500 B.C.[103].

Much further to the north, Dong-Son drums have been found in tombs of the remarkable Metal Age civilisation at Shih-chai-shan in Yünnan, which are of early Han date. There is no doubt that the Dong-Son Style has very close relatives in this area, but the nature of the relationship is still a matter of some dispute. In a recent and important article, Watson[104] has suggested that Yünnan was actually the centre of development of the Dong-Son Style, from where the drums, boot-shaped (pediform) axes and daggers were exported to the rest of Southeast Asia. Because the Shih-chai-shan tombs appear to postdate the Chinese conquest of Tien in 109 B.C., Watson feels that the Dong-Son Style is therefore unlikely to be earlier than *c.* 100 B.C. This view, however, is not supported by the increasing number of radiocarbon dates from Southeast Asia, and furthermore it seems likely that the rulers of Tien were perhaps importing the drums, in order that they could be modified into lidded containers for cowrie shells. Rather than elaborating on this problem, I will merely refer the reader to a number of more detailed discussions[105].

The casting expertise of the metal workers of the Dong-Son Culture is demonstrated by the decorated drums and situlae, which were probably cast complete with decoration by the *cire perdue* (lost wax) method, according to an opinion expressed recently by Helmut Loofs[106]. Although many of the drums retain clear casting seams of the type left by the piece-mould technique, there are some grounds for believing these to be purposefully reproduced in the wax moulds, possibly owing to conservatism in a tradition originating with piece-mould casting. Vandermeersch[107] also supports the use of wax models for drum casting, and a number of rather remarkable human figurines from Dong-Son, in-

cluding the above mentioned dagger handle, and a statuette of a man riding on the back of another man and playing a Vietnamese musical wind instrument known as *khène*[108], were most probably made by the *cire perdue* method. This method seems strangely to be absent from Chinese casting before the third century B.C.[109], and this circumstance could perhaps reinforce suggestions of western influence on Dong-Son metallurgy.

There are a number of other Early Metal Age assemblages from Southeast Asia which are probably related to Dong-Son but which lack the main diagnostic items such as drums and pediform axes. One of the most mysterious of these assemblages is that from Somrong Sen in Cambodia. During his two periods of investigation at this site, Mansuy collected a few bronzes from local inhabitants. Whether all of these were actually dug out of the occupation areas is unknown, but the assemblage includes small bells, one with a rather important spiral relief design paralleled on bells from the Plain of Jars in Laos and Sa-Huynh in South Vietnam (below), a chisel, an arrowhead, a fishhook and a ring. In addition, there is a mould for a broad-bladed knife or cleaver of some kind. But this is not all.

In 1887–8 Somrong Sen was visited by one Ludovic Jammes[110] who 'appears to have been one of the most shameless prevaricators ever to have indulged in archaeology' according to Worman[111], and who is given equally rough treatment in an article by another French prehistorian, L. Finot[112]. Jammes claimed to have found at the site many extended burials with bronze goods, pots, stone bracelets, shouldered adzes, and large numbers of animal bones, particularly rhinoceros. He died at the end of last century, and all that can be located among his collections in Washington are stone adzes, bracelets and beads – no bronze at all. So perhaps we could write him off as a day-dreamer or a liar, except that we have the rather embarrassing proviso that he did manage to convince one of the greatest French prehistorians of his day – Emile Cartailhac – who published in 1890[113] a number of drawings of socketed axes and spearheads, bronze rings with T-sections, and a knife and a bell, both with Dong-Son spiral ornamentation, which were all said to have come from Somrong Sen. No-one knows now where these objects are, but I am personally inclined to accept that Jammes did discover a rich Neolithic and Metal Age burial ground, even though his account is clearly exaggerated in

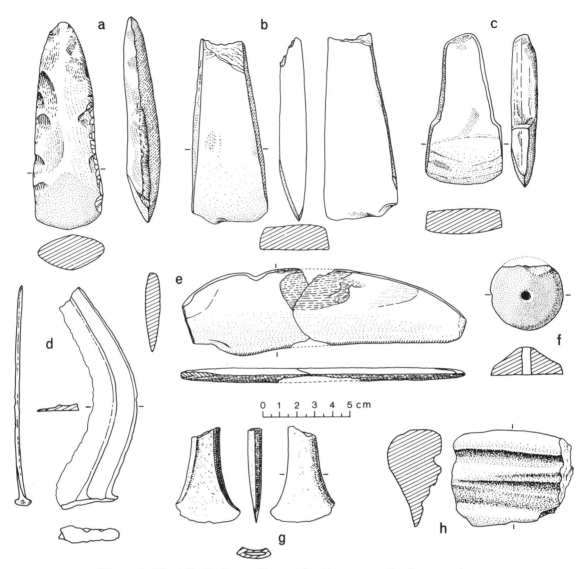

Fig. 7.28. The Mlu Prei assemblage. After Levy 1943. (a–c) stone adzes; (d) bronze sickle; (e) schist reaping knife; (f) clay spindle whorl; (g) socketed bronze axe; (h) grooved sharpening stone.

several other respects.

Other Cambodian assemblages come from three surface sites in the region of Mlu Prei, northern Cambodia[114] (figure 7.28). These assemblages are a confused mixture of Neolithic and Metal Age remains, and for one site (O Yak) there are unverified reports of skeletons with bronze bracelets and glass beads. Otherwise, the assemblages include shouldered and untanged adzes, schist knives, a possible barkcloth beater, schist and clay bracelets (but no earplugs of Somrong Sen type), and clay spindle whorls. Bronzes include a ribbed sickle, splayed socketed axes, and bracelets. There is also an iron chisel and an iron bracelet, and the pottery is both

hand- and wheel-made, with a variety of corded and incised decoration which may relate it to Somrong Sen. In view of the absence of context, however, these sites are of limited value.

Concerning the origins of the Dong-Son Style, we have a choice of several hypotheses which at first sight appear to conflict, but which may well represent something near the truth if considered in combination. The parallels with the Ch'u art of China are clear, but restricted mainly to style motifs. The actual drums of Dong-Son type do not occur north of Yünnan, and the forms of most of the Dong-Son artefacts are un-Chinese. The importance of China in Dong-Son origins was in fact disputed some years ago by Heine

Geldern[115], who argued for a Hallstatt and Caucasian Iron Age origin at about 800 B.C. as a result of direct migration to Yünnan from Europe and western Asia. At first sight this view seems rather extreme, but there are strong similarities, not least in the possible use of *cire perdue*, and it would be wise to allow for at least some diffusion from both Western and Chinese sources. But more recent archaeological evidence is beginning to suggest that Dong-Son is mainly indigenous to Southeast Asia, and it may well be a result of ancestral Vietnamese enterprise. The finds from Non Nok Tha, and the many moulds and axes from other parts of Southeast Asia, suggest that Dong-Son bronze metallurgy has important local roots, and recent radiocarbon-dating of splayed-blade socketed copper axes to *c.* 1300 B.C. from the Hai-men-k'ou site in Yünnan[116] tends to support this view. Furthermore, evidence for bronze-working has now been found in sites along the Red River which are estimated to date back to 2000 B.C.[117], and carbon dates for North Vietnamese sites with metal are now reported from 1400 B.C. onwards. By 1000 B.C. socketed axes, spearheads, pediform axes, sickles and fishhooks were being manufactured at sites such as Dong-Dau and Go-Mun near Hanoi, and Vietnamese archaeologists are rapidly refuting any suggestions of outside influence from China or the west.

In summing up, the Dong-Son Style seems to be the result of radiation from the area of the Dong-Son Culture in North Vietnam. Whether the drums were traded from a small number of workshops, or made locally in several areas, is unknown. But since most of the drums are characterised by a high lead content, it may be that they were made in a limited number of Vietnamese workshops, and the homogeneity of the decoration would tend to support this view. In other parts of Southeast Asia (outside China), bronze-working certainly took place, but may have been confined to simpler forms of tools and ornaments.

We might finally ask who used the drums, and in this respect it may be of significance that two successive local kingdoms were founded in North Vietnam between 257 B.C. and the establishment of a Chinese protectorate in 111 B.C. Both the Thur dynasty (257–208 B.C.) and the Trieu dynasty (208–111 B.C.) were founded by generals of Chinese descent, and if they attempted to establish courts on Chinese models then one does not need to look far for the source of patronage for skilled metalworkers. There is no direct evidence for this view, but it is not unlikely in the light of historical evidence for the commencement of a limited degree of urbanisation in North Vietnam during the Thur dynasty. Chinese historical records indicate that the founder of this dynasty also founded the royal settlement of Co-Loa, 15 kilometres north of Hanoi, in 258 B.C.[118]. The remains of this site still survive as three successive earthen-walled enclosures, the outer enclosing a rough oval of 2800 by 2000 metres, with a smaller enclosure inside, and a rectangular palace enclosure within. None of this site has been excavated, so it is not certain that the remains belong to the Dong-Son Culture, but Bezacier is of the opinion that the defences were laid out in the third century B.C.[119]. This seems to be the only evidence for Dong-Son urbanisation, and clearly the site merits intensive excavation.

It remains for us now to describe a limited number of Metal Age jar burials clearly different from the Dong-Son Culture.

THE METAL AGE JAR BURIAL TRADITION – SOUTH VIETNAM AND LAOS

A limited number of Indochinese Metal Age sites stand out because of their association with jar burial, probably of cremated or previously macerated bone, although osseous material rarely survives in quantity. The sites are unusual because they are the first evidence for jar burial in Mainland Southeast Asia, even though the tradition does go back much earlier in Borneo and the Philippines, as we will see in the next chapter. The lateness of the tradition on the mainland, and the localisation of the pottery (as opposed to stone) jar burials to the Sa-Huynh Culture of South Vietnam suggests that this group may be partly associated with Austronesian Chamic settlement. As we have seen, the Chams are the only Austronesians on the mainland of Southeast Asia apart from the Malays, and their ultimate origins almost certainly lie in the islands. The Laotian jars are of stone, and seem to represent an unrelated development.

We begin with the Sa-Huynh Culture (figure 7.29), which is represented by two groups of sites – four at Sa-Huynh itself, in Quang-Ngai Province, and three around Hang-Gon near Xuan-Loc in Long-Khanh Province. About 500 jars were recovered from the four Sa-Huynh localities in the 1920s and 1930s[120], and they seem to have been buried in clusters, originally perhaps in boats in a Dong-Son type religious

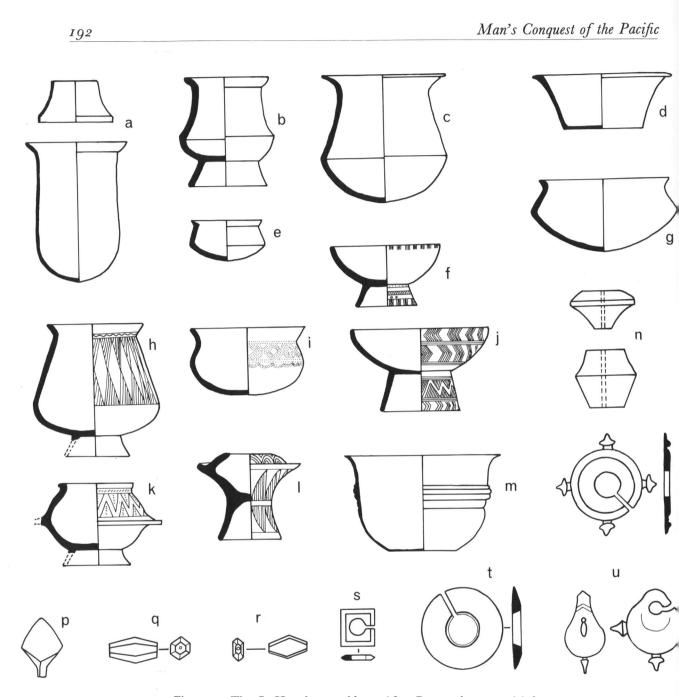

Fig. 7.29. The Sa-Huynh assemblage. After Parmentier 1924. (a) large burial jar, 77 cm high, with lid; (b–l) pottery vessels between 14 and 21 cm diameter, decorated by incision or punctuation; (m) bronze vessel of Dong-Son type, 9 cm diameter; (n) clay spindle whorls, 3.5 cm diameter; (o, s–u) stone earrings – (o) and (u) are of lingling-o type – diameters 2–5 cm; (p) iron hoe 17 cm long; (q, r) facetted carnelian beads, 19 and 15 cm long.

tradition, according to O. Janse[121]. The burial jars are round-based, about 80 cm high on average, usually either plain or cord-marked, and some were covered by trunconical lids which in some cases are decorated with incised rectangular meanders. These jars contained some bone material, which does not appear to have been cremated, and also small pots, beads of glass and carnelian, and a few metal objects. The small pots are of very varied shape and decoration, and include round-based and footed forms with horizontal bands of incised decoration, particularly of triangles and lozenges. There are also a few unusual spool-shaped 'lamps', and pottery spindle whorls. Motifs such as spirals and crosses are absent on the pottery, and it has relatively little resemblance to either the Dong-Son or to any other mainland assemblage, apart perhaps from Somrong Sen where the material is not well dated. It is, however, very close to the Kalanay pottery of the Philippines, of which more later, and some of the decoration is also carried out by stamping with the dentate edge of a marine shell[122], which is similar to some of the dentate stamping in Taiwan and the Philippines. The presence of a red slip on some of the Sa-Huynh vessels also recalls central Philippine Metal Age pottery.

The coloured glass and carnelian beads are of circular, cigar-shaped or facetted lozenge forms (see page 230), and Sa-Huynh has also yielded the penannular earrings of glass or stone, like those of Somrong Sen and Dong-Son. Several of these have the unusual conical projections which equate them exactly with the 'lingling-o' type ear pendants of Luzon, Palawan, Botel Tobago, Hong Kong, and other Metal Age sites in North Vietnam. There is only one bracelet from Sa-Huynh, and that is of bronze, but there are also from the site a bronze goblet and a bell, together with two miniature bells with relief spiral ornamentation (figure 7.35 [n]) which are closely paralleled at Somrong Sen and in north-eastern Laos (see below). Iron is also present, in the form of a few socketed spade-like tools.

The Sa-Huynh site is remarkable because its assemblage clearly has very much in common with the Philippines, perhaps less in common with Somrong Sen, and only limited correlations with Dong-Son. The same applies to the other sites of the Sa-Huynh Culture; Dau-Giay, Hang-Gon 9, and Phu-Hoa[123], which are in the vicinity of Xuan-Loc. Phu-Hoa is the most important, recently rescued during roadworks operations. About 40 partially damaged jars were saved from this site, which occurred in small groups about 50–100 cm below the surface of the ground. These jars contained a typical Sa-Huynh assemblage – bone fragments; incised pottery with Sa-Huynh type decoration; glass and carnelian beads; bracelets of stone, bronze, iron and glass; penannular and lingling-o type white jade earrings; spindle whorls of pottery and iron; and iron socketed picks and unsocketed sickles. In addition there are baked clay pellets of a type found widely on Southeast Asian Neolithic sites (including Spirit Cave), which seem to be for slings or the pellet bow[124]. Phu-Hoa has other interesting characteristics – the absence of stone tools (one stone adze only was found at Sa-Huynh), the wide range of iron artefacts, and the reported presence of charcoal in the jars which may suggest cremation. Apart from a few ceramic idiosyncracies, such as a higher frequency of curvilinear scroll-like decoration on pottery, the site is virtually identical to Sa-Huynh and has two carbon dates between 400 and 700 B.C.

The neighbouring site of Hang-Gon 9, again with an almost identical assemblage, is radiocarbon-dated to between 500 B.C. and 0, and this site has confirmed the practice of cremation, together with the purposeful breakage of pottery grave-goods before placement in the large burial jars. Furthermore, Hang-Gon 9 has produced an animal-headed stone pendant of a kind paralleled exactly at Phu-Hoa, and also in the Tabon jar burial assemblage from Palawan Island in the Philippines (see figure 8.5 [a]). The dates for Phu-Hoa and Hang-Gon 9 are of major significance for dating the appearance of iron in Southeast Asia, and the Phu-Hoa iron sickles are well paralleled in Late Chou China[125], from where the techniques of iron working may originally have spread (but see page 164).

The Sa-Huynh Culture has another rather more problematical representative in the Xuan-Loc area at site Hang-Gon 1, which would appear to be a settlement rather than a burial ground. This site was brought to light by rescue excavation carried out by Edmond Saurin during bulldozing for forestry development[126], and it is on a small headland between two streams. Saurin thinks the settlement area covered about 350 by 150 metres with houses around a central open space, although no actual house remains have been found apart from what appear to be localised occupation deposits. The artefacts include wheel-made plain and paddle-impressed sherds without the elaborate decoration present on the funerary pottery, together with Duff type 2A and 8 adzes, fragments of stone rings, and four complete or partial sandstone moulds for bronze casting, one of which is for a socketed axe with decorative neck rings just like the ones from Non Nok Tha. Another mould is for three penannular earrings, and there is a similar mould for one earring from a neighbouring site at Dau-Giay, which probably belongs to the Sa-Huynh Culture. There appears to be no iron at Hang-Gon 1.

The site in fact presents an important chronological problem. On the one hand, it could be a Sa-Huynh Culture settlement of the first millennium B.C., but on the other hand the parallels with the Non Nok Tha axes suggest that it could be much earlier. To support the latter possibility, a sample of carbonaceous pottery temper has given a date of *c.* 2300 B.C., so Hang-Gon 1 could turn out to be a very important site, although I would be inclined to group it with the Sa-Huynh Culture for the time being on the balance of available evidence, and thus place it within the first millennium B.C.

Other settlement sites of apparent Sa-Huynh affinity have recently been discovered in the Dong-Nai Valley around Bien-Hoa, 20 km north-east of Saigon[127] and these have so far yielded surface finds of incised pottery, shouldered stone adzes, polishing stones, stone bracelets, and baked clay pellets. The two most important sites are at Phuoc-Tan and Ben-Do, and I was fortunate enough to visit the latter in the company of Henri Fontaine in 1974. It is situated, like many other sites in the area, on a low rise above the flood-plain, and the settlement area may have been about 50 metres in diameter. Should future political conditions permit, it would be of great interest to have scientific excavations undertaken on this and other settlement sites in the Mekong Delta region, and we can only admit at the present that we know very little about Neolithic and Metal Age developments in one of the most fertile sectors of Southeast Asia.

There is one other interesting occurrence which seems to relate to the Sa-Huynh Culture, for both the Sa-Huynh and Xuan-Loc sites have a single stone slab grave in their vicinities[128], such graves being prehistorically unknown on the mainland apart from one small group in Malaya. There is of course no guarantee that the slab graves are culturally associated with the jar burial sites, but perhaps the association is more than mere coincidence. The Sa-Huynh example appears poorly preserved, while that at Xuan-Loc is a most impressive structure of worked and slotted slabs, surrounded by a series of notched uprights of unknown significance.

Hence at the end of the pre-Christian era on the mainland there are at least two distinct and contemporary mainland cultures – Dong-Son and Sa-Huynh – with the unstratified assemblages from Somrong Sen and Mlu Prei perhaps forming a third. On grounds of place, date and linguistic history, we may tentatively regard the makers of these three groups as ancestral Vietnamese, Cham, and Mon-Khmer respectively. There is however a fourth group which is more difficult to interpret ethnohistorically, and this is the stone burial jar and megalith complex of northern Laos.

STONE BURIAL JARS AND MEGALITHS OF NORTHERN LAOS

Within the history of archaeology, megaliths have perhaps given rise to as much romantic theorising as any other class of prehistoric monument. As we will see, megalithic monuments are common and widespread amongst the early Austronesian societies of Indonesia and Oceania. But on the South-

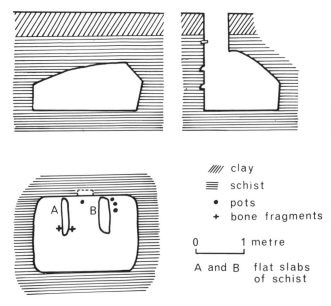

Fig. 7.30. Plan and sections of an underground burial chamber at San Kong Phan, northern Laos, with entrance chimney and steps. After Colani 1935.

Fig. 7.31. A part of the Plain of Jars. From Colani 1935.

east Asian mainland, true megaliths, i.e. monuments of very large stones, are conspicuous by their absence in most areas[129], apart from the one well-described group with which we are now concerned.

The megaliths of Laos were described in 1935 in two lavish volumes by the redoubtable French archaeologist Madeleine Colani[130], who must surely rank as one of the most prolific fieldworkers ever to work in Southeast Asia. They fall into two groups – the megaliths and tombs of Hua Pan Province in the northeast, and the stone jars of Tran Ninh Province in the north-central part of Laos.

The Hua Pan sites are several, but the two most important are those at San Kong Phan and Keo Hin Tan. Both these sites have groups of thin micaschist slabs, some over 3 metres high, together with underground man-made burial pits closed by large discs of the same stone. The burial pits (figure 7.30) consist of excavated chambers reached by 'chimneys' set with stone steps, and some have slabs of stone on their floors which may have once supported a wooden floor, perhaps for a burial, although very few bone fragments and teeth were actually recovered. As in many Southeast Asian burial sites, tropical soil conditions seem to have taken their toll. The artefact

assemblage in and around the tombs and standing stones is rather limited – naturally it includes a number of modern items, but those of apparent antiquity include hand-made undecorated pots with flat, round or ring-footed bases, penannular bronze rings, and micaschist discs of 30 to 40 mm diameter decorated with punctate stelliform designs (figure 7.34). The latter resemble the decorated earplugs of Somrong Sen, but lack the pulley shape, and the majority have central perforations. Little can in fact be said about their use. Otherwise, the absence of iron in the sites may suggest a relatively early date, but it is only possible to guess that it falls somewhere within the first millennium B.C.

It is fairly evident that the Hua Pan sites are burial grounds, and Colani compares them with recent Thai burial places in Thanh-Hoa Province, North Vietnam, where the dead are buried under small huts surrounded by upright stones. In western central China, small underground tombs of this general type appear in the mid-first millennium B.C.[131], but it is not known whether these can be related to the Laotian examples.

The Tran Ninh sites are situated on a grassland plateau about 1000 metres above sea-level, and centre on the famous Plain of Jars at Ban Ang, which has some 250 stone vessels (figure 7.31).

Fig. 7.32. Mushroom-shaped stone at San Hin Oume, 90 cm diameter. From Colani 1935.

There are thirteen sites described by Colani, and the jars themselves are mostly of a rather bulbous cylindrical shape, often with very thick bases, and are worked from soft local stones. In one case, transport of stone from 46 kilometres away is possible, but most were made locally, which is not surprising when one considers that the largest one recorded may weigh about fourteen metric tons! The average size of the jars is around 1.5 metres in height and diameter, but heights and diameters of three metres or more do occur. Some also have rebated rims, perhaps for now-vanished wooden lids to protect the contents. Scattered around the jars on these sites are stone discs – some simple like those at the Hua Pan sites, other strangely complex. These discs do not seal tombs, and neither are they lids for the jars, as Colani has convincingly demonstrated. The complex ones have one plain side, while the other side may either be rounded, or consist of relief concentric circles, or have a foot which gives the whole a mushroom shape[132] (figure 7.32). A few are also decorated with relief quadrupeds (tigers or monkeys?) or spreadeagled human figures (figure 7.33). Remarkable as these objects may be, it is even more remarkable to realise

Fig. 7.33. Stone disc with quadruped, at Keo Tane, 150 cm diameter. From Colani 1935.

that the decorated sides were always placed beneath the disc and hidden in the ground. One disc with a quadruped at the site of Keo Tane sealed two unused quadrangular adzes, and it is clear that the discs as a group served some now obscure ceremonial purpose. Colani suggests that they may be stone copies of Dong-Son drums, perhaps used for calling spirits or the placing of offerings to the dead.

To the north-west of the Plain of Jars are several sites which lack the jars, but which have groups of upright stones instead. Other sites have both jars and uprights, and several have flat stones, called 'dolmens' by Colani, which seal buried pots or stone jars. Unlike the large stone jars, these uprights and 'dolmens' show few signs of being worked to shape. At the site of Thao Kham, which does not have jars, one of these flat 'dolmens' sealed a pot which contained a bronze anthropomorphic figurine (figure 7.34), which could possibly have been from a dagger handle, as it has precisely the same body proportions as the important examples we have already described from Dong-Son and Ha-Dong (p. 187). At another site called Col de Moc Drehun, a similar slab sealed six pots, in two stacks of three each.

In the centre of the Plain of Jars itself, at Ban Ang, stands a small limestone knoll which contains a cave. This cave has two roof vents, both artificially enlarged by man to function as chimneys, and Colani's excavations in the cave floor revealed large quantities of ash and burnt human bone, which suggests very strongly that bodies were cremated here prior to interment in the jars. Some of the jars themselves contain burnt bones in small quantities, but it is not clear how many individuals were placed in each – i.e., whether they were individual graves or communal ossuaries. Without a doubt the whole Tran Ninh complex is unique in mainland Southeast Asia, and has only a remote analogue in the jars of the Sa-Huynh Culture. However, there are parallels in distant Sulawesi, as we will see later, and even more surprisingly, two English explorers reported in 1929 a group of similar sites in the North Cachar Hills of north-eastern India[133]. In a number of sites here there are crude stone jars, mostly consisting of cavities hollowed out of unworked boulders, although there are a few shaped forms like those of Tran Ninh. In addition, Mills and Hutton refer to 'sitting stones', which they describe as 'circular stones, flat on the top but convex underneath, the convex side resting on the ground and the whole propped up with smaller stones around the edge'. These 'sitting stones' quite closely resemble some of the 'dolmens' of South Sumatra,

Fig. 7.34. *Left*, bronze figurine from Thao Kham, Tran Ninh Province, 10.7 cm high. *Right*, schist pendant from Keo Hin Tan, Hua Pan Province, 4.8. cm diameter. From Colani 1935.

and also some of the Tran Ninh discs. It is interesting that many shouldered adzes (Duff type 8) have been found around the Cachar sites, and, despite the distance of over 1200 kilometres between here and Tran Ninh, one is left with the nagging feeling that an unexplained relationship may exist.

The artefacts found in and around the Tran Ninh jars and in the cremation cave relate the sites most closely to Somrong Sen, and rather less closely to Dong-Son or to Sa-Huynh (figure 7.35). The cremation cave included objects which may predate the jars, such as stone rings and Duff type 8 shouldered adzes, and also numerous metal objects, such as bronze bracelets, bronze spiral rings (earrings?), small bronze bells, iron axes, tanged iron knives, and an iron lancehead. Biconical and trunconical spindle whorls of pottery are quite common, a little strange perhaps for a cremation cave, and there is also an unusual clay head, perhaps of a zebu. The jars generally contain little but glass beads, bone fragments, and a few sherds and scraps of iron. Most of the artefacts were recovered by excavating around the jars, and they may have been placed here as offerings. In these situations there are many glass and carnelian beads of spherical or cylindrical shapes – the facetted forms of Sa-Huynh being absent. Also present at some sites are small stone lidded jars, decorated earplugs of Somrong Sen type, perforated axe-like pendants of a form we will meet again on human stone statues in South Sumatra, and miniature bronze bells with spiral and spectacle relief motifs, similar to the above-mentioned small bells of Somrong Sen and Sa-Huynh[134]. Some sites have iron sickles and splayed-blade axes, and bronze was evidently used only for ornaments, rather than for tools or weapons. The pottery is hand-made, often in the form of round-based or footed jars, and complete pots buried near the jars were occasionally covered by a second pot placed upside down over the top, a position reminiscent of some Late Jomon and Yayoi jar burials in Kyushu, Japan[135], and of some Metal Age jar burials in the central and northern Philippines[136], although in both these cases the pots were sometimes used for primary uncremated burials. Incision is the preferred method of ceramic decoration in Tran Ninh, and several sites have a form of wavy or zig-zag comb incision which is paralleled at Oc-Eo (a Funanese city in southern South Vietnam) and in some North Vietnamese Neolithic sites[137], and more distantly perhaps at Sa-Huynh.

It is clear that the northern Laotian sites represent mortuary practices which are so far unique in mainland Southeast Asia. General and specific parallels are close with Somrong Sen, less close with Dong-Son, and very limited with Sa-Huynh, and none of these parallels are strong enough to mask the expression of a distinct Laotian culture of unknown ethnic and archaeological affiliation. One of the most interesting site complexes in Southeast Asia therefore remains shrouded in mystery.

SUMMARY

I have tried in this chapter to survey several spheres of information, which in the present state of our knowledge do not intermesh as well as one might wish. Hence a brief summary might help to tie together some loose ends.

The Early Holocene on the Southeast Asian mainland is dominated by the Hoabinhian technocomplex, with its important innovations of edge-grinding and possibly incipient horticulture. Cord-marked pottery also makes an appearance, and may well have been quite widespread by 5000 B.C. in eastern Asia generally. In central China, the achievements of the Neolithic Yang-shao and Lungshanoid Cultures gave rise to the Shang civilisation of the later second millennium B.C., while in the tropics of Southeast Asia, well developed Neolithic cultures with rice, cattle, and the pottery, adze and ornament types which have occupied so much space in this chapter were present by 3000 B.C. Localised copper and bronze metallurgy was present in Thailand by 3000 B.C., but otherwise the Metal Age as defined by the Dong-Son Culture and its antecedents seems to belong to the second and first millennia B.C. Archaeology perhaps has further to go in Southeast Asia than anywhere else in the world, and the recognition of dated prehistoric cultures has hardly begun. But recent discoveries are showing that many innovations were present in Southeast Asia at least as early as they were elsewhere, and the old view of Chinese cultural domination is being challenged. As far as we know, Southeast Asia did not develop an urbanised civilisation until the period of intensive Indian and Chinese influence at about the time of Christ, although the quality of life for the prehistoric Southeast Asian villager was probably no worse and perhaps much better than that of his Chinese, Sumerian or Egyptian urbanised counterpart.

The sites described in this chapter are a part

of the roots of the Vietnamese, Mon-Khmer, and possibly Thai ethnolinguistic groups. When we turn to the islands of Southeast Asia we enter an Austronesian stronghold, and one which has its own individual archaeological expression from Neolithic times onwards, despite an obvious and deep affinity with the mainland. From the Neolithic cultures of Island Southeast Asia are derived the widely spread Austronesian speakers of Oceania.

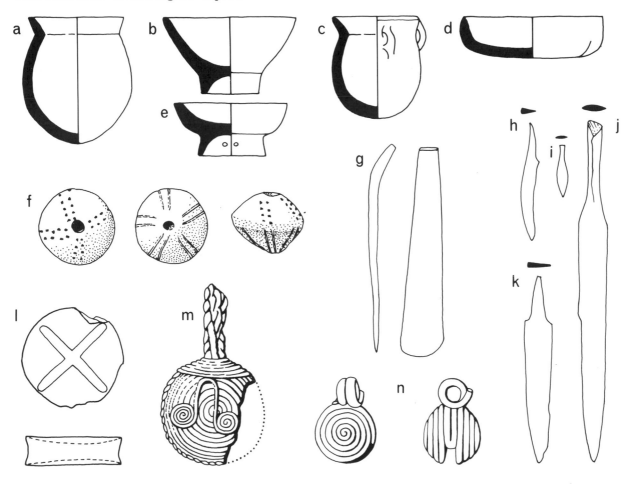

Fig. 7.35. The Ban Ang assemblage, after Colani 1935; (a–e) pottery (x 0.26); (f) spindle whorl of pottery (x 0.52); (g) presumed ploughshare of iron (x 0.26); (h, k) iron blades (x 0.26); (i) iron arrowhead (x 0.26); (j) socketed iron spearhead (x 0.26); (l) pottery ear disc (x 0.52); (m) bronze bell with imitation filigree decoration (x 1.6); (n) bronze bell from Sa-Huynh (x 1.6).

Footnotes

1. e.g. by Dunn 1970; Solheim 1972.
2. Ikawa-Smith 1976.
3. Kokobu 1963; Takamiya 1967; Pearson 1967a; 1969.
4. Chang 1968: 111–12.
5. Chang 1969a: 225; 1972a: 436–441. A recent carbon-14 date on shell of almost 9000 B.C. is reported from Hsien-jen-tung in Kiangsi, apparently in association with cord-marked pottery, although the exact context is not clear. See *JHKAS* 5: 85, 1974.

6. Bard and Meacham 1972; Meacham 1973a; 1973b. See also Maglioni 1952.

7. Chang and Stuiver 1966; Chang 1966; 1967; 1969a; 1972a. Chang (1973) mentions a carbon date of *c.* 3700 B.C. from a corded ware context in southern Taiwan, but few details are available. See also Chang *et al.* 1974.

8. Gorman 1970.

9. Dunn 1964. See also Collings 1940 for similar pottery from Gol Ba'it. Corded pottery appears with Hoa-binhian tools at Laang Spean in Cambodia from 4000 B.C. (Mourer and Mourer 1970.)

10. Cheng 1957.

11. Cord- and basket-marking appear on Philippine and eastern Indonesian ceramics after 1500 B.C., but are not reported before this date.

12. Major sources on Neolithic China are Chang 1968; Cheng 1966; Ho 1969; 1975; Shih H.P. *et al.* 1963; Treistman 1972; Watson 1961; 1965; 1971. Carbon dates are listed in Barnard 1975.

13. Chang 1965: 513.

14. Cheng 1966: 21.

15. Chang's use of the term Lungshanoid has been criticised (e.g. Treistman,1968a), but I use it here in the absence of any better alternative. As Chang himself says, it is 'a working hypothesis based on a subjective inter-pretation of the evidence' (1968: 130).

16. Treistman 1968b.

17. Chang 1968: 139.

18. Chang 1972a: 448.

19. Maglioni 1952.

20. Barnard 1975. Ho (1975: Chapter 2) gives a good summary of the evidence for agriculture and animal husbandry in the Lungshanoid.

21. See references under footnote 7.

22. Solheim 1967a; 1967b; 1968a; 1969; 1970; Bayard 1971a; 1971b; 1972a; Higham 1972; 1975.

23. Higham and Leach 1971; Higham 1975.

24. Gorman and Charoenwongsa 1976.

25. van Esterik 1973; Griffin 1973. Earlier published thermoluminescence dates for Ban Chiang painted pottery (Bronson and Han 1972) are now known to be incorrect (see also Loofs 1974).

26. Wheeler and Maddin 1976.

27. Bayard 1971a; 1972b.

28. Çambel and Braidwood 1970.

29. Barnard (in Barnard ed. 1972) has noted that the Non Nok Tha bronze technology has little in common with Shang bronze technology in China.

30. Higham 1972; Bronson and Han 1972; Solheim 1970: 153. See also Sørensen 1973 for a large assemblage of tanged iron tools from Ongbah Cave, dating probably to the end of the first millennium B.C.

31. Higham 1972. Metal Age deposits in the Ongbah Cave have yielded carbon dates back to 2300 B.C., but these may reflect stratigraphic disturbance (see Tauber 1973).

32. Watson and Loofs 1967; Watson 1968; Loofs 1970.

33. Bayard 1971a.

34. Benedict 1967.

35. Sørensen 1972.

36. Sørensen and Hatting 1967.

37. Sørensen 1965.

38. Parker 1968.

39. Sieveking 1954; Peacock 1959.

40. Compare Malleret 1959; plate Xb with Solheim 1970: plate Ic.

41. Sieveking 1962.

42. Peacock 1964a.

43. Peacock 1959.

44. Dunn 1964; 1966.

45. Sørensen 1967; 1972. Barnard (in Barnard ed. 1972: xxxix) supports a Lungshanoid derivation. Linehan (1968) discusses Malayan stone knives which resemble Chinese Neolithic forms.

46. Trevor and Brothwell 1962.

47. Sangvichien, Sirigaroon, Jorgensen and Jacob 1969.

48. Flatz 1965.

49. Tweedie 1970: 25.

50. e.g. by Heine Geldern 1932.

51. Duff 1970.

52. McCarthy 1940: 40–3.

53. Kokobu 1963: 231.

54. Shih Chang-Ju 1963.

55. Dani 1960: 64.

56. Von Koenigswald 1968b; van Heekeren 1972.

57. Duff 1970: sheet 14.

58. Kokobu 1963: 229.

59. Ling 1962; Lynch and Ewing 1968; Sieveking 1956b; Tolstoy 1972. Having seen some of the Mexican beaters for myself I would strongly support the view of prehistoric contact.

60. Heine Geldern 1932. See also Heine Geldern 1945; 1958.

61. Meacham 1973a; 1973b.

62. Mostly French, and culminating in a peak in the 1920s and 1930s. The majority of the sites are in North Vietnam. See Patte 1936 and Bezacier 1972: 54–73 for general surveys.

63. Malleret 1958–1959; Saurin 1969: 32 (referring to excavations at Minot in Cambodia by B. Groslier).

64. Mourer and Mourer 1970; 1971.

65. Mansuy 1920; 1923. Masashi Chikamori of Keio University in Japan has recently carried out further small excavations on the site.

66. Carbonnel and Delibrias 1968.

67. For some scattered finds see Bezacier 1972; Lafont 1956 (South Vietnam) and Saurin 1952 (Laos).

68. Boriskovsky 1968–71: parts VI and VII; Nguyen 1975.

69. Patte 1924. Fontaine and Delibrias (1973: 32) estimate an age of less than 4000 years for Bau-Tro according to evidence for sea-level changes.

70. Colani 1930.

71. Saurin 1940.

72. Colani 1928.

73. Boriskovsky 1968–71: part VII; Nguyen 1975.

74. Boriskovsky 1968–71: part VII: 234. See also Heine Geldern 1932: 593.

75. e.g. Mansuy and Colani 1925.

76. Mansuy 1920.

77. Mansuy 1920.

78. Condominas 1952; Boriskovsky 1968–71: part VII: 241.

79. Karlgren 1942; Chang 1972b; Watson 1972.

80. Bezacier 1972: 79–82.

81. Chang 1964; 1968: 380–92. See also Chard 1963.

82. Solheim 1964a; 1967c.

83. Finn 1958; Barrett 1973; Meacham 1973a; 1973b.

84. Heanley and Shellshear 1932; Schofield 1940; Davis and Tregear 1960.

85. Maglioni 1938; 1952.

86. See map in Tran van Tot 1969: fig. 2A.

87. Goloubew 1929; Karlgren 1942.

88. Quaritch Wales (1957) has also suggested that the Dong-Son drums are connected with shamanic practices, originally introduced into the region from northern Asia.

89. Goloubew 1929. A bronze statuette of a man wearing a hornbill headdress in a style akin to Dong-Son has been reported by Harrisson from a Kayan village in central Borneo. See Harrisson 1964a; Bezacier 1972: 169–71.

90. Bezacier 1972: 192–212.

91. Janse 1958; Bezacier 1972: 83.

92. Described thus by Chang (1962b).

93. Bezacier (1972: 145) thinks this function is unlikely.

94. See also Karlgren 1942: pl. 9.

95. Shih Chang-Ju 1963.

96. Bezacier 1972: 115.

97. Tran van Tot 1969: pl. 111.

98. Chang 1968: 392.

99. Seligman and Beck 1938.

100. Tran van Tot 1969.

101. Bezacier 1972: appendix 5.

102. Heger 1902; Tweedie 1970; Loewenstein 1956.

103. Peacock 1964b.

104. Watson 1970.

105. von Dewall 1967; 1972; Bunker 1972; Pearson 1962. Other Yünnan finds, now known to be from Shih-chai-shan, are described by Gray 1949–50.

106. Loofs 1976.

107. Vandermeersch 1956.

108. Janse 1958: plates 38, 39.

109. Barnard 1963.

110. Jammes 1891.

111. Worman 1949.

112. Finot 1928.

113. Cartailhac 1890.

114. Levy 1943.

115. Heine Geldern 1937; 1966a.

116. Barnard 1975: date ZK-10. See Saurin 1951–2 for some Laotian finds.

117. Nguyen 1975.

118. Bezacier 1972: 247.

119. Bezacier 1972: 247.

120. Parmentier 1924; Solheim 1959a; Janse 1959; Malleret 1959; Bezacier 1972: 73–7.

121. Janse 1959.

122. Colani 1935: vol. 2: plate 102; Malleret 1959: plates III–V.

123. Fontaine 1971a (Dau-Giay); Fontaine 1972a (Phu-Hoa); Saurin 1973 (Hang-Gon 9).

124. Solheim 1972: 37.

125. Watson 1971: 81.

126. Saurin 1963; 1968a.

127. Fontaine 1971b; 1972b.

128. Parmentier 1924: 314; 1928.

129. For a bibliography of Southeast Asian megaliths see Loofs 1967. The hydraulic works described by Colani (1940) for the Quang-Tri area of North Vietnam could be prehistoric or more likely proto-historic (see Bezacier 1972: 252–3), but they do not appear to have Dong-Son connections. See also Seidenfaden 1944; Wheatley 1965.

130. Colani 1935.

131. Watson 1971:50.

132. cf. Schnitger 1964: 49 for mushroom-shaped stone discs made recently for or to commemorate important women on the island of Nias, western Indonesia.

133. Mills and Hutton 1929.

134. As noted, these small bells with spiral filigree-type decoration are known from Sa-Huynh and Somrong Sen, possibly in late first millennium B.C. contexts. They are also reported from the rich assemblage recovered from the Funanese city of Oc-Eo in South Vietnam (Malleret 1960:219–27), together with comb-incised pottery similar to that from Ban Ang. A date in the early first millennium A.D. for the Tran Ninh sites does seem very likely.

135. Mori 1956; 1963.

136. Solheim 1960.

137. e.g. Mansuy and Fromaget 1924. See also footnote 134.

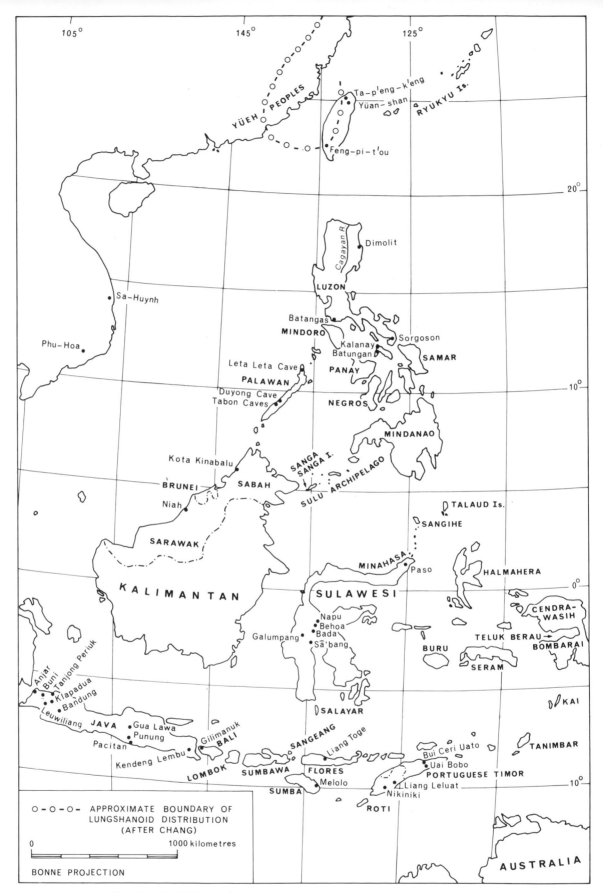

Fig. 8.1 Neolithic and Metal Age sites in Island Southeast Asia. (For Portuguese Timor read eastern Timor.)

CHAPTER 8

Neolithic and Metal Age Cultures of Island Southeast Asia

The islands of Taiwan, the Philippines and Indonesia represent the heartland of the Austronesian world. As we saw in chapter 5, the break-up of the Proto-Austronesian linguistic entity probably took place somewhere in these islands, perhaps between five and seven thousand years ago, and likewise they formed the arena for the developments which led to Austronesian expansion into Oceania and Mainland Southeast Asia. Former hypotheses that the Austronesians expanded from southern China, Vietnam or Malaya do not stand up to modern archaeological and linguistic evidence[1].

However, there is one rather important point which should be clarified here if we are to avoid a terminological quagmire. The traceable homeland of the Austronesian languages and peoples is Island Southeast Asia. But cultural evolution is a continuum, and quite obviously the Austronesians did not spring into being fully formed in this area some five thousand years ago. There must on grounds of simple logic have been peoples who may be called Pre-Austronesian in a taxonomic sense, and it is with these that certain problems arise which are insoluble at present. We cannot take it for granted that Pre-Austronesian languages have been indigenous to Island Southeast Asia for all time, and in chapter 5 I raised the possibility that their speakers spread into the area from either southern China or Japan, well in excess of five thousand years ago. Such movements may have introduced the flake and blade stone tool technologies into Island Southeast Asia, as well as horticulture, although such associations are hard to demonstrate at present. They may also have increased the rate of Mongoloid gene flow, particularly into Taiwan,

the Philippines and Sulawesi.

THE NEOLITHIC CULTURES OF TAIWAN

The Taiwanese Corded Ware and Lungshanoid cultures have been described already in the previous chapter, as both appear to have their ultimate origins on the southern Chinese mainland. I would hypothesise that the Corded Ware Culture may well be associated with speakers of an early Austronesian language ancestral to the present-day Atayalic languages (see page 123), which may represent an initial split from Proto-Austronesian, and which was probably established on the island by 4000 B.C. or earlier. The southern Chinese parallels for the Corded Ware Culture naturally strengthen claims for Pre-Austronesian movements from this area, and may well provide an archaeological edge over Japan, although we cannot necessarily assume that the spread of a new ceramic or blade tool technology will be accompanied by population migration.

Perhaps we should leave problems associated with the conceptually hazy Pre-Austronesians to future researchers, and turn our attention now to some of the more concrete facts of Taiwanese archaeology. Although we have looked at the Corded Ware and Lungshanoid Cultures, these do not represent the totality of Taiwanese Neolithic development. Furthermore, we still have the problem of providing some kind of archaeological identification for the Tsouic and Paiwanic linguistic subgroups.

In the northern part of Taiwan, from the site of Ta-p'en-k'eng and the shell mound of Yüan-shan, in addition to about 18 other sites, come the remains of the Yüan-shan Culture[2].

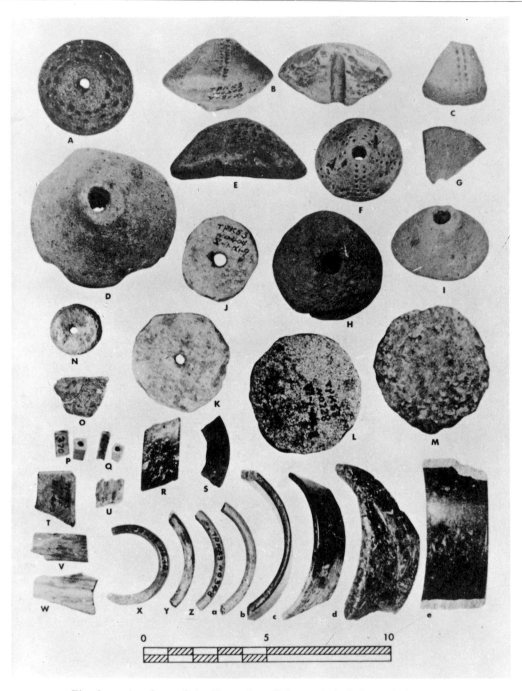

Fig. 8.2a. Artefacts of the Yüan-shan Culture: baked clay spindle whorls and pottery discs (A–N), bronze fragment of uncertain cultural affiliation (O), beads, rings and bracelet fragments of jade or serpentine (P–Z, a–e). From Chang 1969a.

Fig. 8.2b.Artefacts of the Yüan-shan Culture: incised and stamped ceramic decoration. From Chang 1969a.

This dates to between 2000 B.C. and 0, and like its contemporaries in the Philippines is not closely related to the Lungshanoid. Yüan-shan internal development is not well known, for the site of Ta-p'en-k'eng, which has produced the most information, seems to belong mainly to the period between 1000 B.C. and 0. However, present evidence points to an origin from the Corded Ware Culture within Taiwan, combined with a number of distinctive ceramic innovations.

Yüan-shan pottery shows no signs of coiling or wheel manufacture, and has no cord or basket-marked decoration. There are a few bowls, but the most common form at Ta-p'en-k'eng is a globular collared jar with a ring foot, strap handles on the neck, and a lid. The paste is tempered with quartz grit, and fired at a low temperature, most probably in a bonfire. The pots are slipped in a brown or grey wash, and have plain bodies, with simple incised and stamped decoration restricted to the neck region (figure 8.2b). Some of this decoration includes dentate stamped motifs and rows of open circles. Tripod feet and painting are absent at Ta-p'en-k'eng, and cut-outs in ring feet very rare. Despite the loss of the corded decoration, which is in fact a very important negative innovation, the Yüan-shan ceramics can be derived from the Corded Ware, which, as we have seen, is present in the lowest levels of Ta-p'en-k'eng, and which may only be separated from the succeeding Yüan-shan Culture by a fairly small time gap.

Apart from the pottery, Yüan-shan material culture includes quadrangular cross-sectioned adzes, some stepped or shouldered, together with triangular and sometimes perforated slate arrow-heads, grooved net sinkers, and crudely flaked stone hoes. Stone bracelets, and spindle whorls and perforated discs of pottery are also common, but the polished stone knives of Lungshanoid type are rare. Dogs, possibly domesticated, are known from the Yüan-shan shellmound, and burials from the same site do not have shovel-shaped incisor teeth, which may suggest closer affinity with contemporary groups in Island Southeast Asia rather than in mainland China.

So far, the Yüan-shan Culture appears to be restricted mainly to northern Taiwan, and the Lungshanoid to the western coast and southern tip of the island. The east coast of Taiwan, which is still settled by Austronesians today, has a confused archaeological aspect, with possible traces of the Corded Ware Culture, and what appears to be a later culture called the T'ai-yuan

by Pearson[3]. The T'ai-yuan Culture is associated with Yüan-shan pottery types, together with stone cist coffins and groups of standing stones which give it a certain Austronesian aspect, reinforced by probable Austronesian linguistic continuity in the area to the present. If the T'ai-yuan Culture can more definitely be related to the Yüan-shan in the future, it would help to place the Lungshanoid in perspective as an intrusive west coast enclave.

At the end of the first millennium B.C., Taiwan came under the influence of the southern Chinese Geometric pottery cultures (see page 181), and this type of pottery seems to dominate the island, particularly in the west and north, until recent times. Since this does not really concern us, we return to the problems of linguistic and archaeological correlation mentioned above.

However Austronesian languages came to be located on Taiwan, it is fairly clear that they were spoken there by well before 2000 B.C.[4]. The Corded Ware Culture is probably to be associated with early Austronesians (ancestral Atayalic speakers), as suggested above, while the succeeding Yüan-shan and T'ai-yuan Cultures are likely to be connected both with Atayalic and with Tsouic speakers. There is archaeological continuity from the Corded Ware Culture through into the Yüan-shan, and probably the T'ai-yuan as well, although the problems of linguistic relationship between Atayalic and Tsouic are still with us. Whether Tsouic and Atayalic share a common Taiwanese origin, or whether ancestral Tsouic was introduced to the island from outside, are questions which defy a simple answer at present.

Concerning the linguistic status of the Lungshanoid, we must first remember that the Taiwanese member of this culture group is of indisputable Chinese origin. Chang[5] has suggested that its bearers may have spoken ancestral Paiwanic languages, which by the time of Chinese settlement in the seventeenth century A.D. had expanded to cover most of coastal Taiwan. Ferrell[6] has suggested that the Paiwanic languages may not have been in Taiwan for as long as Atayalic and Tsouic, and that they may have come from an unknown outside area. If this outside area could be southern China, then the Lungshanoid could represent a back-migration from a formerly established mainland enclave of Austronesian languages (like Chamic of Vietnam), which has thus given rise to the Paiwanic languages of Taiwan but which is now totally extinct on the mainland. There are in fact Chinese records of southern mainland peoples who may have spoken Austronesian languages (the Yüeh), although the evidence for this linguistic identification is weak[7]. Nevertheless, I put this forward as a hypothesis to explain the Lungshanoid presence in Taiwan, since there are no non-Austronesian languages on the island with which it might otherwise be correlated. We should, of course, remember that the possible Lungshanoid-Paiwanic relationship is no argument for locating Proto-Austronesian in southern China; the dates are simply far too late.

From the evidence discussed above, it should be clear that Taiwan is a potentially vital area for the transmission of cultural innovations from the Asian mainland into the islands. I choose to emphasise the importance of the Corded Ware-Yüan-shan cultural tradition in this respect, rather than that represented by the Lungshanoid, although it has been more common to emphasise the latter in the past[8]. After we have examined the Philippine and Melanesian Neolithic cultures, it should be apparent that they have greater similarities to the Yüan-shan than they do to the Lungshanoid.

NEOLITHIC AND METAL AGE CULTURES IN THE PHILIPPINES

Because of their geographical position between southern China and Melanesia, the Philippines have a marked importance for many aspects of Oceanic prehistory. By Southeast Asian standards they are fairly well-studied archaeologically, and this situation is partly due to a half-century of research carried out by H. Otley Beyer (1883–1966). In 1947 and 1948, Beyer published two detailed works on Philippine prehistory as then understood[9], and presented in these a synthesis which he had already foreshadowed as early as 1932[10]. His theories culminated in 1948 with a rather elaborate series of migrations, based on minute typological variations in adzes and on the ideas contained in Heine Geldern's 'Urheimat' of 1932. Beyer in fact elevated wave-migration theories to their peak of complexity in Southeast Asia, and it is not surprising to find that recent scientific excavations give them very little support[11].

Beyer's scheme involved an Early Neolithic (round or oval axe-adze) culture in three migrant waves between 4000 and 2250 B.C., a Middle Neolithic (shouldered and ridged axe-adze)

culture with several adze variants between 2250 and 1750 B.C., and a Late Neolithic culture with plain and stepped adzes (Duff types 2 and 1A) between 1750 and 250 B.C. This latter culture overlaps with the earliest bronze, between 800 and 250 B.C. Beyer's overall dating for the Neolithic seems to have been a reasonable guess, and his late Neolithic, as with Heine Geldern's Vierkantbeilkultur, does appear to be a general distillation of the main aspects of Philippine Neolithic culture. His Early and Middle Neolithic cultures, like those of Heine Geldern, are of very limited validity. In addition, he made the erroneous assumption that pottery was not made in the Philippines before the Metal Age.

The Late Neolithic as described by Beyer includes many items which are closely paralleled elsewhere in Southeast Asia. We have already described the adzes under Duff's first adze focus, and Beyer, like Duff, believed that Polynesian adzes are to be derived from the Philippines. In addition, the Province of Batangas on Luzon has revealed so many tools of nephrite that Beyer believed that the so-called 'jade-cult' of New Zealand was derived from here – an erroneous assumption, as we shall see. The nephrite artefacts of Batangas offer a large and interesting range – needles and chisels, tanged spearheads like the slate examples of Taiwan, cylindrical and disc-shaped beads, perforated axe-like pendants similar to those from Tran Ninh in Laos, bracelets, plain discs, and the lingling-o earrings. Some ornaments, such as bracelets and beads, are of shell, and glass beads and bronze objects (socketed axes, arrowheads and miniature bells) also occur in some of the Batangas sites. Beyer left precious little stratigraphic information on these finds for posterity, but now we have the benefit of some excellent recent excavations to provide a balance.

The best Neolithic and Metal Age sequence known from the Philippines is that reported by Robert Fox for Palawan[12], and we can use this, together with forays into other areas, to build up a basic cultural sequence for the group. The earliest putative Neolithic assemblage for Palawan, albeit preceramic, is from Duyong Cave in the Tabon region. Here, Fox recovered a flexed male burial which was provided with a stone adze of Duff type 2, four adzes of *Tridacna* shell, two ear discs and a breast pendant made from the perforated bases of *Conus* shells, and six *Arca* shells which seem to have been used as lime containers for betel-nut chewing (figure 8.3). Charcoal from the burial gave a carbon date of

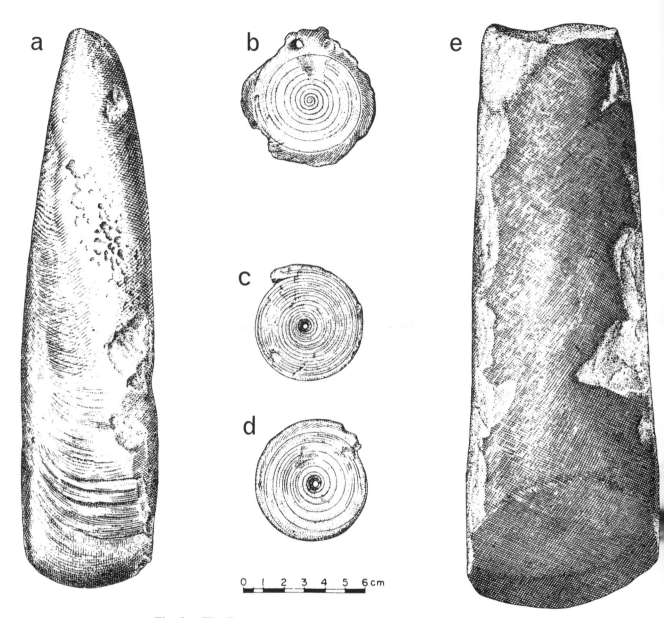

Fig. 8.3. The Duyong Cave preceramic assemblage: (a) shell adze; (b–d)
Conus shell pendants or ear discs; (e) stone adze. From Fox 1970.

2680±250 B.C. (*c.* 3100 B.C. if calibrated), and an associated level in the cave with similar shell implements gave a date of 3730±80 B.C. (*c.* 4300 B.C. if calibrated). Similar shell items have been found elsewhere in Palawan and the Sulu Archipelago, and the Duyong preceramic assemblage is of a date and type which suggests a relationship with the earliest Austronesian settlement of Oceania – particularly Melanesia. This is an important point, for in the chapter on Melanesia (chapter 9) I will suggest that the

earliest Austronesian settlement of this latter area was possibly preceramic as well, and that the main expansion of pottery using peoples into Melanesia did not take place until about 1500 B.C.

In the Philippines, however, the earliest pottery does appear by about 3000 B.C., presumably quite hard on the heels of the Duyong preceramic assemblage. Plain ceramics with a minor red-slipped component are now reported back to about 3000 B.C. from the site of Dimolit in north-eastern Luzon, from the Sulu Archipelago, and from the Talaud Islands in north-eastern Indonesia[13]. Furthermore, the Dimolit site has produced ring feet with small circular cut-outs, and similar sherds are present in Corded Ware sites on Taiwan. Since plain pottery dates back to about 3000 B.C. in southern Sulawesi and Timor also (see below), then it is clear that a widespread ceramic tradition, somewhat different from the corded ceramics of Taiwan and the mainland, had spread through the Philippines and eastern Indonesia by this date. In addition, the Dimolit site also yielded the remains of two surface-floored houses, each about three metres square.

Returning to Fox's Palawan sequence, we find that the first pottery here does not appear until about 1000 B.C., but this could simply represent a local absence of data. The earliest Palawan ceramics belong to a rich tradition of jar burial, which runs through the first millennium B.C., and on into the recent past in some areas. We may refer to this as the Tabon Jar Burial Complex, after Fox[14], who places it straddling the late Neolithic and Metal Ages. The jars are frequently lidded, and were placed on the floors of caves, in situations which of course make stratigraphic analysis difficult. Secondary uncremated burials were placed in the jars after maceration, and the bones are often coated with red haematite. Smaller pots and ornaments were then placed in or around the burial jars as grave-goods, as they were in the Plain of Jars and Sa-Huynh Cultures of the mainland, and in the jar burials of the Talaud Islands to the south (see page 215). It appears that most jars at Tabon contained only one individual, and the skulls are stated to be distinctively Mongoloid. The use of jars is not the only burial method, however, and there are a small number of primary and secondary inhumations as well.

A late Neolithic phase of the Tabon Jar Burial Complex is represented in two caves near Tabon – Ngipe't Duldug and Manunggul chamber A. The former site yielded an assemblage of shell and stone beads, a stepped 1A adze, and a shell scoop and bracelet. Manunggul A, dated by two carbon dates to about 800 B.C., yielded a much more spectacular assemblage of beads of drilled nephrite and other rare stones and shell, together with some remarkable incised and red painted pots, including one with a 'ship of the dead' model with two human occupants on its lid (figure 8.4). This model of course reminds one of the boat symbolism on the Dong-Son drums, as well as of

Fig. 8.4. Jar from Manunggul chamber A, with red-painted and incised motifs and a 'ship of the dead' model on lid. Height 66.5 cm. From Fox 1970.

recent tribal beliefs on Palawan, and Manunggul A clearly represents a very skilled, if localised potting tradition. The splendid position of the cave in a sheer and almost inaccessible cliff well befits its magnificent contents. Another assemblage related to those from Ngipe't Duldug and Manunggul A comes from the Leta Leta cave at El Nido, near the northern tip of Palawan, and this produced shell bead necklaces and shell bracelets, together with very fine pottery including a shallow bowl with an openwork ring foot. Fox believes that the Leta Leta assemblage is late Neolithic, and although Leta Leta and Ngipe't Duldug have not actually produced jar burials, it is nevertheless clear that this mode of burial was developing in or introduced into the Philippines during the late Neolithic, by about 1000 B.C.

The Metal Age jar burial assemblages at Tabon

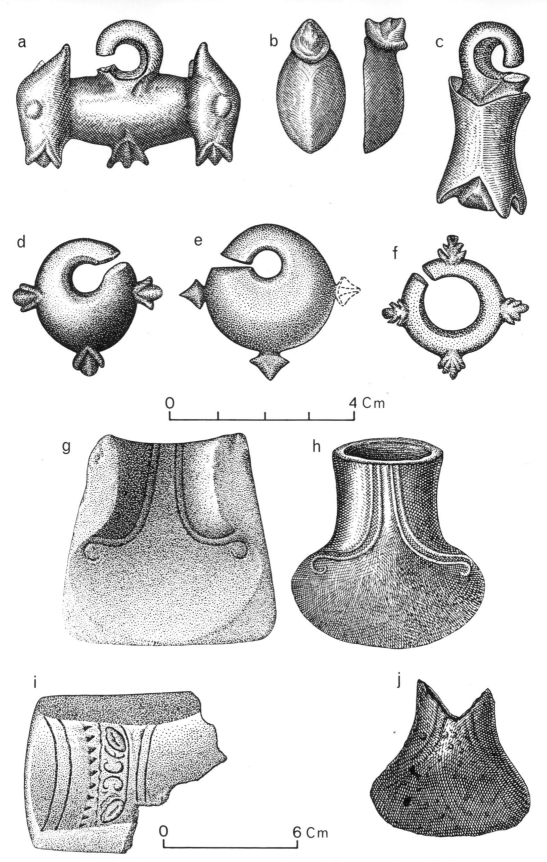

Fig. 8.5. Artefacts from the Tabon Caves: (a-f) ear pendants of jade –
(d–f) are of the lingling-o type; (g–j) baked clay casting valves and socketed
bronze axes. From Fox 1970.

commence about 600–500 B.C., and are divided into two groups by Fox: Early Metal Age, with bronze and glass, and Developed Metal Age, with bronze, glass and iron, the latter being represented in Manunggul chamber B, with a carbon date of *c.* 190 B.C. Although tin is not apparently to be found in the Philippines, the presence of axe moulds shows that local casting was carried out, perhaps using imported mainland tin. The bronzes include socketed axes with splayed and rounded blades, socketed spearheads, tanged arrowheads, knives, and a possible barbed harpoon. To the jade beads of the late Neolithic

are added carnelian and glass forms of Sa-Huynh type, although it is not known whether the glass was manufactured locally. There are also a few gold beads. Jade bracelets and the lingling-o type ornaments appear in many sites, together with a variety of other more unusual jade ornaments (figure 8.5). Shell spoons, beads and scoops continue to be used, and in the later sites, tanged knives and spearheads of iron make an appearance.

The Tabon pottery (figure 8.6) is fairly homogeneous, and all hand-made and fired at low temperatures. The majority of vessels are plain, but

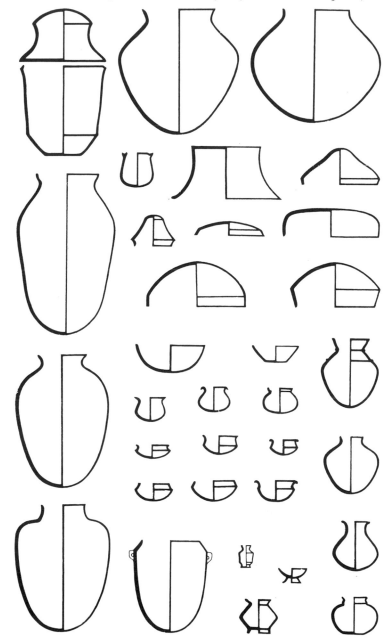

Fig. 8.6. Vessel forms of the Tabon pottery complex. From Fox 1970.

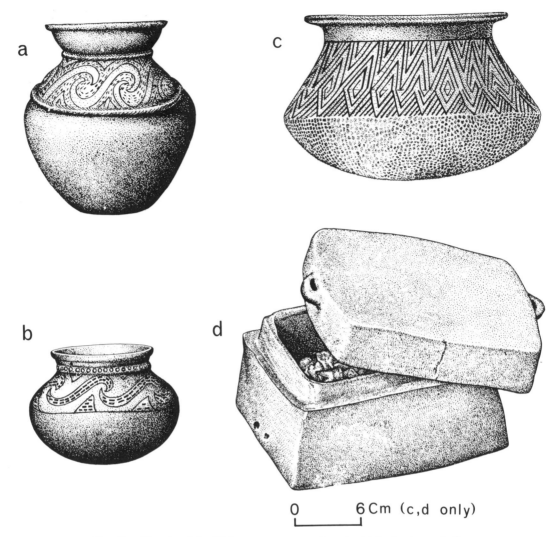

0   6 Cm (c,d only)

Fig. 8.7. Vessels of the Tabon pottery complex: (a, b) incised vessels from Manunggul chamber A, Late Neolithic; (c) incised and paddle-impressed vessel from Diwata Cave, Early Metal Age; (d) pottery container from Bato Puti Cave, containing painted teeth. From Fox 1970.

polished, red-slipped, and carved or bound-paddle impressed vessels are also quite common. Incision is rare, but occasionally occurs in the form of scrolls and triangles (figure 8.7), while painting in red haematite is restricted to the late Neolithic site at Manunggul Cave. Round-based or carinated vessel forms are the most common, and ring feet are rare, tripods absent. The forms and the commonness of cord-marking, particularly in the Neolithic jar burial sites, relate the Tabon pottery most closely to the Niah Cave pottery in Sarawak, of which more later. Resemblances to the Metal Age Kalanay pottery of the central Philippines (below) are not so marked, as cord-marking is absent in the latter. But some of the Tabon burial jars with trunconical lids are paralleled at Sa-Huynh in South Vietnam. In fact, with Sa-Huynh, Kalanay, Niah, Tabon and other sites to be mentioned, we have come upon a major Austronesian jar burial tradition located in the northern and eastern archipelagic zone in the later second and first millennia B.C. This seems to postdate, by only a few centuries, the initial spread of pottery manufacture eastward into Melanesia.

To explain the Tabon Jar Burial Complex, Fox has resorted to a view of successive migrations from the Southeast Asian mainland, despite his disagreements with Beyer's theories. Thus according to Fox, pottery and jade working enter Palawan first, about 1500 B.C., followed by jar burial from Indochina, then bronze, glass, and the lingling-o ornaments, and finally iron. Southern China and Indochina appear to be favoured places of origin, with transmissions via Indonesia and Borneo, or via the northern Philippines. However, while the technologies of bronze and iron may ultimately be a result of contact with the mainland, the Palawan jar burials are earlier than any on the mainland by 500 years. Burial in pottery jars seems to be an indigenous development in Indonesia and the Philippines, with an offshoot represented by the Sa-Huynh Culture in South Vietnam, and the ceramics themselves seem to be ultimately inspired by the Taiwanese Corded Ware and Yüan-shan ceramics. The jar burials are therefore an Austronesian innovation, and they have continued in many western Austronesian areas until recent times[15]. Because the Lapita pottery style which spread from Island Southeast Asia into Melanesia about 1500 B.C. was not associated with jar burial, it is probable that the latter do not commence development much prior to 1000 B.C. – a date which is well supported by the Tabon evidence.

THE LATE NEOLITHIC AND METAL AGES IN THE CENTRAL PHILIPPINES

In the central Philippines, as on Palawan, the first millennium B.C. is also occupied by a tradition of jar burial. However, the island of Masbate has produced pottery which may well predate the use of burial jars, and which relates very closely to the Yüan-shan pottery of Taiwan and to the first Melanesian (Lapita) ceramics. In two caves on a high limestone knoll known as Batungan Mountain, Solheim[16] has recovered assemblages of flake tools, untanged adzes, and many potsherds, of which about 98% were undecorated. The ones which were decorated, however, are of outstanding importance – they are red slipped, and have a motif range including rows of stamped circles, incised scrolls and rectilinear designs, and motifs composed of

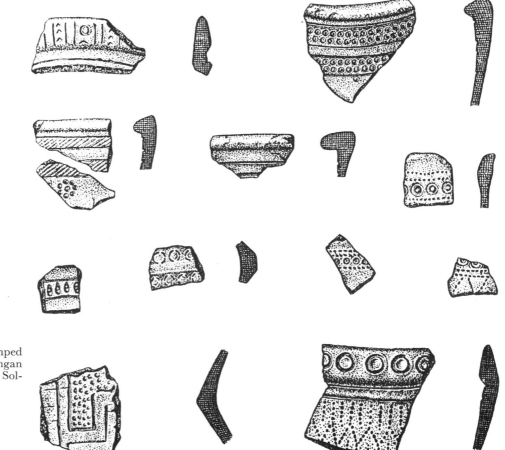

Fig. 8.8. Incised and stamped sherds from the Batungan Caves, Masbate. From Solheim 1968b.

impressed dots arranged in lines (figure 8.8). Some of the incisions also have a white lime infill. This pottery is so far unique in the Philippines, and its resemblances to Yüan-shan pottery from Taiwan and to the earliest ceramics in the Marianas Islands and Melanesia are of profound significance, as we will see later. One of the Batungan caves has yielded a carbon date of *c.* 750 B.C., but the ceramic features suggest that the sites may well be at least 500 years older than this.

The other central Philippine culture to be described dates from the latter half of the first

Fig. 8.9 Pottery of Kalanay type, central Philippines. From Solheim 1959b.

millennium B.C. onwards, and belongs therefore to the Metal Age. This is the Kalanay Culture, again defined mainly by the work of Solheim, who published in 1964[17] a detailed analysis of a large amount of pottery collected from sites in the Philippines by Carl Guthe between 1922 and 1925, as well as his own excavations in the Kalanay jar burial cave on Masbate Island. The sites included within the whole Kalanay Culture may date from about 400 B.C. through to A.D. 1500, but internal developments are not yet clearly differentiated. Solheim has also defined two other ceramic complexes of Metal Age date for the Philippines, and he calls these Bau-Malay and Novaliches. However, there are many problems connected with the interpretation of these two late and insecurely dated pottery styles, and they will not be considered further.

Kalanay ceramics comprise round-based jars, footed dishes, some with cut-outs in the feet, rare tripod vessels, and lids. The vessels are made on a slow wheel, they are often red-slipped, and they frequently have facetted body angles or carinations[18]. The decoration is mainly incised, with triangles, scrolls and rectangular meanders being fairly common, but there is no cord-marking. Some motifs are stamped with the edge of an *Arca* shell, as at Sa-Huynh (figure 8.9c). There can be little doubt that Kalanay is closely related in some way to the Sa-Huynh Culture, and several pots which are very definitely in the Kalanay tradition are known from as far away as Samui Island on the western side of the Gulf of Siam[19]. Since this island is about 1100 kilometres west of Sa-Huynh, and well over 2400 kilometres from the central Philippines, the implications of this find are obviously of great importance.

The Kalanay pottery style also shares motifs with the Dong-Son bronzes, but not with the crude Dong-Son pottery. It is not particularly closely related to the Tabon pottery, which, as noted above, falls closer to the Niah Cave pottery from Sarawak. Associated artefacts in the Kalanay cave itself include a Duff type 2 stone adze, nephrite and glass beads, a bronze miniature bell, iron knives, part of a shell bracelet, and a disc pendant made from a *Conus* shell, like those from the Duyong Cave burial on Palawan.

Although the Kalanay site has no absolute dates, Solheim is inclined to see iron, glass, and perhaps weaving as being introduced into the central Philippines about 400 B.C. Other Kalanay burial and habitation sites in Sorgoson Province, south-eastern Luzon, lack iron and glass, despite

0   5 Cm

Fig. 8.10. Metal Age pottery from Leang Buidane Cave, Talaud Islands, probably mid-late first millennium A.D.

late carbon dates of between 100 B.C. and A.D. 200[20]. There seems little doubt that the Kalanay ceramic style could in fact have continued in production for a very long time in the central Philippines, and this circumstance makes it rather difficult to gauge its exact significance. In a long series of papers commencing in 1959, Solheim[21] has developed a concept of a Sa-Huynh-Kalanay ceramic tradition which includes a large proportion of all the Neolithic and pre-Indianised ceramic assemblages ever recovered in Southeast Asia from Thailand to Irian Jaya. With this view I cannot agree completely, and Solheim's concept seems mainly to be a distillation of the many ceramic features which all Southeast Asian cultures share in common, although the strong parallels between the total assemblages from Sa-Huynh, Kalanay and Tabon are still quite remarkable, and undoubtedly of major culture-historical significance.

As far as the Philippine Neolithic and Metal Age sequence is concerned generally, it is becoming clear that we have first of all the Duyong preceramic shell assemblage, and then a tradition of plain and red-slipped pottery which intrudes over this from about 3000 B.C. down to perhaps 1500 B.C. After this date, decorated pottery of the late Neolithic type appears as at Batungan, with jar burials coming in at about 1000 B.C. The late Neolithic pottery is decorated by incision, stamp-

ing, and sometimes by the old techniques of cord or basket-marking, which seem to have disappeared during the period of production of the earlier plain wares. It is with these decorated ceramics of the period 1500–500 B.C. that the important links with Taiwan (Yüan-shan Culture), eastern Indonesia, the Marianas Islands and Melanesia (Lapita Culture) become visible. The Oceanic pottery is considered later in chapters 9 and 10.

The jar burial cultures, which pass as a continuous tradition into the Early Metal Age about 500 B.C., are so far well represented at Tabon and Kalanay, and of course in the Sa-Huynh Culture of South Vietnam. They are also very well represented in the Talaud Islands to the south of Mindanao, and a brief excursion southwards is now warranted.

The Talaud Islands are linguistically and culturally closely related to the Philippines, even though they now belong politically to Indonesia. Excavations there in 1974 by I.M. Sutayasa and myself were conducted in three caves, and I have already referred above to plain and red-slipped pottery going back to perhaps 3000 B.C., and on page 73 to the preceramic flake and blade industry. The cave deposits in these islands are well stratified and undisturbed, and the plain ware grades, at a date still to be determined, into decorated pottery with close affinities to Tabon and Kalanay (figure 8.10). The later stages of the sequence in the first millennium A.D. contain jar burials together with rich grave goods, including glass, agate and carnelian beads (see page 230), a socketed copper axe and casting moulds of baked clay, pottery earrings, stone earplugs, and shell bracelets. Since our analyses have only just begun I cannot be too precise about the significance of these finds, but it is clear that jar burial sites of the Tabon and Kalanay type continue in use in Talaud until about A.D. 1000.

The Philippine and Talaud cultural developments are well paralleled in other parts of Indonesia, particularly in Sarawak, Sulawesi and Timor, and we can turn to these regions now.

THE NEOLITHIC OF NIAH CAVE, SARAWAK[22]

The Neolithic remains at Niah cover a similar time-span to those from Tabon, and run from the mid-second millennium B.C. down to the appearance of bronze at possibly 250 B.C., or thereabouts. Harrisson dates the Niah adzes of Duff type 2A from *c.* 2500 B.C., and if he is correct then the cave may contain an earlier Neolithic assemblage, although there is no clear sign of this at present. The Neolithic assemblage so far reported has come in the main from burials[23] found in a cemetery area situated behind the main habitation area at the mouth of the cave. These burials are in a different tradition from the earlier preceramic flexed and contorted ones, and as

with most other Southeast Asian Neolithic burials, the extended position now becomes the most common. These extended inhumations are sometimes sprinkled with haematite, and some show signs of burning. They were often placed in shallow trenches, sometimes wrapped in pandanus mats or textiles, and some were in coffins of split tree-trunks or cigar-shaped bamboo caskets. One of the wooden coffins has given a radiocarbon date approximating 500 B.C.

Cremated or less intensely burnt secondary burials are almost as common as primary inhumations, and these are found in wooden coffins, pots, or bamboo caskets. One carved-paddle impressed pot, which contained burnt bone and a small accessory bowl, is radiocarbon-dated to *c.* 1300 B.C. from a piece of burnt wood, and Barbara Harrisson[24] has suggested that the Niah burials as a whole span the period between approximately 1600 and 400 B.C.

Very few of the burials had any grave goods, and only one out of the sixty-six so far reported had an association with bronze. The artefacts which have been found in association include a range of bone pendants and tubular beads, perforated teeth for necklaces[25], shell discs and rings, and a Duff type 2A adze. In shape and decoration, the Niah pottery[26] is very close to the Tabon pottery, and most sherds are either plain or impressed with a cord-bound or carved paddle. The latter is of some interest, both at Niah and at Tabon, because of its contemporary presence in the Geometric pottery styles of southern China. In addition to the above, Niah has also produced unusual spouted vessels[27], and

Fig. 8.11. Three-colour vessel from Niah Cave, Sarawak, with rectangular meander decoration.

some very fine 'three-colour ware', painted in black and red on a cream base, with elaborate designs, such as the rectangular meanders, which are closely paralleled in the Kalanay tradition (figure 8.11). With its high proportion of paddle-impressed decoration, the Niah Neolithic pottery may also be directly ancestral to the 'Bau-Malay' impressed cooking pots which are so common in Borneo and Palawan today[28].

The appearance of the domestic dog and pig in the Niah Neolithic[29], together with the burials of Mongoloid affinity, are two further points of significance reported to date about this site. As far as one can see, the Niah Neolithic has fundamental parallels in the Philippines during the late second and first millennia B.C., although similar parallels in the islands of Indonesia proper to the south are unlikely to be very visible in the present state of knowledge. There are no striking parallels with Malaya[30].

NEOLITHIC SITES IN EASTERN INDONESIA

In south-western Sulawesi, as in the Philippines and Talaud, we see the appearance of plain pottery at about 3000 B.C. in association with a late stage of the Toalean industry (see page 73). Of similar significance are Glover's findings from his excavations in eastern Timor[31], where plain pottery in the form of globular pots and open bowls, some with low ring feet, seems to have been introduced again at about 3000 B.C. This pottery is associated with a shell assemblage comprising bracelets, discs, beads, and adzes, together with a single one-piece fishhook of *Trochus* shell found at the cave of Bui Ceri Uato.

Between 1500 B.C. and A.D. 500, rare sherds appear in the Timor sequence with distinctive incised triangles and rows of interlocking semi-circles, and very similar pottery, so far undated, is known from sites in south-western and central Sulawesi (see below). There are also some similarities with the late Neolithic and Metal Age decorated pottery in the Philippines, but there is too little material from Timor to allow detailed comparison.

Apart from the artefacts, Glover has evidence for the introduction by man of various animal species into Timor, which is of great significance in Southeast Asia where evidence of this type is extremely rare. From about 2500 B.C., bones of pig, an introduced and possibly domesticated species, appear in the Timorese cave record, and perhaps at the same time, although this is less

certain, the dog also appears. By about 1000 B.C., if not before, two further domesticated animals are present – a bovid of undetermined species, and sheep or goat. The two latter cannot be recognised apart from the fragmentary material and either one or both could be present, but both were, until Glover's work, totally unreported from Southeast Asian prehistoric sites. Bovids, in particular the species *Bos indicus*, are known from contemporary and earlier levels at Non Nok Tha in Thailand, but caprovines (sheep and goats) are at present only known from contemporary sites in northern China and in India. It is clear that as far as prehistoric economy is concerned, there is still a very long way to go before even the most rudimentary framework of information can be acquired for Southeast Asia. Especially, perhaps, when we consider three surprising introductions of wild mammals into

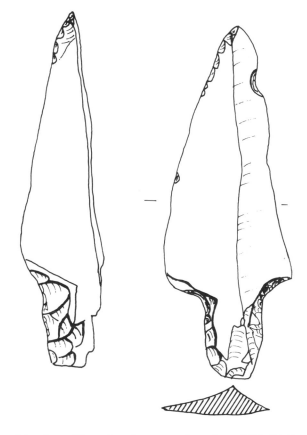

Fig. 8.12. Tanged point 13 cm long from Nikiniki I, Indonesian Timor.

Timor at about 2500 B.C. – the civet cat (*Paradoxurus hermaphroditus*) and the long-tailed macaque monkey (*Macaca iris*) from a westerly source, and the marsupial cuscus (*Phalanger orientalis*) from an easterly source, possibly New Guinea or Maluku. This is one of the very few known cases of transport by man of wild animals in prehistoric times, and of course raises the question of whether the other animals were in fact domesticated at the time of introduction. The pig, introduced into New Guinea by at least 6–7000 years ago, is a special problem in this regard.

Reports of earlier cave excavations in the western part of Timor also deserve brief mention. In two rock-shelters, Nikiniki I and Liang Leluat II[32], some rather unusual tanged points made on elongated blade-like flakes have been recovered (figure 8.12), and these are closely paralleled in Glover's excavation at Uai Bobo I (eastern Timor) where they date from approximately 300 B.C. to A.D. 1200. Nikiniki I has also yielded bifacially flaked adzes of an evidently localised form. From some time in the

first millennium B.C. metal appears to have been introduced into Timor, and from this time the numbers of stone tools in deposits drop markedly.

On the neighbouring island of Flores, flake and small blade industries on chert and obsidian are reported from shelters in the west and centre of the island, together with perforated pearl-shell discs and rare sherds of incised pottery[33]. At Liang Toge[34], an assemblage of this type, without pottery, was associated with pig bones, human skeletal remains diagnosed by T. Jacob as Australomelanesian, and a radiocarbon date of 1600 ± 525 B.C. (*c.* 1800 B.C. if calibrated). At present, this island offers a picture of rather slow development when compared with Timor, but this may of course be due to lack of information. Flores has produced incised and applied-relief pottery which may be Neolithic[35], as has the area around the MacCluer Gulf (Teluk Berau) in Irian Jaya[36], but little is known about the context of these finds.

Apart from the Toalean sites, Sulawesi has so far yielded only two other sites with prehistoric ceramic associations. These are both close together

Fig. 8.13. Stone adzes and points from Kalumpang, west-central Sulawesi. From van Heekeren 1972.

Fig. 8.14. Ceramic decoration from Kalumpang, west-central Sulawesi. From van Heekeren 1972.

on the middle section of the Karama River in central Sulawesi, and consist of two open sites at Minanga Sipakko and Kalumpang[37]. The latter is the most important, and was first tested by van Stein Callenfels in 1933, and later by van Heekeren in 1949. All the finds are from one level, and include Duff type 2A adzes, lenticular cross-sectioned adzes (some tanged or waisted, like the undated examples from Gua Kepah in Malaya), and tanged or plain projectile points of slate and schist, the tanged forms being similar to those from Luzon and Taiwan (figure 8.13). Stone knives, barkcloth beaters, and a possible phallic symbol of baked clay were also found, together with many potsherds, of which about 6% had incised decoration. The designs on this pottery (figure 8.14), particularly the rows of interlocking semicircles, are especially close to those found by Glover in Timor, and also to pre-historic pottery excavated in the Maros region of south-western Sulawesi by Mulvaney and Soejono in 1969[38]. In his excavation report, van Heekeren claimed an age of about 600 years for the site, but this was challenged at the same time by Beyer[39] who suggested at least a B.C. date, which would seem to be confirmed by the ceramic parallels. The site of Minanga Sipakko is similar to Kalumpang.

Despite many uncertainties, one can hardly fail to be impressed by the ceramic similarities expressed within Neolithic and Metal Age cultures from Taiwan and the Philippines, through to Talaud, Sarawak and Sulawesi, and into Timor. The tanged stone points also have a similar distribution, from Japan, southern China, through Taiwan, the Philippines (Luzon), and again into Sulawesi and Timor. At present, these similarities hardly extend to Indochina if one excludes the Sa-Huynh Culture, and nor is there much evidence to extend them to Malaya or western Indonesia at the moment. It is clear that the easterly regions of Island Southeast Asia were linked by related and expanding ceramic Neolithic and Metal Age cultures during the third, second and first millennia B.C., and it is from these that we can trace the expansion of pottery-producing cultures into Oceania. In order to make a little clearer the relationships over time and space, I envisage the following overall sequence for application to Taiwan, the Philippines, and the sites we have been discussing in eastern Indonesia[40]. I would not feel justified in applying it to any other area at present.

Neolithic Period – Early Phase

This includes the Corded Ware Culture in Taiwan, together with the plain and red-slipped pottery from the Philippines, Talaud, the Maros region and Timor. It may well relate to an early expansion of Austronesian-speaking horticulturalists through the region, dating from about 5000 B.C. in Taiwan.

Neolithic Period – Late Phase

This includes the Yüan-shan Culture of Taiwan, the Batungan and early Tabon pottery from the Philippines, and similar decorated pottery from Timor and possibly Kalumpang. It dates from about 2000 B.C. in Taiwan, and perhaps 1500 B.C. further south, and it is the phase during which the first pottery-making peoples move into Micronesia and Melanesia. In its terminal sub-phase, jar burial appears in the Philippines.

Early Metal Period (or Metal Age)

This is the period of the jar burial cultures *par excellence*, particularly at Tabon, Niah, Kalanay, and in the Talaud Islands. It is also the period of bronze, iron, and of glass and carnelian beads of Indian and Malayan origin (see below). It begins about 500 B.C. and lasts to at least A.D. 1000, but its internal chronological developments are unfortunately still obscure.

Late Period

Although not a concern in the present context, this period begins with imported Chinese porcelain from possibly A.D. 1200. Jar burials continue, and many local ceramic styles are reported from the Philippines, and from my own work in northern Sulawesi and the Talaud Islands. The Late Period is intricately tangled with cultures of the ethnographic present, and ceramic styles seem to be rather more complex and diversified than in previous periods, perhaps because of the rapidly increasing rate of foreign contact, particularly Chinese and Moslem.

NEOLITHIC SITES IN WESTERN INDONESIA

The Neolithic of the important large islands of Java and Sumatra is unfortunately still surrounded by almost total mystery. In south-central Sumatra, obsidian flake and blade industries have been found in the Lake Kerinci and Jambi areas, as noted on page 78, and production of these seems to continue after pottery makes its appearance, particularly at the Tianko Panjang cave near Jambi. In the surface collections made around Lake Kerinci[41] the flakes are possibly associated with cord-marked and incised pottery, a pottery earplug of Somrong Sen type, and facetted carnelian beads, all of which have parallels in the Neolithic and Metal Age cultures of Indochina. However, since a bronze armband and part of the tympanum of a Heger type I drum were also found at one of the Kerinci sites, we may be dealing with mixed collections covering a long time span. Of equally unknown context are the flint workshops, scattered over an area of about ten kilometres in diameter around Pacitan and Punung in south-central Java[42]. These seem to have specialised in producing adzes of varying sizes, chisels, and also arrowheads of the rather enigmatic Gua Lawa type (page 76), and they would clearly repay further investigation.

However, our knowledge of prehistoric Java is likely to undergo some transformations in the near future, owing to the growing research programme of the National Research Centre of Archaeology of Indonesia. In western Java, putative Neolithic assemblages with plain, cord-marked or comb-incised pottery are known from highland lake-edge sites near Bandung and Leles, and also at Klapadua, Kramacati and Tanjong Pcriuk in the Jakarta region[43]. Another Neolithic site with plain pottery has been excavated at Kendeng Lembu in eastern Java[44]. Nevertheless, we do not yet have enough information to provide even a skeletal prehistoric framework for Java, although it is my impression that this large and important island will have a sequence (particularly in ceramics) rather different from that of eastern Indonesia and the Philippines. The present gap in knowledge is unfortunate, but the future looks very bright.

To this rather unhelpful corpus, it only remains to add a little insecure evidence for an extension of the jar burial tradition into Sulawesi and Sumba, and possibly Java[45]. At Sa'bang in central Sulawesi a jar-field was excavated many years ago by Willems[46], but unfortunately none of the jars appear to have had any contents, and sherds of Chinese pottery were suspiciously found in the site. At Melolo in eastern Sumba a much richer urnfield was examined at various times in the 1920s and 1930s, and here many large round-based urns were found, containing fragmentary unburnt secondary burials, type 2A adzes, shell bracelets, shell and stone beads, and ·smaller votive pots. Some of the latter are highly polished and very elegant long-necked flasks, with incised geometric and anthropomorphic designs filled in with a white paint (figure 8.15). The date of this urnfield is debatable: van Heekeren has recently opted for a Neolithic date[47], while other authors adopt a Metal Age dating[48]. The flasks are paralleled in heavily disturbed settlement sites around Buni in west Java[49], and also in South Sumatra, and here again both Neolithic or Metal Age contexts are possible. Another jar burial cemetery is recorded from Anjar on the western coast of Java[50], where primary burials were placed in large urns together with smaller funerary pots. The latter look a little like the Philippine Kalanay material, but the general understanding of prehistoric jar burials in Indonesia is really so slight that any conclusions at this stage may be premature.

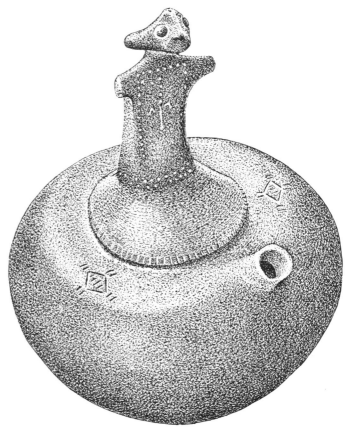

Fig. 8.15. Anthropomorphic flask from Melolo urnfield. From van Heekeren 1958.

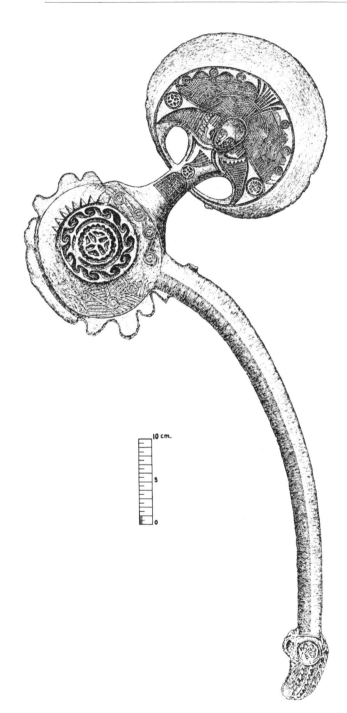

10 cm.

5

0

Fig. 8.16. Ceremonial bronze axe with Dong-Son ornament from Roti. From van Heekeren 1958.

THE METAL AGE OF WESTERN AND SOUTHERN INDONESIA[51]

The Metal Age in the Sunda Islands seems to be of Dong-Son affinity, and can be attributed tentatively to the period between 1000 B.C. and A.D. 500 in the larger western Islands. Even after this date, it is not at all clear what impact developing Indianisation had on indigenous bronze industries, and many objects claimed to have Dong-Son affinity could in reality be fairly recent. The cultural background to the bronze objects of Dong-Son type also remains unknown: findings of moulds for drums (not of Heger type I) and axes at various sites in Indonesia makes some degree of local manufacture certain, but we may also have to contend with trade from the mainland, as well as with the unknown potential for trade and influence to spread in the other direction from Indonesia to Indochina. The picture may also be complicated by direct Chinese contact with western Indonesia after the fifth century A.D.

The Indonesian bronzes resemble those of the Dong-Son style both in form and in composition, particularly in the frequently high lead content. Axes, always socketed as with the mainland types, have been found throughout the archipelago, and many have a distinctive 'swallowtail' upper extremity. Ceremonial axes allied to the boot-shaped axes of Dong-Son are known from Java, and the small island of Roti has yielded three unique and outstanding ceremonial axes with low relief decoration, including Dong-Son circle and tangent motifs and human figures with plumed headdresses (figure 8.16).

Drums of Heger type I are known from many islands to as far east as the Kai Islands, south of the Bombarai Peninsula of Irian Jaya, and three weathered tympani, possibly of this type, have been reported from the Cendrawasih (Vogelkop) Peninsula of Irian Jaya itself[52]. These are the most easterly occurrences of unequivocal Dong-Son artefacts, although western Melanesia does have some evidence for loosely defined 'Dong-Son influences' (see chapter 9). The Indonesian drums generally present classic Dong-Son decorative patterns, together with the animal and bird friezes and the ships of the dead. However, a remarkable drum of Heger type I from the small island of Sangeang, near Sumbawa, has a unique illustration of a raised-floor dwelling with a saddle-roof, within which are people who appear to be in costumes of the Chinese Han dynasty. A panel

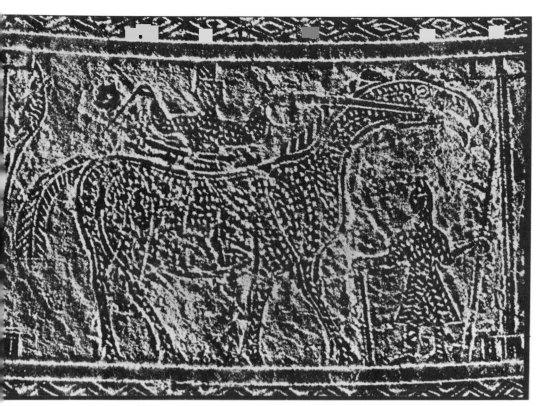

Fig. 8.17. Panel from the Sangeang drum ('Makalamau') showing two figures in non-Indonesian costume, one astride a horse. *c.* A.D. 250. From van Heekeren 1958.

Fig. 8.18. The drum from Salayar Island, showing friezes of elephants and peacocks on the sides. From Karlgren 1942.

elsewhere on the drum shows two men in what appear to be Kusana costumes (from north-western India), one sitting astride a horse, the other standing before the horse and holding a spear and a mace-like object (figure 8.17). Heine Geldern[53] has suggested that this drum was an import into Indonesia from Funan about A.D. 250. Two other remarkable drums, one from the Kai Islands with scenes of men hunting tigers with bows and arrows and lassooing deer, and another from Salayar with friezes of elephants and peacocks (figure 8.18), were evidently imports from the west also, as neither elephants, tigers nor peacocks occur in eastern Indonesia[54]. Two almost identical bronze flasks from Sumatra and

Madura, both decorated with thick spirals in low relief, are also considered to be of Dong-Son affinity by van Heekeren[55], and there is a specimen almost identical from Kandal in Cambodia[56] (figure 8.19).

Recent archaeological work in Java is helping to place the western Indonesian Metal Age in better perspective, and between 1970 and 1973 excavations were undertaken by the Indonesian National Research Centre of Archaeology at a very important site called Leuwiliang (or Pasir Angin) near Bogor. This site is on a hill-top commanding a magnificent vista of the surrounding countryside, and it appears that offerings were ceremonially placed or buried here around

Fig. 8.19. Bronze flasks of possible Dong-Son affinity: *left*, from Lake Kerinci, Sumatra, 51 cm high (from van Heekeren 1958); *right*, from Kandal, Cambodia, 35 cm high (courtesy Dr. H.H.E. Loofs). The Kandal specimen is almost identical to a third flask from Madura Island.

a large natural block of stone. The site may therefore have had primarily a religious function, and objects recovered include obsidian tools, iron daggers and knives, gold ornaments, glass and carnelian beads, and stone axes. Bronzes are also quite plentiful, and include axes, a bell and a bowl. The pottery is mainly plain, but there is some cord-marking and comb-incision. Radiocarbon dates are at present a little puzzling, but indicate use of the site between 1000 B.C. and A.D. 1000[57]. Similar Metal Age assemblages have recently been investigated by Sutayasa in the Buni district, west of Jakarta, here in association with extended burials. As with the Neolithic sites, research is just beginning, but the future looks exciting indeed.

Other bronze finds of outstanding importance in Indonesia include a group of 14 statuettes and 4 baroque bracelets decorated with relief spirals from Bangkinang in South Sumatra[58]. The statuettes are of dancers, and like the anthropomorphic mainland figurines described above (page 187), wear bracelets and anklets, earrings, loincloths, and spiral-shaped breast ornaments. Many other finds of bronze and glass beads throughout western and southern Indonesia, too numerous to mention here, attest to very close relations between Indonesia and Indochina in the Early Metal Age. It is of importance that the

Philippines seem to be much less involved in this relationship, and the bronze drums are totally absent from these islands. Furthermore, megaliths are also generally absent in the Philippines (except in northern Luzon), and it is to monuments of this type, particularly in Sumatra and Java, that we must now turn.

MEGALITHS IN INDONESIA

The megaliths reinforce the evidence from the bronzes: in the later first millennium B.C., a very strong Mainland Southeast Asian-Indonesian linkage of trade and influence existed, from which the Philippines and north-eastern Indonesia, with their related ceramic styles and jar burials, were fairly well isolated. The settlement of Malaya by the Malays may possibly have taken place during this period, although there is very little evidence to suggest when Austronesian speakers first settled western Indonesia. The linguistic evidence would suggest that this westward penetration may have begun before 3000 years ago, but in the absence of information on the Neolithic in this area further surmise is rather pointless. The predominant Mongoloid physical type of western Indonesia may owe much to population movements in the Metal Age, and the rather slim evidence from physical

Fig. 8.20. Moving a megalith, South Nias (before 1939). From Schnitger 1964.

anthropology has been reviewed in chapter 2.

Prehistoric megaliths in Indonesia are known from Sumatra, Java, Bali, Borneo, Sulawesi and Sumbawa, and there are a number of parallel alignments of uprights in south-western Malaya (Malacca and Negri Sembilan) which are similar to recent structures erected by the Kelabits of Sarawak[59]. None are known definitely to be of a pre-metal date, despite claims by Heine Geldern[60] that surviving 'megalithic cultures', particularly on the islands of Nias, Flores and Sumba date back to Neolithic times. However, the wide occurrence of megalithic monuments and statues in Oceania suggests that their origins may go very deep into the Austronesian past, possibly at least into the first millennium B.C. On the other hand, they have been constructed until very recently, both in Oceania and in Indonesia, especially in Nias (figure 8.20), in the uplands of Sarawak

and Kalimantan, and around Kota Kinabalu in Sabah[61]. There is no single function to be ascribed to megalithic structures; while many may be associated with funerary beliefs and rituals to enhance the status of chiefs, the known range of functions in Oceania is very large, and all that appears to be held in common is some connection with the spirit world, via tombs, shrines and statues.

The question of 'megalithic origins' only becomes important if one considers that megaliths express distinctive and recurring cultural characteristics. Hence, in my view, to attempt to derive all Austronesian megaliths from an area such as China[62], or even from the peregrinations of Perry's exotic 'Children of the Sun'[63], may not only be inaccurate, but also unnecessary. Worthy of more consideration is Heine Geldern's view that upright stones, flat slabs supported on

Fig. 8.21. Excavated stone cist at Tegurwangi, South Sumatra. From van der Hoop 1932.

smaller stones, stone seats, terraces, and pyramids predate as a group in origin the slab-grave and stone jar burial complex of the Metal Age. There are some grounds for accepting this view, but no good archaeological evidence. However, it may be significant that the former group is well represented in Oceania, the latter in Indonesia. It is with the latter group that we are mainly concerned here.

Perhaps the finest group of megalithic monuments in Indonesia is situated on the Pasemah Plateau in South Sumatra[64]. This group includes stone blocks with hollowed-out mortars, troughs, groups and avenues of upright stones, terraced 'graves', and slab graves (figure 8.21). Most remarkable are the human statues, carved on large stone blocks, which show a wide range of themes. Men are shown riding on elephants or buffaloes, wearing bracelets, anklets, helmets with peaks at the back, loincloths, tunics and earplugs. One man has a necklace of oblong plaques like the axe-shaped pendants from Tran Ninh (Laos), another has a necklace of facetted beads (figure 8.22), another has a probable band of bells around his shoulder, and, most importantly, one relief shows two men with an elephant, each with a Heger type I drum on his back, and one with a sword (figure 8.23). From these indications, a Dong-Son affinity in the late first millennium B.C. seems clear, and this is loosely supported by the contents of some opened slab graves – glass or carnelian beads (some facetted), bronze spirals, a gold pin, and an iron lancehead.

Possibly remotely related to this Sumatran

Fig. 8.22. Man astride a buffalo, with necklace, helmet and anklets, Pematang, South Sumatra. From van der Hoop 1932.

Fig. 8.23. Relief carving of a man flanking an elephant, carrying a sword and a drum of Heger type I. Batugajah, South Sumatra. From Schnitger 1964.

group are ten slab graves in the state of Perak, Malaya[65], from which were recovered glass and carnelian beads, potsherds with a resin varnish similar to those found with the Kampong Sungai Lang bronze drums (page 189), and some shaft-hole axes or picks of iron, which might have been used by miners of nearby tin sources[66]. These tools are probably contemporary with an industry of very unusual shaft-hole tools of iron, possibly of ultimate Dong-Son derivation, which dates to somewhere in the earlier first millennium A.D. in west-contral Malaya[67].

Whether the slab graves and megaliths of Malaya are connected with the Malay settlement of the peninsula is unknown, but it would seem quite likely. It may be significant that slab graves and stone sarcophagi are also found in eastern Java and Bali[68]. Furthermore, it is of interest that both the pottery jar burials and the slab graves are apparently restricted in prehistoric distribution to Austronesian areas, and that they appear to be indigenous developments; the jar burials in the eastern and northern islands of Southeast Asia together with South Vietnam, the slab graves in the southern and western islands, together with Malaya. As noted above, the most westerly jar burials known at present are from Anjar in western Java, and a Metal Age urn cemetery with Mongoloid burials has recently been excavated by Soejono[69] at Gilimanuk in western Bali. Concerning more distant affinities, there are slab graves from the first millennium B.C. in northern China and Japan, and contemporary pottery jar burials in southern Japan, but there seem to be grounds for invoking diffusion only in the latter case, if at all.

While on the topic of megaliths, there is one other well-described group of stone monuments located in central Sulawesi[70], particularly in the Napu, Behoa and Bada districts (figure 8.24). Most remarkable in these areas are the schematised and simple but massive human statues, some with head bands, curved breast ornaments, and clearly delineated genitalia. Associated with these statues are stone jars, a little like the ones at Tran Ninh (Laos) described on pages 195–196. None of these jars seem to have any surviving contents, but some are decorated with horizontal ribs, and one has a ring of human faces. With these jars are again found stone discs, some with relief knobs or quadrupeds like the Laotian examples, and it is possible that some of these once served as lids.

At first glance, one could postulate a relation-ship between the stone jars of Laos and Sulawesi, but the supervening distance of 3000 kilometres provides so many problems that I would prefer to argue for independent development in the two areas. We have already seen that pottery jar burials are very widespread in the Philippines and north-eastern Indonesia, and very finely decorated stone burial jars with lids were made by the peoples of Minahasa (northern Sulawesi) and Lake Toba (northern Sumatra) in ethnographic times (figure 8.24). In addition, small limestone burial jars are thought to date back to about A.D. 500 in caves in southern Mindanao[71], and local inspiration from a common base of pottery burial jars is not too difficult to conceive.

This survey of Indonesian megaliths has been kept brief because there is so much that remains unknown: not surprising perhaps, when one considers that few modern excavations have been carried out on them. The Neolithic of western Indonesia may be obscure, but so too is the period between the first introduction of metal and the great Indianised kingdom of Srivijaya in the seventh century A.D. Despite the wealth of monuments, valid archaeological interpretation is sadly limited.

To complete this section, we might bring up a matter of art history, which as we will see is of some significance for Oceania. For many years, Heine Geldern[72] held the view that the monumental art styles of Nias, northern Luzon and central Sulawesi were direct survivals of his earlier megalithic complex of the second millennium B.C., while the more ornamental and decorative art styles of central Borneo, central Sulawesi, and the Bataks of Sumatra are survivals of a more recent influence derived directly from the Dong-Son Culture. He also felt that this latter style was dominant in Indonesia on the eve of Indianisation, and that aspects of it still survive in the art of Java. The question of Dong-Son influence in Indonesian art is significant because of the often-claimed survival of Dong-Son motifs in aspects of western Melanesian art. I would not wish to commit myself on the correctness of Heine Geldern's views, particularly on his addition of direct Late Chou influences in Borneo; but we will return to the problem of Dong-Son influence in Melanesia later on.

THE PROBLEM OF BEADS IN SOUTHEAST ASIAN METAL AGE SITES

Beads of imported stones and glass, often in very

Above, large vat with human faces at Behoa, central Sulawesi, from van Heekeren 1958; *above right*, large statue at Behoa, from van Heekeren 1958.

Above, vats and cover with monkey figures at Behoa, from Raven 1926; *right, waruga* at Sawangan, Minahasa, north Sulawesi, with figures in Dutch costume.

Left, vat with lid at Bada, central Sulawesi, from Kaudern 1938; *right*, lidded vat with human face, Samosir Island, Lake Toba, northern Sumatra, from Schnitger 1964.

FIG. 8.24. STONE VATS AND OTHER MONUMENTS IN INDONESIA

large quantities, have been recovered from the great majority of the Metal Age sites described in the last two chapters. Neolithic sites in general seem only to have produced beads in locally occurring substances such as stone and shell. However, many of the characteristic Metal Age beads, of coloured glass, facetted carnelian or etched agate (figure 8.25), are imports which can be traced with a high degree of certainty to India and with lesser certainty to Malaya. The closest Indian parallels, expectably, fall within the time-span between 500 B.C. and A.D. 1500.

The glass beads come in a variety of colours and shapes, and there is no evidence for their presence in Southeast Asia before about 500 B.C. A number of scholars have conducted detailed examinations of these objects in the past, but conclusions concerning dates and origins still seem to be rather hazy. However, a paper published by Lamb in 1965[73] does contain some very exciting conclusions. He notes the similarities in glass beads from contexts of about 2000 years ago in Southeast Asia and southern India, and suggests that there may have been an itinerant class of bead-makers to cater for such dispersed markets. Many of the beads were probably made

in Southeast Asia itself, perhaps from South Indian models, and in addition it appears that scrap glass for the industry may have been imported into western Malaya from the Middle East and the Mediterranean area. Roman trade with South India is well documented, and a small number of polychrome beads from Southeast Asia may actually be of Roman origin. Some of these problems may be approached by chemical analyses and fission-track dating in the future, while at present we have an interesting hint of Indian contact with Southeast Asia some centuries prior to the appearance of the first historical kingdoms[74].

The exotic stone beads are in many cases much easier to interpret than the glass ones, because the complexities of chemical composition are not always of concern. Beads of red carnelian, generally of facetted forms, are very easy to recognise and many were almost certainly imported from the manufacturing centre of Cambay in Gujerat, north-western India[75]. These facetted carnelian beads are reported from literally dozens of sites, ranging in date from the Sa-Huynh Culture (*c.* 500 B.C.?) to contexts around A.D. 1000 in the Talaud Islands. Banded agate

Fig. 8.25. Beads of the Early Metal Period from the Talaud Islands: *top row*, spherical carnelian (*left*) and two facetted carnelians (*right*); *bottom row*, acid-etched agate (*left*) and banded agate (*right*). (See also colour plate.)

beads are also known in smaller quantities, and the Tabon and Talaud jar burials have yielded decorated beads of etched agate which are paralleled precisely in a number of Indian sites back to about 400 B.C. (figure 8.25, lower left)[76]. Naturally, these beads may have remained in use for up to a thousand years, perhaps more, before burial, so as chronological indicators they are of little value. But as indicators of long-distance trade in the period of the Indianised kingdoms they are of inestimable value.

SUMMARY

I have tried in this chapter to throw some light on the prehistory of a long-settled and geographically fragmented region. The difficulties of providing an overall synthesis need hardly be emphasised and I have concentrated mainly on Neolithic sites and on Metal Age sites dating prior to the Indianised kingdoms. Of course, the Metal Age in the islands of the Philippines and eastern Indonesia lasts down to the period of European contact, although I have drawn my own dividing line for convenience at the point where Chinese ceramics enter the record. The prehistory of these eastern islands over the past 1000 years is known in some detail from restricted areas in East Malaysia and the Philippines, but to look at this subject in any detail would expand this chapter to an unacceptable length.

As far as Oceania is concerned, it is the Neolithic period which is of most importance, for this is when the early Austronesian speakers were undertaking their remarkable eastward expansion. The jar burials and megaliths of the Metal Age are of more localised interest, and the archaeological record takes on an increasing degree of local variation as we move forward in time. But for all periods, our greatest difficulties still lie in the large islands of western Indonesia, and it will not be possible to write an integrated prehistory of Indonesia until we know much more about this region.

Footnotes

1. Marschall (1968; 1974) has recently argued that the Austronesian speakers spread from the mainland into Island Southeast Asia after 1500 B.C., and that they brought with them the knowledge of metal-working, wet-rice cultivation, and megalith building. He also implies the absence of a Neolithic in Indonesia, and visualises a direct transition from Palaeolithic to Metal Age. Needless to say, my views as expressed in this chapter are in rather fundamental disagreement with those of Marschall.

2. Chang 1969a.

3. Pearson 1967b; 1969.

4. Ferrell 1969: 73.

5. Chang 1969a: 245–7.

6. Ferrell 1969: 73–4.

7. Ferrell (1969: 3) considers that the Yüeh might have been Austronesians, but Lamberg Karlovsky (1962: 81), Obayashi (1964), Eberhard (1968: 432) and FitzGerald (1972: 1) do not.

8. e.g. by Chang 1964: 374.

9. Beyer 1947; 1948.

10. In *Praehistorica Asiae Orientalis* (1932): 129–35.

11. Evangelista 1967; 1971.

12. Fox 1970.

13. Peterson 1974 (Dimolit); Spoehr 1973 (Sanga Sanga Island, Sulu Archipelago); Bellwood 1976b (Talaud Islands). A site at Lal-lo, in the Cagayan Valley in northern Luzon, has also produced red-slip pottery and stone adzes. No report is yet available, but I understand a radiocarbon date of about 1600 B.C.

to refer to this site (see *Radiocarbon*, 1972: 300–1; Ellen and Glover 1974: 376).

14. Fox 1970: chapters 5–7.

15. e.g. in Indonesia, the Philippines and Taiwan (Solheim 1960), together with Botel Tobago Island (Beauclair 1972).

16. Solheim 1968b.

17. Solheim 1964b.

18. Facetted Kalanay vessels have recently also been found on Samar Island (Tuggle and Hutterer 1972).

19. Solheim 1964c.

20. Fox and Evangelista 1957a; 1957b. These sites contain a very Polynesian-like range of adzes, including Duff types 1A, 2A and 3A.

21. Solheim 1959a; 1959b; 1959c; 1964a; 1966; 1967a; 1967b; 1969.

22. For the Niah reports see footnote 42 in chapter 3.

23. B. Harrisson 1967. Burials similar to and contemporary with those of Niah have been excavated in Magala Cave Mouth E, 8 km to the south (Harrisson B. and T. 1958).

24. B. Harrisson 1968.

25. Harrisson and Medway 1962.

26. Solheim, Harrisson and Wall 1959.

27. Harrisson 1971.

28. Although Solheim (1967c; 1974) derives his 'Bau-Malay' pottery ultimately from southern China, I feel that a local inspiration within Borneo may be more likely.

29. Clutton Brock (1959) for dog, Medway (1973) for pig.

30. Wall 1962.

31. Glover 1972a.

32. Verhoeven 1959; Glover 1972b.

33. Verhoeven 1953.

34. van Heekeren 1967; 1972: 140.

35. Solheim 1966.

36. Röder 1959; Solheim 1962; Ellen and Glover 1974; 370–3.

37. van Heekeren 1950a; 1972: 185–90; Callenfels 1951.

38. Mulvaney and Soejono 1970; 1971.

39. Beyer 1951.

40. Bellwood 1976b.

41. van der Hoop 1940.

42. Callenfels 1932; Heine Geldern 1945: 136–7; Sukendar 1974.

43. Sutayasa 1973.

44. van Heekeren 1972: 173–84.

45. van Heekeren 1958b: 80–3.

46. Willems 1940.

47. van Heekeren 1972: 191.

48. e.g. Heine Geldern 1945: 148. A Metal Age date was originally adopted by van Heekeren (1956b).

49. Soejono 1962; Sutayasa 1972. The Buni sites have ceramic elements which parallel the Sa-Huynh-Kalanay and Bau-Malay ceramic complexes of Solheim (1967c), but they cover an unknown time span.

50. van Heekeren 1956a.

51. See van Heekeren 1958b for a general survey.

52. Elmberg 1959.

53. Heine Geldern 1947.

54. Heine Geldern 1945: 147; 1952: 327–8.

55. van Heekeren 1958b: 34–6.

56. Tran van Tot 1969: pl XII.

57. See Sutayasa 1973. No full report is yet available for Leuwiliang.

58. van Heekeren 1958b: 36–7.

59. Sheppard 1962 for Malaya; Harrisson 1961–2 for Sarawak. For a bibliography of Southeast Asian megaliths see Loofs 1967.

60. Heine Geldern 1937; 1945.

61. Schnitger 1964 for Nias; Harrisson 1958b; 1964; 1973 for Borneo; Harrisson and Harrisson 1971 for Sabah. See also Loofs 1965 for megaliths in northern Luzon.

62. As attempted by Fleming 1962.

63. Perry 1918.

64. van der Hoop 1932. See also J. Peacock 1962 for a sociological interpretation of the Pasemah megaliths as elite symbols within a class society.

65. B.A.V. Peacock 1959; 151–2; Evans 1928; Winstedt 1941.

66. Loewenstein 1956: 55. According to this author, a date well into the first millennium A.D. is quite likely for these slab graves.

67. Sieveking 1956.

68. van Heekeren 1958b: 46–54; Soejono 1969.

69. Soejono 1969.

70. Raven 1926; Kruyt 1932; Kaudern 1938.

71. Kurjack *et al.* 1971.

72. Heine Geldern 1937; 1966a.

73. Lamb 1965.

74. Indian trade contacts with Sumatra are historically dated from the first and second centuries A.D. (Wolters 1967).

75. Arkell 1936; van der Sleen 1958. Some of the spherical carnelians may also have been manufactured in Malaya.

76. Dikshit 1949; 1952.

Fig. 9.1. Map of Melanesia showing archaeological sites. Squares denote Lapita sites, circles are other (non-Lapita) sites.

CHAPTER 9

The Prehistory of Melanesia

East of the Philippines and Maluku, one moves into the Oceanic areas of Melanesia and Micronesia. These two areas comprise a multitude of islands scattered to north and east of the 800,000 square kilometre giant of New Guinea, and both together form a stubby tang which leads to the enormous triangular spearhead of Polynesia. Melanesia, with its great time depth and virtually unrelieved complexity, is the subject of this chapter.

The sole Pleistocene site in New Guinea discovered to date, at Kosipe in the Papuan Highlands, has already been described in chapter 3. The waisted blades and axe-adzes from here probably date to as early as 26,000 years ago, and we have noted that Arnhem Land in Australia has evidence for hafting modification on ground stone-tools at approximately the same time. Taken together, these two areas have in

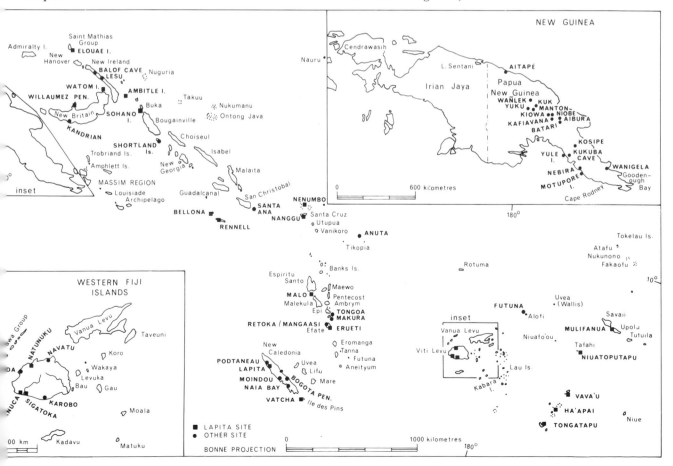

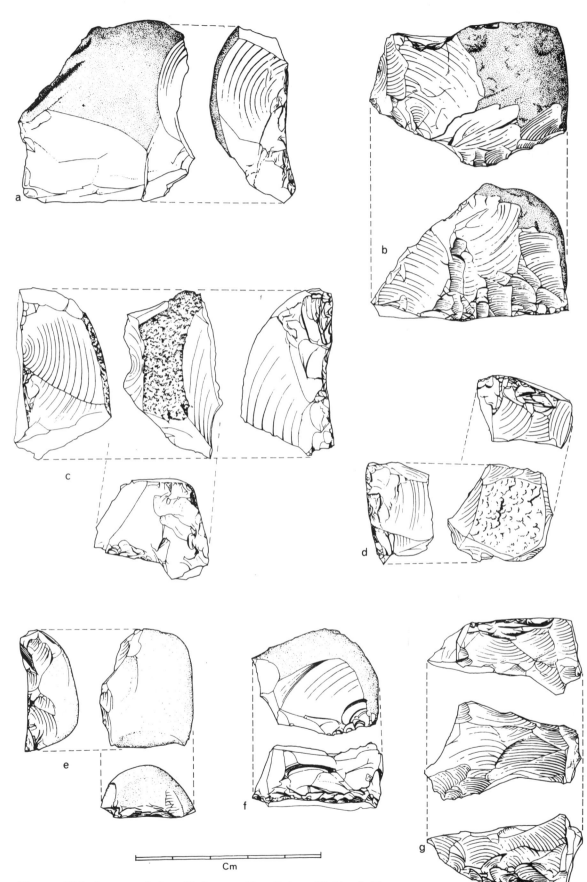

Fig. 9.2. Flaked stone tools from Kafiavana, New Guinea Highlands. From White 1972.

fact produced the earliest evidence for hafting modification in the world. Although tool grinding is not known from Kosipe, it was certainly practiced in New Guinea by 9000 years ago, and may be considerably older than this.

Unfortunately, the Kosipe site is followed by a gap in information which lasts down to about 15,000 years ago. The many sites which are now known from this time onwards are all located in Papua New Guinea, and Irian Jaya is still virtually a complete blank. However, the Papua New Guinea Highlands have produced substantial evidence for a terminal Pleistocene and Holocene prehistoric sequence, mainly from a number of caves and rock-shelters extending about 150 km eastward from Mount Hagen.

One of the most important of these sites, called Kafiavana[1], is a rock-shelter with almost four metres of deposits which go back about 11,000 years or more. At the base, the excavator, J. Peter White, reports a stone industry comprising a few pebble tools, flakes with straight or concave retouched edges, and fragments of ground stone-tools. The pebble tools decrease in numbers in later levels, which may extend almost to the present day, and the proportion of retouch on the flakes also decreases with time, retouch being virtually absent in the Highlands in ethnographic times. The Kafiavana flake industry is characteristic of New Guinea Highland flake industries generally, with their 'small chunky formless tools with a high incidence of step flaking'[2], mostly with unifacial retouch (figure 9.2). White sees these tools mainly as vehicles for cutting edges[3], rather than as tools made to preconceived overall shapes. For some reason, the New Guinea Highlands never received the blade industries which spread into Australia from about 6000 years ago, although there appear to have been some very recent microblade industries along the Papuan coast.

The ground axe-adzes with lenticular cross-sections are present at Kafiavana from about 9000 years ago, and perhaps (in framentary form) from the very basal levels of the site, which could be over 11,000 years old (figure 9.3). The term 'axe-adze' is retained purposefully for the New Guinea Highlands, where these tools recently were sometimes hafted in rotatable handles[4], and so cannot be simply divided into separate classes of axes and adzes. Also from about 9000 years ago (7000 B.C.) marine shells are present, thus documenting the earliest evidence for trade in a commodity which is so important in the Highlands today[5]. Finally, the presence of pig bones from 3000 B.C., or perhaps even 4500 B.C. in the Kafiavana deposits provides valuable information about the date of introduction of this animal into Oceania.

From Kafiavana, we turn to the rather different assemblage from another important rock-shelter, at Kiowa, excavated by Susan Bulmer[6]. Here, some five metres of deposits again extend back over 10,000 years, and an industry of pebble and flake tools, some with edge-glosses caused by cutting plant materials, runs right through to recent times. At some time around 3000 or 4000 B.C., ground lenticular cross-sectioned axe-adzes (like the ones from Kafiavana), unground waisted blades, and a fragment of ground pearl-shell make an appearance, together with pig bones. Strangely enough, the waisted blades here present at Kiowa are absent from Kafiavana, only 30 km away, and they are also absent from two other caves, Aibura and Batari, excavated by White in the Lamari Valley to the east of Kafiavana[7]. Since the Batari deposits go back some 8000 years, it seems that the easternmost New Guinea Highlands were for some reason outside the area of distribution of these artefacts. It is not known what the waisted blades were used for, as they were not made anywhere at European contact. However, since they are often found with axe-adzes, it is likely that these two artefact types had different functions[8], and the waisted blades could in fact have been hoes. We have seen that they are present from over 20,000 years ago at Kosipe, and at the site of Yuku to the north of Mt. Hagen, also excavated by Susan Bulmer[9], flaked waisted blades occur in levels which may be over 10,000 years old. Some of the waisted blades become edge-ground when the first ground axe-adzes appear in the Yuku deposits, around or before 5000 B.C.

The presences of ground axe-adzes and marine shells from at least 7000 B.C., and of pigs from at least 3000 B.C.[10] in the New Guinea Highlands are naturally of great significance. The earliest fully ground axes at Niah Cave in Sarawak are approximately contemporary with those from Kafiavana, and in Timor, pigs are also introduced at about 3000 B.C. Quite clearly, the New Guinea Highlands were not isolated from these developments in the islands to the west, and the axe-adzes and pigs, together with the evidence for forest clearance by about 3000 B.C. from pollen profiles in the Mt. Hagen area[11], all combine in support of the increasing evidence for Highlands cultiva-

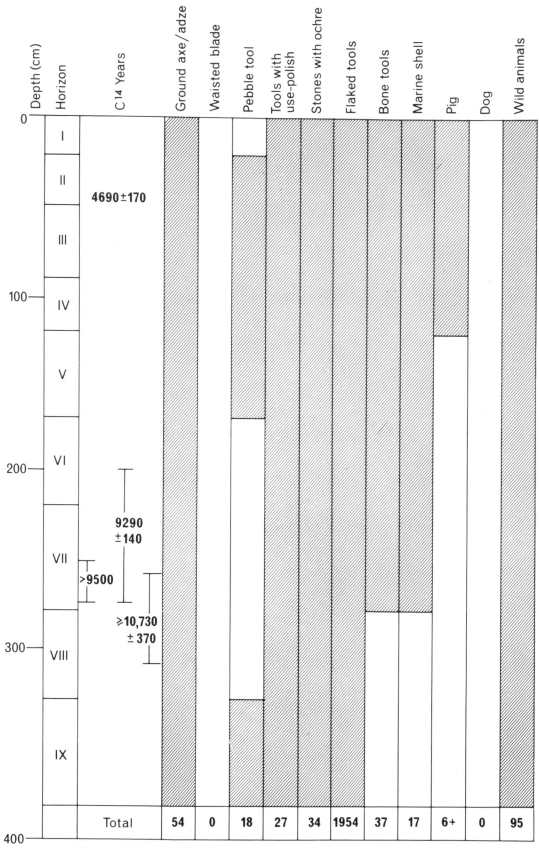

Fig. 9.3. The prehistoric sequence from Kafiavana rock-shelter, New Guinea Highlands. From White 1972.

tion from the fourth millennium B.C. onwards. This evidence is described in more detail below.

In the upper levels of all the Highlands rockshelters, the artefactual assemblages characteristic of recent Highlands cultures make an appearance. Within the past 5000 years the waisted blades have gradually disappeared in the region, and recent industries were based on flake tools and the axe-adzes[12]. At Kiowa, the levels later than 3000 B.C. contain numbers of shell artefacts, and three imported potsherds. At European contact, pottery was made only on the north-eastern periphery of the Highlands, and at no time does its manufacture appear to have spread further inland. At Peter White's Aibura site, shells, potsherds, stone ring fragments, and bones of dog and fowl all make an appearance within the past 800 years, and the fauna from this site suggests an increasing spread of grassland, perhaps through agricultural clearance in the area during the same period. Although one might assume some antiquity for the dog in New Guinea, it is in fact not known from any archaeological

site earlier than about 1000 years ago.

The sequence in the New Guinea Highlands therefore holds some rather interesting surprises, and it is to be hoped that one day comparable material will be recovered from Irian Jaya, where no systematic archaeological work has been carried out to date. The basic flaked stone industry of the Highland sites is of a similar technological standard to that of the earliest sites in Australia, and both the waisted blades and the ground axe-adzes are well paralleled in late Hoabinhian (Bacsonian) contexts in Southeast Asia, and in Australia[13]. At present, Island Southeast Asia has fewer specific parallels (from the caves of Niah and Tabon) with New Guinea than does Australia, but future discoveries will probably redress the balance. It may be noteworthy that in the New Guinea Highlands the degree of retouch on flake tools declines through time, perhaps because of an increasing dependence upon ground tools, while in Australia the flaked stone repertoire becomes more varied over the past 7000 years, despite the similar use of ground

Fig. 9.4. Modern hafted stone axe from the Jimi River. Western Highlands District.

tools. One reason for this may be connected with the development of agricultural activities by the fourth millennium B.C. or earlier in New Guinea, for this is a development which is not seen in Australia.

The development of cultivation in the Highlands has been greatly illuminated by recent research in the Wahgi Valley near Mt. Hagen[14], carried out under the general direction of Jack Golson from the Australian National University in Canberra. Golson began his research at the Manton plantation, where an area of over 300 hectares of peat swamp was drained by ditches, some of which date back to about 300 B.C. The waterlogged ditches produced remains of digging sticks, paddle-shaped spades, and pieces of gourd and pandanus fruit. In the last few years, Golson has moved his research to another plantation called Kuk, where about 150 hectares of swamp were drained in prehistoric times. The Kuk research has been particularly detailed[15].

It appears that, for several millennia, the Kuk swamp was made available for cultivation through the excavation of large linear ditches and smaller subsidiary channels. These ditches and channels would have controlled standing water and the level of the water-table, and would have allowed cultivation of a crop such as taro. Two large linear ditches, both at least 500 metres long and up to 3 metres deep by 4.5 wide, are known to date back to approximately 4000 B.C. (figure 9.5). Similar ditches, generally slightly smaller in cross-section but of at least similar length, were subsequently cut in various parts of the swamp until about A.D. 750, after which there seems to have been a period of abandonment. Unfortunately, neither house remains nor artefacts have yet been found in association with these ditch systems, and even their attribution to taro cultivation is basically hypothetical. However, it is difficult to see what else could have been grown on the site in 4000 B.C., and perhaps we may envisage large rectangular plots of swampland, surrounded by ditches to allow a controlled but fairly wet environment for taro cultivation.

Sometime within the last few hundred years, a new agricultural pattern appears at Kuk. The large linear ditches appear yet again after several centuries of site abandonment, but this time they outline areas criss-crossed with a checkerboard grid of small close-set channels. This is the lay-out for sweet potato cultivation known from other parts of the Highlands (see figure 6.6), and its appearance at Kuk occasions

no surprise. Just when sweet potatoes entered the area is unknown, but Golson feels that it was certainly before any possibility of Spanish or Portuguese transmission. The problem of the sweet potato has been discussed further in chapter 6.

The Kuk ditches naturally take us back to the discussion about intensification of cultivation, already aired on page 145. Quite clearly, labour-demanding systems such as the Kuk drainage channels would not suddenly be developed for no good reason. Needless to say, we can really only make a guess at this point. It could be that the system of shifting cultivation was already under stress by 4000 B.C., and that swamp drainage was developed to increase the food supply. Certainly, the present swamp drainage systems of New Guinea need only short fallows, and they are without doubt very productive. But all this can only be speculation with the present state of knowledge.

Equally speculative are the circumstances surrounding the beginnings of cultivation in New Guinea; were the techniques invented independently, or were they, together with some of the crop-plants, introduced by early Austronesian settlers in coastal areas of the island? It is my own belief that some kind of cultivation may have commenced independently in New Guinea before Austronesians arrived, on the grounds that the latter, who probably were cultivators, were not successful colonisers of New Guinea because quite dense populations of Papuan speakers with their own methods of plant cultivation had probably developed there before them. This matter is raised again in chapter 14, as it is clearly of broad significance.

What Manton and Kuk do tell us is that large and presumably densely settled populations were present in the New Guinea Highlands by perhaps as early as 4000 B.C. This information is markedly at variance with earlier views about demographic history in the area (see page 95), and it does provide a much better context for one of the most enigmatic classes of prehistoric artefacts from New Guinea – the stone pestles and mortars.

What we may, in the absence of a better term, call the 'New Guinea-Bismarcks pestle and mortar complex' is distributed mainly in Papua New Guinea, the Bismarcks, and Bougainville and adjacent islands in the northern Solomons[16]. The complex appears to form something of a typological unit, despite the fact that stone pestles and basins of various kinds are very widespread right

Fig. 9.5. Section through a large drainage ditch (the dark feature seen in the wall of the trench) dating from about 3500 B.C. Kuk plantation, Mt. Hagen.

through eastern Melanesia and Polynesia[17]. However, in these other areas there is no marked typological and stylistic unity until one reaches the distant 'poi-pounder' province of eastern Polynesia.

At present, the pestle and mortar complex is undated, although a fragment of a mortar rim has recently been excavated at a site called Wanlek, near Simbai in the Madang District, from deposits dated to between 3500 and 1000 B.C.[18]. The site also produced lenticular-sectioned axe-adzes, tanged digging tools of slate, and post settings of curved-walled houses, so it looks very much as if this particular fragment can be associated with an agricultural society. However, the mortars and pestles do not appear to have been manufactured at the time of European contact, and in many Highland regions they have been observed in use in ceremonies as 'stone of power', or 'fighting stones', or sometimes as crop fertility stones buried in fields[19]. It is generally assumed on logical grounds that these are not the

original functions of the objects.

Basically, there is no reason to assume any great antiquity for the pestle and mortar complex, and it is described here because it appears to have aceramic associations in most areas. This is of course no reason for assuming that the complex is entirely aceramic or non-Austronesian, but it is generally found in areas where Austronesian languages have not penetrated, with the notable exceptions of New Britain and New Ireland.

In general, the mortars are circular and bowl-shaped, and the internal basins may range from very deep to little more than shallow depressions. Some have short pedestal bases, some may have rows of bosses around their exterior upper surfaces (figure 9.6), and two examples from the Highlands even have lugs left on the rim like the head, wings and tail of a bird. The pestles are generally bulbiform or mushroom shaped, but quite a number have their handles modelled into schematic bird figurines[20] (figure 9.7). Of similar distribution to the mortars and pestles

Fig. 9.6. Bossed stone mortar with bird-head handle, found near Sosointenu village, Kainantu area, Papua New Guinea. Length 37 cm.

Fig. 9.7. Bird-shaped stone pestle from Wonia, Fly Delta, Papua New Guinea. Length 33 cm.

Fig. 9.8. Map showing the distribution of pestles and mortars in New Guinea and the Bismarck Archipelago (as at 1965). The larger symbols indicate concentrations of three specimens. From Pretty 1965.

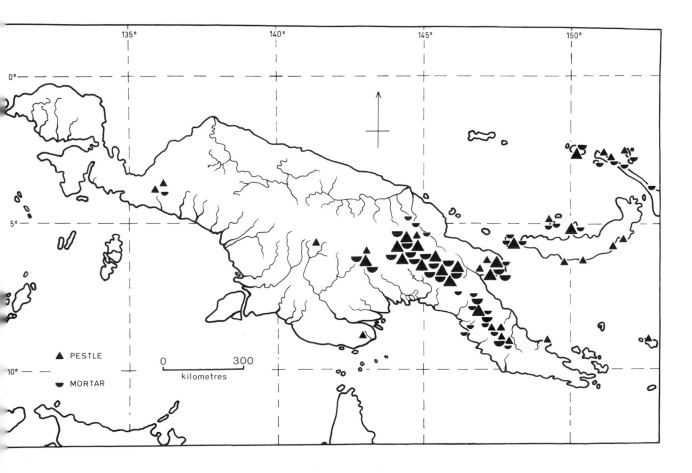

Fig. 9.9. Human head from the Huon Peninsula, Papua New Guinea. Height 21 cm.

are a class of perforated stone clubheads, of various forms including plain discs, flanged discs, knobbed discs, pineapple and sunflower-shaped forms, and battle adzes[21]. Although the majority of these clubs are prehistoric, their production has survived until the present day, particularly amongst the Kukukuku peoples of the upper Watut River area, Morobe District. The perforations, of an hourglass shape in cross-section, are battered through the club by the Kukukuku, and no drill is used[22].

In terms of distribution (figure 9.8), the mortars and pestles are found most frequently in the New Guinea Highlands, especially in the area from Mt. Hagen eastwards to the Chimbu and Eastern Highlands districts[23]; an area of dense population and intensive agriculture for upwards of 6000 years (see above). Their virtual absence in Irian Jaya is a little puzzling, and this situation might reflect lack of research. Further concentrations in Papua New Guinea occur in the Papuan Highlands and on the Huon Peninsula, and from

the latter area comes a remarkable human head with a protruding tongue, enormous rimmed eyes, and a knobbed headdress which resembles a knobbed disc club[24] (figure 9.9). Whether this ever formed the upper part of a pestle is not clear, and is perhaps unlikely.

From New Britain and New Ireland there are numerous pestles and mortars[25], and from Bougainville in the northern Solomons there comes a schematic stone bird head, which may have served as a stopper for a sacred flute rather than as part of a pestle[26]. In Bougainville, the distribution of the pestle and mortar complex seems to come to an end, and at present, one is forced to admit that almost nothing is known of the archaeological context of the most remarkable group of portable stone artefacts found anywhere in Oceania. As to the functions of the mortars themselves, we may accept as most likely the suggestion by R. Bulmer[27] that they were used for the grinding of nuts and seeds. A majority of the mortars have shallow cups which would be ideal for nut grinding, and stone pestles were still used on Buka Island in ethnographic times for the grinding of *Canarium* nuts[28]. In addition, the majority of the pestles and mortars have been found in the Highlands below altitudes of 2000 m, which suggests that they were in use mostly in the period before the introduction of the sweet potato, which has allowed settlement to expand to higher altitudes.

The origins of the pestles and mortars are also obscure, and one can hardly begin to speculate on the presence or absence of pottery or bronze prototypes[29] until some dates are acquired. The bird-shaped terminals do, however, allow us to extend the discussion a little further, and this requires a brief return to the waisted blades and axes, for these are found not only in the Highlands, but do in fact extend in distribution to be roughly coterminous with the pestles and mortars. Flaked waisted blades of chert have been found in undated surface collections inland from Kandrian in south-western New Britain (figure 9.10), together with a chert core and flake industry[30], and waisted blades together with blade-like flakes of chert and volcanic rocks are reported from southern Bougainville[31]. In addition, large numbers of pecked and ground axes from Buka and northern Bougainville have been provided with waists, and also frequently with lugs to aid hafting[32]. Pecked and ground waisted axes have also been found in New Britain[33] and in the southern Solomons, where in the latter area they

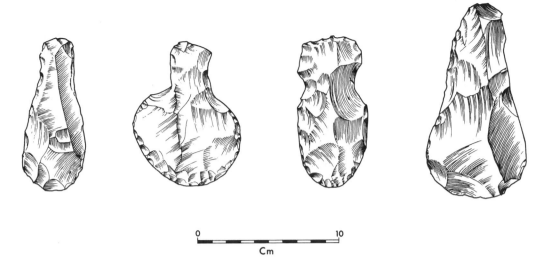

Fig. 9.10. Flaked tools of chert from Kandrian, south-western New Britain. From Golson 1972a.

appear to have been made into recent enthno-graphic times[34].

At first sight, a link between waisted and lugged cutting tools and mortars and pestles may sccm rather tenuous, apart from the roughly similar distribution pattcrns. However, from a locality called Toiminapo on Bougainville Island, there comes a remarkable stone axe which seems to belong with the waisted and lugged Bougainville group[35]. This axe, shown in figure 9.11, has two bird-headed lugs, a row of bosses linking the heads, and an unusual bossed terminal at the butt. The bird's heads and bosses are paralleled on the mortars and pestles, and we have already noted that a stone bird has actually been found on Bougainville. Furthermore, although Toiminapo is on the south coast of Bougainville, the axe does appear to be closely related to the waisted and lugged axes of north Bougainville and Buka. In fact Specht[36] has reported two similar axes from Buka itself. Specht goes further to suggest that the Toiminapo axe is stylistically related to pottery of the incised and applied-relief styles which were current in parts of Melanesia about 2000 years ago. This is of great significance, and while these pottery styles must await later treat-ment, we may conclude here that the mortars and pestles, the pecked and ground waisted and lugged axes, and a Melanesian ceramic style of 2–3000 years ago are all quite possibly related. The waisting technique has a respectable anti-quity of over 20,000 years in New Guinea itself,

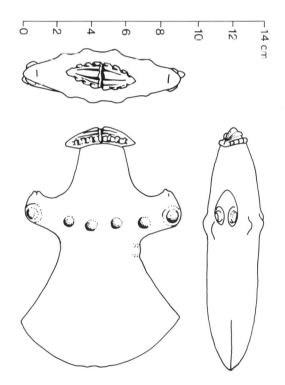

Fig. 9.11. The Toiminapo axe, Bougainville. After Casey 1939.

but the pottery, mortars and pestles are much more recent and could acknowledge a degree of Austronesian influence. It has been suggested that the Toiminapo axe belongs to a group of Melanesian and Polynesian axes and adzes which show Southeast Asian Metal Age influence[37], but as we will see later, there is not really much evidence for Metal Age influence in the Pacific beyond New Guinea and the Bismarcks. For the latter two areas, however, the theory cannot be too easily dismissed.

From the preceramic of New Guinea we have moved, not without good reason, on to a group of recent artefacts which is mainly, but not entirely, aceramic. Before we do move to the ceramic assemblages, we still need to examine the problem of the extent of preceramic settlement in Melanesia. At present, there are only two dated sites outside the New Guinea Highlands which throw light on this matter; Kukuba Cave in the Central District of Papua, where Vanderwal has excavated an industry of notched flakes dating from about 2000 B.C.; and Balof Cave on New Ireland, where White has a flake industry which could be as early as 4000 B.C.[38]. The Papuan speakers who are distributed to as far east as Santa Cruz may originally have migrated prior to Austronesian contact, but this can only be surmise at present. So far, we only have evidence for preceramic settlement to as far as Australia, New Guinea, and the Bismarcks[39].

CERAMIC ASSEMBLAGES IN MELANESIA
THE LAPITA CULTURE

The Austronesian expansion into Melanesia was by no means a simple matter, and the initial migration which introduced the languages ancestral to the present Oceanic subgroup may well have taken place some 5000 years ago. At present, there is no archaeological information whatsoever which may relate to it, and the whole concept of 'initial Austronesian' in Melanesia is purely linguistic. However, we do have archaeological information about the later spread of the Lapita Culture through the area, and about some later influences, all from Island Southeast Asia. Actual migrations of complete ethnic groups from Island Southeast Asia may number only two or three, but the complex mixture of diverse Papuan and Austronesian cultural templates has given rise to the very intricate pattern of variation which we observe today.

There can be little doubt that Austronesians introduced the craft of pottery making into Melanesia, even though many Papuan peoples do make pottery today and many Austronesian do not, particularly within the Bismarcks and Solomons. Two thousand five hundred years ago we can recognise three different types of ceramic decoration in the area – Lapita, incised and applied-relief, and paddle-impressed. The Lapita belonged to a distinct migrant group, the incised and applied-relief poses problems which we will consider in due course, and the paddle-impressed appears to be a development from the first two styles.

In brief, the Lapita Culture is the record of a number of highly mobile groups of sea-borne colonists and explorers, who expanded very rapidly through Melanesia in the mid-late second millennium B.C., and on into Polynesia, whose present inhabitants are almost certainly their direct descendants. The Lapita Culture is therefore intricately involved in the question of Polynesian origins. The Lapita potters were quite possibly the first pottery-making Austronesians to enter Melanesia, and this will be made clear as the discussion is extended to other ceramic styles later. Therefore, archaeological recognition of the importance of the Lapita sites, mainly within the past ten years, may be regarded as one of the most important developments in the study of Oceanic prehistory.

Let us first take a general look at the Lapita site distribution and artefact inventory before we turn to some of the more important sites. The first discovery of Lapita pottery was made on Watom Island, to the north of Rabaul (New Britain), by a Catholic Missionary in 1909[50]. In later years, more sherds were reported from Tonga[41] and the Ile des Pins off New Caledonia[42], but no detailed excavations were carried out until Gifford and Shutler examined the site of Lapita itself, on the Foué Peninsula in north-western New Caledonia, in 1952[43]. Numerous investigations over the past twenty years have now established the distribution of the pottery from northern New Guinea to Samoa, between *c.* 1500 B.C. and the time of Christ, at which time it virtually disappears. In Melanesia, the makers of the pottery are evidently absorbed into surrounding populations after this time, and lose archaeological identity. In Polynesia, the line of ancestry back from the present Polynesians is continuous and unbroken.

The Lapita pottery itself[44] is tempered with sand or crushed shell, and is often fairly friable and fired at low temperatures, perhaps under 850°C, in open bonfires. The tempers serve to differentiate it from most other prehistoric Melanesian ceramics, and some of the sands may have been transported some distance over sea to areas where suitable sands were lacking[45], but the evidence for this at present is not very specific. A few pots appear to have been provided with reddish slips before firing, and on some, the decorations may have been infilled with a white calcareous material for emphasis, although it is usually difficult to separate artificial from naturally deposited infilling. On all sites the greater numbers of sherds are in fact undecorated, and represent in many cases an important class of globular or shouldered cooking pots with narrow necks and short vertical or everted rims. The decorated sherds, which are normally very small and extremely hard to fit together, seem to come mainly from a class of open bowls and beakers, with flat or round bases, sometimes with sharp carinations, sometimes with evenly everted sides (see figure 9.17). In general, the decoration is on the upper surface of the pot, and may often be on the inside as well. Lapita rim forms are more elaborate than those of most later Melanesian ceramics, and rims are often bevelled, grooved, or even provided with flanges which would be added after the body of the pot was finished. Additional items found in small numbers include lugs and strap handles, possible lids and circular pottery discs (bottle stoppers?) and an unusual class of cylindrical or conical pottery objects which may have served as pot supports of some kind (see figure 9.16[e]). There are no examples of tripods or ring feet actually joined to the pots. Lapita manufacturing techniques certainly involve slab building in most areas, together with paddle and anvil finishing, and evidence for ring or coil building is reported from Watom Island[46]. The presence of all these manufacturing techniques in what may be the earliest pottery in Melanesia makes it hard to accept earlier views that the coiling technique was introduced to Melanesia earlier than and separately from the paddle and anvil finishing technique (but see pages 258–9).

It is the decoration of Lapita pottery which endows it with such a high degree of archaeological visibility. This decoration is basically so standardised from New Guinea to Samoa that there can be little doubt that it represents cultural movements unparalleled in Oceanic prehistory before or since. Although actual decorated sherds may represent from only 1% to about 30% of total site inventories, the vast majority of these

Fig. 9.12. Lapita sherd with human face motif from Nenumbo, Gawa, Santa Cruz Islands. From Green 1974a.

Fig. 9.13. Examples of Lapita pottery decoration: (a–e) Ambitle Island; (f–j) Tongatapu; (k, l) Watom Island.

decorated sherds are covered with intricate designs formed by 'dentate stamping', carried out with a range of toothed implements which may basically have resembled tattooing chisels. Tattooing chisels are known from Lapita contexts, but these are of the normal straight kind reported ethnographically in Oceania, and do not encompass the range of dentate stamped curvilinear designs found on Lapita pottery. In fact no definite pottery stamps have been found at all in Lapita sites, so it would appear that a range of wooden toothed objects were used, with straight and curved teeth rows. The ends of the teeth were also cut off square, and not pointed. The motifs are arranged in horizontal bands, and range from rows of simple parallel lines and curves, to motifs of wonderful precision and complexity which in some cases extend to anthropomorphic representations (figure 9.12). Some of the finer forms, which are always geometrically and regularly laid out, include eyes, ropes, arcades, rectangular meanders, interlocking Y's, shield-like designs, stamped circles, and circular concentric arrangements of simple motifs (figure 9.13). Some of the more specific designs have not been found on all sites so far[47], but this hardly detracts from the overall homogeneity of the Lapita pottery.

Apart from the dentate stamping, other Lapita decorative techniques include simple incision, application of strips or nubbins, and rim notching. Quite often several of these techniques will be combined on one pot. In addition, there is a little evidence for the use of a carved paddle in surface finishing, and this will turn out to be rather important in due course. However, the use of a cord-wrapped paddle is most uncommon, and this is a factor which conclusively separates Lapita from any of the Neolithic ceramics of Mainland Southeast Asia[48]. Most of the decorated Lapita pottery would appear to predate 500 B.C., and the last five hundred years down to the birth of Christ are characterised by mainly plain wares through the whole area, with increasing simplification of form, until the style eventually disappears almost completely by the beginning of the first millennium A.D.

The range of Lapita motifs is most closely paralleled in the ceramics from Kalanay Cave on Masbate Island, Central Philippines[49], and to a lesser extent in those from Sa-Huynh in South Vietnam. Both these sites are perhaps a millennium later than the first appearance of Lapita in Melanesia, so the relationship may be better defined as cousinly. The actual ancestry of Lapita is still a little hazy but there are of course fairly close parallels from the contemporary Yüan-shan wares of Taiwan, and the Batungan pottery of Masbate, as discussed in the previous chapter. These parallels include the presence of dentate stamping, shell-edge stamping, incision, circle-stamping, surface-slipping, possible lime infill of designs, carinated body forms, lids and strap handles (Yüan-shan), and absence of painting, cord-marking and tripods. Although the actual design motifs may be closer to the later Kalanay wares, this may reflect some degree of continuing contact between Melanesia and the Philippines in the first millennium B.C. In addition, the incised wares of the first millennium B.C. on Timor, and those of a possible similar date from south-western Sulawesi also have fairly close parallels with Lapita. We may accept that an immediate origin for Lapita lies somewhere in the Philippines or north-eastern Indonesia, between 2000 and 1300 B.C., and the general locality should be pinned down more thoroughly in the near future.

Turning to other aspects of the Lapita Culture, the sites themselves are always in coastal or small offshore island locations. The economy would appear to have been heavily oriented towards marine fishing and shell fishing, and direct evidence for horticulture is so far lacking. Coconut shells are reported in possible association with Lapita pottery at the Watom site[50], as are pig and fowl bones, and one of the Watom sherds has a possible pig-snout design. Pig and fowl are reported from the Reef Islands (Santa Cruz) and possibly Tonga, but evidence for the presence of dogs in the Lapita Culture remains elusive[51]. However, there seems good reason to believe that a wide range of domesticated plants and animals will be demonstrated as research proceeds.

One of the most significant aspects of Lapita economy concerns long-distance inter-island transport of goods. The majority of the Lapita sites have produced small quantities of obsidian (figure 9.14), and spectrographic analyses have shown that a major source of this volcanic glass was at Talasea on the Willaumez Peninsula of northern New Britain[52], from where it was carried to Watom (240 km), Ambitle (500 km), Gawa in the Reef Islands of the Santa Cruz group (2000 km), and the Ile des Pins to the south of New Caledonia (2600 km)[53]. The latter distances are of course quite phenomenal, and I would suggest that

Fig. 9.14. Flakes of Talasea obsidian from Ambitle Island. From Ambrose 1973.

the Lapita potters were highly competent deep-sea voyagers, whose great navigators survive today as some of the illustrious ancestors of Polynesian tradition. Obsidian has also been found on Tongatapu, but the source in this case could be Tafahi Island, in the far north of the Tongan group. In addition to the obsidian transport, oven stones and stones for tool-making (particularly chert) were transported over distances of up to 450 km from the south-eastern Solomons into the coralline islands of the Santa Cruz group[54].

This evidence suggests that the Lapita potters were efficient colonisers, who carried supplies of scarce materials with them in their voyages of discovery. It may also suggest that they carried out some long distance trade, perhaps with other resident populations, either Austronesian or Papuan. But so far, archaeological evidence does not indicate that large quantities of material were

being transported, so some caution is needed in this regard. Nevertheless, in terms of colonisation, we can look to the Lapita pottery makers for the initial settlements of Fiji, Tonga, and Samoa.

The non-ceramic Lapita assemblages have a significance equal to that of the pottery. The untanged stone adzes, with quadrangular, lenticular and plano-convex cross-sections, provide prototypes for the more developed later Polynesian forms. On the other hand, the Lapita shell gear (figure 9.18), which includes adzes, knives, vegetable scrapers, bracelets and necklace units, has rather more in common with later Melanesian assemblages. This makes it clear that Lapita is more than just 'ancestral Polynesian', and to illustrate this point with respect to a final conclusion concerning the significance of the culture, we should now turn briefly to some of the major sites themselves.

MAJOR SITES OF THE LAPITA CULTURE

In the west, a single Lapita sherd has been reported from Aitape on the central northern coast of New Guinea; the only occurrence known so far on this island[55]. Moving eastwards, the important site at Rakival village on Watom Island, off northern New Britain, has recently been excavated by Specht[56], some 60 years after the pioneer collections made by Meyer. The Lapita settlement here seems to have been located on a coastal sand dune, and the pottery almost certainly predates 500 B.C. It has very finely executed close-set designs which include rows of circles and eyes, as well as more complex motifs. An extended headless burial without its skull, and a flexed complete burial were found in the site, but neither had grave goods. Other important Watom artefacts include fragments of shell bracelets, part of a *Trochus* shell one-piece fishhook, and untanged quadrangular and lenticular-sectioned stone adzes.

Elsewhere in the Bismarcks, Lapita pottery has been recovered from a site on Ambitle Island off the south-eastern coast of New Ireland, and on Elouae Island in the Saint Matthias Group[57]. On New Ireland itself, unusual red-slipped pottery has been found dating from *c.* 500 B.C. in refuse mounds in the village of Lesu, together with pig bones, *Tridacna* shell adzes, shell bracelets, obsidian flakes, and sling stones[58]. However, the Lesu pottery is mainly decorated by applied motifs, rather than by dentate stamping or incision, and its relationship to Lapita is not clear.

Further south, on Sohano Island off Buka in the northern Solomons, Specht[59] has excavated late Lapita pottery dating from about 500 B.C., decorated mostly by linear incision rather than by dentate stamping. In the main Solomon Islands there are no Lapita sites reported as yet, although Davenport has reported what may be Lapita plain ware from the first millennium A.D. on Santa Ana Island[60]. However, on the two isolated Polynesian Outliers of Rennell and Bellona to the south of the Solomons, Lapita pottery turns up again[61]. At the site of Sikumango on Bellona, Poulsen has excavated an occupation horizon beneath a low earthen mound, which produced part of a plain carinated Lapita bowl, together with shell adzes and spoons, and perforated flying fox teeth. The pottery is an import, as its temper is not local to Bellona, and Poulsen thinks that this site, dated to about 120 B.C., may document initial Polynesian settlement on the island. This is a matter of some importance, because it may challenge the linguistic hypothesis that the Polynesian Outlier cultures are the result of fairly recent backwash settlements from Triangle Polynesia. On the other hand, it is not unlikely that such backwash movements could already have been taking place by the end of the first millennium B.C., so the Bellonese evidence is not really as contradictory as it might appear.

Perhaps the most spectacular Lapita finds have been made very recently by Roger Green in the Santa Cruz Islands – at the sites of Nanggu on Santa Cruz Island, and Nenumbo on Gawa Island in the Reef Group. These sites date from about 1300–500 B.C., and the pottery demonstrates a wider range of detailed motifs than that from any other site (figures 9.12, 9.15), suggesting that perhaps the origins of Lapita as a distinct style may lie in this general area. Human and bird figurines were also found at these sites, and these are so far unique in Lapita assemblages.

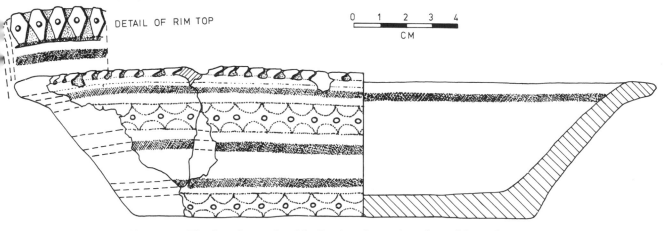

DETAIL OF RIM TOP

0 1 2 3 4
CM

Fig. 9.15. Flat-based vessel with Lapita decoration from Nenumbo, Gawa, Santa Cruz Islands.

Green reports settlements areas of up to 14,000 square metres in size, together with houses, ovens and storage pits[62]. There is also obsidian from Talasea in New Britain, and Green thinks that the sites represent the settlements of mobile traders in an area already settled by Papuan speakers, whose languages are still predominant today on the island of Santa Cruz.

A little to the east of the Santa Cruz group, a predominantly plain ware of evident Lapita affinity has been excavated on the Polynesian Outlier island of Anuta, and this dates to between 1000 B.C. and A.D. 500. In association with the pottery are one-piece fishhooks of *Turbo* shell, adzes of *Tridacna* and *Cassis* shell, and shell bracelets, pendants and small rings. As with Bellona and Rennell, we have the interesting problem of whether this initial Lapita settlement is directly ancestral to the present Polynesian inhabitants of the island. The excavators think not, and that the present Polynesians arrived about 500 years ago, after a period of abandonment lasting from A.D. 500[63]. However, this view has not yet been conclusively demonstrated.

In the New Hebrides, sherds of decorated Lapita pottery dating to 1300–1100 B.C. have been excavated by Hedrick[64] on the island of Malo, in the north of the group, and some of these sherds contain exotic tempers which may have been traded in[65]. In the central New Hebrides, Garanger[66] has recovered a late and mainly undecorated Lapita ceramic assemblage from a site called Erueti on Efate Island, and this dates to *c.* 350 B.C. This site is of great interest, because pottery of the unrelated incised and applied-relief tradition is found both above and below the level with the Lapita, so co-existence is well established by this fairly late date, if not by long before in many areas.

In New Caledonia, the eponymous site of Lapita was first reported between 1900 and 1920[67], and the deposits, which apparently stretch for almost 400 metres along the coast, were excavated by Gifford and Shutler in 1952[68]. Over 30% of the pottery from this site has Lapita decoration, and there is also a small amount of carved-paddle-impressed decoration. The range of Lapita motifs seems to resemble the range from Fiji and Tonga more than that from Watom, and the effects of distance on the overall homogeneity of the assemblage now become visible. The ceramics also include bottle forms, together with pottery discs which may have served as stoppers. Other artefacts fit in well with the general Lapita range, and include shell bracelets, a rectangular shell pendant or necklace unit with two perforations, perforated bivalve net sinkers, cowrie shell caps for octopus lures, and a piece of obsidian. Carbon dates suggest occupation of the site in the earlier first millennium B.C.

Another important Lapita site has been excavated at Vatcha on the Ile des Pins, off the southern end of New Caledonia[69]. The basal level of this site is dated to as early as 2000 B.C., although this date, from radiocarbon analysis of snail shells, does seem surprisingly early. A later level, which also contains incised pottery in a non-Lapita tradition, dates to about 900 B.C. The Vatcha site has several facets of importance; the Lapita pots are very well preserved; what has often been taken to be a lime infill in pot designs has here been shown to be a natural deposit; and a substantial proportion of the pottery has impressions from a carved paddle. As with the Lapita site itself, we will see that this is very important for the origin of the later paddle-impressed ceramic tradition of eastern Melanesia.

The Ile des Pins also provides one of the more unusual archaeological mysteries of the Pacific. The interior plateau of the island contains some 300 earth mounds, and two of these, examined by Golson in 1959[70], proved to contain cylindrical cores of what may be a kind of lime concrete with an ironstone and coral aggregate, over three metres high in the case of one mound. The functions of the concrete cylinders are unknown, and no pottery or other artefacts were found in association. What proportion of the mounds on the Ile des Pins had such cylinders is also unknown, but two similar cylinders are reported from within mounds on the New Caledonian mainland just north of Noumea. Mounds and alignments of lateritic blocks are known from many other areas of New Caledonia[71], but these groups with the cylinders would appear to be unique. Several experimental radiocarbon analyses have been run on concrete and land snail samples, and these give a very odd range of dates between 1000 and 6000 B.C.[72] which may be of questionable value. Furthermore, it is not at all certain that the mounds are man-made, but if they are, then perhaps a Lapita connection may be found, or they may even have been built by some unknown pre-Lapita inhabitants of New Caledonia.

In the Fijian Islands there are three important Lapita sites, all on the large island of Viti Levu. The earliest is at Natunuku[73] in the north-

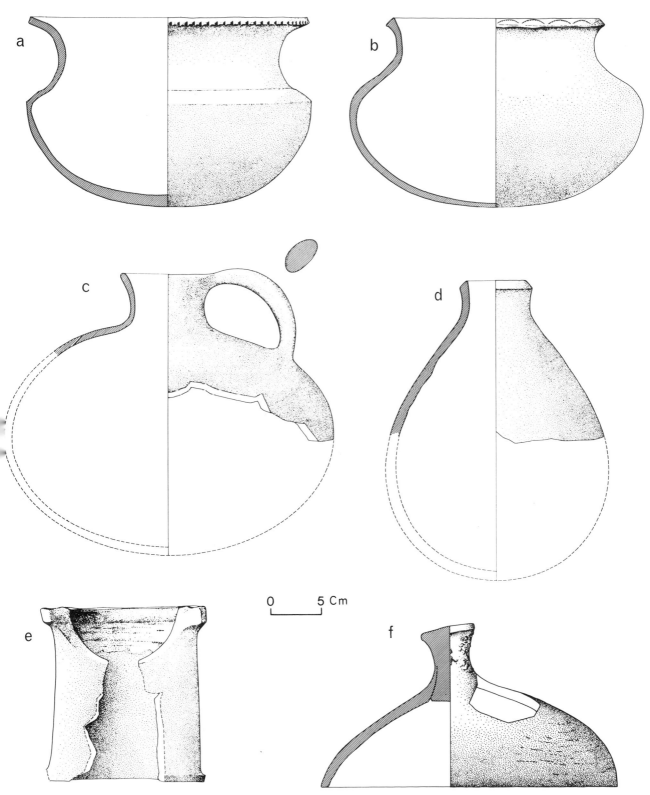

Fig. 9.16. Late Lapita pottery from Sigatoka, Viti Levu, Fiji. (e) is a possible pot-stand; (f) is a lid. From Birks 1973.

western part of the island, where Lapita settlers were established on a coastal sand dune by about 1300 B.C. As befits the early date, the Natunuku decoration is quite complex, and, as at Lapita and Vatcha, there is a small amount of paddle-impression and incision as well. Round on the southern coast of Viti Levu is the second site, a rock-shelter on a small offshore island called Yanuca. This site has produced Lapita pottery with complex decoration dating back to about 1000 B.C., from which Lawrence and Helen Birks have been able to reconstruct a very full range of decorated bowl forms[74]. The third site is on a large sand dune at the mouth of the Sigatoka River[75], not far from Yanuca, and this has a late date of about 500 B.C.

The Sigatoka pottery is almost entirely plain, and flat bases are now virtually absent. The most common pot form is a round-based plain cooking pot, with a vertical or everted rim. There are still a few carinated vessels which retain rare examples of dentate stamping, and the site has also produced sherds from water bottles, ceramic discs which may have served as stoppers, knobbed lids, strap handles, and a number of cylindrical

devices which may have been pot rests[76] (figure 9.16). What may be related forms of pot rests have been found in the other Fijian sites, and on Watom and Tonga.

Sigatoka, like Erueti, clearly represents a very late stage of the Lapita tradition. As Green has pointed out[77] the eastern Lapita sites in Fiji and Tonga show much greater and more rapid degenerative changes in design than sites to the west, and it may be that this reflects a fair degree of isolation after initial settlement (see figure 9.17). Even the Fijian and Tongan groups themselves probably maintained little contact after they were first settled.

Other associated artefacts in the Fijian sites include both quadrangular and plano-convex sectioned untanged adzes from Yanuca and Sigatoka, and shell bracelets and a part of a pearl-shell lure shank of Polynesian type from Yanuca. The latter piece, together with the Watom one-piece hook fragment, a possible hook fragment from Tonga, and the numerous one-piece *Turbo* hooks from Anuta, make up the total of Lapita line fishing gear as known at present.

The actual mechanics of change within the

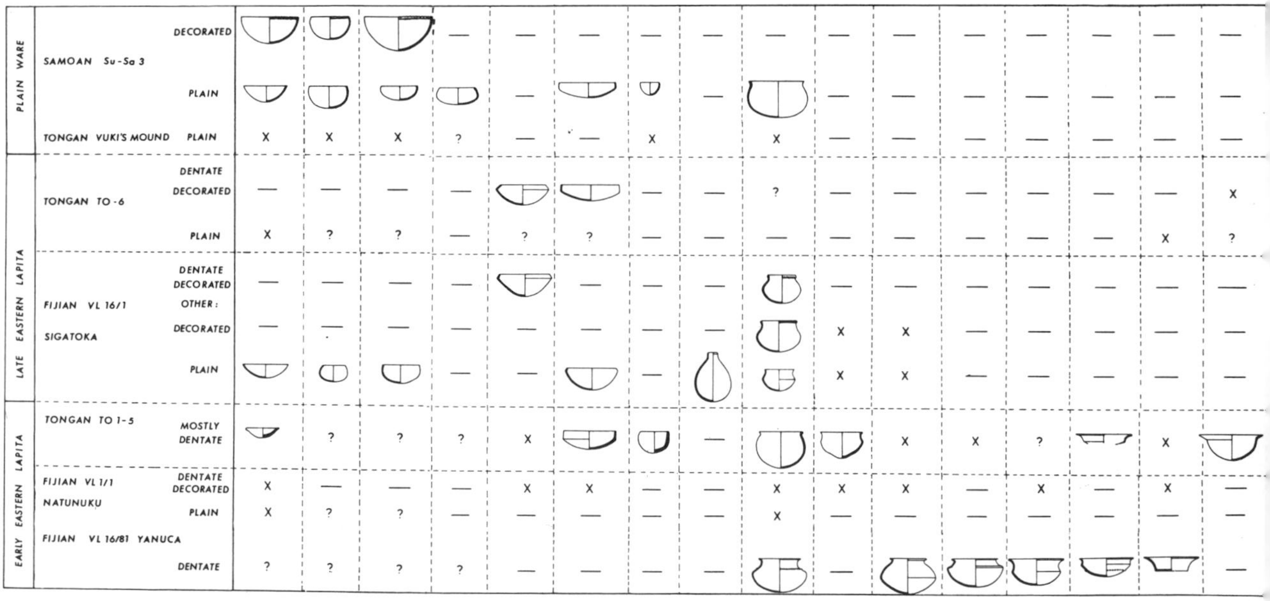

Fig. 9.17. Decorated and plain vessel forms from Fiji, Tonga and Samoa showing change from early decorated Lapita assemblages (*bottom*) to later Samoan plain ware (*top*). X = definite occurrence; ? = probable presence. From Green 1974b.

Lapita style are not particularly well illustrated by the sites discussed so far, because most of them seem to represent short time spans. However, in the Tongan Islands we have a very good ceramic sequence from about 1200 B.C. to perhaps the early first millennium A.D., which is based mainly on excavations by Jens Poulsen in ancient shell middens around the edge of the large lagoon which cuts into the central part of Tongatapu island[78]. Lapita pottery has been found right through the Tongan Islands from Tongatapu, through Ha'apai, Vava'u, and as far as Niuatoputapu in the far north[79]. But the key dated sequence is from Tongatapu.

When Captain Cook visited the Tongan Islands in 1777, he observed the presence of pots which were probably imported from Fiji. There is no evidence that the Tongans made pottery themselves at this time, but Poulsen believed, from the evidence of his excavations, that they did do so until not long before European contact. Subsequent excavations by L.M. Groube have shown that Poulsen's sites had been seriously disturbed, and he has made a very acceptable case for dating the pottery from about 1200 B.C. to early A.D., after which Tonga, like Samoa and the Marquesas Islands, became aceramic. Groube's interpretation is now accepted as correct for the dating, and into this framework can be inserted the details provided by Poulsen, and also by Golson[80].

The decorated Lapita pottery from the middens excavated by Poulsen generally resembles most closely that from Fiji and New Caledonia, which is perhaps to be expected. In early levels up to 12% of sherds may be decorated, and this of course implies that a much higher proportion of actual pots had decoration, as many decorated pots had large plain surfaces. The main early forms are globular pots with collared rims or short vertical or everted rims, together with open bowls, sometimes carinated. Flat bases seem to be confined to the early levels before about 500 B.C., as do the collared rims and carinated pots, while plain globular pots predominate in the later levels. The decoration is mainly by dentate stamping, but as in most other Lapita sites, there are small amounts of shell-edge decoration, appliqué, incision, and rim notching. Groube's excavation of a site called Vuki's mound shows that decoration had disappeared completely by about 400 B.C., and this site provides the best known Lapita settlement pattern for Tonga, consisting of stratified cooking and living floors surrounded by a collar of dumped shell midden. Other ceramic features from Tonga include conical or cylindrical pot-stands, and loop handles. The tempers are not found on Tongatapu itself, but may have come from the neighbouring volcanic island of Eua.

The Tongatapu sites have by far the greatest range of non-ceramic artefacts reported for Lapita sites, and the range encompasses virtually all types so far recorded (figure 9.18). The stone adzes are untanged, and have quadrangular, plano-convex and lenticular cross-sections. In addition, there is a range of adzes, chisels, gouges and scrapers made of shell. Fishing gear includes a one-piece shell fishhook, a gorge made of fish bone, stone and shell net sinkers, and many tops of cowrie shells which are usually interpreted to have belonged to octopus lures. The latter are similar to the ones from the site of Lapita itself, and it is strange that the stone weights are never found, because they are quite common in Polynesian sites where octopus lures were used. Until weights are found in Lapita contexts, one can hardly assume categorically that the important Polynesian octopus lures do in fact have Lapita antecedents. Other artefacts include awls and needles of bone, and a range of files and grindstones of coral and other materials. However, it is the ornament range which is so remarkable a feature of the Tongan sites. These include bracelets and rings of shell, square or rectangular necklace units of perforated shell, whole pearl-shell pendants, beads of shell, stone and bone, and bone tattooing chisels. There are also a few discs of stone, of a kind used for a bowling game in ethnographic contexts in Polynesia.

Until early in 1973, it was thought that the spread of the decorated Lapita pottery ended at Tonga, and that the early ceramics which were taken to the Samoan Islands were undecorated. The general topic of Polynesian ceramics must await the next chapter, but as a result of dredging in the lagoon at Mulifanua, on the western end of Upolu Island in Western Samoa, a number of Lapita sherds were recovered in 1973 from what must have been originally a coastal settlement. Only 8% of the sherds are decorated, with dentate stamped and incised motifs, and all were made locally according to temper analyses. A radiocarbon date of about 1000 B.C. suggests that this site represents the earliest settlement of Samoa[81].

In the northern Tongan islands, the Lapita pottery from the Ha'apai and Vava'u groups and Niuatoputapu is mainly plain, and on present evidence unlikely to be much older than 600–500 B.C. Furthermore, what appears to be plain Lapita pottery has recently been found on the island of East Futuna (Hoorn Island) dated to the late first millennium B.C., and the Futunan language is quite closely related to Samoan. Niuatoputapu may also have had a Samoic language when it was discovered in 1615, although its present linguistic affiliations lie with Tonga[82].

WHO WERE THE LAPITA POTTERS?

Round about 1300 B.C., it is quite clear that people who shared a very homogeneous archaeo-logical culture spread over the 5000 kilometres from New Guinea to Tonga. Available carbon-14 dates suggest that they spread very quickly, and if we bring in the evidence of the obsidian trade, we may infer that their voyaging skills were of no mean order. They may indeed have been the original 'Vikings of the Pacific' – founding heroic figures in the mythologies of the later Polynesians.

To anticipate the next chapter, we should note that the Polynesians, who on archaeological and linguistic grounds settled the Tongan Islands about 1300 B.C. and the Samoan Islands about 1000 B.C., are almost certainly the direct and

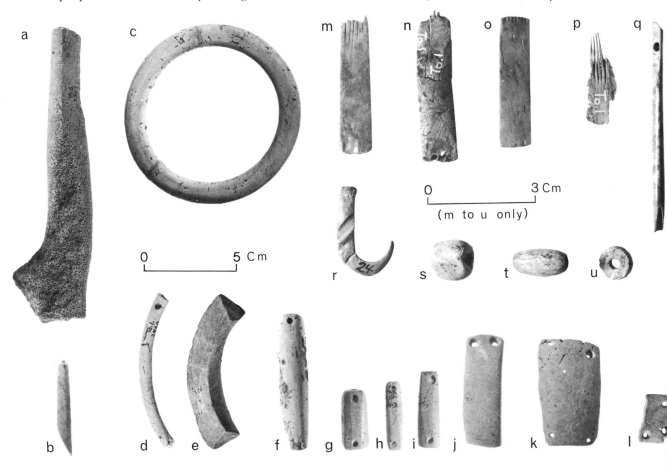

Fig. 9.18. Non-ceramic artefacts of Lapita affinity from Tongatapu: (a) file of branch coral; (b) file of sea-urchin spine; (c) shell bracelet; (d) shell bracelet or pendant fragment; (e) shell bracelet fragment; (f–l) shell ornaments; (m–p) bone tattooing chisels; (q) bone needle; (r) shell fishhook; (s–u) shell beads.

isolated descendants of the Lapita potters. Lapita material culture transmissions to later Polynesian cultures include pottery, shell scrapers and adzes, the prototype Polynesian stone adze kit, tattooing chisels, bowling discs, and a variety of other items, possibly including fishhooks. Oddly enough, the majority of the Lapita ornament types, so well represented in Tonga, do not travel beyond here into Polynesia, although they do survive in the later Melanesian cultures. At about the time of Christ, makers of a predominantly plain variety of pottery settled the Marquesas Islands from Samoa, and their descendants went on in turn to settle the rest of eastern Polynesia over the next thousand years. Therefore we have good reason to assume that the physical type of the Lapita potters was similar to that of the Polynesians, and that the Mongoloid features of their genetic heritage were preserved in the Australoid areas of Melanesia by the social pattern of non-exogamous kinship groups which characterises Polynesia today.

Ceramic features would suggest that the Lapita pottery style has an ultimate origin in north-eastern Indonesia or in the Philippines. When we consider the origins of the actual makers, it seems that two main choices are open. Firstly, there could have been Polynesian-like populations who had already been in Melanesia for a millennium or more speaking Oceanic languages, and who, at some time in the second millennium B.C., came into contact with ceramic societies in Indonesia and the Philippines. As a result they made and traded Lapita pottery, and some settled Polynesia. This explanation is plausible, but there seems to me to be a better one.

The second and by far the best hypothesis is to derive both the Lapita pottery and its makers directly from eastern Indonesia or the Philippines. The actual stylistic combinations that make the Lapita style may have developed within Melanesia, but the period between the initial spread of a ceramic prototype into Melanesia and the eventual settlement of Tonga was probably not more than a few hundred years. One gets the impression that the Lapita potters are themselves intruders into a Melanesia which had been settled by other Austronesians for perhaps at least a thousand years – the linguistic evidence pertaining to the break-up of the Oceanic subgroup would suggest this, and the archaeological evidence might suggest that these initial Austronesians had no pottery. By this hypothesis, the Lapita potters may at first have spoken languages of Western Austronesian type, but in 1500 B.C. or thereabouts the major subgroups of Austronesian would not have diverged to anything like their present extent, and the Lapita potters may not have had great difficulty in communicating with Melanesians who spoke Oceanic Austronesian languages. It is quite possible that the 'Lapita language' formed the common ancestor for the present Eastern Oceanic subgroup in eastern Melanesia and Polynesia, for while this subgroup now belongs with the other Oceanic languages in terms of a number of phonological, lexical and grammatical innovations[83], in total vocabulary it has retained more similarity with Western Austronesian than it has with the other Oceanic subgroups. This was in fact one of the main conclusions from the monumental linguistic analysis of Isidore Dyen[84].

In the first instance, the expansion of the Lapita Culture through Melanesia may have been based on the initiative of small groups of colonists and traders with their families – people who deliberately set out from the first to seek new territories and markets amongst the expanding horticultural societies of early Austronesian Melanesia. By at least 500 B.C. the impetus for colonisation had slackened, perhaps because energies were too busily employed in forging new societies in the big empty island groups of Fiji, Tonga and Samoa. The slackening was of course only temporary, and the longest voyages of discovery ever made by the Polynesians took place in the first millennium A.D. But by 500 B.C., the various widespread components of the Lapita Culture evidently became subject to isolation and ceramic degeneration. In Melanesia, the Lapita makers became absorbed into surrounding Melanesian populations, but their ornament styles and many features of their ceramics lived on, particularly around south-eastern coastal New Guinea and in the Massim district. The Lapita settlers who reached Tonga, and later Samoa, passed on to their Polynesian descendants their aristocratic form of leadership, their Mongoloid genes, and a few features of material culture, particularly adzes, their art style, and perhaps their fishing and voyaging technology.

LAPITA-LIKE ASSEMBLAGES IN MELANESIA

In various parts of western Melanesia there occur ceramic assemblages which are clearly related to Lapita, and which in fact seem to have developed from it at the end of the first millennium B.C. The assemblages from New Ireland and Sohano, which have been described above, may actually be of this type. But a more widespread and well-studied Lapita-derived assemblage is that of the Central District of Papua, where several coastal sites characterised by red-slipped pottery have been found to date to between 0 and A.D. 1200. The two main sites are Nebira 4, 15 kilometres inland from Port Moresby, and Oposisi, on Yule Island about 100 kilometres north-west of Port Moresby.

The site of Oposisi is a hill-top settlement, with dates of between one and two thousand years ago. Its basal levels typify what the excavator, Ron Vanderwal[85], calls the Oposisi Culture, and this seems to belong to the first Austronesian speaking immigrants into the area. The pottery has fairly close resemblances to Lapita, except that the dentate stamping is very rare, but there are red-slipped bowls with shell-impressed and lime infilled decoration (figure 9.19), and plain cooking and water jars. In fact, some of the shell-impression is so similar to the Lapita dentate stamping that an actual Lapita derivation, perhaps from northern New Guinea or the Solomons, can hardly be doubted. On the other hand, a derivation from the west along the southern coast of New Guinea, where there are

neither Austronesian speakers nor Lapita ceramic assemblages, would be most unlikely. Yule Island is almost on the western boundary of the Austronesian languages in southern New Guinea.

The other Oposisi artefacts include Fergusson Island obsidian, while stone adzes with quadrangular cross-sections, and rare triangular-sectioned adzes have been found at a contemporary site on the nearby mainland called Apere Venuna (figure 9.20). In addition, there are perforated pottery net sinkers, shell bracelets, pig bones, human bone beads, and bone spatulae which may have been for taking lime with the chewing of betel nut. The Oposisi Culture continues into what Vanderwal terms the Ravao Culture, and this may be marked by a further minor immigration of people into the area. The red-slipping and shell impressing disappear, burnishing and incision become major decorative techniques, and the Ravao Culture seems to develop continuously through a series of later cultures to about A.D. 1100–1200, with dogs appearing towards the end of this period. Some of the ceramics which follow Ravao, but which predate A.D. 1100–1200, are related to those in the Collingwood Bay and Massim areas of eastern Papua, and it may be that the Austronesians of south-eastern Papua had established

0   10 Cm

Fig. 9.19. Decorated sherds from Oposisi, Yule Island, Papua, *c.* 2000 B.P.

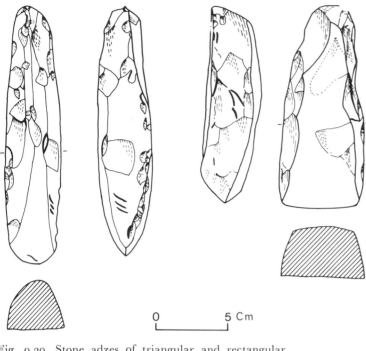

0   5 Cm

Fig. 9.20. Stone adzes of triangular and rectangular cross-section from Apere Venuna, Papua.

Fig. 9.21. Sago storage jar, Aibom village, East Sepik District. Height 4 cm.

long-distance trade routes by this time.

The Nebira 4 site, which consists of a midden deposited at the base of a steep hill, has a sequence from about 2000 years ago to A.D. 1100, which is very like that at Oposisi. Basal Nebira ceramics are red-slipped and shell-impressed, and there are also some painted sherds. Obsidian, shell beads, shell bracelets and pigs are present throughout the levels[86], and 29 burials predating A.D. 1200 were excavated on top of Nebira Hill by Susan Bulmer, some with drilled boars' tusks, necklaces of perforated dog teeth, and shell beads and bracelets[87]. In addition, the Nebira 4 site produced an industry of small flakes and cores which bears some generalised resemblance to the later Australian industries.

In the Yule Island and Port Moresby regions a very different type of comb-incised pottery appears about A.D. 1200, and in the Port Moresby area this may be ancestral to present Motu wares. We will consider these later ceramics in due course, and note here that while there may have been population continuity amongst the Austronesian speakers of Papua for some 2000 years, the picture is certainly complicated by ceramic changes and almost certainly by local population movements.

Fig. 9.22. Pottery manufacture by coiling, Geme village, Talaud Islands, eastern Indonesia. (See also colour plate.)

THE INCISED AND APPLIED-RELIEF CERAMICS OF MELANESIA

Very soon after the first appearance of the Lapita Culture, other apparently unrelated Melanesian ceramics make an appearance as well. These ceramics belong to a tradition characterised by incised and applied-relief decoration, and have baggy pot shapes which bear little resemblance to the Lapita forms, although some diffusion of design elements between the two traditions apparently did occur. The origins of the incised and applied-relief wares are at present unknown, although, like the Lapita, they might be derived from Indonesia or the Philippines by separate movements into Melanesia.

However, there is one important matter which can conveniently be aired at this point. The incised and applied-relief wares are generally made by coiling or ring building, while the Lapita ceramics are dominated by the slab building technique. It has been pointed out many times since 1930 that the coiling method of pottery manufacture is the main one associated with both the Austronesian and the Papuan ceramic industries of ethnographic times in western Melanesia, and the possibility of a Japanese Jomon or central Chinese origin for the technique has often been mooted[88], coiling being a major technique in the Neolithic pottery of both these areas. There is no direct proof for this viewpoint, but it is of interest that many of the Melanesian ceramics (excluding Lapita), with their baggy

Fig. 9.23. Incised and applied-relief pottery in Melanesia: *top*, early Mangaasi vessel, Mangaasi, Efate, New Hebrides – from Garanger 1971; *bottom*, sherds of Sohano style from Buka, Solomon Islands.

0   5 Cm

0   10 Cm

or pointed-based pot forms, do not find very close parallels in Southeast Asia where coiling is said to be found only rarely. Some of the remarkable ethnographic pots from the Sepik River (figure 9.21) and New Caledonia would demonstrate this point very well. It is therefore possible that many of these western Melanesian wares, unrelated to Lapita, have descended from ceramic industries so far unknown which were introduced from the north, although I would personally hesitate to accept a conclusion of this nature myself. I have observed coiling in the Talaud Islands of eastern Indonesia (figure 9.22), and Sutayasa[89] has described the technique for central Java, so I would suspect that the commonly held view that coiling was virtually absent in prehistoric Indonesia may well be oversimplified. Having aired this well-enshrined problem, let us return to our primary subject matter.

The most detailed archaeological information on the incised and applied-relief wares comes from Buka Island in the northern Solomons, and from the central New Hebrides. In the latter area, the French archaeologist José Garanger[90] has excavated distinctive ceramics on the islands of Efate, Tongoa and Makura, which belong to what may be termed the Mangaasi Culture. These wares develop from at least 700 B.C. to about A.D. 1600, although on Tongoa and Makura the pottery disappears about A.D. 1200, when new peoples arrive in the area.

The Mangaasi pottery is coiled and made from naturally tempered clay, and shows no signs of paddle and anvil finishing. The forms comprise spherical baggy pots with simple direct rims (figure 9.23), and there are none of the Lapita characteristics such as slipping, dentate stamping, or complex rim forms. The early Mangaasi pottery, which lasts into the first millennium A.D., has rich incised designs and liberally applied cordons and nubbins. In the lower levels of the Mangaasi site, on Efate Island, there are many handles, including some zoomorphic forms which may suggest relationships with the New Guinea and Bismarcks mortar and pestle complex (figure 9.24). I have already mentioned these relationships in the earlier part of this chapter in connection with the decorated Toiminapo axe. In the late Mangaasi ware, which develops continuously from the early ware and which seems to be widespread by about A.D. 800, the relief designs fade, incision becomes dominant, and the handles disappear. On Makura and Tongoa, a pottery with plain exterior but stab-incised interior appears with the later Mangaasi wares, and Garanger terms this Aknau ware. Its origin is unknown, but it may have been made in an area since annihilated by a massive volcanic eruption at about A.D. 1400. There is also the important point that some late Lapita pottery is found with the Mangaasi wares in the site of Erueti on Efate at about 350 B.C. (see page 250), although the Mangaasi levels at the site go back earlier.

The Mangaasi assemblage includes, from its early phases, bones of pig, lenticular cross-sectioned stone adzes, and bracelets and adzes of *Tridacna* shell. There appear to be no dogs or fowls. Pottery like the Mangaasi ware is found on surface sites elsewhere in the northern New Hebrides, but the closest parallel sequence comes from Jim Specht's excavations on the island of Buka in the northern Solomons, and on the tiny island of Sohano offshore from Buka[91].

The earliest style here which is characterised by incised and applied-relief designs is called the Sohano style by Specht, and this is found on Sohano Island and at Hangan village on Buka Island. It appears from about 500 B.C., if not earlier, and is contemporary in the later 1st millennium B.C. with the late Lapita pottery described above. This late Lapita pottery disappears at about the time of Christ, but the Sohano style continues unbroken into a later style, which belongs in the first millennium A.D., and which Specht calls the Hangan style.

Both the Sohano and Hangan wares, which therefore cover the period from perhaps 500 B.C. to A.D. 800, are coiled and, unlike the Mangaasi wares, finished with paddle and anvil. However, like the Mangaasi they have tempers and spherical baggy shapes which clearly set them apart from the Lapita wares. Their decoration is like that of the Mangaasi style, with punctation, incision and appliqué, often organised into triangular panels (figure 9.23). Rows of stamped circles are common in the Sohano style, and this is a possible borrowing from Lapita. Artefacts found with Sohano and Hangan styles include shell adzes and bracelets, sea urchin spine files, and shell bonito lure shanks.

Pig and dog were present from the Sohano phase, and this is perhaps the earliest occurrence of the rather enigmatic dog in Melanesian archaeology. Little else is known about the economy of these early Melanesian potters, either on Buka or in the New Hebrides, but we may perhaps see them as sedentary horticulturalists with whom the Lapita potters shared a contemporary existence in the first millennium B.C. So far, Buka and the New Hebrides have the only good sequence from island Melanesia for the incised and applied-relief wares, although they are present in other undated sites in northern New Guinea and the Bismarcks. Incised and applied-relief pottery has also been excavated in southern Bougainville by John Terrell, but the affiliations of this are not yet reported.

The evidence we have for western Melanesia (i.e. excluding Fiji and New Caledonia) suggests, therefore, that ceramics of two styles dominate in the period 1000 B.C. to A.D. 1000. These are the Lapita style and derivatives, and the incised and applied-relief styles. After A.D. 1000 many changes take place, possibly connected, possibly not. They must wait until the Fijian and New Caledonian areas have been considered, for here again we have some evidence for the presence of incised and applied-relief styles contemporary with Lapita, but the picture is complicated by an initial dominance of sherds decorated with carved-paddle-impressions.

THE NON-LAPITA PREHISTORY OF NEW CALEDONIA AND FIJI

The decoration of pottery by striking the surface with a carved paddle or die is common from the first millennium B.C. onwards from southern China (see figure 7.19) right through into the

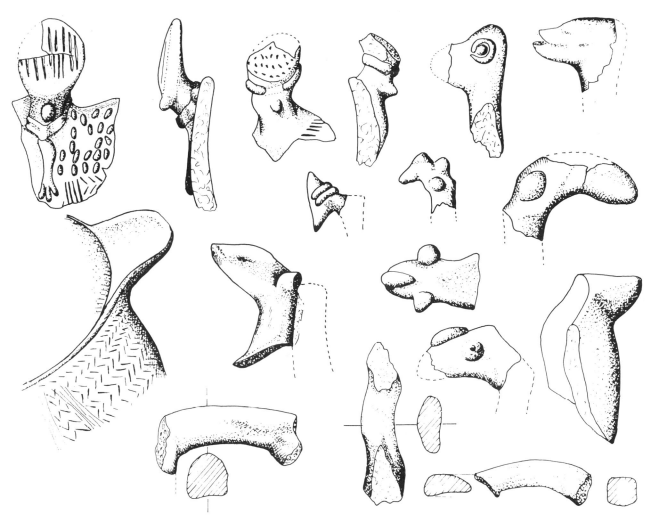

Fig. 9.24. Early Mangaasi handles from the central New Hebrides. From Garanger 1971.

Philippines and eastern Indonesia. On the other hand, it is generally absent or of very late date in western Melanesia. For instance, G.J. Irwin has shown that it belongs to the recent past in the Shortland Islands[92], and there are some undated and probably recent sherds of this type from Efate, in the central New Hebrides[93]. Therefore it is strange that it should be present in both New Caledonia and Fiji from almost 1000 B.C. Because of the presence of some carved paddle decoration on Lapita sherds in eastern Melanesia, particularly at the sites of Lapita, Boirra and Vatcha in New Caledonia, it may be that this ware develops partially out of the Lapita repertoire[94], even though the Lapita itself continues as a contemporary tradition for almost 1000 years. On the other hand, many of the

paddle-impressed sherds do have some incised and applied-relief decoration, which in time becomes dominant at the expense of the paddle-impression.

In order to explain the paddle-impressed wares, we need to resort to a fairly complex hypothesis. New Caledonia was settled by Lapita potters by at least 1000 B.C. (excluding for the moment the possibility of a preceramic occupation), and at about the same time by other groups who may have had some knowledge of the incised and applied-relief pottery. These latter people adopted paddle-impression from the Lapita potters and emphasised its importance into a major decorative technique, but otherwise retained the pot forms and some decorative motifs from the incised and applied-relief tradition. By

700 B.C., makers of this paddle-impressed pottery had already moved across to Fiji, and in New Caledonia and Fiji the paddle-impressed wares are dominant, besides the Lapita, through the first millennium B.C., after which the incised decoration swings gradually back into fashion. The tempos of replacement are different in the two areas; in New Caledonia it appears (on rather poor evidence) to be a gradual continuous change, while in Fiji there are more rapid changes at about A.D. 1100.

In New Caledonia, the Lapita and the paddle-impressed pottery appear at about the same time, unless one accepts the 2000 B.C. date for Lapita at Vatcha (above). At a site on Naia Bay, about 25 km north-west of Noumea, paddle-impressed pottery seems to be made right through the first millennium B.C., and no Lapita is present at all[95]. Together with the paddle-impressed pottery, which forms the great bulk of all decoration at the site, there are a few sherds of incised pottery, with some of the simpler incised motifs which occur in the Mangaasi and Sohano styles. At another site called Podtanean[96], near the site of Lapita, paddle-impressed sherds are present as the sole form of decoration in levels dated prior to A.D. 250. Although the New Caledonian sequence is very poorly understood at present, we may perhaps sketch in later developments as follows. After about A.D. 250 the paddle-impression declines markedly, and becomes totally absent in the Naia Bay sites, but continues to fairly recent times in very small proportions elsewhere. The incision gradually becomes dominant, although it should be remembered that in most sites well over 90% of the sherds are actually plain, and the incision was restricted to narrow zones around the rims and upper bodies of the pots. Dates for sites with a predominance of the incised ware, which also has simple relief motifs like the Mangaasi pottery in the New Hebrides, range from about A.D. 300 to 1600[97]. There also appear to be some regional differences within the tradition; northern New Caledonia tends to have a lot of comb-incision, which elsewhere in Melanesia becomes very important in the past 1000 years (below), and the north also has many rims with small suspension holes. In the south-west, handles are common from some 2000 years ago, and incised designs like those in the Mangaasi style also occur[98]. In addition, at Moindou, on the west coast of the island, flat-based and carinated pottery with applied garlands around the rims has been found at a depth of 6.5 metres,

under a thickness of 3 metres of alluvium[99]. This pottery is undated, but it looks like an isolated Lapita survival.

New Caledonian ethnographic pottery, which was made only in the northern part of the island, was coiled and unslipped, round based and often glazed with *Agathis* gum. It had some incised and relief decoration, and a number of pots were provided with rather spectacular reliefs of human faces and lizards, rather like the reliefs on Sepik River (figure 9.21) and Markham Valley pottery. These features have not been traced archaeologically, although most of the ethnographic pottery had rim suspension holes and no handles, like the prehistoric pottery in the northern part of the island[100]. In addition, there is no pedigree yet for the beautiful greenstone maceheads that New Caledonians made until recently, even though these are amongst the finest examples of stoneworking in the Pacific. Many of the later incised ware sites contained shell tools, bracelets, and land snail fishhooks, but there are few innovations and indeed many losses from the earlier Lapita assemblages.

Racially and linguistically, New Caledonia is a complex place. There is not the homogeneity which characterises Fiji, and the above archaeological story is probably only a scratch on the surface. Settlement by Lapita potters and other ceramic Austronesians about 1000 B.C. seems fairly certain, and the island has probably been fairly isolated since then; there were no pigs or dogs here for instance at European contact. Archaeologically, New Caledonia and Fiji present almost identical pictures from the ceramic evidence, yet it is clear that New Caledonia should have more to tell than Fiji. Whether the island had preceramic settlers remains uncertain, and I have described the ambiguous evidence from the concrete-cored mounds above. But awareness of the diversity within New Caledonia led the French geologist Avias in 1949 to reconstruct successive migrations of Tasmanoids, white-skinned Ainoids, Melanesians, and finally Polynesians to the island[101]. Make-believe certainly, and we can today restrict ourselves to a consideration of diverse settlers from within the Melanesian ethnic area. One group of settlers without pottery probably did reach New Caledonia in the past (but not necessarily before 1000 B.C.), even if they cannot yet be identified archaeologically. In the southern Hebrides, another area, like New Caledonia, of high linguistic diversity outside the Eastern Oceanic

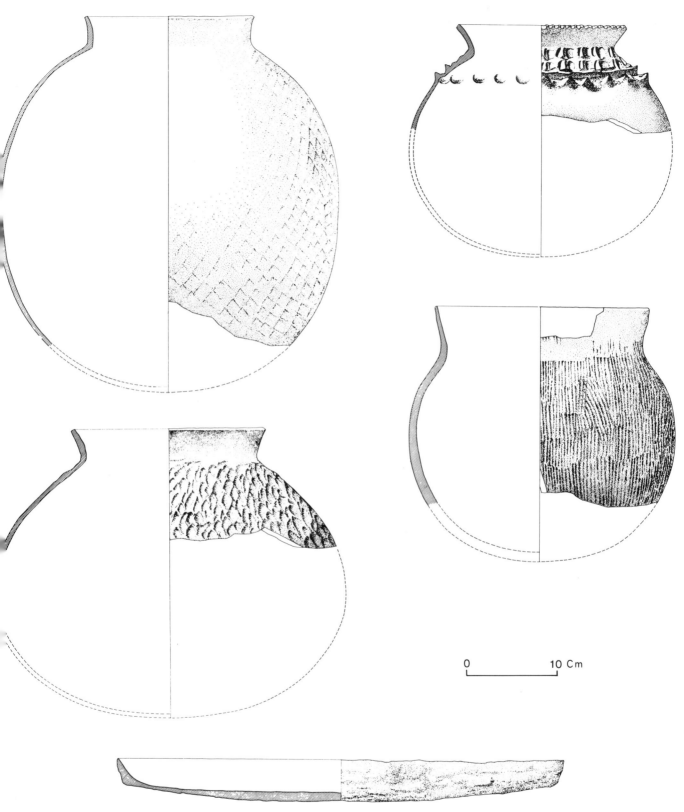

Fig. 9.25. Paddle-impressed pots from Sigatoka, Viti Levu, Fiji. From Birks 1973.

subgroup, Richard Shutler has found evidence of aceramic settlement going back to at least 500 B.C.[102]. From the islands of Tanna, Futuna and Aneityum, and particularly the two former islands, assemblages characterised by burials with shell bead necklaces and pendants, together with stone and shell adzes, have been recovered from many sites. On Futuna the burials are reported back to A.D. 300, but how these relate to the present Polynesian settlers of this island is not known. Shutler's evidence shows, therefore, that there were other peoples besides the potters in first millennium B.C. eastern Melanesia. Whether Austronesian or Papuan, such aceramic groups surely reached New Caledonia as well, to contribute to the ethnic diversity, but to remain archaeologically invisible. On the other hand, there is no sign that they ever got to Fiji.

The first people to settle Fiji were almost certainly the Lapita potters, whose genes still survive amongst the coastal Fijians and Lau Islanders of today. Soon after their arrival, it would appear that other Melanesian populations arrived, and settled the interiors of the larger islands, as well as mixing with their Lapita predecessors. Perhaps this second group came from New Caledonia with paddle-impressed pottery, and their language was probably sufficiently close to that of the Lapita settlers to allow formation of a single ancestral dialect chain for the two closely related languages which exist in the Fijian Islands today. In the Yanuca rockshelter on Viti Levu, paddle-impressed pottery occurs, without Lapita, in a level dated to about 700 B.C., and this actually predates the late Lapita pottery found in the Sigatoka dunes which dates to about 500 B.C. Above the Lapita level at Sigatoka there is a clearly defined level of paddle-impressed pottery, again with no Lapita at all, and this dates to about A.D. 200[103]. This pottery consist mainly of globular cooking pots, paddle-impressed and with some rim notching or incision, and there are also a few very crude flat-bottomed dishes which may have been for salt evaporation (figure 9.25 bottom). In Fiji there is little overlap in form or association between the Lapita and the paddle-impressed wares, and this does give the impression that the development of the latter took place outside Fiji, and most probably in New Caledonia.

The paddle-impressed pottery is found right through the Fiji group; up to 65 kilometres inland on Viti Levu[104], on Taveuni and Vanua Levu, and at least as far as Kabara Island in the Southern Lau group[105]. At the important site of Navatu in northern Viti Levu, Gifford[106] excavated deposits with paddle-impressed pottery spanning the period from about 50 B.C. to A.D. 1100, with the impressed sherds forming over 50% of the totals from some levels. The main forms were globular and carinated cooking pots, and a very small amount of incision was present, as in the paddle-impressed assemblages generally in New Caledonia and Fiji. Pig, chicken, and cannibalized human bones, together with shell adzes and bracelets were also found at Navatu, and at another site called Karobo on the south coast of Vitu Levu, remains of Tahitian chestnuts, candlenuts and pandanus fruits were found with paddle-impressed pottery[107]. The stone adzes from these paddle-impressed pottery sites show a clear development towards the lenticular cross-sections which dominate later prehistory in most of Melanesia, although as might be expected, Fiji is certainly not lacking in some of the adze forms distinctive of Polynesia[108].

What appears to be a fairly simple sequence in Fiji undergoes marked change at about A.D. 1100. As well as excavating the site of Navatu, Gifford in 1947 also excavated a site called Vuda on the west coast of Viti Levu. According to traditions of *yavusa* origin (see page 101) remembered by many of the peoples of Viti Levu, a very important ancestral figure named Lutunasobasoba came with his followers and landed at Vuda[109], probably about A.D. 1500–1600 according to genealogies, but perhaps a few centuries earlier if we allow for some genealogical abbreviation. The people of Lutunasobasoba then moved inland to the Nakauvadra Mountains, and from there established *yavusa* over much of Viti Levu. Some may eventually have gone to Vanua Levu, where some groups still trace *yavusa* origins to eastern Viti Levu. According to most scholars, the people of Lutunasobasoba are to be reckoned as immigrants from outside Fiji, but their exact origins are traditionally unknown. With this knowledge in mind, we can see that Gifford's excavations at Vuda are of some importance. The site contained levels dating from about A.D. 1100 to European contact, which were characterised from the start by a sharp drop in the amounts of paddle-impressed pottery, a corresponding slight increase in the amount of incised ware and a large increase in plain ware. The main forms are globular cooking pots and narrow-necked water jars, and the amount of incision increases gradually through time, and more markedly at about the period of European contact. Green and Shaw[110] have called the period from 1100 to European contact the Vuda phase, and the ethnographic period, with its diversified and remarkable wares, some of which almost certainly reflect European influence[111], the Ra phase.

From sites on Taveuni Island, Everett Frost[112] has evidence for ceramic changes at about A.D. 1100 which parallel those on Viti Levu, and he feels that these are sufficient to postulate a definite migration into Fiji at this time. The paddle-impression declines sharply, although it does survive in minimal amounts, and a range of incised, applied and shell impressed motifs come to the fore. Our best explanation for the widespread ceramic change, given the full and convincing traditional evidence above, is to postulate a migration from the late Mangaasi area in the central New Hebrides at about A.D. 1100, and we will return to the later prehistory of this island group below. In Fiji, the newcomers may have arrived in small unco-ordinated groups, because they do not appear to have had much impact on the Fijian language or physical type, although they have of course impressed themselves on the traditional corpus of knowledge.

Whatever the exact contribution of the new arrivals to the ethnic pattern in Fiji, they do seem at least to have increased the degree of hostility between local groups. Frost's excavations revealed that from 1100 onwards large numbers of earthwork forts were constructed on Taveuni, and these are either on the tops of steep ridges and defended by short transverse ditches, or they are on flatter ground and defended by circular ditches, broken by causeways. Some contain twenty or more house platforms of earth, and some of the circular enclosures are linked together in complex groups. They are nearly all in areas near the coast which would allow permanent habitation, and only a very few are in remote inland situations. This description of the Taveuni forts would also apply to the hundreds of others elsewhere in Fiji, particularly on the islands of Viti Levu[113], Vanua Levu and Wakaya[114]. On Viti Levu, there may be over 1000 of them, mainly in the south-eastern part of the island in areas of intensive taro cultivation. Many of these forts were used in the nineteenth century wars between Bau and Rewa, but a lot are definitely prehistoric, despite the absence of detailed excavation. The ridge and ring ditch forms are again the basic types, and many of the latter are multivallate. Banks may be inside

or outside the ditches in both forms, and in lowland areas of Viti Levu the ditches were often flooded to serve as moats. House mounds, sometimes stone-faced, and sometimes linked by causeways, are present in virtually all of the Viti Levu sites, and the prevailing impression is that a large proportion of the Fijian population lived in these defended areas for upwards of 700 years.

We have now taken the New Caledonian and Fijian sequences through to the period of European contact. We will return to them briefly later to consider rock art and stone structures,

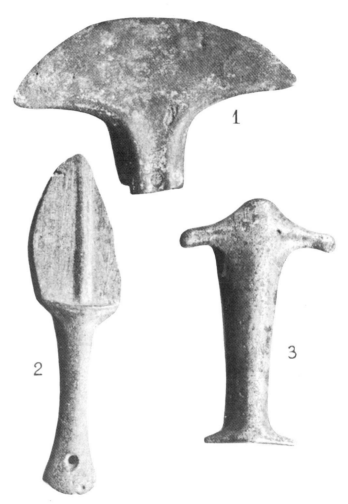

Fig. 9.26. Bronze objects from Kwadaware, Lake Sentani; (1) socketed axe 11.9 cm wide; (2) spearhead(?) 13.7 cm long; (3) brass dagger handle 10 cm long. From De Bruyn 1959.

but for the meantime we must return to western Melanesia to examine the changes of the past 1500 years. In relative terms, the first 2000 years of Melanesian ceramic history appear simple; perhaps this reflects lack of knowledge. By contrast, the last 1500 years present a picture of considerable complexity.

SOUTHEAST ASIAN METAL AGE INFLUENCES IN WESTERN MELANESIA

Metal Age influences in western Melanesia have been proposed at various times in the past, although the evidence ranges from fairly acceptable to frankly doubtful. Three eroded Dong-Son drum tympani which still retain their central twelve-rayed stars are today in the possession of the Mejbrat people in central Cendrawasih, Irian Jaya[115], but these are the only objects reported from western Melanesia which may be accepted as actual imports from the west. Much weaker evidence for Dong-Son influences comes from further east in northern New Guinea, from a burial mound in a village called Kwadaware, on a small island in Lake Sentani[116]. Some years ago, socketed axes and spearheads, as well as a brass oil burner and a brass dagger with an iron hilt were found in this mound by the villagers (figure 9.26). But none of these items is obviously Dong-Son in the strict sense of the word, and we may have to do with an indigenous metal industry established by Indonesian traders sometime within the past 1500 years.

The possibility of Dong-Son influence behind the pestle and mortar complex, and behind the axes and adzes with waists or splayed blades which are found widely in Melanesia, has been considered above. Without more archaeological evidence the question must rest open, but a few axes of stone or obsidian which are very strongly splayed at the cutting edge have been found in New Guinea, and here a Metal Age influence may be likely[117], although we are still in the realms of hypothesis. Direct archaeological evidence of widespread influence in Melanesia from what is in fact a very poorly defined Dong-Son Culture anyway, is virtually negligible.

If we turn to the possibility of influence from the Philippines, the prospects become slightly more exciting. Let us consider the practice of jar burial, which in Melanesia is known only from Cape Rodney on the south-eastern coast of Papua, in several islands in the Massim District including the Trobriands[118], and on southern

0   10 Cm

Fig. 9.27. Sherd with channelled decoration from Wanigela, Collingwood Bay, Papua.

Bougainville[119]. On Bougainville, John Terrell has excavated an urn-cremation in a thick painted pot of unknown ceramic affinity, while in Papua, the jar burials appear to have been uncremated. Some of the Massim jar burials are in pots with incised scrolls which suggest Dong-Son parallels to Golson[120], but here we have the problem that jar burial in Island Southeast Asia is by no means well correlated with the Dong-Son bronzes. In fact we find much closer parallels in the ceramics of the Philippine Metal Age, after 1500 years ago, and recent archaeological evidence from south-eastern Papua takes on relevance here.

The archaeological evidence comes from work by Brian Egloff in Collingwood Bay, and by Peter Lauer in the Massim Islands[121]. Some of the Trobriand burial pots, and a good deal of surface collected material from the Trobriand and D'Entrecasteaux Islands, appears to have been traded into the area from potteries on Collingwood Bay, sometime before 500 years ago. In historic times, the Trobrianders, who have no clay to make their own pottery, acquired nearly all of their pottery from the Amphlett Islanders via the *Kula* trade cycle. Hence, the present form of the island-based trade cycle is a recent phenomenon, and much stronger mainland links were present in the past. In Collingwood Bay itself, Egloff excavated three artificial mounds of uncertain function at a village called Wanigela, and these mounds contained pottery with complex channelled, incised, shell-impressed and punctate decoration (figure 9.27) covering the period A.D. 700–1400. This is the type of pottery which was traded to the Trobriands, and amongst the earliest pieces, which may go back into the early first millennium A.D., are sharply carinated or flanged bowls, often profusely provided with triangular cut-outs on rims or flanges. An almost complete pot of this kind was recovered from a site a few kilometres inland from Collingwood Bay, with a high ring-foot with rectangular cut-outs (figure 9.28). Similar pottery was collected at Wanigela early in this century[122], and one does not have to look very hard to find good Philippine Metal Age parallels for it, particularly in the Novaliches pottery complex as defined by Solheim (see page 214).

The Wanigela sites have also produced *Conus* shells incised with spirals and scrolls (figure 9.29), although no jar burials are yet known from this particular area. Nevertheless, what we do have is good evidence in south-eastern Papua for an association of elements otherwise rare or absent in·Melanesia: jar burials, Philippine-type pottery, and distinctive scroll and spiral motifs (I do not include Bougainville in this complex, and have no suggestions concerning the origins of jar burial here). Other Wanigela artefacts are more in the Melanesian tradition; bone lime spatulae and needles, shell bracelets and necklace units, lenticular cross-sectioned adzes, and a perforated stone clubhead. But the presence of Island Southeast Asian traders in south-eastern Papua about 1500 years ago is a likely hypothesis, and it is quite strongly supported by Capell's (albeit disputed) linguistic evidence[123] that south-eastern Papua was subjected to migrations from central Sulawesi and the Philippines at about this time. The contact may have lasted some time, but was evidently not accompanied by any permanent settlement of large magnitude. I do not wish to suggest that the contact was directly with the central Philippines, due to the distances involved, and future work in eastern Indonesia may reveal ceramic complexes of Novaliches type which would be a more likely source.

What we really see from the above is that there are archaeological and ethnographic features in western Melanesia which suggest contacts with areas west of New Guinea. Generally, scholars subsume these influences under the general term 'Dong-Son', but more detailed research shows that the picture is in fact more complex than this. The art evidence provides similar misty vistas which have intrigued culture historians for many years.

The art historians who have had most to say about the history of Melanesian art have been frankly diffusionist in outlook. The common procedure is to trace specific artistic manifesta-

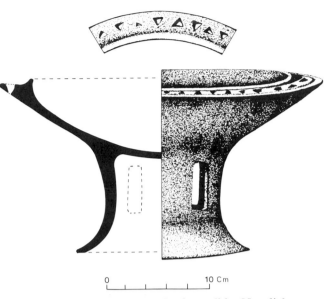

0   10 Cm

Fig. 9.28. Pedestalled vessel of possible Novaliches affinity (central Philippines), Wawa gardens, Rainu, Collingwood Bay. From Egloff 1971b.

Fig. 9.29. Incised *Conus* shell from Collingwood Bay.

tions in all areas of Oceania back to sources in Shang and Chou China, Dong-Son, or India. The first two sources are by far the most popular. I am personally unable to share such views; I can see that there are meaningful parallels, but the facts of archaeology make such long range direct diffusion impossible. The Pacific cultures share with the east Asian cultures a complex resistant set of artistic motifs which possibly extend back to a time when Austronesian expansion into Oceania was not even dreamt of. Some of these artistic motifs were isolated in a study carried out under the direction of Douglas Fraser[124], and they are widely present in a number of areas, including Shang and Chou China, Sumatra and Borneo, the middle Sepik region of New Guinea, New Zealand and other scattered Pacific Islands, British Columbia, and central America and Peru. The motifs include, amongst many, protruding tongues on human figures[125], human masks on the gable ends of houses, human figures flanked by 'heraldic' animals, and a preoccupation with bilateral symmetry, particularly in the human form. Either one has a multitude of migrations to account for their occurrence, or one traces the whole complex back to a common east Asian source, which probably existed by at least 6000 years ago. Many of these motifs, which do of course attain complexities which can only be hinted at here, were certainly present by Proto-Austronesian times in Southeast Asia, as Ch'en Ch'i-lu has shown for Taiwan and other Austronesian areas[126]. Heine Geldern groups them into his Old Pacific style[127], and he suggests origins for the complex in neolithic northern Eurasia, although it is hard to see why he rules out a Chinese or Southeast Asian origin. We may of course never know the exact origin of the Old Pacific Style, but we do know that it was taken by the first Austronesian migrants across the whole Pacific, where it was subjected to development in isolation, a modicum of local diffusion, and, in some areas, a nineteenth century efflorescence made possible by the introduction of steel tools. The vast majority of art objects in museums are of course far removed from being prehistoric, and there are many pitfalls here for the unwary.

For me, Heine Geldern's Old Pacific style is a crucial concept; a real entity which lies at the base of all Pacific art. Millennia of isolation have led to the tremendous variations which lead art historians to bring in their diffusionistic models, and some diffusion in later periods there certainly

has been, as we have seen above in connection with New Guinea. But some of the art historians writing prior to the development of archaeology in the region did develop some rather extraordinary hypotheses. To take an illustrative example, Heine Geldern suggested in 1937[128] that there had been direct links between the Marquesas Islands and China prior to 600 B.C., and he later suggested links between New Zealand and the Yüeh peoples of southern China in the third century B.C.[129]. He even went on to suggest that New Zealand Maori art could not be Polynesian, and was 'a barbarised art, but an art which could only have been born in a high civilisation'[130]. This tends to reduce the issue to little more than a value judgement; the New Zealand Maori were far removed from the Yüeh in time and space, and any credit for their artistic achievement goes to them and to their more distant Austronesian ancestors.

Another rather complex explanation for Pacific art history has been presented by Fraser[131], who has developed and extended some of Heine Geldern's theories. Fraser recognises the antiquity of a fairly simple Papuan art style in New Guinea, characterised by the use of masks and curvilinear motifs, but the succeeding Austronesian art styles are given a rather bewildering variety of sources, and a brief summary is rendered impossible. As an example, he regards Hawaiian art as the product of influences from China, Japan, India and Dong-Son, but recent archaeological work would make an explanation of this kind very hard to uphold.

Diffusionists have not of course had the only say. The opposite viewpoint has been taken by Levi-Strauss in connection with the phenomenon of bilateral symmetry[132]. He suggests that this develops independently in different societies, when a three dimensional human face is represented in a two dimensional design. This is particularly the case when the face has tattoos, for a frontal representation in true perspective would not of course show the designs in their full glory. There is logical sense in this explanation, but perhaps it swings too much to an extreme. The spread of bilateral symmetry from an Old Pacific ancestor still seems to be an acceptable conclusion.

All this of course stemmed from an initial discussion of Metal Age and Dong-Son influence in Melanesia. However one wishes to define Dong-Son, a number of art historians have shown clearly that elements such as 'soul-boats', spirals, and bird headed canoe prows are present quite widely in western Melanesia. Traces of what may be an art complex which is somehow related to the designs on the Dong-Son drums have been noted in the Sepik area, the Admiralties, New Ireland, and the Trobriand Islands[133], and with the latter we are back to the archaeological evidence related above. East Indonesian or Philippines traders of the Metal Age, with or without Dong-Son influences, would appear to have made their presences felt, but perhaps to no further east than the Solomons.

COMB-INCISED POTTERY IN MELANESIA

From about one thousand years ago there is a sudden appearance of curvilinear comb-incision in prehistoric pottery from New Guinea to Fiji. Perhaps this reflects another more recent period when Indonesian or Philippine traders penetrated into western Melanesia. Comb-incision as a decorative technique has a respectable distribution in Neolithic and Metal Age sites in Southeast Asia, and, significantly, is common in the Philippines right through the past two thousand years[134]. The Melanesian occurrences are too specific in time and technique to imply coincidence, and comb-incision is virtually absent in earlier periods. As we will see, its occurrence becomes later as one moves east, so a direct Southeast Asian influence all the way to Fiji can

hardly be countenanced. Local population movements within Melanesia need of course cause no surprise, but what is hard to explain is why the comb-incision should have been adopted so widely.

In the west, comb-incised ware seems to replace the older Lapita-derived styles in the Yule Island area about A.D. 1200 (figure 9.30), and Vanderwal argues for new arrivals in the region at this time[135]. Near Port Moresby there appears to be a similar sequence, with the Lapita-derived wares fading out around A.D. 1200, and comb-incised and painted wares appearing in midden deposits on Motupore Island at about the same time. These comb-incised ceramics seem to grade into the present-day Motu pottery, which is now mainly undecorated[136]. On linguistic grounds it is hard to imagine the Motu coming from very far afield to central Papua in recent times, and we may have a situation where a single population has been adapting its ceramic industry to outside influences for about 2000 years. This may be the case around Yule Island too. For instance, there is continuity in the presence of painted pottery around Port Moresby from 2000 years ago almost to the present, and this is a specific design technique which is very rare elsewhere in Melanesia. People with comb-incised wares, and also Massim traders who were transmitting their wares to the Port Moresby area some 700 years ago[137], may well have caused widespread changes

0   10 Cm

Fig. 9.30. Comb-incised pottery in Melanesia: *left*, Orourina, Yule Island; *right*, Buka, northern Solomons.

in an indigenous ceramic tradition.

Allen's excavations at Motupore have also documented certain very important aspects of Motu non-ceramic cultural evolution. It seems that about A.D. 1000–1200, the inland Papuan-speaking peoples of central Papua expanded to the coast, and forced the coastal Austronesians into the highly specialised fishing and pottery-trading economy which was characteristic of the ethnographic Motu. The Motupore site, which consists of an occupation area and midden, contained evidence for intensive net fishing, and the making of shell beads, and it may be assumed that fish, necklaces and pots were traded to the inland peoples in return for wallabies, the bones of which were found in large numbers in the site. Allen's view is that the Motu immigrated into the area from an unknown outside source and replaced the earlier Austronesians, but I feel that Motu culture is simply the product of major economic and ceramic changes caused by a complex of population movements and influences at around A.D. 1100. Oddly enough, although it may be coincidental, there is a lot of evidence for cultural upheaval in the New Hebrides and Fiji at about the same time (see below and page 265).

Eastwards from central Papua, comb-incised wares are widely reported in eastern Papua, in southern New Ireland, and in the northern Solomons, where Specht[138] traces them to the late first millennium A.D. in his Buka sequence (figure 9.30). Here, the style is grafted on to the existing Sohano/Hangan incised and applied-relief style, and continues on in direct ancestry to modern Buka pottery. In the New Hebrides, however, the style is only present on Malekula, where it is not dated, and elsewhere in the northern New Hebrides the incised and applied-relief styles have survived into ethnographic times. Today, pottery is only made on Espiritu Santo in the New Hebrides, but it is not clear how this relates to prehistoric styles in the area, and it is unusual in having a red slip[139]. On New Caledonia, comb-incision makes an appearance at an unknown date in the incised and applied-relief wares in the northern part of the island, and in Fiji it makes a fairly major impact at about the time of European contact, or a little before, and survives as an important decorative element in modern Fijian ceramics[140].

The widespread appearance of comb-incision may be coincidence, but I suspect not. Its eastward spread over a period of some 500 or more years may not involve major population displacement, but it is a fact of Melanesian culture history which deserves at least some attention.

HUMAN SACRIFICE IN THE NEW HEBRIDES

In the central New Hebrides, on the islands of Efate, Makura and Tongoa, the Mangaasi pottery fades out of existence sometime after A.D. 1200, and new people who did not make pottery arrived on the scene. As we have seen, some of the late Mangaasi potters evidently moved to Fiji, perhaps expelled by the new arrivals, or perhaps driven away by a cataclysmic volcanic eruption which shattered a once large island into the present tiny Shepherd Islands to the south of Tongoa. This eruption probably took place about A.D. 1400[141].

We now come to one of the most astounding archaeological discoveries ever made in the Pacific. The people of Efate still retain detailed traditions of the arrival, sometime before the volcanic eruption, of a group of titled and high ranking individuals who spread out over Efate, Makura and Tongoa, and introduced a form of matrilineal social organisation into the area[142]. One of these men was called Roy Mata, and he established himself with his followers on north-eastern Efate. When he died, he was buried, according to tradition, on a small island called Retoka off the western coast of Efate, together with a number of faithful followers from the clans under his influence, who sacrificed their lives voluntarily. In addition, other individuals were killed forcibly and buried with the retinue.

In 1967, the French archaeologist José Garanger was led by informants to a group of small standing stones on Retoka island, and commenced excavations. The results were quite startling. The body of a man, who can hardly be any other than Roy Mata himself, was found extended on its back in a pit which also contained, to his left, a man and woman side by side, to his right a single male, and across the feet of these four parallel bodies, a young girl. Between the legs of Roy Mata lay a bundled secondary burial, possibly of a predeceased wife. The pit was marked on the ground surface by two large slabs of stone, and by a number of large marine shells. Around it were slightly shallower burials of 35 individuals, of which 22 comprised men and women buried together in pairs (figure 9.31). In Garanger's words, the women 'seemed always to be seeking the protection of their companion, clasping him by the neck, waist or arm, with their legs frequently interwoven with those of the man, and their fingers and toes clenched'[143] (figure 9.32). Burials of pigs and scattered cannibalised human bones attested to some of the rites which must have accompanied this mass burial, and it seems that the men may have been stupefied with kava before burial, while the women were in many cases buried alive and conscious.

Nearly all of the burials were associated with personal ornaments, with some being very much richer than others, and some having even more ornaments than Roy Mata himself. Individual preferences seem to have differed widely, but the overall range of artefacts is quite surprising. Necklaces were formed of hundreds of tiny shell beads, interspersed with perforated cones made from whale-teeth, bone 'reel' ornaments, or perforated shells. One necklace also had a perforated calcite bird-head pendant. Armbands,

skirts or loincloths of tiny shell beads affixed to some kind of backing adorned many of the bodies, and bracelets of recurved pig tusks and of *Trochus* shell adorned many arms, one woman having no less than 34 of the latter. Bundles of perforated cowries and other decorative shells were strung around ankles, arms or shoulders, perhaps as a form of dancing costume (figure 9.32). A few graves also contained shell adzes.

The collective sepulture of Roy Mata has a carbon date of A.D. 1265±140, which of course supports the traditions perfectly. This graveyard is, however, not unique, for Garanger found other similar ones on the island of Tongoa, which was settled traditionally from Efate after the great volcanic eruption of *c.* 1400. At three sites on this island smaller burials of known chiefs with attendant sacrifices were excavated, with similar

Fig. 9.31. The collective burial of Roy Mata, Retoka Island, Efate, central New Hebrides. From Garanger 1972.

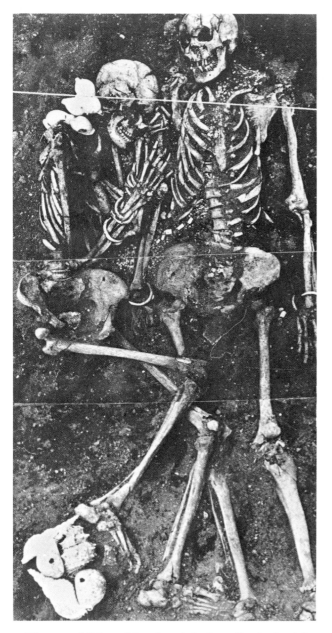

Fig. 9.32. Male and female pair in the collective burial of Roy Mata. Ornaments include pig tusk bracelets, perforated shells, and small shell discs, probably once mounted on fabric. From Garanger 1972.

ornaments and stone markers, and carbon-14 analyses show a date around A.D. 1400 to be reasonably certain for them. Clearly, the central New Hebrides underwent marked cultural change with the arrival of Roy Mata and his people, and traditions derive them from the south, although Garanger prefers a northern origin on the archaeological evidence. Without ceramics this problem is difficult to resolve, and sacrificial burial on this scale is rarely reported from anywhere else in Oceania. However, there is a recorded observation from Uvea (Wallis Island) of a chiefly burial laid across the legs of eight sitting corpses, with an extra body at the head and the foot[144], and sacrificial burial at the death of a chief is also reported from Truk in the Carolines[145]. In addition, the sacrifice of one or more wives to accompany a dead chief to his grave was not at all uncommon in Oceania according to ethnographic accounts[146], although we have few reports of anything approaching the extravagance of Roy Mata.

STONE STRUCTURES AND ROCK ART IN MELANESIA

Stone structures, often rather splendidly termed Megaliths, are found in scattered localities all over Melanesia. House platforms, burial places, and ceremonial or burial complexes of upright stones seem to form the majority of sites, and very few have been examined archaeologically. In 1950, a monumental survey of Melanesian megaliths by Alfonse Riesenfeld made its appearance[147], and this will certainly serve as a sourcebook for many years. Unfortunately, however, Riesenfeld was obsessed with the view that all stone structures, however trivial, belonged to a single related group of migrants whom he called 'stone-using immigrants'. His theoretical framework has never really been accepted, but it does at least deserve a comment.

Riesenfeld, like many historical ethnologists before him[148], felt that Melanesia was settled by migrant waves with differing cultures, and that these waves could be identified from the distribution of ethnographic elements. For him, Melanesia was settled firstly by aceramic Papuans, secondly by his stone-using immigrants who came in via western Micronesia, and finally by dark-skinned Melanesians, who came in at least two waves; one to eastern Melanesia, and another with the betel-chewing habit to western Melanesia[149]. He attempted to reconstruct the culture of his stone-using immigrants in intense detail;

they had coiled pottery, bows and arrows, wore hats, were not cannibals, built megaliths, introduced pigs, coconuts and other crops, and had secret societies. Their religion involved shark and bonito cults, and the croton, dracaena and cordyline plants were considered sacred. Their myths encompassed white-skinned superhumans, creator snakes, sky people, and adulterous brothers. The people themselves were actually Mongoloids, entering Melanesia through Indonesia, the Philippines and Micronesia, after about A.D. 800.

What Riesenfeld has done is perhaps to isolate some of the elements in Melanesian culture which are basically early Austronesian; the stone structures, pigs, coconuts, and coiled pottery. On the other characteristics archaeology can throw no light, but there is no real evidence that they form a coherent complex, or that most of them were not perhaps already in Melanesia by at least 1000 B.C. This may be particularly true of the stone structures, which had certainly spread to as far as Easter Island by initial settlement there about A.D. 500, and it is stone structures which are the major crux of Riesenfeld's argument. The total absence of stone structures in the New Guinea Highlands argues for a high degree of Austronesian correlation, but this does not mean that all stone structures in Melanesia were built by Austronesian speakers, for they most certainly were not.

From Riesenfeld's survey, together with more recent ones, we can get a good idea of the distribution of stonework in Melanesia. The constructions are generally very simple, and show few resemblances to the great temple structures of eastern Polynesia. The simplicity of Melanesian stonework would suggest that local innovation has played a large part behind its very irregular distribution, and no great historical significance can be attributed to the sporadic appearance of features such as house pavements or platforms. On the other hand, there are some more unusual classes of stone structure which we might briefly describe.

Circles and alignments of small upright stones are particularly widespread, although we probably do not need to invoke diffusion to explain them. Circles of uprights are reported for southeastern New Guinea, particularly by Williams and Egloff[150] for Goodenough Bay, where they are associated with circular pavements, and with rock engravings of circles and spirals very like those on New Caledonia (figure 9.34 [w–z]).

There is some evidence that such stone circles served as meeting or burial places, and Williams noted skulls covered with pots buried in one of them.

Circles and squares of small spaced upright stones are also known on southern Bougainville[151] where they were evidently used to enclose cremation burials, either buried in pots or scattered on the ground. Monuments of the 'dolmen' kind – capstones raised above the ground on small blocks – were also used sometimes in southern Bougainville to cover uncremated secondary burials. The square burial enclosures of uprights on southern Bougainville may find a parallel in the remarkable rectangular slab-lined burial enclosures in the Trobriand Islands[152]. These are massive structures (figure 9.33) with walls up to 4 metres high, which were used for burial (rite unknown), and which often contain pedestalled sherds of Collingwood Bay origin, perhaps from the late first millennium A.D. (see page 266). Superficially, these structures resemble some Polynesian monuments, but functionally they are undoubtedly of local origin.

Moving into central Melanesia, we find circles of upright stones on Eddystone Island in the Solomons and on Malekula in the New Hebrides, together with more complex alignments and 'dolmens' on the latter[153]. The island of San Cristobal in the southern Solomons would appear to contain a unique type of burial monument, if we can rely on somewhat contradictory descriptions by Fox[154]. He reported a number of stone-faced rectangular mounds called *heo*, up to 13 by 20 metres in area by 7 metres high, some with a vertical shaft leading down from the top of the mound to an underground burial chamber. Corpses were laid on beds in these chambers, and washed frequently by an attendant until the flesh had rotted. After this, the skull was placed under a small dolmen which was constructed on top of the mound. While simple stone-faced grave mounds are known from other parts of Melanesia, the San Cristobal *heo* as described are clearly special in many ways. Unfortunately, recent research on the island has failed to confirm Fox's accounts[155], and one is left with a suspicion that they were exaggerated for the benefit of an archaeological clientele who were intent on demonstrating world-wide migrations from Egypt.

In the Fijian Islands a new type of monument makes an appearance, known as the *naga* enclosure on Viti Levu, where it occurs only in the central part of the island, mainly in the upper

Sigatoka and Wainimala Valleys[156]. The *naga* enclosures were used for male initiation ceremonies and circumcision, amongst other things, and Palmer's[157] recent survey has shown them to consist of long walled avenues divided internally into separate rectangular enclosures by cross-walls. It may be that each division was used by a particular kin group for its own private ceremonies. On Vanua Levu, we have the benefit of detailed surveys by Parke[158] of eight sites which are very similar to the Viti-Levu *naga*. These consist of rectangular open spaces up to 170 metres long and 10 metres wide, lined by earth and stone walls. The longitudinal walls often have entrance gaps, and upright pillars set into them, together with stone-faced earthen platforms across the ends and along the sides. Some of the

sites simply consist of two parallel walls, while others have the whole set of features in quite complex arrangements. The Vanua Levu sites differ mainly from those on Viti Levu in the absence of cross walls, and they do in fact come fairly close to some of the ceremonial structures of Polynesia, in particular the *tohua* dancing floors of the Marquesas, which we will examine in chapter 12.

In general, a survey of stone structures in Melanesia at the present stage of archaeological knowledge tells us little. The corpus can be extended to include mounds and alignments of lateritic blocks on New Caledonia, some of the latter forming serpent motifs, circles and curves[159]. We have already observed that some of the mounds on the Ile des Pins may have Lapita

Fig. 9.33. Part of a rectangular slab-lined burial enclosure in Museu village, Kitava Island, Trobriand Islands.

associations, but the others, which seem best developed on the Bogota peninsula on the east coast of New Caledonia, may well be much later. We might also add stone fortification walls across valleys on New Caledonia, and stone walls surrounding villages on Santa Cruz Island[160]. Earthwork forts, apart from Fiji, are otherwise very rare in Melanesia.

Like the evidence for stone structures, that for rock art is rather scattered and inconclusive. The most common modes of expression are red and black painting and line engraving, and the majority of motifs seem to fall into anthropomorphic and 'geometric' categories – the latter of course being a hold-all term for a large range of motifs of unknown meaning. The world-wide motif of the hand stencil, which may well be one of the most ancient forms of artistic expression indulged in by man, occurs right through Melanesia from New Guinea to Fiji[161], although I know of no examples in New Caledonia, where engraving seems to be the only reported technique. Depictions of simple human forms are also widespread, as are various zoomorphic motifs such as lizards and other quadrupeds. It seems that very little research has been done so far on stylistic analysis of these motifs, and perhaps the fundamental problem is the virtual impossibility of dating them.

However, there are a number of motifs, mostly engraved, which are quite widespread in western Melanesia and Australia, and which are dominated by circular and curvilinear arrangements (figure 9.34). In Melanesia, these are best recorded in New Caledonia, and comprise rayed circles, spirals, crosses in curvilinear 'envelopes', many other enveloped geometric designs, stick figures of human beings, zigzags, 'flowers', and a whole range of intriguing motifs which might well be derived from parts of the human body. They are found on engraved rocks over the greater part of the island[162]. The range is in fact quite surprising, and the New Caledonians have left the finest range of rock engraving known from the Pacific, except perhaps for the Marquesas Islands. A rather more restricted range of motifs in the New Caledonian range is reported from New Hanover (crosses in envelopes)[163], Goodenough Bay (where circles, spirals and crosses in envelopes are found on the uprights of the stone circles)[164], and from the New Guinea Highlands. The presence of similar curvilinear engravings in Australia argues for a long antiquity of the group in general, although specific con-clusions about all kinds of rock art in Melanesia must await a good deal more research.

THE MELANESIAN PAST

Behind the present-day ethnic pattern in Melanesia lie the lives of many millions of past members of the human species. If we wish, we can divide these into the Papuans, who have inhabited western Melanesia for 30,000 years or more, and the Austronesians, who entered the area from about 5000 years ago in several groups. Of the latter, it seems clear that at least two separate groups were involved; an initial group who may have had no pottery, and a later group, perhaps more Mongoloid than the initial settlers[165], with the pottery known as Lapita ware. Whether the spread of the incised and applied-relief pottery was through yet another migration from outside Melanesia is not clear, but I suspect that it was not. The Lapita potters had little impact in a long-term sense in Melanesia, but some of them travelled on to become Polynesians. The Austronesians who settled and remained in Melanesia very rapidly became diversified into a myriad of local ethnic groups, mainly dominated by unilineal kinship reckoning, weakly developed leadership, and often by intense inter-group hostility. Perhaps they had these social characteristics before they came to Melanesia, or perhaps they were simply 'conquered' by the resident Papuans. Whatever the answer, the resulting Melanesians of ethnographic times were the most heterogeneous peoples in the Pacific, and the ones who resisted European penetration the longest.

Finally, we might ask if the combined results of modern archaeology, linguistics, and physical anthropology can really tell us the 'truth' about Melanesian culture history. Without really detailed research, it would appear that the results given in this chapter, which are based mainly on archaeology, do not correlate very obviously with the multiple migration waves postulated by the historical ethnologists of the past; by men such as Graebner, Rivers, Deacon and Riesenfeld[166]. It has become fashionable in these hopefully more objective days to reject many of these old theories, but I suspect that with further intensive research in all fields, certain aspects of them may one day be shown to be valid in the context of modern knowledge. We will meet the same problems of equating new knowledge with old ideas in Polynesia, and of course in many cases

CURVILINEAR   ENVELOPED   RAYED   HUMAN

Fig. 9.34. Rock engravings in Melanesia (bb, gg painted in red and white);
(a–r) New Caledonia (after Chevalier 1958–9; 1963–5; Luquet 1926:
Oriol 1948); (s, u, aa) Normanby Island (after Williams 1931); (t,v)
New Hanover (after Lampert 1967); (w-z) Goodenough Bay (after
Williams 1931; Egloff 1970); (bb–hh) Sogeri, Papua (after Williams 1931).

the old ideas simply have to be discarded. But I regret that I have been unable to pursue Melanesian historical ethnography in more depth in this chapter, although I feel that at present it might add unnecessary confusion to the newly emerging picture provided by archaeology and linguistics.

Footnotes

1. White 1971; 1972a.
2. White 1969: 19.
3. White 1967.
4. Bulmer S. and R. 1964: 53.
5. Hughes 1971.
6. S. Bulmer 1963–4; 1964; 1966; 1975; Bulmer S. and R. 1964. For a recently excavated sequence, like that from Kiowa, in the Western Highlands, see Christensen 1975a.
7. White 1972a.
8. See White 1971: 48, for a discussion of this.
9. Bulmer S. and R. 1964; S. Bulmer 1975; Allen 1972a.
10. S. Bulmer (1975) has recently claimed pig at Kiowa from about 10,000 years ago. If this claim is verified, it could be of outstanding significance.
11. Powell 1970. See also Hope and Hope 1974.
12. See Strathern 1969. The axe-adzes are basically lenticular in cross-section, but recent Western Highlands (especially Wahgi and Jimi Valleys) axe-adzes most commonly have planilateral cross-sections, i.e. lenticular with squared-off edges (Bulmer S. and R. 1964: 73). The hafted axe-adze shown in figure 9.4 is of this type.
13. For Australia see McCarthy 1940, and also 1949a (waisted hammers from Queensland); Lampert 1975 (waisted tools from Kangaroo Island, South Australia).
14. Golson et al. 1967; Allen 1970; 1972a; Powell 1970.
15. Jack Golson: Communication through A.N.U. Seminar series, 1975.
16. Specht 1967: 494.
17. e.g. Etheridge 1916–7 for the northern New Hebrides.
18. S. Bulmer 1973.
19. Bulmer R. and S. 1962; Rappaport 1967: 123; Berndt 1954.
20. Holtker 1951.
21. Bulmer S. and R. 1964; Pretty 1964.
22. Blackwood 1950: 34–6.
23. Bulmer S. and R. 1964; McCarthy 1949b; Wirz 1951; Pretty 1965: fig. 1; Schmitz 1966.
24. Schuster 1946.
25. Specht 1966; Riesenfeld 1955.
26. Neich 1971.
27. R. Bulmer 1964.
28. Specht 1974b.
29. Schmitz (1966) is in favour of Indonesian bronze prototypes for some of the New Guinea Highland stone mortars.
30. Chowning and Goodale 1966; Shutler and Kess 1969.
31. Nash and Mitchell 1973. Blade-like flakes are apparently only otherwise known in Melanesia from the Admiralty Islands, where they are of obsidian.
32. Specht 1969: vol. 1: 271ff.
33. Davenport 1972: 182.
34. Riesenfeld 1950b.
35. Casey 1939.
36. Specht 1969: vol. 1: 278.
37. Riesenfeld 1950b; 1954–5.
38. Vanderwal 1973; White 1972b.
39. See also Riesenfeld 1952.
40. Meyer 1909; 1910; Cassey 1936.
41. McKern 1929.
42. Lenormand 1948.
43. Gifford and Shutler 1956.
44. General reviews of Lapita pottery; Specht 1968; Golson 1968; 1971c; 1972a; 1972b; Green 1973; Mead et al. 1973.
45. Dickinson and Shutler 1971; 1974. Sand temper of Fijian origin has been identified in one sherd from the Ha'apai Islands in Tonga.
46. Specht 1968: 128.
47. Specht 1968: 130–2.
48. Hedrick 1971: plate I illustrates two cord-marked sherds from Malo Island, but these are the only ones reported to my knowledge from Lapita contexts.
49. Solheim 1959b: fig. 1.
50. Specht 1968: 125–6.
51. Crem 1975. Dog bones are reported from the Sikumango site on Bellona (page 249), but this site falls at the very end of the Lapita time span.
52. Key 1969.
53. Ambrose and Green 1972; Ambrose 1973.
54. Green 1973: 335; Ward and Smith 1974.
55. Golson 1969a: 49.
56. Specht 1968.
57. White and Specht 1971; Ambrose 1973 (Ambitle); Egloff 1975 (Elouae). Ambrose (personal communication) has dated the Ambitle site to the first millennium A.D. by obsidian hydration dating.
58. White 1972b.
59. Specht 1969; 1972.
60. Davenport 1972.

61. M. Chikamori; personal communication for Rennell; Poulsen 1972 for Bellona.
62. Green 1973; 1974b.
63. Kirch and Rosendahl 1973. For comments see Davidson 1974c.
64. Hedrick 1971; Green 1976: 82.
65. Dickinson 1971.
66. Garanger 1972; Hebert 1963–5.
67. Avias 1950: 122.
68. Gifford and Shutler 1956.
69. Golson 1959–62; 1971c: 75; Frimigacci 1966–70; Frimigacci: report to IX Inqua Congress, Christchurch, December 1973.
70. Golson 1961b.
71. Avias 1949.
72. Rafter *et al.* 1972: 651.
73. Shaw 1973.
74. Birks and Birks 1973.
75. Birks 1973; Birks and Birks 1973.
76. Birks and Birks 1968; see also Gifford 1951: plate 18c, for recent conical potrests from Fiji.
77. Green 1974b.
78. Poulsen 1967; 1968.
79. Kaeppler 1973; Davidson 1971a; Rogers 1974.
80. Groube 1971; Poulsen 1967; Golson 1969a.
81. Green 1974c; 1976: 82.
82. Biggs (1972: 150) for Niuatoputapu; Kirch (1976) for East Futuna.
83. Pawley 1972.
84. Dyen 1965. The linguist Andrew Pawley (1972: 141) feels that the spread of the Lapita Culture postdates the break-up of the Eastern Oceanic subgroup, but I feel that the two events are more closely correlated in time.
85. Vanderwal 1973.
86. Allen 1972b.
87. S. Bulmer 1971.
88. Schurig 1930; Heine Geldern 1932; MacLachlan 1938; Solheim 1952; 1968c; S. Bulmer 1971; Palmer 1972.
89. Sutayasa 1974.
90. Garanger 1971; 1972.
91. Specht 1969; 1972. See also Kaplan 1973.
92. Irwin 1973: 229; Irwin 1974.
93. Garanger 1972: 32.
94. As suggested by Groube (1971) and by Frimigacc[i] (1976).
95. This is site TON–7, excavated by C. Smart, which has carbon dates of 905 ± 90 and 115 ± 110 B.C. (Golson 1971c; 76; Polach *et al.* 1968). I am indebted to R. Vanderwal for permission to see the unpublished material from this site.
96. Gifford and Shutler 1956.
97. Polach *et al.* 1968; Gifford and Shutler 1956.
98. Gifford and Shutler 1956: 71; Avias 1950; Golson 1972a; 565 ff; Chevalier 1966–1970.
99. Avias 1950: 122.
100. Avias 1950.
101. Avias 1949.
102. Shutler and Shutler 1966; Shutler 1970.
103. Birks 1973; Palmer 1968a.
104. Palmer 1968b.
105. Smart 1965.
106. Gifford 1951.
107. Palmer 1965.
108. e.g. Palmer 1969a; 1969b.
109. Capell and Lester 1940–2; Gifford 1951; Riesenfeld 1950a: 575.
110. Green 1963a; Shaw 1967.
111. Palmer 1971a.
112. Frost 1974.
113. Palmer 1967a; 1967b; 1969c.
114. Palmer 1967a.
115. Elmberg 1959.
116. DeBruyn 1959; 1962.
117. Seligman 1915; Heider 1969; Bulmer and Tomasetti 1970; Christensen 1975b.
118. Lyons 1922; Egloff 1972.
119. Recent fieldwork by John Terrell.
120. Golson 1972a: 581 ff.
121. Egloff 1971a; 1971b; Lauer 1970b.
122. Seligmann and Joyce 1907; Joyce 1912. Furthermore, at Itlopan on Buka Island, two small monoliths have been carved with bands of sunken triangles rather like those on the Wanigela pottery described above (Riesenfeld 1950a: plate 2), although it seems rather optimistic to expect a direct connection between the two areas.
123. Capell 1943.
124. Fraser 1967.
125. Badner 1966.
126. Ch'en Ch'i-lu 1972.
127. Heine Geldern 1966b.
128. Heine Geldern 1937: 180.
129. Heine Geldern 1966b.
130. Heine Geldern 1937: 202.
131. Fraser 1962; see also Fraser 1972; Speiser 1941.
132. Levi-Strauss 1963: chapter 13.
133. Spiegel 1971; Badner 1972.
134. Gifford 1951: 237.
135. Vanderwal 1973.
136. F.J. Allen, personal communication; 1972b.
137. S. Bulmer 1971.
138. Specht 1969.
139. M.E. Shutler 1971.
140. Palmer 1971a.

141. Garanger 1972: 98–9.

142. Garanger 1972: 25–6, 59–77.

143. Garanger 1972: 76.

144. Poncet 1948. See also Villaret 1963.

145. Lessa 1962: 367 (from Benjamin Morrell, 1822–31).

146. e.g. Hale 1846: 64–5 for Fiji; Wilson 1799: 236 for Tonga; Maning 1948: 200 for New Zealand. Tippett (1968: 60) also records sacrificial burials of living persons beneath house posts in Fiji.

147. Riesenfeld 1950a.

148. see Rosenstiel 1953–4.

149. Riesenfeld 1947.

150. Williams 1931; Egloff 1970.

151. Thurnwald 1934–5; John Terrell, personal communication.

152. Austen 1939; Ollier *et al.* 1968; 1970.

153. Riesenfeld 1950a: 93.

154. Fox 1919; 1924.

155. Roger Green; personal communication.

156. Fison 1885; Joske 1889.

157. Palmer 1971b.

158. Parke 1971–2.

159. Avias 1949.

160. Moresby 1876: 86.

161. e.g. Röder 1939; Garanger 1972: fig. 51; Paine 1929.

162. Luquet 1926; Oriol 1948; Avias 1949; Chevalier 1958–9; 1963–5.

163. Lampert 1967.

164. Williams 1931; Egloff 1970.

165. As suggested by Howells 1973a: 210.

166. See particularly Rivers 1914; Deacon 1934; Rosenstiel 1953–4.

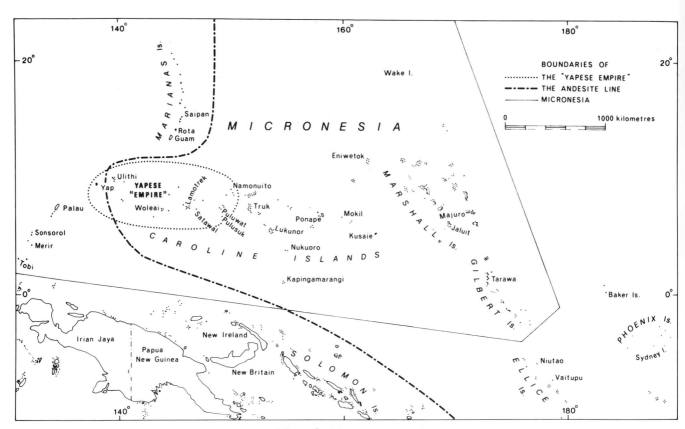

Fig. 4.8. Map of Micronesia.

CHAPTER 10

The Prehistory of Micronesia

Micronesia forms the northern half of that stubby tang which leads into the enormous triangular spearhead of Polynesia (see figure 4.8). It does not appear to offer such a degree of complexity as Melanesia to its south, partly because the islands are very small and the patterns of diversity within the archipelago do seem to be fairly orderly. But the greater part of Micronesia is still an archaeological blank, and we are certainly not in a position to close down the dossier and stamp it 'solved'.

Physically, the Micronesians are predominantly of Mongoloid phenotype. There has been gene flow from Melanesia into Yap and the Palaus in particular, but this has not obscured the basic continuity in Mongoloid phenotype from Indonesia and the Philippines, through Micronesia and into Polynesia. In 1938, one of the most outstanding Polynesian scholars of all time, Sir Peter Buck (Te Rangi Hiroa), drew what was then the obvious conclusion[1]. The Polynesians had migrated eastward through Micronesia, but because they could not take domesticated plants and animals through the atolls (apart from coconuts and a few other hardy species of plants), they were obliged to acquire these later on through contacts with Melanesia, via Fiji and Samoa, after the tenth century A.D.

Buck's hypothesis has retained sporadic support through the years, particularly through a monumental ethnographic study of Oceanic fishing gear prepared in 1955 by Bengt Anell[2]. Anell pointed out, quite correctly, that the shell one-piece bait hooks and the shell trolling lures of Polynesia (see chapter 11) were well paralleled through Micronesia, but hardly paralleled at all in Melanesia. Furthermore, the Micronesian and

Polynesian forms were also present in Japan and in northern Eurasia, so it seemed likely that they were transmitted by migrations down from these regions which by-passed Melanesia and Southeast Asia.

More recently, Roger Duff[3] has given further support to a Micronesian migration route for the Polynesians by claiming that the distinctive tanged Polynesian adzes were derived from the Philippine area by transmission through Micronesia (where, incidentally, adzes of this type have never been found), and W.W. Howells has lent his weight to the argument from the viewpoint of a physical anthropologist[4]. I should make it clear at this point that it is very hard to disprove the 'Micronesian route' in any absolute sense, and there is no reason why some transmission should not have taken place from Micronesia to Polynesia. But I feel that the role of Micronesia in this respect is small, and I regard the immediate Polynesian ancestry, both linguistically and archaeologically, as firmly established in Melanesia. I have given some reasons for this in connection with the Lapita Culture in chapter 9, and I will return to the matter again in chapter 11. But a few specific reasons for my attitude will not be amiss here.

When first set out, the overall hypothesis of a Micronesian migration route into Polynesia made good logical sense, until the contrary indications began to appear. Firstly, archaeologists discovered the Melanesian Lapita Culture with its ancestral Polynesian adze forms; a particularly robust coffin nail. Just as robust is the linguistic evidence (see chapter 5) that the languages of western Micronesia (the Palau and Marianas Islands) are of Indonesian or Philippine origin, while those of eastern (Nuclear) Micronesia, with the possible exception of Yapese, are probably quite closely related to the Eastern Oceanic subgroup, and thus may have been derived from the New Hebrides or some adjacent area in central-eastern Melanesia. The Nuclear Micronesian languages certainly do not form a continuum with the Polynesian, although there is likely to be a rather remote cousinly relationship.

Any doubts about driving these coffin nails home would be dispelled by the evidence of material culture collected by the German ethnologist Gerd Koch in the Gilbert and Ellice Islands[5]. The Gilberts are in the south-eastern corner of Micronesia, and their neighbours to the south are the Polynesian Ellice Islands. Between the two groups, according to Koch, runs a sharp but certainly not unbreached cultural boundary: 'cultural traits held in common between the two groups are relatively few, so that one can scarcely speak of a transitional region or of a bridge for migrations within the context of Oceanic settlement history'[6].

The results of all the non-archaeological evidence as known at present therefore suggest the following hypotheses for Micronesian prehistory:

1. Western Micronesia, comprising the Palau and Marianas Islands, was settled directly from Indonesia or the Philippines. The island of Yap is a possible third member of this division.
2. Eastern (Nuclear) Micronesia and Polynesia were settled from a similar region in eastern Melanesia, possibly connected with the Lapita Culture. Items such as fishhooks which they share in common may reflect this common origin, as there are shell hooks and lures in the Lapita Culture (see chapter 9) which were of course unknown to Anell in 1955. However, the possibility of a Japanese origin for Micronesian and Polynesian fishing gear is still open.
3. Despite the basic dual origin of the Micronesian cultures, there has been a great deal of contact between all the Micronesian Islands and with those of western Polynesia, as Koch has shown clearly for the Gilbert and Ellice Islands. The 'Yapese Empire' (see page 106) also, of course, straddles a marked linguistic boundary within Micronesia.

The division between western and eastern Micronesia is not only marked linguistically. The islands of western Micronesia are mostly volcanic, while those of eastern Micronesia are mostly atolls (except for Truk, Ponape and Kusaie in the Carolines). As may be expected, prehistoric pottery was only made in the western division, and has never been found anywhere in the eastern. Rice was observed by Magellan on Guam in 1521[7], and may have been grown elsewhere in the Marianas, but it is not known from any other part of Micronesia. Dogs and pigs were apparently absent in the Palau Islands[8], and perhaps in the Marianas too[9], while the Carolines had only dog and fowls, and the Marshall and Gilbert Islands only the fowl[10].

Having given such fundamental matters a brief airing, we may now turn to the archaeology.

WESTERN MICRONESIA – THE MARIANAS ISLANDS

Although the Marianas Islands comprise a chain of 15 volcanic and raised coral islands, only the southern four – Saipan, Tinian, Rota and Guam – have been investigated archaeologically. The most important work, by Spoehr on Saipan and Tinian[11] and by Reinman on Guam[12], has produced a relatively long and coherent sequence. This begins with a type of pottery called 'Marianas Red' by Spoehr, which seems very likely to be of central Philippine origin at about 1500 B.C. Marianas Red is thin and red-slipped, usually plain, and a few vessels seem to have had flat bases and carinations. On Saipan and Tinian a few rare sherds have lime-infilled decoration in the form of rows of stamped circles (figure 10.1), together with lines and zig-zags seemingly made by a process akin to dentate stamping. The parallels with the sherds recovered by Solheim from Batungan Cave 2 on Masbate Island in the central Philippines[13] are remarkably close, and as we have seen (page 213), the latter approach 1000 B.C. in date. The Batungan sherds have similar red slipping, lime infill, decorative designs and rim forms, and if they are not ancestral to the Marianas Red they are at least very close cousins. There is no reason to relate the Marianas Red directly to the less similar Lapita pottery to the south, although both types may have a similar ultimate origin in Island Southeast Asia.

On Saipan, the Marianas Red pottery has been found in an open site called Chalan Piao, associated with a carbon-14 date from an oyster shell of 1527±200 B.C. (*c.* 1800 B.C. if calibrated)[14], and the shell was actually found at a depth of only 0.5 metres in a site which was almost 2 metres deep. The date may be suspect, since it is not certain that the shell is associated food refuse, and the only other date we have for Marianas Red is from Nomna Bay, on Guam[15], where it dates from at least 100 B.C. In the Laulau rock-shelter on Saipan, Marianas Red pottery was found with extended burials in sand-lined pits, and associated artefacts in this and other sites include shell beads and bracelets, *Tridacna* shell adzes, stone adzes of Duff type 2A, and stone adzes with circular cross-sections (Duff type 6: an unusual type also present in the Philippines and Polynesia).

By about A.D. 800, the Marianas Red ware seems to have given way to a plain unslipped ceramic, and we enter what Spoehr has termed the 'Latte Phase of Marianas Culture'[16]. The *latte* of the Marianas are amongst the most remarkable examples of stone architecture in Oceania, and consist of two parallel rows of uprights of coral or volcanic rock, with generally hemispherical capstones set on their tops[17] (figure 10.2). The rows are usually a little under 4 metres apart, but lengths can range up to 22 metres (in the case of an example with 14 pillars on Rota), and heights, with capstones, up to 5.5 metres (in the case of the House of Taga on Tinian; figure 10.3). Early Spanish accounts report the existence of houses on stone pillars, and it seems that some of the large ones may have been men's houses or canoe sheds. In this connection, Thompson has suggested that the hemispherical capstones served as rat guards[18]. Quite often the *latte* occur singly but village groups seem to have occurred fairly frequently; the Taga site on Tinian originally had a row of 18 *latte*, and clusters of up to 30 are reported from Guam[19]. On Rota, a quarry in coral limestone for the uprights and capstones still survives[20], and the cutting of the rock was assisted here by the use of fire to cause crumbling.

The earliest carbon-14 date for a *latte* comes from the Blue site on Tinian, of A.D. 900[21]. As far as is known, the *latte* were certainly in use from this time until the seventeenth century, when the Spanish resettled all surviving Chamorros on Guam, except for a handful remaining on Rota. These structures give every appearance of being indigenous developments in the Marianas, and the only outside similarities lie in reports of stone pile houses in the Palau Islands and possibly on Yap. In basic principle, the form is simply a translation into stone of the raised pile houses of Island Southeast Asia.

The pottery associated with the *latte* is all plain (Marianas Plain ware of Spoehr), and

seems to comprise open bowls and plates. There is no slipping, but a miniscule number of sherds have been found with cross-hatch incision or cord-marking, the latter being of outstandingly rare occurrence anywhere in Oceania. Other associations include stone adzes with circular or lenticular cross-sections, *Tridacna* and *Terebra* shell adzes (both common in Micronesian ethnographic collections), stone pounders and mortars, possibly for rice and taro preparation, stone grooved weights for fishnets, shell beads and bracelets, and shell one-piece fishhooks. The assemblage belongs to a late date when most of Micronesia shared a fairly basic range of stone

Fig. 10.1. Incised and lime-infilled sherds of Marianas Red pottery. From Spoehr 1957.

Fig. 10.3. Standing *latte* pillars with capstones, 5.5 metres high, in the house of Taga, Tinian. From Thompson 1932.

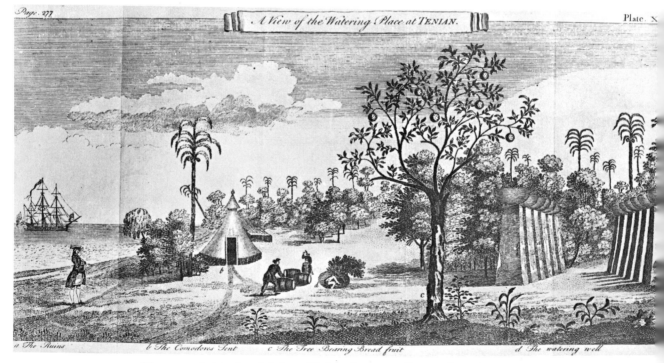

A View of the Watering Place at TENIAN.

Page 277   Plate X

a The Ruins   b The Comodores Tent   c The Tree Bearing Bread fruit   d The watering well

Fig. 10.2. A *latte* (at right) on Tinian, drawn on George Anson's voyage of 1740–44.

and shell gear[22], and it contains little of obvious typological significance. Whether pigs and dogs were present in the *Latte* Phase is unknown.

Excavations in a number of sites have also shown that extended burials were often placed between the upright rows, and these are sometimes headless, suggesting that the skulls were taken away for ritual purposes. The teeth of these burials are stained from betel-nut chewing, and one, from the Blue site on Tinian, showed symptoms of yaws – a pre-European disease which was spread through most of Oceania, except perhaps for New Zealand and Easter Island[23].

The results from archaeology in the southern Marianas have shown that these islands were probably settled from Island Southeast Asia at about the same time that Lapita settlers penetrated into Melanesia. The colonisers of Saipan, Tinian and Guam seem, in fact, to have sailed from the central Philippines in the mid-second millennium B.C., some time before the jar-burial cultures began to develop in that area. Unfortunately, however, only the Marianas have so far provided such useful evidence, and the other islands of western Micronesia are still hiding their basic secrets.

THE ISLAND OF YAP

Physically, the Yapese demonstrate a greater number of Australoid phenotypic characters than the Chamorros of the Marianas, and this may reflect proximity to western Melanesia as a source of gene flow. At European contact, the island was at the head of a most impressive chain of trade and tribute which ran for some 1100 km eastwards through the Carolines, as has been described in chapter 4. Early European visitors were also impressed by the great variety of stone architecture, particularly the faced and paved platforms, sometimes with two tiers, for god houses and men's houses[24]. Lining the paths which led to these structures were, and often still are, rows of wheel-shaped discs of stone money (figure 4.9), and similar discs also lean against the terrace faces. This money was cut from aragonite quarried in the Palau Islands and transported by canoe to Yap (see page 106), and one of its functions appears to have been the purchase of concubines for the mens' houses. Just why the Yapese chose to stow their wealth in such a form is not known, but one may perhaps regard the discs as gigantic versions of the shell discs which are strung together as currency in several areas of western Oceania.

The only archaeological work reported from Yap is that by the Giffords[25], carried out in 1956. The Giffords investigated a number of stone monuments, including hexagonal-shaped house platforms and a structure which looked a little like a very wide *latte* without capstones. As far as one can tell, all these monuments are fairly recent, and the earlier phases of Yapese prehistory are only known from portable artefacts. Throughout the first millennium A.D. a type of pottery like the Marianas Plain ware of the *Latte* Phase was made on the island, and this has been found with *Tridacna* shell adzes, shell bracelets, shell scrapers, and a perforated bone disc which could be a forerunner of the stone money. No sites are yet known from the island with a B.C. date, but they will almost certainly be found in the future.

By about A.D. 1000, pottery of the ethnographic type made on Yap makes an appearance, and Gifford calls this 'laminated ware' as it tends to split longitudinally, rather like shale. It was made in recent times by low caste villagers[26] and was built up from a lump of untempered clay, using a cowrie shell for rubbing and a bamboo knife for scraping. The paddle and anvil do not appear to have been used, and neither does the coiling method. The absence of coiling from any of the prehistoric ceramics of Yap or the Marianas Islands may be significant, in view of the rarity of this method in the Philippines and Indonesia. As the pottery of the Palau Islands was coiled (see below), this may reflect a greater degree of contact with western Melanesia.

The late laminated ware of Yap is simpler and cruder than the earlier 'unlaminated ware' of Marianas Plain affinity, and it has been found with the widespread late Micronesian shell assemblage of *Tridacna* and *Hippopus* adzes, *Terebra* gouges, shell knives and peelers, and shell disc beads. Coral taro pounders were also made on Yap, as in the Marianas, but were not found in any excavations. Two other ethnographic traits of potential interest are pottery lamps, and the practice of infant burial in two jars buried mouth-to-mouth adjacent to menstrual houses[27]. These traits almost certainly reflect some degree of Island Southeast Asian influence in Yapese culture, but when and whence they reached the island remains unknown.

So far, our knowledge of Yap tells us that a portable assemblage like that of the *Latte* Phase in the Marianas was established by the beginning of the first millennium A.D., although the two areas are quite different in their uses of stone for architectural purposes. It is unlikely that Yap remained unsettled until this late date, but further surmise on this question is rather pointless at present. As a final point, pigs and dogs seem never to have been present on the island, but fowls were present from the earliest known sites.

THE PALAU ISLANDS

The Palau Islands, in the south-western corner of Micronesia, consist of a number of raised coral islands and atolls to north and south of a large volcanic island called Babeldaob. At European contact, they were divided between a number of matrilineal chiefdoms, similar to those in the Carolines to the east. Because of their geographical position they have received drift voyages from Sulawesi, Halmahera and Mindanao in the past, and it may be from these islands that their original settlers first came. The Palaus have also been in extensive contact with Melanesia to the south, particularly with New Guinea and the Admiralty Islands, and this is evidenced by phenotype and by a number of cultural traits such as nose piercing and the importance of female tattooing[28]. As with Yap and the Marianas, the Palauans did not have pigs or dogs at European contact, although they did have fowls. They were also using glass money (figure 10.4) in the form of beads and segments of bracelets, and there is some evidence that these have an immediate origin in the central Philippines in the second millennium A.D.[29]. Ultimate Roman or Chinese origins have been suggested for some of these glass objects, but they have never really been demonstrated.

Our knowledge of Palau archaeology comes from work carried out by Douglas Osborne in 1954[30]. Osborne surveyed archaeological remains on most of the islands, but only carried out very limited excavations. From one of these excavations, covering about 14 square metres, he bravely attempted. to construct a cultural sequence for the Palaus, but was hampered particularly by the absence of any absolute dates. For the following excursion into Palauan culture history I therefore use the basic data provided by Osborne, but organise it according to slightly different criteria[31].

At European contact, the Palauans were making a simple kind of coiled pottery, with a temper of ground sherds. Finishing was carried out with a wooden paddle, and sometimes a pottery object of mushroom shape was used for smoothing, but no anvil was used apart from the hand. Osborne found large quantities of this pottery, mainly from bowl and jar forms, on surface sites right through the Palaus, and it has no known outside parallels. It is mostly undecorated and unslipped, but a very few sherds were crudely painted in red, or slipped or incised, the incisions sometimes being filled with haematite. No dated scheme of development is known for it, although it is clear that Osborne is quite correct to speak of a Palauan ceramic unity.

The sherd tempered ware in fact occurs in all the collections made by Osborne, from about 160 surface sites in all. Only two sites, one on Koror Island, the other on Aluptaciel Island, have produced evidence for a chink in the facade. Sherds of a very different sand tempered ware were recovered from these two sites, and a few of them were decorated by punctate stamping or basket impression. An anvil also appears to have been used in their manufacture, and despite the absence of a date, a Philippine origin would cause no surprise, although the evidence of the glass money might suggest that this could be quite recent.

So far, archaeology has therefore thrown little light on the question of Paluan origins. However, Osborne was able to survey a number of the rather impressive monuments of the group, of which the foremost are the huge terraced hills (figure 10.5). These appear each to be focussed on a central earthen platform, sculptured from the hill summit, which may have served as a defensible citadel. Around and below the central platforms

Fig. 10.4. Palauan money of glass beads and bracelet segments.

are earthen terraces, dug probably to remove a widespread and sterile layer of bauxite in order to expose fertile subsoil for taro cultivation. Some of the terraces are up to 100 metres wide, but they have no defensive features like the banks which sometimes exist on the tops of the citadels. Therefore, these terrace sites appear to have served both defensive and agricultural functions, and are without parallel anywhere else in Oceania. The terraced forts of New Zealand are an unrelated and rather different development (see chapter 13).

Other Palauan monuments comprise stone pavements and platforms for houses, a structure comprising two rows of upright monoliths with slotted tops rather like a Marianas *latte*, and several large stone anthropomorphic carvings, of which one, at Aimeong on Babeldaob Island (figure 10.6), resembles the anthropomorphic carvings on Unea Island off north-western New Britain[32]. This is another possible instance of a Palauan parallel with western Melanesia. Portable objects found on Palauan surface sites include untanged stone adzes with oval or circular cross-sections, *Terebra* and *Tridacna* shell adzes, stone pestles, and shell bracelet fragments and knives. Fishing gear, which was made of turtle shell in ethnographic times, does not appear to have survived archaeologically.

Fig. 10.6. Head of andesite at Aimeong, Babeldaob Island, 60 cm high.

Fig. 10.5. A terraced hill in the Palau Islands.

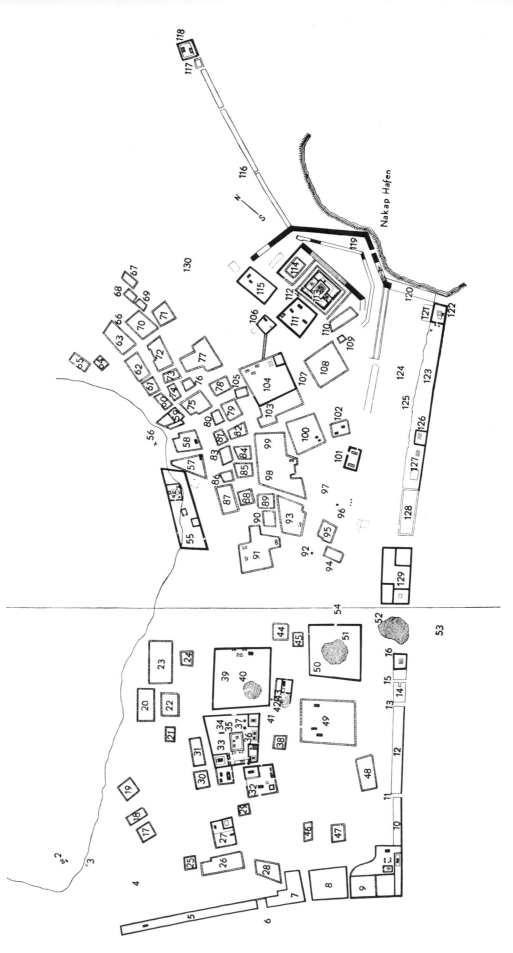

Fig. 10.7. Hambruch's plan of Nan Madol. Madol Pah lies to the left, Madol Powe to the right. 33–36 comprises Pahn Kedira, 113 is Nan Douwas. From Hambruch 1936.

EASTERN MICRONESIA – THE CAROLINE ISLANDS

There is no prehistoric sequence yet available for any of the Micronesian islands in the extensive Caroline chain, which may seem a little strange when one considers that two of them, the volcanic islands of Ponape and Kusaie, contain stone monumental remains which are amongst the most magnificent of any surviving in the whole of Oceania. The ruins on Ponape in particular rank with the statues on Easter Island as fuel for the lunatic fringe of archaeology[33], and as recently as 1970 a serious claim was made that they were survivors from a drowned Pacific continental civilisation[34]. Since the author of this view seems to have been totally unaware of the existence of Hambruch's fundamental report on the Ponapean ruins, we can hardly take him seriously. The ruins of Ponape, called Nan Madol, are in fact by no means as mysterious as many popular writers would have us believe, and we will begin our description with them.

Nan Madol may best be described as a small town and ceremonial centre, comprising 92 artificial platforms built up from the shallow lagoon on the eastern side of Ponape (see the plan, figure 10.7). The ruins were first reported in 1835, and later in 1857 by an American named L.H. Gulick, who noted that they covered half a square mile in area, and suggested that they were built by the ancestors of the present Ponapeans[35]. A little later, the first outline plan of the ruins was prepared by the German settler J. Kubary[36], and this was used as the basis for further work, or more properly ransacking, by a somewhat insensitive Englishman named F.W. Christian who visited the island in 1896[37]. Christian upset the local inhabitants of the area around Nan Madol so much that he appears to have been lucky to escape with his life, after shovelling out the contents of several rather venerated tombs. He also made the erroneous statement that the complex covered 11 square miles, and this was even repeated in print as recently as 1962[38]. In fact, the ruins cover an area of 70 hectares (0.7 square kilometres or about 0.2 square miles), so Gulick made a much closer estimate in 1857. Nan Madol did indeed suffer rather badly from mis-reporting, until the excellent and seemingly accurate survey carried out by Paul Hambruch in 1910[39]. Although Hambruch used tape and compass methods, his report contains no obvious faults and is the basis of the following description.

The Nan Madol platforms are of coral rubble faced with basalt retaining walls, and generally have rectilinear ground plans. The facings may be of basalt prisms which outcrop in the northern part of the island, laid in a 'header and stretcher' formation (figure 10.8), or they may be of larger cruder blocks packed with rubble. The majority of the platforms are simply flat-topped, and may originally have supported pole and thatch

Fig. 10.8. Nan Douwas – outer wall at west corner.

dwelling houses. The gaps between them are flooded at high tide, and the town is thus interlaced by a network of canals like a small-scale Venice.

The platforms are arranged in two main groups, the northern one being a priestly and burial area called Madol Powe, the southern being a royal dwelling and cult area called Madol Pah. On one side the town abuts against an island, while most of the remainder of its rectangular boundary is marked by two lines of rectangular platforms forming a breakwater, with canoe channels left between. The longer of these breakwaters is 1400 metres long, while the shorter is 500 metres long. The short northern edge was apparently left open to the elements, and a number of structure in the complex in fact appear to have been left unfinished.

The more important platforms, for royal or ceremonial use, generally have high enclosure walls of basalt prisms which rise above the basic level of the platforms, to a height of 11 metres in one case. These walls are the spectacular elements which have always caught the eyes of visitors, and they are mostly of the cribwork formation with headers and stretchers of prismatic basalt. Before we describe individually some of the more important of these enclosures, it is necessary to review briefly the traditional history of Nan Madol.

Traditionally, Nan Madol belongs to recent history, and its partially unfinished nature supports this. It was built when the separate chiefdoms of Ponape, with their matrilineal descent, were unified under the leadership of the Sau Deleur dynasty. After an unknown but possibly short period of time, the Sau Deleur dynasty was overthrown by invading Kusaieans, and the island broke up at first into three independent districts, and then into the five districts present at European contact. The site was finally abandoned in the early nineteenth century, possibly owing to depopulation caused by introduced diseases[40]. The total history of the site is unlikely to go back more than a few centuries, but there is no reason to assume any European influence behind its design.

Returning to the more important islands, we begin in Madol Pah in the south, with the platform called Pahn Kedira, the 'place of announcements'. This trapezoidal island supported an enclosure wall up to 5 metres high, broken by entrance gaps, with a three-tiered platform in the centre which probably supported a wood

and thatch temple covering approximately 24 by 10 metres. Along one side of the temple platform stands a row of stone mortars for crushing *kava*, which was not chewed during preparation on Ponape or Kusaie as it was in Polynesia. In three corners of the enclosure there are further subsidiary courtyards which contain house platforms, traditionally for the ruling Sau Deleur and his family, and there is also a small bathing pool dug down to the reef within the fill of the main platform. The majority of the other platforms in the southern area seem to have been for the dwellings of nobility, but one of them was reserved specifically for the growing of fruits for offerings, and another contained an enclosure for sacred eels. These eels were fed on turtles raised in an artificial basin in the northern complex.

The northern part of Nan Madol (Madol Powe) consists of a number of platforms which appear to have served as priests' dwellings, and these are flanked on the east by the most magnificent monument of all – the chiefly burial enclosure of Nan Douwas. This structure, and rightly so, has been a photographer's delight since the days of F.W. Christian, and it would be no exaggeration to say that it is one of the most remarkable pieces of prehistoric stone architecture known from anywhere in Oceania. The basal foundation of the structure is 1.75 metres high, and covers about 60 by 65 metres. It is flanked to its east by a separate and massive protective wall, 10.5 metres thick and 4.5 metres high. The platform itself is surrounded on the top by an outer courtyard wall up to 8.5 metres high (figure 10.8), with an inner raised gallery running around it for the exposure of corpses before burial (figure 10.9). Within this outer enclosure are three tombs built of basalt prisms (figure 10.10), the northern one recorded as nearly 5 metres deep by Christian, and an inner courtyard enclosure wall 4 metres high, with further raised galleries and a decorative projecting cornice around its top. This inner enclosure contains another tomb constructed of basalt prisms, 12 by 8 metres in area by almost 3 metres deep, which was dug out in 1896 by Christian. Traditionally, this central tomb belonged to the successive rulers of the Sau Deleur dynasty, and Christian's list[41] of the voluminous loot which he dug out from it shows that these chiefs were not ill-provided. He records 'a quart of circular rose-pink (shell) beads . . . eighty pearl-shell shanks of fishhooks. . . five ancient *Patkul* or shell-axes of sizes varying from 2½ feet to 6

Fig. 10.9. Nan Douwas – inner gallery around the outer enclosure wall.

Fig. 10.10. Nan Douwas – the roof of the tomb in the north section.

inches . . . five unbroken carved shell-bracelets of elegant design . . . a dozen antique needles of shell . . . thirty or forty large circular shells, bored through the centres, and worn as a pendant ornament on the breast. . . fragments of bone, portions of skulls and bits of shell-bracelets, a couple of small shell gouges, a piece of iron resembling a spearhead', and what appears to have been a piece of obsidian.

Fortunately, we are not completely dependent on Christian for a description of artefacts recovered from Nan Madol, as Hambruch has given an excellent illustrated account (figure 10.11). To Christian's list we may also add shell necklace spacers of various shapes, bracelets of *Tridacna* and *Conus* shell, adzes of *Tridacna* and *Terebra*, and a single untanged stone adze with a lenticular cross-section. Despite the presence of volcanic stone on Ponape, this island and the other Carolines all depended heavily on shell for tools, as did the Banks and New Hebrides Islands to the south. Hambruch also pointed out that the pearl-shell lure shanks (figure 10.11[e]) might have served as currency.

Apart from Nan Madol, there are many other surviving pieces of prehistoric handiwork on Ponape, including walled burial enclosures, house platforms, and inland terraced settlements which appear to be defensive[42]. But there is nothing to match Nan Madol, which clearly served as a very special elite area for a population of perhaps 1000 people. There are similar but less spectacular structures on the island of Kusaie, in particular a large rectangular walled enclosure called Pot Falat on the islet of Lele[43], with walls up to 10 metres high (figure 10.12), and we may of course remember that the conqueror of the Sau Deleur dynasty, a man named Isoh Kelekel, is stated to have come from Kusaie with his followers. Christian thought that Pot Falat was built by intrusive Malays or Japanese, but this is hardly a view to be taken seriously, especially as Christian also thought that Nan Madol was built by Negritos (after Kubary). There seem to me to be no reasons to disbelieve Ponapean tradition, which states quite clearly that the builders were well-organised indigenous Micronesians.

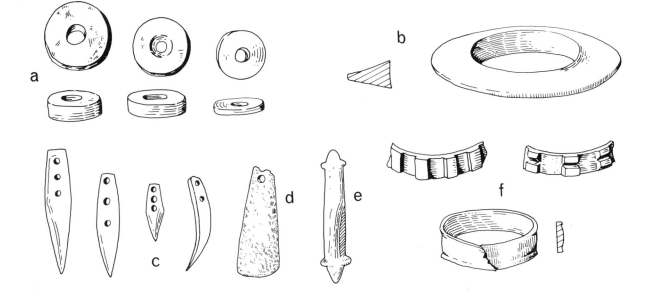

Fig. 10.11. Shell artefacts from Nan Madol: (a) beads (x 0.8); (b) *Tridacna* bracelet (x 0.4); (c, d) necklace spacers (x 0.8); (e) pearl-shell lure-shank, possibly used as currency (x 0.4); (f) *Conus* bracelet (x 0.8) and two fragments of carved *Tridacna* armrings (x 0.4). After Hambruch 1936.

EASTERN MICRONESIA — NUKUORO ATOLL

The atoll of Nukuoro is the only eastern Micronesian island to have received any modern archaeological attention, by Janet Davidson from the Auckland Museum[44]. Although the island is strictly a Polynesian Outlier, and its inhabitants speak a Polynesian language (see page 129), its archaeology is considered here because it is mainly of Micronesian affinity as far as artefacts are concerned.

Nukuoro is a rather small and isolated atoll, which lies about 200 km south of the main sweep of the Caroline chain. In 1965, Miss Davidson excavated within the confines of the only village on the island, where several centuries of continuous habitation had produced deposits up to 3 metres deep; a most unusual archaeological phenomenon for an atoll environment. Radiocarbon dates indicate that the locality was first settled between A.D. 1300 and 1500, and occupation has continued to the present. It is not known whether the island was uninhabited prior to *c.* 1300, but this could be the case.

The most numerous objects found in the excavations were unbarbed one-piece fishhooks of

Fig. 10.12. Stonework at Pot Falat, Kusaie. From Christian 1899.

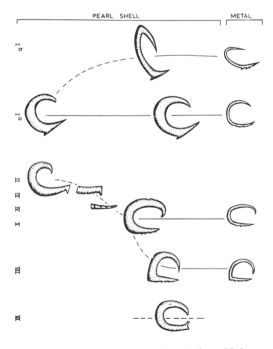

Fig. 10.13. Stylistic change in fishhooks from Nukuoro, *c.* A.D. 1300 to recent times. From Davidson 1968.

pearl-shell, which showed definite stylistic changes over time (see figure 10.13). There were also a small number of fragments of pearl-shell lure hooks, and the range of Nukuoro fishing gear seems to combine both Micronesian and Polynesian stylistic characteristics, as one might expect. Ornaments include shell disc beads, triangular pendants, and bracelets, all in a Micronesian rather than a Polynesian tradition. Adzes made from *Terebra* and *Tridacna* shells also fall into the general Micronesian and northern Melanesian range (figure 10.14). Despite the Polynesian linguistic affinity of Nukuoro, it is of interest to note that in terms of excavated artefacts it fits quite conformably with the other Carolinean atolls. Perhaps the first Polynesian settlers adopted from their Micronesian neighbours what was, after all, a material culture long adapted to the fairly spartan environments of the atolls.

The Nukuoro excavations were too limited to yield any evidence of the prehistoric village pattern, but two items of economic importance were brought to light; bones of dog, an animal not present on the island in ethnographic times, were found in the lower levels; and the rat bones, also present from the lower levels, were of the Micronesian species *Rattus rattus mansorius* rather than of the more widespread Melanesian and Polynesian *Rattus exulans*[45]. Nukuoro culture, in

many respects, is an interesting example of a creation which cannot simply be dichotomised as Micronesian or Polynesian.

As we will see in chapter 11, the Carolineans certainly had the navigational knowledge to maintain contact between all the islands along the chain, and it is therefore not surprising that a simple hand loom for weaving banana and *Ficus* fibre, perhaps of Indonesian origin (see page 104), should be found on many islands along it. Such looms also reached Nukuoro, the Santa Cruz and Banks Islands, and many of the Polynesian Outliers in Melanesia[46].

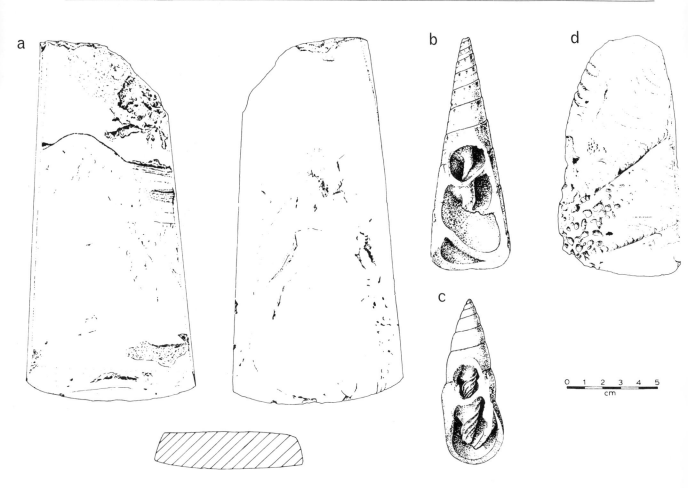

Fig. 10.14. Shell adzes from Nukuoro: (a) *Tridacna maxima*, made from solid portion; (b) *Tridacna maxima*, made from ventral lip; (c) *Terebra maculata;* (d) *Mitra mitra*. From Davidson 1971b.

SUMMARY

In terms of culture history, the only extensive prehistoric sequence in Micronesia, with possible Philippine origins, is known from the southern Marianas group. The sequences of Yap and the Palaus seem to represent local and later developments, which probably do not extend back much beyond 2000 years. For eastern Micronesia, the archaeological picture does not add much to the general historical hypothesis given at the beginning of this chapter.

As we have seen, the degree of variation in the Micronesian artefact assemblage, at least that portion which survives archaeologically, is very limited. Pottery of course varies, as do shell fishhooks, but in general the widespread use of shell imposed an intractable medium on the prehistoric artisan. Stone tools are not common, even on the volcanic islands, and Micronesian stone adzes are generally of the simple untanged oval or lenticular cross-sectioned forms characteristic of Melanesia (Duff types 2F and 2G). Tanging and waisting are virtually unrecorded.

We might finally air the hypothesis that eastern Micronesian cultural origins are at least partially derived from the Lapita Culture. This would explain the many close similarities with Polynesia, and it would also explain the differences between the two areas as being caused by some 2000 to 3000 years of virtual separation. Environmental factors are obviously to be taken into account as well, for Polynesian culture generally is most characteristically developed on volcanic islands, while eastern Micronesia is a zone of atolls *par excellence*. It is therefore quite obvious why stone tools and pottery are rare or absent in this region, but I would not be surprised to hear one day that Lapita pottery has been discovered on Truk, Ponape or Kusaie. Perhaps an archaeologist will go and have a look in the not too distant future.

Footnotes

1. Buck 1938.
2. Anell 1955. See also Spoehr 1952.
3. Duff 1970: 16.
4. Howells 1973a.
5. Koch 1961; 1965; 1966.
6. Koch 1965: 201.
7. Barrau 1960.
8. Osborne 1966: 29.
9. Spoehr 1957: 25.
10. Urban 1961: map 1.
11. Spoehr 1957; Pellett and Spoehr 1961.
12. Reinman 1968a; 1968b.
13. Solheim 1968b.
14. Spoehr 1957: 66.
15. Reinman 1968b.
16. Spoehr 1957: 171.
17. For descriptions of *latte* see Thompson 1932; 1940; Spoehr 1957; Beaty 1962.
18. Thompson 1940.
19. Reinman 1968a.
20. Spoehr 1957: 102–6.
21. Spoehr 1957: 85.
22. Examples of this widespread assemblage are given by Matsumura (1918). It includes shell earrings and bracelets, necklaces of shell discs, shell knives and scrapers, splayed pounders of coral and volcanic stone, and shell fishing gear.
23. Pirie 1971–2.
24. Christian 1899; Matsumura 1918; Beauclair 1967a.
25. Gifford and Gifford 1959.
26. Beauclair 1966.
27. Beauclair 1966; 1967b.
28. Osborne 1966: 472–3; Matsumura 1918.
29. Force 1959; Osborne 1966: appendix I.
30. Osborne 1958; 1966. I understand that a report on more recent work by Professor Osborne will soon be in press. For a brief account of earlier Japanese investigation in the Palaus, see Chapman 1968.
31. Osborne has proposed a cultural sequence for the Palaus going back to *c.*2000 B.C., but the dates are based mainly on guess work. He also dates the terraces and stone monuments generally to the period A.D. 900–1400, and claims that the terraces were out of use by 1600.
32. Riebe 1967.
33. This statement is not a criticism of the work of Heyerdahl on Easter Island, and I certainly would not wish to include him in any lunatic fringe. Easter Island is discussed more fully in chapter 12.
34. Morrill 1970.
35. Gulick, reproduced in Morrill 1970.
36. See Hambruch 1936: abb. 1.
37. Christian 1899. See also Christian 1897.
38. By Brandt 1962.
39. Hambruch 1936. See also Chapman 1968 for Japanese reports on Nan Madol.
40. Fischer 1964.
41. Christian 1899: 89–90.
42. Davidson 1967a.
43. Christian 1899: 171.
44. Davidson 1967b; 1968; 1971b.
45. Davidson 1971b.
46. Riesenberg and Gayton 1952.

Bateau des îles Carolines.

Fig. 11.1. Outrigger canoe with asymmetrically cross-sectioned hull from
the Caroline Islands, drawn by Louis Choris in 1815.

CHAPTER 11

The Prehistory of Polynesia: Part One

In chapter 9, we saw that the first settlers of Polynesia made their homes in the Tongan Islands soon after 1500 B.C. There seems no reason to doubt that these people had large seaworthy canoes, and they must have had some knowledge of navigation. Over the next 2000 years, their descendants settled the remainder of Polynesia, and visited almost every speck of land in the great triangle formed by Hawaii, Easter Island and New Zealand. We commence this chapter with a review of perhaps the most popular aspect of the Polynesian story.

CANOES AND THEIR NAVIGATION

One of the major inventions of the Austronesians, prior to their dispersal into Oceania, was the balancing outrigger to give stability to a canoe. In Island Southeast Asia, the usual procedure is to place an outrigger along either side of the hull, while in Oceania, a single outrigger, always kept to windward of the hull, is the almost universal form. The single outrigger may be subject to less stress in heavy seas than the double, and it never seems to have been of importance in the close-set archipelagoes of Island Southeast Asia, except in the Andaman and Nicobar Islands, and on the small Indonesian Islands of Nias and Mentawei. As one might expect, the great feats of ancient navigation were carried out by the Oceanians, who carried fast and manoeuvrable sailing canoes to their highest development.

Thanks to a monumental corpus prepared by A.C. Haddon and James Hornell[1], any interested reader can find out as much about Oceanic canoe construction at European contact as the world of scholarship will probably ever know. The single outrigger canoe with a dug-out or carvel-built hull was found everywhere in Oceania, except for a few peripheral regions of Polynesia such as Mangareva and the Chatham Islands. The Micronesians, more than any other Oceanians, developed this type of canoe into the most advanced sailing machine in Oceania, by the use of deep and asymmetric V-sectioned hulls to restrict leeward drift, and by the use of a true triangular lateen sail which could be swung from one end of the canoe to the other when direction was changed (figure 11.1). These Micronesian canoes did not have separate bows and sterns, but could be sailed either end forward, simply by swinging the sail right around on the central mast. Platforms down the centres of the canoes and on the lee sides gave ample space for passengers and cargo, and in terms of speed and windward sailing ability[2] the Micronesian canoe may well have been unequalled. Variants of this type of canoe were also used in the Santa Cruz Islands of Melanesia, and the Oceanic lateen sail, probably a Micronesian invention, was also in use on double canoes in Fiji and in New Caledonia, and by the Mailu of southeastern Papua.

Melanesia, as in all ethnographic matters, is a complex area. Double outrigger canoes of Indonesian type are found in a few western areas, including the Cape York Peninsula of Australia, and the Solomon Islanders specialised in an outriggerless form of plank-built canoe, which may also be of eastern Indonesian origin. Elsewhere, the normal single outrigger type was virtually universal, sometimes with square sails in some western areas. In general, there are considerable variations in development throughout

Melanesia; the New Hebrides, for instance, retained simple dug-out hulls, sometimes with added washstrakes, and simple dug-outs, often without sails at all, were widespread in northeastern New Guinea. On the other hand, an isolated island like New Caledonia had true double canoes with Oceanic lateen sails and reversible ends, and many of the coastal traders of western Melanesia also developed excellent sailing craft. The largest and finest canoes in Melanesia were the *drua* of Fiji, which appear literally to have been a cross between the outrigger sailing canoes of Micronesia and the much larger double forms of Polynesia (figure 11.2). *Drua* were in fact double canoes, but the windward hull was shorter than the leeward. The use of the Oceanic lateen sail and reversible ends gave the mobility associated with the Micronesian canoes, although the technique of constructing the hull with an asymmetric cross-section did not spread from Micronesia further than the Ellice Islands. In the early nineteenth century, Fijian canoes could transport up to 200 men, and at the time of European contact they were rapidly replacing the more conventional Polynesian double canoes of Tonga and Samoa.

In Polynesia, the single outrigger canoe is again an almost universal form, although the Mangarevans were only constructing log rafts

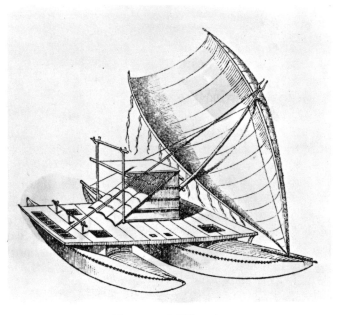

Fig. 11.2. A Fijian *drua*.

(with sails) at contact, and the Moriois of the Chatham Islands had developed flat-bottomed craft made from bundles of flax or fern. In New Zealand, the single outrigger and double canoes had faded in popularity by the time of Captain Cook, and had been virtually replaced by single-hulled dug-out canoes. Addition of washstrakes and elaborately carved bows and sterns led to the giant monohulled war-canoes for which the Maori were so well-known (figure 11.3).

However, the hallmark of Polynesian voyaging in most areas was the double canoe with equal-sized[3] hulls of symmetrical cross-section, and perhaps the best known of these were the great war canoes and sailing canoes of the Society Islands (figure 11.4), which could be up to 30 metres long, with enormous raised and carved sterns up to 8 metres or more in height, and, in one case, an observed seating capacity for 144 paddlers. Cook and Banks have given us some excellent descriptions of these superb craft, and in 1774 Cook saw a fleet of 160 double war canoes with paddlers, and 170 small sailing transport canoes in attendance; he estimated a total crew of 7760 men. This fleet was mustering before a planned attack on Moorea, and it is of interest that the Society Islanders had developed the art of naval warfare into a major weapon of aggression. The Boraborans had recently defeated the Raiateans by this means, and it appear that opposing canoes were brought together for the warriors to fight in twos or fours on raised stages, being replaced as they fell. These stages were constructed especially for warriors, and apparently chiefs and priests as well, while the paddlers do not appear to have taken part in the fighting. Special canoes to transport the dead and also to carry portable *marae* platforms of timber are also known to have been used. Cook's view of the Tahitian fleet seems to have made a very deep impression on him, and it is unfortunate that he was never able to watch actual combat taking place.

The Polynesian double canoes were generally provided with definite bows and sterns, and were sailed by the slower method of tacking (i.e. steering the boat round on to a new course), rather than by changing ends. The Tuamotuans appear to have been the only Polynesians to develop reversible ends and the Oceanic lateen sail, and it may be that this development was independent of that in Micronesia and Melanesia. A more primitive lateen sail for bow-and-stern canoes was in use in Tonga and Samoa, but

Fig. 11.3. Single-hulled New Zealand war canoe, drawn on Cook's first voyage by Sydney Parkinson.

Fig. 11.4. Painting by the Hawaiian artist H. Kawainui Kane of a Tahitian double canoe (*pahi*).

A War Pahi of Tahiti

otherwise the Polynesians had only developed the less efficient fixed sail and vertical mast. However, while the Micronesians may have excelled in manoeuvrability, the Polynesians certainly excelled in size, and their canoes were the means of transporting large numbers of people over very sizeable stretches of ocean. How did they do it? No other question of Polynesian culture history has generated so much emotion and vituperative argument.

In order to review this thorny topic, we may begin at the beginning. The first useful comments about Polynesian navigation were not made until the late eighteenth century, and here is the most flattering, made by Andia y Varela, a Spaniard who visited Tahiti in 1774–5. Varela was able to interview a Tahitian sailing master who accompanied him on a voyage to Lima, and he found out how the Tahitians used sunrise and sunset positions for a horizon compass, and how they made careful observations of wind and wave directions on beginning a voyage. His observations apply only to voyages in which the direction of the destination was already known (i.e. not to exploratory voyages) and he continues as follows:

He (i.e. the navigator) proceeds out of port with a knowledge of these (conditions), heads his vessel according to his calculation, and aided by the signs the sea and wind afford him, does his best to keep steadily on his course. This task becomes more difficult if the day be cloudy, because of having no mark to count from (i.e. the sun's position) for dividing out the horizon. Should the night be cloudy as well, they regulate their course by the same signs; and, since the wind is apt to vary in direction more than the swell does, they have their pennants, (made) of feathers and palmetto bark, to watch its changes by and trim sail, always taking their cue for a knowlege of the course from the indication the sea affords them. When the night is a clear one they steer by the stars; and this is the easiest navigation for them because, these being many (in number), not only do they note by them the bearings on which the several islands with which they are in touch lie, but also the harbours in them, so that they make straight for the entrance by following the rhumb of the particular star that rises or sets over it; and they hit it off with as much precision as the most expert navigator of civilised nations could achieve[4].

These techniques were used for navigation from Tahiti to Raiatea (200 km), and to other islands further afield which Varela does not name. They do, of course, refer to known courses between islands which were in fairly regular contact, and Varela's description does not automatically imply that the Tahitians were capable of long-distance exploratory navigation during which they could always keep track of position. No early European explorer indicates this, not even Captain Cook, who was, in fact, less complimentary about Polynesian navigation than Varela by the time of his third voyage (1776–80). In the Tongan Islands in 1777, he observed that the local canoes could sail at 'seven knots or mile in an hour', and then went on:

In these Navigations the Sun is their guide by day and the Stars by night, when these are obscured they have recourse to the points from whence the Wind and waves of the Sea come upon the Vessel. If during the obscuration both the wind and the waves shift . . . they are bewildered, freqently miss their intended port and are never heard of more[5].

A little before he made this observation, Cook had visited the island of Atiu in the southern Cooks, and had found there five survivors of a drift voyage from Tahiti during which 15 people had died. He noted:

This circumstance very well accounts for the manner the inhabited islands in this Sea have been at first peopled; especially those which lay remote from any continent and from each other[6].

Varela and Cook were both able to interview qualified Polynesian navigators[7], and their statements are quite clear on the methods used and the difficulties associated with them. They were also able to collect equally valuable evidence about Society Island geographical knowledge. In 1769, Cook collected the names of 130 islands known to the Raiatean navigator Tupaia, and was able to position 74 of them on a map. Today, about 45 of them are reckoned to be identifiable[8]. According to Lewthwaite, Tupaia knew the names of most Polynesian islands to as far west as Fiji, with the exceptions of New Zealand, Hawaii, Mangareva and Easter Island. How he came to acquire this knowledge is another question, for there is no evidence that the Tahitians were voyaging outside the Society and northwestern Tuamotu Islands at European contact, and the Duff missionaries in 1797 were told that they were unable to sail further than Raiatea or Huahine[9]. Therefore, much of the information could reflect folk memory and the chance arrivals of drift voyagers[10].

In 1772, the Spaniard Boenechea[11] was given the names of sixteen islands by a Tahitian, and this list certainly includes at least one island in the southern Cooks (Atiu). When the missionary John Williams officially discovered Rarotonga in 1823, he was able to affirm that the southern Cook Islanders and the Society Islanders did have at least some knowledge of each other's existence[12]. But no sooner had the first European explorers set foot on their new found islands than the rot of contamination set in. Polynesians quickly assimilated European geographical knowledge, and naturally wove it into their traditions. In 1774–5 another Spaniard[13] collected further island names from Tahiti, only two years after Boenechea. This time the list includes the Society Islands and many of the Tuamotus, together with some of the southern Cooks and Australs, and also a place called Ponamu, which can only be the South Island of New Zealand, described to Captain Cook as Te Wahi Pounamu (the place of greenstone) in 1769. The Tahitians can only have acquired the term from Cook or his men, and so within five years prehistory was very rapidly changing into protohistory, with many attendant dangers for later scholarship.

As far as inter-island voyaging at European contact is concerned, there is good information that the Society and Tuamotu Islanders were in frequent contact, as were the Tongans, Samoans and Fijians, together perhaps with the Ellice Islanders and Rotumans[14]. All other groups appear to have been isolated, particularly those such as New Zealand, Hawaii and Easter Island. Therefore, the Polynesians were not making long-distance voyages of exploration at European contact, and neither were any of the other Oceanic peoples. But what of the more distant prehistoric past, when the islands were first settled?

With this question the matter becomes rather complex, partly because so many authors have been unwilling to accept Cook and Varela at face value. By the late nineteenth century, Polynesian scholarship had entered its 'romantic phase', and tales of mighty voyages from one end of Oceania to the other were appearing frequently, particularly in the pages of the *Journal of the Polynesian Society*, then edited by

S. Percy Smith. In 1898–9 Smith published the first edition of his now famous book *Hawaiki: The Whence of the Maori*[15], and exploratory navigated voyages from Indonesia to Hawaii and eastern Polynesia became accepted as fact. In 1923, Elsdon Best penned the following in a phase of romantic but rather unscientific fervour:

> For, look you, for long centuries the Asiatic tethered his ships to his continent ere he gained courage to take advantage of the six months' steady wind across the Indian Ocean; the Carthaginian crept cautiously down the West African coast, tying his vessel to a tree each night lest he should go to sleep and lose her; your European got nervous when the coast-line became dim, and Columbus felt his way over the Western Ocean while his half-crazed crew whined to their gods to keep them from falling over the edge of the world: but the Polynesian voyager, the naked savage, shipless and metalless, hewed him out a log dugout with a sharpened stone, tied some planks to the sides whereof with a string, put his wife, children, some coconuts, and a pet pig on board, and sailed forth upon the great ocean to settle a lone isle two thousand miles away – and did it[16].

In the climate generated by Smith and Best, navigated return voyages over vast distances were acceptable, although most scholars, even Elsdon Best, were fully aware of the importance of involuntary drift voyages. In 1934, Roland Dixon[17] was quite happy to accept 2000 miles as the limit of non-stop Polynesian voyaging. But the pendulum was already showing signs of a swing – back towards the common-sense of Cook and Varela. In 1924, John Bollons, an experienced sea captain, made the following observation:

> It is amazing how boldly the landsman has launched the Polynesian out into the – at that time – infinite ocean; described the voyage, the seaworthiness of the canoes, the cargo carried, the manner in which the canoes were hove-to in bad weather, and the navigating by stars and the rising and setting of the sun. How simple it all is, or seems to be, when one is living ashore[18].

The problem, as seen from our present vantage point, was that writers like Smith and Best were taking Polynesian traditions at their face value, without taking into account the fact that many of these traditions were collected a century after initial European contact. Polynesian traditions were not accurately recorded accounts by eye-witnesses, although the scholarly community as a whole was unwilling to recognise this until well after 1930. By the 1950s, the pendulum was swinging rapidly, and the result was a controversial work by Andrew Sharp, published in final form in 1963[19].

Sharp's view was that Polynesia was settled mainly by one-way voyaging, i.e. by voyagers who had no real means of tracking their course, and who could not have returned to their homelands, even had they wanted to. Whether the voyages were intentional or unintentional is of no practical importance; exiles, drift voyagers and voluntary emigrants alike could all indulge in one-way voyaging. Two-way voyaging was, of course, practised between close-set islands, but the only good records of two-way voyaging between islands over 150 km apart without intervening islands come from the Society-Tuamotu and western Polynesian regions, as we have seen above. Islands such as Hawaii, Easter Island, New Zealand, the Marquesas, most of the Cooks, and many others had no regular outside contacts except by one-way voyaging. Sharp's main arguments were that the Polynesians had no methods for determining longitude, and were unable to reckon displacement caused by currents, which can flow at up to 40 km a day, or by winds. In other words, no Polynesians would know their positions at sea after a few days in unknown waters.

In 1968, Sharp's views were supported by a more detailed analysis published by Kjell Akerblom[20]; not only were longitude reckoning and displacement by winds and currents major problems, but Akerblom also pointed that the use of zenith stars for latitude reckoning was probably unknown to Polynesians as well[21]. Long distance two-way voyaging, with fully stocked expeditions following in the wake of explorers, was not considered to be a viable concept for any part of prehistoric Oceania, and the accumulated archaeological knowledge of the past 20 years does not allow us, unfortunately, to contradict this view.

But this is not all. There are many facets of Oceanic voyaging which do demonstrate great skill and daring, albeit based on knowledge of an empirical rather than heuristic derivation. Firstly, Polynesia was almost certainly not settled by a succession of blind drifters. In the Polynesian

area, the currents to north and south of the Equator move from east to west at up to 40 km a day, and there is only a narrow belt of west-east flowing current between latitudes 4° and 10°N[22]. The trade winds also blow from east to west, except during summer periods when they may be replaced by intermittent westerlies. As might be expected, the vast majority of real drift voyages recorded in Polynesia have been from east to west[23], although west-east drifts are common in Micronesia, as the Carolines especially are in the latitude of the west-east flowing countercurrent[24]. Accordingly, the sailing trip from Melanesia into Polynesia is very much 'uphill'.

Just how uphill has recently been shown by a most ingenious computer analysis[25], which involved the simulation of over 100,000 drift voyages, using wind and current data from Meteorological Office records in England covering the whole area from Melanesia to the American coast. The drifts were started from specific islands within this region (mostly in Polynesia), and successful ones were those which reached another island within an allotted survival time. The results of this exercise showed, as expected, that the highest drift possibilities are in an east to west direction, particularly from Tonga to Fiji, Samoa to the Ellice Islands, the northern Cooks to the Tokelaus, Pitcairn to Mangareva and the eastern Tuamotus, and from Rapa to the Australs and southern Cooks. All these drifts have over 20% probability, and many others with above 10% have a general east-west trend, with localised northing and southing. Several of the Polynesian Outliers in northern Melanesia are also well placed to receive drifts from western Polynesia.

All this is, of course, expectable, and Thor Heyerdahl showed many years ago that drift voyages into Polynesia are feasible from the east. However, in the light of today's knowledge, we can say that the settlers of Polynesia certainly did not come from the east, and the currents from Peru which reach Polynesia actually give little hope of a successful drift unless one starts some 500 km offshore, as the computer survey demonstrated[26]. It further demonstrated some very important points: it is almost impossible to drift into the Polynesian triangle from any outside land area, and it is almost impossible to drift some of the major settlement voyages which the Polynesians are now known to have made – from Fiji to Tonga, from Samoa to the Society or Marquesas Islands, and from islands in central

Polynesia to Hawaii, Easter Island and New Zealand. On statistical grounds, these islands were probably first settled by exploratory canoes which were deliberately sailing at up to 90° into the wind. Many of these voyages were probably one-way, although by sailing into the wind on the outward voyage, it would in theory be easier to return home downwind, so two-way exploratory voyaging over short distances cannot be ruled out.

We will, of course, never know exactly how the individual islands of Polynesia were settled. But we do know that once a basic geographical knowledge of an area with close-set islands was established, then two-way voyaging, for a variety of motives, would commonly be established. The contact zones of Oceania in ethnographic times have been described by David Lewis[27], and he has demonstrated that there were several large ones in Micronesia, western Polynesia, and the Society-Tuamotu area, while in other regions there is much more localisation. Some Melanesians, particularly the south-east Papuans and the peoples of the Santa Cruz Islands, were very skilled navigators, although their horizons were mainly limited by the exigencies of local trade. Inter-island trade in Polynesia was of much less significance, and here major motives seem to have been conquest, prestige, and also the exploitation (for birds and fish) of uninhabited atolls and sand-cays[28]. Similar motives apply to Micronesia, and here there is the large Carolinean voyaging sphere focussed on the island of Yap.

It is from Micronesia that we have our best knowledge of the techniques for two-way voyaging between known destinations available to Oceanians, and the Carolineans in prehistoric times were evidently capable of making return voyages from the central Carolines to the Marianas Islands – distances of up to 700 km. These Micronesian voyaging techniques, particularly in the central Carolines, have recently been studied in detail by Thomas Gladwin and David Lewis[29]. Carolinean canoe captains are trained in schools of navigation, where they learn the large body of empirical knowledge which enables them to reach other islands. These other islands are, of course, known already from prior visits, and the techniques are not used for pure exploration, although some of them certainly may have been in the past. Carolinean navigators choose definite seasons of the year for sailing, they align their courses on horizon stars, and by taking backsights on landmarks, natural or

artificial, on their starting islands[30]. While at sea they take careful note of wave directions and swell intersection patterns (particularly in the Marshalls), sunrise and sunset positions, reef positions, homing birds at dusk, cloud formations, and a variety of other natural phenomena. But as Gladwin points out, the body of theory used in the Carolines is really specific to that area, and the same proviso applies to the Marshalls, where a number of different techniques were used. In other words, the techniques work perfectly well in their localised areas of use, and some of them were no doubt available to the Lapita voyagers who colonised through Melanesia into western Polynesia prior to 1,000 B.C. But to suggest that they could be used for non-stop two-way voyages from one end of Oceania to the other would, of course, be going much too far, and the zones of regular contact have probably changed little since Lapita times.

However, the intensity of the desire for colonisation of new islands may have waxed and waned at various times, and it may have been at a fairly low ebb at the time of European contact. Polynesian traditions do indicate that many voyages of exploration and settlement took place in the later first and early second millennia A.D., and archaeology gives some support to this for such areas as Hawaii, New Zealand and the Cook Islands, as we will see in due course. Indeed, since this chapter was submitted to the publisher, a two-masted double canoe called the *Hokule'a* was sailed by the very techniques mentioned above from Maui in the Hawaiian Islands to Tahiti. The canoe, 18 metres (60 feet) long, carried a crew of 15 men, plus a cargo of traditional foods and livestock. Its course was partially into the wind[31], but Tahiti was reached successfully after 35 days, and a trip of almost 5000 kilometres. Although no detailed appraisal of the results of the voyage (which was in fact a return voyage, since the canoe sailed back to the Hawaiian Islands) is yet available, it is quite clear that the *Hokule'a* will make a significant impact on the study of Polynesian voyaging[32].

THE WHENCE OF THE POLYNESIANS: THEORISTS GALORE

As one of the most far-flung peoples of the earth, the Polynesians have given rise to more than their fair share of theorising about origins. For over two hundred years, theories have come forth; multitudinous, confusing, contradictory, and ranging in tenor from scholarly to charlatanic and even lunatic fringe. Since the majority of these theories have recently been reviewed by Howard[33], I do not wish to load the reader with too many tedious details, but there are a number of rather interesting high-points, as well as a sobering moral. And the latter is that no real progress was made into the question of Polynesian origins until archaeology made its belated appearance in the 1950s. Before this, over 100 years of wrangling with spurious traditions and a random smatter of ethnography had lead to a rate of progress which one might, perhaps pessimistically, regard as nil. When the *Kon-Tiki* hit the headlines in 1947, Polynesian historical ethnology was in a more confused state than it had been in 1847.

During the golden age of exploration in the late eighteenth century, the prevailing opinion was that the Polynesians came from the west, and that they were related to the peoples of Micronesia, Indonesia, the Philippines, and Madagascar – peoples whom today we would, of course, recognise as Austronesian speakers[34]. In general, there was little major deviation from this view for many years, and it is no accident that with the passage of time it has turned out to be the correct one. The early explorers had no preconceptions, and were fortunate enough to see the South Seas as they really were before the crushing weight of colonialism descended upon them.

The early nineteenth century missionaries seem to have been in general accord with the explorers, but they did toss in a few, at first trivial, misconceptions which were eventually to bedevil later workers. John Williams[35] agreed on a Southeast Asian origin, but also felt some Indian influence to be worthy of consideration; whether from the subcontinent itself or from Indonesia he did not make clear. William Ellis[36] took a rather different tack; while agreeing that both Polynesians and American Indians came from Asia, he felt that the former had crossed the Bering Straits and then swung back from America with the prevailing winds and currents to settle Polynesia through the Hawaiian Islands. With his emphasis on the difficulty of sailing from west to east in tropical Polynesia, Ellis anticipated in a most exact fashion some of the theories of Thor Heyerdahl.

If we look at the range of ideas in print by 1850, we will see that almost all the well-known theories of later years had made an appearance in one rudimentary form or another. Even a

sunken continent theory had appeared in 1837[37], but this particular year is more significant in my mind for the appointment of a 20-year-old American, Horatio Hale, to the American Exploring Expedition which researched its way through Polynesia in a very systematic fashion between 1838 and 1842. Hale's report, published in 1846[38], is a highlight of nineteenth century scholarship. From a base of linguistics and traditions, he anticipated present views by over a century.

Hale placed the Polynesian homeland in Maluku, and specifically on the island of Buru for linguistic reasons. Polynesians from here settled Fiji, from where they were driven by Melanesians to Samoa and Tonga. From Samoa, people moved to New Zealand and the Society Island about 3000 years ago. From Tonga, people moved to the Marquesas a little later, and the Marquesans later settled Hawaii, probably about 1500 years ago. Rarotonga was settled from Samoa and the Society Islands, and Mangareva and Rapa settled from Rarotonga. Hale agreed with the later view of Cook that the South Seas were settled by drift voyagers, but unlike Ellis, he emphasised the importance of periodic westerly winds. Of course, some of Hale's migrations are now known to be incorrect, and some of his traditional dates were wrong. But as an example of systematic reconstruction his work far exceeds that of many of his successors.

Through the remainder of the nineteenth century progress in unravelling Polynesian origins was slow. Differing views appeared in print, including one which derived the Polynesians from a human line which evolved in New Zealand[39]. However, scholars were beginning to place more and more emphasis on the traditions recorded from Polynesians themselves. It was widely held in the late nineteenth century that the Polynesians were a dying race, and, not surprisingly, their numbers had declined drastically since the arrival of Europeans. This situation appears to have given rise to a degree of morbid romanticism, coupled with a lack of judgment within the scholastic community.

The Polynesians undoubtedly had traditions about their origins when Europeans first arrived amongst them. Unfortunately, systematic recording was not undertaken, because explorers generally made short visits and they were not fluent in Polynesian languages. By the time people began to record traditions seriously in the mid-nineteenth century, it was already too late to account for massive contamination – not only from the Bible[40], but from travelling Polynesians themselves. One has only to scan Cook's journals to see how the Raiatean Tupaia was welcomed as an enthralling story-teller in New Zealand in 1769, and a specific case of contamination has already been given on page 301. Within a few years of European discovery a new kind of geographical knowledge was spreading like wildfire, and it spread even more quickly as Polynesians joined European ships in large numbers well before the year 1800, and as stray Europeans settled in as beachcombers. And not only geographical knowledge, but the whole fabric of Polynesian oral tradition was fundamentally altered by a veritable barrage of new information. By the time scholars in the late nineteenth century began to look at Polynesian traditions in serious detail, not even the Polynesians themselves really knew what was pre-European and what was not. Even William Ellis, writing as early as 1830 about the Hawaiian Islands, was describing a society which had changed much more than he realised from its prehistoric forebear[41].

Polynesian oral tradition is a vast topic which I cannot hope to cover properly in a book which is primarily on archaeology[42]. Lest I appear too pessimistic, I should point out that many traditions, particularly those relating genealogical information, can have considerable historical validity, and I will refer to examples below which are well supported by archaeology. My main contention is not that traditions are right or wrong in any absolute sense, but that by their very nature and by the ways in which they have been used[43], they have never given an overall reliable view of Polynesian prehistory and may never be expected to do so at this late date.

The two major scholars of traditions in the late nineteenth century who deserve attention are Smith and Fornander. The former, writing in 1878–80[44], felt that the Polynesians were white Caucasoids ('Aryans' in the terminology of the day), who were strongly influenced by Mesopotamian civilisation and who had intermarried with Dravidians in southern India. They moved to Indonesia, and were pushed out from here in the first and second centuries A.D. by the incoming Indian civilisation. They then moved to Fiji, and into Polynesia, where they settled Hawaii and other areas by A.D. 600. Fornander's rather uncritical use of place-names and Polynesian traditions influenced by (unknown to him) Biblical teachings led him right away from the sound foundations laid by Hale, with

whom he recorded disagreement.

Smith first published his *Hawaiki* in 1895–6, but the ideas therein were repeated several times by him in later years[45]. He came closer to the truth than Fornander, and used traditions mainly from Rarotonga, while Fornander collected most of his information from Hawaii. Smith derived the Polynesians from a Caucasoid population in India, who departed for Indonesia about 400 B.C. From here, the Polynesian legendary figure Maui explored Polynesia about A.D. 50, and Tonga and Samoa were settled, through Fiji, about A.D. 450. Following this, a different wave of Polynesians (called by Smith the Maori-Rarotongans) sailed from Fiji through Samoa to settle the rest of Polynesia between A.D. 650 and 900. These people took Negrito slaves with them from Indonesia and Melanesia, and Smith equated the latter with the Manahune of Tahiti and Hawaii (see below). Both Smith and Fornander thought that there was another major phase of internal Polynesian voyaging in the thirteenth and fourteenth centuries, and traditions and archaeology in central Polynesia do, in fact, suggest that this view may be correct. Indeed, by using genealogies to give dates, Smith presented a picture for central and eastern Polynesia which is very close to the modern view, despite his upholding of the myth of a Caucasoid origin in India[46].

Smith, in my view, ranks with Hale as a major contributor of the nineteenth century, although I have subjected him to some criticism in the earlier section on voyaging. He and his predecessors seem to have held the general view that Polynesia was settled by one group of peoples; namely, the Polynesians, although Smith did of course try to separate them into two streams. However, many of his successors with their remarkable ethnic and racial wave theories reduced the first half of the twentieth century to a nadir of chaos.

In 1895, the ball started to roll when John Fraser[47] suggested from linguistic evidence that Polynesia was first settled by two black races from India, and then by the Caucasoid Polynesians, also from India. The former were credited by Fraser with the construction of the large stone structures on Ponape and Easter Island, on the grounds that 'the black races everywhere – in India, Babylonia, Egypt – have shown a liking for hugeness of architecture'. Such a theory was not unusual for its time, but worse was to come. In 1907, J. Macmillan Brown[48] produced one of the strangest theories of all time, apparently from a base of guesswork, prejudice, muddled thinking and erroneous facts. He believed that Polynesia was first settled by Caucasoid peoples with primitive Aryan languages, who moved across landbridges from Japan to Easter Island during the last Ice Age. Megalith-building Caucasoids then sailed into Polynesia from north Asia before the sixth century B.C., without women or pottery. More Caucasoids finally came in from Indonesia a little later, with agriculture.

In 1924, Brown elaborated his theory in an absolutely astounding work on Easter Island, and suggested that this island was once a burial place for the great chiefs of a Polynesian empire situated on a now-sunken continent. Amongst other things, these remarkable Polynesians seem to have founded the greater part of prehistoric American civilisation. Finally, Brown produced a third work in two volumes in 1927, in which he reproduced his sunken continent theory and showed how imperial Polynesians had fled into the benighted areas of Melanesia and Indonesia when their continent sank. Anyone reading Brown today can hardly fail to be struck with absolute amazement, as well as no small degree of puzzlement.

Happily, and for obvious reasons, no-one took Brown very seriously. In 1911 and 1912[49] William Churchill presented his linguistic analyses as evidence for Polynesian origins, and rejected the Indo-European (Aryan) and Semitic hypotheses of earlier scholars. He was content to trace the Polynesians to Indonesia, whence they moved into Polynesia in two major streams. The first (Proto-Samoan) travelled in two separate migrations through Melanesia about 2000 years ago to settle virtually all points of Polynesia, and then a later stream (the Tongafiti) came in, perhaps through Micronesia, to overlay the previous Proto-Samoans at about A.D. 1200. Churchill believed that incoming Malays drove the Polynesians out eastwards, and in the process borrowed many words from their languages. He did not therefore regard Malayo-Polynesian (Austronesian) as a true linguistic family.

Smith, Churchill, and also Williamson[50] seem to have agreed rather loosely on two Polynesian movements into Polynesia, and they did not pay much attention to possible non-Polynesian racial substrata. The views of Fraser and Brown were more extreme in this respect, and the rather complex wave theories which they favoured were given an unfortunate boost in the 1920s by the results from craniology. We have already reviewed

Sullivan's ideas of Negroid, Caucasoid and Mongoloid waves in Polynesia (page 48), and a similar theory was published by Dixon in 1920[51], although he placed more emphasis on the Mongoloid component than Sullivan. Intricate details need hardly concern us here, but it does seem to me that by 1925 the linguists, traditionalists, and physical anthropologists were producing irreconcilable theories from their isolated disciplines. A synthesist was clearly called for.

The best candidate for this title, although his views are now known to be wrong, was Ralph Linton, who in 1923[52] concluded a detailed survey of Marquesan material culture with a view of Polynesian origins based on ethnology, physical anthropology, and a little traditional material. Linton adopted Dixon's conclusions from physical anthropology, and postulated first a settlement of Melanesian Negroids, then Caucasoids who travelled through Micronesia to hybridise with the Negroids, and finally Indonesians (presumably Mongoloids), who complicated the hybrid even more but got through in fairly pure form to settle the outposts of Hawaii and New Zealand. Like most of the theories I have reviewed, Linton's was very much more complex than I indicate here, and like the others it seems to have attracted few followers. Everyone wanted his own theory in the halcyon days before archaeology.

A few years after Linton, E.S.C. Handy[53] published a simpler theory which was based, like the theories of Smith, Churchill and Williamson, on two strata. The first stratum (his Indo-Polynesian) was of Vedic, Hindu and Southeast Asian origin, mainly of Caucasoid race, and it introduced the gods Tane, Tu and Rongo throughout Polynesia. The second migration (his Tangaloa-Polynesian) came in about A.D. 600, and its strong Buddhist content linked it with ethnic groups in southern China. Tangaloa was another widespread Polynesian god, and his adherents in this later migration established themselves as chiefs in Samoa, the Society Islands (in the district of Opoa on Raiatea), and in the Hawaiian Islands. They appear to have had little influence elsewhere, but in the Society and Hawaiian Islands they drove the members of the first migration inland, and the latter later became known as *manahune*. However, according to Cook and Banks, the term *manahune* simply referred to Tahitian commoners in the late eighteenth century, and Katherine Luomala[54] was later able to show that Handy's linking of the term with an early wave of settlers was invalid.

Luomala's analysis was not published until 1951, and in the meantime another two-stratum theory similar to Handy's was published in 1938 by Peter Buck[55]. Buck thought that the Polynesians were of mixed Caucasoid and Mongoloid origin, and that they migrated from Indonesia through Micronesia (see page 281) in two waves; the first being later submerged in the second (and dominant) aristocratic wave which established itself on Raiatea in the Society Islands. Perhaps unfairly, this 1938 work is the one most frequently associated with the name of Peter Buck, but he did in fact publish a much more detailed and modified version in 1944, and I wish to return to this later.

It is quite clear from our present vantage point in time that the scholars of the first half of the twentieth century were busily debating how many strata there were in Polynesia, and where they came from, but generally getting nowhere in terms of an acceptable and stable theory of Polynesian origins. Some viewed the Polynesians as a relatively homogeneous group, others searched for Negroids, Caucasoids and Mongoloids, but very few would have been willing to accept fewer than two clear-cut strata at the very least. The time was over-ripe for dissent, and one of the strongest dissenters was social anthropologist Ralph Piddington.

In 1939[56], Piddington strongly attacked the prevailing ideas about diffusion and the view that cultures never changed except when externally influenced. He felt the culture area concept (that the area of a trait or complex corresponds directly to its age), which had been originally propounded by American ethnologist Edward Sapir, had been naively misused in Polynesia to bolster sharply differentiated strata of settlement. Even Sapir himself, writing as early as 1916, had written an unheeded warning:

> The notion of a culture stratum, composed of a large number of elements that are technically independent of each other, journeying without great loss of content, as though isolated in a hermetically sealed bottle, from one end of the world to the other is unthinkable and contradicts all historical experience[57].

Piddington summed up his survey of Polynesian historical ethnology as follows:

> ... the most that historical ethnology can ever do is to offer us a vast number of alternative possibilities, without any hope of ever knowing which is the correct interpretation; this is seen from the most cursory glance at the achievement of over forty years of historical speculation, which has resulted in nothing more than a number of utterly divergent theories of origin, and of alleged parallels with Polynesian culture in other ethnographic areas[58]. We may expect that if any light is in the future cast upon the problem of Polynesian origins, it will be by archaeology rather than by ethnology[59].

Piddington's warning did not go unheeded. In 1944, Peter Buck produced a detailed and very valuable analysis of central Polynesian culture[60], and challenged Handy's rather simplistic two-stratum theory for exactly the same reasons covered in the quote from Sapir given above; in other words, cultural traits could evolve within Polynesia, and did not automatically have to come in a hermetically sealed bottle from some exotic homeland. Buck's own theory, as given in this work, was perhaps the finest of its day, and was soundly based on a tremendous knowledge of traditions and material culture. He was wisely cautious about ultimate origins and dates, and only committed himself to an initial migration into Polynesia through Micronesia, by people without domestic plants and animals. This was the only major migration to enter Polynesia from outside, and Buck felt obliged to reject a Melanesian route on racial and cultural grounds. These early settlers reached all of Polynesia, with the exception of Easter Island, and some of them were able to develop a highly ranked society with a strong priesthood (of the god Tangaroa) on the island of Raiatea. This chiefly society was able to dominate Tahiti and the other Society Islands, and eventually spread its influence through the rest of eastern Polynesia, including Easter Island, by a series of migrations between the twelfth and fourteenth centuries. However, Tonga and Samoa were not influenced by Raiatean culture, although the domestic plants and animals were spread from Fiji through Samoa to Raiatea at some time before the dominance of the latter island in eastern Polynesia.

Buck's idea of a Micronesian migration route was later supported by Spoehr[61], and more recently by Howells and Duff (see page 281), although the tide of archaeological and linguistic evidence has now swung rather heavily against it. Twenty years ago, however, it was in great favour, and held out right to the end of the period of ethnological theorising in the early 1960s. For instance, in 1952, Robert Heine Geldern[62] claimed three strata for Polynesia, with an early Walzenbeile settlement which reached New Zealand, a later settlement from the Philippine-Taiwan region through Micronesia at about the time of Christ, and a final Hindu-Buddhist wave which he recognised in a number of special chiefly customs. In 1961, C.A. Schmitz[63] published a further two-stratum theory, in which his early wave, Southern Austronesian, entered Melanesia from eastern Indonesia, and there mingled with preceeding non-Austronesian settlers to form an 'Austro-Melanid' mixed culture, which went on to settle Polynesia. A later and separate wave, called Northern Austronesian, later entered Polynesia through Micronesia. In a slightly diluted form Schmitz' theory could, in fact, be made to fit well with the picture for Melanesia presented by modern linguistics and archaeology.

By 1960, a single origin for Polynesian culture was accepted by the great majority of scholars. Linguistics and archaeology were beginning to dominate the field at the expense of ethnological studies, and rightly do. However, I do not wish to give the impression in this section that I am deliberately denigrating historical ethnology; it

played a tremendous role in shaping the field for Polynesian archaeology, and despite its errors it was simply a normal product of its day. One particular piece of historical ethnology has, in fact, always seemed to me to be basic for modern Polynesian archaeology, and that was published by Edwin Burrows in 1938[64].

Burrows decided to take a detailed look at the distribution of specific ethnographic traits (both social and material) across Polynesia. He found that differences in distribution allowed him to define two major culture areas – western Polynesia, and central-marginal Polynesia (figure 11.5). Western Polynesia comprises Tonga, Samoa, and adjacent groups; central Polynesia includes the Hawaiian, Society, southern Cook, Austral and Tuamotu Islands; and marginal Polynesia includes the Marquesas Islands, Easter Island, and New Zealand. More recent scholars have tended to lump central and marginal Polynesia together as eastern Polynesia, and I will be using this term frequently below in a cultural sense. Burrows also recognised a grouping called intermediate Polynesia, which included the atolls of the northern Cook, Tokelau, and Ellice Islands, and as later pointed out by Vayda[65], these atolls had small vulnerable populations who were open to in-

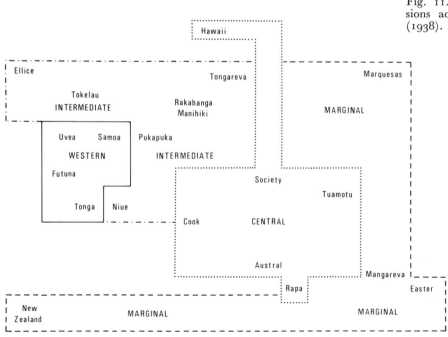

Fig. 11.5. Polynesian cultural divisions according to Edwin Burrows (1938).

fluences from both western and eastern Polynesian sources.

The divisions established by Burrows, although based on ethnographic criteria, have remained of great importance for archaeologists to the present, and are of fundamental significance in Polynesian prehistory. He implied, quite correctly, that the cultures of western Polynesia had undergone development separately from those of central-marginal Polynesia, and vice-versa. Several items widely present in central-marginal Polynesia were virtually absent in western Polynesia, such as tanged adzes, simple shell bait hooks for fishing, stone food pounders, and human figures carved in stone or wood. The two regions also had contrasting techniques of barkcloth manufacture, house building, canoe building, kinship terminology and religion. Even more important from an archaeological view-point, the temples of central-marginal Polynesia consisted of open courts with platforms and upright pillars (generally referred to as *marae*), while the temples of western Polynesia consisted of large houses, sometimes raised on earth or stone platforms. Burrows' distinctions were not meant to be absolute, and as examples, one can find references to occasional god-houses in central-marginal Polynesia, and to tanged adzes and human figure carvings in western. But the western-eastern division was, and still is, of basic significance.

Burrows also argued against the multi-stratum theories, and suggested that the distribution of culture traits was more likely to reflect processes such as diffusion, local development, and abandonment, rather than to reflect superimposed strata through time. He felt that the Polynesians had a unified origin, but he did suggest that eastern Polynesia was strongly influenced from Micronesia, and western from Melanesia. The eastern Polynesian fishhooks with their strong Micronesian parallels[66] might give some support to this view, as we will see later.

Having now run the gamut of what we might call 'establishment' historical ethnology, we can turn to the more contentious question of contacts between the Americas and Polynesia. A large number of scholars before 1950 had investigated this field, and most remained fairly reserved about the possibility of massive trans-Pacific contact in any direction[67]. The few who were prepared to commit themselves strongly seem to have felt that Polynesians went to the Americas, rather than vice-versa. Thor Heyerdahl, one of the most

remarkable men ever to turn his attention to Polynesian prehistory[68], turned the tables on all previous theories and brought the Polynesians before millions of readers throughout the world.

As a young man Heyerdahl had spent a year in the Marquesas Islands, and felt certain that the Polynesians were in no small degree of American ancestry. When he suggested that peoples from Peru and Ecuador had sailed into Polynesia on balsa rafts with the prevailing winds and currents, his learned friends informed him that balsa rafts would very quickly get waterlogged and sink. This argument did not convince Heyerdahl, and in 1947[69] he and his companions constructed a balsa raft, the *Kon-Tiki*, in the harbour at Callao, on the lines described by early sixteenth century chroniclers for rafts observed sailing along the coasts of Ecuador and northern Peru. After being towed for 80 kilometres out of Callao harbour by a tug, they sailed directly with the winds and currents for 101 days until they crash-landed on the atoll of Raroia in the Tuamotus. Many people laughed, Heyerdahl achieved world-renown, and I personally think he proved a very important point – South American Indians could have reached Polynesia.

In 1952 [70], Heyerdahl presented his theory in detail. Following the views of some of his predecessors, he felt that the Polynesians could not possibly have migrated through Melanesia, or even through the atolls of Micronesia, and he felt with Churchill that the Polynesian languages were unrelated to Malay. In fact, he fell into the usual pre-archaeological trap – because Melanesia and Polynesia are culturally and racially different now, they have always been completely separate worlds. He also accepted the traditional dates which placed the Polynesian migrations within the past 1000 years, and pointed out that as there were no Sanscrit words in Polynesian languages, the Polynesians themselves could not have come from Southeast Asia, although he does seem to have agreed on an ultimate pre-American origin in this region.

Heyerdahl thought that Polynesia had first been settled by white-skinned Caucasoid settlers from South America at about A.D. 800. They probably found an earlier wave of Melanesians already in possession, unless they actually sailed to Melanesia and brought them back as slaves (Heyerdahl was evidently convinced of the total inferiority of the Melanesians). These Caucasoids perhaps originated in North Africa, moved to the Americas to found civilisations there, and then established

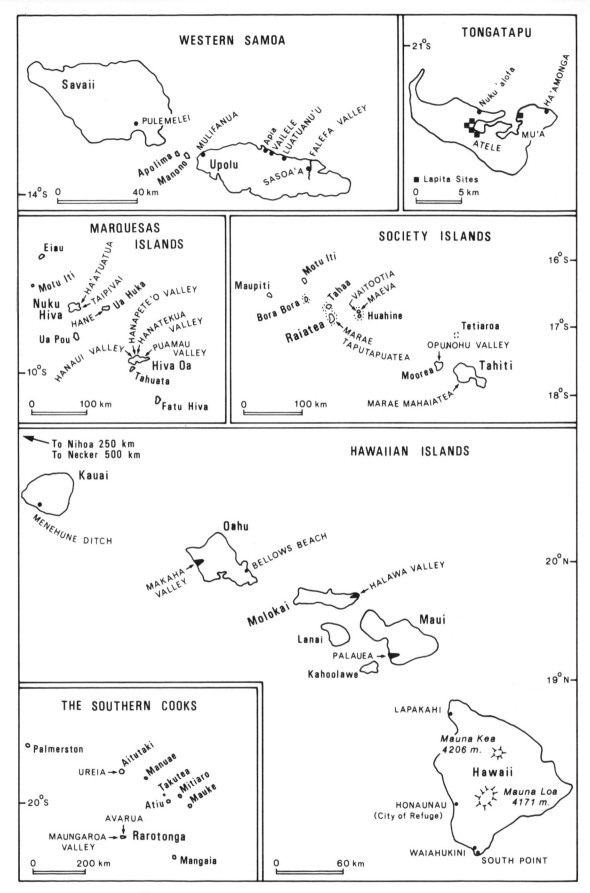

Fig. 11.6. Island groups and archaeological sites in Polynesia.

themselves around the famous area of Tiahuanaco in Bolivia, seat of one of South America's classic civilisations. Under their leader Con Ticci Viracocha, later to be deified as a creator god, they were eventually expelled north through Peru to southern Ecuador, from where they sailed into the Pacific never to return. They settled most areas of Polynesia, and carved their own images in the statues on Easter Island.

A little later, between A.D. 1100 and 1300, the ancestors of the present Polynesians sailed into the Hawaiian Islands from British Columbia, from where they had been driven by expanding Salish tribes. These Polynesians were equated with Kwakiutl Indians by Heyerdahl, and he thought they had sailed from Hakai Strait in British Columbia, as this word seemed to be the same as that for the eastern Polynesian homeland – *Hawaiki*.

Heyerdahl bolstered his arguments with botanical data, and attempted to add coconuts, gourds, yam beans and dogs to the list of American introductions into Polynesia (in addition to the more acceptable sweet potato and wild cotton). He assembled an incredible number of ethnographic parallels between Polynesia and America, many of dubious validity, and overcame the linguistic problem by stating that the language of Tiahuanaco was extinct, and the later Incas, whose language (Quechua) was totally unrelated to Polynesian, did not settle Polynesia anyway.

Not surprisingly, the literature of the 1950s was very liberally peppered with anti-Heyerdahl statements. Heine Geldern[71] isolated a vital logical flaw; if the Polynesians could not sail into Polynesia upwind from the west (as Heyerdahl claimed), then how did they manage to bring crops such as taro, yam and banana, together with the pig and the chicken, from Melanesia to eastern Polynesia? Even Heyerdahl accepted these crops as Indo-Malayan in origin. Another rather impassioned review was presented by Suggs in 1960[72], but we will look at the tail end of the story later in the light of modern Easter Island and Peruvian archaeology. Heyerdahl might have been off the mark, but the hypothesis of some American contact with Polynesia is not to be taken too lightly.

After Heyerdahl, Polynesian origin theories settled down under the guiding hand of archaeology to form the modern view. In 1960, Robert Suggs[73] was able to use archaeological evidence to support his hypothesis that the Polynesians originated in southeast China, and were pushed out from there by Shang expansion. This view would now need heavy revision, but is along the right lines. In 1967, Roger Green[74], was able to use developing knowledge of Lapita sites in Melanesia and western Polynesia to place the immediate origins of the Polynesians squarely in eastern Melanesia. The rest of the story lies in the rest of this chapter.

THE PREHISTORY OF WESTERN POLYNESIA

We have seen already (chapter 9) how Lapita potters established themselves in Tonga before 1200 B.C., and how they went on from there to settle Samoa by about 1000 B.C. In both Tonga and Samoa the Lapita pottery loses its decoration after about 400 B.C. and finally disappears from production about the time of Christ. The Lapita Culture of these two areas in the first millennium B.C. forms the foundation for the Polynesian societies observed by early European explorers, and we will now turn to the tracing of this line of development.

It is not my purpose here to repeat the details of the Lapita Culture, and I intend instead to look at post-Lapita developments in Samoa and Tonga in this section. We will see that these two areas did in fact develop rather different cultures, despite their proximity and known voyaging contacts, and we will see also that the Samoans seem to have been the main instigators in the settlement of eastern Polynesia. By European contact, the Tongan and Samoan Islands had developed rather different societies and material cultures, and Tonga seems to have retained its Lapita heritage a little more tenaciously.

To begin with Tonga, we have first of all an unfortunate gap in knowledge extending through the first millennium A.D. No excavations coherently cover this period, and there are no traditions and apparently no surface monuments. As this period may well have been a formative one for the Tongan society of Cook's day[75], the gap is to be regretted. Tongan society in 1777 was one of the most highly stratified in Polynesia – Cook observed commoners stooping to touch the sole of a chief's foot as he passed, or putting their heads between his feet if he was seated, and the Duff missionaries in 1797 observed how a chief simply rode his double canoe over the smaller canoes of commoners in order to reach the English ship[76]. Tongan society was ordered along the basic ramage lines typical for Polynesia, but by European contact had generated enough prestige rivalry to become a stratified society in Goldman's classification (see page 110)[77].

Traditionally[78], the senior ruling line of Tonga was the Tui Tonga dynasty, which had a genealogy back to about A.D. 950, and by about A.D. 1200 would seem to have dominated some parts of Samoa as well as the whole Tongan group from its home district of Mu'a, on Tongatapu. By about 1500 secular rule was passed to the Tui Ha'a Takalaua dynasty, with the Tui Tonga line retaining some sacred powers until the mid-nineteenth century. The secular power passed again from the Tui Ha'a Takalaua to the Tui Kanokupolu line about 1600, and the latter still retains it today, in the person of King Taufa'-ahau Tupou IV. Traditions also suggest that Tongan warriors dominated Uvea (Wallis Island), Futuna (Hoorn Islands), and Rotuma in times past, and they seem generally to have been the widest ranging navigators in western Polynesia. By Cook's time they were still visiting Samoa, and bringing back weapons, mats and pottery from Fiji, although the inhabitants of the latter group seem to have inspired them with some trepidation.

Archaeologically, the past two thousand years in Tonga are aceramic. A large number of surface monuments belong to this period, although all those with traditional or carbon-14 dates fall within the past 1000 years only. On traditional grounds, one of the earliest monuments is said to be the massive trilithon called the Ha'amonga-a-Maui (figure 11.7), located in eastern Tongatapu, which was constructed by the eleventh Tui Tonga (*c*. A.D. 1200) to symbolise his two sons and the bonds between them. It consists of two shaped coral uprights, each claimed by McKern to weigh 30–40 tonnes, and these each have deep notches in their upper surfaces to support a well-shaped lintel. The top of the lintel has a cup and grooves carved into it, and the present King of Tonga has suggested that these may have been used for recording equinoxes from star positions. Other large upright slabs of coral of unknown use stand nearby.

The other surface monuments of Tonga consist mainly of mounds. These were described in detail by McKern in 1929[79], and he classified them into three groups; mounds for chiefs to rest upon (*esi* – also used for kava drinking according to Cook); mounds for the chiefly sport of pigeon snaring, sometimes with pits sunk into their tops; and burial mounds. The burial mounds were further subdivided into three groups: small earthen burial mounds for commoners; circular earthen burial mounds for chiefs with internal coral-slab tombs (*fiatoka*); and the large rectangular burial mounds of the Tui Tonga dynasty, usually terraced and stone-faced, and known as *langi*.

The *esi* and the *fiatoka* types of mound were described by Cook on his second and third voyages, and some of the latter had houses built on top for corpses and carved wooden figures. A little later, Wilson[80] saw another *fiatoka* with a house on top over a coral burial cist, and it seems from the early accounts that these structures served both as chiefly burial places and as god-houses for religious observances. Some of the ones seen by Cook were certainly stone-slab- or

Fig. 11.7. The Ha'amonga-a-Maui, Tongatapu Island. (See also colour plate.)

wood-faced as well. However, as Davidson[81] has pointed out, none of the early visitors recorded the term *langi*, so it may be that this term is of quite recent origin. The majority of the *langi* (28 out of 45 recorded) are around the Tui Tonga ceremonial centre at Mu'a, on Tongatapu. The more spectacular of these monuments have up to five low steps faced with shaped slabs of coral (figure 11.8), and the remarkable Paepae-o-Telea, traditionally dated to the sixteenth century, has two terraces of shaped slabs up to 1.3 metres thick with bases stepped back at ground level (figure 11.9). Some of the corner stones are actually carved into an L-shape.

More recently, Janet Davidson has surveyed a number of mounds in the Vava'u Group in northern Tonga, and in 1964 she excavated two earthen burial mounds at 'Atele on Tongatapu[82]. These both dated back 1000 years or so, and each contained over 100 extended or slightly flexed inhumations laid in pits and covered with white sand. Some had also apparently been wrapped in black *tapa* cloth. As a result of her investigations Davidson feels that McKern's classification of mounds is unsatisfactory, as his types cannot be clearly differentiated in the field, and are thus unusable unless traditional or archaeological information regarding function is available, which is rarely the case.

The settlement pattern in Tonga at European contact, as described by Cook and Wilson, consisted of scattered dwellings in fenced gardens with neat gateways, separated by roads and tracks (figure 11.10). There may have been some localised nucleation around chiefly establishments, but there are no records of planned villages, and this is in accord with the general pattern of prehistoric Polynesian settlements. However, Tongatapu did have one major ceremonial centre at Mu'a[83], where the establishments of the Tui Tonga and Tui Ha'a Takalaua families were situated in an enclosure on the edge of the Tongatapu inland lagoon. This enclosure, approximately 400 by 500 metres in size, was surrounded on the inland side by a substantial ditch and bank, and it contained numerous house platforms for chiefs, their families and retainers.

Fig. 11.8. A *langi* faced with coral slabs, Mu'a, Tongatapu. (See also colour plate.)

Fig. 11.9. Facing of dressed coral blocks on the Paepae-o-Telea, Mu'a, Tongatapu. Note the carved step at ground level. (See also colour plate.)

Fig. 11.10. Fenced gardens on Tongatapu. Drawn by L. de Sainson on the voyage of Dumont D'Urville, 1826–9.

and priests. In the centre was a large rectangular open space (*malae*), and several of the massive *langi* tombs were situated both inside and outside the enclosed area. Traditionally, Mu'a became the seat of the Tui Tonga line in the eleventh century, while the defences were constructed about 1400, and another large defended enclosure for the Tui Kanokupolu family was annexed to the south in the seventeenth century. As far as is known, Mu'a has the only example of a prehistoric earthwork fortification known in Tonga.

Tongan material culture at European contact may have retained some degree of its Lapita inheritance, particularly in the dominance of simple untanged adzes, in the survival of long units as necklace elements[84], and in the relative absence of shell fishing gear, apart from a few rare trolling hooks which might have been introduced at a late date from eastern Polynesia. That ethnographic Tongan society is a direct descendant of its Lapita forebear seems an acceptable hypothesis, and there is no traditional or archaeological information to suggest any marked cultural break in the Tongan prehistoric sequence.

If we now move from Tonga to Samoa, we move from flat coralline islands to high volcanic ones, and to a prehistoric culture which seems to have been the parent for the scattered island cultures of eastern Polynesia. Samoa may well be *Hawaiki* – a traditional homeland remembered by many of the eastern Polynesians. In this connection, it may be no coincidence that one of

the islands of Western Samoa is called Savai'i – the Samoan dialectal equivalent of Hawaiki.

Modern Samoa is of course divided into two countries – Western Samoa and American Samoa, and it is the former which has produced the vast bulk of our archaeological knowledge, as a result of work carried out between 1962 and 1967 by a team of archaeologists under the direction of Roger Green and Janet Davidson[85]. Western Samoa also contains the two largest and most important islands – Savai'i and Upolu.

We saw on page 253 that sherds of decorated Lapita pottery have recently been recovered from the lagoon at Mulifanua on Upolu, unfortunately without stratigraphic context. These date from about 1000 B.C., and obviously confirm the presence of actual Lapita settlers in Samoa. However, the stratigraphic record established for Western Samoa by Green and Davidson does not begin until about 300 B.C., and by this time Samoan pottery was virtually plain. It went out of use completely soon after the time of Christ, as it did in Tonga, and after this time the Samoan archaeological record consists mainly of house mounds and other monuments, together with non-ceramic artefacts. We may therefore divide Samoan prehistory into two working divisions – ceramic (*c.* 1000 B.C.–A.D. 200) and aceramic (A.D. 200–ethnographic present).

Knowledge of the ceramic phase comes mainly from two localities[86] on Upolu; at Sasoa'a in the inland Falefa Valley, and at Vailele just east of Apia. The Vailele region is characterised by a very liberal scatter of earthen mounds, presumably mainly for houses, which cover almost one square kilometre. Several of these mounds were partly excavated and shown to be aceramic, but two of them were built over earlier soil layers (without evidence for mounding) which contained pottery, adzes, and carbon samples giving dates between 300 B.C. and A.D. 200[87]. The Sasoa'a site, 3 kilometres inland in the Falefa Valley, produced similar material from an occupation layer stratified beneath an abandoned nineteenth century hamlet, and odd sherds have been found in sites as far as 6 km inland in the same valley, suggesting that a substantial population was present on the island by at least the time of Christ.

The pottery from Vailele and Sasoa'a is all plain, apart from occasional rim notching, and the reconstructed forms consist almost entirely of simple round-bottomed bowls which, despite some initial disagreement[88], are now agreed to be late and simplified descendants of the earlier Lapita forms. All the tempers are of local Samoan sands, and there seems to be a clear evolution from a fine thin ware, best represented at Sasoa'a, to a coarse thick ware more common at Vailele. The stone adzes found with the pottery are of considerable importance; like the Tongan ones all are untanged, and the quadrangular and plano-convex cross-sections found in adzes from Lapita sites continue. However, the oval cross-sections which were of some importance in Tonga fade out in Samoa, and a new cross-section of great importance in eastern Polynesia – the triangular – makes its appearance (figure 11.11). As Green has pointed out[89], these changes in adze design in Samoa may well reflect the crossing of the andesite line (see page 280) which runs between Tonga and Samoa. As Samoa is in the Oceanic geological region, with its predominantly basaltic rocks, it seems likely that the enforced concentration on these more tractable basalts could have led to the development of the more angular adze forms characteristic of Samoa and eastern Polynesia generally (excluding New Zealand).

The early Samoan adze kit is in fact directly ancestral and very similar to the early adze kits in the Marquesas and Society Islands in eastern Polynesia[90], and the early Samoan assemblages also anticipate early eastern Polynesian assemblages in the absence of shell ornaments and in the appearance of stone weights for octopus lure

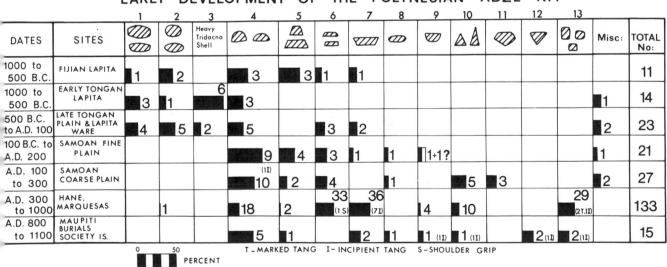

Fig. 11.11. Early adze assemblages from Fiji, western and eastern Polynesia illustrating the development of the Polynesian adze kit through cross-sections. Note the appearance of the triangular form no. 10 in Samoa and eastern Polynesia. From Green and Davidson 1974.

hooks[91]. These important continuities between Samoa and eastern Polynesia, and the corresponding discontinuities between Tonga and Samoa around 2000 years B.P., have led Green to state the following: 'The process of becoming Polynesian began in Tonga. . . but arrival at a truly Polynesian ancestral complex was achieved in Samoa and other Oceanic islands in West Polynesia'[92]. The other Oceanic islands referred to by Green are probably Uvea and Futuna, and the latter has in fact produced late Lapita pottery, as we saw on page 254.

Therefore, towards the end of the ceramic phase, settlers from Samoa or adjacent islands (but not Tonga) set off to found an initial settlement in eastern Polynesia, and we will return to this subject later. But for the past two thousand years Samoa, like Tonga, has had an aceramic prehistory in its own right, and to this, and the Samoa of the early nineteenth century, we turn now.

The aceramic prehistory of Samoa is mainly known from surface monuments such as stone or earthen mounds, terraces, and a few earthwork forts. In the Luatuanu'u and Falefa Valleys on northern Upolu, as well as around Vailele, a large number of such structures have been surveyed and partly excavated. They tend to occur in clusters along valley bottoms and lower slopes, although some attain fairly high elevations, and they comprise agricultural terraces, paved house terraces or platforms with oval kerb settings which once marked the wall positions, and a small number of earthwork forts. One such fort in

the Luatuanu'u Valley was constructed along a steep-sided ridge about 700 metres long, terraced in places, and defended by two parallel banks set across the lower approach line. Some of the terraces have pits which may have been for breadfruit storage (similar pits are reported from the ceramic layers at Vailele), and a carbon date from excavations on this site suggests that parts of it may have been constructed by as early as A.D. 400. If this is so, then this fort is the earliest dated example in Polynesia, as fort building in the two major countries of development – namely, Fiji and New Zealand – does not appear to begin until about A.D. 1100.

The Samoan settlement pattern throughout prehistory was evidently not nucleated, although some earlier writers had erroneously assumed that the planned villages recorded from 1830 onwards were present in prehistoric times[93]. It now appears that these, as in many parts of Polynesia, developed with the advent of European shipping, traders and missionaries, the process perhaps being aided by depopulation. Prehistoric settlement was fairly evenly dispersed in coastal and the more fertile inland areas, and from early European sources analysed by Davidson[94], it appears that the main types of structure would have been dwelling houses and meeting houses (*fale tele*) built on raised platforms of various sizes, an open space for ceremonies known (as in Tonga) as a *malae*, and god-houses (*fale aitu*). The dwelling and meeting houses were usually round-ended, sometimes circular (see figure 4.11), and these shapes are known to go back to the ceramic period from the excavations at Sasoa'a. The god-houses are very poorly recorded, but Davidson[95] has located an early missionary account of what may have been a god-house, with two corpses on a canoe-like bier, together with a wooden image inside it. On Savai'i and Upolu the archaeologists have located a number of star-shaped mounds built of earth or stone blocks (figure 11.12), and these could possibly have supported god-houses as well, although there is an early missionary reference to one being used for pigeon-snaring by chiefs for divinatory purposes[96], and we have already seen that some mounds were used for this purpose in Tonga. However, Samoa does not appear to have any large burial mounds of Tongan type, and neither Tonga nor Samoa have the open-air temple structures (*marae*) which are so important in eastern Polynesia.

Unfortunately, it has proven very difficult to

Fig. 11.12. Perspective sketch of star mound at Vaito'omuli, Savai'i. From Scott 1969.

date these surface monuments, particularly in the absence of pottery, although most of those investigated date to within the past 1000 years, and rebuilding processes and time would quickly hide or remove earlier ones. One of the most splendid mound groups in Samoa is to be found in the district of Palauli in south-eastern Savai'i, centred on a huge flat-topped mound of stone blocks known as the Pulemelei[97]. This covers 60 by 50 metres at the base, and rises 12 metres in height (figure 11.13). At either end is a slightly sunken ramp to the top, together with a pavement, and numerous other platforms, roads and stone walls surround it as would befit a major ceremonial centre. On top of the Pulemelei are postholes and an oval of small stone cairns, but the function of the mound is uncertain. However, one might expect that major communal structures, particularly a large community house (*fale tele*), may once have stood on top. The Pulemelei, as it stands today, is probably the largest surviving man-made mound in Polynesia.

By the time of European contact, the Samoan type of society described on page 111 had presumably developed, and we have already noted that in its emphasis on councils and election to titles it stands apart from all other Polynesian societies. Early European records on Samoa are unfortunately very few, and little definite is known until missionary records begin in the 1830's. In recent years, a number of scholars have argued over the exact nature of Samoan kinship and political structure, with Sahlins[98] and Ember[99] suggesting that kinship units were highly fragmented into localised and independent land-holding groups, and Freeman[100] stating that they were organised more along normal Polynesian ramage lines with paramount chiefs. Archaeology cannot of course throw direct light on a dispute of this kind, but by showing that dispersed settlement of normal Polynesian type was the norm in prehistory, it may indicate that a ramified social structure was in fact more important in the past than it was at European contact. Both Ember[101] and Goldman[102] have suggested this to be the case.

It is very hard now to explain the unique developments in Samoan social and political organisation from archaeological and ecological evidence, and many of the developments may of course reflect the actions of far-sighted individuals rather than long-term social trends. That the Samoans were a fairly dynamic people in prehistoric times seems clear – they were almost

Fig. 11.13. Perspective view of the Pulemelei mound, Savai'i. From Scott 1969.

certainly responsible for initial settlement in eastern Polynesia, and they are still one of the most successful Polynesian nationalities in the Pacific today, having held out very strongly against European domination in the past.

For later prehistory in the rest of western Polynesia, knowledge is virtually absent. Godhouses and open *malae* are quite widely reported, and some islands, such as Niutao (in the Ellice Islands), Alofi, Uvea and Anuta are reported to have settings of upright stone slabs, as in many of the eastern Polynesian religious structures[103], so it is clear that Burrow's distinctions between western and eastern Polynesia are not absolute in this sense. Green[104] has recently brought together the sources on early settlement patterns in western Polynesia and the Outliers, and reports the presence of quite heavily nucleated villages on several islands (Futuna, Atafu in the Tokelau Islands, Tikopia, Nukuoro and Kapingamarangi), although it is not always clear whether these developed after European contact or whether they do have prehistoric validity.

Anyway, with western Polynesia behind us, we can now turn to the ultimate and final achievement of Austronesian settlement – eastern Polynesia.

THE EARLY EASTERN POLYNESIAN CULTURE (C. A.D. 300–1200)

Although a good deal of archaeological information has become available for the Samoan and Tongan groups in recent years, western Polynesia still has some way to go before it catches up with the wealth of information known from eastern Polynesia. Excellent archaeological sequences are available for the Marquesas and Hawaiian Islands, Easter Island, the southern Cooks, and New Zealand, and because of the underlying homogeneity of eastern Polynesian culture it is not difficult to relate these sequences to each other in some detail.

Polynesian culture, looked at as a whole, has clearly been channelled through a number of bottlenecks. The initial Polynesians, in a geographical sense, settled Tonga before 1200 B.C., and then Samoa soon afterwards. After a further 500–1000 years of relative isolation in Samoa, initial settlers moved to some point in eastern Polynesia. During these centuries of relative isolation in western Polynesia, it is clear that a number of major cultural changes took place which were not reflected in the contemporary cultures of Melanesia, and these changes lie partly at the base of the distinctive Polynesian linguistic and ethnographic entity observed at European contact. One cannot of course explain all of Polynesian culture in this way, for the greater part was more probably inherited directly from the Lapita forebear, which was later to be heavily modified in Melanesia by cultural competition. Nevertheless, the concept of two successive cultural bottlenecks in Tonga and Samoa has obvious relevance for Polynesia as a whole, and for eastern Polynesia as a sub-area.

But this is not all, for the islands of eastern Polynesia were not all settled independently from Samoa. Eastern Polynesian cultures share certain linguistic traits and ethnographic traits such as shell fishhooks, tanged adzes, stone food pounders, and open-air temples with courts and platforms, all absent in western Polynesia. Naturally, one cannot assume that these traits developed several times through pure coincidence, and one is forced to assume another bottleneck, this time in eastern Polynesia itself, where these traits developed independently of western Polynesia during several further centuries of isolation. On present evidence, the most likely location for this bottleneck, which I will call the eastern Polynesian primary dispersal centre[105], would appear to be the Marquesas Islands.

During the first millennium A.D., all the major groups of eastern Polynesia for which we have information were settled. And where relevant excavations have been carried out, the assemblages of this early period share a degree of homo-geneity which leads me to group them together into an Early Eastern Polynesian Culture. These assemblages have a number of unique items not present in Tonga or Samoa, as well as many items which obviously do reflect a western Polynesian ancestry. We saw above how shell ornaments characterised the Lapita Culture in Tonga, but were absent in Samoa; so too, they are absent in eastern Polynesia (with minor exceptions). The earliest eastern Polynesian adzes are untanged, like Samoan and Tongan examples (although tangs develop very quickly), and the cross-sections show obvious continuity with Samoa, being rectangular, trapezoidal, triangular, and plano-convex[106]. Octopus lures (figure 11.14 [i]), shell adzes and chisels, shell paring knives, tattooing chisels and pottery also continue directly from western to early eastern Polynesia[107]. On the other hand, items unique to early eastern Polynesia include whale-tooth and bone reel ornaments, stone food pounders, and shell fishing gear. The latter is so important for archaeology that a short digression is needed.

Archaeological fishhooks in eastern Polynesia fall into two major groups (figure 11.14); bait hooks used for angling, and lure hooks which do not take a bait and which are usually towed along behind a moving canoe near the surface of the water. The bait hooks are generally of shell, bone or stone (stone ones seem to be restricted to Easter Island and Pitcairn), while turtle shell, wood (for catching shark and ruvettus) and coconut shell examples are known ethnographically. They may be made of one piece of material, or of two, in which case the shank and point are made separately and lashed together at the base. The lure hooks generally have a fish-shaped shank of pearl-shell or some other brightly coloured shell (e.g. *Haliotis* shell in New Zealand), and they have a curved point, of pearl shell, turtle shell or bone, lashed on to the base (figure 11.14 [1]). These lure hooks are used to catch voracious surface swimming fish such as the bonito, and are often termed 'bonito spinners'.

The archaeological fishhooks of the central Polynesian islands (Marquesas, Societies, and Cooks especially) are generally of pearl-shell, and the bait hooks are made in one piece, being of circular form (the so-called rotating hook) or U-shaped (the jabbing hook). Because shell is rather an intractable material, barbs are uncommon, except on specific islands such as Pukapuka and in some parts of Micronesia. In the Hawaiian islands, Easter Island and New

Zealand shell was used rarely, being generally replaced by bone. Bone is a stronger material than shell, and lent itself in these three areas to the production of two-piece bait hooks of larger size (such hooks being absent in central Polynesia), although the one-piece forms were also made (figure 11.14 [a–d, j, k]). The bone forms could also take barbs more easily. However, lure hook shanks were rarely made of bone, and the New Zealanders adapted to the use of stone for lure shanks in early sites, while the Easter Islanders dropped the use of lure hooks altogether. The Hawaiians could, of course, fall back on pearl-shell for this type of hook.

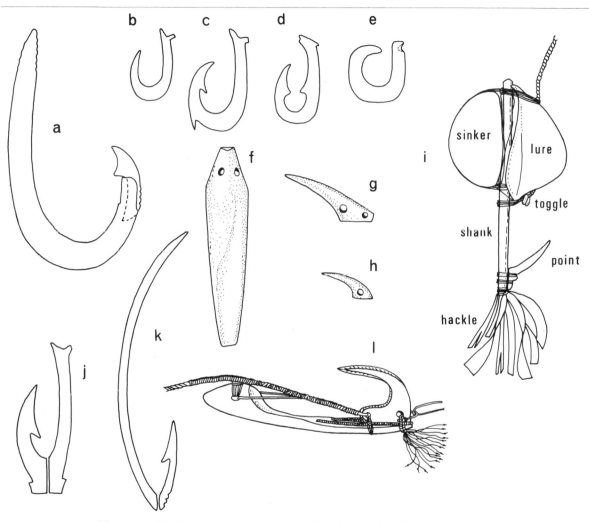

Fig. 11.14. Fishing gear from eastern Polynesia: (a–d, j, k) one and two piece bait-hook types from Hawaii (after Emory, Bonk and Sinoto 1959); (e) early form of Marquesan rotating hook of pearl-shell (after Sinoto 1970); (f) pearl-shell lure shank from Hane, Marquesas (after Sinoto 1967); (g, h) pearl-shell lure points from Hawaii and Borabora (after Sinoto 1967); (i) octopus lure of Hawaiian type showing positions of sinker, cowrie shell lure, and point (after Emory, Bonk and Sinoto 1959); (l) complete lure hook of pearl-shell from Pukapuka, showing details of lashings (after Beaglehole 1938).

The fishhooks of Oceania do show a bewildering typological variety, particularly the bait forms. This is not entirely coincidence, and Reinman has shown in two excellent articles[108] just why a fishhook is more than a mere bent pin. I cannot hope to summarise all of Reinman's information here, but he stresses the complexity of marine ecology and fish habits, as well as the importance of the raw material used in hook manufacture. As examples, circular forms of bait hook are best for shell, while bone will take a U-shape and barbing more easily. Incurved points on bait hooks are best for nibbling fish, while outcurved points suit voracious species better. Barbs are valuable for catching deep-sea fish, as they are held on the hook for longer.

The distribution of shell and bone fishing gear is another interesting topic. The bait hooks and bonito spinners are fairly universal in eastern Polynesia, with a few localised exceptions. They are also found widely in Micronesia, especially in the Carolines, and the forms here link up with eastern Polynesia through occurrences in the Ellice and Tokelau Islands. However, they are almost totally absent in western Polynesia, apart from the bonito spinners which are found in the ethnographic assemblages of Samoa and Tonga, but which may be late introductions. In Melanesia, shell bait and lure hooks are found in the Solomons and around eastern New Guinea, but in forms which are only rather remotely related to those of eastern Polynesia. Other localised developments of one-piece shell hooks in New Caledonia, eastern Australia, California and northern Chile may bear little relationship to Polynesia, although some kind of diffusion in these cases is obviously very possible[109]. Finally, Southeast Asia seems to have had only thorn hooks ethnographically, and this area, together with most of Melanesia, relied more on shallow-

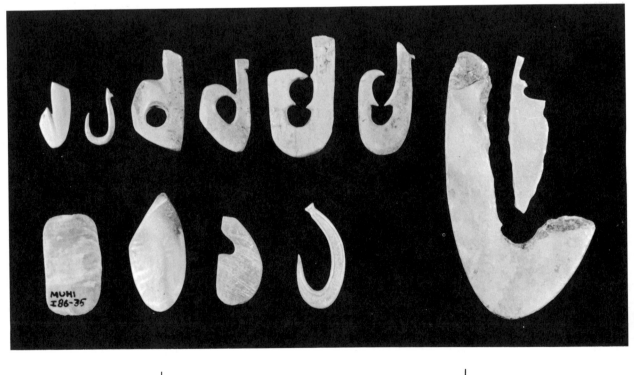

Fig. 11.15. Stages in the manufacture of one-piece hooks of pearl-shell; Hawaii, Tuamotu, Marquesas. From Sinoto 1967.

water trapping, netting and poisoning.

The details of these distributions may be culled from a monumental survey by Anell[110], who has suggested that the eastern Polynesian forms may have been derived from Japan, through Micronesia. Bone bait hooks, often barbed, are known from Neolithic sites in Japan and northern Asia, although there are no lure hooks in Japan, these being found only in some north Eurasian regions and in Oceania. Skinner[111] has also discussed possible north Pacific elements in Polynesian culture, and suggests that such things as slate knives, net and line sinkers, and harpoons (the latter found archaeologically in New Zealand, the Marquesas and Mangareva) may have diffused from the north too.

Now all this brings up a rather important consideration, for not all scholars, even today, agree on the totality of a Lapita origin for Polynesian culture. My own inclination is to give heavy stress to the Lapita Culture, which does of course have a small number of occurrences of shell bait and lure hooks (chapter 9) which in my view can quite adequately be considered as ancestral Polynesian and Micronesian forms. The same applies to adzes, although Duff[112] has attempted to derive the tanged eastern Polynesian forms directly from the Philippines, through Micronesia, despite the fact that these forms are absent in this area as they are in Melanesia and western Polynesia. Duff's argument has been refuted by Green[113], who has shown how tanging in eastern Polynesia develops independently of the tanging applied to adzes in Southeast Asia. Nevertheless, we may still need to reckon with perhaps a little diffusion into eastern Polynesia from an area such as Japan, perhaps through Micronesia, and evidently independent of the Lapita Culture and western Polynesia. Let us now return from this digression to our main topic – the Early Eastern Polynesian Culture.

The story, as we know it at present, seems to begin in the Marquesas Islands. These are rugged cliff-girt islands without reefs, and are relatively infertile by Polynesian standards. Most of the prehistoric settlement was concentrated in the bottoms of deep and narrow gorge-like valleys, and the earliest sites are found along the backs of the beaches, and in coastal rock-shelters. In 1956 and 1957 Robert Suggs conducted the first modern excavations here, and found, in beach deposits behind Ha'atuatua Bay on Nuku Hiva Island, an early assemblage which he thought dated to about the time of Christ, and which he related to antecedents in eastern Melanesia and western Polynesia. The assemblage included shell bait and lure hooks, mainly untanged adzes, shell vegetable peelers, a few plain potsherds, and bones of pig and dog. According to Suggs[114], it represented an initial settlement in the Marquesas from the west by a purposeful and well-equipped expedition. To an extent, Suggs was quite right on this point, but recent excavations at Ha'atuatua by Yosihiko Sinoto[115] have shown that Suggs confused several periods of occupation in his excavations, and the site has consequently passed into a kind of limbo. Whether the Marquesas really were settled at the time of Christ still remains uncertain.

It is thanks to Sinoto that we now have a very acceptable sequence for the Marquesas, and this comes mainly from his excavations in an open site behind the beach of Hane Valley, on Ua Huka Island[116]. He has also derived additional information from beach and rock-shelter excavations in the Hanaui and Hanatekua Valleys of northern Hiva Oa, and I was fortunate enough to work with Sinoto on these sites in 1968. Sinoto divides Marquesan prehistory into four phases, and for the moment our interest is with the first two; Phase I (Initial Settlement) – A.D. 300–600; Phase II (Developmental) – A.D. 600–1300.

The Phase I artefacts at Hane were associated with remains of rectangular timber houses and stone pavements, and, despite the importance of rounded house forms in Samoa, these have not been found so far in the Marquesas[117]. The artefacts themselves (figures 11.16, 11.17, 11.18) included simple adzes of Samoan types, but now differentiated by the presence of a few tanged examples, together with shell chisels and coconut graters, tattooing needles of bone or shell, breast pendants of perforated pearl-shells, and small perforated shell discs which may have formed parts of head-dresses. Pearl-shell fishhooks were present from the beginning, mainly of circular forms in Phase I, and a small amount of porpoise bone was in use as well. The lure hooks were of the important early eastern Polynesian type shown in figure 11.14 [1], mostly with a proximal extension at the base of the point. And last, but certainly not least, we have a few sherds of crude plain pottery like that from Ha'atuatua, and it is now known that pottery was only present at the very beginning in the Marquesas, and that it died out very quickly, presumably before the end of Phase I. Recent temper analyses by Dickinson and Shutler[118] have brought up the absolutely as-

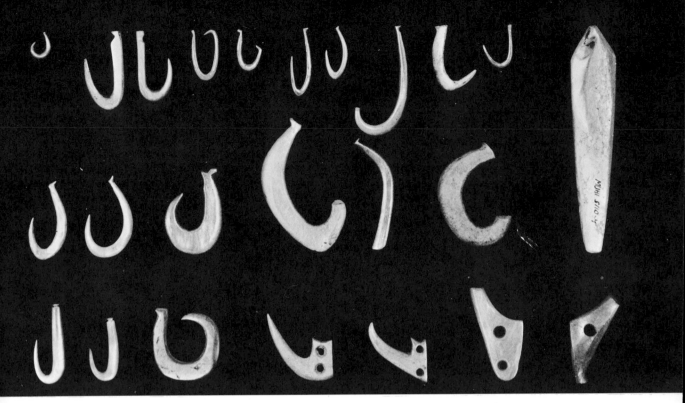

Fig. 11.16. Fishhooks of pearl-shell from the Hane site, Ua Huka. From Sinoto 1966.

Fig. 11.17. Early Eastern Polynesian artefacts from the Hane site, Ua Huka: (a) whale tooth reel ornament; (b–e) whale tooth pendants; (f) pearl-shell harpoon; (g) bone harpoon; (h–k) pendants of teeth and pearl-shell; (l–o) tattooing needles of pearl-shell, except (n), bone. From Sinoto 1966.

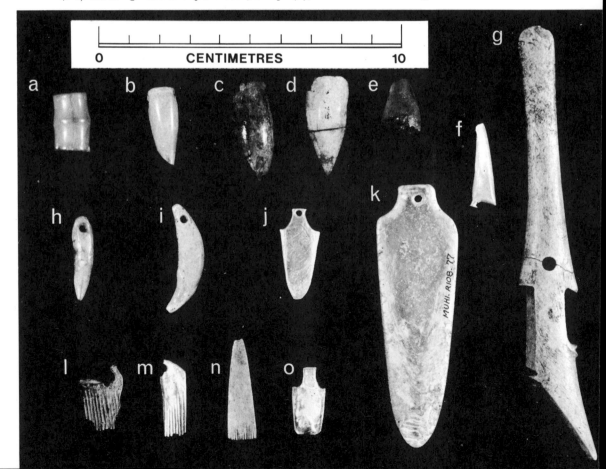

tounding possibility that two Marquesan sherds (one from Ha'atuatua, one from Hane) actually have sand tempers from the Rewa Delta on Viti Levu, Fiji. If this is so then a direct western origin for early Marquesan culture becomes almost a certainty, and the voyaging capabilities of Polynesians of two thousand years ago become rather dramatically enhanced.

Other Phase I artefacts at Hane include octopus lure sinkers like the ones from Vailele in Samoa, possible bone cloak pins, and small necklace ornaments of a very important kind (figure 11.17 [b–e]), made from shaped and perforated whale teeth. In Phase II these artefacts evidently develop with few changes, except that jabbing hooks tend to replace rotating hooks, and a few items such as harpoons, whale tooth reel ornaments, shell paring knives and stone food pounders make an appearance.

What we see, in short, is an Early Eastern Polynesian assemblage in the Marquesas which dates from about A.D. 300, and as such is so far the earliest known from eastern Polynesia. We will examine the question of priority again later, but it should be noted at this point that the early Marquesan assemblage cannot simply be derived straight from Samoa. The fishing gear, the ornaments and the tanged adzes do indicate a prior development outside Samoa, but whether this development took place in the Marquesas Islands themselves or some other island group we cannot really say at present.

Concerning the economy of the early settlers of the Marquesas, it appears from analyses of midden materials by Patrick Kirch[119] that fish, porpoises, turtles and sea birds were all of great importance in Phase I, but declined rapidly in importance during Phase II, most probably due to overexploitation. On the other hand, horticulture and shellfishing seem to increase in importance in Phase II and thereafter, and Kirch suggests (unlike Suggs) that the pig, dog and rat were not introduced until the end of Phase I. At any rate, the trend in the Marquesan economy is similar to that claimed for Hawaii and New Zealand, with initial coastal settlement and emphasis on exploitation of various native resources giving way gradually to both coastal and inland settlement with a predominantly horticultural economy, no doubt with increasing population density. It is of course almost certain that horticulture was known to the first settlers, but with small populations and abundant natural resources they would probably have found it more convenient not to indulge in the heavy labour of forest clearing and horticulture until the changing ratio of human population to natural resources forced them to do so (see page 145). And it may of course have forced them to do so very quickly – at least within a century or two – if reconstructions of population growth in other parts of Polynesia are any guide[120].

To date, the Hane assemblage remains the centre-piece of the Early Eastern Polynesian Culture, and it does owe its existence in some ways to environmental conditions in the Marquesas, which have enforced localisation of settlement and hence the formation of deeply

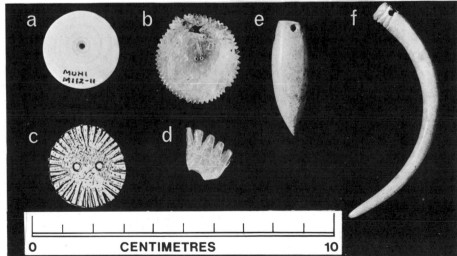

Fig. 11.18. Ornaments from eastern Polynesia: (a) *Conus* disc, Hane, Ua Huka; (b) pearl-shell disc, Hane, Ua Huka; (c, d) pearl-shell discs from Ha'atuatua, Nuka Hiva; (e) whale tooth pendant, Hane, Ua Huka; (f) perforated pig tusk, Hawaii.

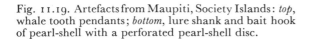

Fig. 11.19. Artefacts from Maupiti, Society Islands: *top*, whale tooth pendants; *bottom*, lure shank and bait hook of pearl-shell with a perforated pearl-shell disc.

stratified deposits within small areas. In the much more expansive landscapes of the Society and Hawaiian Islands, more limited luck has been forthcoming to date, but enough is known for a pattern to be visible.

In the Society Islands, the main site of the Early Eastern Polynesian Culture is a burial ground located on a small coral islet in the lagoon of Maupiti Island, where 16 burials with grave-goods were excavated in 1962 and 1963[121]. The burials were extended or flexed, and the goods included adzes like the ones from Hane, but with a higher percentage (about 25%) provided with tangs; pearl-shell lure hooks and one-piece hooks, again very close to the Marquesan forms; shaped whale-tooth pendants; a perforated whole pearl-shell pendant; and a perforated shell disc. (figure 11.19). All these items are very closely paralleled in Phases I and II at Hane, although Maupiti probably correlates with Phase II in time, having radiocarbon dates between A.D. 800 and 1200.

Since 1973, another site with an assemblage of the Hane and Maupiti type has been excavated by Sinoto at Vaitootia, in Fare village on the island of Huahine[122]. As well as the adzes, fishhooks and other shell artefacts, this site has produced whalebone and wooden hand-clubs of the *patu* type used by the New Zealand Maoris (page 403), and also what may be a simple religious structure consisting of a single basalt upright on a coral base. The lower waterlogged layer in the site also yielded remains of two wooden storehouses raised on stone and wooden piles, together with fragments of sennit, coconut shell, pandanus keys, and gourds. Radiocarbon dates suggest that the site may date between A.D. 850 and 1150, although Sinoto prefers a slightly earlier date on typological grounds.

One very important point about these early Society Island assemblages concerns their astonishing similarity to that from the best known early burial ground in New Zealand, at Wairau Bar in Marlborough Province. New Zealand prehistory is a topic for chapter 13, but the Maupiti burial orientations and the artefacts are all so closely paralleled at Wairau Bar that a direct Society Island origin for the first settlers of New Zealand is very likely.

In the Hawaiian Islands, assemblages similar but not identical to the Marquesas-Society Island types were established by about A.D. 600. Occupation levels dating to between A.D. 600 and 1000 at Bellows Beach on Oahu[123] have produced fishhooks, adzes and a shell coconut grater of Early Eastern Polynesian type, together with bones of pig, dog and rat. At the mouth of the Halawa Valley on Molokai Island[124], a similar assemblage has been found in association with successive round-ended houses (figure 11.20) dating to between A.D. 600 and 1200. Both the Halawa site and Bellows Beach produced flakes of a basaltic glass which can be dated by a technique known as hydration-rind dating (a similar technique is used for dating obsidians), and these dates provided a useful independent confirmation of the carbon dates for the sites[125]. Whether the Halawa houses can be related directly to similar round-ended houses in Samoa is not certain, as the form appears to be absent in the Marquesas. However, round-ended forms are dominant in Easter Island and the Society Islands at slightly later dates, as we will see below.

In the Ka'u District at the southern end of the island of Hawaii, excavations were carried out in the 1950s on two important sites; a rock-shelter at Waiahukini, and a series of beach deposits at South Point. Vast numbers of fish-hooks were found in these sites, which have lent themselves to a fairly elaborate typological study using seriation methods[126]. An astonishing total of 59 radiocarbon samples were submitted from the two sites for dating, and the results might perhaps be described as variable in the wildest sense. Nevertheless, rough agreement seems to have been reached that the main lower level at Waiahukini dates to between A.D. 750 and 1250, while the lower level at South Point might date from about A.D. 1000[127].

The two sites between them produced over 2600 whole or broken fishhooks, mainly of the bait type, with bonito spinners being present but much rarer than in central Polynesia. Most of the hooks were of bone, with pearl-shell used mainly in the early levels, and, as we noted above, many of the Hawaiian bait hooks of bone were made in two pieces (sometimes with a wooden shank) and have parallels in the bone-using areas of Easter Island and New Zealand. As in the Marquesas, the early one-piece bait hooks are predominately of the rotating type, while the jabbing hooks become more common later. Also present are stone sinkers for octopus lures of the 'coffee-bean' type present in stage II in the Marquesas. Typological analyses show clearly that the earlier bait hooks, both one and two-piece, tend to have grooved line attachments and

Fig. 11.20. Part of a round-ended house with pavement at one end, Halawa dune site, Molokai. From Kirch 1971a.

lashing areas, while the later ones (after A.D. 1300) tend to be knobbed. However, this typological sequence is apparently local to the island of Hawaii, and the early hooks from Bellows Beach and Halawa are knobbed.

The Early Eastern Polynesian assemblage from Hawaii clearly shows some marked differences from the assemblages of the Marquesas and Society Islands, despite the suggestions by Green[128], and Emory and Sinoto[129] that Hawaii was first settled from the Marquesas. While the one-piece bait hooks and the lure hooks may be similar to central Polynesian forms, other features such as the use of barbs and the two-piece bait hooks are not. In addition, the shaped whale-tooth pendants[130], bone reels and per-forated shell discs have not been found at all in Hawaii. This may mean that there are earlier sites still to be found in the group, and it is not without the bounds of possibility that the Hawaiian Islands could themselves be the prim-ary dispersal centre for eastern Polynesia. At present, the case for Marquesan primacy is not completely watertight.

This in fact brings us to a rather crucial question; can we hope to isolate the exact pattern of early eastern Polynesian settlement at all? It is fairly clear that as we go back in time in eastern Polynesia, so the assemblages converge more and more until they reach hypothetical unity in the primary dispersal centre. Because the assemblages did not differentiate to any great extent until well after the islands were settled[131], it is clear that we are in a very unsound position to draw migration arrows on maps. The Marquesas stand as the primary dispersal centre at present because they have the earliest carbon dates and the best conditions for preservation. But while identification of the Marquesas may be correct, this is obviously a situation where one discovery elsewhere could overturn the whole framework.

The best known and most recent framework for the settlement of eastern Polynesia to date is given in the diagram illustrated here as figure 11.21, which I have taken from a recent article by Sinoto. My use of this diagram does not mean that I agree with all the arrows, for the reasons I have given above. Marquesan primacy is not totally established, and the theories of double movements to Hawaii and New Zealand need further examination, as we will see below. For the present, we can accept this diagram as a working hypothesis only.

It is necessary here to re-cap a little on what I have defined as the Early Eastern Polynesian Culture. Its component artefacts are best

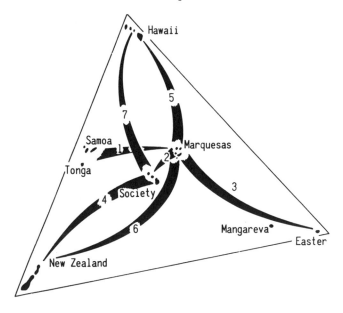

Fig. 11.21. The pattern of Polynesian settlement as reconstructed in 1968. From Sinoto 1968.

illustrated from the Marquesas Islands and Maupiti, and the range as known from Hawaii is, so far, less complete. The Wairau Bar assemblage from New Zealand probably represents settlement of this area towards the end of the time-span of the culture, before it was broken up by regional differentiation. It seems to have been established in the southern Cooks by A.D. 900, to judge from my own findings on Aitutaki Island[132], and it undoubtedly spread in some form to Easter Island, although little is known of the Early Period there in terms of artefacts. For the other areas of eastern Polynesia we know very little, although Green[133] has postulated settlement of Mangareva from the Marquesas, possibly about A.D. 1000 on the evidence of fishhooks.

As I have defined this culture it obviously has no sharply marked end, and its break-up into the regional Polynesian cultures observed at European contact of course began as soon as the various islands of eastern Polynesia were settled from the primary dispersal centre. I simply use the term 'Early Eastern Polynesian Culture' to include the relatively homogeneous assemblages of the area prior to about A.D. 1200, as after this approximate date there seems to be good traditional and archaeological evidence for increasing isolation. But it should not be forgotten that eastern Polynesian cultural development is a continuum, and any temporal division of it will naturally be chosen in terms of convenience for research workers. We have no foreign invasions or periods of marked economic change (except possibly in New Zealand) to mark out our temporal phases for us.

Finally, the Early Eastern Polynesian Culture does show certain trends in development, with the disappearance of pottery in the Marquesas, the increasing importance of tanged adzes, typological changes in fishhooks, and perhaps the more marked importance of shaped whale-tooth pendants and bone reel ornaments coming towards the end. We do not need to postulate any marked developments in economy, apart from a possible increasing dependance on horticulture as natural resources were depleted, and pigs, dogs and rats were certainly present in the primary dispersal centre, although the status of the chicken is uncertain. One major problem remains; to clear up the obvious gap between the earliest Marquesan assemblage and its presumed parent in Samoa.

Footnotes

1. Haddon and Hornell 1936–8. Excellent illustrations of Oceanic canoes are given by Dodd 1972, and Lewis 1972. See also Doran 1974.

2. Lewis (1972: chapter 10) discusses Oceanic voyaging canoes and their capabilities. See also Bechtol 1963.

3. Banks (in Beaglehole 1962: 319) describes what may have been a Fijian type of canoe in Tahiti, with unequal hulls 15.5 and 10 metres long. This example appears to be unique in eastern Polynesia.

4. Corney 1913–9, Vol. II: 285–6.

5. Beaglehole 1967, part I: 164.

6. Beaglehole 1967, part I: 87.

7. The Raiatean navigator Tupaia accompanied Cook on part of his first voyage.

8. Dening 1963; Lewthwaite 1966b.

9. Wilson 1799: 203.

10. This observation was made by Anderson during Cook's third voyage.

11. Corney 1913–9, Vol. 1: 306.

12. Williams 1838: 88.

13. Gayangos, in Corney 1913–9, part II: 187–94.

14. Lewthwaite 1967; Sharp 1963: 32.

15. Smith 1898–9.

16. Best 1923a: 8.

17. Dixon 1934.

18. Bollons 1924.

19. Sharp 1963. An earlier version of this book (Sharp 1956a), in which Sharp stressed accidental rather than one-way voyaging, was criticised in detail from a traditionalist viewpoint by Parsonson (1963).

20. Akerblom 1968.

21. Boulinier and Boulinier (1972) provide a contrary argument for accepting the use of zenith stars.

22. Voitov and Tumarkin 1967.

23. Dening 1963.

24. Riesenberg 1965.

25. Levison, Ward and Webb 1973; see also review by Bellwood 1975b.

26. Levison, Ward and Webb 1973: 47.

27. Lewis 1972: map 2.

28. Dening 1963.

29. Gladwin 1970; Lewis 1972.

30. See also Hilder 1963 on navigational stones in the Gilberts, and Williams 1838: 97 on backsighting on landmarks in the southern Cooks.

31. The advantages of north-south sailing in an area with prevailing easterly winds have been discussed by Heyen (1963).

32. For some of the background to the *Hokule'a* see Finney 1967. I owe my present knowledge of the canoe to Herb Kane, Ben Finney, and David Lewis, and I was fortunate enough to be living in Honolulu while the trip was underway. Some specifications for the canoe are as follows (in British measurements): overall size 60 by 15 feet, with two hulls, each 3.5 feet wide and 5 feet deep; deck 10 by 8 feet; laden weight approximately 25,000 lbs. Sennit lashings and mat sails were used, while the hulls were of modern materials. The cargo included one dog, two chickens and one pig, plus traditional foodstuffs intended for planting. All arrived in Tahiti in good form, except for the taro. I have no information about the results of the return voyage.

33. Howard 1967.

34. e.g. Banks (for 1769) in Beaglehole 1962, part I: 372; part II: 37; Varela (for 1774) in Corney 1913–9, part II: 256–7; Wilson 1799–86. Cook held the same view.

35. Williams 1838: chapter 29.

36. Ellis 1969a: 122. Colenso (1868) held a similar but more extreme view.

37. Howard 1967: 49.

38. Hale 1846.

39. By Lesson – See Howard 1967: 53–4.

40. Barrere 1967.

41. See Kelly 1967.

42. Many articles have been written on the value of traditions and genealogies. See especially Buck 1926; Stokes 1930; Luomala 1951; Piddington 1956; Robertson 1956; 1962; Suggs 1960b; Barrère 1967; Bellwood 1977a. The matter is discussed further in connection with New Zealand on pages 382ff.

43. For an interesting case of exaggeration, see the Samoan and Rarotongan traditions recorded by Stair (1895).

44. Fornander 1878–80.

45. Smith 1898–9 (3rd ed. 1910); 1921.

46. Mesopotamian and Indian origins for the Polynesians were also favoured by Elsdon Best (1923b).

47. Fraser 1895.

48. Brown 1907; 1924; 1927.

49. Churchill 1911; 1912.

50. Williamson 1924, Vol. 1.

51. Dixon 1920.

52. Linton 1923.

53. Handy 1928; 1930a; 1930b.

54. Luomala 1951.

55. Buck 1938. Buck's view was partially anticipated by Shortland in 1868.

56. Piddington 1939.

57. Sapir 1916: 49.

58. Piddington 1939: 339.

59. Piddington 1939: 335.

60. Buck 1944: especially pp. 473–7.

61. Spoehr 1952.

62. Heine Geldern 1952.

63. Schmitz 1961.

64. Burrows 1938.

65. Vayda 1959.

66. Anell 1955.

67. e.g. Nordenskiold 1933; Dixon 1934; Emory 1942; Buck 1938; Heine Geldern 1952; Hornell 1945.

68. Jacoby 1967.

69. Heyerdahl 1950.

70. Heyerdahl 1952. For summaries see Heyerdahl 1968.

71. Heine Geldern 1952.

72. Suggs 1960a: chapter 16.

73. Suggs 1960a.

74. Green 1967. See also Emory 1959. Other recent general articles on Polynesian origins include Marshall 1956; Ferdon 1963; Golson 1959b; Bellwood 1975a.

75. Cook visited the Tongan Islands on his second and third voyages (see Beaglehole 1967; 1969).

76. Wilson 1799: 234–5.

77. Goldman 1970: chapter 12.

78. For Tongan traditional history see Gifford 1919; Claessen 1968.

79. McKern 1929.

80. Wilson 1799: 241.

81. Davidson 1971a.

82. Davidson 1969b.

83. McKern 1929: 92–101; Green 1970b: 16.

84. Kaeppler 1971.

85. Green and Davidson 1969; 1974.

86. Two other sites in north-west Upolu have recently been reported by Jennings (1976).

87. These early levels at Vailele were first excavated by Golson in 1957 (see Golson 1959b; 1969b).

88. Summarised in Green 1972a.

89. In Green and Davidson 1974: 142.

90. Green 1971a.

91. Green and Davidson 1969: 134–5; and see Poulsen 1970 for shell artefacts.

92. Green 1972a: 84–5; Green 1968.

93. Sahlins 1958; see survey by Davidson 1969a.

94. Davidson 1969a.

95. Davidson 1969a: 66.

96. Davidson 1969a: 67.

97. Scott 1969.

98. Sahlins 1958.

99. Ember 1959; 1962. See also Williams 1838: 454.

100. Freeman 1964.

101. Ember 1966.

102. Goldman 1970: Chapter 11.

103. Burrows 1938: 77–8; Kirch and Rosendahl 1973: 28.

104. Green 1970a.

105. Bellwood 1970.

106. Emory 1968; Green 1971a.

107. Poulsen 1970; Green 1968: 104.

108. Reinman 1967; 1970. See also Sinoto 1967 for manufacturing techniques.

109. For diffusion through transport of fishhooks in fish stomachs, see Landberg 1966. Fishhooks from the north coast of Chile are particularly close to Polynesian forms, and fall into the same categories of one– and two-piece bait hooks and lure hooks. See Willey 1971: figures 3–10, 4–5, 4–6, 4–7.

110. Anell 1955.

111. Skinner 1968.

112. Duff 1959; 1970.

113. Green 1971a.

114. Suggs 1961a: 60–65; 1961b.

115. Sinoto 1966a; 1968a.

116. Sinoto 1970.

117. Suggs claimed to have found round-ended houses at Ha'atuatua, but the evidence is inconclusive.

118. Dickinson and Shulter 1974.

119. Kirch 1973.

120. e.g. Groube 1970 for New Zealand.

121. Emory and Sinoto 1964.

122. Sinoto 1975, and personal communication. See also Gérard 1975 for recent finds (including a reel-shaped ornament) on Moorea.

123. Pearson, Kirch and Pietrusewsky 1971; Kirch 1974.

124. Kirch 1971a; Kirch and Kelly 1975.

125. Barrera and Kirch 1973; Kirch 1974.

126. Emory, Bonk and Sinoto 1968.

127. Emory and Sinoto 1969; Green 1971b.

128. Green 1966.

129. Emory and Sinoto 1964.

130. Cox 1967.

131. Operation of the 'founder effect' (Vayda and Rappaport 1963) might have caused some initial small-scale variation from island to island.

132. Bellwood 1977a.

133. Green, unpublished notes, University of Auckland.

CHAPTER 12

The Prehistory of Polynesia: Part Two

LATER EASTERN POLYNESIAN PREHISTORY (c. A.D. 1200–1800)

For the last 600 years of Polynesian prehistory we have quite clear evidence from archaeology, linguistics and ethnology that cultural differentiation was taking place at an appreciable rate in eastern Polynesia. The ethnological evidence, particularly that pertaining to material culture, is available in great detail from many sources, and it is not my purpose here to document inter-island variation in such subjects as clothing, woodcarving, pastimes, weaving methods, or the many other cultural traits which are virtually invisible in the archaeological record. The latter in itself is a sufficient illustrator, particularly in such categories as adze and fishhook typology, temple and house architecture, stone carving, and a wide range of lesser archaeological phenomena. The absence of pottery, never found in eastern Polynesia except in the basal Marquesan levels, is naturally something of a drawback for archaeological analysis, but not an insuperable one. Why pottery making should have been discarded by sedentary and populous agricultural societies is not very clear, and raw materials are not lacking except on atolls. The Tongans never adopted pottery making from their Fijian neighbours after the extinction of Lapita pottery, and baking and roasting necessarily replaced boiling in Polynesian cuisine. Wooden bowls, coconuts, bamboos and gourds were used for water storage, and while one could sit down and imagine numerous reasons for the demise of Polynesian pottery, none are ever likely to find acceptable proof.

Among the more interesting manifestations of later Polynesian culture are the stone temple structures, or *marae*. From the Early Eastern Polynesian Culture there is the single basalt upright at Vaitootia in the Society Islands, described on page 324, and it may be that this is a forerunner of the later and more complex examples. On Easter Island there are a number of very remarkable stone platforms dating to before A.D. 1000 (see pages 366–7), and contemporary structures of this kind may also have been quite widespread in central Polynesia, although no direct evidence has survived. As far as eastern Polynesia is concerned generally, it seems likely that the initial settlers held their religious ceremonies in god-houses, similar to the ones used ethnographically in western Polynesia. Before movements out of the primary dispersal centre in eastern Polynesia had taken place, the god-house was evidently relegated to a subsidiary function of storage of paraphernalia, while the focus for rituals became a line of upright stones, a small platform, or a combination of the two. This focus was almost certainly termed an *ahu*[1], and quite simple structures still called by this term survived at European contact in New Zealand and the northern Marquesas Islands, as we will see below.

However, the peoples of the central Polynesian Islands – southern Marquesas, Tuamotus, Societies, Australs and Cooks – frequently elaborated on the simple *ahu* plan either by placing platforms or lines of upright slabs across the ends of large rectangular courts, which could be anything from a cleared rectangle covered with sand to a finely paved and walled courtyard, or by constructing complex arrangements of terraces. In these islands the term *ahu* was retained for the platform itself, but the term *marae* came into general use for the whole structure, and this term is the general one used by archaeologists today to refer to the whole class of stone religious structures in eastern Polynesia. The term *marae* (or *malae* in Samoa and Tonga) refers to an open space in the centre of a settlement in New Zealand and western Polynesia, so it looks as if the central Polynesians at a fairly late date (almost certainly after A.D. 1000) combined the secular *malae* and the sacred *ahu* into a single community structure. As we will see later, the *marae* of each island do in themselves vary greatly in design, but we can nevertheless see a pattern which most probably does reflect historical development[2].

If the *marae* provide a very valuable source of information for the later phases of eastern Polynesian prehistory, then so too do adzes. In the early sites such as Hane and Maupiti, the adzes tend to be very varied in such characters as tanging and cross-section, and the adze makers seem to have been experimenting with a whole range of possibilities. By about A.D. 1300, however, we find a pattern of stabilisation beginning, and several island cultures begin to specialise in one form of adze at the expense of all others. The later adzes of Polynesia have been classified

by Duff[3], and we have seen already how his classification applies to the adzes of Southeast Asia. In Polynesia there are a few differences – for instance, the shouldered, pick and beaked adzes are not found – but the type 1 (tanged quadrangular) and type 2 (untanged quadrangular) adzes are very important, as they are in the Philippines-Taiwan-South China region. However, Polynesian forms which are not common in Southeast Asia include types 3 and 4 (with triangular cross-sections), and the rare type 5, which has a tang chipped from the side rather than the front of the adze (the so-called 'side-hafted adze').

By A.D. 1200 the adzes with plano-convex cross-sections had dropped from the eastern Polynesian inventory, and the quadrangular and triangular forms dominate the field from here on. The Hawaiians concentrated almost entirely on the tanged 1A adze, the Maoris on the untanged and hammer-dressed 2B (often made of hard andesites which were unavailable in the tropical Polynesian islands), and the central Polynesians of the Society, Tuamotu, Austral and southern Cook Islands concentrated on the tanged type 3A adze (figure 12.1 [b]). To a lesser extent the Marquesans appear to have specialised in the

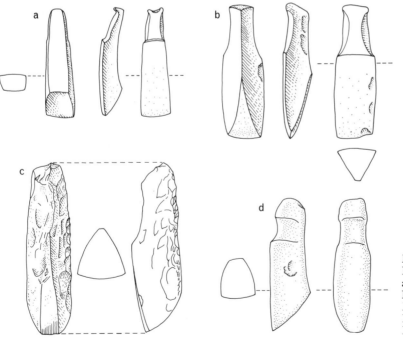

Fig. 12.1. Adze types of eastern Polynesia (after Duff 1959, except (c) after Suggs 1961): (a) Duff type 1A, Nassau, northern Cook Islands; (b) Duff type 3A, Society Islands; (c) Duff type 4A, Marquesas Islands; (d) Duff type 4D, Easter Island.

tanged type 4A adze (figure 12.1 [c]). What we see is an increasing tendency towards specialisation, with the central Polynesians being linked into a well-defined group possessing the type 3A. Cutting across this specialising trend we can perhaps pick up a few traces of diffusion; for instance, Duff[4] has stressed the importance of a particular type of 1A adze which has relief lugs left on the poll (figure 12.1 [a]), and this is found in small numbers in the Society, Austral and Cook Islands and New Zealand. Duff feels that the form was diffused from the Society Islands at about A.D. 1100–1400.

The trends in cultural development and change in eastern Polynesia are well reflected in *marae* and adzes, and we will look at other types of archaeological information for individual islands below. What is fairly clear in later prehistory is that the central islands (Societies, Australs, Tuamotus and southern Cooks) retain a good deal of cross-contact, while the peripheral islands (Hawaii, Marquesas, Easter and New Zealand) develop numerous idiosyncracies in their isolation. It is now time to look at the individual cultures themselves.

THE MARQUESAS ISLANDS

The early Europeans who visited the Marquesas Islands found themselves among one of the healthiest populations in Polynesia. Captain Cook observed 'The Inhabitants of these Isles are without exceptions as fine a race of people as any in this sea.'[5] The Marquesan environment, with its limited supplies and proneness to drought, seems to have produced a normally well-fed, but fairly egalitarian society, with populations divided into narrow but isolated valleys. Each valley had its chiefs and priests, but paramount chiefs with authority in more than one valley do not seem to have existed. The valley populations were frequently on very hostile terms with their neighbours, and warfare, cannibalism and human sacrifice were undoubtedly common in the eighteenth century. Some observers also reported mountain strongholds defended by earthworks (figure 12.2) and palisades, with raised platforms ('fighting-stages') inside for hurling missiles down on to the enemy[6]. Forts of this kind are otherwise rare in eastern Polynesia, with the marked exceptions of New Zealand and Rapa.

Fig. 12.2. Rock-cut ditch of fort above Taiohae, Nuku Hiva, Marquesas. (See also colour plate.)

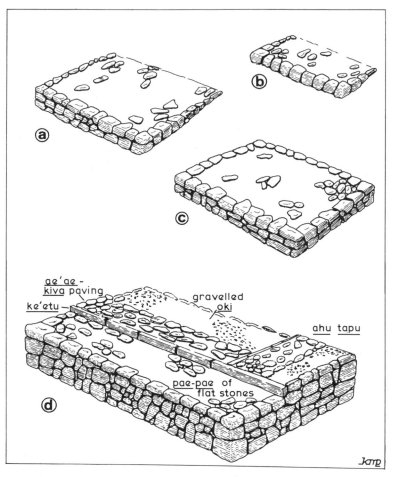

Fig. 12.3. Types of house platforms (*paepae*) in the Marquesas Islands. (d) has a separate raised sleeping area at the back, faced with cut slabs of red tuff (*ke'etu*). From Bellwood 1972a.

The Marquesas are particularly well-supplied with accounts by Europeans covering the period 1595 to 1840, and some of the more famous observers include Quiros (1595), Cook and the Forsters (1774), Marchand (1791), the Duff Missionaries (1797), Fanning (1798), Porter (1813), and Krusenstern, Lisiansky and Langsdorff (1804). Early residents include Edward Robarts (1797–1804), the missionary William Crook (1797–9), and the renowned Herman Melville (*c.* 1842)[7]. These writers all give valuable accounts of the social and material culture of the Marquesas, but the first comprehensive ethnographies of the group were not produced until the 1920s, by Linton and Handy[8].

The prehistoric development of Marquesan culture is quite well-known, and the islands have long been of interest to archaeologists owing to the presence of massive stone constructions and statues. Naturally, the surviving examples of these constructions belong to the final phases of prehistory, because constant rebuilding by an expanding population would leave few untouched survivals from an earlier era. If there are such survivals they may never be located, and we know very little about stone construction in the Marquesas prior to about A.D. 1300.

The later period of Marquesan prehistory has been divided by Sinoto[9] into Phases III (Expansion – A.D. 1300–1600) and IV (Classic – A.D. 1600–1800). Artefact changes are not especially marked through this period, but the Duff type 4A adze tends to become dominant, and the shaped whale-tooth pendants disappear, while reel-shaped ornaments (figure 11.17 [a]), similar to examples found commonly in New Zealand (page 388) may become more important in Phase III. Amongst the one-piece fishhooks the jabbing form replaces the rotating, and the points of the bonito spinners lose their proximal extension, as they do in the Society and Hawaiian Islands at about the same time. Dogs become extinct in Phase III for some unknown reason, and evidence for cannibalism may indicate an increasing population, in accord with expectancies. A phase IV assemblage has recently been excavated in Hanapete'o Valley, Hiva Oa, and we see here the complete dominance of jabbing hooks, together with imitation whale-tooth pendants made of cowrie shell[10]. At European contact real whale-teeth were status items, worn only by high-ranking individuals[11], and by this time there is no evidence for the artificial shaping found in the Phase I and II examples.

The large stone structures, so characteristic of eighteenth century Marquesan culture, make their appearance in Phase III, although simple pavements are present earlier at the Hane site. The larger dwellings, frequently recorded by earlier voyagers, were raised on high rectangular platforms (*paepae*) sometimes exceeding thirty metres in length, and comprised a paved front verandah with an inner gravelled sleeping area (figure 12.3 [d]), the two often being separated by a step faced with cut slabs of red tuff. The house itself had a very steep rear roof which reached down to the *paepae* surface, while the front roof sloped more gently down to eaves about two metres above the pavement. Associated with some of the dwelling houses, particularly on Hiva Oa, would be a high stone platform for an embalming house for the dead. The chiefly establishment comprised a number of structures[12], including dwellings for attendants, warriors and old men, as well as two very important ceremonial structures – the *me'ae* and the *tohua*.

The term *me'ae* as used in the southern Marquesas is the equivalent of the term *marae*, used more widely to mean temple in central Polynesia. The southern Marquesan *me'ae* comprise complex

and very irregular groupings of terraces, with *paepae* built on the terraces for the houses of priests and sacred paraphernalia. The priests' houses are recorded as having unusual obelisk shapes, up to twenty metres high on Hiva Oa[13]. In the northern Marquesas, particularly on Nuku Hiva, the temples were much simpler structures, consisting of a house on a single raised platform. As noted above, the term *ahu* was retained for these structures. A rather magnificent description of one of these structures in Taipivai Valley, Nuku Hiva, has been given to us by Herman Melville;

> Here and there, in the depths of these awful shades, half screened from sight by masses of overhanging foliage, rose the idolatrous altars of the savages, built of enormous blocks of black and polished stone, placed one upon another, without cement, to the height of twelve or fifteen feet, and surmounted by a rustic open temple, enclosed with a low picket of canes, within which might be seen, in various stages of decay, offerings of breadfruit and coconuts, and the putrefying relics of some recent sacrifice.[14]

The structure described by Melville seems to have been a fenced enclosure rather than a house, but god-houses are described by other early nineteenth century writers[15] sometimes with images inside, and the northern Marquesas do

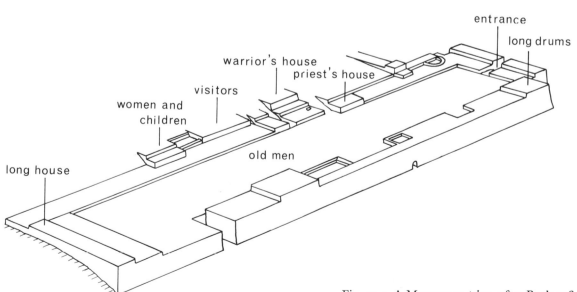

Fig. 12.4. A Marquesan *tohua*, after Buck 1964.

long house

women and children

visitors

warrior's house

priest's house

old men

entrance

long drums

rank closely with western Polynesia in possessing god-houses of this type, which are not recorded elsewhere in eastern Polynesia with the exception of Hawaii. Melville seems to have made a mistake in his reference to polished stone, unless he was simply referring to a water worn appearance. Actual cut stone was used only for the low slab facings of house floors in the prehistoric Marquesas, and there is none of the elaborate shaping that one meets on Easter and a few other Polynesian islands.

The *me'ae* of the Marquesas seem to have been of two functional types – mortuary and public – according to Linton and Handy[16]. The mortuary *me'ae* were usually in secluded places, and often had lined pits set into them for the placing of bones. The public *me'ae* near the chiefly establishments were generally associated with splendid ceremonial structures known as *tohua*, which were a unique Marquesan development. These *tohua* consisted of rectangular flat areas, sometimes built into hillsides by terracing, which were used for ceremonies. Around them were raised platforms of various sizes used by spectators and high-ranking personages (figure 12.4). Sir Peter Buck[17] has given an excellent imaginative reconstruction of a ceremony in one of these *tohua*, but again we turn to Melville for a shorter but equally evocative quote:

> In the midst of the wood was the hallowed 'hoolah-hoolah' ground – set apart for the celebration of the fantastic religious ritual of these people – comprising an extensive oblong 'pi-pi', terminating at either end in a lofty terraced

altar, guarded by ranks of hideous wooden idols, and with the two remaining sides flanked by ranges of bamboo sheds, opening towards the interior of the quadrangle thus formed. Vast trees, standing in the middle of this space, and throwing over it an umbrageous shade, had their massive trunks built round with slight stages, elevated a few feet above the ground, and railed in with canes, forming so many rustic pulpits, from which the priests harangued their devotees[18].

The *tohua* described by Melville was in the Taipivai Valley on Nuku Hiva, and this island was the focus of the largest structures of this kind. In 1957 one of the largest Taipivai *tohua*, named Vahangeku'a[19], was surveyed and test-excavated by the American archaeologist Robert Suggs. It was built on an artificial terrace cut into a hillside, 170 by 25 metres in area, faced by a 3 metre high wall of enormous stones on the downhill side (figure 12.5). The plaza is surrounded by massive raised *paepae*, many with the upper surfaces stepped to support houses, and Suggs has estimated that the amount of earth used in the basic terrace alone would be about 9,000 cubic metres[20]. This huge structure was evidently built over several centuries and reached its final form at about the time of European contact.

Suggs did make a rather brave attempt to excavate and date a number of stone structures on Nuku Hiva, but was rather thwarted by the lack of associated artefacts and carbon samples. The essence of stratigraphy is burial, and as stone

Fig. 12.5. Lower terrace walling of the *tohua* Vahangeku'a, Taipivai Valley, Nuku Hiva. (See also colour plate.)

structures tend to sit rather stubbornly on top of the ground for several centuries they are notoriously difficult candidates for successful archaeological dating. So in 1968, when I was working with Yoshiko Sinoto on Hiva Oa Island, I decided to see what information could be gleaned from stone structures without resorting to excavation. A lead in this respect had been given by Marimari Kellum-Ottino[21], who had carried out detailed surveys of stone structures in Hane Valley on Ua Huka. I used a plane-table to survey every stone platform, wall, terrace and store-pit in the valley of Hanatekua on Hiva Oa, and, while amassing a rather indigestible mass of data about the structures themselves, I was also able to draw a few conclusions of more general interest[22]. Firstly, the valley fell clearly into three sections. The lower part was mainly under plantations of coconut, and possibly other trees as well, and had few dwellings. There may have been two small *tohua* here, now destroyed. The middle section had many dwellings near a large stone-walled fort, together with many small walled plantations for breadfruit trees, and pits for the storage of fermented breadfruit – a Marquesan hedge against famine. The largest *me'ae* were also in this middle section. The upper section was rather narrow and restricted, and seems mainly to have been given over to terraces for tuber cultivation. It seems that the bulk of the population was clustered in the middle of the valley, perhaps for defence and protection from tidal waves, and they kept their precious breadfruit trees close-by, this being the major food throughout the Marquesas. The houses were not tightly clustered into anything like a village, and were fairly evenly distributed about 50 metres apart, as with the general non-nucleated pattern observed throughout the Marquesas Islands.

The other exercise I attempted in Hanatekua was to estimate the population of the valley from its food-producing capacity, and then use the derived figure to acquire an estimate for the total Marquesan population at about 1800. I suspect from this analysis that the total Marquesan population was not much over 30,000, despite much higher estimates by early explorers. Nevertheless, we are still left with the fact of a shocking drop in population to under 4000 persons by 1900 – a dismal advertisement for the advantage of European civilisation.

Finally, we may note one other achievement of the prehistoric Marquesans – the carving of large stone anthropomorphic statues. Such statues,

Fig. 12.6. Marquesan stone statue in the Taipivai Valley, Nuku Hiva. (See also colour plate.)

often of red tuff and up to 2.5 metres high, were placed in various positions on or in the faces of platforms or ceremonial structures, particularly on the islands of Nuku Hiva and Hiva Oa. Squat, bent-kneed and usually goggle-eyed, with flaring nostrils, thick wide lips, and hands placed on tummies, these statues represent one of the peaks of the stone carvers' art in Polynesia (figure 12.6). They are undoubtedly overshadowed by the massive statues of Easter Island, but only otherwise paralleled by similar large statues on the island of Raivavae in the Australs. Elsewhere in Polynesia, especially in some of the Hawaiian and Society Islands, the only stone statues produced were of much smaller size.

In 1956, two of the best known Marquesan statue groups, in the Taipivai Valley on Nuku Hiva and the Puamau Valley on Hiva Oa, were investigated by Ferdon and Heyerdahl[23]. Associated carbon dates suggested that these large and well-carved statues dated to about A.D. 1500, quite late in the Marquesan sequence. Heyerdahl compared them with similar large statues from San Agustin in Colombia, and claimed influence from this area to the Marquesas and Raivavae about A.D. 1500. However, while the similarities noted by Heyerdahl are to the point, I cannot see that the Marquesan statues are much different from smaller wooden and stone examples from other parts of Polynesia – a little wooden fisherman's god from Rarotonga is, in my opinion, almost an exact parallel (figure 12.17). The problem of possible South American influence in Polynesia is nevertheless rather a thorny one, and we will return to it later in connection with Easter Island.

It only remains to note that the Marquesas, like many other Polynesian islands, are quite rich in rock engravings. These include stylised and goggle-eyed human masks, spread-eagled human figures, dogs and fish, and they are obviously in the same tradition as the petroglyphs from Hawaii and Easter Island in particular, although one can trace parallels back through Oceania to at least as far as New Caledonia. Since no-one has ever made chronological sense of the myriad petroglyphs of Oceania, I do not propose to follow the matter further. Leaving the Marquesans to rest, we can now turn our attention to the traditional centre of eastern Polynesian affairs.

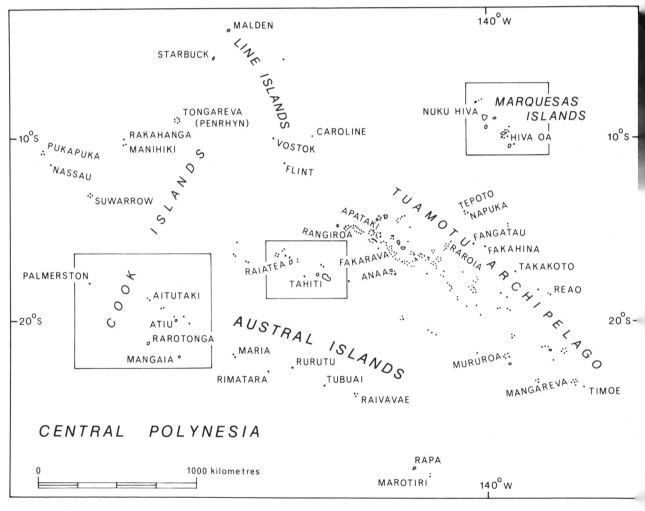

Fig. 12.7. Map of central Polynesia. For insets see figure 11.6.

CENTRAL POLYNESIA – THE SOCIETY, TUAMOTU, AUSTRAL AND SOUTHERN COOK ISLANDS

Throughout this chapter I have been using the term central Polynesia to refer to the islands of the Society, Austral, Tuamotu, and southern Cook groups, and it is well established that these islands at European contact shared sufficient linguistic and cultural homogeneity for them to be identified as a secondary culture area within eastern Polynesia. The central Polynesian grouping was set out in some detail by Burrows in 1938[24], although he chose to include the Hawaiian Islands, while I feel these are sufficiently discrete in cultural terms to merit separate consideration.

Linguistically, the languages of the central Polynesian islands belong to the Tahitic subgroup of eastern Polynesian (see chapter 5), and the common proto-language may have broken up only about 1000 years ago. While it seems likely that the proto-language was originally developed in the Society Islands, this cannot be proven conclusively, although it does look as though the southern Cook and Austral Islands were uninhabited until the late first millennium A.D. The Society Islands certainly have the strongest archaeological and traditional evidence for primacy.

The homogeneity of ethnographic material culture in central Polynesia was established most fully by Buck in 1944[25]. He did not consider the Tuamotu Islands in much detail, probably for lack of information, although we do know from the Spaniards who visited Tahiti in 1774–5[26] that the Tahitians claimed fourteen islands in the north-western Tuamotus as tributaries, and these islands included the large and important atolls of Apataki, Rangiroa, Fakarava and Anaa. The Tahitians evidently acquired coconuts, fish, birds, pearl-shell, dogs and mats from this area. Buck was able to list many items widespread in the Society, Austral and southern Cook Islands which were absent or rare elsewhere in Polynesia, and these included special forms of coconut graters, food pounders, wooden seats, ponchos, slit gongs, the Duff type 3A adze, and several other items. His analysis also tended to suggest that the southern Cooks and Australs had been in particularly intensive contact, especially through the island of Mangaia.

Buck's observations were of course fairly expectable. The central Polynesian islands are fairly close together, and we have many records of drift voyages, particularly from the Societies to the southern Cooks. The missionary John Williams was quite astonished to find that a Tahitian woman had arrived on Rarotonga sometime between 1797 and his official discovery of the island in 1823, and had told the Rarotongans wonderful stories about Captain Cook, metal tools, and Jehovah and Jesus Christ. So excited were the Rarotongans that they even built a *marae* to Jehovah and Jesus Christ[27]. In addition to information of this type, we have the accounts of Tahitian geographical knowledge (see above) which indicate that the Tahitians knew most of the islands of central Polynesia, and there is strong traditional evidence in support which we will examine in due course.

Naturally, however, regular contacts were not kept up throughout the area right through prehistoric times, and the southern Cook and Austral Islands were individually fairly well isolated, each showing quite marked cultural differences in some respects (particularly *marae* architecture). The only area of very frequent inter-island voyaging seems to have been within the Society Islands, and here the islands are close enough together to be intervisible (even across the 180 km gap between Tahiti and Huahine)[28]. The small islands of Mauke, Mitiaro and Atiu in the southern Cooks also seem to have been in regular contact, with political dominance being wielded by Atiu at European contact over a minor hegemony[29].

Having established the scene, we may now turn to each of the island groups in more detail, beginning with the Society Islands – once described as 'the hub of Polynesia' by Peter Buck.

THE SOCIETY ISLANDS

The Society Islands are divided into two groups; Leeward, including the important islands of Raiatea, Tahaa, Borabora and Huahine; and Windward, including Tahiti itself, and Moorea. These are all volcanic islands of great natural beauty, and at European contact were inhabited by what may be considered a single ethnic group. Modern anthropologists have no hesitation in recognising Society Island society as amongst the most stratified in Polynesia, with an upper class of powerful chiefs (*ari'i*), a class of lesser chiefs and landholders (*ra'atira*), and commoners (*manahune*). Although society was most probably originally organised along Polynesian ramage lines, with all members linked genealogically and the chiefly lines claiming seniority of descent, it is quite clear that by European contact these links had been broken, and a relatively endogamous chiefly class had established itself over localised bilateral groups of commoners, as in Hawaii[30]. As King noted on Huahine in 1777:

> there is not perhaps a single instance where merit or abilities have rais'd a low man to a high rank amongst them; the Classes keep seperate & distinct from one another[31].

As if to prove the point, a high chief of Huahine at the time was a boy aged about 10, and one of his chiefly contemporaries on Tahiti was aged only about 9.

According to Goldman, the main ways by which a commoner could achieve status in the Society Islands were through military distinction or by the grades in the Arioi Society. The latter was a particularly interesting institution, most highly developed in the Societies, but with cognate institutions in the Marquesas, southern Cooks, Tuamotus and Australs. The society was said to have been founded on the island of Raiatea in the sixteenth century, and was sacred to the god Oro. Its members were patronised by local chiefs, and in the Societies they moved around the districts and islands giving dramatic and choral performances. They practised infanticide; the women were compared by Buck to European actresses who could not afford to have children if they were to fulfil their engagements, and they also seem to have indulged in a degree of promiscuity which most early writers tended to gloss over. It has in fact been claimed by several authors that the society was based on a fertility cult[32].

The early explorers have given us most of our definite information about the Arioi. Banks (in 1769) was disgusted by their free sex, and stated that members who had children were expelled from the society unless the baby was given away or killed. Cook in 1774 saw 60 canoe loads of Arioi sailing from Huahine to visit their brethren in Raiatea, and Wilson in 1797 recorded that one man of chiefly rank had destroyed eight children in order to preserve his rank within the society. Wilson also noted that many plantations on Tahiti were situated inland, in order to escape the depradations of Arioi members.

The explorers of the late eighteenth century left so many observations, particularly about Tahiti, that I cannot hope to compress everything into a few pages. But let us stay with them for a while longer to see one of the most magnificent societies of Polynesia in operation[33].

In 1769, the island of Tahiti was divided amongst a number of independent chiefdoms, although Cook mistakenly thought that Tu, chief of the Pare district, was king of the whole island. The chief of Pare did, however, have control of the atoll of Tetiaroa, about 40 km north of Tahiti, which was exploited for fish and other resources. Banks saw 25 canoes come in from Tetiaroa with a supply of fish to Pare in 1769. In the Leeward Societies, Raiatea was the island of highest traditional status, indeed in the whole Society group, and Cook was told of its former eminence, while Varela was told a tradition in 1774 that Tahiti was settled from this island. Wilson (1797) tells how mythology was taught regularly on Raiatea, and how its priests established themselves in positions of great importance on Tahiti. Ellis, writing in 1830, related that the first humans as well as the great god Oro, son of Ta'aroa, were born in the sacred district of Opoa, where still stands today the *marae* Taputapuatea, one of the major religious centres of Polynesia. However, by 1767, Raiatea had declined in secular power, and its districts were under the control of appointees of the high chief of the neighbouring island of Borabora.

None of the explorers failed to notice the power of the chiefs in the Society Islands, on a par with their counterparts in Tonga and Hawaii. Only chiefs were allowed to wear a special girdle of red or yellow feathers; they presided over human sacrifices, were carried from place to place on the backs of retainers, and subjects had to bare the upper parts of their bodies before them (unlike Tonga, there was evidently no prostration). Any house entered by the chief (except his own) had to be burnt afterwards with all its belongings, owing to the tremendous strength of the *tapu* surrounding him. Chiefs controlled land distribution, and frequently called for tribute from the lesser orders, although much of the tribute was quickly channelled back to the people through feasts and gifts, apart from that dissipated amongst retainers and the Arioi grades. If a chief struck a union with a commoner, infanticide was the usual rule for any offspring, but if the union was deemed to be in order then the eldest son would inherit his father's title on birth (hence the very young chiefs mentioned above), and the father would thereafter act as regent until his son reached maturity. Chiefs were also entitled to eat pork frequently, and to a simple form of mummification after death. Naturally, these

Fig. 12.8. The *marae* Mahaiatea. From J. Wilson 1799.

privileges applied mainly to the *ari'i* class, and the *ra'atira*, while certainly not without power, would have more fulfilled the role of landed gentry and advisory council members for the *ari'i*, and were probably not 'fatt and lusty' as the latter appeared to Captain Cook.

Paramount chiefs are individuals of some interest to anthropologists, not least because they do control large concentrations of manpower and resources. In Tahiti we can see the material effects of this in the great temples and war fleets (see above) – the prerogatives of highly stratified and populous[34] societies. As Banks pointed out, 'The greatest pride of an inhabitant of Otaheite is to have a grand *Marai*', and Banks himself was fortunate enough to see the grandest of them all just after its completion; the *marae* Mahaiatea, constructed by the chieftainess Purea of Papara district at the peak of her power, before her defeat by the warriors of Taiarapu in 1768. Banks was very excited by this *marae*, recording 'we no sooner arrivd there than we were struck with the sight of a most enormous

pile, certainly the masterpiece of Indian architecture in this Island so all the inhabitants allowd. Its size and workmanship almost exceeds belief'[35].

The platform of Mahaiatea measured 81 by 22 metres at the base, and rose as a stepped pyramid with 11 steps, each 1.2 metres high, making a total height of 13.5 metres. The steps were faced with courses of squared volcanic stones, over a basal course of coral blocks, and the platform was placed at the end of a sizeable walled court 115 metres long[36]. Banks was truly amazed at the amount of labour needed to quarry and fetch the stones, and then to dress them to shape, and it is a tragedy that this monument is now virtually destroyed, although even in Banks' day the ground beneath the platform had evidently subsided under the weight, so some of the destruction may have arisen from natural causes. Very fortunately, the site was visited again in 1797, and we have an accurate drawing from this time which shows clearly the structure of the platform, although the court enclosure wall has been erroneously replaced by a fence (see figure 12.8). The measurements made in 1797 differ from those of Banks, and the total height may in fact have been about 15.5 metres.

The *marae* of the Society Islands were first described in detail by Emory in 1933[37]. He clearly demonstrated the differences between the Windward and Leeward Island structures, the former having *ahu* (platforms) of coursed basalt or coral blocks, sometimes dressed into shape, while the latter have *ahu* faced with upright slabs of reef coral. He divided the Windward *marae* into three types, the first (and possibly the earliest) being the type most commonly found inland on Tahiti and Moorea, with a small *ahu* with uprights on top and in front, set at one end of a walled or unwalled court (figure 12.9). The second type is an intermediate form between the inland type and the larger coastal type, the latter having a stepped *ahu* right across one end of a walled court, with stone uprights restricted to the court only. The *marae* Mahaiatea, described above, is the largest known example of this coastal type.

Emory viewed the series inland-intermediate-coastal as chronological, and on a general level this sequence may well be correct. However, it is clear that at least the coastal and inland types were in use together at European contact, so that their occurrences probably reflected social ranking. The coastal forms were generally built by chiefs in favourable coastal locations, while the simpler kinds were either joined to coastal *marae* as subsidiary shrines, or apparently built by lesser ranking members of society in inland plantation areas. Green and Green[38] have recently analysed the detailed descriptions referring to coastal *marae* by Bligh (1792) and Cook (1777),

and have shown that the coastal *marae* with stepped *ahu* were used by high chiefs, and that they may have developed in the eighteenth century with the spread of the cult of Oro from Raiatea. The inland types, which have close parallels in the Tuamotu and Hawaiian Islands (see below), are almost certainly of earlier date as an architectural form, while the coastal ones are unique to Tahiti and Moorea.

The Leeward Island *marae* do not show the same variety as those in the Windwards, and have more simple *ahu* (only two stepped ones are known). In addition, the courts are rarely walled. The famous *marae* of Taputapuatea on Raiatea, centre of the worship of Oro, is of the normal Leeward type, with an *ahu* faced with large coral slabs up to 4 metres high, covering an area of 40 by 7 metres. Clam shells recently taken from the fill of this *ahu* have given a carbon date in the seventeenth century[39]. At Maeva village, on the island of Huahine, there stands a remarkable cluster of no less than 25 *marae* of this type (figure 12.10), and several of these have recently been restored by Bishop Museum personnel from Honolulu.

From late eighteenth century accounts we have a lot of information about the uses of the *marae* and their component parts (figure 12.11). The court uprights were used as backrests for participants and to represent ancestral spirits, and were sometimes covered with cloth. The *ahu* was sacred to the gods, who seem to have been represented by carved wooden boards (*unu*) or stone slabs set up on top. Other structures such as round-ended priests' houses, raised wooden platforms for sacrifices, sacrifice pits, and small portable god-houses for religious paraphernalia

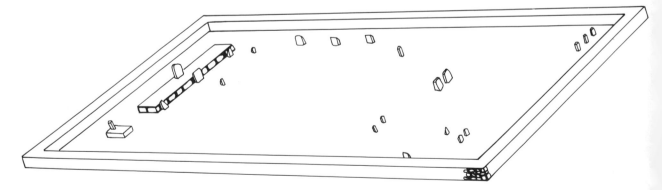

Fig. 12.9. *Marae* of Tahitian inland type (sketch). After Emory 1933.

Fig. 12.10. Two-tiered *marae* platform of Leeward Island type, *marae* Manunu, Maeva, Huahine. (See also colour plate.)

Fig. 12.11. A *marae* scene observed on Tahiti during Cook's third voyage (drawn by J. Webber). An *ahu* with skulls and carved *unu* is in the background, and a human sacrifice lies in the foreground.

(including human skulls) have all been recorded. Human sacrifices and the bodies of important chiefs were buried in *marae*, although the former were sometimes left to rot in the open air, cannibalism being unrecorded for Tahiti. Other stone structures in the Society Islands include horned platforms for the chiefly sport of archery[40] (figure 12.12), and low kerbed house foundations. Tahitian houses are recorded up to the remarkable length of 130 metres, and those of high-ranking persons seem generally to have been round-ended.

Despite its obvious splendour, we unfortunately have very little archaeological knowledge to throw light on the evolution of Society Island culture. We do, however, have a number of now-outdated non-archaeological theories, the best known perhaps being that by Handy[41]. His view was that the Society Islands were first settled by a simple egalitarian type of society which he called Old Tahitian, and then later, about the seventh century A.D., a new migration arrived – the Ari'i stratum – bringing the aristocratic tradition with its complexity of status institutions. Buck's 1944 theory[42] was similar to that of Handy, although he only accepted one basic migration into the area, after which the Ari'i concentrated themselves on Raiatea and imposed their society on the surrounding islands, including Tahiti, after receiving their domesticated plants and animals from Melanesia via Samoa. Both Buck and Handy placed a lot of stress on the role of Raiatea, and this is justified to an extent in the light of the late eighteenth century records. However, Luomala[43] has pointed out that the traditional evidence for actual political domination by Raiatea

is weak, and the idea of a conquest of the large island of Tahiti may not be very sound. Perhaps we should view Raiatea as a centre of religious innovation, but express reserve about the possibility of secular domination.

Archaeological sites in the Society Islands which postdate the Early Eastern Polynesian Culture consist mainly of house sites, *marae*, and a few coastal middens. Such middens excavated at the mouth of the Opunohu Valley on Moorea[44] have yielded assemblages going back to about A.D. 1100, and the artefacts here, while different from those at Maupiti, are almost certainly in the same unbroken evolving tradition. The Opunohu adzes are mainly tanged and of Duff types 4A and 3B, while the Maupiti adzes were more varied and mainly untanged. Furthermore, such Early Eastern Polynesian items as the shaped whale-tooth pendants and shell discs are absent from the Moorean sites, although this could be due simply to the absence of burials. Just when ornaments of this kind finally disappeared is unknown. Other Opunohu items such as a shell gouge, a shell coconut grater, and the bonito spinners continue the early Polynesian tradition, and there is at present no artefactual evidence which would suggest any sharp discontinuity in the evolution of Society Island culture.

It remains only to mention some intensive settlement pattern work carried out by archaeologists on Tahiti and Moorea[45], as the results of the Moorean work especially do throw a lot of light on the nature of society at European contact. Society Island settlements were not nucleated, and as in most other parts of Polynesia were simply scattered amongst plantations on coastal flats and in valley bottoms, with periodic clustering around chiefly establishments and *marae*. In the Opunohu Valley, on Moorea, Roger Green and colleagues have surveyed several hundred structures in inland clusters two or three kilometres from the coast, and these include agricultural terraces, small rectangular dwelling houses and larger round-ended community houses, and many *marae*. The latter fall into Emory's coastal and inland groups, but with so much variation that Green has established a new classification dividing them into 12 types[46]. Excavations on some of the sites showed that most belonged to the eighteenth century and were probably in use at European contact, but one round-ended house was dated to the thirteenth century, so occupation of this inland portion of the valley may have begun at this time.

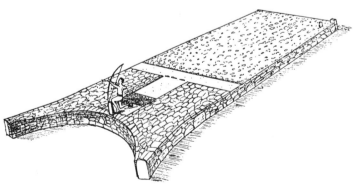

Fig. 12.12. Horned archery platform in the Papenoo Valley, Tahiti. From Emory 1933.

From ethnohistorical sources and the surveys, Green has suggested that at least two maximal ramages dwelt in the valley, and he has, to my mind very convincingly, attempted to correlate the stone structures with the hierarchies in the ramage systems. There is one very fine *marae* with a stepped *ahu*, of Emory's coastal type, and this, on the basis of well-documented parallels in Tahiti (see above), is connected by Green with the highest ranking chiefly line. It is probably no coincidence that this *marae* is also in the most densely settled portion of the valley. Other *marae*, of increasing simplicity, are associated by Green with lesser ramage segments (*mata'eina'a*) or individual family groups, and the *mata'eina'a* also used the round-ended houses for community activities or as chiefs' dwellings. Commoners apparently had rectangular houses of smaller size.

As one would expect, structures associated with low-ranking segments of society, such as individual extended families, are much more common than those associated with larger ramage segments. Amongst the *marae*, the single example of highest status is ranked above eight of lesser ramage segment status, and 47 which, according to Green, are of individual extended family status. The whole exercise, which I cannot describe in full here, is an excellent example of how a well-preserved settlement pattern can enable archaeologists to throw a great deal of light on the structure of a prehistoric society. It also shows how this structure is reflected in simple geography, with settlement clusters located away from the main chiefly focus being apparently of lesser rank. Of course, the idea that the complexity or size of a stone structure necessarily relates exactly to the rank of its builder is not always going to be correct, but with a very large sample of sites, which Green has, the proposed correlations do become much more convincing, particularly when balanced against ethnohistorical data.

THE TUAMOTU ARCHIPELAGO

To the east of the Society Islands lies a remarkable belt of low coral atolls, stretching for about 1300 km from north-west to south-east. The largest atolls in this chain are set fairly close together in the north-west, within reach of contact from Tahiti, while moving south-eastwards the islands get smaller and further apart. Most of the far south-eastern atolls were in fact uninhabited or only very sparsely populated at European contact, and one of these islands, Mururoa, has recently attained a questionable fame as a site for atomic bomb tests. Beyond the south-eastern Tuamotus lies Mangareva, comprising a number of small

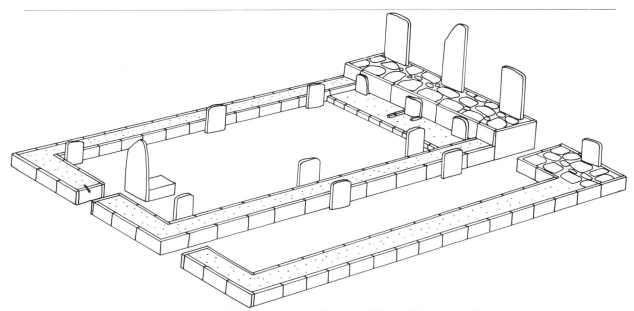

Fig. 12.13. *Marae* Mahina-i-te-ata, Takaroa Island, Tuamotus. Length 10 metres. After Emory 1934a.

volcanic islands within a lagoon. Because of its isolation Mangareva had evolved a prehistoric culture which differed in some respects from that in the Tuamotus generally.

Most of our archaeological knowledge of the whole region is restricted to *marae*, and it is thanks again to Kenneth Emory that we have excellent records of many of these structures[47]. Remains of dwelling sites and stratified archaeological deposits do not seem to have survived, and this is not surprising on these barren coralline islands with their sparse and scattered populations. Mangareva is an exception here, and excavations were undertaken here some years ago by Roger Green[48], who found fishhooks and other material dating back to about A.D. 1200, and concluded that the group had been settled from the Marquesas. Emory was also of this opinion[49], although it seems on geographical grounds that Mangarevan culture should be as closely related to the Tuamotus as it is to the Marquesas.

The Tuamotuan *marae* as described by Emory are basically of the Tahitian inland type. The general pattern consists of a low *ahu* with upright slabs, usually three, in a line on top (figure 12.13). Courts tend to be unpaved and unwalled, although there are many exceptions, and the courts generally have uprights set up within them. On Takakoto, Fakahina and Fangatau atolls some of the coral uprights were shaped into forms which could, with a little imagination, be described as anthropomorphic, and, astounding as it may seem, similar shaped uprights which are very obviously in the same tradition are found in *marae* on the isolated atoll of Penrhyn, some 1800 km to the north-west (see below).

Not all the Tuamotu islands have *marae* which conform to the general pattern, and considerable local diversity is one of the characteristics of this class of Polynesian architecture. On Reao, the *marae* have high and well-constructed *ahu* with many uprights on top, and the *ahu* sometimes have a lower *ahu* abutting directly in front, the whole facing into a walled court. On Tepoto Island one *marae* surveyed by Emory was without *ahu* or court, and consisted simply of two parallel lines of uprights, some with little individual platforms in front to serve as seats. On Mangareva there are unfortunately very few surviving *marae* remains, but one fine example was surveyed by Emory on the neighbouring atoll of Temoe, consisting of an *ahu* with two steps set into its front, facing an unwalled court. This *ahu* had no uprights on it at all, and is another good example

of the great variation which one gets in the basic Polynesian *marae* pattern.

The Tuamotuan *marae* in their most common form, as found in the north-western islands, are obviously similar to the inland *marae* of Tahiti, but this may not mean that all the Tuamotus were necessarily settled from this source. However, we do know from Emory's analysis of *marae* usage in the Tuamotus[50] that the *marae* here served the same functions as their counterparts in Tahiti; they reflected rank and population distribution, and their appendages, such as uprights, godhouses, storehouses and *tapu* refuse pits, all fitted the Society Islands functional pattern.

THE AUSTRAL ISLANDS

The Australs comprise a number of very isolated volcanic islands in the vicinity of the Tropic of Capricorn, south of the Societies. Four islands of the group – Rimatara, Rurutu, Tubuai and Raivavae – are each about 200 km apart in a rough east-west line, and if one looks at figure 12.7 one will see that they form a geographical continuum with the southern Cooks, the whole forming a thin chain of islands running from north-west to south-east for over 2500 km. Culturally, the southern Cooks and Australs formed a continuum in late prehistory, and I have referred to Buck's detailed analysis of material cultures above. All these islands shared the Duff type 3A adze as a dominant form, as did the Societies to a lesser extent, and even in *marae* types we can see that neighbouring islands right through the chain do share specific similarities; Mangaia and Rurutu certainly do so, and Rimatara might fit between them, except that this is the only island in the chain about which virtually nothing is known. I should point out that Rapa, isolated 500 km away from the other Australs, does not fit into this cultural chain, and as might be expected developed some quite interesting local idiosyncracies, not least of which are its spectacular terraced forts.

If we exclude Rapa for the moment, most of our knowledge of prehistory in the group centres on *marae*, except for Rurutu, which has been the scene of detailed work by French archaeologist Pierre Verin[51]. Beginning with *marae* architecture, we see that the simplest structures are in the eastern islands of Tubuai and Raivavae, while from Rurutu into the southern Cooks they tend to become more complex. The Raivavae *marae* consisted of paved rectangles surrounded by upright slabs up to 4 metres high forming a kind of fence, and did not have *ahu*[52]. One of them, *marae* Unurau, was approached by a slab-lined avenue 150 metres long, which had two stone statues flanking its commencement. Raivavae is an island famous for its huge stone statues, up to 2.7 metres high, and in fact ranks second after Easter Island on the Polynesian scale of stone statue sizes, with the Marquesas coming a close third. One of the Raivavae *marae* was excavated by the Norwegian Expedition in 1956[53], and several statue fragments were found in association with it, although apparently not in their original positions. The *marae* of Tubuai seem to have been fenced on only three sides[54], and are simpler versions of the Raivavae ones, again without *ahu*.

The island of Rurutu is perhaps most famous for a wooden god, shown in figure 12.14 and now in the British Museum. In 1821, a party of Rurutuans was driven by a storm from Tubuai to the Society Islands, and from here the missionary John Williams returned them to their home with two Raiatean deacons, who were to introduce Christianity to Rurutu. When these two men returned to Raiatea they had with them the wooden god, which was displayed during one of the London Missionary Society services. Williams described it as follows:

> One in particular, Aa, the national god of Rurutu, excited considerable interest; for, in addition to his being bedecked with little gods outside, a door was discovered at his back, on opening which, he was found to be full of small gods; and no less than twenty-four were taken out, one after another, and exhibited to public view. He is said to be the ancestor by whom their island was peopled, and who after death was deified[55].

Why the Rurutuans appear to have had no knowledge of the great Society Island gods Ta'aroa and Oro is not clear, and may simply be due to isolation. At any rate, A'a is undoubtedly one of the most magnificent pieces of wood sculpture to have survived from central Polynesia.

While it appears that some of the Rurutu *marae* were like the ones on Tubuai[56], many seem to have been more complex, and this is particularly true of those in the remarkable prehistoric village at Vitaria, on the north-western coast of the island, investigated in great detail by Verin. Vitaria is a unique site in Polynesia by any standards, comprising at least 60 houses running in roughly parallel lines for about half a kilometre.

Fig. 12.14. Wooden carving of A'a, Rurutu.

Verin seems to feel that he has only uncovered about half of the area, so it could be that we are here dealing with a prehistoric ribbon of houses up to one kilometre in length, aligned locally along parallel streets and around plazas. Given the extreme rarity of village clustering of this kind in Polynesia I am at a loss to explain the situation, unless it be connected with extreme localisation of resources, coupled with chronic warfare (although the village does not appear to be defended). Since there are other reported villages on Rurutu like Vitaria, there may be a strong element of cultural choice involved as well.

The Vitaria houses are all round-ended, and the kerb settings which once outlined their walls are placed on top of rectangular stone-faced earthen terraces. The village as it survives is certainly very late prehistoric, but Verin did excavate an occupation level below one house which gave a carbon date of about A.D. 1050. Scattered amongst the houses, and sometimes sharing house terraces, are the *marae*, about fourteen in total, which generally comprise one or more paved rectangular courts, with or without *ahu*, and surrounded by spaced uprights of basalt. Many of the house terraces also have uprights set in rows along the fronts of their terraces, perhaps to serve as casual backrests.

The artefacts found at Vitaria are of the general late central Polynesian types; Duff type 3A adzes, stone food pounders, and one-piece fishhooks of shell. Bonito spinners were absent, as they were generally in late prehistory in the Australs and southern Cooks. Unfortunately, Verin was not able to provide a dated sequence of changes in artefacts or *marae*, although this is a problem which still affects most areas of central Polynesia.

To finish the Australs, we turn to isolated Rapa, an island just outside the tropics, and without coconuts, breadfruit, pigs, dogs or chicken at European contact. Its population depended heavily on wet-field taro grown in terraces of a kind very common in Polynesia, particularly in the southern Cook, Austral and Hawaiian Islands (see chapter 6). We know little about their prehistoric culture, and the islanders did not make the Duff type 3A adzes or shell fishhooks which characterised the rest of central Polynesia in late prehistory. Instead, they developed two unique adze forms, one being a Duff type 1, often with a knob left on the poll, and the other being a type 2 with a scarfed grip, paralleled rather remotely in the scarfed adzes of type 4 found commonly on Easter Island (see figure

12.1 [d]). Of Rapan *marae* and houses we know virtually nothing, but we do know that the inhabitants of this rugged and barren little island practised frequent warfare amongst themselves, and they developed some very remarkable methods of defence. Endemic warfare within Polynesia was not unique to Rapa – the Mangaians, the Marquesans and the Easter Islanders appear to have had a remarkable penchant for it – but none of the other eastern Polynesians (excluding the Maoris) attempted to build earth-work forts with anything like the finesse of the Rapans.

The Rapan forts[57] are at ridge junctions high in the knife-edge terrain of the island, and comprise central sculpted towers surrounded by lower terrace arrangements – either in rings, or radial lines, or both. Some of the terraces and towers are stone-faced, and when very steep they have climbing stones set into their faces. The central towers are generally too small for dwellings, and may have been used by chiefs when coordinating defences during an attack. However, the lower terraces presumably did have dwellings, and in the fort of Morongo Uta (figure 12.15), cleared by the Norwegian expedition in 1956, the lower terraces were divided by cross-walls into separate dwelling areas, and also fenced in by low walls along their front edges. Some of them had little shrines cut into their back walls for miniature *marae* comprising parallel rows of tiny upright basalt prisms – rather touching symbols of Polynesian religion at the family level (figure 12.16).

Owing to rain and hasty excavation methods, the Norwegian expedition found no house remains at Morongo Uta, but their reconstruction of the site, shown in figure 12.15, seems to be reasonably acceptable. The round-ended houses are certainly conjectural, and it is not certain that this was the prehistoric shape for Rapa. Artefacts from the site included adzes of the Rapan types, together with stone food pounders, and it dates to somewhere between A.D. 1650 and 1800. Another unfortified site on Rapa produced a carbon sample dated to about A.D. 1300, and this is the earliest yet for the island. Just when Rapa was settled and where from remains unknown, but the most likely source would be in the Australs to the north.

THE SOUTHERN COOK ISLANDS

The southern Cooks comprise nine islands, of which four – Rarotonga, Aitutaki, Mangaia and

Fig. 12.15. Reconstruction of a Rapan terraced fort, Morongo Uta. From Heyerdahl and Ferdon (eds.) 1965.

Fig. 12.16. Miniature *marae* in the Morongo Uta fort, set into a terrace wall. From Heyerdahl and Ferdon (eds.) 1965.

Atiu – will be discussed here. These are all volcanic islands, but Mangaia and Atiu have raised coral circumferences, as does Rurutu. Ethnographically, they are among the better known Polynesian islands, having been particularly well served by such prolific writers as Peter Buck and the nineteenth century missionary William Wyatt Gill. Percy Smith also based his great work on Polynesian migrations on traditions collected on Rarotonga[58]. Furthermore, a lot

Fig. 12.17. Wooden fisherman's god from Rarotonga, 32 cm high.

of archaeology has been carried out in these islands, by the Canterbury Museum from Christchurch, and more recently by myself when based at the University of Auckland[59].

According to the traditions collected by Smith, the southern Cooks were probably settled about A.D. 8–900. Buck, in his major work of 1944, felt that they were only settled about 600 years ago, from the Society Islands at the beginning of the period of Raiatean dominance. My own work suggests that Smith was nearer the mark, as in 1970 I excavated a coastal midden at Ureia on Aitutaki, which yielded a Duff type 4A adze and shell fishhooks dating to about A.D. 950. This is the earliest site in the Cooks, and it suggests that these islands were settled, perhaps from the Societies, during the later span of the Early Eastern Polynesian Culture. This of course is many centuries later than initial settlement in the Marquesas, but Cook Island culture as we know it (together with Austral Island culture) does equate quite happily with the later first millennium A.D. culture of the Society Islands.

The southern Cooks are also the closest eastern Polynesian islands to Samoa, and it is not surprising that very good traditional evidence survives for a Samoan settlement on Rarotonga about A.D. 1300, in the person of the chief Karika. Karika arrived on Rarotonga with a Tahitian contemporary named Tangi'ia, and these two men founded the main chiefly lines of the island[60]. By a stroke of good luck, a cache of adzes of definite Samoan form (Duff type 4E) was found near the main settlement of Avarua on Rarotonga some years ago, and when I excavated this site in 1972 I found that the adzes were probably associated with a dwelling unit consisting of a rectangular house with associated cookhouse, and shell fishing gear of eastern Polynesian type, all dating to between A.D. 1250 and 1450. These Samoan-type adzes are known only from the cache, and most of the other adzes from the site are of the common central Polynesian type 3A, which seems to have been established as the dominant form on the island by at least 1400. However, the site does provide some evidence in support of an important tradition, and we may perhaps see a small Samoan intrusion into a culture of eastern Polynesian type, round about 1300. This intrusion did found a very important chiefly line, even if the overall impact of Samoan material culture on Rarotonga was clearly negligible.

As a result of my work in the southern Cooks, I

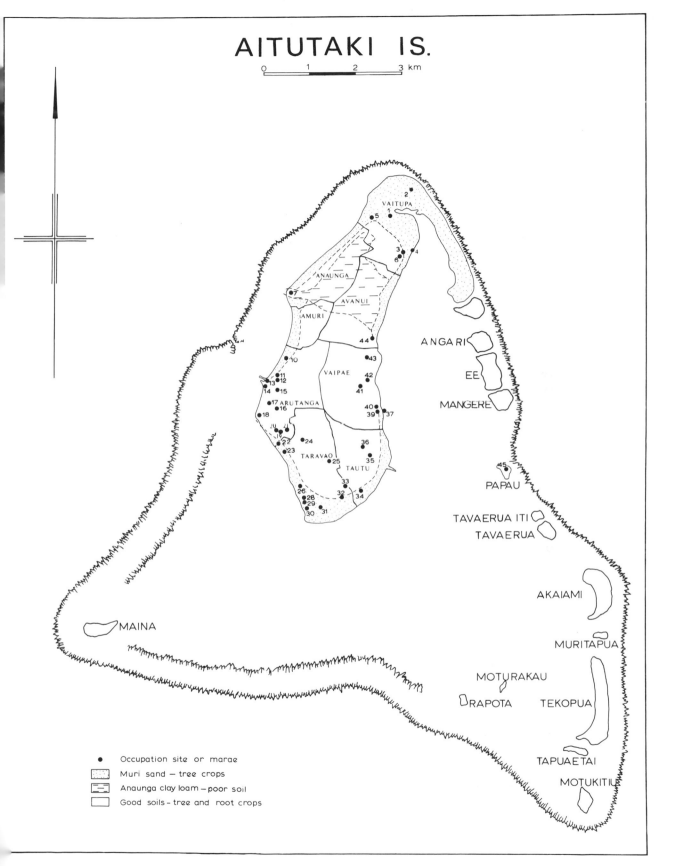

AITUTAKI IS.

0 1 2 3 km

Occupation site or marae
Muri sand – tree crops
Anaunga clay loam – poor soil
Good soils – tree and root crops

Fig. 12.18. The pattern of prehistoric settlement on Aitutaki. From Bell-wood 1971a. Ureia is the dot marked 10.

did of course find lots of artefacts, and survey and excavate lots of monuments. Suffice it to say that the artefacts fit into the central Polynesian pattern as we know it over the past 800 years or so, and let us look at some broader issues concerning settlement and resource distribution[61], and meaning in *marae* variation. The earliest settlements on Rarotonga and Aitutaki, as the only islands in the Cooks with prehistoric sequences, lie on the coasts. As one would expect, small initial populations were exploiting marine and lowland resources, and in the case of Rarotonga, almost certainly planting their taro in coastal swamps. They had a few domestic animals – the pig on Rarotonga and Atiu, the chicken on Aitutaki, but none of the other islands had any domestic animals at all. This suggests a lack of planned large-scale settlement, although it seems probable that most of the important crop plants were present.

As population increased, the house sites and *marae*, which were not normally nucleated in the southern Cooks, increased in number and spread themselves along boundaries between resource zones, which ecologists call ecotones. On Aitutaki, resources are zoned in a very approximate concentric pattern, with inland garden soils, coastal sandy soils for coconuts, and then the lagoon stocked with fish. The Aitutakians spread their settlements in a very commonsense way along the boundary between the coastal coconut soils and the inland garden soils, and thus minimised the distances they would need to traverse to produce and collect their food (figure 12.18). A similar pattern prevailed on Rarotonga, and here the ecotone between the rich coastal strip and the inland hills and valleys was marked by a line of settlement along a continuous paved road known as the Ara Metua (the parent path). On Mangaia, the barrenness of the island meant that most food came from highly localised taro swamps, so here of course the settlements were fairly tightly clustered around these swamps. Because of the restricted occurrence of resources in Mangaia, warfare was very frequent, with successful warriors gaining control of sections of the island and redistributing land to their followers. Losers made the best of it in the wilderness, an option not open to losers on the low and fertile island of Aitutaki, from which they probably just sailed away. Rarotonga was a little different.

On a small island like Aitutaki, it is probable that population increased quickly to put most of the surface into utilisation, and then proceeded to stabilise its numbers through warfare, infanticide, or even voluntary restriction on numbers of births. On a larger and more mountainous island like Rarotonga, excess populations of later prehistory were able to utilise previously uninhabited inland valleys for settlement, and this is what we see in the Maungaroa Valley on the western side of the island. Here, during surveys and excavations undertaken between 1968 and 1970[62], were found the remains of 78 house pavements and *marae*, quite tightly clustered into four groups, with one group being perched high on a defensible ridge above the valley. The four groups were constructed between about A.D. 1600 and 1823, although some small-scale earlier settlement is suggested by a carbon date of A.D. 1300 from an earlier site near the head of the valley.

In 1823, the missionary John Williams recorded that the people of the Maungaroa Valley had been driven inland by their more successful neighbours, and were not even allowed to go to the sea to fish. The Maungaroa Valley settlements are therefore a good example to illustrate population growth and pressure, as well as enforced nucleation both for defensive purposes and to leave as much of the cultivable land as possible free for cultivation – the settlements are all confined to rocky and useless areas, or to man-made terraces on steep slopes. This is Polynesian crowding on a small island in one of its most extreme forms, and it parallels evidence from some of the other and larger volcanic islands of Polynesia, where we see increasing inland settlement (not necessarily for defensive purposes) in later prehistory.

The Maungaroa sites have survived because, like those in Opunohu, they are in a marginal situation today. I discussed above how Green used the sites in the Opunohu Valley to illustrate the nature of Moorean society and its internal structure, and I could do the same to a lesser extent with the Maungaroa data. However, I am simply using the Maungaroa data to illustrate population increase and pressure and its effects on settlement distribution. The reader may accept that Rarotongan society was very like that of Moorea, and its *marae* reflect the island's ranking system, although this was rather less stratified than that in the Societies.

Finally, to describe the Maungaroa sites themselves, they comprise house pavements of T or rectangular shape (see figure 12.19) clustered in small groups around *marae* of very varied form. Some *marae* are terraced, others flat, some have

Fig. 12.19. Excavated T-shaped house platform in the Maungaroa Valley, with sketch reconstruction of house.

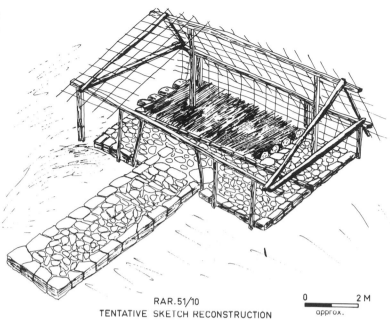

RAR.51/10
TENTATIVE SKETCH RECONSTRUCTION

0   2 M
approx.

platforms, others do not, and uprights are distributed according to no clear pattern. Rarotongan *marae* do not conform to any particular design, although some are similar to Tahitian inland *marae*. Relative isolation has obviously led to a great proliferation of form, and the same is true of Aitutaki, where the *marae* are unique in Polynesia, and consist generally of parallel lines of upright basalt pillars, without courts or *ahu* (figure 12.20). On Mangaia and Atiu they are totally different again – simple earthen platforms here, faced with coral slabs, and with upright pillars at intervals set into the facings. There is no regularity in *marae* architecture in the southern

Cooks[63], and anyone attempting to trace cultural origins from this source of evidence would conclude that the southern Cook Islanders were an extremely diverse amalgam – a conclusion which is obviously at variance with the evidence of linguistics and material culture, not to mention traditions and social structure. *Marae* forms can fluctuate at whim, and in the present state of our knowledge we are better to use them as indicators of societies and population distributions, rather than as indicators of cultural origin.

This does not mean that inter-island links are invisible archaeologically – I have evidence for very similar Arioi house structures with attached

Fig. 12.20. Line of basalt uprights averaging 2 metres high, forming part of a large *marae* at Paengariki, Aitutaki. (See also colour plate.)

marae on Mangaia and Rurutu, and Mangaia and Aitutaki also have some very close similarities in archaeological structures. Likewise, one of the *marae* on Rarotonga is very close to one on Rangiroa Island in the Tuamotus, and all these examples may represent small-scale inter-island voyages in late prehistory, like the voyager Karika who landed on Rarotonga from Samoa. But these tell us little about the evolution of the cultural mainstream for each island, which was quite clearly impervious to such minor intrusions. Cultural evolution is concerned with whole populations and long term trends, and I will have more to say about this when we come to the Hawaiian Islands.

THE ISOLATED MYSTERY ISLANDS

Scattered throughout Polynesia are a number of small isolated islands which have traces of prehistoric settlement, but which had no inhabitants at European contact. I discuss these here together as they represent a phenomenon of interest; I do not suggest that they were closely related culturally in any meaningful way. The most famous mystery island is Pitcairn[64] – a tail end to one of the greatest stories of the Pacific owing to its settlement by the *Bounty* mutineers in 1790. Pitcairn had at least three stone platforms at this time, and some of them were associated with stone statues[65], now alas, destroyed or dispersed apart from a single fragment. The island has also produced pig bones, stone fishhooks, petroglyphs, and stone adzes of a bewildering variety which are best matched in the Archaic adze assemblages from New Zealand. Yet the statues and stone fishhooks seem to point to Easter Island rather than New Zealand, so Pitcairn may have been settled and abandoned more than once in prehistoric times. Both Pitcairn and neighbouring Henderson Island have recently been visited by Yosihiko Sinoto, and he has evidence for initial settlement going back to about A.D. 1100[66].

Moving westwards, we find that two isolated atolls in the Cook Islands – Palmerston and Suwarrow – once had prehistoric occupants[67], and the same applies to the Kermadec Islands, with possible occupation from the southern Cooks in the fourteenth or fifteenth century[68]. Even little Norfolk Island, far to the west, has produced stone tools which may be of New Zealand Maori origin[69].

Scattered along the equatorial zone in rather remote isolation are a number of atolls belonging to the Phoenix and Line groups. None of these islands had human populations at European discovery, yet at least four and possibly several more of them have prehistoric remains[70]. Howland, Washington and Christmas Islands have little that is particularly diagnostic, but Fanning and Malden do. Malden has house pavements, *marae* and slab-lined graves which indicate to me clear evidence of settlement from the atoll of Penrhyn, 500 km to the south-west in the northern Cooks. Fanning has a slab-lined enclosure and shell fishhooks which I would also trace to Penrhyn, although Emory and Finney seem to agree on a Tongan origin. We don't really know enough to be very dogmatic about this.

Other remote and once-inhabited islands occur in the Hawaiian group too, but we will look at these later. The point I wish to make is that all the islands I have mentioned are isolated, and are most unlikely to have served as impermanently inhabited supply islands for a larger neighbour – there are dozens of examples in this latter class scattered through the Marquesas, Tuamotu, Society and Cook Islands, but there is no reason to include these in the class of mystery islands.

Why were these islands abandoned? Lack of water may have been the answer on the equatorial atolls, but this will not explain Pitcairn or Norfolk Island. Canoe loads of men only, who lived their lives and died without heirs? Lost voyagers who called in to recuperate, and then followed the call of homesickness? Epidemics? Demographic instability? Bloodthirsty quarrels resulting in mass murder (and don't forget the *Bounty* mutineers reduced their own numbers rather drastically by this means on Pitcairn)? Or mass suicide? I am afraid I really don't know, but the problem is still a very fascinating one.

Having mentioned the connections between Malden Island and Penrhyn, I might mention the northern Cooks briefly here for the sake of completeness. Pukapuka, Manihiki, Rakahanga and Penrhyn are all atolls, which had thriving Polynesian cultures at contact. Pukapuka is the most easterly outpost of western Polynesia, having apparently a Samoic language, but many cultural features which place it in an expectable intermediate position. The other three are culturally eastern Polynesian, and Manihiki and Rakahanga, being only 40 km apart, were once utilised on a rotational basis by a single population. Penrhyn is the only one of the group with extensive archaeological remains, investigated by Buck in 1929, and by myself in 1972[71]. These include paved and gravelled house floors, slab-lined enclosures for fish-storage and possibly salt evaporation, and numerous *marae*, some with very large mounds of shattered coral oven stones, derived from the cooking of turtles for ceremonies. The *marae* have rectangular courts enclosed by spaced uprights, often shaped into a rough human form like the ones mentioned above in the Tuamotus, and a few have *ahu* in addition. Penrhyn also has some oddities including circular *marae*, and a dry stone construction about one metre high, built in the form of a human being (figure 12.21). This monument is absolutely unique in the whole Pacific to my knowledge. My own excavations on Penrhyn did not produce a coherent sequence, but there are signs of settlement going back to about A.D. 1200. Most of the stone structures are more recent than this, and the *marae* were still in use in 1853 when E.H. Lamont was shipwrecked there; the first European to land on the island and record his experiences[72]. A few years after Lamont the island population was decimated by brutal slave-raiders 'recruiting' from Peru, and the same hideous fate was even more tragically to befall the remarkable culture of Easter Island, to be described below.

THE HAWAIIAN ISLANDS

The Hawaiian Islands stretch in a scattered line for some 3000 kilometres, although human habitation was confined to the southern third of this chain in prehistoric times, between the large volcanic island of Hawaii (over 10,000 sq. km.) and the tiny speck of Necker Island. The major inhabited islands between these two are Maui, Molokai, Lanai, Oahu and Kauai. At European contact the Hawaiian Islands were probably the most populous in Polynesia, with a possible population of 200,000 people[73].

When Captain Cook discovered the Hawaiian Islands in 1778 the society was clearly stratified under a class of powerful chiefs. Unfortunately, Cook had no Polynesian interpreters with him at the time (as he did have on his two earlier voyages), and his observations are therefore somewhat imprecise. However, the islands seem to have been under the control of four major chiefdoms, located on Hawaii, Maui, Oahu and Kauai, with the most powerful being on Hawaii and Maui according to Cook. As we know from

history[74], the arrival of Europeans seems to have precipitated the developments which Goldman[75] thinks were about to happen in some form even without outside stimulus; Kamehameha of Hawaii defeated his arch-rivals on Maui and Oahu in 1795, and thus gained control over all the islands except Kauai. By 1810 he was king of a unified Hawaiian kingdom.

The chiefly system which Cook observed was clearly of the same order as that of Tonga or Tahiti, being characterised by human sacrifice,

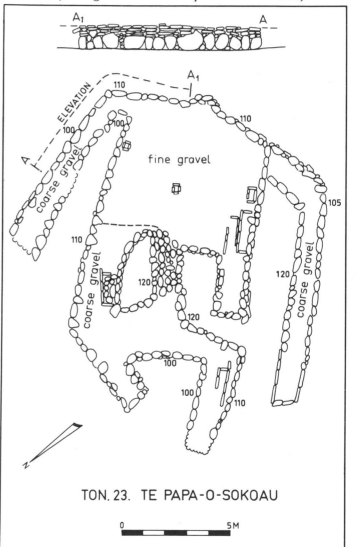

TON. 23. TE PAPA-O-SOKOAU

0   5M

Fig. 12.21. Stone monument, said to be a refuge *marae*, on Penrhyn Island, northern Cooks.

chiefly arrogance, and the prostration of commoners. Chiefly regalia was particularly splendid,
comprising beautiful cloaks and helmets set with
red and yellow feathers. The helmets, with their
unusual crested form, suggested to Cook that
the Hawaiian Islands had previously been visited
by Spaniards, but this now seems most unlikely[76].
We do not need to look to stray Europeans to
explain Hawaiian cultural development before
1778.

The Hawaiian society described for the contact
period by Goldman[77] comprised an intermarrying
chiefly class for each island which could even
resort to brother-sister marriage to preserve
pedigree, stratified over a mass of commoners
who simply dwelt in localised bilateral kinship
groups, without pedigree or widespread genealogical links, and without any strong ranking
amongst themselves. There even seems to have
been a special pariah group at the bottom of
society. The commoners could own land, but could
be dispossessed at whim by the chiefs, who were
able to redistribute land to their favoured followers
and relatives. This is of course the despotic and
feudal type of system that one associates with the
archaic civilisations elsewhere in the world – an
early version of the state, with kinship heterogeneity and high mobility replacing kinship
connectedness and the land-holding ramified
chiefdom. It seems to me, however, that Goldman
may be reading too much from the society of
early nineteenth century Hawaii, which clearly
was of this type; the pre-Cook society may well
have been a much more kin-based affair, like
that of Tahiti. Changes in Hawaii in the forty
years between the descriptions of Cook and Ellis
were very rapid indeed[78].

Nevertheless, Goldman's conclusions concerning the extent of the transformation of Hawaiian
society from the traditional type of Polynesian
organisation are still very pertinent:

> The allocation of chiefly office as a reward for
> political services and without reference to the
> genealogical relationship of the appointed chief
> to his constituency was a more solidly estab-
> lished principle in Hawaii than anywhere else
> in Polynesia. The ranks of chiefs constituting
> a general corps of potential administration,
> as in a European monarchy, were fully detached
> from their genealogical network, except for
> purposes of establishing their own rank. It
> was undoubtedly this thorough cleavage be-
> tween chiefs and the people working the land

that disrupted and transformed so completely
a segmentary organisation originally rooted in
kin and based on orderly subdivisions of the
genealogical network[79].

Goldman feels that this transformation took place
between A.D. 1100 and 1450 from the evidence of
traditions, and we will see later that there is
indeed archaeological evidence in support of
this.

Turning now to the origins of Hawaiian culture,
there is a certain amount of traditional evidence
which could indicate an initial settlement from the
Society Islands, particularly Tahiti (or 'Kahiki'
in local parlance), some 30–40 generations ago,
or early in the second millennium A.D.[80]. This
evidence remained acceptable to scholars for
many years, until the archaeological results of
the 1960s began to point to the Marquesas as a
more likely source, and to relegate the Society
Islands to a secondary role. The early notched
Hawaiian fishhooks, the octopus lure sinkers, and
a special kind of food-pounder made on Kauai
(the 'stirrup' pounder) were all thought to be of
Marquesan origin, while the later bait hooks of
the South Point sequence with their knobbed line
attachments were thought to indicate new introductions from the Society Islands[81]. However,
Cordy[82] has recently presented a sensible
argument against this dual origin of Hawaiian
culture, and the so-called 'Tahitian' fishhooks
are in fact present in small numbers in the very
earliest Hawaiian sites. We are left with a single
origin for Hawaiian culture, i.e. that of the founder
population, and for reasons I have given above
(page 325) we are unable at present to pinpoint
this origin with certainty, although the Marquesas remain the best bet.

The artefacts of the later part of the Hawaiian
sequence are in fact quite acceptable lineal
descendants of those of the earlier sites which
date to before A.D. 1000. The South Point sequence
shows a reasonable continuity in the typological
changes in fishhooks (see page 325) from Early
Eastern Polynesian times, and the Duff type 1A
adze probably becomes dominant by A.D. 1000
in Hawaii generally. Most of the late sites contain
a range of undiagnostic items such as grindstones,
coral files, bone tools, octopus lures of cowrie
shell, fishnet weights and so forth, and there is
little sign of any change in any of these through
time. One important ornament form which
appears in late sites is the hook-shaped breast
pendant made of cachalot whale-tooth (the *lei*

niho palaoa), and this is a type unique to the Hawaiian Islands, although it may have some remote connection with the shaped whale-tooth pendants of the Early Eastern Polynesian Culture in central Polynesia and New Zealand[83].

The most exciting aspect of present-day Hawaiian archaeology is not really connected with artefacts, but more with surveys and excavations of ancient temples, settlements and cultivation systems. Hawaii is a rich state by Pacific standards, and it supports many archaeologists; the result of this is that several fully integrated investigations of whole valleys have been carried out, to the general benefit of our understanding of prehistoric Hawaiian society.

Remains of ancient endeavour litter the Hawaiian landscape in the remoter coastal and valley areas – house terraces, stone temple complexes (known in Hawaii as *heiau* rather than *marae*), stone field boundaries, earth and stone burial platforms[84], and stone trackways[85], to name just a few of the major categories. Since the islands have no coral reefs, fish are not always in plentiful supply, and to overcome this difficulty the Hawaiians built elaborate funneled fish-traps, and also stone walled fish storage areas which could enclose up to 200 hectares of shallow coastal lagoon, with specially constructed grills to let small fry pass in and out[86]. Slab-lined enclosures were also built near the coast for the evaporation of salt from sea-water[87], and loss by seepage was countered by lining the pans with leaves.

Agricultural sites include stone-faced terrace complexes for growing wet-taro, and on Kauai Island there is a rather remarkable irrigation canal (the 'Menehune' Ditch) which is banked along one side with very finely cut blocks of stone[88]. Oddly enough, this seems to be the only example of the use of cut stone in Hawaii, as only unshaped blocks were used in *heiau* construction. Other agricultural remains comprise

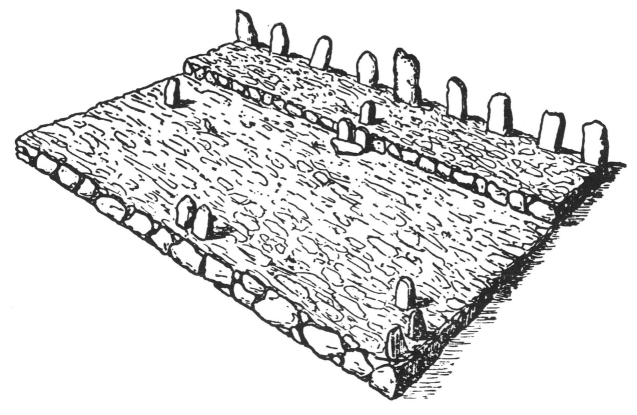

Fig. 12.22. Sketch of a typical Necker Island *marae*. From Emory 1928a.

walled fields for sweet potatoes, and stone clearance mounds and shelter foundations.

The *heiau* of the main Hawaiian islands are complex and varied structures, consisting of terraces, walls and platforms in so many arrangements that almost no two are alike. I will describe some of these sites later, but firstly I want to turn to some remarkable discoveries on the isolated islets of Necker and Nihoa, respectively 500 and 250 km west of the nearest island (Kauai), and each about 1 km in total length. Neither of these islands had populations at European contact, and neither have reliable water supplies, yet both are virtual museums of ancient Hawaiian culture. In 1923 and 1924, they were visited by Kenneth Emory of the Bishop Museum[89], who surveyed no less than 15 *heiau* on Nihoa, 33 on Necker, as well as lots of house and cultivation terraces. Despite their appalling barrenness, both islands had clearly supported sizeable populations in prehistoric times, but whether of drift voyagers, exiles, pilgrims or voluntary settlers no-one knows. Nihoa was apparently remembered in Hawaiian traditions, but Necker was totally unknown to the Hawaiians at European contact.

The surface of the treeless rock of Necker is dotted with *heiau* of a very standardised form – probable indications that the island was settled by a single related group of people rather than by casual and intermittent stray voyagers. These *heiau* (figure 12.22) comprise an upper terrace with a line of uprights along the back, and a lower terrace with a fairly standardised setting of uprights, as shown in the figure. According to Emory, no less than 28 of the 33 *heiau* are very close to this plan. A number of remarkable male figures of stone, with beaming round faces, erect posture and straight hanging arms in typical Hawaiian style were also collected from the island in the nineteenth century, apparently all from one *heiau*, although the exact context is now unknown. As Emory has pointed out, these have facial similarities with certain Marquesan figures, although this probably reflects a common eastern Polynesian heritage rather than a direct cultural transmission.

In addition to the *heiau*, a cave on Necker has yielded a number of items, including Duff type 1A adzes, octopus lure sinkers and sandstone bowls of local rock, and wood from this cave has given a carbon date in the late eighteenth century[90]. It is not inconceivable that a small group of people were blown to the island several centuries ago, perhaps as early as A.D. 1400 if

the Nihoa dates are any guide (see below), and that they were unable to get off because their canoe was wrecked. Since there is no timber on the island, they and their descendants may have eked an existence for several centuries in total isolation, before dying out for some unknown reason not too long before European discovery. It is quite conceivable that each generation would build *heiau* to exactly the same pattern in such isolation, as they would not of course have knowledge of any other form, and it is perhaps through an explanation of this kind that we can explain the phenomenal number of *heiau* on the island. My imagination can only lead me to the rather horrifying picture of a small group of men and women, with children, cut off in utter isolation and ignorance for centuries on a desolate piece of wind-swept rock one kilometre long. Such a picture of death in isolation has even intrigued some of the great writers of our time, particularly John Updike, who has blended a little Herman Melville with the ruins on Fanning Island into a very evocative reconstruction[91].

The great significance of the Necker remains for archaeology is that they seem to have been fossilised from some early date, perhaps before A.D. 1500. The *heiau* are nothing like the ones on the main Hawaiian islands, which have of course been rebuilt and modified to such an extent that there are probably no *heiau* left there surviving untouched from such an early period. Stone uprights, so common on Necker, are almost entirely absent elsewhere in the group. But as Emory has pointed out, the inland *marae* of Tahiti and those of the Tuamotus are very like the ones on Necker, and simple and ancient forms may well have continued to be constructed right through the sequences in these two areas. Whether the Necker type of structure was originally introduced into the Hawaiian Islands from the Societies, or even the Marquesas (as Emory has since claimed) remains unknown – they are simply indicators that Hawaiian culture was once much closer to central Polynesian culture than it was at European contact, and it seems quite possible that the type was once widespread right throughout the Hawaiian Islands.

The remains on Nihoa are a little different from those on Necker – the *heiau* here consist of more complex terrace arrangements with parallel rows and varied settings of uprights. There are some sites a little like the Necker ones, but generally they are more like the usual Hawaiian terraced structures, except in the presence of so many upright pillars. These sites have produced a similar assemblage to that from the cave on Necker, including the unusual stone bowls which are unique to Nihoa and Necker, but otherwise all the artefacts are of fairly standard Hawaiian types. One site on Nihoa has a rather uncertain carbon date falling somewhere between A.D. 800 and 1500[92], and it looks as if the island was settled from the same source as Necker (i.e. Kauai?), but perhaps a little later in time.

The *heiau* of the main Hawaiian islands[93] have broken away fairly completely from the standardised court and *ahu* pattern of much of central Polynesia, and Rarotonga and the southern Marquesas are the only areas of equal variety known to me. Oddly enough, the first *heiau* ever described for the Hawaiian Islands – that at Waimea on Kauai, visited by Cook in 1778 – is actually one of the closest known to the Tahitian pattern (it is therefore unfortunate that the site of this *heiau* is no longer known). In the drawing by Webber

(figure 12.23), we see a paved and walled court with a low platform across the end. On the platform are what appear to be five wickerwork representations of gods, together with two carved wooden boards like the three shown standing in the court. These were carved with human faces, and the flaring tops probably represented head-dresses; surprisingly, their outline is closely paralleled by some of the shaped coral uprights on the *marae* of Penrhyn (see page 353), but whether this is mere coincidence I cannot say. Also on or behind the platform is an oracle tower, which would once have been covered with *tapa* cloth (felted barkcloth), and into which the priest would have climbed to communicate with the god. These oracle towers were seen all along the Kauai coast by Cook in 1778, and are found nowhere else outside the Hawaiian Islands, unless the obelisk-shaped priests' houses on Marquesan *me'ae* can be regarded as cognate.

In the court of the Waimea temple stands a

Fig. 12.23. *Heiau* at Waimea, Kauai, drawn by J. Webber in 1778. The carved figures are discussed further in Cox and Davenport 1974: 66.

platform for offerings, a strange carving with an
elongated headdress, a house, and a stone upright.
The latter is rather unusual, as stone uprights
are found hardly anywhere apart from Nihoa
and Necker. The house, as we know from another
drawing by Webber, was 12 metres long, and
contained two wooden statues. Cook also recorded
that chiefs and human sacrifices were buried in
the *heiau*.

Another *heiau* seen by Cook, this time on the
island of Hawaii, was a rather different affair,
consisting simply of a large raised platform, with
a railing round the top set with human skulls.
Inside were three houses, an offering platform,
several wooden statues, and what may have been
a disposal pit for *tapu* offerings. This *heiau* seems
to have been rather like the one described by
Ellis in 1823 at Honaunau on the west coast of
Hawaii[94], which comprised a thatched house, in

a fenced and paved enclosure, containing the
bones of chiefs, tied in bundles, together with
numerous chiefly garments, red-feather images,
and wooden carved figures. More wooden images
were placed both inside and outside the fence,
and this structure, called the Hale-o-Keawe, has
recently been reconstructed for visitors (figure
12.24).

The *heiau* described by Ellis was actually in
one corner of one of the most remarkable structures found in the Hawaiian Islands, known
as the City of Refuge, or Pu'uhonua. This was
enclosed by a massive wall up to 4 metres high,
which ran in two sections at right angles, each
200 metres long, to cut off a roughly rectangular
area on a peninsula. Ellis reported images set
into holes along the top of the wall, and three
heiau platforms inside. One of these, the *heiau*
Alealea, has recently been reconstructed (as

Fig. 12.24. The reconstructed Hale-o-Keawe and part of the wall of the
Pu'uhonua, Honaunau, Hawaii.

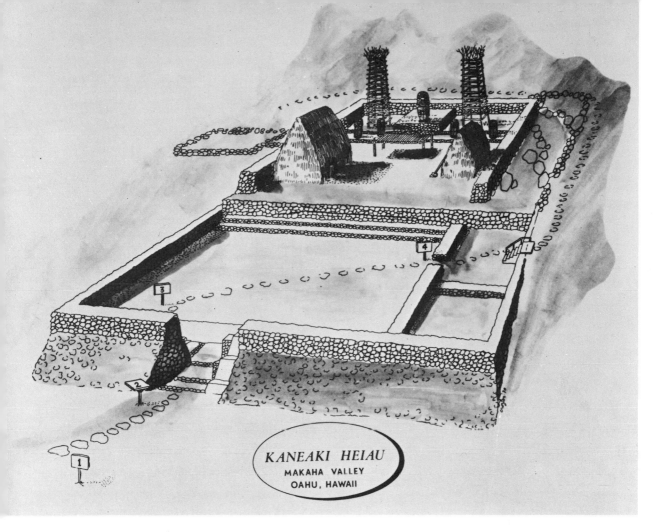

KANEAKI HEIAU
MAKAHA VALLEY
OAHU, HAWAII

Fig. 12.25. The reconstructed *heiau* Kaneaki, Makaha Valley, Oahu.

has the wall itself), and the archaeologists concerned found that it had undergone seven phases of accretion to an original minor platform, eventually to become a massive platform of almost 40 by 20 metres, and 2.4 metres high[95]. Traditionally, the whole Pu'uhonua complex could have been built as early as A.D. 1450, although this date has not been verified archaeologically.

As described by Ellis, the City of Refuge was a place to which fugitives of all kinds could flee for guaranteed priestly protection – clearly it was an indicator of a strong authority able to enforce some kind of law and order, and even to protect murderers from vengeance. Several structures of this kind are known from the Hawaiian Islands and other parts of Polynesia[96], and the concept of having a haven for fugitives appears to be quite a basic one in Polynesian society. However, the Pu'uhonua, now reconstructed and open to tourists, is by far the most

splendid surviving example.

The archaeological remains of *heiau* on the main Hawaiian islands, particularly Hawaii and Oahu, are quite well described in the literature[97]. They range from small platforms or small walled enclosures which may have served as family or fishermen's shrines, to huge complexes of multi-level terraces, sometimes walled, and often supporting numerous supplementary platforms for the various houses and other wooden structures which once graced the court. One of these *heiau* has recently been reconstructed in the Makaha Valley on Oahu, and one can see in figure 12.25 the main court with its sacred house, drum house, offering platform, idols and oracle towers. In a site such as this we may imagine that a whole multitude of rites and rituals would have been carried out to ensure the general well-being of the local society and its chiefs.

Concerning the general distribution of settlements in Hawaii, we know from Cook that they could be either dispersed, or sometimes clustered into villages which might contain up to 200 houses. Most of the Hawaiian islands seem to have been divided, as in fact were most Polynesian islands, into radial landholding units which included a valley, a piece of coastline, and some inland hill country. The ideal form for one of these units, called an *ahupua'a*, seems to have been something like a pie-segment, with the broad base being along the coast. An *ahupua'a* would also ideally be exploited by one large group of related families, who would have equal access to all the resource zones.

A number of large-scale archaeological projects have recently been undertaken in *ahupua'a* units to recover details of settlement patterning and land use, in order to throw light on the general cultural evolution of local units and Hawaiian society as a whole. On Maui, the coastal section of an *ahupua'a* unit at Palauea has been investigated by Kirch[98], who has located a cluster of late prehistoric sites 10 to 20 metres apart which may have formed the settlement of a related group of families. These structures, comprising small walled enclosures and platforms, seem to have belonged to a men's house, together with dwelling and storage houses and working areas. Nearby is a ceremonial complex consisting of a *heiau* and a small shrine, and Kirch thinks that this served as a focus for a number of family groups spread throughout the *ahupua'a*.

Kirch's survey was limited to the coastal section of an *ahupua'a*, and on Oahu a somewhat complementary survey has been carried out in the Makaha Valley[99], with a concentration on the inland agricultural structures within the valley itself. The Makaha Valley is about 7 kilometres long and 1–2 kilometres wide, and being on the drier side of Oahu its lower part has a low rainfall and a long dry season. The upper part is considerably wetter. The lower part of the valley seems to have been used for seasonal cultivation of sweet potatoes, dry taro, and other non-irrigated crops such as gourds and sugar cane. The whole area is scattered with rock heaps piled up during clearance of the ground, and most of the cultivation took place on low terraces built along the slopes to hold the movement of soil and run-off. Amongst the terraces are the rough stone foundations, usually L or C shaped, for temporary field shelters, and in a few places there are better built walled enclosures or terraces for more permanent houses, shrines, and *heiau*.

The largest *heiau* is actually in the middle of the valley, and this is the restored *heiau* Kaneaki shown in figure 12.25. The investigations in this *heiau* showed that it had six phases of accretion, beginning with a small terrace built about A.D. 1550. Radiocarbon dating in the lower valley showed that some of the agricultural areas were probably in use from about A.D. 1100, although the area under cultivation has almost certainly been increased since then.

The upper Makaha Valley, with its higher rainfall, was used for wet-taro cultivation in stone-faced irrigated terraces. These upper terraces may have been fed by stream water or by the channeled collection of ground-water from the higher slopes, and they cover an area of about 9 hectares, being in the largest cases up to 1000 square metres in individual size. Also in the upper valley were scattered kerb-settings or platforms for houses, as well as stone mounds and upright stones which are thought to have had religious functions. Excavations in one of the taro terraces revealed an early period of use, carbon-dated to about A.D. 1400, and this may well date the first intensive use of this upper section.

The Makaha results fit quite well with those recovered from other surveys. In the Halawa Valley, on the wetter north-eastern side of Molokai[100], irrigated taro fields inside the valley were established from about A.D. 1500, about 300 years after the coastal site of the Early Eastern Polynesian Culture (see page 325) had been abandoned. In the Lapakahi area[101], a dry region of fairly even slope on the north-western side of Hawaii, coastal settlement was established at about A.D. 1300, while between 1400 and 1600 the area of coastal settlement expanded and agricultural complexes were constructed on the inland slopes. Lapakahi is so dry that there is a belt of uncultivable territory about 2 km wide between the coastal settlements and the upland zone where rainfall is high enough to support cultivation (without irrigation), and this uncultivated zone seems to have been utilised mainly for trails. In the cultivation zone itself there are rectangular gridded field systems with earth and rock boundary walls, the fields averaging 10 by 30 metres in size. Ethnohistoric records indicate that sweet potatoes were grown in this zone, and actual remains of tubers have been found in excavations inside the stone foundation walls of temporary shelters. In the wetter areas higher up the slopes it appears that breadfruit, banana and taro could be grown as well. Dates for this upland agricultural system begin at about A.D. 1400, and a sound sequence has been based on hydration-rind dates for basaltic glass. I mentioned use of this technique in the Early Eastern Polynesian site at Halawa, and to my mind it ranks as perhaps the major scientific development in recent Hawaiian archaeology, superseding even carbon dating in accuracy and relatively easy abundance of the dateable medium.

Now all this information about field walls and taro terraces may seem somewhat overwhelming, and indeed it would be if it were simply amassed to no purpose. However, several Hawaiian archaeologists are now looking for trends which run through the data on a broad scale in order to raise hypothesis about Hawaiian cultural development. The Hawaiian islands are perhaps the best known part of Polynesia in terms of archaeology, with the exception of New Zealand, and obviously if we cannot pose useful hypotheses here we have little chance of doing so elsewhere.

It may be noted, for instance, that the increase in valley utilisation which seems to have taken place about A.D. 1100–1300 corresponds nicely with Goldman's view from traditions that the transition from a traditional to a stratified society took place at about this time. In 1969, Newman[102] suggested that the prehistory of the island of Hawaii itself could be divided into four periods, which he termed Settlement, Early Swidden, Late Swidden and Permanent Agriculture. Through these four periods Newman wove the trends of population increase, increasing stratification and specialisation within society, increasing importance of agriculture over marine exploitation, and increasing degradation of the natural environment. These are likely to be very long term trends, and the periods therefore not sharply divisible on a presence-absence basis. Wet-taro cultivation may well be dominant in the final period of prehistory, but the techniques were almost certainly known even to the first settlers of the Hawaiian Islands[103], as they were to most of the other early Polynesians.

The most recent synthesis of Hawaiian prehistory is by Cordy[104], who emphasises the important distinctions between the wetter windward sides of islands and the drier leeward sides. The Hawaiian islands are large enough to have this kind of rainfall distinction, which is of course much less important in the smaller Polynesian islands. Cordy has three periods for Hawaiian prehistory: (1) Initial Settlement Period with small permanent settlements in the wet windward areas and favourable leeward areas with good water supplies; (2) New Adaptation Period with a spread into the drier leeward agricultural areas (such as Makaha and Lapakahi); and finally (3), the Complex Chiefdom Period with the highly ranked ethnographic society developing after A.D. 1600, stimulated by increasing population pressure on resources.

Naturally, these hypotheses are only tentative, and will certainly be revised in the future. But they are beginning to make sense, and it is interesting to note how they correspond with data from elsewhere in Polynesia; for instance, inland settlement on Rarotonga and Moorea seems to begin at about A.D. 1300, as it does in many of the Hawaiian valleys. There clearly are observable trends in Polynesian prehistory, particularly in the field of population growth and its relationship to increasing agricultural and societal complexity.

It only remains for me to note that the Hawaiian Islands have a rich repertoire of rock petroglyphs – humans, spread-eagled 'birdmen'[105], dogs, other fauna, and a rich range of circles and other geometric motifs[106] – before passing to the climax of this chapter; Easter Island.

EASTER ISLAND

Easter Island is without doubt the enigma of Polynesia. On the one hand it has the most magnificent stone monuments and statues in the whole of Oceania; but on the other hand its prehistoric culture was utterly destroyed before outsiders had any chance to make reliable records. Records of course there are, but because they are so unreliable and contradictory they have allowed Easter Island to be the subject of unprecedented batterings by the lunatic fringe, and to have its name linked with such garbled trivia as sunken continents and astronauts. Fortunately, however, not all is at the level of the 'popular' press, and some of the research carried out on the island since 1914 has been of excellent standard, particularly that by the Franco-Belgian expedition in 1934–5 and by the Norwegian team under Thor Heyerdahl in 1955–6[107].

Easter Island is small and isolated even by Polynesian standards, being almost 2000 kilometres from Pitcairn, its nearest once-inhabited neighbour in Polynesia, and almost 4000 kilometres from the coasts of Peru and Chile. The island has a triangular shape (figure 12.26) with a total length of 25 km and has been built around a number of volcanic craters. Three of these: Rano Aroi, Rano Kao and Rano Raraku, contain freshwater lakes.

We know from the eighteenth century explorers that the Easter Islanders had chickens, but no pigs or dogs. They cultivated sweet potatoes, yams, taro, bananas, sugar cane, gourds, and the paper mulberry tree, all of westerly origin apart from the Andean sweet potato (see page 140). As the island lies outside the tropics, coconut and breadfruit were not grown. The crater lakes supported a number of plants, including the *totora* reed (*Scirpus riparius*), used for housing materials and swimming floats, and other plants such as *Polygonum acuminatum* and *Cyperus vegetus*, all with origins in South America. The same origin applies to the small and important *toromiro* tree (*Sophora toromiro*), almost the only source of

wood left to the islanders in late prehistory.

As is well-known, Heyerdahl has used these American plants as evidence for contact between Easter Island and South America[108], together of course with the sweet potato, and he has also accepted a report that chili peppers (again an American plant) were growing on the island in 1770. He has linked the list of American plants on Easter Island into a total list of 22 species which he thinks may have been introduced by man from the Americas into various parts of eastern Polynesia, and these also include cotton and the coconut. Since some of these are discussed in chapter 6, I will not repeat myself, except to note that the majority are not important food plants, and that their antiquity in Polynesia may long exceed that of man[109]. Emory[110] has pointed this out as a distinct possibility, and has also thrown doubt on the report of chili peppers on

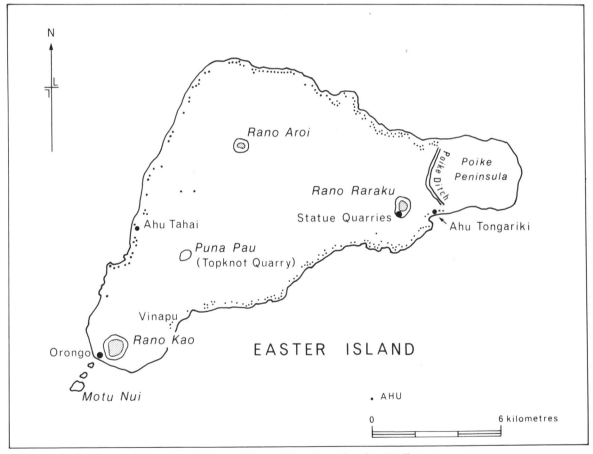

Fig. 12.26. Map of Easter Island, partly after Mulloy 1970.

Easter Island. Since none of the early explorers mentioned the really important American cultigens such as maize, beans or squashes, it seems to me that the sweet potato remains the only good potential piece of botanical evidence for prehistoric contact between Polynesia and America, but even this could have been of natural introduction.

Before I review the long debate about American influence on Easter Island any further, I wish first to look at the ethnology and archaeology of the Island in a purely descriptive sense. Between 1722 and 1862 a number of European voyagers called at the island; most stayed only one or two days, and none appear to have had any useful grasp of the language. Through this period the culture of the island was in evident decline, poor in food resources and with a decreasing population. In 1862 a most fearful disaster took place, when about 1000 Easter Islanders were captured by slavers and taken to Peru. Within a short time 900 were dead, and under strong representation from Britain and France the remainder were repatriated, with smallpox. Fifteen reached home alive, the disease spread, and by 1877 only 110 people remained on the island, after a number had been recruited for plantation work on Tahiti[111]. In the mid-eighteenth century the population may have been about 3000 persons, so this is perhaps the most dreadful piece of genocide in Polynesian history. And as the islanders died so their culture died with them – the first outside resident of the island came in 1863 (a French missionary), and he, not surprisingly, was under constant threat of losing his life. By the time detailed observations were made in the 1880s the old culture was virtually dead, although perhaps we should be thankful that at least something was recorded.

The first European to visit Easter Island was the Dutchman Roggeveen[112], on Easter day in 1722. He was quite impressed with the fertility of the island, and thought it 'might be made into an earthly Paradise, if it were properly worked and cultivated; which is now only done in so far as the inhabitants are obliged to for the maintenance of life'. He noted the remarkable slit and distended earlobes of the inhabitants, which they often plugged with ornaments; this type of of ear piercing was in fact common throughout Polynesia, except in Mangareva and Hawaii[113]. The now-famous statues each had a basket of stones (a topknot?) on its head, and Roggeveen thought they were made of sticky clay and

pebbles. He also stated that the inhabitants 'kindle fire in front of certain remarkable tall figures they set up; and, thereafter squatting on their heels with heads bowed down, they bring the palms of their hands together and alternately raise and lower them'. This supplicating behaviour was probably occasioned by the arrival of the Dutchmen in their mysterious giant ships[114], but the prayers appear to have fallen on deaf ears, as about .12 of the islanders were killed during the visit. Roggeveen also noted that Easter Island canoes were made of many small boards lashed together, and the island had no heavy or thick timber by this time. It appears from modern evidence that serious environmental degradation was well under way by 1722, and pollen samples do indicate that the island was quite heavily forested when man first arrived[115]. Statue carving also seems to have ceased by Roggeveen's time.

Therefore, a major cultural decline had apparently set in on Easter Island before 1722, and the situation seems progressively to worsen with later voyagers. A Spanish expedition under Gonzalez arrived in 1770[116], and found most of the island uncultivated, with no large trees. Some of the commoners were living in caves, and the Spaniards gave different estimates for the population between 900 and 3000 persons. It has recently been suggested that Easter Island might at one time have supported 10,000 persons[117], in an earlier and happier era. The Spaniards recorded the statues with their topknots properly, and noted that human bones were placed on top of the latter. They saw one of the large basket-work figures erected near the statues during memorial feasts (*paina*), and it is of interest here that Banks saw a similar figure used during public entertainment on Tahiti in 1769[118]. Finally, the Spaniards staged a formal procession and ceremony of annexation, during which the islanders called out the name of their chief god, Makemake, and appended their pictographic signatures to an official document. One of these signatures was identical to the bird-man pictographs of the nineteenth century script, of which more below.

In 1774 the island was visited by Cook and the Forsters[119]; the island appeared so barren to Cook that he only stayed one full day, and his shore party was only able to find stagnant water. The population was now thought to be about 700, of whom two-thirds were men. By this time many of the statues had toppled over, but whether

Fig. 12.27. An Easter Island scene, drawn by Duché de Vancy in 1786.

they were in this state in 1770 is not clear from the Spanish account. George Forster recorded that the statues were set up to represent deceased chiefs, after whom they were actually named – a very significant piece of information. He also described the boat-shaped thatched houses and gave his conviction that the islanders were Polynesians.

When the French navigator La Pérouse visited the island in 1786[120] the population had evidently recovered to number about 2000, and food was very plentiful. In fact, it looks as though some internal upheaval had taken place just before the arrival of Cook, and many of the women and children were probably in hiding, thus rendering his population estimate of 700 souls of dubious validity. La Pérouse spent only 10 hours on the island, but his engineer has provided the best illustrations extant from the eighteenth century, and we have excellent descriptions of the statues on their platforms (*ahu*), as well as of three house types; a stone oval form with a corbelled roof; an underground oval form shaped from a natural cave, and approached down a ramp and steps; and the more common elongated boat-

shaped houses, with low roofs of arched timbers set into holes in stone kerbs, thatched with rushes. One of these boat houses was 108 metres long, and was described as 'forming a village by itself'. The inaccurate but rather romantic drawing of two disdainful statues on their *ahu*, here reproduced in figure 12.27, was also made on La Pérouse's visit.

After 1786 little of importance was recorded about the island until the 1860s. In 1864 the missionary Eugene Eyraud gave the first report about a mysterious script (*rongorongo*) carved on wooden boards kept in the houses. At that time no-one seemed to know the meanings of the symbols, and I will come back to this genuine 'mystery' of Easter Island again below. In 1866 the first report was given of the remarkable 'bird-man ceremony', during which members of the tribal groups in military ascendance each appointed a servant to swim with a reed float to the small island of Motu Nui, about 1.5 km off the south-western tip of the main island. Here, the servants awaited the arrival of migratory sooty terns, which laid their eggs on the island. The first servant to find an egg called out to watchers on the mainland, and his master was placed in *tapu* seclusion for several months, evidently as the representative of the great god Makemake. The ceremony was repeated yearly until about 1867, but whether the unfortunate servants who did all the work ever received any reward is unclear.

Traditions of origin held by the islanders were not recorded in any detail until the 1880s. The founding chief was a man called Hotu Matua, who according to Thomson[121] came from a scorched land to the east 57 generations before. However, different versions of the story bring him from the west at a much later date[122], and it is no longer possible to know which, if any, of these traditions is the valid one. It is my own suspicion that none are valid, and the same applies to the traditions about another ancestor called Tuu-ko-ihu, and about two groups of people variously called 'Long Ears' and 'Short Ears', or 'heavy-set people' and 'slender people'[123]. There may be some untraceable historical sources for these traditions, and J. Macmillan Brown managed to weave them into an incredible ethnographic fairy-tale in 1924[124]. Heyerdahl[125] has also used them in a popular work on Easter Island, but to my mind they all add untold confusion to a situation which can only now be illuminated by straight archaeology. For this reason I will not refer to traditions in the coming discussion.

The Easter Island society observed by Europeans was not of the highly stratified Tahitian variety, and George Forster regarded it as quite egalitarian. Instead, it was dominated by small independent warring tribes, who probably spent a good deal of their time fighting over scarce resources, as in other ecologically poor Polynesian islands such as the Marquesas or Mangaia. Political power was concentrated in the hands of a rather unstable warrior class at contact, although the traditional leading *ariki* line, vested in the Miru family, still retained a degree of ceremonial prestige. Goldman[126] classifies Easter as an Open society, with the original land-holding ramages being dispersed through frequent warfare and upheaval. The situation was complicated even more by the presence of the 'Bird-man' with his high sanctity, but it does appear that these Bird-men belonged to the dominant warrior group anyway, and so they probably did not unduly complicate a basic dual division of prestige between the *ariki* line and the warrior class.

The orthodox opinion on Easter Island origins at present is that the first settlers came from the Marquesas[127], although insufficient is known of the early period of settlement on the island to allow certainty. Linguistically, the Easter Island language seems to have split off from a source in eastern Polynesia before A.D. 500 – remarkably early considering the extreme isolation of the island. The archaeology supports this early date, and Easter Island material culture lacked the food pounders and tanged adzes which had developed by A.D. 1000 in central Polynesia. The Easter adze kit[128] was in fact dominated by simple untanged quadrangular forms, and by an unusual triangular-sectioned form with a grooved lashing grip (Duff type 4D – see figure 12.1 [d]). It looks very much as though the island was settled at a relatively early date and thereafter isolated until 1722, and in making this statement I am of course supporting the view that the remarkable developments in Easter Island culture resulted purely from internal stimuli, so perhaps we should now look at some of these developments in the light of archaeology.

The first detailed survey of Easter Island monuments was made by Thomson in 1886, although he unfortunately sullied his otherwise good name by badly damaging a number of sites in an enthusiastic hunt for treasure and information. In 1914 a British expedition under Katherine Routledge carried out more detailed work, but most of the detailed records of this expedition have since been sadly mislaid[129]. In 1934–5 a Franco-Belgian expedition under Métraux and Lavachery recorded ethnography and petroglyphs, and systematic archaeological excavation was begun by the Norwegian expedition under Heyerdahl in 1955–6[130]. Since then several Americans have worked on the island, in particular William Mulloy of the University of Wyoming, who was originally a member of the Heyerdahl expedition. The results of all this work are voluminous to say the least, and the following description can only be a distillation of the major points.

The coasts of Easter Island are littered with the remains of about 300 stone platforms called *ahu* – equivalents of the central Polynesian *marae*, although the latter word seems to have come into use in central Polynesia after the initial settlers of Easter had departed. The *ahu* associated with the stone statues generally comprise a rectangular platform which abuts on its landward side on to a sloping ramp, which in turn leads into a cleared but usually unwalled rectangular court (see figure 12.28). The ramps often extend for a long distance on either side of the central platform to form wings. The largest of the *ahu*, the now-destroyed *ahu* Tongariki, had a central platform about 45 metres long, and a total length, with the two wings, of about 160 metres. The central platform supported a record number of 15 massive statues, all prostrate (except for one statue base) by about 1860, which seems to have been the latest date when any might have been left standing anywhere on the island.

Naturally, many of the *ahu* as they are now represent several stages of rebuilding and accretion, and at the late date when the statues were toppled they were used and modified entirely for burials. In addition, special burial *ahu* were built in late prehistory which were never associated with statues – these are the boat-shaped and wedge-shaped (or semi-pyramidal) types of Routledge. The more famous 'image *ahu*' with the statues belong to earlier phases of prehistory, to which we now turn.

As a result of its excavations in 1955–6, the Norwegian expedition divided Easter Island prehistory into three periods: Early Period A.D. 400–1100; Middle Period 1100–1680; Late Period 1680–1868. We know very little about the Early Period outside the field of *ahu* architecture, but for the two later periods the picture is much clearer, and it was during the Middle Period that the haughty but standardised statues for which Easter is so famous were produced.

At the present time I know of only two *ahu* which I would regard as unequivocally of the Early Period. The first, examined by Heyerdahl's team, is *ahu* 2 at Vinapu, which had a central platform 36 by 4 metres in area, raised three metres in height, and faced on its seaward side with massive vertical slabs of rough stone filled and levelled with dry-stone work. This abutted on its inland side on to a long sloping ramp with wings, and beyond this was a cleared court surrounded on two sides by an earthen bank. A carbon date of about A.D. 850 was obtained from beneath this bank. The neighbouring *ahu* I of Vinapu was claimed to belong to the Early Period as well[131], but in view of Golson's excellent rein-

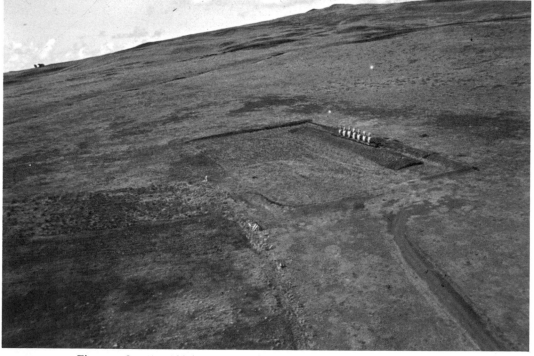

Fig. 12.28. *Ahu* Akivi: a restored Middle Period structure showing a complete arrangement of statues, ramp and earth-walled court. (See also colour plate.)

terpretation of some of the results of the Heyerdahl expedition[132], I consider this to be a much later Middle Period structure.

The other Early Period *ahu* is *ahu* Tahai, constructed as a similar winged platform at about A.D. 700, and faced with cut stone[133]. From Vinapu II and Tahai we know two very important things: religious structures of the basic eastern Polynesian plan (platform and court) were being constructed on Easter Island by as early as A.D. 700 – the earliest dates by far for Polynesia – and we also know that cut stone was in use. Whether Easter Island was originally precocious in these respects we may never know, for its inhabitants reused and added to the same basic structures for upwards of one thousand years, while their cousins in most other parts of Polynesia appear to have innovated new forms much more rapidly. In its isolation, Easter Island culture, like that of Necker Island, seems to have been singularly conservative despite its high technical ability.

There are certain other *ahu* which are thought to belong to the Early Period, some being simple platforms without wings, but quite a few having cut stone. No statues stood on the platforms at this time, but some may have stood in the courts. An aberrant kneeling statue was found by the Heyerdahl expedition in the Rano Raraku quarry, and claimed to belong to the Early Period, but I see no very good reason for this dating. The same applies to the 'solar observation device', comprising four small holes pecked in to the bedrock at the ceremonial village of Orongo (to

be described below), and said to be an Early Period structure with astronomical significance. I do not find this a very convincing structure, although Mulloy has recently claimed another example near the Middle Period platform of *ahu* Huri a Urenga, and it could well be significant that both Vinapu II and Tahai have solar-solstice orientations, as do several later *ahu*[134]. Nevertheless, the exact functions of the Early Period *ahu* can only remain a matter of surmise, and it seems to me that they may have begun as community structures with a range of uses, but were gradually transformed into burial places and chiefly memorials from the Middle Period onwards.

Apart from the *ahu*, the only other structure of possible Early Period date is a rectangular kerbed house floor near the rim of the Rano Kao crater, excavated by McCoy[135]. This is associated with an obsidian flake industry, and may date to about A.D. 1000. It may be that the rectangular house form was established early on the island, while the universal boat-shaped form of later prehistory developed sometime in the Middle Period. However, some of the drilled stone kerbs of the type used to support the thatched boat-shaped houses of the ethnographic period have been found re-used as building material in Middle Period *ahu* (figure 12.29), so it does seem possible that the form could have been present in the Early Period as well.

During the Middle Period most of the *ahu* appear to have had wings, and some of the

Fig. 12.29. Drilled house kerbs re-used in the Middle Period *Ahu* Heki'i.

Fig. 12.30. Shaped and fitted facing blocks at *Ahu* Vinapu I. (See also colour plate.)

Early Period structures, such as Vinapu II and Tahai, were rebuilt to support the massive stone busts. The Heyerdahl expedition thought that the Early and Middle Periods were separated by quite a sharp break, but it has since been shown that the pattern of change is more a gradual trend, so the dividing line at A.D. 1100 may be rather academic. Dates for Middle Period *ahu* with wings and statues range from about A.D. 1000 to 1600[136], and during this period we find burial chambers inserted into the *ahu* ramps and small slab-lined cists for cremation burials set into the plazas. Since there appears to be no evidence for Early Period burials in *ahu*, this change is probably significant.

The peak of Middle Period craftsmanship was attained in the *ahu* Vinapu I, which was probably constructed about 1500, and which has an absolutely outstanding seaward face of precisely cut and fitted stones (figure 12.30). Both Vinapu I and II received their statue busts – six for Vinapu I, nine for Vinapu II, all set in landward-facing lines. Since about 100 of the *ahu* have one or more of these statues (figure 12.31), we can now give them our undivided attention.

Easter Island has about 600 large statues[137], of which over 150 remain unfinished in their quarries – mute testimony to some unknown disaster which halted all work. The quarries are located inside and outside the crater rim of the Rano Raraku volcano, and here the giants were cut from the rock – an andesitic tuff – and partly dressed to shape with stone mauls. The

very clear evidence left in the quarries shows that they were initially modelled in the living rock, with trenches cut around for access for the carvers, and kept attached to the rock by uncarved spines left down their backs. When the modelling was almost finished the spines were severed, and the statues lowered by ropes caught round holes and protuberances in the rock, to be erected upright at the foot of the talus slopes below. About 70 statues still stand in these positions inside and outside the crater, now buried almost to their heads by the downward movement of thousands of tons of quarry rubble. Here, in a temporary standing position, they were finished, apart from the carving of the eyes, and a number were embellished with symbols to represent tattooing and what may be loincloths. When one realises that the statues were carved from vertical as well as horizontal rock-faces, and that the largest unfinished giant is no less than 20 metres long, one can hardly fail to be struck by the tremendous skill and daring of the workers. Broken statues attest to accidents, and the presumed human death toll will never be known.

After the statues were dressed at the base of the talus, they were then moved along cleared roads to the *ahu* for erection with their topknots, which were carved separately from a quarry in the crater of Punapau volcano. People have puzzled for years how the statues were moved, and wilder theories range from aerial ropeways to conveniently timed volcanic eruptions propelling them through the air. However, what I think may well be the answer has been recently worked out by William Mulloy, in a remarkably clever piece of reconstruction[138]. He feels that a huge forked sled was attached to the front of each statue, held partly in place by the protruding belly and chin. The sled protected the finished statue from contact with the rough ground, and the statue was then moved by an ingenious system of leverage using a bipod. If and when the *ahu* was finally reached, (and several broken statues still lie along access tracks) the topknot would be lashed to the head of the statue, and both raised together by a complex method using levers and ramps. Since I cannot describe all the details here, I refer the reader to Mulloy's article, which should be enough to stimulate anyone's do-it-yourself dreams.

The largest statue ever erected on an *ahu* had a total height, with topknot, of 11.5 metres, and weighed almost 100 tonnes. This one, according to Mulloy, would have taken 30 men one year to carve, 90 men two months to move the 6 kilometres from the quarry, and 90 men three months to erect. It may be no small wonder that the statue carving came to a sudden and dramatic halt, for of course the island may have been stripped of all sizeable timber after a few centuries, and this would cause construction necessarily to stop. One has only to recall the eighteenth century accounts of the island's lack of timber. Furthermore, the statue discussed by Mulloy was not the biggest on the island – I have already mentioned the 20 metre giant left unfinished in the quarry, and one erected at the base of the talus was found to be no less than 11.4 metres high when excavated by the Norwegian expedition in 1956. Another giant at the base of the talus had been damaged during finishing, and after becoming partly buried some later carvers had actually cut another small bust out of its

Fig. 12.31. Re-erected statues at *Ahu* Akivi.

Fig. 12.32. 20-tonne statue restored with topknot at *Ahu* Ko te Riku.

head, giving a most peculiar combination when exposed to view by modern excavation!

The Easter statues are of an extremely standardised type, and show no evident sign of evolutionary variation. Most have elongated earlobes, one at least with an earplug (a very small minority have normal ears), and the heavy foreheads, enormous noses and pointed chins probably need little introduction. All those erected on *ahu* have flat bases cut across their midriffs (i.e. they are busts rather than complete figures), and the hands extend with enormously long fingers across their tummies. The hand position is typical of Polynesian carving, but the busts in their general form are clearly a product of local evolution on the island. One statue with a squatting posture, unusual for Easter Island but typical for Polynesia generally, was found in the Rano Raraku talus by the Norwegian expedition, but claims that this is a prototype for the *ahu* images are not supported by any stratigraphical evidence. However, Easter Island wooden figures have affinities both with the images and with other Polynesian carvings, and the *ahu* images can be little more than the result of intensive local specialisation. It has been suggested that the statues indicate the custom of head-deformation[139], or even a widespread disease caused by malfunctioning of the endocrinal glands[140], but I suspect this is taking faith in realism a little too far.

It appears to me that the islanders in the Middle Period might have developed quite rapidly a desire to portray deceased chiefs or gods through statues. Although Forster reported that they represented chiefs, we cannot be certain that this was the original inspiration, and they could in fact have represented gods like the upright slabs on the *ahu* of central Polynesian *marae*. Emory has suggested that the statues may gradually have replaced simple slab prototypes[141], and this development may have been stimulated by a process which Sahlins has called 'esoteric efflorescence'[142], which really boils down to an increasing obsession with an esoteric domain of culture, caused by degradation of the environment and a decreasing number of outlets for communal energy and labour. Whether Sahlins' view be acceptable or not, it seems that statue carving began abruptly, continued for several centuries with precise standardisation, and then stopped abruptly. Carbon dates from the Rano Raraku quarries span the period A.D. 1200–1500, so we could have at least 300 years to account for the island's 600 statues.

Most of the recorded range of house types on Easter Island make an appearance in the Middle Period, and these include the common boat-shaped form with drilled kerb-stones, as well as circular forms with dry-stone walls and presumably thatched roofs. The latter also provided sheltered plots for cultivation when not in use for dwellings. Houses may occur singly or in groups, and Thomson claims to have seen a village of stone-walled houses 1.6 kilometres long[143], although there are no reports of anything as large as this surviving today. Nevertheless, it is clear that Easter Island did have quite

Fig. 12.33. Partially buried statues beneath the Rano Raraku quarries. (See also colour plate.)

Fig. 12.34. Restored houses in the village at Orongo.

large clustered settlements in prehistory, and the best known one which still survives is the ceremonial village of Orongo, high on the crater rim of Rano Kao, where the would-be birdmen and their supporters used to gather during the annual egg-gathering competition.

The Orongo village was built sometime in the sixteenth century[144], although there does appear to have been some limited Early Period occupation on the site. The village has about 48 oval corbelled houses[145] (figure 12.34), with narrow entrance tunnels and dark interiors lined with upright slabs. The walls may be up to 2 metres thick, and the interiors about 1.5 metres high. As the situation is exposed and cold, the roofs were often insulated with layers of soil on their outsides. The houses are tightly clustered in lines and around plazas, and quite often several rooms were constructed inside one single structure. One of the rooms contained a statue of the *ahu* type, made of a hard stone which does not occur on Rano Raraku, and this has relief carvings on its back representing a girdle, birdmen, and double-bladed paddles. It now graces the entrance to the Museum of Mankind in London.

Carved on the rocks near the Orongo village are many representations of birdmen (figure 12.35), similar to the ones on the back of the statue. The bird represented seems to be the frigate bird rather than the sooty tern, and the rather odd-looking anthropomorphic figures are sometimes shown clutching eggs. In the absence of a better explanation one might regard these petroglyphs as commemorating successful birdmen, earthly representatives of the god Makemake, and Heyerdahl has suggested[146] that the British Museum statue may have represented Makemake himself. However this may be, mention of petroglyphs gives me an excuse to note the quite surprising range on Easter Island[147], although not all of course are necessarily Middle Period. These include (apart from the birdmen) birds, fish, turtles, large-eyed human faces, crescentic neck ornaments called *rei miro*, and vulvas. Several of the symbols turn up in the treaty signed with the Spanish in 1770, and also in the *rongorongo* script. Most of them are widely paralleled in other parts of Polynesia; for instance, the human faces in the Marquesas and the birdmen in the Hawaiian Islands[148], and they are yet further examples of a very basic stratum of Polynesian rock-art – a class of evidence which has never really lent itself to successful archaeological analysis in the absence of any widely applicable dating method. The petroglyphs are found in many parts of the island, and in particularly secluded places, such as caves or the interiors of the Orongo houses, rock paintings have survived as well.

Middle Period sites have produced a number of artefacts, but perhaps we can look at these in connection with the Late Period, to which we now turn. The Heyerdahl expedition commenced the Late Period from A.D. 1680, one of several genealogical dates for a war fought between the rather enigmatic 'Long Ears' and 'Short Ears'.

Fig. 12.35. Carved birdmen and large eyed human face, Orongo. (See also colour plate.)

It is said that the 'Long Ears' defended themselves behind a line of ditches across the Poike peninsula in the east of the island, and that they placed brushwood in the ditches with the gruesome intention of driving in the 'Short Ears' and burning them alive. The 'Short Ears' managed to sneak around the back and hoist the 'Long Ears' with their own petards, so to speak, with the result that only one of the latter survived.

The 'Poike Ditch' itself is a most unusual earthwork, and comprises 26 sections of disconnected ditch, each five metres wide and three or four deep, running in a line for about 3 kilometres. The ditches are separated by uncut causeways, and my own impression is that this is not a defensive structure at all, and it may well be partly a natural feature. Emory[149] has in fact pointed out that the ditches could have been used as sheltered cultivation areas for bananas, sugar cane and taro. However, during their excavations in the fill of one of the ditch sections, Heyerdahl's team found that it had been in use some time during the seventeenth century on the evidence of a carbon-14 date and obsidian hydration dates[150]. So the tradition of the battle could have some historical validity, and perhaps we could compromise and have a battle story in which one side attempted to defend itself behind a pre-existing line of cultivation hollows.

The Late Period on Easter Island is marked by an absence of statue carving, and the only new *ahu* seem to have been small structures specifically for burials. We may perhaps picture a scene of increasing warfare, and decreasing resources, with a culmination in the period of statue-toppling between 1770 and 1860. Tanged obsidian spearheads (*mataa*) make a sudden and plentiful appearance in the Late Period to give support to a view of increasing warfare (figure 12.36).

The *ahu* during the Late Period were used entirely for burials. Many of them had contained burial cists during the Middle Period, but in the Late Period, burials, presumably after exposure on wooden biers, were laid on the pavements and covered with piles of small stones. Other burials were inserted into chambers and cists constructed beneath the fallen statues, and over time the once-splendid *ahu* were converted into shapeless heaps of small stones, bones and fallen statues. Burials analysed from these Late Period mantles have all turned out to be of Polynesian morphology[151].

The house forms of the Late Period were a direct continuation from the Middle, although

the circular forms may have been less common, and there is more evidence for occupation in refuge caves. Tall masonry towers with corbelled internal chambers known as *tupa* (fig. 12.37) were in use now, if not earlier, and functional explanations for these unusual structures cover turtle-spotting, burial or dwelling places (the latter being most likely), and fishermens' shrines.

The artefacts of both the Middle and Late Periods form a homogeneous group of basic Polynesian type – stone adzes, fishhooks of bone and stone (but no bonito spinners), stone bowls, obsidian tools, and several minor categories including grindstones and basalt knives. None of these artefact types have South American antecedents, and the important Andean archaeological categories of pottery, metalwork, and pressure-flaked stone tools are absent. The ethnographic assemblages do of course contain certain types unique to Easter, but this is true of all Polynesian Islands. Even such strange features as the hugely

Fig. 12.36. Obsidian *mataa*, 9 cm long.

distended ear-lobes and the topknots on the statues have numerous well-authenticated Polynesian parallels[152].

Having summarised the Easter Island archaeological record, it is perhaps time to turn in more detail to the whole question of South American contacts with Polynesia, because it is this question which of course sent the Heyerdahl expedition to Easter Island in the first place. On page 309 I reviewed the theories of Heyerdahl concerning American settlements in Polynesia as published in 1952. At this time he had two major waves, the first being white-skinned Caucasoids expelled from the Tiahuanaco region in southern Peru and Bolivia, the second being the Polynesian movement from British Columbia. After his work on Easter Island, he suggested[153] that during the Early Period the island was settled by peoples of Tiahuanaco origin, with sun-worship and the god Makemake. At the end of the Early Period the island may have been abandoned, but fresh Peruvian settlers arrived at the beginning of the Middle Period with a birdman cult and an ancestor memorial cult represented by the statues on the *ahu*. During the Middle Period the true Polynesians arrived, perhaps from the Marquesas, and the two groups coexisted until the Late Period, when the Polynesians wiped out the South Americans, and established the society observed in the eighteenth century.

Heyerdahl of course made some useful points, but I feel that even before going to Easter Island he was determined to demonstrate the existence of a superior Caucasoid group as a substratum in Polynesia, and to his own satisfaction he naturally did so. Another problem is that the archaeological and ethnographic facts from South America and eastern Polynesia are so numerous, so diverse, and so varying in their degrees of significance and reliability that any well-read person could make a very good case for American contact with Easter Island, and no-one could prove him wrong with one hundred percent certainty. As I will indicate, I do not think that Heyerdahl was necessarily completely wrong, but the inexorable recovery of information from 1956 to the present has made the possibility of major American influence on Easter Island and Polynesia increasingly remote.

Many articles have been written against Heyerdahl's views[154] in recent years, and for me to summarise them all and to cover every class of evidence would undoubtedly bore the reader to tears. Heyerdahl has worked through every available archaeological fact from Easter Island in his efforts to find American parallels, but I will limit myself to what I feel are the most significant topics.

Firstly, the language of Easter Island is Polynesian, and probably (but not certainly) has been spoken on the island since before A.D. 500. The so-called non-Polynesian numerals collected by the Spaniards on Easter in 1770 are undoubtedly the result of garbling through total non-comprehension of the language[155], and the Easter Island language has no known words of South

Fig. 12.37. *Tupa* with entrance passage and tower near *Ahu* Heki'i. (See also colour plate.)

American origin.

Secondly, skeletal evidence from the island is all Polynesian, although admittedly it comes only from the Late Period. If there were Peruvians on the island in the Early Period, we have no skeletal evidence for them.

Thirdly, all the portable artefacts ever recovered from Easter Island are either of clear Polynesian type, or sufficiently trivial to have been developed on the island through 1500 years of prehistory. I have made this point above, and while I realise that Heyerdahl has argued the opposite, I find his knowledge of Polynesian assemblages rather biased. No South American artefacts of any kind have ever been found on the island.

Fourthly, Heyerdahl's evidence for a sun-cult in the Early Period seems to be an over-romantic interpretation of some fairly shaky and poorly dated archaeological evidence. Furthermore, none of the Easter Island statues resemble Tiahuanaco styles any more than they do other Polynesian styles, and with a rather simple technology there are only so many shapes which a monolithic stone statue can take. The postures which the two areas hold in common can be found right through Southeast Asia, Oceania, and into the Americas. They probably represent a common inheritance of very high antiquity.

Other features such as double-bladed paddles, wall-paintings of weeping eyes, stone house types, birdmen symbols and the obsidian *mataa* most probably represent local forms with coincidental parallels in South America, and one can in fact find scattered parallels for all these things in various parts of Polynesia. However, before the reader says I have an irrational bias against Thor Heyerdahl because his evidence is so much more interesting, let me list a few points on which I could agree with him.

The sweet potato came from the Andean region, but whether direct to Easter Island or via some other Polynesian island is unknown, and there is always the chance of a natural introduction. Heyerdahl has also pointed out that the American lake plant *Polygonum acuminatum* makes an appearance in Easter Island pollen diagrams with the first evidence for clearance of forest by man, so it might have been introduced at this time, although the evidence is far from conclusive[156]. Some of the stone house types could have been introduced from Peru, but again one might expect the use of stone to develop independently with degradation of the forests, and the only Early Period houses in evidence were of timber superstructure.

The Early Period *ahu* with their faces of cut stones are contemporary with the use of cut stone in Classic Period Tiahuanaco (about A.D. 600), and the very finely fitted masonry of

Fig. 12.38. Cast of a section of *rongorongo* script on a piece of European ash (*Fraxinus excelsior*), total length one metre.

Vinapu I is contemporary with similar polygonal-block masonry in Inca Peru (about A.D. 1500). This may be pure coincidence, but it also may not, and having seen the relevant Inca sites myself I would incline to give Heyerdahl the benefit of the doubt over Vinapu I. It could well be Inca-inspired, although it is the only one of the 300 *ahu* on the island for which this claim can be made.

However, the cut-stone facings and the plants are the only lines of evidence which I feel give Heyerdahl any support at the present day, and even this support is still very debatable. A Peruvian specialist has recently deflated most of Heyerdahl's points from the Peruvian side as well[157], by pointing out that the Tiahuanaco coastal cultures had no maritime tradition, and that the nearest region where sea-going rafts were made is over 1000 kilometres to the north in southern Ecuador. Heyerdahl did counter these points in his 1952 book, but modern evidence is putting him more and more out on a limb. However, if I were asked whether I thought that South American Indians had ever reached Easter Island directly I would reply in the affirmative. I would genuinely like to see some more acceptable evidence of American contact in eastern Polynesia generally, if only to liven up some of the problems. And we still have one knotty problem left to consider.

In 1864 the missionary Eyraud wrote to his superiors about inscribed wooden boards kept in the houses on Easter Island, which the people apparently did not know how to read. A few of these have survived to the present day (figure 12.38), and the script is carved with about 120 elements, many based on birdman or human symbols. The script as a whole is called *rongorongo*, and the lines of characters run alternately right-left and left-right, in a pattern known as reversed boustrophedon, after the manner in which an ox ploughs a field.

Several attempts have been made to wring translations of the tablets from the Easter Islanders themselves, but none have achieved any notable degree of success. Some of the symbols occur in petroglyphs, and in the signatures on the Spanish treaty of 1770, so we do not necessarily require an exotic introduction to explain it. Views on its status vary; Métraux[158] thought it was simply a pictographic and mnemonic aid for chanting, and that the symbols were mainly of ornamental and religious value. This certainly seems to have been the way the script was used

in the nineteenth century, but it is conceivable that by this time many of the meanings of individual signs had been forgotten, and the last priests who knew the script may have died as a result of the Peruvian slave raids.

However, recent scientific attempts at decipherment have been made by Russian and German scholars, and some success has been claimed[159]. Thomas Barthel, a German pictographer, has claimed that the script has about 120 symbols which were combined into 1500–2000 composite forms. He thinks the script was basically ideographic rather than pictographic, and that some of the symbols had phonetic values as well. Barthel has also claimed that the contents of the tablets include the names of gods, creation themes, liturgical songs, calendrical data, genealogies, and even bibliographies of other tablets. In addition, some are stated to contain information on statues and *ahu*, and on the origins of the Easter Island population. Barthel thinks Easter was first settled from the Marquesas Islands, and then by Hotu Matua and his followers who came from Raiatea about A.D. 1400, bringing the script with them. While I do not have the necessary linguistic knowledge to criticise Barthel's conclusions in detail, it does seem to be that he has placed undue weight on a view of Polynesian prehistory which is a little out of date and not supported by recent archaeological findings. This does not mean that his general ideas about the script are wrong, and it could indeed be a script (albeit only a partial script according to Barthel) rather than just a simple series of mnemonic and ornamental pictures. I would not be very willing to commit myself to one viewpoint or another at the present stage of research.

Similar problems surround the origins of the script. Wilder theories of the past traced it to the Indus Valley in Pakistan or to the rulers of a lost Pacific continent, and Heyerdahl has claimed in more sensible vein[160] that it has an Andean origin. On the other hand, Barthel has pointed out that pre-Spanish scripts are not definitely reported from South America, and those of historic times are not likely to be related to the Easter Island *rongorongo*. In fact, the question looms of whether the Easter script is prehistoric at all, as it may have developed due to emulation of European writing. I find the latter prospect very likely, and the boustrophedon method is the simplest form which gives a continuous line of writing across a large space. Emory[161] thinks that the script evolved from observation of the Spanish treaty of annexation in 1770, and that it was probably developed to 'fix' chants into some concrete form which would store *mana* and prestige. I tend to agree with him, and this explanation need not necessarily conflict with that of Barthel, since it is still very likely that the priests who had developed the script were no longer alive to describe it after the Peruvian raids. The ninety years between the Spanish visit and the slave raids could in theory provide sufficient time for such a development to take place. In addition, it is rather difficult to see any reason for development of a true script in prehistoric times on Easter Island, and if one had been developed we might expect to find traces of it carved on stone. Such traces are completely absent, except for the individual pictographs.

So we finish with a view of Easter Island cultural evolution comprising a few initial settlers who increase their numbers, build their monuments, degrade the environment of the island, fight, destroy, and finally puzzle the majority of outsiders who try to understand. Easter Island prehistory may therefore look rather dull – no fleets of Viracochas or Incas, no sunken continents – but this may reflect one of our misconceptions about prehistory. Is excitement to be measured in terms of migrations, or is it not even more exciting that a group of isolated Polynesians could evolved such a magnificent prehistoric record by using their own ideas, brawn and procreative ability, rather than someone else's? Too many anthropologists in the past have held the view that all good things come from a very few areas, and that most of these areas were inhabited by Caucasoids. I am aware that the majority of archaeologists have not thought this way for many years, but it is perhaps time the change spread more widely to the general public. The peoples of Oceania deserve the credit for their achievements, not the peoples of some imaginary Mediterranean colonial enterprise.

Footnotes

1. The term *ahu* is Proto-Polynesian, meaning 'to pile up, to heap up' (Walsh and Biggs 1966: 2). The Easter Islanders also retained the term *ahu* for their temples, but these were not of the simple type mentioned for New Zealand and the Marquesas (see pages 365–366).
2. For *marae* generally see Emory 1943; 1970.
3. Duff 1959; Figueroa and Sanchez 1965. See also Groube and Chappell 1973.
4. Duff 1959; 1968a.
5. In Beaglehole 1969: 372–3.
6. Forster 1777, part II: 10; Porter 1823; Suggs 1961: 27.
7. For bibliographic references see Dening 1974; Bellwood 1972a.
8. Linton 1923; Handy 1923.
9. Sinoto 1970.
10. Skjølsvold 1972.
11. Porter 1823: 83.
12. See Handy 1923: 43.
13. Handy 1923: 231.
14. Melville 1959: 113.
15. e.g. Ferdon 1965: 121.
16. Handy 1923: 231; Linton 1925: 31.
17. Buck 1964: 163–8.
18. Melville 1959: 113.
19. Suggs 1961a: 30–38. Linton (1925-114) calls the site Uahakekua.

20. Suggs 1960a: 124.
21. Kellum-Ottino 1972.
22. Bellwood 1972a.
23. See Heyerdahl and Ferdon (eds.) 1965: 117–51.
24. Burrows 1938.
25. Buck 1944.
26. Corney 1913–9, part II: 187–94.
27. Williams 1838: 90–1.
28. According to Cook, in Beaglehole 1969: 390.
29. Williams 1838: 73–5.
30. Goldman 1970: Chapter 9. For a masterly account of all aspects of Tahitian society see Oliver 1974.
31. King, in Beaglehole 1967: 1386–7.
32. For general descriptions of the Arioi, see Williamson 1939; Henry 1928; Goldman 1970.
33. I do not give references in this section, but take my observations mainly from Cook, Banks, the Spanish expeditions (1772–5), Wilson, and Ellis. See also Lewthwaite 1964 and 1966a, and Oliver's general survey (1974).
34. The Tahitian population in 1797 was 16,050 persons approximately (Wilson 1799: 215).
35. Beaglehole 1962, part I: 303.
36. See Emory 1933: 73.
37. Emory 1933.
38. Green and Green 1968.
39. Sinoto 1966b: 49.
40. One on Huahine has been dated recently to *c.* A.D. 1600 (Sinoto 1966: 49).

41. Handy 1930b.
42. Buck 1944: 521.
43. Luomala 1951: 62.
44. Green *et al.* 1967.
45. Garanger 1964; 1968 for Tahiti, Green *et al.* 1967 for Moorea.
46. Green 1961.
47. Emory 1934a; 1939a; 1947; Garanger and Lavondes 1966.
48. Unpublished notes, University of Auckland.
49. Emory 1939a: 50.
50. Emory 1947.
51. Verin 1969.
52. See Emory 1970: 80–3.
53. Skjølsvold 1965.
54. Aitken 1930.
55. Williams 1838: 37–8. See also Verin 1969: 282–3.
56. Emory 1970: 84.
57. See Heyerdahl and Ferdon 1965: reports 2–4.
58. For references to these works, see Bellwood 1977a.
59. Trotter ed. 1974; Bellwood 1974, 1977a.
60. See Williams 1838: 165–9 for the earliest record of this story.
61. Bellwood 1971a.
62. See Bellwood 1977a.
63. Bellwood 1970.
64. See Heyerdahl and Skjølsvold 1965; Emory 1928b; Green 1959; Lavachery 1936; Gathercole 1964.
65. Records of these structures are unfortunately very imprecise – see Lavachery 1936.
66. Sinoto 1973.
67. Bellwood 1977a.
68. Duff 1968b.
69. McCarthy 1934.
70. Emory 1934b; 1939b; Finney 1958. Maude (1963: 173) thinks once-inhabited Sydney Island was abandoned because of the high salinity of the lagoon and the lack of fish.
71. Buck 1932a; Bellwood 1977a.
72. Lamont 1867.
73. Schmitt 1971.
74. Hopkins 1862; Kuykendall 1947: chapter 3.
75. Goldman 1970: 200.
76. Dahlgren 1916.
77. Goldman 1970: chapter 10.
78. Kelly 1967.
79. Goldman 1970: 241.
80. Ellis 1969b: 430; Buck 1957:1; Emory 1959.
81. Sinoto 1968: 116–7; Emory 1970: 90.
82. Cordy 1974a.
83. Cox 1967.
84. e.g. Tainter 1973.
85. Apple 1965.
86. Summers 1964
87. Ellis 1969b: 356.
88. Bennett 1931.
89. Emory 1928a.
90. Emory and Sinoto 1959.
91. Updike 1965: 167–9.
92. Emory 1970: 88.
93. For general descriptions see Buck 1957; Bennett 1931; McAllister 1933.
94. Ellis 1969b: 164; Ladd 1969c.
95. Ladd 1969a; 1969b.
96. Anell 1956.
97. e.g. Bennett 1931; McAllister 1933.
98. Kirch 1971b.
99. Green (ed.) 1969; 1970d; Ladd and Yen 1972; Ladd 1973.
100. Griffin *et al.* 1971; Kirch and Kelly 1975.
101. Griffin *et al.* 1971; Newman 1972; Tuggle and Griffin 1973.
102. Newman 1969.
103. As pointed out by Yen 1973: 81; 1974: 315.
104. Cordy 1974b; 1974c.
105. Barrow 1967.
106. e.g. Emory 1924; Cox 1970.
107. Major works covering Easter Island include Thomson 1889; Routledge 1919; Métraux 1940; Heyerdahl and Ferdon 1961; 1965; Heyerdahl 1968b; Englert 1970.
108. Heyerdahl 1966; 1968b: 51–74.
109. Heyerdahl (1968b: 160) has stated that *Polygonum* first appears in an Easter Island pollen profile when evidence for forest clearance begins, but this may not necessarily mean that man had just introduced it from South America. The clearing process itself could have encouraged its growth in hitherto forested areas around the lake.
110. Emory 1972: 62–3; see also Pickergill and Bunting 1969.
111. Métraux (1940: 20–3) gives a figure of 111, but I understand the correct figure to be 110 (Grant McCall: personal communication).
112. See Corney 1908: 3–25.
113. Dening 1960: Table I.
114. Suggested by Englert 1970: 121.
115. Heyerdahl 1968a: 134; 1968b: 159–60.
116. Corney 1908.
117. McCoy 1971.
118. For a discussion of these basket-work figures see Luomala 1973: 40–4.
119. Beaglehole 1969; G. Forster 1777, Volume I.
120. Heyerdahl and Ferdon 1961: 56–64.
121. Thomson 1889: 526.

122. Métraux 1940: 90.

123. Englert 1970: 93.

124. Brown 1924.

125. Heyerdahl 1958.

126. Goldman 1970: Chapter 6.

127. e.g. Métraux 1957: 238; Suggs 1960a: 186; Barthel 1961; Emory 1970: 91.

128. Métraux 1940: 272; Figueroa and Sanchez 1965; Emory 1968: 161.

129. Routledge did publish two important works in 1919 and 1920.

130. See Heyerdahl and Ferdon 1961, from which many of the points in the following discussion are taken. Also Smith 1962.

131. Mulloy 1961.

132. Golson 1965.

133. Ayres 1971.

134. Mulloy 1975a.

135. McCoy 1973.

136. Ayres 1971.

137. For detailed descriptions see Routledge 1919; Métraux 1940; Skjølsvold 1961; Mulloy 1970. Mulloy (1973) has suggested that there could once have been as many as 1000 statues on the island.

138. Mulloy 1970.

139. Brown 1924: 16.

140. Chauvet 1935.

141. Emory 1943; 1970, but disputed by Lavachery 1951.

142. Sahlins 1955.

143. Thomson 1889: 486.

144. Ferdon 1961.

145. Routledge 1920. Many of these houses have recently been restored; see Mulloy 1975b.

146. Heyerdahl 1961: 511.

147. Lavachery 1939.

148. See Barrow 1967.

149. Emory 1963a.

150. Evans 1965.

151. Murrill 1968.

152. Skinner 1967.

153. See Heyerdahl 1968a; 1968b. For an interesting anticipation of Heyerdahl's views see Thomson 1871: 45.

154. e.g. Suggs 1960a; Golson 1965; Lanning 1970; Emory 1972.

155. Métraux 1936.

156. See footnote 109.

157. Lanning 1970.

158. Métraux 1940: 399–405.

159. Butinov and Knorozov 1957; Barthel 1971.

160. Heyerdahl 1965.

161. Emory 1972.

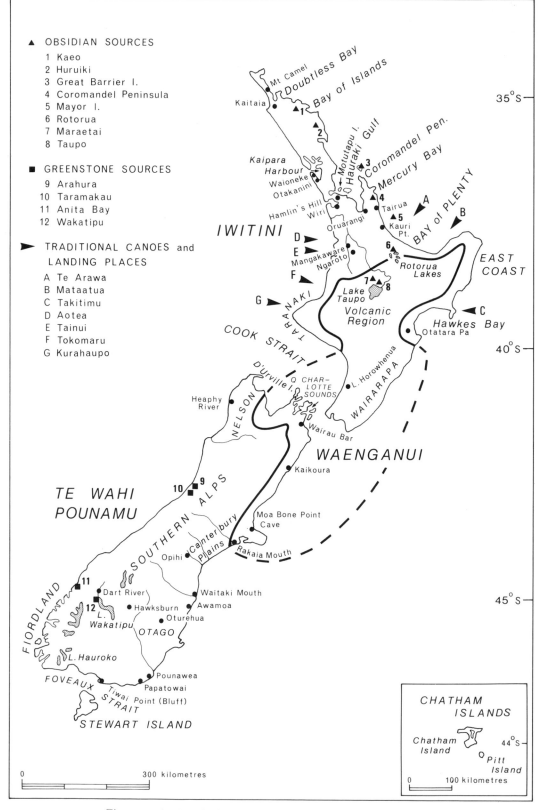

▲ OBSIDIAN SOURCES

1 Kaeo
2 Huruiki
3 Great Barrier I.
4 Coromandel Peninsula
5 Mayor I.
6 Rotorua
7 Maraetai
8 Taupo

■ GREENSTONE SOURCES

9 Arahura
10 Taramakau
11 Anita Bay
12 Wakatipu

► TRADITIONAL CANOES and LANDING PLACES

A Te Arawa
B Mataatua
C Takitimu
D Aotea
E Tainui
F Tokomaru
G Kurahaupo

Fig. 13.1. Archaeological and traditional map of New Zealand.

CHAPTER 13

The Prehistory of New Zealand

New Zealand provides an interesting arena for prehistory, despite its apparent isolation. With over 250,000 square kilometres of land it is bigger than all the rest of Polynesia put together, and it was also the only large temperate land mass to be settled by Austronesian horticulturalists. Furthermore, it has a more detailed archaeological record than any other area covered in this book[1].

So let us look at the country in a little more detail, particularly from the viewpoint of its early Polynesian settlers, who probably arrived at some point between A.D. 750 and 1000[2]. The three main islands (North Island, South Island and Stewart Island) stretch for about 1300 kilometres from north to south, between 34° and 47° South latitude. The climate ranges from warm temperate to cool temperate, and the variation from north to south is sufficient to impose considerable complexity in economic organisation. The main tropical crops such as coconut, banana, and breadfruit would not grow, although the taro, yam and gourd seem to have enjoyed a limited degree of success in the North Island. The paper mulberry tree also acquired a very precarious foothold, but barkcloth was very rare by Captain Cook's day, and in the Bay of Islands it was apparently used only for ear ornaments. However, one hardier plant did gain a more important foothold, and this was the Andean sweet potato – the *kumara* of the Maoris. Even this was limited mainly to the coasts of the North Island and the northern part of the South Island, to as far south as the Christchurch region. Since the first settlers also failed to introduce pigs and chicken, it is clear that prehistoric Maori economy was by necessity far removed from that of the tropical Polynesians[3].

In 1949, two New Zealand geographers, Lewthwaite and Cumberland, devised a tripartite division of New Zealand into three main environmental provinces[4]. The northern province of Iwitini ('many tribes') comprises the whole area north of and including the inland Waikato, together with the coastal regions of Taranaki and the East Coast down to Hawkes Bay. This province is warm and relatively frost-free, and with its extensive fertile volcanic soils and large harbours it probably supported over 80 percent of New Zealand's population in the eighteenth century. To the south of Iwitini lies Waenganui ('transitional'), and this includes the southern part of the North Island and the northern and northeastern fringes of the South. Generally a frostier region at the limits of *kumara* cultivation, it might have supported about 15 percent of New Zealand's population in the eighteenth century. Finally, the province of Te Wahi Pounamu ('the place of greenstone'), the greater part of the South Island, was beyond the range of Maori horticulture and populated by rather scattered food gatherers.

In pre-human times, New Zealand was primarily a forested country, except for the high mountain chain of the South Island and the volcanically active interior of the North Island. Few resources were available on the acid andesitic ash cover of the latter area, and settlement was necessarily restricted. Otherwise, the North Island was mostly clothed in semi-tropical rain forest which would supply birds, berries, and a wide range of native vegetable foods. Many parts of the South Island also supported forest, but here the ecologically favourable podocarp forests which dominated in the North Island gradually gave way southwards and westwards to more barren beech forests. The rain-shadow area of the Canterbury Plains probably supported a podocarp forest and grassland mosaic which would have been a major habitat for extinct land birds (moa) in early days, although this mosaic rapidly succumbed, as did the moa, to man and his fire[5].

From the great range of native vegetable foods, a small number are known to have been of particular importance[6]. *Karaka* trees (*Corynocarpus laevigatus*) were often planted around settlements for their edible berries. The massive rhizome of the cabbage tree (*Cordyline terminalis* – a possible non-native) was cooked for up to two days in large earth ovens to caramelise the starch. But the major native food was without doubt the rhizome of the fern, *Pteridium esculentum*. This rather stringy product was baked and pounded to assist extraction of the edible starch from the tough fibres, and it could be easily dried and stored after the harvest on raised wooden platforms (*whata*). In the highly seasonal climate of New Zealand food storability was a major factor, as we will see in the case of the sweet potato. The fern rhizome liked good well-drained soil, and like the sweet potato seems to have flourished best in the warmer parts of the North Island, where it was partly cultivated by man and even transported as food over considerable distances. It was used as a fallow crop for sweet potato, and also seems to have been grown in specially made clearings kept open by frequent firing. As well as being resistant to fire, the rhizomes could also be cropped much more frequently than any of the introduced food plants without causing severe soil exhaustion[7].

Of the introduced plants[8], the taro seems to have had a limited success as a slow-maturing crop in sheltered areas, but the plant of greatest ritual and social importance for the Maori was the sweet potato. This was less productive by weight than the fern rhizome and much more difficult to grow, but was undoubtedly considered superior in terms of taste and texture. It needed light friable soil of high fertility, and seems to have grown best on the mature volcanic or alluvial soils of the northern part of the North Island, although even here, particularly in the Waikato region, thousands of hectares had to be lightened and aerated by the addition of thousands of tons of quarried sand or gravel[9]. In addition, soil regeneration under the regime of shifting agriculture practised in temperate New

Zealand was rather slower than in the humid tropics, and fallow periods of more than ten years could be necessary. Furthermore, the sweet potato needed elaborate frost-free subterranean storage if seed tubers were to survive the winter, and the pits used for this storage provide a valuable class of archaeological features to which we will return later.

Seasonal availability of these foods of course varied considerably[10]. In the horticultural areas of Iwitini and Waenganui the sweet potato would be planted in spring and harvested in autumn, while the fern rhizome would be at its best for harvest in early summer. Fishing and shellfishing went on all year, with dogs and occasional men as extra protein. Food gathering and birding could continue during the winter, but at this time the value of stored foods was at a premium. Visiting, feasting and warfare seem to have been activities most popular after the autumn harvests, when food availability would be at its highest[11].

When Captain Cook first landed in New Zealand in 1769, it is possible that the country supported a colourful and warlike population of between 100,000 and 150,000 people[12]. These were divided into about 40 tribes, and in social organisation and language they had retained their Polynesian ancestry in a very clear-cut and decisive fashion, as we saw in chapters 4 and 5. However, technology had seen marked changes, and subsistence economy a major transformation, and it is with the prehistoric record of these developments that we will be concerned most in this chapter.

THE VIEW FROM TRADITION

Before we do turn to some of the more prosaic facts of modern archaeology, we should at least take a brief look at some of the romantic beliefs of an earlier age. When Europeans first arrived in New Zealand they occasionally questioned Maoris about their origins, but very few seem to have made any recorded headway. Sir Joseph Banks was told in 1769 that the Maori homeland was called Heawye, and lay to the north of New Zealand, in an area of many islands. This, of course, can only be the legendary homeland Hawaiki, a name very widespread throughout eastern Polynesia. Unfortunately however, no-one else seems to have attacked the problem with any vigour for a tragic lapse of seventy years, during which time Maoris and Polynesian islanders were hobnobbing about traditional matters with great gusto – a development which had already begun with Tupaia in 1769. So by the late 1830s, when serious recording about traditional matters began, we can only expect to find massive contamination through increasing communication, education, and perhaps even nostalgia in a rapidly changing world. What the Maoris really knew in 1769 about their origins we will never know.

Anyway, a brief review of the course of traditional history is still in order, and it does seem reasonable to assume that much valid information may have been retained in priestly families for several generations after Cook. A good deal of this information seems to have revolved around the arrivals of ancestors in named canoes. Horatio Hale, who visited the Bay of Islands around 1840[13], was told that the first Maori arrivals came in four canoes called Tainui, Te Arawa, Horouta and Takitumu, which landed at various remembered points around the Iwitini coastline. Hamlin, writing about the same area in 1842[14], gave the canoe names as Tainui, Arawa, Matátua and Kuraawhaupo, and stated that no Maoris could tell him the dates of arrival. Hamlin also mentioned an important Northland tradition to the effect that New Zealand was first explored (but not settled) by a man named Kupe. Finally, Sir George Grey, writing in the same period[15], stated that New Zealand was first found by Ngahue, and then settled by six canoes, named Tainui, Matatua, Takitumu, Kurahaupo, Tokomaru and Matawhaorua. Something like a coherent tradition, albeit with a few rough edges, was starting to make its appearance. Also appearing at this time were traditions of large flightless birds (moas), whose bones were being found in certain areas[16], and even still being used for making fishhooks by some eastern North Island tribes.

Canoe traditions continued to be repeated sporadically through the rest of the nineteenth century, and it also became clear from surviving genealogies that the main time of arrival was probably around the fourteenth century[17]. By the end of the century it was commonplace to write of the initial discovery of New Zealand by Kupe or Ngahue, followed by settlement by a major 'Fleet' of seven or so canoes[18].

But there is much more to traditional history than the now well-known Fleet. As early as 1866, J.A. Wilson[19] had claimed a pre-Fleet settlement in New Zealand, of non-horticulturalists whom he called the 'Maui Nation'. These people settled the North Island, spoke Maori, and were eventually over-run by their close cousins the 'Hawaiki Maoris', who arrived with the Fleet. Wilson's Fleet actually included 11 canoes, and he even noted an account written between 1836 and 1841 which gave the names of 22! No wonder that the careful William Colenso was constrained to write in 1868:

> In all this mythical rhapsody there is scarcely a grain of truth; and yet some educated Europeans have wholly believed it. The New Zealanders themselves, however, never did so. The names of the canoes and of the leaders are nearly all figurative names suitably coined in the New Zealand tongue, and given after the event. . .[20]

Unfortunately, Colenso seems to have attracted few disciples, perhaps because people at that time knew that traditions were the only available key to the past, apart from the nascent discipline of archaeology. And if the traditions were to provide an acceptable Maori history, then they had to be tidied up. This rather fundamental task was carried out by Percy Smith in 1915[21], when he published translations of traditions collected about 1865 from a *whare wananga* (school of learning) in the Wairarapa District of the southern North Island. Smith imposed his own ideas rather heavily on the resulting narrative, but came up with the following record of events:

1. Initial exploration by Kupe, from Rarotonga, about A.D. 925. No permanent settlement.
2. Initial settlement by the '*tangata whenua*' (people of the land), who were a mixed Melanesian-Polynesian group from western Polynesia with a Polynesian language. They settled only the North Island, and later the Chathams (about A.D. 1175).
3. Polynesians arrive under Toi and Whatonga, about A.D. 1125, followed by another settler called Manaia.
4. The Fleet arrives about A.D. 1350 from Tahiti.

Although Smith did not provide details of all the Fleet canoes, the accepted number soon became fixed at seven; particularly the *Tainui, Tokomaru, Kurahaupo, Te Arawa, Matatua, Aotea* and *Takitimu* (or *Takitumu*). Other canoe names recorded from various parts of New Zealand were attributed to periodic arrivals not directly connected with the main Fleet, and in fact there never was any complete agreement amongst scholars about the exact composition of the latter. Despite integration of the concept into the beliefs of many Maori communities, and its almost fossilised position in school and popular books, the Kupe-Toi-Fleet chronology has been systematically dismantled in recent years. A long and thoughtful debate carried out in the pages of the *Journal of the Polynesian Society* from 1956 to 1969 examined the whole issue of traditions from top to bottom[22], finally to produce an unfavourable verdict from the viewpoint of the Fleet. Roberton, a respected scholar of Maori tradition, was obliged during this period to alter his view from acceptance of the Fleet to rejection, while retaining the *Tainui* and *Te Arawa* canoe traditions as valid sources of history. Sharp, his main protagonist, proposed the major view that the Fleet traditions simply referred to internal population movements within New Zealand. More recently, Simmons[23] has systematically dismantled the historicity of Smith's *whare wananga* narrative, and the Kupe-Toi-Fleet traditions can no longer be considered as valid representations of New Zealand prehistory.

However, let us beware at this point. As we will see, the date for Kupe correlates very well with the approximate archaeological date for the settlement of New Zealand, and the date for the Fleet correlates with the commencement of Classic Maori culture in the North Island, to be discussed below. These traditions do undoubtedly contain some valid historical information, and it will be possible to return to them when we come to the archaeological reconstruction of New Zealand prehistory later on. The traditions in themselves are not automatically wrong, and the fault lay far more in the interpretations of them by European scholars.

The point is emphasised even more with the so-called *tangata whenua* settlement of Melanesian-like peoples, believed by Smith to have settled the North Island after the visit of Kupe. Best[24] rather irresponsibly stirred up the concept of inferior Melanesian settlers called Maruiwi (or Mouriuri) in the North Island, later to be amalgamated into and exterminated by the superior Polynesian Maoris. For a while this view attracted followers, and Keyes has quite recently proposed some rather more scholarly evidence, without the old overtones of inferiority, for Melanesian and western Polynesian settlement in New Zealand, centering his arguments on possible Melanesian prototypes for a number of items of material culture[25]. However, the bulk of evidence is now against direct Melanesian settlement in New Zealand, although Maori culture does of course share many common retentions with Melanesia[26]. Best's sources were in fact strongly attacked many years ago by Williams and Skinner[27], and his reconstruction labelled the 'Maruiwi myth', so the whole issue may be safely laid to rest.

THE COMING OF ARCHAEOLOGY

While the armchair traditionalists were wrestling with their genealogies, other more energetic natural scientists were busy laying the foundations of field archaeology in New Zealand. From 1838 onwards, moa bones and traditions about these flightless birds were being recovered, and New Zealand's first excavation occurred in 1847 when the geologist Mantell excavated moa bones at a site called Awamoa in north Otago[28]. In 1859–60 a moa egg was found with a human skeleton at Kaikoura, and later sold in England for £120![29] In 1869, the geologist Julius von Haast carried out his first excavation on a prehistoric campsite at the mouth of the Rakaia River in Canterbury[30], and first coined the now widely used term 'Moa-hunter'.

At Rakaia, von Haast found moa bones, ovens, flaked stone tools, and a few pieces of obsidian imported from Mayor Island in the Bay of Plenty. He felt that the Maoris really knew nothing about the moas, and that their rather slim traditions actually referred to cassowaries, known by them from their earlier migrations through New Guinea. Moas belonged to a much more remote era, contemporary with the mammoths and cave bears of Europe (i.e. late Pleistocene in present terminology, although von Haast was unable to give specific dates). The Moa-hunters were Polynesian autochthones from a Pacific continent, and inhabited New Zealand when it was a single land-mass, long before the arrival of the Maoris. They did not polish stone tools, use greenstone, or practise cannibalism, and their dogs he considered feral.

In 1872, von Haast turned his attention to the Moa Bone Point Cave near Christchurch[31]. Here he was obliged to modify his ideas a little, for he found polished stone tools in the Moa-hunter levels, together with wooden posts[32], but no shellfish. The latter were present in the higher and recognizably Maori levels of the cave, and von Haast was quick to notice this difference, together with the absence of moa remains in

Fig. 2.3. New Hebridean children at Ebao village, Efate.

Fig. 2.4. Fijian women at Sigatoka village, Viti Levu.

Fig. 2.5. Indonesian street scene at Banjarmasin, Kalimantan Selatan (Borneo).

Fig. 2.6. Polynesian family at Vaipa village, Aitutaki, southern Cook Islands.

Fig 4.6. A northern Abelam ceremonial house, Sepik District. For a discussion of the painted designs see Forge 1973.

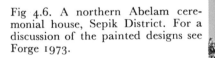

Fig. 4.7. A village on Kiriwina Trobriand Islands. The tall structure at centre left is a yam-storage house (see also figure 6.4).

Fig. 4.12. Circular houses in a Samoan village at Matautu, Upolu.

ig. 6.4. A yam store-house on Kiriwina,
robriand Islands.

Fig. 6.7. Swamp cultivation of taro on Mangaia, Cook Islands.

Fig. 6.8. 'Staircase' terracing for taro cultivation on Rarotonga, Cook Islands.

Fig. 8.25. Beads of the Early Metal Period from the Talaud Islands: *top row*, spherical carnelian (*left*) and two facetted carnélians (*right*); *bottom row*, acid-etched agate (*left*) and banded agate (*right*).

Fig. 9.22. Pottery manufacture coiling, Geme village, Talaud Islands eastern Indonesia.

Fig. 11.7. The Ha'amonga-a-Maui, Tongatapu Island.

Fig. 11.8. A *langi* faced with coral slabs, Mu'a, Tongatapu.

Fig. 11.9. Facing of dressed coral blocks on the Paepae-o-Telea, Mu'a, Tongatapu. Note the carved step at ground level.

Above. Fig. 12.2. Rock-cut ditch of fort above Taiohae, Nuku Hiva, Marquesas.

Right. Fig. 12.6. Marquesan stone statue in the Taipivai Valley, Nuku Hiva.

Below left. Fig. 12.5. Lower terrace walling of the *tohua* Vahangeku'a, Taipivai Valley, Nuku Hiva, Marquesas.

Below right. Fig. 12.10. Two-tiered *marae* platform of Leeward Island type, *marae* Manunu, Maeva, Huahine.

Fig. 12.20. Line of basalt uprights averaging 2 metres high, forming part of a large *marae* at Paengariki, Aitutaki.

Fig. 12.30. Shaped and fitted facing blocks at *Ahu* Vinapu I, Easter Island.

Fig. 12.33. Partially buried statues beneath the Rano Raraku quarries, Easter Island.

Fig. 12.28. *Ahu* Akivi: a restored Middle Period structure showing a complete arrangement of statues, ramp and earth-walled court.

Fig. 12.35. Carved birdmen and large-eyed human face, Orongo, Easter Island.

Right. Fig. 12.37. *Tupa* with entrance passage and tower near *Ahu* Heki'i.

Below left. Fig. 13.3. A reconstruction of the large moa *(Dinornis maximus)*.

Below right. Fig. 13.18. The Lake Hauroko burial, South Island of New Zealand.

the latter. However, his initial and rather extreme views about the Moa-hunters were quickly dealt with by a vociferous opposition, led partly by his own assistant MacKay, who felt that the moas had been exterminated by Maoris who arrived sometime before the Fleet, perhaps about 1350 years ago[33]. MacKay was supported by many other scholars[34], and by 1879 von Haast himself was forced to subscribe to the popular view: the Moa-hunters, basically, were simply the first Maoris[35]. So ended the rather flamboyant early phase of New Zealand archaeology.

After the excavations of von Haast, who for his day could be considered a careful excavator and recorder, a marked decline seems to have affected the fortunes of archaeology in New Zealand. Little further work was carried out until the 1920s and 1930s, when a rather unsystematic and destructive phase of excavation was perpetrated on Moa-hunter sites in the Otago region[36]. A high standard of ethnological reconstruction was achieved by H.D. Skinner during this period, and one of his major contributions was to differentiate between the 'Southern Culture' of the South Island and Chatham Islands, and the 'Northern Culture' of the North Island. The former was regarded by Skinner as fundamentally Polynesian, the latter as having both Polynesian and Melanesian traits, particularly in art styles[37]. And while direct Melanesian influences on New Zealand are no longer considered seriously, Skinner did make an initial and fundamental division between the two cultural 'poles' visible in New Zealand; poles which I will refer to below as the Archaic and Classic Phases of the New Zealand Eastern Polynesian Culture. With this cue, we can now turn to the modern archaeology.

THE NEW ZEALAND PREHISTORIC SEQUENCE

The foundation work of the modern period of New Zealand archaeology was published by Roger Duff in 1950, and entitled *The Moa-Hunter Period of Maori Culture*[38]. Partly as a result of his earlier excavations at the remarkable burial ground of Wairau Bar in Marlborough Province, Duff concluded that New Zealand prehistory was Polynesian right through, and that the Maori culture observed by Cook in 1769 was preceded by a lineal ancestral culture which he called 'Moa-hunter', after von Haast. The Moa-hunters arrived from the Society Islands some time before A.D. 1000, and Duff went on to conclude that 'Moa-hunter culture merged in-sensibly and unconsciously into Maori culture, indeed became Maori culture, and that in the isolated South Island the time lag of this process was more marked'[39].

Maori culture, according to Duff, developed mainly in the southern part of Iwitini, and from there spread over the North Island and into the northern part of the South Island. Maoris of the Moa-hunter Period lacked cultivation, warfare, weapons and forts, and Duff therefore retained the Fleet concept to introduce horticulture into the North Island about A.D. 1350, and thus to provide the necessary fillip for the development of Maori culture. Duff's two period division still holds today, although it has been modified in several aspects, particularly those concerning horticulture and warfare.

In 1959, Jack Golson presented a rather different terminology from that of Duff, albeit based on a fairly identical two-phase division[40]. Golson coined the term 'New Zealand Eastern Polynesian Culture' for the whole span of prehistory, and divided it into two phases: Archaic and Classic (or Classic Maori). These terms are still in common use in the literature, and I will be using them in the North Island context below.

The Duff and Golson classifications are the only two which have really been applied to the whole of New Zealand, although more detailed culture-historical frameworks have been proposed for the Auckland region and the South Island, and we will be returning to these later. Two-phase divisions of the Duff-Golson type do of course tend to polarise what may in fact be a quite complex trend in cultural development, and they are based very heavily on artefacts. But, on the other hand, they do provide a rather necessary degree of simplicity which is valuable if not abused.

THE ORIGINS OF THE MAORIS

For Golson and succeeding New Zealand archaeologists, the Kupe-Toi-Fleet concept of successive arrivals from outside New Zealand has not proved very viable. The prevailing view now is that New Zealand was settled once, and that most of its cultural development is indigenous. The inhabitants of any later canoes arriving at odd points around the coastline would not have had any marked impact on the already established settlers, and items once attributed to the Fleet, such as horticulture, warfare and certain weapon types, are almost certain to have been present from the beginning. This means that the origin of the Maoris is really focussed on the first arriving canoes.

The Archaic Phase in New Zealand is represented by a range of artefacts paralleled very closely in the Maupiti and Vaitootia sites in the Society Islands, and in the earlier levels of the Hane site in the Marquesas (see pages 321–324). These sites, and the earliest sites in New Zealand, date to the centuries around and before A.D. 1000, and there is little reasonable doubt that the first Maori settlers came from some part of central Polynesia, from an area encompassing the Marquesas, Society, Cook and Austral Islands. It is not possible to be more specific than this owing to cultural convergence in eastern Polynesia as one goes back in time. However, Roger Green has suggested that a shank of a trolling hook made of pearl-shell (figure 13.2), found in an Archaic site at Tairua on the Coromandel Peninsula of the North Island, may be of direct Marquesan origin[41], and he has suggested a Marquesan settlement on the north-eastern coast of the North Island in the tenth or eleventh century. Sinoto also supports a Marquesan settlement on other artefact similarities[42], although many New Zealand Archaic sites, particularly Wairau Bar, find closer parallels in the Maupiti assemblage from the Societies. It could be that New Zealand was settled by more than one group, roughly at the same time, and this hypothesis does not necessarily pose any challenge to a unitary and indigenous development of New Zealand culture after initial settlement. What is apparent, from available radiocarbon dates, is that once New Zealand was settled people spread over the coastal areas, with a fairly homogeneous artefact assemblage, very quickly. Sites dated to around A.D. 1000–1100 occur right through from north to south, and there are as yet no indications for earliest settlement in any one particular locality.

MAN AND THE MOAS

If the early settlers in New Zealand found them-

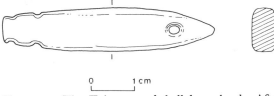

Fig. 13.2. The Tairua pearl-shell lure shank. After Green 1967a.

selves without many of their tropical foods and fibres[43], they did at least have the advantage in the early days of a sizeable avifauna[44]. Unfortunately, this was not an advantage which was to be very long-lived, owing to a rather tragic rate of extinction which may have been due both to human and to natural causes. By the seventeenth century the flightless moa were all but extinct[45], and so was the eagle *Harpagornis moorei* which probably depended upon them for food. Other avian extinctions in Maori prehistory include a giant rail (*Aptornis otidiformis*), a flightless goose (*Cnemiornis calcitrans*), a swan (*Chenopis sumnerensis*), a coot (*Palaeolimnas chatamensis*), a hawk (*Circus eylesi*), and a crow (*Palaeocorax moriorum*).

The moas comprise 6 genera, with between 20 and 22 species[46], and there is little doubt that they were of considerable economic importance in some parts of New Zealand in the first few centuries of settlement. In addition, their bones, together with those of the extinct swan, were very frequently used for fishhooks and ornaments. The species ranged in size from small birds of kiwi size to giants up to 3 metres in height (*Dinornis maximus* – figure 13.3), and all six genera were still surviving when man first appeared, although the medium-sized *Eurapteryx* seems to have been the most common. It has been suggested that

Fig. 13.3. A reconstruction of the large moa *Dinornis maximus*. (See also colour plate.)

moas had solitary habits and laid single eggs, so their island paradise would very quickly have been devastated by the combined actions of men and dogs.

Concerning moa habitats, Simmons[47] has suggested that the majority of them were forest and forest-edge dwellers, and that they lived mainly on foods provided by the podocarp forests. The more barren beech forests of parts of the South Island evidently did not support large populations, and the North Island moa populations were also small owing to the increasing replacement of the podocarp forests by less favourable broadleaf forests, from a time perhaps prior to the arrival of man[48]. Indeed, North Island Archaic sites quite often have very few or no moa bones at all, and this circumstance has led to criticisms of Duff's term 'Moa-hunter' in terms of its universal validity.

The greatest populations of moa appear to have lived down the eastern side of the South Island, in a pre-human mosaic of forests and grassland. Some of the larger species may in fact have been grassland dwellers; it is rather difficult to imagine *Dinornis maximus* making successful headway in New Zealand rain forest, although its food may have come mainly from forest edges. Certainly, after the destruction of the Canterbury forests by man between about A.D. 1100 and 1350 the moa populations undergo a

sharp decline, so tussock grassland alone was probably not a favourable environment for them. On the other hand, before the forest destruction, the Canterbury and Otago coast supported what was almost certainly the densest concentration of moas and human settlements in New Zealand, as we will see below.

But was man alone (or with his dogs) responsible for the demise of the moa? David Simmons does not think so and suggests that the moa gene pool might have been reduced in the late Pleistocene when these birds were confined to small areas of forest, and that they may never have fully recovered their prior vigour. So man may merely have added the finishing touches, albeit with a rather heavy hand.

THE ARCHAIC PHASE IN THE SOUTH ISLAND

The Archaic Phase, equivalent to the Moa-hunter Period of Duff, witnessed initial settlement of the whole of New Zealand by settlers with a characteristically Early Eastern Polynesian material culture. In the North Island it is overlain by the Classic Maori Phase, developing from about A.D. 1300 onwards. Over the greater part of the South Island the Archaic Phase continues until European contact. The terms Archaic and Classic are therefore taken to refer to cultural patterns and not to time periods.

Fig. 13.4. Reconstruction of burial 2 (male) at Wairau Bar, with necklaces of reels and imitation whale teeth (*top left*), a necklace of drilled porpoise teeth (*next to skull*), 14 argillite adzes, and a drilled moa egg.

The most spectacular site of the New Zealand Archaic lies on a narrow spit which forms a bar across the mouth of the Wairau River, in the province of Marlborough, South Island. This site, with an estimated 15–20 acres of occupation, was excavated by Jim Eyles and Roger Duff between 1939 and 1952[49]. Although the excavation methods used do not allow reconstruction of the settlement plan, it certainly comprised shell middens, ovens, pits of unknown function (sweet potato storage seems unlikely), and burials. The latter lie on the inland side of the occupation area, and some contained assemblages of unparalleled richness.

The most important burials were those of males in extended positions, often buried with perforated whole moa eggs which may have served as water bottles (figure 13.4). Seven of the richest burials were in fact clustered in a single group. Female burials were more frequently in a crouched position, with few or no goods. Some burials lacked skulls, others had apparently been exhumed and then reburied, and certain bones were very probably removed for ancestor rituals and to make ornaments for relatives. Several burials were also provided with moa joints, and at least one was laid in a wooden coffin, perhaps a canoe section. A radiocarbon date from the site suggests a date around A.D. 1125.

The goods found with the burials (see figure 13.6), particularly the high status males, are of tremendous importance, and the whole assemblage is greatly increased in number by the artefacts recovered from the occupation areas of the site during excavation. No less than 121 reel units for necklaces were found, carved from moa bone (*Eurapteryx*), whale ivory, dentalium shell, or even human bone. Other necklaces were made of small shark teeth (figure 13.5) or whale teeth, and the latter could be perforated and used with their shape unmodified, or they could be shaped into peg-like forms generally referred to as 'imitation whale-tooth pendants'. These imitation forms were usually made from moa or human bone, more rarely of true whale teeth, and a rather surprising total of 131 were recovered from the Wairau site. These ornament forms are of course very closely paralleled in contemporary assemblages from the Marquesas and Society Islands, as we saw in Chapter 11.

Other more utilitarian Wairau artefacts include possible cloak pins made from whale ribs, needles and awls of bird bone, bone or stone tattooing needles, and bone bird spears and harpoons (figure 13.6). However, perhaps the most spectacular of the Wairau artefacts are the adzes, of which 207 were recovered in total, one very rich male burial being provided with no less than fourteen (figure 13.4). Some of the adzes were very large and showed no signs of usage, so either

Fig. 13.5. Part of burial 29 at Wairau Bar showing shark tooth necklace and adzes *in situ*. From Duff 1956.

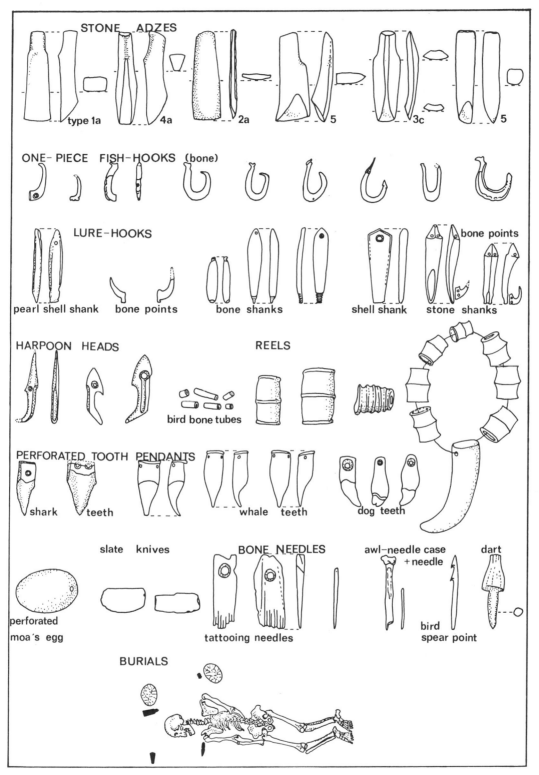

Fig. 13.6. The New Zealand Archaic assemblage; a composite illustration from several sites. From Green 1974a.

they were made especially for the burials, or perhaps they served some ceremonial usage in the society. The majority were made of a very fine argillite of the kind which outcrops on D'Urville Island and in the Nelson Mineral Belt[50], and they encompassed almost the whole range of New Zealand variety, with the notable exception of the Classic Maori type 2B (Duff terminology). Tanged adzes of types 1A and 4A, together with untanged adzes of type 2A were the predominant forms, and one of the horned 1A adzes attained a remarkable length of 45 centimetres.

The Wairau Bar fishing gear comprised one-piece bait hooks of moa bone or seal ivory, and trolling hooks with stone or bone shanks and bone points. Only two points of composite bait hooks were found, this type being more popular in later sites. The fishing gear is clearly paralleled very precisely in contemporary Society Island and Marquesan sites, although the absence of pearl shell in New Zealand obviously necessitated the use of stone and bone. The same central Polynesian parallels apply to the adzes, with the proviso that the Wairau site does have a higher proportion of tanged adzes, and is thus clearly preceded by the earlier part of the Marquesan sequence in typological terms.

So far, the richness of Wairau Bar is unique, and it may have been an important chiefly burial ground for quite a wide area. Sites of similar Archaic type do cluster thickly along the eastern seaboard of the South Island, and some are even larger than Wairau; one at the Rakaia River mouth covers about 20 hectares, another at the Waitaki River mouth covers about 60. All these sites of early date have produced more limited assemblages of Wairau type, although some unusual ornament types not known from Wairau have been found at other places. These include the so-called 'chevroned amulets' (figure 13.8), disc-shaped stone pendants, and 'hybrid reels' of stone, the latter with possible Cook Island parallels[51].

A basic cultural sequence for the South Island has been built up by Simmons[52], utilising information from excavations and museum collections. He divides the South Island Archaic Phase into three periods – Early, Middle and Intermediate, with a final Late Period representing Classic Maori intrusion from the north. The Early Period (A.D. 1000–1200) includes the Wairau midden material, and other well-known South Island sites including the Waitaki River mouth, Pounawea and Papatowai[53]. At this time man would have been spreading through a relatively rich environment, with birds (including moa), forest foods and undepleted marine resources to make up for the loss of horticulture. Material culture is of the Early Eastern Polynesian type represented at Wairau and Maupiti, with the wide New Zealand adze range being present. Specialised stone industries include awls made in the Cook Strait and Foveaux Strait regions, and a very fine blade industry in Otago made on quartzite. The latter has been subjected to a multivariate statistical analysis by Leach[54], and he has raised the possibility of its introduction from an area outside eastern Polynesia, although a local development seems not unlikely, given

0   5 Cm

Fig. 13.7. Stages in the manufacture of New Zealand one-piece hooks of bone. Compare figure 11.15.

Polynesian adze-making skills. These quartzite blades are found mainly in Otago and Southland, and the same distribution applies to a class of polished slate knives[55], again probably representing a local development.

In Simmons'· Middle Period (1200–1400), a decline in forest cover and moa numbers takes place in the eastern South Island, although the human population may now have been at its highest, and there is a greater concentration on marine resources, including sea mammals. Amongst the adzes, the types 1A and 4A increase in importance, the blades and slate knives continue in use in the south, and greenstone first comes into use. Amongst the fishhooks[56] a number of important changes take place; one-piece bait hooks decrease in importance, and greater numbers of composite ones appear, mainly with wooden shanks and bone points, sometimes barbed (figure 13.13 [n]). The stone trolling hook shanks used for catching the barracouta (*Thyrsites atun*) are replaced by bone forms, and then finally give way to a simpler form with a wooden shank and simple point, known commonly as thc 'barracouta lurc' (figurc 13.13 [r]). Some ornament types, such as the reels and the imitation whale-tooth pendants, seem to disappear by the end of the Middle Period.

The Intermediate Period of Simmons (1400–1800 in the south, 1400–1550 in the north) witnessed a decline in resources and human population and perhaps an increasing dependence on fish and shellfish. Adzes of Duff type 2A and an unclassified spade-shouldered form now dominate in the southern sites, and barracouta lures and bait hooks with barbed points, both one- and two-piece, characterise the fishing gear. Harpoons, slate knives and quartzite blades now finally disappear. Overall, the Intermediate Period appears to represent the sad result of human over-exploitation of resources, although there is also the possibility of adverse climatic change (discussed below) to be taken into account.

The Late Period in the South Island equates with the Classic Maori Phase in the North, and appears to be inaugurated in the Canterbury-Marlborough region after about 1550, with the arrival of the Ngai Tahu tribe from the eastern North Island. Sweet potato cultivation, pit storage thereof, and earthwork forts were introduced into the northern coastal fringes (actually part of Waenganui) during this period, but the southern South Island (Murihiku)

apparently had to wait for such developments until the introduction of the white potato after 1769. Simmons has suggested[57] that Cook may have introduced this hardy and useful plant to Queen Charlotte Sound about 1769, and that it was then spread into Murihiku by Canterbury Maoris. Whatever the answer, it is clear that the Classic Phase in the South Island saw the spread of a whole new range of artefacts, which we will describe in due course when we look at the North Island sequence.

ECONOMY, SETTLEMENTS AND TRADE IN THE SOUTH ISLAND

Arguing from the presumed absence of horticulture in the South Island (excluding southern Waenganui) prior to the Late Period, it seems

Fig. 13.8. One of a pair of chevroned amulets made from whale tooth, Aniseed, Kaikoura (cast). Length 14 cm.

rather unlikely that sites in this area would ever have been settled all year round by permanently sedentary populations, except in areas of outstanding resource potential. Seasonal movement seems in fact to have lain at the base of the economy, as it did in ethnographic times[58], and the very large sites on the east coast may represent successive annual habitations by quite large groups during particular seasons, perhaps the winter. Houses and storage facilities may have stood with reasonable permanency in such situations, despite the fluctuations in population. From Cook's accounts of Queen Charlotte Sound we know that sites were abandoned quite frequently, and houses and palisades[59] simply left standing, perhaps for future use.

So far, little concrete evidence for winter utilisation of particular sites has been recovered by archaeologists, but some smaller midden sites in Southland have recently been diagnosed as summer camps by analysis of migratory bird bones and growth rings in shellfish[60]. Summer appears to have been the season of population dispersal with the exploitation of microenvironments, and it may also have been the season when groups would venture into the inhospitable areas of Fiordland[61] and central Otago. In the latter area, sites such as Oturehua (about A.D. 1100) and Hawksburn (about A.D. 1500) were probably used as camps for the quarrying of stone for tools (particularly quartzite), but the majority of these inland sites seem to have been abandoned with the decline of forest and the moas[62]. The quartzite blade industries also disappear around A.D. 1550.

Concerning the layouts of the sites themselves, it must be admitted rather sadly that very little is known, owing to the poor standards of excavation prevailing before the 1950s. Older reports contain hints of house floors, but otherwise leave much to be desired. A recent excavation on an Archaic site at the mouth of the Heaphy River in the north-western South Island[63] has, however, provided an interesting plan. An area of about 20 by 20 metres was partly excavated, and found to contain a small shell midden, a dense cluster of successive earth ovens arranged roughly like a horseshoe, and three small stone pavements. The latter may have been used for wood or stone working, and no evidence was found that they were ever roofed. Although postholes were scattered through the site, they formed no meaningful patterns. The site is dated to about A.D. 1500, or perhaps earlier, and contains moa remains, and

an Archaic assemblage with large quantities of obsidian from the Mayor Island source in the Bay of Plenty.

Another South Island site of great potential interest is situated in the Dart River Valley near Lake Wakatipu, and has been described briefly[64] as having twenty small mounds (about 2 by 1 metre), paved with gravel or stone and connected by paved pathways. A carbon date suggests a date of about A.D. 1500, and this unique site might well repay excavation. It also appears to have been used for the working of greenstone from the local Wakatipu source.

The picture we have of the South Island in the Archaic Phase suggests seasonally mobile groups, moving not only on foot but also by efficient river and ocean-going canoes. This mobility also seems to have encouraged a certain amount of trade, which is attested from the very earliest sites right through to European times, with a possible lapse occurring in the period of decreased population between A.D. 1500 and 1800. For instance, obsidian from the Mayor Island source was traded right down to Bluff[65] in quite large quantities from a time perhaps very soon after initial settlement, and a smaller amount from the Taupo source was distributed likewise.

The South Island was also the source of the fabled greenstone, or nephrite, so valuable in Classic Maori culture when sawn and polished into adzes, war-clubs and ornaments. In the Archaic Phase it was little used, although small numbers of artefacts have been found at Wairau Bar, and the Rakaia and Heaphy River mouths. In the former case some could be of Classic origin, but the latter two assemblages are certainly Archaic, and it is interesting that here the nephrite is mostly flaked to shape like other stone materials, rather than sawn. Sawing may thus be a local technique developed mainly in the Classic Maori Phase.

The main greenstone sources were located in the valleys of the Arahura and Taramakau Rivers in Westland, near the northern head of Lake Wakatipu, and in Milford Sound[66]. The latter source seems to have been the least important, the two Westland ones the most, and it may have been these two which led Cook's Queen Charlotte Sound informant in 1770 to describe the South Island as 'Tovy-poinammu' (presumably Te wahi pounamu, the place of greenstone). The Poutini Ngai Tahu tribe which inhabited the Westland coast in ethnographic times located its permanent winter camps near to the Arahura and Taramakau sources[67], and presumably exploited the greenstone for trade purposes whenever opportunity presented itself.

Other stone materials traded all over New Zealand include a range of metamorphic rocks, generally described as 'argillites', which were quarried from several localities in the Nelson Mineral Belt, and particularly from D'Urville Island[68]. These argillites were traded for adze making throughout the Archaic Phase, but seem to have given way to greenstone in the Classic. Otago quartzites from various sources were also traded locally for the making of the Murihiku blade industries. However, despite the evidence for both local and long-distance trade in New Zealand, it seems unlikely that Maori society, whether Archaic or Classic, ever supported specialist and itinerant traders. The goods moved rather than the people, probably by the kind of reciprocal exchange between neighbouring communities and individuals which is so characteristic of ethnographic trade in Melanesia. (See chapter 4.)

THE ROCK ART OF THE SOUTH ISLAND[69]

New Zealand, like many other Polynesian islands, has a very fine heritage of rock art. The great majority of the sites – perhaps 95 percent of the four hundred or so recorded throughout the country, are situated in the South Island. And the greatest concentrations here are in the limestone areas of Canterbury and north Otago, where the art is found on cliffs, overhangs and rock-shelters, although it has never been found to date in deep inaccessible caves like some of the rock art of Europe or Australia.

The South Island art is drawn rather than painted, by using dry pigments, most commonly red and black, and it is stylistically quite homogeneous. Human and animal representations are common, and include dogs, birds (including moa) and fish, together with somewhat enigmatic creatures generally called *taniwha*. Perhaps the most famous group of *taniwha*, in great demand as a design for stamps, ashtrays and other tourist bric-a-brac, comes from the Opihi shelter in south Canterbury (figure 13.9). The drawings can be simply outlined, or partly or completely filled in with pigment, and the animals may be portrayed in both side-on or spreadeagled poses. Spreadeagled bird-like figures with long narrow wings form one intriguing group (figure 13.10 [b]), sometimes, perhaps erroneously, interpreted as 'birdmen'. In general, much of the New Zealand rock art is quite closely paralleled in other parts of Polynesia, particularly the Hawaiian Islands, and there is no sign of any extra-Polynesian

1M

Fig. 13.9. The Opihi '*taniwha*' charcoal drawing, South Canterbury. From Trotter and McCulloch 1971.

Fig. 13.10. Various designs in South Island rock drawing (not to scale): (a) fish, South Canterbury; (b) 'birdman', Frenchman's Gully, South Canterbury; (c) moa, Timpendean, North Canterbury; (d) human figure with chevron pattern alongside (compare figure 13.17), North Otago; (e) human figure with (?) *patu*, North Otago; (f) human figure, South Canterbury; (g) men in canoe, South Canterbury; (h) dog, North Canterbury; (i) dog (?), North Otago; (j) dog, South Canterbury. From Trotter and McCulloch 1971.

influence.

The purpose of the South Island rock art remains unknown, although there is no real reason to assume that it all had religious motivation. Certainly, the tradition had died out several hundred years before European contact, and quite a large number of excavated and dated sites fall exclusively into the period between A.D. 1000 and 1500. After this time the forest of the eastern South Island had virtually disappeared, the inland areas where the rock art was mostly situated were no longer visited, and the human population, to judge from the small number of later sites, declined rather rapidly. Cumberland has given a graphic if perhaps exaggerated description of the consequences of this forest destruction, which provides a rather thought-provoking sequel to the prehistory of the South Island:

> The ghostly remnants of the forest and the bones of destroyed avifauna littered the ground for centuries, despite repeated firing of the tussocks. . . Rivers rose in flood and carried unwonted burdens of debris. . . The Waimakariri spread its load of sand and shingle twelve feet deep over twenty-five thousand acres in the vicinity of the present Christchurch; it interred a standing forest . . . buried the settlements of the moahunters living in the vicinity, and destroyed much of the evidence of their occupance[70].

But while the population of the South Island declined, that of the North Island was forging the new and dynamic cultural form which we now know as Classic Maori.

THE ARCHAIC PHASE IN THE NORTH ISLAND

The Archaic sites of the North Island, like those of the South, are almost entirely coastal in distribution, although there is some very limited evidence for slight inland settlement in the Waikato and Lake Taupo regions. As far as one can tell, the North Island sites represent the same type of seasonally mobile economy as those of the South, but there is an added complication. Sweet potato horticulture was feasible, and evidently practised in some areas. In Duff's 1956 scheme for New Zealand prehistory, the Archaic was rated as entirely non-horticultural, and it could then be assumed that the plant had been introduced by the Fleet. However, subsequent loss of faith in the Fleet concept, plus new excavations, have served to change this view.

New Zealand is on the very limit of the sweet potato range; it could only be grown with decreasing success to as far south as the southern limit of Waenganui[71]. The plant had to be grown seasonally, and protected from winter cold and frosts during storage. Ideal winter storage conditions are generally assumed to have been continuous temperatures between about 12° and 16°C, together with high humidity, and in recent prehistoric times in all horticultural areas these conditions could only be provided in thickly roofed rectangular pits dug in the ground (figure 13.26), or in smaller lidded bell-shaped ones. These structures will be described in more detail later, as they are primarily a Classic Maori phenomenon. However, we may note here that pits of both the bell-shaped and rectangular types are known from Archaic sites of the twelfth and thirteenth centuries A.D. on the Coromandel Peninsula[72], and possible agricultural soils for taro or sweet potato have been claimed for Archaic contexts from the Bay of Islands, and from as far south as D'Urville Island[73]. Therefore it is very likely that the sweet potato was present in New Zealand from the first settlement[74].

Now, there are important matters which arise here in connection with a widely postulated climatic deterioration in New Zealand after about A.D. 1300[75]. Assuming that an adverse climatic change did take place, as this does seem to be the present trend of informed opinion, then the sweet potato may not have needed underground storage at the time of its earliest introduction into Iwitini, perhaps before A.D. 1000. In fact, Yen[76] had already pointed out some years ago that pit storage was too complex a technique to have been invented overnight, and that if the first plants brought to the country were to survive, then it is likely that the climate at the time of settlement was warmer than now. This leads us straight into the hypothesis that the techniques of pit storage for sweet potato were developed owing to climatic deterioration in late Archaic Iwitini, and this is certainly what the archaeological record suggests; there may also be the factor of successful pit storage lying partially behind the success of the Classic Maori expansion evident from the fourteenth century onwards, especially if the technique had not spread very widely in Archaic times. However, this is a question which will concern us more a little later.

The further effects of the climatic deterioration are difficult to determine, and in the South Island it does look as though men and their fires, rather than climatic deterioration, were the major agents of environmental degradation. In the North Island it is not clear just how much forest had been cleared in the Archaic Phase, but it does seem possible that increasing clearance and erosion was causing increasing deposition of sediments around the coasts of the North Island[77]. Recent archaeological work in the Wairarapa district has provided some rather graphic evidence for such man-induced changes.

The Wairarapa district, at the southern end of the North Island, is today a fairly cold and exposed area of Waenganui. Yet during the Archaic phase, between about A.D. 1100 and 1400, archaeologists from Otago University[78] have found evidence for a flourishing horticultural system, presumably of sweet potato, associated with roughly rectangular field systems bounded by low walls of stones removed from the soil. After A.D. 1400 there is evidence for the environmental degradation in the form of deforestation and erosion, and the horticulture apparently ceases. The climate also becomes more rugged, and many of the Archaic beach settlements are abandoned.

The Wairarapa evidence probably indicates a failed attempt to establish a horticultural economy in a climatically marginal area, although how one apportions the blame between man and climate is not entirely clear. In the warmer parts of the North Island we do not have evidence for such marked changes, but it could well be that, under generally worsening conditions at the end of the Archaic Phase, some of the Archaic populations of Iwitini were becoming more vulnerable to conquest by more successful groups. Again, herein may lie a clue to explain the success of the later Classic Maori economy, with its emphasis on protective pit storage for the sweet potato.

Concerning Archaic economy generally in the North Island, the issue may be a little more complex than in the South Island because of the unknown regional importance of horticulture. Most North Island Archaic sites appear, from the limited evidence available, to represent the same kind of fishing, shellfishing, hunting and gathering populations as those in the South, although there are none as large as the giant spreads of occupation along the South Island's east coast. Thanks to a stimulating analysis by Wilfred Shawcross, we can look at the economy of one North Island site in some considerable detail.

This site is called Mount Camel[79], and lies at the mouth of the Houhora Harbour, near the far northern tip of the North Island. The settlement originally covered about 1.5 hectares, on a platform a little above high water mark. Shawcross excavated a living floor covering about 100 square metres, which was associated with a cluster of ovens, and evidence for butchering, fish scaling, cooking, fishhook manufacture, and the manufacture of bone and ivory ornaments. The artefact assemblage, dating to between A.D. 1150 and 1260 approximately, was particularly rich in one-piece fishhooks of bone, adzes of Archaic type, and ornaments including reels, whale teeth, and bird bone tubes. Also from the site are trolling hook shanks, harpoons, and tattooing chisels.

The economic analysis was undertaken on some 21,000 bones, of fish, seal, dolphin, dog, rat and moa. Shellfish were insignificant, although it could be that the inhabitants ate them at seasonal camps elsewhere. The fish were mainly snapper (*Chrysophrys auratus*), a common denizen of the Iwitini coasts, and caught with the one-piece bait hooks and nets. Trolled fish, such as the *kahawai* (*Arripis trutta*) were much less common. From the survival statistics of the bones, Shawcross was able to demonstrate that some snapper were probably dressed on the site and their bodies taken and eaten elsewhere, while the moas appear to have been dressed at kill sites and brought back to the site without their lower legs. The large sizes of the snapper also indicated that the inhabitants were exploiting a population not previously exploited heavily by man, and they evidently fed many of the smaller ones to dogs, to judge from an analysis of coprolites.

The next and most important stage of the analysis was to estimate the weights of meat of the different species represented in the site, and Shawcross actually goes further than this to estimate energy from meat weight for diagrammatic purposes (figure 13.11). As will be seen, fish are most numerous in terms of individuals, but seals provided the most meat. And since the site was apparently occupied during the summer season, Shawcross goes on to suggest that it might have supported a family of five individuals for about twelve six-month seasons.

The Mount Camel analysis is obviously an excellent start, although we do not yet know exactly where a site such as this fits into the Archaic site hierarchy; were most Archaic sites of this type, or are there a number of functional, seasonal, and size classes? How important are

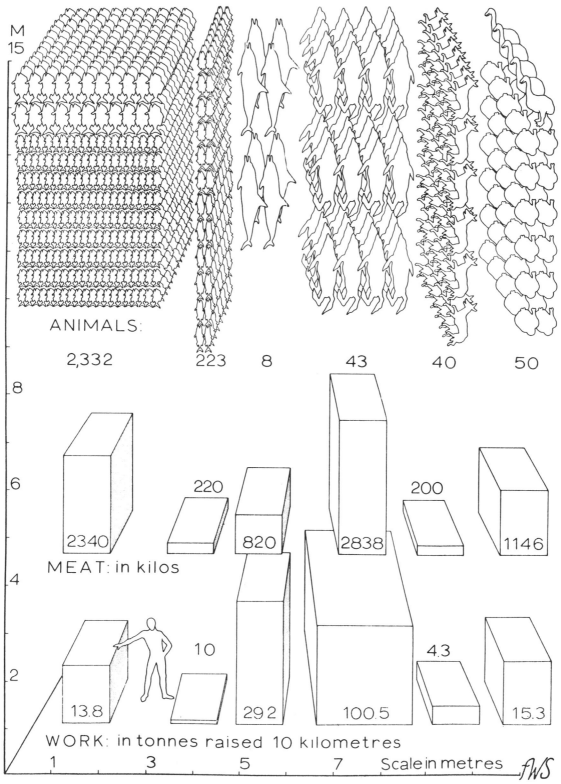

M
15

ANIMALS:

2,332   223   8   43   40   50

8

6   220   200

2340   820   2838   1146

MEAT: in kilos

4

10

2

13.8   29 2   100.5   4.3   15.3

WORK: in tonnes raised 10 kilometres

1   3   5   7   Scale in metres   *fWS*

Fig. 13.11. Diagrammatic representation of meat weights and energy equivalents from the Mount Camel excavations. *Left to right*: snapper; trevalli and *kahawai*; dolphins; seals; dogs; moa. From Shawcross 1972.

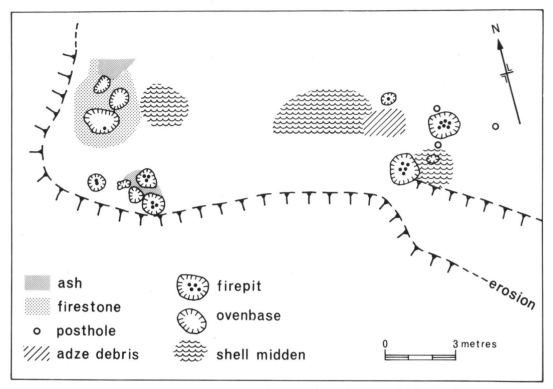

Fig. 13.12. Plan of Archaic campsite at Tairua, Coromandel Peninsula.
After K. Jones 1973.

the factors of horticulture and seasonal movement? These are all major problems for future
research, and at present there is only one other
North Island site with useful evidence on settlement layout, and this is at Tairua, on the Coromandel Peninsula[80]. Here, excavations over an
area of about 24 by 6 metres have revealed a
camp (figure 13.12), dating to about A.D. 1100,
with separate areas for ovens, shellfish and
obsidian flake dumping, butchering, adze flaking,
and dwellings. The total area of this site may
originally have been about 25 metres square, thus
much smaller than Mount Camel. So at least we
are beginning to look at a range of site sizes.

Concerning the North Island artefact assemblages, there is little to say except that they are
very similar to those of the South Island. There
are minor differences, for instance the use of
Cookia sulcata (Cook's turban) shell for fishhooks
on the Coromandel peninsula[81], and the frequency
of dorso-ventrally perforated lure shanks along
the eastern coast of Iwitini[82]. Fishhooks do show
small differences in shape between the North and

South Islands, not least because the fish being
caught were sometimes of differing species. Some
South Island stone tool forms, such as the slate
knives and the quartzite blades, were also absent
in the North. However, the argillites from
Nelson and D'Urville Island were certainly
traded to the North Island from earliest times.

Trade in the North Island Archaic has recently
been illuminated considerably by analyses of
obsidian. The archaeological study of New
Zealand obsidians, both for sourcing and hydration dating, was pioneered in the early 1960s by
Roger Green[83]. So far, the hydration dating has
provided some valuable support for the radiocarbon chronology, but the most recent advances
have been in the field of sourcing. Techniques
used include emission spectroscopy[84], atomic absorption spectrophotometry and flame photo-
metry[85], X-ray fluorescence spectrography[86], and
density measurements[87]. Grahame Ward has
recently identified no less than 45 separate
possible sources of obsidian, all in the northern
half of the North Island, and these fall mostly

into eight major areas, as shown on figure 13.1. These areas may be listed as Northland (Kaeo and Huruiki), Great Barrier Island, Coromandel Peninsula, Rotorua, Maraetai, Taupo and Mayor Island.

Of these sources, it appears that the Mayor Island one was first utilised, and its products traded all over New Zealand. The Taupo sources were located soon afterwards, and also traded to as far south as Bluff, but in smaller quantities. In this regard, the Mayor Island sources do seem to produce the best quality flaking material in New Zealand, of a distinctive translucent green colour. The dates of discovery of the other sources are not known, but many of them may only have been exploited during the Classic Phase. Patterns and directions of trade still remain to be studied; while Mayor Island obsidians were traded far and in quantity, those from the other sources seem to decrease sharply in importance with distance from the source. Gift exchange along lines of tribal relationship seems to be indicated, and there are indications that some tribes in Classic times were unable for political reasons to exploit the sources in closest proximity[88]. The overall chronological pattern seems to be an overwhelming dominance of Mayor Island material in the earliest sites, even those adjacent to other sources[89], followed by piecemeal competition from these other sources and increasing regionalism.

To close this section on the North Island Archaic, we should examine briefly the evidence for internal subdivision and development. Green[90] has presented three divisions of his Eastern Polynesian Culture (equivalent to Golson's Archaic Phase) in the Auckland Province; namely, Settlement, Developmental, and Experimental. These three phases develop through increasing permanence and complexity of settlements, increasing importance of horticulture, and a decreasing range of avifauna[91]. Green also noted the importance of shellfish from rocky-shore environments in the Archaic, and their gradual replacement by species from the more productive mud-flat environments in the Classic. His model is not accepted by all scholars[92], mainly due to its evolutionary implications, but there is a certain amount of evidence in its support, and no-one has yet attempted to replace it.

THE CLASSIC MAORI PHASE

At some time between A.D. 1300 and 1500, a new cultural configuration spreads through Iwitini, characterised by the construction of earthwork forts, the frequent use of storage pits for sweet potato, and a new artefact suite. The configuration also spreads through Waenganui, although perhaps a little later than in the north. It appears to stop, doubtless significantly, at around the southern limit of sweet potato cultivation. The only evidence for its spread into Te Wahi Pounamu comes late in the eighteenth century, and at this time there is evidence for European-introduced stimuli, particularly the white potato (see page 391).

The new configuration is of course what we know as Classic Maori, and its generation undoubtedly took place in Iwitini. Classic Maori culture is fairly homogeneous in Iwitini and Waenganui, and possibly 80% of the sites and population were located in the former, more fertile, area. The degree of homogeneity is such that it has clearly not evolved independently in several places, and the most likely explanation for it seems to be transmission from a source region, followed by local adaptation. What was the nature of this transmission?

I might as well state at the outset that this problem has never been fully solved. At no excavation ever undertaken in New Zealand has anyone found evidence for an evolutionary transition from Archaic to Classic. Of course, the two do share features in common, and as we noted above, pit storage for sweet potato is undoubtedly a transmission from the Archaic, although evidence for its use is, perhaps significantly, much more widespread in the Classic. In addition, there are certain types of artefact which continue in use through the two phases with no important modification. But the differences, which are major, cannot be glossed over simply as a slight case of adaptation, and neither can we fall back on migrations from Polynesia; there is no archaeological evidence for this, and, according to the traditional scholars, no more Fleet.

It is my personal belief that a transition from Archaic to Classic does exist, but in an area where very little excavation has so far been undertaken. And I also believe that Classic Maori culture was spread by population movement and conquest, rather than by simple diffusion of a new and attractive life-style (which the Classic Maori life-style may not necessarily have been).

My beliefs in this matter are not original. As

early as 1956, Sharp[93] had suggested that the so-called Fleet migrations referred to population movements within New Zealand. More recently, Groube and Simmons[94] have carried this idea much further, by suggesting that the Fleet traditions really refer to migrations from Northland to all the coastal areas of Iwitini lying south of Auckland, particularly Taranaki and the Bay of Plenty. Simmons[95] has postulated that three main periods of migration might have taken place, and has attempted to associate the terraced form of earthwork fort (described below) with the first, about A.D. 1300, and the ring ditch type of fort with the second, before A.D. 1450. The third migration comprised several groups, moving also between 1300 and about 1450. Simmons has related the tribal canoe traditions to the origins of the Classic Maori tribes of Iwitini in some detail, and his ideas clearly have a good deal of merit. We might note at this point that forts (*pa*) have never produced any substantial evidence for presence in the Archaic; they invariably produce Classic assemblages, and all excavated examples postdate A.D. 1300.

This same potential correlation of earthworks and the spread of Classic Maori culture has been examined in more detail by Groube[96], and his conclusions are generally very similar to those of Simmons. Groube suggests that there may have been initial migrations from north-eastern Northland, perhaps associated with the Tainui and Te Arawa canoe traditions (see figure 13.1 for traditional landing places), and he follows these with a major migration phase revolving around the other main canoe traditions in the fifteenth century. This second migration was associated in particular with the movement of Awa tribes from north-western Northland to the Taranaki and Bay of Plenty districts, and Groube noted the important occurrence in only these three areas of the distinctive ring ditch type of fortification. The correlations are beginning to look very convincing, and both Groube and Simmons have I think demonstrated the likelihood of considerable population expansion from Northland between 1300 and 1500.

A little later on I will return to the forts in more detail, and will simply ask the reader for the present to take the differences between the terraced and ring ditch forms on faith. We must also consider why the postulated migrations from Northland might have taken place, after presenting the actual material remains of the Classic phase in a little more detail.

THE CLASSIC MAORI ARTEFACT ASSEMBLAGE

The Classic Maori artefact assemblage (figure 13.13) is naturally best known from the records of early explorers[97] and museum collections, although excavations in recent years have expanded the picture considerably and also added the important dimension of time-depth. The major definition of the Classic assemblage was made by Golson in 1959[98], and remains basically accurate today. From our present vantage point the artefactual changes from Archaic to Classic Maori do seem rather abrupt, but we do need to bear in mind that future discoveries could give a picture of more gradual changes in fashion in certain classes of object. The Classic assemblage also includes many objects made of organic materials found in swamps and from ethnographic collections, and in these cases we generally have no information about possible Archaic forebears.

Classic adzes show a very abrupt change from the Archaic forms; the earlier diversity gives way entirely to the untanged and fully ground adze of Duff type 2B, and the aspect of ceremonialism witnessed by the magnificent adzes from Wairau Bar seems to disappear. Classic sites produce these 2B adzes in quantity, and generally no other forms, and this late phenomenon of standardisation and apparent mass production is paralleled by the predominance of the Duff type 3A adze form in central Polynesia. The use of greenstone for adzes also increases markedly.

Fishing gear also shows marked changes, and, as in the South Island, the one-piece bait hooks fade rapidly in importance in the later sites, and are replaced almost completely by two-piece barbed forms[99]. The Archaic types of harpoons and trolling hooks also virtually disappear, and a wooden-shanked form of trolling hook with a shell inlay, used for catching the *kahawai* (*Arripis trutta*) is present in ethnographic collections (figure 13.13 [q]), although it has not so far survived from Classic excavations. Net fishing was evidently of great importance in the Classic Phase, with nets recorded up to 500 fathoms (about 900 metres) long[100].

As with the adzes, the changes in ornament styles appear to be quite marked (figure 13.14). Necklaces are replaced by single pendants worn round the neck or in the ear, and the reels and imitation whale teeth seem to disappear quite suddenly before the end of the Archaic Phase. The Classic forms are generally of bone, whale ivory or greenstone, and two particular forms,

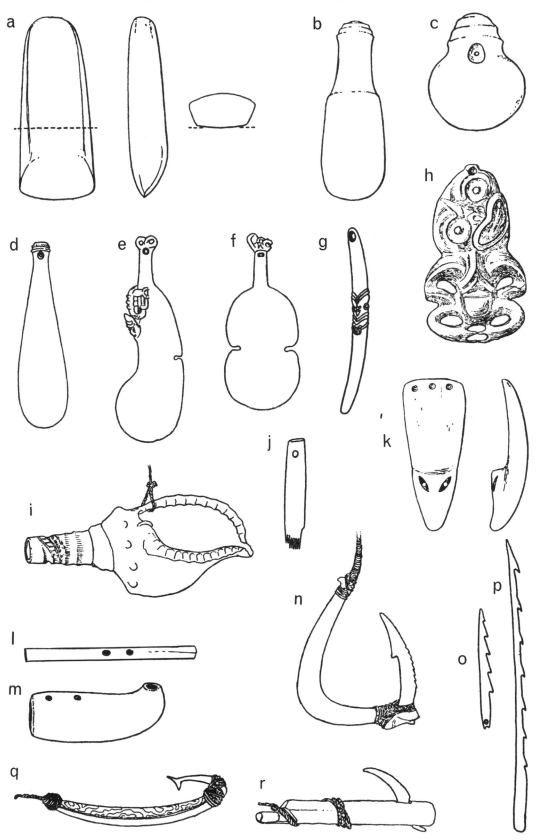

Fig. 13.13. Artefacts of Classic type (not to scale):
(a) adze of Duff type 2B; (b) stone flax pounder;
(c) stone fish-net sinker; (d-f) hand clubs of stone
or whalebone: *patu*, *wahaika* and *kotiate* respectively;
(g) bone cloak pin; (h) greenstone (nephrite)
hei tiki; (i) shell trumpet; (j) bone tattooing
chisel; (k) whale tooth pendant (*rei puta*); (l)
flute of wood or bone; (m) nose flute of stone,
wood or bone; (n) two-piece bait hook with
wooden shank and bone point; (o, p) bird spear
points of bone; (q) *kahawai* lure with *Haliotis*
shell strip on wooden shank and point of bone; (r)
barracouta lure with wooden shank and bone
point. After Golson 1959a.

Fig. 13.14. Tattooed Maori man wearing wooden comb, ear pendant and whale tooth *rei puta* pendant. Drawn by Sydney Parkinson on Cook's first voyage.

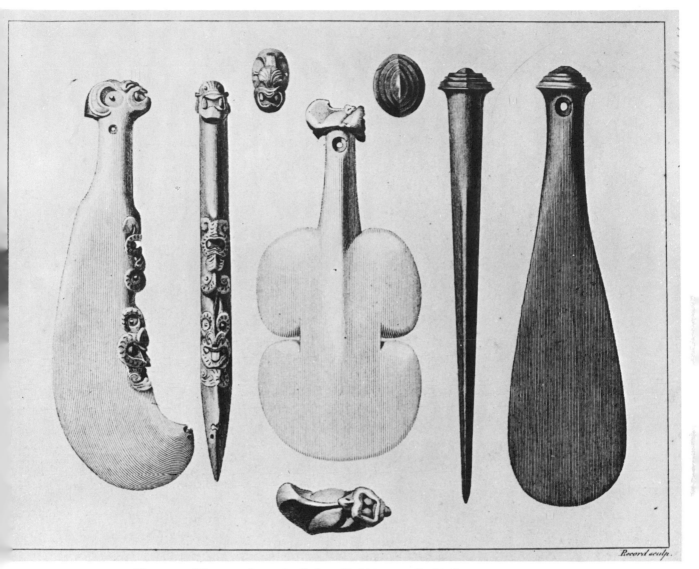

Fig. 13.15. Weapons drawn by Sydney Parkinson on Cook's first voyage: *left to right, wahaika* (front and side), *kotiate, patu onewa* (front and side).

the whale tooth *rei puta* and the greenstone *hei tiki* (figure 13.13 [h]) are well-known from ethnographic collections, and both Cook and Banks saw them being worn. The *hei tiki* is particularly common in nineteenth century collections, and many were made from obsolete greenstone adzes after the introduction of metal tools[101].

Weapons form another important class of artefacts in the Classic, particularly the spatulate hand-clubs generally known as *patu* (or *mere* when made in greenstone). These were also made sometimes in whalebone, especially the notched and decorated variants known as *kotiate* and *wahaika* (figure 13.15). The *patu* weapons were used with a thrusting motion to split off the top of the skull, and it was probably a *patu* duel which was witnessed by Roux in 1772, when the unfortunate loser lost the top of his skull above the eyes[102]. Other Classic weapons include various wooden staff forms, including the *taiaha*, the *tewhatewha*, and the *pouwhenua*. These wooden forms are known from Classic swamp and lake-bed assemblages[103], but have not so far been found in Archaic sites. Simple *patu* of whalebone were, however, present in the Archaic[104], and they are also known from the site of Vaitootia in the Society Islands (page 324), so New Zealand, with the Chathams and Easter Island, may have

403

retained an Early Eastern Polynesian form right through the prehistoric sequence. Nevertheless, the apparent efflorescence of forts and weapon types in the Classic undoubtedly reflects a major indigenous development of a warring spirit which was probably only weakly developed in the Archaic.

Other Classic artefacts known mainly from ethnographic collections and without Archaic antecedents include musical instruments (flutes and shell trumpets) and hair combs, although in both cases the Archaic absence may simply reflect lack of discovery. A unique assemblage of wooden Maori combs was excavated some years ago by Wilfred Shawcross, from a swamp beside the fort at Kauri Point, near Tauranga in the Bay of Plenty[105]. The combs, about 330 pieces comprising about 187 complete specimens, had been ceremonially deposited in a small plank-lined enclosure at the edge of the swamp, doubtless for reasons connected with the sacredness of the human head in Maori belief. With the combs were over 13,000 flakes of obsidian[106], perhaps used for scarification or hair cutting, and these had in some cases been deposited in textile packages, gourds or wooden bowls. A study of the distribution of the combs by depth showed that flat-topped forms preceded the round-topped type shown in figure 13.14, although there was

no evidence for sharp fashion change at any point in time. A few specimens had finely carved human faces on their upper parts, but the majority were either provided with schematic knobs or notches, or were plain. Oddly enough, the decorative changes did not show such an orderly chronological relationship as did the overall shapes, and the finest designs seem to have been more a result of good craftsmanship than fashion.

Reference to the wooden combs from Kauri Point leads me to a brief resumé of Classic material culture in wood, for naturally only a very small proportion of the total object range has survived in archaeological sites. Lake bed discoveries in Lake Horowhenua (near Levin) and Lake Mangakaware (Waikato), as well as ethnographic collections[107], illustrate the total variety very well. Apart from magnificent wood carvings, we have a range of everyday tools including horticultural implements, bowls, weapons, paddles and canoes, palisade posts and house timbers, burial chests, adze and chisel handles, fishhook shanks, childrens' tops, adze and knife handles, and fern rhizome beaters, to list only a few of the more common categories.

Maori art, with its unusual emphasis on scroll and spiral ornamentation (figure 13.16), is without close parallel elsewhere in Polynesia, although the human figure motifs do of course belong to a

Fig. 13.16. A masterpiece of Classic Maori carving: canoe prow carved near Otaki in the 1830s (compare figure 11.3).

Fig. 13.17. Wooden lintel of presumed Archaic date from Kaitaia, Northland. Scale in feet. From Trotter and McCulloch 1971.

general Polynesian continuum. Despite earlier claims for parallels in China and British Colum-bia[108], it now looks as though the style is an in-digenous New Zealand development, and Mead[109] has recently suggested that it develops with the beginning of the Classic Maori Phase as a validator, perhaps conscious, of the new social order and patterns of land ownership. In his view, Archaic art would probably have resembled more the intricate zoned style represented on Lapita pottery, perhaps with only a slight degree of curvilinearity. The best piece of assumed Archaic wood carving comes from a swamp at Kaitaia, and its rather simple design (figure 13.17) is paralleled in the so-called 'chevroned pendants' (figure 13.8), also of assumed Archaic provenance. North Island rock art seems to have no Archaic representatives, and the few examples known are mainly engravings of spirals and canoes in what

appears to be a Classic mode.

Classic burial methods show a fairly definite trend away from the Archaic extended position, towards flexed earth burial for commoners, and secondary cave burial for higher ranking per-sonages, the pattern of seclusion being necessary in a society where one's enemies might use one's bones for the ignominious purpose of making fishhooks. Bone boxes of sewn planks, sometimes carved in Northland, also come into vogue. The most splendid example of a cave burial was found recently on an island in Lake Hauroko[110], in the remote south-west of the South Island (doubtless the reason for its survival). It com-prised the skeleton of a woman, still propped in a sitting position on a bier of sticks, and wrapped in a woven flax cloak with bird feather edgings and a dogskin collar (figure 13.18). The lady was laid to rest sometime in the seventeenth century,

Fig. 13.18. The Lake Hauroko
burial. (See also colour plate.)

and hence may not strictly be classifiable as Classic Maori in this region, although the method of burial may generally belong to the later part of New Zealand prehistory. Another, and better known, aspect of Maori death is the steaming and drying of tattooed heads, an honour originally reserved for chiefs and warriors in the days when only they had facial tattooing, but debased after 1815 when tattooing spread to commoners and the European curio trade began to make heavy demands[111].

CLASSIC MAORI SETTLEMENTS AND ECONOMY

While our knowledge of Archaic settlements does little more than allow us to classify them as large or small camps, apparently without defences, the Classic Maori record is very much fuller. The earthwork forts (*pa*) are very obvious features of the landscape, and their areas are easily measured. These *pa* seem to be the key nodes of the Classic settlement pattern in Iwitini and Waenganui, and they integrate with a range of undefended smaller sites which seem to have functioned as dwelling places, sweet potato storage magazines, shell midden dumps, or combinations of these and other functions, on a seasonal basis.

Several authors have attempted to classify and describe *pa* in the past[112], but the most recent overview has been presented by Groube[113]. He suggests that there may be between 4000 and 6000 *pa* in New Zealand, the vast majority in Iwitini. Areas within defences (including terracing) range from 0.1 to 50 hectares, and densities rise to between 1 and 1.5 per square kilometre in the most favourable areas. Groube's classification for *pa*, expressed in its most simple terms, separates out three major groups on style of defence. These are terraced *pa* (class 1), promontory or ridge *pa* with short transverse ditches (class 2), and ring ditch *pa* (class 3).

The terraced *pa* of class 1 form a somewhat diffuse group without ditch and bank defences, and the terraces consist simply of flats cut into hill-slopes. The largest *pa* recorded in New Zealand is of this type – Otatara *pa* in Hawkes Bay, at a little under 50 hectares – but the finest examples were built on the many extinct volcanic cones which now protrude from the urban landscape of Auckland city (figure 13.19). These sites are a little difficult to explain because none were described in detail by early European explorers, and it is not really clear just how the defences

were organised, if indeed they were used for defence at all in many cases. Excavations on the terraces of *pa* in this class have produced sweet potato storage pits and ephemeral traces of houses, and some may well have had palisades along their outer edges. The age and origin of the form is also unknown; they occur quite widely throughout the whole North Island, and Groube[114] has suggested that they may represent a bunching of population into large sites early in the Classic Phase, although this view really lacks verification at present. As we noted above, Simmons has attempted to associate them with his earliest Classic migration out of Northland, although here again we are on shaky ground, and they may in fact reflect nothing more than the presences of rounded hills and volcanic cones.

Groube's second class – the promontory and ridge forts – seems certainly to be distributed according to topographical rather than cultural factors. Good narrow steep-sided promontories and ridges could easily be defended by digging ditches and banks, often multiple, across the lines of easiest approach. Indeed, class 2 *pa* occur throughout the settled areas of Iwitini and Waenganui, and generally tend to be small and obviously designed for defence. Our two best early descriptions of *pa* in fact belong with this class; one by Cook and Banks in Mercury Bay (1769), and the other by Lieutenant Roux in the Bay of Islands (1772). The Cook account is so interesting that it deserves a full quote:

This village is built upon a high Promontory or point on the North side and near the head of the Bay. It is in some places quite inaccessible to man, and in others very difficult, except on that side which faced the narrow ridge of the hill on which it stands. Here it is defended by a double ditch, a bank and 2 rows of Picketing, the inner row upon the Bank; but not so near the Crown but what there was good room for men to Walk and handle their Arms between the Picketing and the inner Ditch. The outer Picketing was between the 2 Ditches, and laid sloping with their upper ends hanging over the inner Ditch. The Depth of this Ditch from the bottom to the Crown of the bank was 24 feet.

Close within the inner Picketing was erected by strong Posts a stage 30 feet high and 40 in length and 6 feet broad. The use of this stage was to stand upon to throw Darts at the Assailants, and a number of Darts lay upon it for that purpose. At right angles to this Stage

Fig. 13.19. One Tree Hill, Auckland. Terraced *pa* on a volcanic cone. (Whites Aviation photo.)

Fig. 13.20. View inside a New Zealand *pa*, drawn by J. Webber on Cook's third voyage.

the Inside of a HIPPAH in NEW ZEELAND.

and a few paces from it was another of the Construction and bigness; this stood likewise within the Picketing, and was intended for the same use as the other – viz., to stand upon to throw stones and darts upon the Enemy as they advanc'd up the side of the Hill where lay the Main way into the place. It likewise might be intended to defend some little out-works and Hutts that lay at the Skirts on this side of the Hill. These outworks were not intended as advanced Posts, but for such of the Inhabitants to live in as had not room in the Main works, but had taken Shelter under it.

Besides the works on the land side above described the whole Village was Pallisaded round with a line of pretty strong Picketing run round the Edge of the hill. The ground within having not been level at first, but laid Sloping, they had divided it into little squares and Leveled each of these. These squares lay in the form of an Amphitheatre, and were each of them Pallisaded round, and had communica-tion one with another by narrow lanes and little gateways, which could easily be stoped up, so that if an Enemy had forced the outer Picketing he had several others to incounter before the place could be easily reduced, supposing them to defend everyone of the places one after another.

The main way leading into this fortification was up a very steep part of the Hill and thro' a narrow passage about 12 feet long and under one of the Stages. I saw no door nor gate, but it might very soon have been barricaded up. Upon the whole I looked upon it to be very strong and well choose Post, and where a small number of resolute men might defend them-selves a long time against a vast superior force, Arm'd in the manner as these People are. These seem'd to be prepared against a Siege, having laid up in store an immense quantity of Fern roots and a good many dry'd fish; but we did not see that they had any fresh Water nearer than a brook which runs close

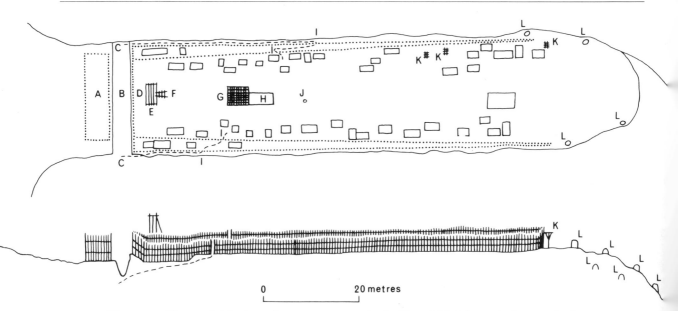

Fig. 13.21. Plan and side view of a promontory *pa* in the Bay of Islands, made in 1772 during the visit of Marion Du Fresne: (A) outer palisaded work; (B) dry ditch; (C) entrance paths; (D) rampart; (E) fighting stage; (F) ladder to fighting stage; (G) rack on which to place the weapons; (H) house of the chief, serving also as a store for the weapons; (I) gates; (J) stake having a very hideous head in the shape of a box; (K) trellises supported by stakes on which to place fern roots for drying; (L) small houses for seine nets, and they have some of the same shape to store potatoes, yams and fern roots which are, like their dwellings, waterproof.

The original map also refers to a latrine and a large storehouse for provisions and nets, but I am unable to locate these. After Kelly 1951, Groube 1964b.

under the foot of a hill, from which I suppose they can at times get water, tho' besieged, and keep it in gouards until they use it[115].

Banks[116] noted a few further points of interest; the internal palisaded enclosures numbered 20, each with between one and fourteen houses, and an area of about 0.2 hectares inside the *pa* was also planted with gourds and sweet potatoes.

For the Roux account we do not need to give a long quote, as we have a contemporary map[117] (figure 13.21). This shows a rectangular palisaded outworks to protect the approach to the ditch, and like the Mercury Bay *pa*, the ditch is also covered by a fighting stage, and the entrances placed rather deviously. The houses are ranged between the palisades and the flat inner open space (the *marae*) inside the *pa*, and this open space contains a carving, weapon rack and chief's house. At the end of the *pa* are racks for fern rhizomes and latrines, the latter apparently being a universal feature of Classic Maori sites[118], otherwise unknown in Polynesia. One might note that this map may not be entirely

accurate – considerable hostility accompanied the French visit to the Bay of Islands in 1772 and about 250 Maoris were killed – and as a point of interest another contemporary account suggests that there might have been additional storehouses for food and nets in the central area. It is also interesting that neither Cook nor Roux ever mention sweet potato storage pits, although this could simply be lack of observation.

A number of *pa* in Groube's second class have been excavated in recent years, and perhaps the most interesting results may come from recent excavations by Aileen Fox[119] at Tirimoana *pa* in Hawkes Bay. Here, excavations have produced the post holes of palisades, a house 11.8 by 4 metres in size, storage pits, and two phases of defended occupation perhaps extending right through the Classic Phase.

Returning to Groube's classification, his third class of *pa* is the ring ditch type, which usually consists of a roughly rectangular area, deliberately flattened or terraced in steeper areas, surrounded on two or more sides by ditch and bank defences. Sometimes the defences may be doubled on weak

Fig. 13.22. The ring ditch *pa* at Kauri Point, Bay of Plenty.

sides, and these sites rarely exceed 2 hectares in size. They are often the most distinctive of the New Zealand *pa*, and generally owe to human rather than natural defensive measures much more than those of the other two classes. As noted on page 400, Groube has tied in this form with the migrations of Awa tribes from Northland early in the Classic Phase, and they are only found in large numbers in north-western Northland, and along the coasts of Taranaki and the Bay of Plenty, on opposite sides of Iwitini. However, this distribution is not absolutely clear-cut, and could be modified in the future[120].

Pa of Groube's class 3 have been well studied by excavation, particularly at Otakanini and Waioneke *pa* on the shores of the South Kaipara Harbour[121], and at Kauri Point *pa* (figure 13.22) near Tauranga in the Bay of Plenty[122]. Otakanini *pa* covers an area of 1.8 hectares on a small island in the southern part of the Kaipara Harbour, and some preliminary terracing seems to have begun as early as the fourteenth century, together with the digging of pits for sweet potato storage. Around A.D. 1500 the defended area was divided into two sections – possibly an inner citadel and an outer annexe – and the inner citadel in the area of the excavations was defended by a massive fighting stage built on an artificial scarp, with posts sunk about 2 metres into the ground. Later in the sixteenth century, and possibly associated with the arrival of new peoples in the South Kaipara region (the Ngati Whatua), these defences were remodelled into a ditch and bank with two fighting stages on top, as shown in figure 13.23. The entrance at this time was along the top of the ditch and then back along a passageway between two palisade rows, and both the entrance and the stages at Otakanini clearly recall the descriptions of Cook and Roux. Although no inner areas of the *pa* were excavated, some economic evidence was obtained from the very large shell-middens surrounding the defences, and it may be that the site was occupied all year round, but with a fluctuating population.

Kauri Point, although a little more complex than Otakanini, perhaps because a larger area was excavated, shows a similar pattern of development. The earliest level on the site, dating from about the fourteenth century, consisted of a horticultural soil and a few store pits, and this was soon replaced by two groups of simple terraces. Following this, a ring ditch *pa* was built on the site, defended by sea cliffs on two sides and ditches and banks on the other two, the latter

being double on the line of easiest approach. After a following period when the ditches were filled with shell midden, a new threat made its appearance and the site was refortified with a single ditch and bank over only half of its former area. The ditch was later doubled (figure 13.22), again along the line of easiest approach, and these two final periods may belong to the eighteenth century. The inside of the *pa* in the defensive periods contained very large numbers of intercutting storage pits, and Ambrose has suggested that it may have functioned primarily as a defended storage area at certain times. We will return to this general question of *pa* function later.

The site at Waioneke has again a similar sequence to Otakanini and Kauri Point, with early store pits followed by a large ring ditch *pa*, perhaps at about A.D. 1600, and finally a much smaller ring ditch defence at about the time of European contact. Certainly, it appears from these results that terracing precedes the ditch and bank defences in origin, and it also seems that there may be a tendency for sites to be reduced to small citadels in later prehistory, although not enough is known to support generalisations about trends in population size or intensity of warfare. Not all excavated sites of Groube's class 3 fit this pattern anyway, although we do have enough of a pattern for them to suggest imposition in areas where formerly only terraced forms existed, and the Groube hypothesis of Awa migration may stand up well to future testing. Just where the promontory and ridge forms fit into all this is not known, because so far they have shown no particular geographical or chronological orientations[123].

So far, of course, we have been discussing *pa* built on dry land and defended by earthworks. However, in certain North Island regions endowed with shallow lakes and swamps, such as the Waikato, the Hauraki Plains, and Lake Horowhenua, we find a most unusual but archaeologically rewarding type of fortification. As the Rev. Richard Taylor reported in 1872, some of the Lake Horowhenua sites were built,

first by driving long stakes into the lake to enclose the required space then by large stones being placed inside them, and all kinds of rubbish being thrown in to fill up the centre, upon which an alternative stratum of clay and gravel was laid until it was raised to the required height, on which the houses were then erected, and the *pa* surrounded with the usual fence[124].

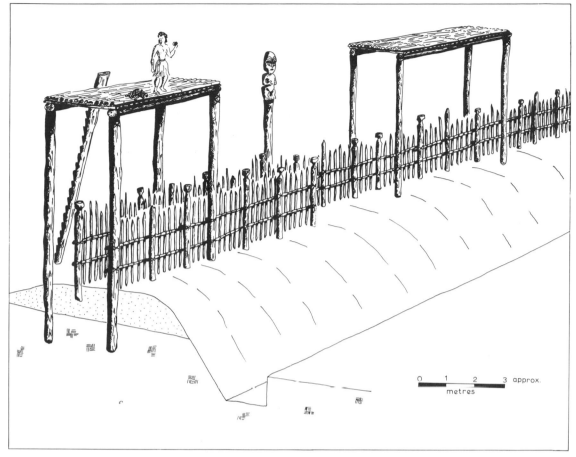

Fig. 13.23. Two fighting stages reconstructed from excavations at Otakanini
pa, South Kaipara Harbour. From Bellwood 1971b.

Some of these Horowhenua lake *pa* have been described in more detail by Adkin[125], and similar multi-layered artificial mounds have been discovered in the swampy Hauraki Plains[126]. The largest numbers of them occur in the Waikato district, on the edges of numerous small peaty lakes. The Waikato sites seem to have been built out of swamps rather than shallow standing water, and consist of floor-layers of quarried sand or clay laid one above the other, separated by layers of occupation debris in the form of charcoal, shellfish, and decomposing organic rubbish. These sites are generally under 0.5 hectares in size and up to about three metres in greatest depth. Surrounding palisade foundations often survive in the swamps around the sites, and some sites appear to have been defended by as many as six parallel palisade lines in areas of weakness.

Waikato swamp *pa* have been excavated on the edges of Lake Ngaroto[127] and Lake Mangakaware[128], and the latter site, being partially waterlogged during the past, has preserved very clear

evidence for settlement lay-out (figure 13.24). The Mangakaware *pa* (*c.* A.D. 1500–1800) covered about 0.2 hectares, and was built up with sand lenses from a patch of swamp on the edge of the lake. Massive timber palisades driven up to three metres into the ground formed the defences, with a double row on the vulnerable landward side. The *pa* was entered through a very narrow palisaded passage similar to that reconstructed for Otakanini, and quite a number of broken weapons and ornaments were found in this passage, together with human bone and red ochre. Evidently there had been a battle centred on the very spot, and excavations in one area inside the *pa* revealed clear traces of cannibalism. Whether the attackers or the defenders won the day we will perhaps never know.

The inside of the *pa* was centred on an open space (*marae*), functionally similar to that described by Roux for the Bay of Islands *pa* (page 409). Many hearths were found in this open area, but no houses, these being grouped into a semi-

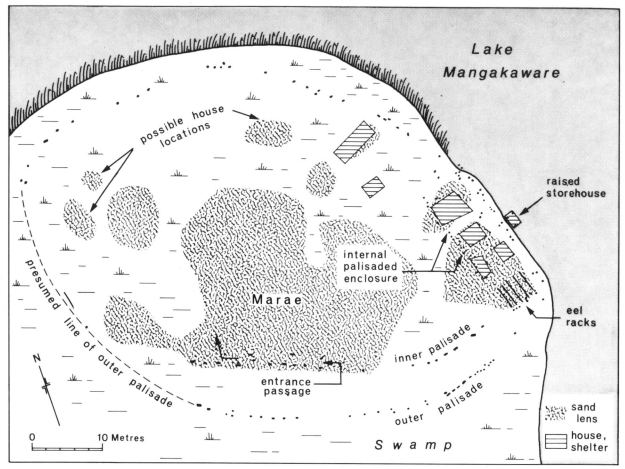

Fig. 13.24. Plan of the excavated swamp *pa* by Lake Mangakaware, Waikato.

circle of six or more backing on to the palisades on the lakeward side of the *pa*. The finest house, 6 metres long by 2.20 wide, was built of planks and (presumably) thatching, and because so many complete house timbers were found in the bed of the lake it is possible to reconstruct the framework of the house as in figure 13.25. The notch and tenon method of linking rafters and wall posts is well described in the ethnographic literature[129]. The other houses were smaller than this one, and built either of planks or small tree-fern posts. A possible separation between winter and summer houses could also be made – the former with strong walls, many hearths for heating, and thick brushwood bedding on the floors. Summer houses, on the other hand, seem to have been more flimsy and perhaps not fully enclosed, and floored with flax mats. Analysis of remains of berries and seeds also supported these conclusions, although the separation between winter and summer houses is not to be taken as too clearly demarcated, for both types were

undoubtedly standing and thus in use all year round, so it would be more correct to say that the intensity of use varied from season to season.

Economic analyses from the Mangakaware excavations suggest that the site was settled all year round, but by a fluctuating population, many of whom would disperse to look after sweet potato and fern plantations in the summer, and even to travel to the sea (40 kilometres away direct) to get fish and shell-fish. As noted on page 404, an enormous number of wooden artefacts were recovered from the bed of the lake, both by the excavated *pa* and by other *pa* elsewhere on the shoreline, and these illustrate most graphically the wide range of activities carried out on the sites. However, none of these swamp *pa* were of course suitable for the excavation of sweet potato storage pits, or for that matter of defensive ditches. For these reasons they may not always be obvious features of the landscape for field archaeologists.

Having surveyed the types of *pa*, we may now

see how they fit into the overall pattern of Classic settlement. Classic settlement in the North Island was certainly spread over a much wider area than that of the Archaic, and although the great majority of sites are still within 10 kilometres of the sea, dense settlement now took place in important inland regions such as the Waikato and Rotorua districts. Within this settlement network the *pa* served various functions, some being large tribal centres and others merely fortified hamlets, some being settled all year round and others being perhaps little more than fortified storage places[130]. The environmental locations of *pa* also vary considerably, with the largest tending to be in areas of good horticultural soils and near large harbours with their abundant fish and shellfish resources. Many of these sites are associated with enormous dumps of marine shellfish, and there are good grounds for suggesting that marine resources in the Classic tended to outweigh the forest and avian resources which were apparently so important in the Archaic.

The *pa* probably formed defended nodes for populations using a wide range of much smaller seasonal settlements. These include coastal shellfish dumps, probably used by a few families for just a few seasons[131], and small hamlet clusters of storage pits and houses, sometimes with burials and working floors. Sites of the latter kind constructed on small terraces have recently been excavated at Hamlin's Hill near Auckland[132], and at two localities on Motutapu Island in the Hauraki Gulf[133]. The inhabited areas of Iwitini are in fact well littered with such small pit and terrace sites, and until a few years ago it was commonly held[134] that the pits were the remains of subterranean houses.

Now, this necessitates a brief discussion of these pits and their functions. Pits, whether for stores or dwelling houses, were never commented upon by the earliest explorers, although there is ethnographic evidence for use of the rectangular types for storage[135], and some have been used thus until quite recently by Maori communities. The bell-shaped types were undoubtedly used for storage, owing to their small size.

However, the rectangular forms can be up to 10 metres in greatest dimension, and sometimes have multiple post rows inside to support a roof, which, from ethnographic observations, would have been ridged with its eaves resting on the ground around the pit. The roof was then covered with a thick layer of soil to insulate the contents

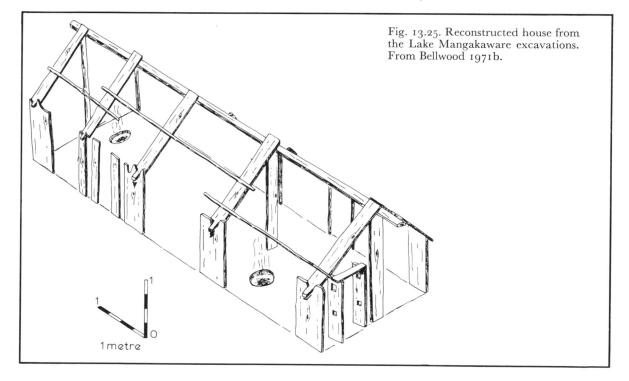

Fig. 13.25. Reconstructed house from the Lake Mangakaware excavations. From Bellwood 1971b.

1 metre

of the pit and to maintain a constant temperature (figure 13.26). Clearly, many of these large pits could have served as houses, and many were inhabited during later stages of their life, as witnessed by hearths and other traces of occupation in their fills. Hence Roger Green[136], for a large undefended pit complex at Kauri Point near Tauranga, suggested that the pits might have served both storage and dwelling functions, and this type of compromise solution could in fact hold for certain sites.

Nevertheless, recent work has not provided much support for the pit-dwelling theory, and

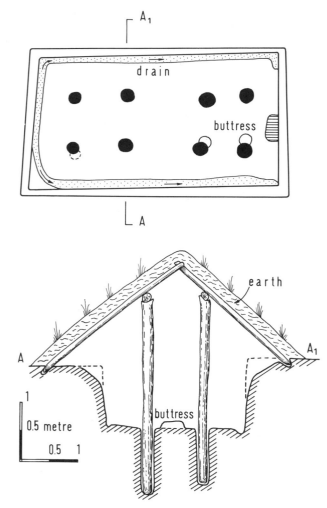

Fig. 13.26. Plan and reconstructed cross-section of sweet potato storage pit at Taniwha *pa*, Waikato. After A. Fox 1974, with minor modifications.

Ambrose's detailed evidence from the Kauri Point *pa*[137] suggests that the pits here were dug for storage, and maintained in a fungus-free state by annual fumigation from hearths lit in their bases. After fumigation, the charcoal from the hearths was scooped out and replaced with a wad of clay. So it seems a reasonable working hypothesis that remains of dwelling refuse in pits will probably relate to a stage after the original storage function was served. In the most recent and comprehensive survey of these pits, Aileen Fox[138] has accepted a storage function, and it should also be noted that the large ones often have small 'bin-pits' let off to one side, perhaps for the separate storage of seed tubers for the following year's planting.

While on the topic of horticultural manifestations in the Classic Maori phase, there are large areas of prehistoric fields still surviving in the North Island, particularly on the rich volcanic soils of Auckland and Northland, where lumps of scoria were collected from the soil and built into mounds and low linear boundary walls, rather similar to the field systems in the Hawaiian Islands. Such systems do not survive on stone-free soils, although in these cases it is sometimes possible to observe traces of drainage ditches, and many terrace systems may have had horticultural functions as well[139].

Agnes Sullivan[140] has recently estimated that perhaps 2000 hectares of the rich volcanic soil of the Auckland Isthmus may once have supported stone boundary alignments and mounds, and an excellent area of about 280 hectares still survives at Wiri, on the Manukau Harbour south of Auckland, in association with a terraced *pa* which has dated occupation back to about A.D. 1300. These fields are not systematically rectangular, but rather roughly defined by alignments, mounds, and topographic features. It is possible that they were used for sweet potatoes and fern rhizomes in a long-term cycle of cropping and fallow, although Maoris apparently did have methods of increasing soil fertility by burning brushwood on fields and raking in the ash[141].

Observations by early explorers give us some idea of contemporary patternings of the various kinds of site mentioned. The journals of Cook and Banks (1769–70) provide a lot of valuable information, particularly for the eastern coast of Iwitini between Hawkes Bay and the Coromandel Peninsula. Areas of up to 80 hectares were reported under cultivation, divided into neat rectangular plots, although details of crops being grown are not given. Large numbers of *pa* were observed, particularly around the densely settled Bay of Plenty, while house clusters of varying size, some fenced and some open, were apparently quite widely distributed across the countryside. However, there were quite obviously some marked regional differences: Hawkes Bay was described as prosperous and peaceful, and without forts, while the equally prosperous Bay of Plenty to the north seems to have had a high density of forts. On the other hand, the Coromandel Peninsula and Queen Charlotte Sounds were described as without cultivation, although forts were certainly present (see page 392). Banks also gives us our only early description of a religious structure in New Zealand; a square of stones around a basket of fern rhizomes hung on a spade[142], seen in the Hawkes Bay region. New Zealand does in fact lack structures similar to the eastern Polynesian *marae*, although there are simple lines of standing stones (*tuahu*) in some areas, particularly around Rotorua.

The French accounts of the visit of the De Surville expedition to Doubtless Bay in 1769[143], and of the visit of the Du Fresne expedition to the Bay of Islands in 1772[144], are equally illuminating. One of the Doubtless Bay accounts refers to a pattern of large fortified *pa* with houses arranged on terraces, and then small hamlets and individual houses, some of circular shape, scattered through the countryside. In times of danger all the people moved into the *pa* and abandoned the dispersed huts. This is the same pattern as that observed by Cook, and it is clear that the *pa* contained the majority of the thick walled winter sleeping houses, while in summer 'many of them live dispers'd up and down in little Temporary Hutts, that are not sufficient to shelter them from the weather'[145].

The accounts of the Bay of Islands in 1772 give a similar picture, and here no less than 26 fortified *pa* were probably occupied in the vicinity of the French anchorage, although it is apparent that in such situations the very presence of strange outsiders would cause an unusual concentration of population in defensible places. The French accounts are sufficiently detailed to allow the conclusion that:

The 1772 population (in the Bay of Islands) were a settled fishing community, practising agriculture, and living in fortified settlements, or nucleated unfortified areas associated with these. Their economy was based on the production of a limited supply of root crops, particularly *kumara*, and their diet consisted chiefly of fernroot and fish. Restricted mobility of groups smaller than the village population varied seasonally, depending on the size of the labour force necessary for a particular task. The defended *pa* was thus occupied continuously, though at any one time small groups would have been absent[146].

This quote encapsulates the Classic Maori economy for perhaps the majority of the more fertile and populous areas of Iwitini.

Finally, we might turn briefly to general questions of the origin and development of Classic Maori culture. Attempts to subdivide the Classic Maori Phase into several subphases have not so far met with success, and in the general absence of firmly dated local sequences there is in fact some disagreement on the course of its internal evolution. So we will not tarry with the problem here. However, the circumstances of the origin and spread of Classic Maori culture are much more restricted in time and place, and Groube[147] has suggested that peoples may have been obliged to leave the Northland region and settle further south owing to a shortage of cleared land. The importance of cleared land in tribal disputes was pointed out some years ago by Vayda[148], and since the damp sub-tropical forests of Northland would not be easy to clear, then it would be reasonable to expect a strong tribe with an increasing population to eject one of its less fortunate neighbours, who would in turn either migrate elsewhere to eject someone else, or turn to clearing fresh forest. Assuming a period of considerable population growth in Iwitini in the fourteenth and fifteenth centuries, and this is a central assumption behind Groube's theory, then population movement could be expected, particularly out of a small and restricted area such as Northland. This argument seems quite attractive to me, and it should be noted that Groube stresses the importance of cleared land, rather than overpopulation in an absolute sense. Iwitini was still quite heavily forested in places at European contact, and clearly the Maoris could have increased their population had they cleared the whole country. They never did this, presumably being fully acquainted with the law of diminishing returns. Warfare and migration were simpler and more effective measures of maintaining a population balance, and one of the reasons for the success of the migrations may have been connected with the successful use of pit storage for sweet potato, as mentioned earlier on page 395.

So we have now traced the Maoris through to the time of European contact, and to the period of major cultural changes following 1800. Muskets, metal tools, new crops, pigs, whaleboats, and, not least, missionaries, wrought enormous changes in Maori society in the period between 1810 and 1840. Unfortunately, most of the best-known accounts of New Zealand date from this period, and are thus of limited value for prehistoric reconstruction. This is of course why I have stressed the accounts of the period 1769–1772 so heavily in this chapter – they caught prehistory 'alive'.

THE CHATHAM ISLANDS[149]

The Chatham Islands are of particular interest in a Polynesian context. Discovered in 1791, they supported a population of about 2000 people[150] living in total isolation. These people had no horticulture, no domesticated animals, and never had the benefit of a moa population. They had indeed cleared most of the forest from the islands and were exploiting large areas of fern rhizomes, but there is no evidence from early records for permanent settlements, or even permanent dwelling structures, and the account of discovery only mentions 'arbours' formed under growing trees. Current archaeological work from the University of Otago should fill out this rather barren picture considerably, and a life-style similar to that of the Murihiku Maoris is at least expectable. Nevertheless, the Chatham Islanders (Moriois) are in a class of their own as the only Polynesian hunter-gatherers totally cut off from contact with horticultural peoples. They represent the utter limits of Polynesian colonisation.

Traditionally, the islands were settled about A.D. 1100–1200, and Moriori material culture is very closely related to that of the South Island of New Zealand. Artefacts collected include the whole range of New Zealand Archaic adze types, together with reel ornaments, imitation whale tooth units, shark tooth necklace units, bird spears, and harpoons. Bait fishing gear was like that of New Zealand, with one- and two-piece forms, although trolling hooks appear to have been absent. All this suggests settlement of the islands from a South Island source during the Archaic Phase, followed by considerable isolation. However, the isolation may not have been absolutely complete, as certain Classic Maori forms such as Duff type 2B adzes are found quite commonly, and two tools of Mayor Island obsidian (not conclusively known to be prehistoric) have recently been reported[151]. In addition, a double line of small standing stones has been reported from one site[152], and this may be related to some of the smaller *marae* structures of eastern Polynesia.

SUMMARY

Owing to its temperate climate, New Zealand required unprecedented adaptations from its Polynesian settlers. On the evidence of artefacts these people were of undoubted eastern Polynesian origin, and probably reached the new land a little prior to A.D. 1000. The economy of the Archaic Phase was based mainly on fishing, gathering, and the hunting of moas (particularly in the South Island), while horticultural activities, mainly confined to the sweet potato, were highly restricted. The settlements of this phase consisted on present evidence of seasonally occupied and undefended camps, and the South Island may have supported a population larger than at any time prior to European settlement.

After the thirteenth century, the North and South Islands undergo rather different cultural developments. The South Island, together with the Chathams, maintains an economy based on fishing and gathering, and the Archaic artefact types undergo only limited modification. The North Island, on the other hand, becomes the scene for the development of Classic Maori Culture, characterised by new artefact types, fortified settlements, and a dense population subsisting to a greater extent on the cultivated sweet potato than in Archaic times. It is possible that an unfavourable climatic change, by stimulating the development of pit-storage methods for the sweet potato, could have given an economic advantage to the more northerly inhabitants of the North Island. From the archaeological record, it seems that they were not slow to use this advantage to develop and spread the fairly uniform Classic Maori Culture observed in the North and northern South Islands by the first European visitors. The expansion of this Classic Maori Culture may also be closely connected with the Fleet traditions recorded after 1840 in the North Island.

The New Zealand prehistoric sequence therefore reveals economic and cultural changes of an order unprecedented elsewhere in Polynesia.

There are no archaeological signs that these changes were stimulated by outside contacts, and the prehistorian is faced with an unusual closed system which presents one of the most interesting arenas for research in the Pacific.

Footnotes

1. Active Departments of Prehistory are located in the universities of Auckland and Otago, and in numerous museums, particularly Auckland, Canterbury and Otago (Dunedin).

2. Recent claims for a B.C. settlement in Hawkes Bay have not to my knowledge been substantiated, and the possibility of earlier non-Polynesian settlement in New Zealand seems slight. The earliest carbon dates go back about 1000 years (see Shawcross 1969; McCulloch 1973).

3. For Polynesian adaptations to New Zealand generally, see Green 1974a.

4. Lewthwaite 1949; Cumberland 1949. Only Te Wahi Pounamu has status as a traditional Maori name, being recorded by Cook.

5. Cumberland 1961; 1962a; 1962b.

6. On New Zealand food plants generally see Colenso 1880; Cumberland 1949; Buck 1958; Firth 1959; Hamel 1974.

7. For the economic significance of the fern rhizome see K. Shawcross 1967.

8. On Maori agriculture generally see Best 1925.

9. Taylor 1958.

10. Firth 1959; Leach 1969; Cassels 1972.

11. Vayda 1960: 77–8.

12. Pool 1964; Shawcross 1970a.

13. Hale 1846: 146.

14. Hamlin 1842.

15. Grey 1965.

16. Colenso 1846; Duff 1956: chapter 9.

17. Shortland 1868.

18. e.g. Wallace 1886; Ngata 1893; Hamilton 1896–1901: 29–37.

19. Wilson 1866; 1894.

20. Colenso 1868: 404, see also Travers 1871.

21. Smith 1915.

22. See Roberton 1956; Sharp 1956b; Piddington 1956; Roberton 1957; Sharp 1958; Roberton 1958; Pei te Hurinui 1958; Sharp 1959; Roberton 1959; Simmons 1966; Roberton 1966; 1969. For further debate on traditions see Adkin 1960; Keyes 1960; Golson 1960.

23. Simmons 1969a.

24. Best 1915, see also Downes 1933.

25. Keyes 1967.

26. As pointed out by Skinner (1916; 1924).

27. Williams 1937; Skinner 1923.

28. Mantell 1872.

29. Hutton 1891.

30. Haast 1871. For modern information about this site, which dates to *c.* A.D. 1400, see Trotter 1972b.

31. Haast 1874.

32. One of these posts has since given an unusually early carbon date of A.D. 780 ± 65 (Duff 1963: 28).

33. MacKay 1874.

34. See Hutton 1891; Downes 1915.

35. For general surveys of this early period of New Zealand archaeology see Davidson 1967; Duff 1968c; and the *N.Z. Arch. Assn. Newsletter*, Vol. 15, Part 1, 1971.

36. See H. Leach 1972.

37. Skinner 1921; 1924; 1974.

38. Duff 1956 (first edition 1950). See also Duff 1947, and Duff 1963 for a more recent view.

39. Duff 1956: 194.

40. Golson 1959.

41. Green 1967a.

42. Sinoto 1968b. In addition to similarities mentioned, strong Cook Island parallels are shown in a wooden 'godstick' from a swamp at Katikati, Bay of Plenty (Simmons 1973b), and also in the stone 'hybrid reels' of Waenganui (Duff 1956: Chapter 4).

43. The major New Zealand plant for fibres, basketry, etc., was the native flax *Phormium tenax* – a common swamp plant.

44. For lists see Scarlett 1972.

45. *Megalapteryx* may have survived until later in Fiordland; see Duff 1956: 75–6.

46. Falla 1964; Simmons 1968a. The genera are *Dinornis, Anomalopteryx, Megalapteryx, Pachyornis, Emeus* and *Euryapteryx*.

47. Simmons 1968a. See also Gregg 1972.

48. Simmons 1969b. McFadgen (1974) correlates the broadleaf expansion with the decline of the moas, as these birds when numerous may have kept the forest floor free of broadleaf seedlings. Concerning the scarcity of moas in the North Island, H. Leach (1974) reports that they were probably extinct in the Wairarapa district before the arrival of man.

49. Duff 1956.

50. Walls 1974.

51. Duff 1956: chapter 4.

52. Simmons 1967; 1973a.

53. For Pounawea and Papatowai see Lockerbie 1959.

54. B.F. Leach 1969.

55. Lockerbie 1959; Orchiston 1971.

56. On fishhook typology in the South Island see Hjarno 1967.

57. Simmons 1967. .

58. See H. Leach 1969.

59. Palisaded sites were only present in the northern part of the South Island.

60. Higham 1970; Coutts and Higham 1971; Coutts and Jurisich 1972. The shellfish growth-ring method is still experimental; see Coutts 1974.

61. Coutts 1969.

62. Ambrose 1968.

63. Wilkes and Scarlett 1967.

64. Simmons 1973c.

65. Reeves and Armitage 1973.

66. Duff 1956: chapter 7; Coutts 1971.

67. H. Leach 1969.

68. Walls 1974.

69. For full descriptions of rock art see Trotter and McCulloch 1971; Trotter 1971; Ambrose 1970.

70. Cumberland 1962b: 163–4.

71. Law 1969.

72. Golson 1959; Parker 1962; Green 1972a; Davidson 1974a; 1975.

73. Groube 1968; Wellman 1962.

74. As suggested by Law (1970).

75. Climatic change around A.D. 1300 was strongly supported until the early 1960s, after which the issue became considerably more cloudy; see Gorbey 1967; Molloy 1969; Law 1970. Prevailing opinion now seems to accept that an adverse change did take place; see Park 1970; H. Leach 1974.

76. Yen 1961.

77. McFadgen 1974.

78. H. Leach 1974. See also Leach and Leach 1971–2.

79. Shawcross 1972; 1975.

80. Smart, Green and Yaldwin 1962; Jones 1973. This site also produced the pearl-shell lure shank mentioned on page 386.

81. Jolly and Murdock 1973.

82. Green 1967a.

83. Green 1964.

84. Green, Brooks and Reeves 1967.

85. Armitage, Reeves and Bellwood 1972.

86. Ward 1973; 1974.

87. Reeves and Armitage 1973.

88. e.g. Armitage, Reeves and Bellwood 1972: 419.

89. e.g. near Lake Taupo and on Great Barrier Island (Law 1972; 1973).

90. Green 1970a (first edition 1963).

91. Decreasing ranges of avifauna are indicated clearly at the Sunde Site on Motutapu Island (Scott 1970) and at the Hot Water Beach Archaic site (Leahy 1974: 62).

92. See Groube 1967a for criticisms.

93. Sharp 1956.

94. Simmons 1969b; Groube 1970.

95. Simmons 1971.

96. Groube 1970.

97. e.g. Shawcross 1970b for collections made on Captain Cook's first voyage.

98. Golson 1959. See also Golson 1957a; Groube 1969.

99. e.g. at Oruarangi and Paterangi in the Hauraki Plains 192 composite hook points were found, but only 2 one-piece hooks. See Shawcross and Terrell 1966.

100. Beaglehole 1962, Part I: 444. See also Best 1929 for ethnographic Maori fishing methods.

101. Skinner 1966; Groube 1967b.

102. McNab 1914: 395.

103. e.g. Adkin 1948; Bellwood 1977b.

104. Adkin 1948: 69–72.

105. Shawcross 1964b.

106. Shawcross 1964a. North Island stone flake assemblages, whether in basalt or obsidian, are generally amorphous and without retouch (e.g. Bellwood 1969), although obsidians particularly are amenable to functional analysis through the study of use wear (Morwood 1974).

107. Adkin 1948 (Horowhenua); Bellwood 1977b (Mangakaware). See also Duff 1961b for a swamp assemblage at Waitara, near New Plymouth.

108. e.g. Heine Geldern 1966; Badner 1966.

109. Mead 1975.

110. Simmons 1968b; Trotter 1972a.

111. Orchiston 1967.

112. e.g. Best 1927; Golson 1957b. A well illustrated book on Maori fortifications is now available by Aileen Fox (1976).

113. Groube 1970.

114. Groube 1967: 19.

115. Reed 1969: 61–2.

116. Beaglehole 1962, Part I: 433.

117. Reproduced in Kelly 1951; Groube 1964b; Kennedy 1969.

118. For an excavated example see Bellwood 1972b: 275.

119. Fox 1975.

120. For descriptions of some class 3 *pa* in North Taranaki see Buist 1964. For criticism of Groube's classification see Gorbey 1971.

121. Bellwood 1971b; 1972b (Otakanini); McKinlay 1971 (Waioneke).

122. Golson 1961; Ambrose 1962; Ambrose – unpublished paper read at NZAA Conference, New Plymouth 1967.

123. Except perhaps at Castor Bay (Auckland), where a ditched promontory *pa* was superimposed over a larger terraced *pa* at about A.D. 1550 (Green 1970b; Davidson 1974b).

124. Taylor 1872: 101–2.

125. Adkin 1948.

126. Teviotdale and Skinner 1947; Shawcross and Terrell 1966.

127. Shawcross 1968.

128. Bellwood 1971b; 1977b.

129. Firth 1926.

130. On the rather complex topic of *pa* function see Green 1970a; Bellwood 1971b; and an important unpublished M.A. thesis by L.M. Groube (1964a).

131. See the excellent analysis of such a coastal midden by Shawcross (1967; 1972) and Terrell (1967).

132. Davidson 1970a.

133. Davidson 1970b; Leahy 1970; 1972; Davidson 1972.

134. e.g. by Duff 1961a for pits in a promontory *pa* in Marlborough Province.

135. Maning 1948: 181; Best 1916; Colenso 1868: 47.

136. Green 1963b.

137. Ambrose – unpublished paper read at NZAA Conference, New Plymouth 1967.

138. Fox 1974.

139. Wilson 1921 for swamp drainage ditches; McNab 1914: 361 and McNab 1969 for terraces.

140. Sullivan 1974; and paper presented at ANZAAS Congress, Canberra 1975.

141. Yate 1835: 156; Rigg and Bruce 1923.

142. Beaglehole 1962, part II: 34.

143. See McNab 1914.

144. See McNab 1914; Roth 1891. For a good archaeological commentary on the French visits, see Kennedy 1969.

145. Reed 1969: 147.

146. Kennedy 1969: 167–8.

147. Groube 1970.

148. Vayda 1956; 1960: 113.

149. For ethnographic descriptions see Skinner 1923; Skinner and Baucke 1928.

150. Richards 1972.

151. B.F. Leach 1973.

152. Simmons 1964: 67.

CHAPTER 14

Some Problems for the Future

Now that we have hopped our way through two million years and sixteen thousand west-to-east kilometres of prehistory, we should perhaps take a final opportunity to look back over some of the major themes of the story. It goes without saying that there are many more regions to be investigated, and many more techniques of information recovery to be perfected. As a result, the details of the prehistoric record will no doubt be improved immeasurably in the fairly close future. But there will always be broad themes of fundamental underlying significance which will never cease to provoke discussion.

Two of these themes, both closely related, concern the expansions of Mongoloid populations and Austronesian languages over the greater part of our area of concern. These are major success stories of human prehistory, and while the two themes are not necessarily identical, they are certainly closely related as far as Island Southeast Asia and Oceania are concerned. The corollary, of course, is why the two expansions have not been so successful in New Guinea and western Melanesia.

Perhaps we can provide a framework for a hypothesis concerning the success of these two groups. If we begin about 40,000 years ago, then we can suggest from the information given in chapter 2 that the present Mongoloid and Australoid populations had already begun to differentiate, in the north and south of eastern Asia respectively. Both groups were presumably separated by clinal populations in what is now Mainland Southeast Asia. From the archaeological record of the northern regions of Eurasia, it is clear that late Pleistocene populations, and presumably the early Mongoloids, were successful

projectile-hunters and gatherers in a zone with a very high biomass of animal life. Their numbers and economy may have allowed the formation of quite large seasonal settlements, and the germs of a ranked form of social organisation to ensure control may have been developing at this time. To the south, the Australoid populations of Java could also have occupied parkland and savanna zones with high biomasses during glacial peaks[1], but here we have no very clear traces of any technology for successful hunting. Presumably, the late Pleistocene peoples of Indonesia were sparsely settled hunters and food gatherers, with a fairly stable population and economy.

If the Mongoloids of central and northern China were, as suggested, successful and expanding populations, then they may have established a flow of Mongoloid genes into populations lying to the south. One does not need to posit a large-scale migration of projectile-hunters, since there is no archaeological evidence for this. But we do have the possible spread of flake and blade industries from Japan through to the Philippines and eastern Indonesia, and a degree of southward population movement early in the Holocene is quite possible. A long-term and inexorable result of such population movement, however small, could have been a steepening of the cline between Mongoloids and Australoids, with the advantage going to the Mongoloids.

Let us now turn to the environmental changes at the end of the Pleistocene. As the sea began to rise from its glacial minimum, so the shallow surface of the Sunda shelf was gradually drowned. Shallow seas tend to support high biomasses of fish and shellfish, and the shallow seas of the Sunda shelf region allowed the people we now term late Hoabinhians to adopt a semi-sedentary existence, evidenced today by a small number of surviving shell-mounds (see chapter 3). And an increasing degree of sedentism, as shown from ethnographic data by Harris[2], tends to allow an increasing population. Infanticide, prolonged lactation, and the need to carry children over large distances tend to cause wide spacing of births amongst hunter-gatherers. A semi-sedentary existence in a reduced size of territory would reduce the significance of these factors, and children could be born more frequently.

So we now have a theoretical situation in which a clinal population would be increasing its numbers, possibly on the northern part of the Sunda shelf, at the end of the Pleistocene Epoch. But as the population grew, so the land disappeared beneath the sea. Between 14,000 and 7000 years ago more than three million square kilometres of land on the Sunda shelf were drowned. At first sight, a rise in sea-level spread over 7000 years or more might seem too slow a transformation to have had any effect upon human economic systems, but there are three very important points to be considered. Firstly, the Sunda Shelf is well over 800 kilometres wide in some directions, and even with regular eustatic rise coastlines might have been receding locally at a rate of one kilometre every six years. Secondly, the eustatic rise was probably irregular, and localised speeding up is possible. Thirdly, some outer north-eastern parts of the shelf could have sunk 50 metres or so due to tectonic movement[3], although it is not known whether this movement would be contemporary with the eustatic rise.

However one assesses these three pieces of evidence, there can be little doubt that coastal populations on the Sunda Shelf were obliged to move owing to an inexorable encroachment by the sea. Some groups may have moved several times during the course of a single generation, so is it possible that local temporary land shortage may have induced demographic pressure, and perhaps systematic cultivation? The full answer to this question may never be known, since details of natural resources and population densities in an area now beneath the sea may always remain unknown. However, explanations of this general demographic kind have been put forward to explain agricultural intensification in many parts of the world, and the hypothesis as applied to Southeast Asia at least deserves a brief statement[4].

If the hypothesis is correct, then Southeast Asia would be established as an early and independent focus of plant domestication, possibly on a chronological level with early cereal domestication in western Asia. Furthermore, if plant cultivation then spread widely throughout Mainland Southeast Asia and southern China, with a consequent increase in Mongoloid populations, then the cline between Mongoloids and Australoids would be steepened still further. By 5000 B.C. the archipelagoes of Southeast Asia had attained their present configurations, and Austronesian speaking populations with developing techniques of canoe construction and navigation could commence their expansion through Taiwan into the Philippines and eastern Indonesia. Of course, the predominantly Mongoloid phenotype of the Austronesians need not imply that the expansion of the Austronesians is coterminous with the expansion of the Mongoloids; the latter were doubtless expanding long before we have any linguistic trace of the former, who probably represent quite a late phenomenon in relative terms.

By the time iron tools and wet-rice cultivation appear on the scene, some time before 2000 years ago, the Mongoloid takeover of South-east Asia may have been virtually complete, and the Polynesians had almost reached Easter Island. However, it would be simplistic to explain the expansion of the Austronesian speaking Mongoloids into Oceania purely on the grounds of population growth through plant cultivation alone. Even in recent times large islands such as Borneo and Sumatra had quite sparse populations. One cannot simply ignore the fact that the settlers of Oceania had a desire to explore and probe the unknown, despite the impossibility of subjecting this desire to anything approaching scientific proof.

The success of the Austronesian speakers in dominating Indonesia and the Philippines may be impressive, and even the Philippine Negritos and the recently-discovered Tasaday cave-dwellers of southern Mindanao speak Austronesian languages. On the other hand, one cannot claim the same success for New Guinea, where the boot, so to speak, is on the Papuan foot. Austronesians have gained a few toe-holds along the north and south-eastern coasts of the island, but no more. It seems to me that the best explanation for this is to postulate that the New Guineans developed techniques of plant cultivation before Austronesians arrived, and thus developed populations of sufficient size to resist penetration.

Admittedly, the New Guinea Highlands are geographically isolated, and this circumstance may have been important too. A high incidence of malaria in coastal New Guinea might also have taken its toll of the newcomers. And we also have to explain why plant cultivation should develop in New Guinea independently of Southeast Asia. But since we now have evidence for plant cultivation in the New Guinea Highlands from 4000 B.C. we are forced to consider the possibility of independent development, even if a simple explanation is lacking.

Another major theme, this time mainly of Oceanic significance, concerns the origins of the Polynesians. I have stressed the formative role of the Lapita Culture of Melanesia, since this does fit the archaeological and linguistic requirements with considerable precision. W.W. Howells[5] has recently made a detailed case for the early movement of the Polynesians through Micronesia, but in my opinion this is rather difficult to uphold. However, there is now general agreement that Polynesian origins are to be sought amongst the early Austronesian cultures of Island Southeast Asia, and at least we may be spared the time-wasting task of reading about stray Egyptians or white-skinned culture heroes in the future. But one problem does remain, and this concerns the apparent clash between the archaeological and the linguistic evidence. The archaeology states clearly to me that ancestral Polynesians journeyed quite quickly from eastern Indonesia through to Polynesia in the second millennium B.C. The linguistic evidence suggests that the Polynesian languages have an ancestry dating from about 3000 B.C. in Melanesia. There is obvious conflict here, and it will hopefully be resolved in the near future.

Another problem with the Polynesians concerns the origin of their quite elaborate form of social and genealogical ranking, and this problem applies to Micronesia as well. Ranking systems of this kind are not found generally in Melanesia or Island Southeast Asia, but the widespread occurrence of aristocratic concepts in Polynesia must mean that these concepts are of Proto-Polynesian antiquity at least. They probably go back to a society ancestral to both Polynesian and Nuclear Micronesian societies, but we simply do not know whether they were brought from Southeast Asia or developed somewhere around the Eastern Oceanic homeland in Oceania. I feel the former to be most likely, since there are social systems akin to the Polynesian type in Taiwan, and this circumstance could take us back to Proto-Austronesian times.

Some scholars have tried to show that the Polynesian chiefdoms developed in Oceania. As an example, Rappaport has suggested that they could reflect an increasing need for managerial control in small island situations where populations were densely distributed and possibly expanding[6]. In support of this view, we can see clearly that where populations are both large in an absolute sense and densely distributed, as in Tahiti, the Hawaiian Islands and Tonga, the aristocratic process is intensified. This is part of the background to all man's early civilisations, and needs no further emphasis. In such situations, chiefs and incipient kings may be needed to control land tenure, law and order, and the orderly circulation of produce and commodities.

But, the sceptic might ask, why are there large and dense populations in Melanesia and Island Southeast Asia which have not developed chiefdoms? Relatively egalitarian societies can expand to very large numbers, and the New Guineans seem mainly to have managed with Big Men and free enterprise trade. Hence I think there is more to Polynesian aristocracy than just a large population squeezed on to a small island, although I don't quite know what this ingredient is. All I can do is to push the problem back into the mists of time.

The problems which I have just described are large ones, and their solution will require all the techniques which modern archaeology can provide. In terms of the basic culture history of Southeast Asia and Oceania, the record is now quite rich, despite the presence of some major gaps. But once we look beyond culture history into the sphere of process – the why and how rather than the where and when, then the scope becomes virtually limitless.

Footnotes

1. Glacial period environments in Java are discussed by Verstappen 1975.
2. Harris, 1974.
3. Haile 1971: 338.
4. Bellwood 1976a; see also Barrau 1974; Gorman 1974.
5. Howells 1973.
6. Rappaport 1964: 168.

Glossary

Aceramic without the use or presence of pottery.

Affine a relative through marriage.

Agnate a blood relative in the male line.

Ambilineal a system of descent (as in Polynesia) whereby a person can inherit from father or mother, but in general terms not equally from both (the Polynesians placed strong stress on the male line). (See page 84.)

Avunculocal post-marital residence with the maternal uncle of the husband.

Bilateral a system of descent wherein a person inherits from both parents equally. (See page 84.)

Boustrophedon writing which goes from left to right and right to left, with alternate lines inverted.

Brachycephaly relative broad-headedness; having a value of over 81 on an index of breadth ÷ length × 100 measured on the skull.

Calibration of radiocarbon dates Radiocarbon dates, especially for the period before 1000 B.C., do not correlate precisely with solar years in our own calendar. This important fact was established by dating the growth rings of the long-lived California bristlecone pine, and for details the reader is invited to consult R. M. Clark, A calibration curve for radiocarbon dates, *Antiquity* 49:251-266, 1975. The procedure is too complex for a brief description here, but radiocarbon dates older than 3000 years are *younger* than solar dates, and require increments from an approximately-known scale if they are to fit our own B.C. / A.D. system.

Carination a sharp angle in the side profile of a pot, usually at the greatest diameter. (See figure 9.15.)

Cline a geographical gradient in the frequency of occurrence of a human physical characteristic (e.g. a blood-group gene, skin colour, stature, etc.).

Cognate a blood relative.

Coprolites faeces preserved in archaeological deposits.

Cultigen a cultivated plant which has diverged genetically from its wild progenitor owing to domestication and selection by man.

Diachronic emphasising the dimension of time.

Dolichocephaly relative long or narrow-headedness; a value of under 75 on the skull (see *brachycephaly*).

Endogamy (endogamous) the restriction of marriage to members of the same class or local group.

Epicanthic fold an outer fold of skin over the upper eyelid; a characteristic of Mongoloid populations.

Eustatic pertaining to the level of the oceans (excluding tidal variations).

Exogamy (exogamous) the restriction of marriage to persons outside one's class or local group.

Extended burial burial with the body laid out to its full length.

Flexed burial burial on the side with bent legs; the legs can be drawn up into the chest in extreme cases.

Inhumation earth burial.

Lens an archaeological layer of localised extent, shaped in a generalised way like an optical lens (i.e. thick in the middle, and tapering away around the edges).

Matriline (matrilineal) a descent group which traces its ancestry through the female line.

Mesocephaly a value of 75-80 on the skull (see *brachycephaly*).

Moiety one of two *exogamous unilineal* divisions of a tribe, itself usually divided into *sibs*.

Palynology the study of pollens preserved in soils, usually as a guide to vegetation history.

Patriline (patrilineal) a descent group which traces its ancestry through the male line.

Patrivirilocal post-marital residence with the husband's father.

Petroglyph a rock-carving.

Phenotype (phenotypic) the actual form of an individual human or animal, being the result of interaction between genetic endowment and environment.

Phratry an *exogamous unilineal* division of a tribe, itself usually divided into *sibs* (see also *moiety*).

Phylogeny (phylogenetic) an evolutionary scheme of development (or 'family-tree'), ideally based on genetic similarities between related life forms.

Polyandry marriage in which a woman may have more than one husband at the same time.

Polygyny marriage in which a man may have more than one wife at the same time.

Preceramic prior to the manufacture and use of pottery.

Ramage an *ambilineal* descent group, internally stratified according to genealogical criteria. Well developed in Polynesia. (See page 84.)

Ruvettus a large tropical deep-water fish, *Ruvettus pretiosus*.

Sib a *unilineal* grouping of several lineages, found typically in Melanesia. (See page 84.)

Situla a bronze vessel shaped like a bucket.

Steatopygia unusually fatty buttocks in females.

Technocomplex a group of archaeological cultures characterised by assemblages sharing the same general families of artefact types. A technocomplex results from widely diffused responses to common factors in environment, economy and technology.

Unilineal *matrilineal* or *patrilineal* descent.

Uxorilocal post-marital residence with the wife's family.

Virilocal post-marital residence with the husband's family.

Bibliography

ABBREVIATIONS USED

A	Anthropos
AA	American Anthropologist
AJPA	American Journal of Physical Anthropology
AP	Asian Perspectives
APAMNH	Anthropological Papers of the American Museum of Natural History
APAO	Archaeology and Physical Anthropology in Oceania
APAS	Asian and Pacific Archaeology Series
BAIM	Bulletin of the Auckland Institute and Museum
BEFEO	Bulletin de l'École Française d'Extrême-Orient
BIEAS	Bulletin of the Institute of Ethnology, Academia Sinica
BMFEA	Bulletin of the Museum of Far Eastern Antiquities
BPBMB	Bernice P. Bishop Museum Bulletin
BPBMM	Bernice P. Bishop Museum Memoir
BPBMOP	Bernice P. Bishop Museum Occasional Paper
BPBMSP	Bernice P. Bishop Museum Special Publication
BSEI	Bulletin de la Société des Études indochinoises
BSGI	Bulletin du Service Géologique de l'Indochine
CA	Current Anthropology
CMB	Canterbury Museum Bulletin
DMB	Dominion Museum Bulletin (Wellington)
DMM	Dominion Museum Monograph (Wellington)
EM	Études mélanésiennes
FMJ	Federation Museums Journal
JEAS	Journal of East Asiatic Studies
JFMSM	Journal of the Federated Malay States Museum
JHKAS	Journal of the Hong Kong Archaeological Society
JMBRAS	Journal of the Malaysian Branch of the Royal Asiatic Society
JPNGS	Journal of the Papua New Guinea Society

JPS	Journal of the Polynesian Society
JRAI (JAI)	Journal of the Royal Anthropological Institute
JRSNZ	Journal of the Royal Society of New Zealand
JSO	Journal de la Société des Océanistes
MSGI	Memoir du Service Géologique de l'Indochine
NZAAM	New Zealand Archaeological Association Monograph
NZAAN	New Zealand Archaeological Association Newsletter
NZJS	New Zealand Journal of Science
OUMPA	Otago University Monographs in Prehistoric Anthropology (formerly Studies in Prehistoric Anthropology, Department of Anthropology, University of Otago)
PAR	Pacific Anthropological Records
PJS	Philippine Journal of Science
PPS	Proceedings of the Prehistoric Society
RAM	Records of the Australian Museum
RAIM	Records of the Auckland Institute and Museum
RCM	Records of the Canterbury Museum
RFM	Records of the Fiji Museum
ROMA	Records of the Otago Museum, Anthropology
RPNGM	Records of the Papua New Guinea Museum
SMJ	Sarawak Museum Journal
SWJA	Southwestern Journal of Anthropology
TNZI	Transactions of the New Zealand Institute
TRSNZ	Transactions of the Royal Society of New Zealand
UISPP	Union International des Sciences Préhistoriques et Protohistoriques
WA	World Archaeology
WBKL	Wiener Beiträge zur Kulturgeschichte und Linguistik

ADKIN G.L. 1948 *Horowhenua*. Wellington: Polynesian Society Memoir 26.

—— 1960 An adequate culture nomenclature for the New Zealand area, *JPS* 69:228–38.

AIGNER J. 1973 Pleistocene archaeological remains from South China, *AP* 16:16–38.

AIGNER J.S. and W.S. LAUGHLIN 1973 The dating of Lantian man and his significance for analysing trends in human evolution, *AJPA* 39:97–109.

AITKEN R. 1930 *Ethnology of Tubuai*. BPBMB 70.

AKERBLOM K. 1968 *Astronomy and navigation in Polynesia and Micronesia*. Stockholm: Ethnographical Museum Monograph 4.

ALEXANDER J. and D.G. COURSEY 1969 The origins of yam cultivation, in Ucko P. and G.W. Dimbleby (eds.), *The domestication and exploitation of plants and animals*, p. 405–425. London: Duckworth.

ALKIRE W.H. 1960 Cultural adaptation in the Caroline Islands, *JPS* 69: 123–50.

—— 1965 *Lamotrek atoll and inter-island socio-economic ties*. Illinois Studies in Anthropology 5, Urbana.

—— 1972 *An introduction to the peoples and cultures of Micronesia*. Addison-Wesley Modular Publication 18.

ALLEN B. 1971 Wet field taro terraces in Mangaia, Cook Islands, *JPS* 80: 371–8.

ALLEN J. 1970 Prehistoric agricultural systems in the Wahgi Valley – a further note, *Mankind* 7:177–83.

—— 1972a The first decade in New Guinea archaeology, *Antiquity* 46: 180–90.

—— 1972b Nebira 4: an early Austronesian site in central Papua, *APAO* 7: 92–124.

ALLEN M. 1972 Rank and leadership in Nduindui, northern New Hebrides, *Mankind* 8: 270–82.

ALMEIDA A. de and G. ZBYSZEWSKI 1967 A contribution to the study of the prehistory of Portuguese Timor lithic industries, *APAS* 1: 55–68.

AMBROSE W. 1962 Further investigations at Kauri Point, *NZAAN* 5:56–66.

—— 1968 The unimportance of the inland plains in South Island prehistory, *Mankind* 6:585–93.

—— 1970 Archaeology and rock-drawings from the Waitaki gorge, central South Island, *RCM* 8:383–437.

—— 1973 3000 years of trade in New Guinea obsidian, *Australian Natural History*, Sept. 1973:370–3.

AMBROSE W. and R.C. GREEN 1972 First millennium B.C. transport of obsidian from New Britain to the Solomon Islands, *Nature* 237:31.

ANELL B. 1955 *Contribution to the history of fishing in the southern seas*. Uppsala: Studia Ethnographica Upsaliensia 9.

—— 1956 The Polynesian cities of refuge, *Orientalia Suecana* 5:189–209.

APPLE R. 1965 *Hawaiian archaeology: trails.* BPBMSP 53.

ARKELL A.J. 1936 Cambay and the bead trade, *Antiquity* 10:292–305.

ARMITAGE G.C., R.D. REEVES and P.S. BELLWOOD 1972 Source identification of archaeological obsidians in New Zealand, *NZJS* 15:408–20.

ARMSTRONG W.E. 1928 *Rossel Island.* Cambridge University Press.

ASHTON P.S. 1972 The Quaternary geomorphological history of western Malesia and lowland forest phytogeography, *in* Ashton P. and M. (eds.) 1972:35–49.

ASHTON P. and M. (eds.) 1972 *The Quaternary era in Malesia.* University of Hull, Department of Geography, Miscellaneous series 13.

AUDLEY-CHARLES M.G. and D. A. HOOIJER 1973 Relation of Pleistocene migrations of pygmy stegodonts to island arc tectonics in Eastern Indonesia, *Nature* 241:197–8.

AUSTEN L. 1939 Megalithic structures in the Trobriand Islands, *Oceania* 10:30–53.

AVIAS J. 1949 Contribution à la préhistoire de l'Océanie: les tumuli des plateaux de fer en Nouvelle-Calédonie, *JSO* 5:15–50.

—— 1950 Poteries canaques et poteries préhistoriques en Nouvelle-Calédonie, *JSO* 6:111–40.

AYRES W.S. 1971 Radiocarbon dates from Easter Island, *JPS* 80:497–504.

BADNER M. 1966 The protruding tongue and related motifs in the art styles of the American Northwest Coast, New Zealand and China, *WBKL* 15:1–44.

—— 1972 Some evidences of Dong-Son derived influence in the art of the Admiralty Islands, *in* Barnard N. (ed.) 1972, vol. 3, p. 597–630.

BALL S.C. 1933 *Jungle fowls from the Pacific Islands.* BPBMB 108.

BANDI H.G. 1951 Die obsidianindustrie der Umgebung von Bandung in Westjava, *in Südseestudien*, p. 127–61. Basel: Museum für Volkerkunde.

BARBETTI M. AND H. ALLEN 1972 Prehistoric man at Lake Mungo, Australia, by 32000 years B.P., *Nature* 240:46–8.

BARD S.M. and W. MEACHAM 1972 Preliminary report on a site at Sham Wan, Lamma Island, Hong Kong, *AP* 15, 2:113–26.

BARNARD N. 1963 Review article, in *Monumenta Serica* 22, fascicle 2:213–255.

—— 1975 *The first radiocarbon dates from China.* Revised edition. Monograph on Far Eastern History 8, Australian National University.

—— (ed.) 1972 *Early Chinese art and its possible influence in the Pacific Basin.* 3 volumes. New York: Intercultural Arts Press.

BARNES J.A. 1962 African models in the New Guinea Highlands, *Man* 62:5–9.

BARNETT H.G. 1960 *Being a Palauan.* Holt, Rinehart and Winston.

BARRAU J. 1956 *L'agriculture vivrière autochthone de la Nouvelle-Calédonie.* Noumea: South Pacific Commission.

—— 1958 *Subsistence agriculture in Melanesia.* BPBMB 219.

—— 1960 Plant exploration and introduction in Micronesia, *South Pacific Bulletin* 10, part 1:44–7.

—— 1961 *Subsistence agriculture in Polynesia and Micronesia.* BPBMB 223.

—— (ed.) 1963 *Plants and the migrations of Pacific peoples.* Honolulu: Bishop Museum Press.

—— 1965a Histoire et préhistoire horticoles de l'Océanie tropicale, *JSO* 21:55–78.

—— 1965b Witnesses of the past: notes on some food plants of Oceania, *Ethnology* 4:282–294.

—— 1968 L'humide et le sec, *in* Vayda A.P. (ed.) 1968: 113–32.

—— 1970 La région indo-pacifique comme centre de mise en culture et de domestication des végétaux, *Journal d'Agriculture Tropicale et de Botanique Appliquée* 17, 12:487–503.

—— 1974 L'Asie du Sud-Est, berceau cultural, *Études Rurales* 53–56:17–39.

BARRERA W.M. and P.V. KIRCH 1973 Basaltic glass artefacts from Hawaii, *JPS* 82:176–87.

BARRÈRE D. 1967 Revisions and adulterations in Polynesian creation myths, *in* Highland G. *et al.* (eds.) 1967: 103–19.

BARRETT C.J. 1973 Tai Wan reconsidered, *JHKAS* 4:53–9.

BARROW T.E. 1967 Material evidence of the bird-man concept in Polynesia, *in* Highland G. *et al.* (eds.) 1967: 191–214.

BARTH F. 1952 The southern Mongoloid migration, *Man* 52:5–8.

BARTHEL T. 1963 Review of Heyerdahl T. and E.N. Ferdon (eds.) 1961, *AA* 65:421–4.

—— 1971 Pre-contact writing in Oceania, *in* Seboek T. (ed.) 1971:1165–1188.

BARTLETT H.H. 1962 Possible separate origin and evolution of the ladang and sawah types of tropical agriculture, *Proceedings 9th Pacific Science Congress*, vol. 4:270–3.

BARTSTRA G.J. 1974a Short account of the 1973 investigations on the Palaeolithic Patjitan culture, Java, Indonesia, *Berita Prasejarah* 1:23–6.

—— 1974b Notes about Sangiran, *Quartär* 25:1–12.

—— 1976 *Contributions to the study of the Palaeolithic Patjitan Culture, Java, Indonesia, Part 1.* Leiden: E. J. Brill.

BAUMGARTEN A., E. GILES and C.C. CURTAIN 1968 The distribution of haptoglobin and transferrin types in northeast New Guinea, *AJPA* 29:29–37.

BAYARD D.T. 1966 *The cultural relationships of the Polynesian Outlier.* Unpublished M.A. thesis, University of Hawaii.

—— 1970 Excavations at Non Nok Tha, northeastern Thailand, 1968: an interim report, *AP* 13:109–44.

—— 1971a *An early indigenous bronze technology in north-east Thailand: its implications for the prehistory of east Asia.* Expanded version of paper presented at 28 Congress of Orientalists, Canberra, January 1971 (mimeo.).

—— 1971b *A course towards what? Evolution, development and change at Non Nok Tha, northeastern Thailand.* Unpublished Ph.D. thesis, University of Hawaii.

—— 1972a *Non Nok Tha: the 1968 excavations.* OUMPA 4.

—— 1972b Early Thai bronze: analysis and new dates, *Science* 176:1411–2.

BEAGLEHOLE E. and P. 1938 *Ethnology of Pukapuka.* BPBMB 150.

BEAGLEHOLE J.C. (ed.) 1962 *The Endeavour Journal of Joseph Banks 1768–1771.* 2 volumes. Sydney: Trustees of the Public Library of New South Wales.

—— (ed.) 1967 *The Journals of Captain James Cook: the voyage of the Resolution and Discovery 1776–1780.* 2 volumes. Cambridge: Hakluyt Society.

—— (ed.) 1969 *The Journals of Captain James Cook: the voyage of the Resolution and Adventure 1772–5.* Cambridge: Hakluyt Society.

BEATY J. 1962 The mystery of the Marianas latte stones, *Pacific Discovery* 15, part 1:8–12.

BEAUCLAIR I. de 1946 The Keh Lao of Kweichow and their history according to Chinese records, *Studia Serica* 5:1–44.
—— 1963 Stone money of Yap Island, *BIEAS* 16:147–60.
—— 1966 On pottery of Micronesia, Palauan lamps and Mediterranean lamps in the Far East, *BIEAS* 21:197–214.
—— 1967a On religion and mythology of Yap Island, Micronesia, *BIEAS* 23:23–36.
—— 1967b Infant burial in earthenware pots and the pyramidal grave on Yap, *BIEAS* 24:35–9.
—— 1968 Social stratification in Micronesia: the low-caste people of Yap, *BIEAS* 25:45–52.
—— 1972 Jar burial on Botel Tobago, *AP* 15:167–76.
BECHTOL C. 1963 Sailing characteristics of Oceanic canoes, *in* Golson J. (ed.) 1963:98–101.
BELLWOOD P.S. 1969 Excavations at Skipper's Ridge, Opito Bay, Coromandel Peninsula, North Island of New Zealand, *APAO* 4:198–221.
—— 1970 Dispersal centres in East Polynesia, with special reference to the Society and Marquesas Islands, *in* Green R.C. and M. Kelly (eds.) 1970:93–104.
—— 1971a Varieties of ecological adaptation in the southern Cook Islands, *APAO* 6:145–69.
—— 1971b Fortifications and economy in prehistoric New Zealand, *PPS* 37:56–95.
—— 1972a *A settlement pattern survey, Hanatekua Valley, Hiva Oa, Marquesas Islands.* PAR 17.
—— 1972b Excavations at Otakanini Pa, South Kaipara Harbour, *JRSNZ* 2:259–91.
—— 1974 Prehistoric contacts in the Cook Islands, *Mankind* 9:278–80.
—— 1975a The prehistory of Oceania, *CA* 16:9–28.
—— 1975b Review of Levison M., R.G. Ward and J.W. Webb 1973, *in Journal of Interdisciplinary History* VI/1:154–7.
—— 1976a Prehistoric plant and animal domestication in Austronesia, *in* Sieveking G. de G., I. H. Longworth and D. E. Wilson (eds.), *Problems in economic and social archaeology*, p. 153–68. London: Duckworth.
—— 1976b *Indonesia, the Philippines and Oceanic prehistory.* Paper presented at IXᵉ Congrès UISPP, Nice, September 1976.
—— 1977a *Archaeological research in the Cook Islands.* PAR forthcoming.
—— 1977b *Archaeological research at Lake Mangakaware, Waikato, 1968–70.* NZAAM forthcoming.
BENDER B. 1971 Micronesian languages, *in* Seboek T. (ed.) 1971:426–65.
BENEDICT P.K. 1942 Thai, Kadai and Indonesian: a new alignment in South-eastern Asia, *AA* 44:576–601.
—— 1966 Austro-Thai, *Behavior Science Notes* 1:227–61.
—— 1967 Austro-Thai studies, *Behavior Science Notes* 2:203–32, 232–46, 275–336.
BENNETT W.C. 1931 *Archaeology of Kauai.* BPBMB 80.
BERGMAN P.A.M. and P. KARSTEN 1952 Fluorine content of Pithecanthropus and of other species from the Trinil fauna, *Koninklijke Nederlandse Akademie van Wetenschappen, Proceedings Series B*, vol. 55:150–2.
BERNATZIK H.A. 1947 *Akha und Meau.* Innsbruck: Wagner'sche Univ. – Buchdruckerei.
BERNDT R.M. 1954 Contemporary significance of prehistoric stone objects in the eastern Central Highlands of New Guinea, *A* 49:553–87.
BEST E. 1915 Maori and Maruiwi, *TNZI* 48:435–47.
—— 1916 *Maori storehouses and kindred structures.* DMB 5.
—— 1923a *Polynesian voyagers.* DMM 5.
—— 1923b The origin of the Maori, *JPS* 32:10–20.
—— 1925 *Maori agriculture.* DMB 9.
—— 1927 *The Pa Maori.* DMB 6.
—— 1929 *Fishing methods and devices of the Maori.* DMB 12.
BEYER H.O. 1947 Outline review of Philippine archaeology by islands and provinces, *PJS* 77:205–374.
—— 1948 *Philippine and east Asian archaeology and its relation to the origin of the Pacific Islands population.* National Research Council of the Philippines, Bulletin 29.
—— 1951 A tribute to van Stein Callenfels, *JEAS*: 77–81.
—— 1955 The origin and history of the Philippine rice terracers, *Proceedings 8th Pacific Science Congress*, vol. 1:387–97.
—— 1956 The relation of tektites to archaeology, *Proceedings 4th Far Eastern Prehistory and the Anthropology Division of the 8th Pacific Science Congresses combined*, 2nd fascicle, section 1, p. 371–415.
BEZACIER L. 1972 *Le Viêtnam: de la préhistoire à la fin de l'occupation chinoise.* Paris: A. and J. Picard.
BIASUTTI R. 1959 *Le razze e i popoli della terra.* 3rd revised edition, 4 volumes. Unione Tipografico, Editrice Torinese.
BIGGS B.G. 1965 Direct and indirect inheritance in Rotuman, *Lingua* 14:383–415.
—— 1967 The past twenty years in Polynesian linguistics, *in* Highland G. *et al.* (eds.) 1967:303–21.
—— 1971 The languages of Polynesia, *in* Seboek T. (ed.) 1971: 466–505.
—— 1972 Implications of linguistic subgrouping with special reference to Polynesia, *in* Green R.C. and M. Kelly (eds.) 1972:143–52.
BIJLMER H.J.T. 1939 *Tapiro Pygmies and Pania mountain Papuans.* Leiden: E.J. Brill.
BIRDSELL J.B. 1949 The racial origin of the extinct Tasmanians, *Records of the Queen Victoria Museum* 2:105–22.
—— 1967 Preliminary data on the trihybrid origin of the Australian Aborigines, *APAO* 2:100–55.
—— 1972 *Human evolution.* Chicago: Rand McNally.
BIRKS L. 1973 *Excavations at Sigatoka dune site, Fiji.* Fiji Museum Bulletin 1.
BIRKS L. and H. 1968 Early pottery objects from Fiji. *JPS* 77:296–9.
BIRKS L. and H. 1973 Dentate stamped pottery from Sigatoka, *in* Mead S.M. *et al.* 1973:6–18.
BLACKWOOD B. 1950 *Technology of a modern stone age people in New Guinea.* Pitt Rivers Museum, Occasional Papers in Technology 3.
BLOOM A.L. 1971 Glacial-eustatic and isostatic controls of sea level since the last glaciation, *in* Turekian K.T. (ed.) 1971:355–80.
BLUNDELL V.M. and P. BLEED 1974 Ground stone artefacts from late Pleistocene and early Holocene Japan, *APAO* 9:120–33.
BLUST R.A. 1974 Eastern Austronesian: a note, *Working Papers in Linguistics* 6, no. 4, p. 101–7. Department of Linguistics, University of Hawaii.
—— 1976 Austronesian culture history: some linguistic inferences and their relations to the archaeological record, *WA* 8:19–43.
BOLLONS J. 1924 Polynesian navigators: a seaman's view, *New Zealand Herald*, May 24, 1924.
BOOTH P.B. and H.W. TAYLOR 1974 *An evaluation of genetic distance analysis of some New Guinea populations.* Paper given at Australian Institute of Aboriginal Studies Conference, Canberra, May 1974.
BOOTH P.B. and A.P. VINES 1968 Blood groups and other genetic data from the Bismarck Archipelago, New Guinea, *APAO* 3:64–73.

BORISKOVSKY P.I. 1967 Problems of the Palaeolithic and of the Mesolithic of South East Asia, *APAS* 1:41–6.
—— 1968–1971 *Vietnam in primeval times.* Published in 7 parts in Soviet Anthropology and Archaeology, vols. 7(2):14–32; 7(3):3–19; 8(1):70–95; 8(3):214–57; 8(4): 355–66;9(2):154–72; 9(3):226–64.
—— 1971 New problems of the Palaeolithic and Mesolithic of the Indochinese peninsula, *APAO* 6:102–6.
BOSERUP E. 1965 *The conditions of agricultural growth.* London: Allen and Unwin.
BOULINIER G. and G. 1972 Les Polynésiens et la navigation astronomique, *JSO* 28:275–84.
BOWLER J.M., R. JONES, H. ALLEN, and A.G. THORNE 1971 Pleistocene human remains from Australia: a living site and human cremation from Lake Mungo, western New South Wales, *WA* 2:39–60.
BOWLER J.M., A.G. THORNE and H.A. POLACH 1972 Pleistocene man in Australia: age and significance of the Mungo skeleton, *Nature* 240:48–50.
BRACE C.L. 1964 A non-racial approach towards the understanding of human diversity, *in* Montagu M. (ed.) 1964:103–52.
BRACE C.L., H. NELSON, and N. KORN 1971 *Atlas of fossil man.* New York: Holt, Rinehart and Winston.
BRANDT J.H. 1962 Nan Matol: ancient Venice of Micronesia, *Archaeology* 15:99–107.
BRONSON B. and M. HAN 1972 A thermoluminescence series from Thailand, *Antiquity* 46:322–6.
BROOKFIELD H.C. 1962 Local study and comparative method, *Annals of the Association of American Geographers* 52:242–54.
—— 1964 Ecology of Highland settlement, *AA* 66(4), part 2:20–38.
BROOKFIELD H.C. and P. BROWN 1963 *Struggle for land.* Melbourne: Oxford University Press.
BROOKFIELD H.C. with D. HART 1971 *Melanesia: a geographical interpretation of an island world.* London: Methuen.
BROOKFIELD H.C. and P. WHITE 1968 Revolution or evolution in the prehistory of New Guinea Highlands, *Ethnology* 7:43–52.
BROTHWELL D.R. 1960 Upper Pleistocene human skull from Niah caves, Sarawak, *SMJ* 9:323–49.
BROWN J.M. 1907 *Maori and Polynesian: their origin, history and culture.* London: Hutchinson.
—— 1924 *The riddle of the Pacific.* London: Fisher Unwin.
—— 1927 *Peoples and problems of the Pacific.* 2 volumes. London: Fisher Unwin.
BROWN P. 1960 Chimbu tribes: political organisation in the Eastern Highlands of New Guinea, *SWJA* 16:22–35.
BROWN P. and H.C. BROOKFIELD 1967 Chimbu settlement and residence, *Pacific Viewpoint* 8:119–51.
BRYAN E.H. 1963 Discussion, *in* Fosberg F.R. (ed.) 1963:38.
BUCK, Sir Peter 1926 The value of traditions in Polynesian research, *JPS* 35:181–203.
—— 1932a *Ethnology of Tongareva.* BPBMB 92.
—— 1932b *Ethnology of Manihiki and Rakahanga.* BPBMB 99.
—— 1934 *Mangaian Society.* BPBMB 122.
—— 1938 *Vikings of the sunrise.* New Zealand: Whitcombe and Tombs (1964 reprint).
—— 1944 *Arts and crafts of the Cook Islands.* BPBMB 179.
—— 1957 *Arts and crafts of Hawaii.* BPBMSP 45.
—— 1958 *The coming of the Maori.* Wellington: Whitcombe and Tombs.
BUIST A.G. 1964 *Archaeology in North Taranaki, New Zealand.* NZAAM 3.

BULMER R.N.H. 1964 Edible seeds and prehistoric stone mortars in the Highlands of East New Guinea, *Man* 64:147–50.
—— 1971 The role of ethnography in reconstructing the prehistory of Melanesia, *in* Green R.C. and M. Kelly (eds.) 1971: 36–44.
BULMER R.N.H. and S. 1962 Figurines and other stones of power among the Kyaka. *JPS* 71:192–208.
BULMER S. 1963–4 Prehistoric stone implements from the New Guinea Highlands, *Oceania* 34:246–68.
—— 1964 Radiocarbon dates from New Guinea, *JPS* 73:327–8.
—— 1966 Pig bones from two archaeological sites in the New Guinea Highlands, *JPS* 75:504–5.
—— 1971 Prehistoric settlement patterns and pottery in the Port Moresby area, *JPNGS* 5(2): 29–81.
—— 1973 *Notes of 1972 excavations at Wanlek.* Working Papers 29, Department of Anthropology, University of Auckland.
—— 1975 Settlement and economy in prehistoric Papua New Guinea, *JSO* 31:7–76.
BULMER S. and R.N.H. 1964 The prehistory of the Australian New Guinea Highlands, *AA* 66(4), part 2:39–76.
BULMER S. and W. TOMASETTI 1970 A stone replica of a bronze socketed axe from the Eastern Highlands of Australian New Guinea, *RPNGM* 1:38–41.
BUNKER E.C. 1972 The Tien culture and some aspects of its relationship to the Dong-Son culture, *in* Barnard N. (ed.) 1972, vol. 2: 291–328.
BURKILL I.H. 1953 Habits of man and the history of cultivated plants in the Old World, *Proceedings of the Linnean Society of London* 164, 1:12–42.
BURLING R. 1965 *Hill farms and padi fields.* Prentice Hall.
BURROWS E.G. 1938 (1970) *Western Polynesia: a study of cultural differentiation.* Ethnologiska Studier 7 (reprinted 1970 by University Bookshop, Dunedin).
—— 1939 Breed and border in Polynesia, *AA* 41:1–21.
BUTINOV N.A. and Y.V. KNOROZOV 1957 Preliminary report on the study of the written language of Easter Island, *JPS* 66:5–17.
CALLENFELS P.V. van Stein 1932 Les ateliers néolithique de Punung et Patjitan, *in Hommage du Service Archéologique des Indes Néerlandaises au Ier Congrès des Préhistoriens d'Extrême-Orient à Hanoi,* p. 25–9.
—— 1936 The Melanesoid civilisations of East Asia, *Bulletin of the Raffles Museum,* Series B, 1:41–51.
—— 1938 Mededeelinginen het Proto-Toaliaan, *Tijdschrift voor Indische Taal- en Volkenkunde* 68:579–84.
—— 1951 Prehistoric sites on the Karama River, *JEAS* 1:82–97.
CALLENFELS P.V. van Stein and I.H.N. EVANS 1928 Report on cave excavations in Perak, *JFMSM* 12:145–60.
CALLENFELS P.V. van Stein and H.D. NOONE 1940 A rock-shelter excavation at Sungai Siput, Perak, *in* Chasen F.N. and M.W.F. Tweedie (eds.) 1940:119–25.
ÇAMBEL H. and R.J. BRAIDWOOD. 1970 An early farming village in Turkey, *Scientific American* 222:51–6.
CAMPBELL B.G. 1967 *Human evolution.* Heinemann.
CAPELL A. 1943 *The linguistic position of southeastern Papua.* Sydney: Australasian Medical Publishing Co. Ltd.
—— 1962 Oceanic linguistics today, *CA* 3:371–428.
—— 1964 Comments, *CA* 5:385.
—— 1969 *A survey of New Guinea languages.* Sydney University Press.
—— 1971 The Austronesian languages of Australian New Guinea, *in* Seboek T. (ed.) 1971:240–340.

CAPELL A. and R.H. LESTER 1940–2 Local divisions and movements in Fiji, *Oceania* 11:313–41; 12:21–48.

CARBONNEL J.-P. and P. BIBERSON 1968 Industrie osseuse et présence humaine dans le gisement pléistocene inferieur du Phnom Loang (Cambodge), *Academie des Sciences, Comptes Rendues Série D* 267:2306–8.

CARBONNEL J.-P. and G. DELIBRIAS 1968 Premières datations absolues de trois gisements néolithiques cambodgiens, *Academie des Sciences, Comptes Rendues Série D* 267: 1432–4.

CARBONNELL V.M. 1963 Variations in the frequency of shovel-shaped incisors in different populations, *in* Brothwell D. (ed.), *Dental Anthropology*, p. 211–34. Pergamon Press.

CARTAILHAC É 1890 Les bronzes préhistoriques et les recherches de M. Ludovic Jammes, *L'Anthropologie*, part 1 6:41–50.

CARTER G.F. 1950 Plant evidence for early contacts with America, *SWJA* 6:161–82.

CASEY D.A. 1936 Ethnological Notes, *National Museum Melbourne, Memoir* 9:90–7.

CASEY D.A. 1939 Some prehistoric artefacts from the Territory of New Guinea, *National Museum Melbourne, Memoir* 11:143–50.

CASSELS R. 1972 Human ecology in the prehistoric Waikato, *JPS* 81:196–247.

CAVALLI-SFORZA L.L. 1974 The genetics of human populations, *Scientific American* 231:80–9.

CAVALLI-SFORZA L.L., I. BARRAI and A.W.F. EDWARDS 1964 Analysis of human evolution under random genetic drift, *Cold Spring Harbour Symposium on Quantitative Biology* 29:9–20.

CHAGNON N.A., J.V. NEEL *et al.* 1970 The influence of cultural factors on the demography and pattern of gene flow from the Makiritare to the Yanomama Indians, *AJPA* 32:339–50.

CHAMPNESS L.T. *et al.* 1960 A study of the population near Aiome, New Guinea, *Oceania* 30:294–304.

CHANG K.C. 1962a New evidence on fossil man in China, *Science* 136:749–60.

—— 1962b Major problems in the culture history of South-east Asia, *BIEAS* 13:1–26.

—— 1964 Prehistoric and early historic culture horizons and traditions in South China, *CA* 5:359, 368–75, 399–400.

—— 1965 Relative chronologies of China to the end of Chou, *in* Ehrich R. (ed.), *Chronologies in Old World Archaeology*, p. 503–26. University of Chicago Press.

—— 1966 Preliminary notes on excavations in Formosa 1964–5, *AP* 9:140–9.

—— 1967 The Yale expedition to Taiwan, *Discovery* 2, part ii:3–10.

—— 1968 *The archaeology of ancient China.* Revised edition. Yale University Press.

—— 1969a *Fengpitou, Tapenkeng, and the prehistory of Taiwan.* Yale University Publications in Anthropology 73.

—— 1969b Review article, on *Changpinian: a newly discovered preceramic culture from the agglomerate caves on the east coast of Taiwan,* by Wen-hsun Sung. *AP* 12:133–6.

—— 1970 The beginnings of agriculture in the Far East, *Antiquity* 44:175–85.

—— 1972a Neolithic cultures in the coastal areas of Southeast China, *in* Barnard N. (ed.) 1972, vol. 2:431–458.

—— 1972b Major aspects of Ch'u archaeology, *in* Barnard N. (ed.) 1972, vol. 1:5–52.

—— 1973 Radiocarbon dates from China: some initial interpretations, *CA* 14:525–8.

CHANG K.C. and collaborators 1974 Man in the Choshui and Tatu river valleys in central Taiwan, *AP* 17:36–55.

CHANG K.C. and M. STUIVER 1966 Recent advances in the prehistoric archaeology of Formosa, *Proceedings of the National Academy of Science* 55:539–43.

CHAPMAN D.R. 1964 On the unity and origin of the Australasian tektites, *Geochimica et Cosmochimica Acta* 28:841–80.

CHAPMAN P. 1968 Japanese contributions to Micronesian archaeology and material culture, *in* Yawata I. and Y.H. Sinoto (eds.) 1968:67–82.

CHAPPELL J. 1966 Stone axe factories in the New Guinea Highlands, *PPS* 32:96–121.

—— 1968 Changing duration of glacial cycles from lower to upper Pleistocene, *Nature* 219:36–40.

—— 1974 *Aspects of late Quaternary paleogeography of Australian-East Indonesian region.* Paper given at Australian Institute of Aboriginal Studies Conference, Canberra, May 1974.

CHARD C. 1963 Check-stamped pottery in northern and eastern Asia, *Proceedings 9th Pacific Science Congress*, vol. 3:3–7.

CHASEN F.N. and M.W.F. TWEEDIE (eds.) 1940 *Proceedings of the Third Congress of Prehistorians of the Far East.* Singapore: Government Printer.

CHAUVET S. 1935 *L'île de Pâques et ses mystères.* Paris: Éditions 'Tel'.

CH'EN Ch'i-lu 1972 The aboriginal art of Taiwan and its implication for the cultural history of the Pacific, *in* Barnard N. (ed.) 1972, vol. 2:395–430.

CHÊNG Tê K'un 1957 *Archaeological studies in Szechwan.* Cambridge University Press.

—— 1959 *Archaeology in China: Prehistoric China.* Cambridge: Heffer.

—— 1966 *New light on prehistoric China.* Cambridge: Heffer.

CHEVALIER L. 1958–9 Nouveaux pétroglyphes du Nord Calédonien, *EM* 12–13: 82–99.

—— 1963–5 Nouveaux pétroglyphes du Sud Calédonien, *EM* 18–20:22–33.

—— 1966–70 Les élements de prehension de la poterie calédonienne, *EM* 21–5:45–54.

CHILD R. 1964 *Coconuts.* London: Longmans.

CHILDE V.G. 1957 *The dawn of European civilisation.* 6th edition. London: Routledge and Kegan Paul.

CHOWNING A. 1963 Proto-Melanesian plant names, *in* Barrau J. (ed.) 1963: 39–44.

—— 1968 The real Melanesia: an appraisal of Parsonson's theories, *Mankind* 6, 12:641–52.

—— 1973 *An introduction to the peoples and cultures of Melanesia.* Addison-Wesley Module in Anthropology 38.

CHOWNING A. and J.C. GOODALE 1966 A flint industry from southwest New Britain, Territory of New Guinea, *AP* 9:150–3.

CHRETIEN C.D. 1956 Word distribution in southeastern Papua, *Language* 32:88–108.

CHRISTENSEN O.A. 1975a Hunters and horticulturalists: a preliminary report of the 1972–4 excavations in the Manim Valley, Papua New Guinea, *Mankind* 10(1): 24–36.

—— 1975b A tanged blade from the New Guinea Highlands, *Mankind* 10(1):37–8.

CHRISTIAN F.W. 1897 On the outlying islands, *TNZI* 30:93–109.

—— 1899 *The Caroline Islands.* London: Methuen.

CHURCHILL W. 1911 *The Polynesian wanderings.* Carnegie Institution of Washington.

—— 1912 *Easter Island: the Rapanui speech and the peopling of southeast Polynesia.* Carnegie Institution of Washington.

CLAESSEN H. 1968 A survey of the history of Tonga: some new views, *Bijdragen tot de Taal- Land- en Volkenkunde* 124:505–20.

CLARKE D.L. 1968 *Analytical archaeology*. London: Methuen.

CLARKE W.C. 1966 Extensive to intensive shifting cultivation: a succession from New Guinea, *Ethnology* 5:347–59.

—— 1971 *Place and people*. Canberra: Australian National University Press.

CLUTTON BROCK J. 1959 Niah's Neolithic dog, *SMJ* 9:143–5.

CODRINGTON R.H. 1891 *The Melanesians*. Oxford.

COEDES G. 1967 *The making of South East Asia*. London: Routledge and Kegan Paul.

—— 1968 *The Indianised states of Southeast Asia*. Canberra: Australian National University Press.

COLANI M. 1927 *L'âge de la pierre dans la province de Hoa-Binh (Tonkin)*. MSGI 14, fascicle 1.

—— 1928 *Notice sur le préhistoire du Tonkin: station de Cho-Ganh, atelier*. BSGI 17, fascicle 23–37.

—— 1929 Quelques stations hoabinhiennes: note préliminaire. *BEFEO* 29:261–72.

—— 1930 Recherches sur le préhistorique indochinoises. *BEFEO* 30:299–422.

—— 1935 *Mégalithes du Haut-Laos*. 2 volumes. Publications de l'école française d'Extrême-Orient nos. 25, 26.

—— 1940 *Emploi de la pierre en des temps reculés: Annam-Indonesie-Assam*. Publication des Amis du Vieux Hué, Hanoi: Imprimerie d'Extrême-Orient.

COLE F.C. 1945 *The peoples of Malaysia*. New York: Van Nostrand.

COLENSO W. 1846 An account of some enormous fossil bones, of an unknown species of the class Aves, lately discovered in New Zealand, *Tasmanian Journal of Natural Science, Agriculture, Statistics* 2:81–107.

—— 1868 On the Maori races of New Zealand, *TNZI* 1:339–424.

—— 1880 On the vegetable foods of the ancient New Zealanders before Cook's visit, *TNZI* 13:3–19.

COLLINGS H.D. 1940 Neolithic pottery from Sungai Siput, Perak, *in* Chasen F.N. and M.W.F. Tweedie (eds.) 1940:126–30.

CONDOMINAS G. 1952 Le lithophone préhistorique de Ndut Lieng Krak, *BEFEO* 45:359–92.

CONKLIN H.C. 1954 An ethnoecological approach to shifting cultivation, *Transactions of the New York Academy of Sciences*, 2nd Series, vol. 17:133–42.

—— 1961 The study of shifting cultivation, *CA* 1:27–61.

COON C.S. 1962 *The origin of races*. London: Jonathan Cape.

—— 1966 *The living races of man*. London: Jonathan Cape.

COON C.S. and J.M. ANDREWS 1943 *Studies in the anthropology of Oceania and Asia*. Papers of the Peabody Museum of American Archaeology and Ethnology, vol. 20.

CORDY R.H. 1974a The Tahitian migration to Hawaii *ca.* 1100–1300 A.D. – an argument against its occurrence, *NZAAN* 17:65–76.

—— 1974b Cultural adaptation and evolution in Hawaii: a suggested new sequence, *JPS* 83:180–91.

—— 1974c Complex rank cultural systems in the Hawaiian Islands: suggested explanations for their origin, *APAO* 9:90–109.

CORNEY B.G. 1908 *The voyage of Captain Don Felipe Gonzalez to Easter Island 1770–1*. Hakluyt Society Series 2, vol. 13.

—— (ed).) 1913–19 *The quest and occupation of Tahiti by emissaries of Spain during the years 1772–6*. 3 volumes. Hakluyt Society.

COURSEY D.G. 1972 The civilisations of the yam, *APAO* 7:215–33.

COUTTS P.J.F. 1969 The Maori of Dusky Sound: a review of the historical sources, *JPS* 78:178–211.

—— 1971 Greenstone: the prehistoric exploitation of bowenite from Anita Bay, Milford Sound, *JPS* 80:42–73.

—— 1974 Growth characteristics of the bivalve *Chione stutchburyi*, *New Zealand Journal of Marine and Freshwater Research* 8:333–9.

COUTTS P.J.F. and C.F.W. HIGHAM 1971 The seasonal factor in prehistoric New Zealand, *WA* 2:266–77.

COUTTS P.J.F. and M. JURISICH 1972 *An archaeological survey of Ruapuke Island*. OUMPA 5.

COWAN H.K.J. 1965 On Melanesian and the origin of Austronesian, *CA* 6:217.

COWGILL G.L. 1975 On causes and consequences of ancient and modern population changes, *AA* 77:505–25.

COX J.H. 1967 The lei niho palaoa, *in* Highland G. *et al.* (eds.) 1967:411–24.

—— 1970 *Hawaiian petroglyphs*. BPBMSP 60.

COX J.H. and W. DAVENPORT 1974 *Hawaiian sculpture*. Honolulu: University of Hawaii Press.

CRAM L. 1975 Prehistoric fauna and economy in the Solomon Islands, *in* Castell R.W. and G.I. Quimby (eds.), *Maritime adaptations of the Pacific*, p. 247–54. The Hague: Mouton.

CRANSTONE B.A.L. 1961 *Melanesia: a short ethnography*. London: British Museum.

CROCOMBE R.G. and M. (eds.) 1968 *The works of Ta'unga*. Canberra: Australian National University Press.

CUMBERLAND K.B. 1949 Aotearoa Maori: New Zealand about 1780, *Geographical Review* 39:401–24.

—— 1961 Man *in* nature in New Zealand, *New Zealand Geographer* 17:137–54.

—— 1962a 'Climatic change' or cultural interference? *in* McCaskill M. (ed.), *Land and Livelihood*, p. 88–142. Christchurch: New Zealand Geographical Society.

—— 1962b Moas and men: New Zealand about A.D. 1250, *Geographical Review* 52:151–73.

CURTAIN C.C. 1976 On genetic markers in Oceania, *CA* 17:530–1.

CURTAIN C.C. *et al.* 1962 Thalassemia and abnormal hemoglobins in Melanesia, *AJPA* 20:475–83.

CURTAIN C.C. *et al.* 1971 The ethnological significance of the gammaglobulin (Gm) factors in Melanesia, *AJPA* 34:257–71.

DAHL O.C. 1951 *Malagache et Maanyan*. Oslo.

—— 1973 *Proto-Austronesian*. Scandinavian Institute of Asian Studies Monograph 15.

DAHLGREN E.W. 1916 *Were the Hawaiian Islands visited by the Spaniards before . . . . . 1778?* Stockholm: Almquist and Wiksells.

DAMM H. 1951 Methoden der Feldbewässerung in Ozeanien, *Südseestudien*: 204–34. Basel: Museum für Volkerkunde.

DANI A.H. 1960 *Prehistory and protohistory of eastern India*. Calcutta: Mukhopadhyay.

DARLINGTON P.J. 1957 *Zoogeography: the geographical distribution of animals*. New York: Wiley.

DAVENPORT W. 1962 Red feather money, *Scientific American* 206:94–103.

—— 1964 Social structure of Santa Cruz Island, *in* Goodenough W.H. (ed.) *Explorations in cultural anthropology*, p. 57–94. McGraw-Hill.

—— 1972 Preliminary excavations on Santa Ana Island, eastern Solomon Islands, *APAO* 7:165–83.

DAVIDSON J.M. 1967a Preliminary archaeological investigations on Ponape and other eastern Caroline islands, *Micronesica* 3:81–95.

—— 1967b An archaeological assemblage of simple fishhooks from Nukuoro Atoll, *JPS* 76:177–96.

—— 1967c Midden analysis and the economic approach in New Zealand archaeology, *RAIM* 6:203–28.

—— 1968 Nukuoro: archaeology on a Polynesian Outlier in Micronesia, *in* Yawata I. and Y.H. Sinoto (eds.) 1968: 51–66.

—— 1969a Settlement patterns in Samoa before 1840, *JPS* 78:44–82.

—— 1969b Archaeological excavations in two burial mounds at 'Atele, Tongatapu, *RAIM* 6:251–86.

—— 1970a Salvage excavations at Hamlin's Hill, N42/137, Auckland, New Zealand, *RAIM* 7:105–22.

—— 1970b Excavation of an 'undefended site', N38/37, on Motutapu Island, New Zealand, *RAIM* 7:31–60.

—— 1970c Polynesian Outliers and the problem of culture replacement in small populations, *in* Green R.C. and M. Kelly (eds.) 1970:61–72.

—— 1971a Preliminary report on an archaeological survey of the Vava'u Group, Tonga, *in Cook Bicentenary Expedition in the South-west Pacific*, p. 29–40. Royal Society of New Zealand Bulletin 8.

—— 1971b *Archaeology on Nukuoro Atoll*. BAIM 9.

—— 1972 Archaeological investigations on Motutapu Island, New Zealand, *RAIM* 9:1–14.

—— 1974a A radiocarbon date from Skipper's Ridge (N40/7), *NZAAN* 17:50–2.

—— 1974b Radiocarbon date for Rahopara pa (N38/20) at Castor Bay, Auckland, *NZAAN* 17:144–5.

—— 1974c Cultural replacements on small islands: new evidence from Polynesian Outliers, *Mankind* 9:273–7.

—— 1975 The excavation of Skipper's Ridge (N40/7), Opito, Coromandel Peninsula, in 1959 and 1960, *RAIM* 12:1–42.

DAVIS S.G. and M. TREGEAR 1960 Man Kok Tsui, archaeological site 30, Lantau Island, Hong Kong, *AP* 4:183–212.

DAY M.H. 1965 *Guide to fossil man*. London: Cassell.

DAY M.H. and T.I. MOLLESON 1973 The Trinil femora, *in* Day M.H. (ed.), *Human evolution*, p. 127–54. London: Taylor and Francis.

DEACON A.B. 1934 *Malekula*. London: Routledge.

DE BRUYN J.V. 1959 New archaeological finds at Lake Sentani, *Nieuw Guinea Studien* 3:1–8.

—— 1962 New bronze finds at Kwadaware, Lake Sentani, *Nieuw Guinea Studien* 6:61–2.

DENING G.M. 1960 *East Polynesian prehistory*. Unpublished M.A. thesis, Melbourne University.

—— 1963 The geographical knowledge of the Polynesians and the nature of inter-island contact, *in* Golson J. (ed.) 1963: 102–131.

—— 1974 *The Marquesan journal of Edward Robarts, 1797–1824*. Canberra: Australian National University Press.

DENTAN R.K. 1968 *The Semai*. New York: Holt, Rinehart and Winston.

DEWALL M. von 1967 The bronze culture of Tien in southwest China, *Antiquity* 41:8–21.

—— 1972 Decorative concepts and stylistic principles in the bronze art of Tien, *in* Barnard N. (ed.) 1972, vol. 2:329–72.

DICKINSON W.R. 1971 Temper sands in Lapita style potsherds in Malo, *JPS* 80:244–6.

DICKINSON W.R. and R. SHUTLER 1971 Temper sands in prehistoric pottery of the Pacific Islands, *APAO* 6:191–203.

—— 1974 Probable Fijian origin of quartzose temper sands in prehistoric pottery from Tonga and the Marquesas Islands, *Science* 185:454–7.

DIFFLOTH G. 1974 Austro-Asiatic languages, *Encyclopaedia Britannica, 15th edition, Macropaedia* 2:480–4.

DIKSHIT M.G. 1949 *Etched beads in India*. University of Poona Press.

—— 1952 The beads from Ahichchhatrā, U.P., *Ancient India* 8:33–63.

DIXON R.B. 1920 A new theory of Polynesian Origins, *Proceedings of the American Philosophical Society* 59:261–7.

—— 1932 The problem of the sweet potato in Polynesia, *AA* 34:40–66.

—— 1933 Contacts with South America across the southern Pacific, *in* Jenness D. (ed.) 1933. 313–54.

—— 1934 The long voyages of the Polynesians, *Proceedings of the American Philosophical Society* 74:167–75.

DOBBY E.H.G. 1961 *Southeast Asia*. University of London Press.

DOBZHANSKY T. 1963 Biological evolution in island populations, *in* Fosberg F.R. (ed.) 1963:65–74.

DODD E. 1972 *Polynesian seafaring*. Lymington: Nautical Publishing Co. Ltd.

DORAN E. 1974 Outrigger ages, *JPS* 83:130–40.

DOUGLAS G. 1969 Check list of Pacific Oceanic islands, *Micronesica* 5:327–464.

DOWELL M.F., P.B. BOOTH and R.J. WALSH 1967 Blood groups and hemoglobin values amongst the Ewa Ge and Orokaiva peoples of the Northern District of Papua, *APAO* 2:47–56.

DOWNES T.W. 1915 New light on the period of the extinction of the moa (according to Maori record), *TNZI* 48:426–34.

—— 1933 Maruiwi, Maori and Moriori, *JPS* 42:156–66.

DUFF R. 1947 The evolution of native New Zealand culture: moa-hunters, Moriories and Maoris, *Mankind* 3:281–91, 313–22.

—— 1956 *The moa-hunter period of Maori culture*. 2nd edition. Wellington: Government Printer.

—— 1959 Neolithic adzes of eastern Polynesia, *in* Freeman J.D. and W.R. Geddes (eds.) 1959: 121–48.

—— 1961a Excavations of house pits at Pari-Whakatau pa, Claverly, *RCM* 7:269–302.

—— 1961b The Waitara swamp search, *RCM* 7:303–26.

—— 1963 Aspects of the cultural succession in Canterbury-Marlborough, with wider reference to the New Zealand area. *TRSNZ* (general) 1:27–37.

—— 1968a Archaeology of the Cook Islands, *in* Yawata I. and Y.H. Sinoto (eds.) 1968:119–32.

—— 1968b Stone adzes from Raoul, Kermadec Islands, *JPS* 77:386–401.

—— 1968c A historical survey of archaeology in New Zealand, *APAS* 2:167–90.

—— 1970 *Stone adzes of Southeast Asia*. CMB 3.

DUNN F.C. 1964 Excavations at Gua Kechil, Pahang, *JMBRAS* 37:87–124.

—— 1966 Radiocarbon dating of the Malayan Neolithic, *PPS* 32:352–3.

—— 1970 Cultural evolution in the late Pleistocene and Holocene of Southeast Asia, *AA* 72:1041–54.

DUTTA P.C. 1966 The kitchen middens of the Andaman archipelago, *in* Sen D. and A.K. Ghosh (eds.), *Studies in Prehistory*, p. 179–94. Calcutta: Mukhopadhyay.

DUTTON T.E. 1969 *The peopling of central Papua*. Pacific Linguistics, Series B, Monograph 9.

DUY N. and N.Q. QUYEN 1966 Early Neolithic skulls in Quynh-Van, Nghe-An, North Vietnam, *Vertebrata Palasiatica* 10:49–57.

DYEN I. 1953 Review of Dahl 1951, *Language* 29:577–90.

—— 1956 Language distribution and migration theory, *Language* 32:611–27.

—— 1962 The lexicostatistical classification of the Malayopolynesian languages, *Language* 38: 38–46.

—— 1965a *A lexicostatistical classification of the Austronesian languages*. International Journal of American Linguistics, Memoir 19.

—— 1965b Formosan evidence for some new Proto-Austronesian phonemes, *Lingua* 14:285–305.

—— 1971a The Austronesian languages and Proto-Austronesian, *in* Seboek T. (ed.) 1971:5–54.

—— 1971b The Austronesian languages of Formosa, *in* Seboek T. (ed.) 1971:168–99.

EBERHARD W. 1968 *The local cultures of south and east China*. Leiden: E.J. Brill.

EGGAN F. 1967 Some aspects of bilateral social systems in the northern Philippines, *in* Zamora M.D. (ed.) 1967: 186–201.

EGLOFF B. 1970 The rock carvings and stone groups of Goodenough Bay, Papua, *APAO* 5:147–56.

—— 1971a *Collingwood Bay and the Trobriand Islands in recent prehistory*. Unpublished Ph.D. thesis, Australian National University.

—— 1971b Archaeological research in the Collingwood Bay area of Papua, *AP* 14:60–64.

—— 1972 The sepulchral pottery of Nuamata Island, Papua, *APAO* 7:145–63.

—— 1975 Archaeological investigations in the coastal Madang area and on Eloaue Island of the St. Matthias Group. *RPNGM* 5.

EINZIG P. 1966 *Primitive money*. 2nd edition. Oxford.

ELBERT S.H. 1953 Internal relationships of Polynesian languages and dialects. *SWJA* 9:147–73.

—— 1967 A linguistic assessment of the historical validity of some of the Rennellese oral traditions, *in* Highland G. et al. (eds.) 1967:257–88.

ELLEN R.F. and I.C. GLOVER 1974 Pottery manufacture and trade in the central Moluccas, Indonesia, *Man* (new series) 9:353–79.

ELLIS W. 1969a *Polynesian researches: Polynesia*. 1831 edition reissued by Charles E. Tuttle.

—— 1969b *Polynesian researches: Hawaii*. 1842 edition reissued by Charles E. Tuttle.

ELMBERG J.E. 1959 Further notes on the northern Mejbrats (Vogelkop, western New Guinea), *Ethnos* 24:70–80.

EMBER M. 1959 The non-unilineal descent groups of Samoa, *AA* 61:573–7.

—— 1962 Political authority and the structure of kinship in aboriginal Samoa, *AA* 64:964–71.

—— 1966 Samoan kinship and political structure: an archaeological test, *AA* 68:163–8.

EMERY K.O., H. NIINO and B. SULLIVAN 1971 Post-Pleistocene levels of the East China Sea, *in* Turekian K.T. (ed.) 1971:381–90.

EMORY K.P. 1924 *The island of Lanai*. BPBMB 12.

—— 1928a *Archaeology of Nihoa and Necker Islands*. BPBMB 53.

—— 1928b Stone implements of Pitcairn Island, *JPS* 37:125–35.

—— 1933 *Stone remains in the Society Islands*. BPBMB 116.

—— 1934a *Tuamotuan stone structures*. BPBMB 118.

—— 1934b *Archaeology of the Pacific Equatorial Islands*. BPBMB 123.

—— 1939a *Archaeology of Mangareva and neighbouring atolls*. BPBMB 163.

—— 1939b *Additional notes on the archaeology of Fanning Island*. BPBMOP 15, no. 17.

—— 1942 Oceanian influence on American Indian culture: Nordenskiold's view, *JPS* 51:126–35.

—— 1943 Polynesian stone remains, *in* Coon C. and J. Andrews (eds.) 1943:9–21.

—— 1947 *Tuamotuan religious structures and ceremonies*. BPBMB 191.

—— 1959 Origin of the Hawaiians, *JPS* 68:29–35.

—— 1963a East Polynesian relationships, *JPS* 72:78–100.

—— 1963b Review of Heyerdahl T. and E.N. Ferdon (eds.) 1961, *AA* 28:565–7.

—— 1968 East Polynesian relationships as revealed through adzes, *in* Yawata I, and Y.H. Sinoto (eds.) 1969:151–70.

—— 1970 A re-examination of East-Polynesian marae: many marae later, *in* Green R.C. and M. Kelly (eds.) 1970:73–92.

—— 1972 Easter Island's position in the prehistory of Polynesia, *JPS* 81:57–69.

EMORY K.P., W.J. BONK and Y.H. SINOTO 1968 *Hawaiian archaeology: fishhooks*. BPBMSP 47.

EMORY K.P. and Y.H. SINOTO 1959 Radiocarbon dates significant for Pacific archaeology, *Pacific Science Association Information Bulletin* 11, no. 3, supplement 1959, p. 13.

EMORY K.P. and Y.H. SINOTO 1964 Early eastern Polynesian burials at Maupiti, *JPS* 73: 143–60.

EMORY K.P. and Y.H. SINOTO 1969 *Age of the sites in the South Point area, Ka'u, Hawaii*. PAR 8.

ENGLERT S. 1970 *Island at the centre of the world*. London: Hale.

EPSTEIN T.S. 1968 *Capitalism, primitive and modern: some aspects of Tolai economic growth*. Manchester University Press.

ERDBRINK D.P. 1954 Mesolithic remains of the Sampung stage in Java: some remarks and additions, *SWJA* 10: 294–303.

ESTERIK P. van 1973 A preliminary analysis of Ban Chiang painted pottery, northeast Thailand, *AP* 16:174–94.

ETHERIDGE R. 1916–7 Additions to the ethnological collections, chiefly from the New Hebrides, *RAM* 11:189–203.

EVANGELISTA F. 1967 H.O. Beyer's Philippine Neolithic in the context of postwar studies in local archaeology, *in* Zamora M.D. (ed.) 1967: 63–87.

—— 1971 Type-sites from the Philippine Islands and their significance, *in* Green R.C. and M. Kelly (eds.) 1971: 28–35.

EVANS C. 1965 The dating of Easter Island archaeological obsidians, *in* Heyerdahl T. and E.N. Ferdon (eds.) 1965:469–95.

EVANS I.H.N. 1928 On slab built graves in Perak, *JFMSM* 12:111–20.

EVANS P. 1971 *Towards a Pleistocene time scale*. Geological Society of London Special Publication 5, supplement part 2, p. 121–356.

FAIRSERVIS W.A. 1971 *The roots of ancient India*. New York: Macmillan.

FALLA R.A. 1974 The moa, *New Zealand's Nature Heritage* 1, part 3: 69–74.

FERDON E.N. 1961 The ceremonial site of Orongo, *in* Heyerdahl T. and E.N. Ferdon (eds.) 1961:221–56.

—— 1963 Polynesian origins, *Science* 141:499–505.
—— 1965 Surface architecture of the site of Paeke, Nukuhiva, *in* Heyerdahl T. and E.N. Ferdon (eds.) 1965:117–22.
FERRELL R. 1969 *Taiwan aboriginal groups: problems in cultural and linguistic classification*. Monograph 17 of the Institute of Ethnology, Academia Sinica. Taipei.
FIGUEROA G. and E. SANCHEZ 1965 Adzes from certain islands of eastern Polynesia, *in* Heyerdahl T. and E.N. Ferdon (eds.) 1965:169–254.
FINN D.J. 1958 *Archaeological finds on Lamma Island*. Ricci Publications, University of Hong Kong.
FINNEY B. 1958 Recent finds from Washington and Fanning Islands, *JPS* 67:70–2.
—— 1967 New perspectives on Polynesian voyaging, *in* Highland G. *et al.* (eds.) 1967:141–66.
FINOT L. 1928 Ludovic Jammes, préhistorien, *BEFEO* 28:473–9.
FIRTH R. 1926 Wharepuni: a few remaining Maori dwellings of the old style, *Man* 26:54–9.
—— 1957 A note on descent groups in Polynesia, *Man* 57:4–8.
—— 1959 *Economics of the New Zealand Maori*. Wellington: Government Printer.
—— 1960 Succession to chieftainship in Tikopia, *Oceania* 30:161–80.
—— 1963 Bilateral descent groups: an operational viewpoint, *in* Schapera I. (ed.) *Studies in kinship and marriage*, p. 22–37. Royal Anthropological Institute Occasional Paper 16.
FISCHER J.L. 1964 Abandonment of Nan Matol (Ponape), *Micronesica* 1:49–54.
FISON L. 1885 The nanga, or secret stone enclosure of Wainimala, Fiji, *JAI* 14:14–30.
FITZGERALD C.P. 1972 *The southern expansion of the Chinese people*. Canberra: Australian National University Press.
FLATZ G. 1965 Hemoglobin E in south-east Asia, *in Felicitation volumes of Southeast Asian Studies*, p. 91–106. Bangkok: Siam Society.
FLEISCHER R.L. and P.B. PRICE 1964 Fission track evidence for the simultaneous origin of tektites and other natural glasses, *Geochimica et Cosmochimica Acta* 28:755–60.
FLEMING M. 1963 Observations on the megalithic problem in eastern Asia, *BIEAS* 15:153–62.
FLINT R.F. 1971 *Glacial and Quaternary geology*. New York: Wiley.
FONTAINE H. 1971a Renseignements nouveaux sur la céramique du champ de jarres funeraires de Dau-Giay, *BSEI* 46:3–6.
—— 1971b Enquête sur le néolithique du bassin inferieur du Dong-Nai, *Archives géologiques du Viêt-Nam* 14:47–116.
—— 1972a Nouveau champ de jarres dans le province de Long-Khanh, *BSEI* 47:397–486.
—— 1972b Deuxième note sur le 'néolithique' du bassin inférieur du Dong-Nai, *Archives géologiques du Viêt-Nam* 15:123–9.
FONTAINE H. and G. DELIBRIAS 1973 Ancient marine levels of the Quaternary in Vietnam, *JHKAS* 4:29–33.
FORCE R.W. 1959 Palauan money, *JPS* 68:40–4.
FORGE A. 1972 Normative factors in the settlement size of Neolithic cultivators (New Guinea), *in* Ucko P.J., R. Tringham and G.W. Dimbleby (eds.), *Man, settlement and urbanism*, p. 363–76. London; Duckworth.
—— 1973 Style and meaning in Sepik art, *in* Forge A. (ed.) *Primitive art and society*, p. 169–92. Oxford University Press.

FORNANDER A. 1878–80 *An account of the Polynesian race*. 2 volumes. London: Trubner.
FORSTER G. 1777 *A voyage round the world. . . . during the years 1772, 3, 4, and 5*. 2 volumes. London.
FOSBERG F.R. (ed.) 1963 *Man's place in the island ecosystem*. Honolulu: Bishop Museum Press.
FOX A. 1974 Prehistoric Maori storage pits: problems in interpretation, *JPS* 83:141–54.
—— 1975 Tirimoana pa, Te Awanga, Hawkes Bay: interim report, *NZAAN* 17:163–70.
—— 1976 *Prehistoric Maori fortifications*. Auckland: Longman Paul.
FOX C.E. 1919 Further notes on the *heo* of the Solomon Islands, *JPS* 28:103–5.
—— 1924 *The threshold of the Pacific*, London: Kegan Paul.
FOX R. 1967 Excavations in the Tabon Caves and some problems in Philippine chronology, *in* Zamora M.D. (ed.) 1967:88–116.
—— 1970 *The Tabon Caves*. Manila: National Museum Monograph 1.
FOX R. and A. EVANGELISTA 1957a The Bato Caves, Sorgoson Province, Philippines, *JEAS* 6:49–55.
—— 1957b The cave archaeology of Cagraray Island, Albay Province, Philippines, *JEAS* 6:57–68.
FOX R. and E.H. FLORY 1974 *The Filipino people* (map). Manila: National Museum of the Philippines.
FRAKE C.O. 1956 Malayo-Polynesian land tenure, *AA* 58:170–3.
FRASER D. 1962 *Primitive art*. New York.
—— 1972 Early Chinese artistic influence in Melanesia? *in* Barnard N. (ed.) 1972, vol. 3:631–54.
—— (ed.) 1967 *Early Chinese art and the Pacific Basin*. New York: Columbia University.
FRASER J. 1895 The Malayo-Polynesian theory, *JPS* 4:241–55.
FREEMAN J.D. 1955 *Iban agriculture*. London: Her Majesty's Stationery Office, Colonial Research Studies 18.
—— 1961 Review of Sahlins 1958, *Man* 61:146–8.
—— 1964 Some observations on kinship and political authority in Samoa, *AA* 66:553–68.
FREEMAN J.D. and W.R. GEDDES (eds.) 1959 *Anthropology in the South Seas*. New Plymouth: Avery.
FRIEDLAENDER J.L. 1970 Anthropological significance of gamma globulin (Gm and Inv) antigens in Bougainville Island, Melanesia, *Nature* 228:59–61.
—— 1971a Isolation by distance in Bougainville, *Proceedings of the National Academy of Science* 68:704–7.
—— 1971b The population structure of south-central Bougainville, *AJPA* 35:13–25.
FRIEDLAENDER J.S. *et al.* 1971 Biological divergences in south-central Bougainville, *American Journal of Human Genetics* 23:253–70.
FRIMIGACCI D. 1966–70 Fouilles archaéologiques à Vatcha (près de Vao), Île des Pins, *EM* 21–25:23–44.
—— 1976 *La Poterie imprimée au battoir en Nouvelle-Calédonie: ses rapports avec le Lapita*. Paper presented at IXe Congrès U.I.S.P.P., Nice, September 1976.
FROMAGET J. 1940a Les récentes découvertes anthropologique dans les formations préhistoriques de la Chaine Annamitique, *in* Chasen F.N. and M.W.F. Tweedie (eds.) 1940:51–9.
—— 1940b La stratigraphie des dépôts préhistoriques de Tam Hang, *in* Chasen F.N. and M.W.F. Tweedie (eds.) 1940:60–71.
FROST E.L. 1974 *Archaeological excavations of fortified sites on Taveuni, Fiji*. APAS 6.

GABEL N. 1955 *A racial study of the Fijians*. University of California: Anthropological Records 20.

GAJDUSEK D.C. 1964 Factors governing the genetics of primitive human populations, *Cold Spring Harbour Symposium on Quantitative Biology* 29:21–35.

—— 1970 Psychological characteristics of stone age man, *Engineering and Science* 33:26–33, 56–62.

GALLUS A. 1970 Expanding horizons in Australian prehistory, *Twentieth Century* 24:1–8. Melbourne.

GARANGER J. 1964 Recherches archéologiques dans le district de Tautira, *JSO* 20:5–21.

—— 1967 Archaeology and the Society Islands, *in* Highland G. *et al.* (eds.) 1967:377–96.

—— 1971 Incised and applied-relief pottery, its chronology and development in southeastern Melanesia, and extra areal comparisons, *in* Green R.C. and M. Kelly (eds.) 1971:53–66.

—— 1972 *Archéologie des Nouvelles Hébrides*. Paris: Office de la Recherche Scientifique et Technique Outre-Mer.

GARANGER J. and A. LAVONDES 1966 Recherches archéologiques à Rangiroa, archipel des Tuamotus, *JSO* 22:25–65.

GARN S.M. 1961 *Human races*. Springfield, Illinois: Thomas.

GARVAN J.M. 1963 Negritos of the Philippines. *WBKL* 14.

GATES R.R. 1961 The Melanesian dwarf tribe of Aiome, New Guinea, *Acta Geneticae Medicae Gemellologiae* 10:277–311.

GATHERCOLE P. 1964 *Preliminary report on archaeological fieldwork on Pitcairn Island, January–March 1964*. Unpublished manuscript.

GEERTZ C. 1963 *Agricultural Involution*. Berkeley: University of California Press.

GEERTZ H. 1963 Indonesian cultures and communities, *in* McVey R. (ed.), *Indonesia*, p. 24–96. Yale University Press.

GÉRARD B. 1975 Moorea, Afareaitu site 1, *Bull. de la Société des Etudes Océaniennes* 16(5)525–35.

GERBRANDS A.A. 1967 *Wow-Ipits*. The Hague: Mouton.

GHOSH A.K. 1971 Ordering of lower Palaeolithic traditions in South and South-east Asia, *APAO* 6:87–101.

GIFFORD E.W. 1929 *Tongan society*. BPBMB 61.

—— 1951 *Archaeological excavations in Fiji*. University of California: Anthropological Records 13, part 3 (p. 189–288).

—— 1952 *Tribes of Viti Levu and their origin places*. University of California: Anthropological Records 13, part 5 (p. 337–76).

GIFFORD E.W. and D.S. 1959 *Archaeological excavations in Yap*. University of California: Anthropological Records 18, part 2 (p. 149–224).

GIFFORD E.W. and R. SHUTLER 1956 *Archaeological excavations in New Caledonia*. Univeristy of California; Anthropological Records 18, part 1 (p. 1–148).

GILES E., E. OGAN and A.G. STEINBERG 1965 Gamma-globulin factors (Gm and Inv) in New Guinea; anthropological significance, *Science* 150:1158–60.

GILES E., R.J. WALSH and M. BRADLEY 1966 Microevolution in New Guinea and the role of genetic drift, *Annals of the New York Academy of Science* 134:655–65.

GILES E., S. WYBER and R.J. WALSH 1970 Microevolution in New Guinea – additional evidence for genetic drift, *APAO* 5:60–72.

GILL W.W. 1876 *Life in the southern isles*. London: Religious Tract Society.

GILSON R.P. 1970 *Samoa 1830 to 1900*. Melbourne: Oxford University Press.

GITEAU M. 1958 Aperçu sur le civilisation du Fou-Nan, *France-Asie* 15-356–68.

GLADWIN T. 1970 *East is a big bird: navigation and logic on Puluwat Atoll*. Harvard University Press.

GLOVER I. 1969 Radiocarbon dates from Portuguese Timor, *APAO* 4:107–12.

—— 1971 Prehistoric research in Timor, *in* Mulvaney and J. Golson (eds.) 1971:158–81.

—— 1972a *Excavations in Timor*. 2 volumes. Unpublished Ph.D. thesis, Australian National University.

—— 1972b Alfred Buhler's excavations in Timor – a reevalution, *Art and Archaeology Research Papers* 2:117–42. London: Institute of Archaeology.

—— 1973a Late stone age traditions in South-East Asia, *in* Hammond N.D. (ed.), *South Asian archaeology*, p. 51–66. London: Duckworth.

—— 1973b Island Southeast Asia and the settlement of Australia, in Strong D.E. (ed.), *Archaeological theory and practice*, p. 105–29. London: Academic Press.

—— 1975 Ulu Leang Cave, Maros: a preliminary sequence of post-Pleistocene cultural development in South Sulawesi, *Archipel* 11:113–54.

GLOVER I. and E.A. 1970 Pleistocene flaked stone tools from Timor and Flores, *Mankind* 7:88–90.

GOLDMAN I. 1970 *Ancient Polynesian society*. University of Chicago Press.

GOLOUBEW V. 1929 L'âge du bronze au Tonkin, *BEFEO* 29:1–46.

GOLSON J. 1957a New Zealand archaeology 1957, *JPS* 66:271–90.

—— 1957b Field archaeology in New Zealand, *JPS* 66:64–109.

—— 1959a Culture change in prehistoric New Zealand, *in* Freeman J.D. and W.R. Geddes (eds.) 1959:29–74.

—— 1959b Archéologie du Pacifique Sud, résultats et perspectives, *JSO* 15:5-54.

—— 1959–62 Rapport sur les fouilles effectués a l'île des Pins (Nouvelle Calédonie) de Décembre 1959 à Février 1960, *EM* 14–17:11–23.

—— 1960 Archaeology, tradition and myth in New Zealand prehistory, *JPS* 69:380–402.

—— 1961a Investigations at Kauri Point, Katikati, *NZAAN* 4:13–41.

—— 1961b Report on New Zealand, western Polynesia, New Caledonia and Fiji, *AP* 5:166–80.

—— (ed.) 1963 *Polynesian navigation*. Wellington: Polynesian Society Memoir 34.

—— 1965 Thor Heyerdahl and the prehistory of Easter Island, *Oceania* 36:38–83.

—— 1968 Archaeological prospects for Melanesia, *in* Yawata I. and Y.H. Sinoto (eds.) 1968:3–14.

—— 1969a *Lapita pottery in the south Pacific*. Paper given at Wenner-Gren Symposium on Oceanic Culture History, Sigatoka, Fiji, August 1969.

—— 1969b Archaeology in Western Samoa 1957, *in* Green R.C. and J.M. Davidson (eds.) 1969:14–20.

—— 1971a Both sides of the Wallace Line: Australia, New Guinea. and Asian prehistory, *APAO* 6:124–44.

—— 1971b Australian Aboriginal food plants: some ecological and culture-historical implications, *in* Mulvaney D.J. and J. Golson (eds.) 1971:196–238.

—— 1971c Lapita ware and its transformations, *in* Green R.C. and M. Kelly (eds.) 1971:67–76.

—— 1972a Both sides of the Wallace Line: New Guinea, Australia, Island Melanesia and Asian prehistory, *in* Barnard N. (ed.) 1972, vol. 3:533–96.

—— 1972b The Pacific islands and their prehistoric inhabitants, *in* Ward R.G. (ed.), *Man in the Pacific Islands*, p. 5–33. Oxford University Press.

GOLSON J., R.J. LAMPERT, J.M. WHEELER, and W.R. AMBROSE 1967 A note on carbon dates for horticulture in the New Guinea Highlands, *JPS* 76:369–71.

GOODENOUGH W. 1955 A problem in Malayo-Polynesian social organisation, *AA* 57:71–83.

—— 1961 Migrations implied by relationships of New Britain dialects to central Pacific languages, *JPS* 70:112–36.

GORBEY K. 1967 Climatic change in New Zealand archaeology, *NZAAN* 10:176–82.

—— 1971 Review of Green R.C. and M. Kelly (eds.) 1970, *NZAAN* 14:67–8.

GORMAN C.F. 1970 Excavations at Spirit Cave, north Thailand: some interim interpretations, *AP* 13:79–108.

—— 1971 The Hoabinhian and after: subsistence patterns in Southeast Asia during the late Pleistocene and early Recent periods, *WA* 2:300–20.

—— 1974 Modèles a priori et préhistoire de la Thailande, *Études Rurales* 53–6: 41–71.

GORMAN C. and P. CHAROENWONGSA 1976 Ban Chiang: a mosaic of impressions from the first two years, *Expedition* 18 (4): 14–26.

GOULD R.A. 1971 The archaeologist as ethnographer: a case from the Western Desert of Australia, *WA* 3:143–78.

GRACE G.W. 1955 Subgrouping of Malayo-Polynesian: a report of tentative findings, *AA* 57:337–9.

—— 1959 *The position of the Polynesian languages within the Austronesian (Malayo-Polynesian) language family.* International Journal of American Linguistics Memoir 16.

—— 1964 Movements of the Malayo-Polynesians 1500 B.C. – 500 A.D.: the linguistic evidence, *CA* 5:361–68, 403–4.

—— 1966 Austronesian lexicostatistical classification: a review article, *Oceanic Linguistics* 5:13–31.

—— 1967 Effect of heterogeneity on the lexicostatistical test list: the case of Rotuman, *in* Highland G. *et al.* (eds). 1967:289–302.

—— 1968 Classification of the languages of the Pacific, *in* Vayda A.P. (ed.) 1968:63–79.

—— 1971 Languages of the New Hebrides and Solomon Islands, *in* Seboek T. (ed.) 1971:341–58.

GRAY B. 1949–50. China or Dong-Son, *Oriental Art* 2:99–104.

GRAYDON J.J. *et al.* 1958 Blood groups in Pygmies of the Wissellakes in Netherlands New Guinea, *AJPA* 16:149–59.

GREEN R.C. 1959 Pitcairn Island fishhooks in stone, *JPS* 68:21–2.

—— 1961 Moorean archaeology: a preliminary report, *Man* 61:169–73.

—— 1963a A suggested revision of the Fijian sequence, *JPS* 72:235–53.

—— 1963b An undefended settlement at Kauri Point, Tauranga district, *Historical Review, Whakatane Historical Society* 11:143–56.

—— 1964 Sources, ages and exploration of New Zealand obsidian, *NZAAN* 7:134–43.

—— 1966 Linguistic subgrouping within Polynesia: the implications for prehistoric settlement, *JPS* 75:3–35.

—— 1967a Sources of New Zealand's East Polynesian Culture: the evidence of a pearl-shell lure shank, *APAO* 2:81–90.

—— 1967b The immediate origins of the Polynesians, *in* Highland G. *et al.* (eds.) 1967:215–40.

—— 1968 West Polynesian prehistory, *in* Yawata I. and Y.H. Sinoto (eds.) 1968:99–110.

—— (ed.) 1969 *Makaha Valley Historical project; interim report I.* PAR 4.

—— 1970a *A review of the prehistoric sequence in the Auckland Province.* 2nd edition. Dunedin: University Bookshop.

—— 1970b Settlement pattern archaeology in Polynesia, *in* Green R.C. and M. Kelly (eds.) 1970:13–32.

—— 1970c Investigations at Castor Bay Point Pa, Takapuna, New Zealand, *NZAAN* 13:2–22.

—— (ed.) 1970d *Makaha Valley historical project: interim report 2.* PAR 10.

—— 1971a Evidence for the development of the early Polynesian adze kit, *NZAAN* 14:12–44.

—— 1971b The chronology and age of the sites at South Point, Hawaii, *APAO* 6:170–6.

—— 1971c Anuta's position in the subgrouping of Polynesia's languages, *JPS* 80:355–70.

—— 1972a Revision of the Tongan sequence, *JPS* 81:79–86.

—— 1972b Additional evidence for the age of settlements at Sarah's Gully, Coromandel Peninsula, *NZAAN* 15:89–93.

—— 1973 Lapita pottery and the origins of Polynesian culture. *Australian Natural History*, June: 332–7.

—— 1974a Adaptation and change in Maori culture, *in* Kuschel G. (ed.), *Ecology and biogeography in New Zealand*, p. 1–44. The Hague: Junk.

—— 1974b Sites with Lapita pottery: importing and voyaging, *Mankind* 9:253–9.

—— 1974c Pottery from the lagoon at Mulifanua, Upolu, *in* Green R.C. and J.M. Davidson (eds.) 1974:170–5.

—— 1976 *New sites with Lapita pottery and their implications for an understanding of the settlement of the western Pacific.* Paper presented at the IXᵉ Congrès U.I.S.P.P. Nice, September 1976.

GREEN R.C., R.R. BROOKS and R.D. REEVES 1967 Characterisation of New Zealand obsidians by emission spectroscopy, *NZJS* 10:675–82.

GREEN R.C. and J.M. DAVIDSON (eds.) 1969 *Archaeology in Western Samoa.* Volume 1. BAIM 6.

—— 1974 *Archaeology in Western Samoa.* Volume 2. BAIM 7.

GREEN R.C. and K. 1968 Religious structures (marae) of the Windward Society Islands, *New Zealand Journal of History* 2:66–89.

GREEN R.C., K. GREEN, R.A. RAPPAPORT, A. RAPPAPORT, and J.M. DAVIDSON 1967 *Archaeology on the island of Mo'orea, French Polynesia.* APAMNH 51, part 2.

GREEN R.C. and M. KELLY (eds.) 1970 *Studies in Oceanic culture history.* Volume 1. PAR 11.

—— 1971 *Studies in Oceanic culture history.* Volume 2. PAR 12.

—— 1972 *Studies in Oceanic culture history.* Volume 3. PAR 13.

GREENBERG J.H. 1971 The Indo-Pacific hypothesis, *in* Seboek T. (ed.) 1971: 807–76.

GREGG D.R. 1972 Holocene stratigraphy and moas at Pyramid Valley, North Canterbury, New Zealand, *RCM* 9:151–8.

GRESSITT J.L. (ed.) 1963 *Pacific basin biogeography: a symposium.* Honolulu: Bishop Museum Press.

GREY, Sir George 1965 *Maori mythology.* (First edition 1855). New Zealand: Whitcombe and Tombs.

GRIFFIN P.B., T. RILEY, P. ROSENDAHL and H.D. TUGGLE 1971 Archaeology of Halawa and Lapakahi: windward valley and leeward slope, *NZAAN* 14:101–12.

GRIFFIN R.S. 1973 Thailand's Ban Chiang: the birthplace of civilisation? *Arts of Asia*, Nov.–Dec.:31–4.

GRIGG D.B. 1974 *The agricultural systems of the world.* Cambridge University Press.

GROUBE L.M. 1964a *Settlement patterns in New Zealand prehistory.* Unpublished M.A. thesis, University of Auckland.

—— 1964b *Archaeology in the Bay of Islands 1964–5.* Dunedin: Anthropology Department, University of Otago.

—— 1967a Models in prehistory: a consideration of the New Zealand evidence, *APAO* 2:1–27.

—— 1967b A note on the Hei Tiki, *JPS* 76:453–8.

—— 1968 Research in New Zealand prehistory since 1956, in Yawata I. and Y.H. Sinoto (eds.) 1968:141–9.

—— 1969 From Archaic to Classic Maori, *Auckland Student Geographer* 6:1–11.

—— 1970 The origin and development of earthwork fortification in the Pacific, in Green R.C. and M. Kelly (eds.) 1970: 133–64.

—— 1971 Tonga, Lapita pottery, and Polynesian origins, *JPS* 80:278–316.

—— 1973 Review of King J. and P.J. Epling 1972, *Journal of Pacific History* 8:233–6.

—— 1975 Archaeological research on Aneityum, *South Pacific Bulletin* 25(3):27–30.

GROUBE L.M. and J. CHAPPELL 1973 Measuring the differences between archaeological assemblages, in Renfrew C. (ed.), *The explanation of culture change*, p. 167–84. London: Duckworth.

GROVES C.P. 1976 The origin of the mammalian fauna of Sulawesi (Celebes), *Zeitschrift für Säugertierkunde* 41: 201–16.

GROVES M. 1963 Western Motu descent groups, *Ethnology* 1:15–30.

GROVES M. et al. 1958 Blood groups of the Motu and Koita peoples, *Oceania* 28:222–38.

GUDSCHINSKY S. 1964 The ABC's of lexicostatistics (glottochronology) in Hymes D. (ed.), *Language in culture and society*, p. 612–23. New York: Harper and Row.

GUIART J. 1956 L'organisation sociale et coutoumière de la population autochthone de la Nouvelle-Calédonie, in Barrau J. 1956: 17–44.

—— 1963 *Structure de la chefferie en Mélanésie du sud.* Paris: Institute d'Ethnologie.

HAAST, J. von 1871 Moas and moa hunters, *TNZI* 4:66–107.

—— 1874 Researches and excavations carried on, in, and near the Moa-bone Point Cave, Sumner Road, in the year 1872, *TNZI* 7:54–85.

HADDON A.C. and J. HORNELL 1936–8 *The canoes of Oceania.* 3 volumes. BPBMSP 27, 28 and 29.

HAILE N.S. 1971 Quaternary shorelines in West Malaysia and adjacent parts of the Sunda shelf, *Quaternaria* 15: 333–43.

HALE H. 1846 *United States Exploring Expedition 1838–42: ethnography and philology.* Philadelphia: Lea and Blanchard.

HAMBRUCH P. 1936 Ponape: die Ruinen, in Thilenius G. (ed.), *Ergebnisse der Südsee-Expedition 1908–1910.* Volume II, B7–3, Ponape: 3–113.

HAMEL J. 1974 The Maoris and plants, *New Zealand's Nature Heritage* 1, part 7:182–7.

HAMILTON A. 1896–1901 *The art workmanship of the Maori race in New Zealand*, Wellington: New Zealand Institute.

HAMLIN J. 1842 On the mythology of the New Zealanders, *Tasmanian Journal of Natural Science, Agriculture, Statistics* 1:254–64, 342–58.

HANDY E.S.C. 1923 *The native culture in the Marquesas.* BPBMB 9.

—— 1928 Probable sources of Polynesian culture, *Proceedings 3rd Pacific Science Congress*, vol. 2:2459–68.

—— 1930a *The problem of Polynesian origins.* BPBMOP 9, part 8.

—— 1930b *History and culture in the Society Islands.* BPBMB 79.

HANSON F.A. 1970 *Rapan lifeways.* Boston: Little, Brown.

HARDING T.G. 1967 *Voyagers of the Vitiaz Straits.* Seattle: University of Washington Press.

HARRIS D.R. 1972 The origins of agriculture in the tropics, *American Scientist* 60:180–93.

—— 1973 The prehistory of tropical agriculture: an ethnoecological model, in Renfrew C. (ed.), *The explanation of culture change*, p. 391–417. London: Duckworth.

—— 1974 *Settling down: an evolutionary model for the transformation of mobile bands into sedentary communities*, Paper given at Evolution of Social Systems Seminar, London, May 1974.

HARRISSON B. 1967 A classification of stone-age burials from Niah Great Cave, Sarawak, *SMJ* 15:126–155.

—— 1968 A Niah stone-age jar-burial C14 dated, *SMJ* 16:64–6.

HARRISSON B. and T. 1968 Magala – a series of Neolithic and Metal Age burial grottos at Sekaloh, Niah, Sarawak, *JMBRAS* 41, part 2:148–75.

HARRISSON T. 1937 *Savage civilisation.* London: Gollancz.

—— 1957 The Great Cave of Niah: a preliminary report, *Man* 59:161–6.

—— 1958a Niah: a history of prehistory, *SMJ* 8:549–95.

—— 1958b Megaliths of central and western Borneo, *SMJ* 8:394–401.

—— 1959a *The peoples of Sarawak.* Kuching: Government Printing Office.

—— 1959b New archaeological and ethnological results from Niah Cave, Sarawak, *Man* 59:1–8.

—— 1961–2 Megaliths of central Borneo and western Malaya, compared, *SMJ* 10:376–82.

—— 1963 100,000 years of stone age culture in Borneo, *Journal of the Royal Society of Arts* 112:74–91.

—— 1964a Imun Ajo': a bronze figure from interior Borneo, *Artibus Asiae* 27:157–71.

—— 1964b Inside Borneo, *Geographical Journal* 130:329–36.

—— 1967 Niah Caves, Sarawak, *APAS* 1:77–8.

—— 1970 The prehistory of Borneo, *AP* 13:17–46.

—— 1971 Prehistoric double spouted vessels excavated from Niah Caves, Borneo, *JMBRAS* 44, part 2:35–78.

—— 1973 Megalithic evidences in East Malaysia, *JMBRAS* 46, part 1: 123–40.

—— 1975 Tampan: Malaysia's Palaeolithic reconsidered, in Bartstra G.J. and W.A. Casparie (eds.), *Modern Quaternary research in Southeast Asia*, p. 53–70. Rotterdam: Balkema.

—— 1976 *The Upper Palaeolithic in Malaysia (Malaya and Borneo) and adjacent areas: gateways to the Pacific?* Paper presented at IXᵉ Congrès U.I.S.P.P., Nice, September 1976.

HARRISSON T. and B. 1971 *The prehistory of Sabah.* Kota Kinabalu: Sabah Society.

HARRISSON T., D.A. HOOIJER and Lord MEDWAY 1961 An extinct giant pangolin and associated mammals from Niah Cave, Sarawak, *Nature* 189:166.

HARRISSON T. and Lord MEDWAY 1962 A first classification of prehistoric bone and tooth artefacts, *SMJ* 10:335–62.

HAUDRICOURT A.G. 1965 Problems of Austronesian comparative philology, *Lingua* 14:315–29.

—— 1970 Les arguments géographiques, écologiques et semantiques pour l'origine des Thai, *in Readings in Asian topics*, p. 27–34. Scandinavian Institute of Asian Studies, Monograph 1.

HAU'OFA E. 1971 Mekeo chieftainship, *JPS* 80:152–69.

HEANLEY C.I.M. and J.L. SHELLSHEAR
1932 A contribution to the prehistory of Hong Kong and the New Territories, *in Praehistorica Asiae Orientalis*, p. 63–76. Hanoi: Imprimerie d'Extrême-Orient.

HÉBERT B. 1963–5 Contribution a l'étude archéologique de l'ile d'Efaté et des iles avoisinantes, *EM* 18–20:71–98.

HEDRICK J.D. 1971 Lapita style pottery from Malo Island, *JPS* 80:5–19.

HEEKEREN H.R. van 1949 Rapport over de ontgraving van de Bola Batoe, nabij Badjo (Bone, Zuid-Celebes), *Oudheidkundig Verslag 1941–7*: 89–108. Bandung.

—— 1950a Rapport over de ontgraving te Kamasi, Kalumpang (West Centraal-Celebes), *Oudheidkundig Verslag 1949*: 26–48. Bandung.

—— 1950b Rock paintings and other prehistoric discoveries near Maros (South West Celebes), *Laporan Tahunan 1950*: 22–35. Dinas Purbakala Republik Indonesia.

—— 1956a Notes on a proto-historic urn-burial site at Anjar, Java, *A* 51:194–200.

—— 1956b *The urn cemetery at Melolo, East Sumba (Indonesia)*, Berita Dinas Purbakala 3, Djakarta.

—— 1958a The Tjabenge flake industry from South Celebes, *AP* 2:77–81.

—— 1958b *The Bronze-Iron Age of Indonesia*. The Hague: Martinus Nijhoff.

—— 1967 A Mesolithic industry from the Toge Caves, Flores, *in* Jacob T. 1967:157–9.

—— 1972 *The Stone Age of Indonesia*. 2nd edition. The Hague: Martinus Nijhoff.

HEEKEREN H.R. van, and E. KNUTH 1967 *Archaeological excavations in Thailand. Volume 1: Sai Yok*. Copenhagen: Munksgaard.

HEGER F. 1902 *Alte Metalltrommeln aus Südost-Asien*. Leipzig.

HEIDER K. 1967a Speculative functionalism: archaic elements in New Guinea Dani culture, *A* 62:833–40.

—— 1967b Archaeological assumptions and ethnographic facts, *SWJA* 23:52–64.

—— 1969 The Dong-Son and the Dani: a skeuomorph from the West Irian Highlands, *Mankind* 7:147–8.

HEINE GELDERN R. von 1932 Urheimat und früheste Wanderungen der Austronesier, *A* 27:543–619.

—— 1937 L'art prébouddhique de la Chine et de l'Asie du sud-est et son influence en Océanie, *Revue des Arts Asiatiques* 11:177–206.

—— 1945 Prehistoric research in the Netherlands Indies, *in* Honig P. and F. Verdoorn (eds.), *Science and Scientists in the Netherlands Indies* p. 129–67. New York.

—— 1946 Research in South-east Asia: problems and suggestions, *AA* 48:149–75.

—— 1947 The drum named Makalamau, *India Antiqua*, 1947:167–79. Leiden.

—— 1952 Some problems of migration in the Pacific, *WBKL* 9:313–62.

—— 1958 Correspondence, *JPS* 67:170–1.

—— 1966a Some tribal art styles of Southeast Asia: an experiment in art history, *in* Fraser D. (ed.), *The many faces of primitive art*, p. 165–221. Prentice Hall.

—— 1966b A note on relations between the art styles of the Maori and of ancient China, *WBKL* 15:45–68.

HENRY T. 1928 *Ancient Tahiti*. BPBMB 48.

HEYEN G.H. 1963 Primitive navigation in the Pacific, *in* Golson J. (ed.) 1963:64–80.

HEYERDAHL T. 1950 *The Kon-Tiki expedition*. London: Allen and Unwin.

—— 1952 *American Indians in the Pacific*. London: Allen and Unwin.

—— 1958 *Aku-Aku*. London: Allen and Unwin.

—— 1961 General discussion, *in* Heyerdahl T. and E.N. Ferdon (eds.) 1961:493–526.

—— 1965 The concept of *rongo-rongo* among the historic population of Easter Island, *in* Heyerdahl T. and E.N. Ferdon (eds.) 1965:345–386.

—— 1966 Discussions of Transoceanic contacts: isolationism, diffusionism, or a middle course? *A* 61:689–707.

—— 1968a The prehistoric culture of Easter Island, *in* Yawata I. and Y.H. Sinoto (eds.) 1968:133–40.

—— 1968b *Sea routes to Polynesia*. Edited by K. Jettmar. London: Allen and Unwin.

HEYERDAHL T. and E.N. FERDON (eds.) 1961 *Reports of the Norwegian Archaeological Expedition to Easter Island and the East Pacific, volume I: archaeology of Easter Island*. School of American Research and Museum of New Mexico, Monograph 24, part 1, Santa Fe, New Mexico.

—— 1965 *Reports of the Norwegian Archaeological Expedition to Easter Island and the East Pacific, volume 2: miscellaneous papers*. School of American Research and Kon-Tiki Museum, Monograph 24, part 2. Stockholm.

HEYERDAHL T. and A. SKJÖLSVOLD 1965 Notes on the archaeology of Pitcairn, *in* Heyerdahl T. and E.N. Ferdon (eds.) 1965:3–8.

HIGHAM C.F.W. 1970 The role of economic prehistory in the interpretation of the settlement of Oceania, *in* Green R.C. and M. Kelly (eds.) 1970:165–74.

—— 1972 Initial model formation *in terra incognita*, *in* Clarke D.L. (ed.), *Models in archaeology*, p. 453–76. London: Methuen.

—— 1975 Aspects of economy and ritual in prehistoric northeast Thailand, *Journal of Archaeological Science* 2:245–88.

HIGHAM C.F.W. and B.F. LEACH 1972 An early centre of bovine husbandry in Southeast Asia, *Science* 172:54–6.

HIGHLAND G. *et al.* (eds.) 1967 *Polynesian culture history: essays in honor of Kenneth P. Emory*. BPBMSP 56.

HILDER B. 1963 Primitive navigation in the Pacific, *in* Golson J. (ed.) 1963:81–97.

HJARNO J. 1967 Maori fish-hooks in southern New Zealand, *ROMA* 3.

HO P-T. 1969 The loess and the origin of Chinese agriculture, *American Historical Review* 75:1–36.

—— 1975 *The cradle of the East*. Chinese University of Hong Kong and University of Chicago.

HO R. 1960 Physical geography of the Indo-Australasian tropics, *in Symposium on the Impact of Man on Humid Tropics Vegetation*, p. 19–34. Unesco: Science Co-operation Office for Southeast Asia.

HOCART A.M. 1915 The dual organisation in Fiji, *Man* 15:5–9.

HOGBIN H.I. 1935 Native culture of Wogeo, *Oceania* 5:308–37.

—— 1947 Native trade around the Huon Gulf, *JPS* 56:242–55.

HOGBIN H.I. and C.H. WEDGEWOOD
1953 Local grouping in Melanesia, *Oceania* 23:242–76, 24:58–76.

HOLLYMAN K. 1959 Polynesian influence in New Caledonia: the linguistic aspect, *JPS* 68:356–89.

HOLMES L.D. 1974 *Samoan village*. New York: Holt, Rinehart and Winston.

HOLTKER G. 1951 Die Steinvögel in Melanesien, *in Södseestudien*, p. 235–65. Basel: Museum für Volkerkunde.

HOOIJER C.R. 1969 *Indonesian prehistoric tools: a catalogue of the Houbolt collection*. Leiden: Brill.

HOOIJER D.A. 1950a *Man and other mammals from Toalian sites in south western Celebes*. Verhandelingen der Koninklijke Nederlandische Akademie van Wetenschappen, Afdeling Natuurkunde, Tweede Sectie 46, 2, p. 1–158.

—— 1950b Fossil evidence of Australomelanesian migrations in Malaysia? *SWJA* 6:416–22.

—— 1952 Australomelanesian migrations once more, *SWJA* 8:472–77.

—— 1958 The Pleistocene vertebrate fauna of Celebes, *AP* 2:71–6.

—— 1962 Pleistocene dating and man, *Advancement of Science* 18:485–9.

—— 1963 Further 'Hell' mammals from Niah, *SMJ* 11:196–200.

—— 1967–8 Indo-Australian pygmy elephants, *Genetica* 38:143–62.

—— 1968 The middle Pleistocene fauna of Java, *in* Kurth G. (ed.) 1968:86–90.

—— 1969 The Stegodon from Flores, *Koninklijk Nederlands Akademie van Wetenschappen, Proceedings Series B,* vol. 72:203–210.

—— 1975 Quaternary mammals west and east of Wallace's Line, *in* Bartstra G.J. and W.A. Casparie (eds.), *Modern Quaternary Research in Southeast Asia*, p. 37–46. Rotterdam: Balkema.

HOOP A.N. van der 1932 *Megalithic remains in South-Sumatra*. Zutphen: Thieme.

—— 1940 A prehistoric site near Lake Kerinchi, Sumatra, *in* Chasen F.N. and M.W.F. Tweedie (eds.) 1940:200–4.

HOOPER A. 1968 Socio-economic organisation of the Tokelau Islands, *8th Congress of Anthropological and Ethnological Sciences*, vol. 2:238–40. Tokyo and Kyoto.

HOPE G.S. and J.A. PETERSON 1975 Glaciation and vegetation in the high New Guinea mountains, *in* Suggate R.P. and M.M. Cresswell (eds.), *Quaternary Studies*, P. 155–62. Wellington: Royal Society of New Zealand.

HOPE J.H. and G.S. 1974 *Palaeoenvironments for man in New Guinea*. Paper given at Australian Institute of Aboriginal Studies Conference, Canberra, May 1974.

HOPKINS M. 1862 *Hawaii: the past, present and future of its island-kingdom*. London: Longman.

HORNELL J. 1945 Was there Pre-Columbian contact between the peoples of Oceania and South America? *JPS* 54:167–91.

—— 1946 How did the sweet potato reach Oceania? *Journal of the Linnean Society* 53:41–62.

HOSSFELD P. 1964 The Aitape calvarium, *Australian Journal of Science* 27:179.

HOWARD A. 1967 Polynesian origins and migrations: a review of two centuries of speculation and theory, *in* Highland G. *et al.* (eds.) 1967:45–102.

HOWELLS W.W. 1933 *Anthropometry and blood types in Fiji and the Solomon Islands*. APAMNH 33, part 4.

—— 1943 The racial elements of Melanesia, *in* Coon C.S. and J.M. Andrews (eds.) 1943:38–49.

—— 1966 Population distances: biological, linguistic, geographical and environmental, *CA* 7:531–40.

—— 1970 Anthropometric grouping analysis of Pacific peoples, *APAO* 5:192–217.

—— 1973a *The Pacific Islanders*. New York: Scribner's Sons.

—— 1973b *Cranial variation in man*. Papers of the Peabody Museum, Harvard University, vol. 67.

HSU J. 1966 The climatic conditions in north China during the time of *Sinanthropus, Scientia Sinica* 15:410–14.

HUGHES D.R. 1967 Osteological evidence suggestive of the origin of the Mongoloid peoples, *APAS* 1:1–10.

HUGHES I. 1971 *Recent Neolithic trade in New Guinea*. Unpublished Ph.D. thesis, Australian National University.

HUTTON F.W. 1891 The moas of New Zealand, *TNZI* 24:93–172.

IKAWA-SMITH F. 1976 On ceramic technology in East Asia, *CA* 17:513–5.

IRWIN G.J. 1973 Man-land relationships: an investigation of prehistoric settlement in the islands of the Bougainville Strait, *APAO* 8:226–52.

—— 1974 Carved paddle decoration of pottery and its capacity for inference in archaeology: an example from the Solomon Islands, *JPS* 83:368–71.

IVENS W. 1930 *The island builders of the Pacific*. London: Seeley, Service.

JACOB T. 1967a Recent *Pithecanthropus* finds in Indonesia, *CA* 8:501–4.

—— 1967b The sixth skull cap of *Pithecanthropus erectus, AJPA* 25:243–60.

—— 1967c *Some problems pertaining to the racial history of the Indonesian region*. Utrecht: Drukkerij Neerlandia.

—— 1972a The absolute date of the Djetis beds at Modjokerto, *Antiquity* 46:148.

—— 1972b The problem of head hunting and brain eating among Pleistocene men in Indonesia, *APAO* 7:81–91.

—— 1972c New hominid finds in Indonesia and their affinities, *Mankind* 8:176–81.

—— 1974 *Early populations in the Indonesian region*. Paper given at Australian Institute of Aboriginal Studies Conference, Canberra, May 1974.

JACOBY A. 1967 *Señor Kon-Tiki*. Chicago: Rand McNally.

JAMMES L. 1891 L'âge de la pierre polie au Cambodge d'après de récentes découvertes, *Bulletin de Géographie Historique et Descriptive*, 1891:35–52. Paris.

JANSE O.R.T. 1958 *The ancient dwelling-site of Dong-Son (Thanh-Hoa, Annam)*. Archaeological Research in Indo-China volume 1, Institut Belge des Hautes Études Chinoises.

—— 1959 Some notes on the Sa-Huynh complex, *AP* 3:109–11.

JENNESS D. (ed.) 1933 (1972) *The American aborigines, their origin and antiquity*. 1972 reprint. New York: Russell and Russell.

JENNINGS J.D. (ed.) 1976 *Excavations on Opolu, Western Samoa*, PAR 25.

JOLLY R.W.G. and P. MURDOCK 1973 Further excavations at site N40/2, Opito Bay, *NZAAN* 16: 66–72.

JONES K. 1973 Excavations at Tairua (N44/2) 1958–64: a synthesis. *NZAAN* 16:143–9.

JONES R. 1973 Emerging picture of Pleistocene Australians, *Nature* 246:278–81.

JOSKE A.B. 1889 The *nanga* of Viti Levu, *Internationales Archiv für Ethnologie* 2:254–71.

JOYCE T.A. 1912 Note on prehistoric pottery from Japan and New Guinea, *JRAI* 42:545–6.

KAEPPLER A.L. 1971 Eighteenth century Tonga: new interpretations of Tongan society and material culture at the time of Captain Cook, *Man* (new series) 6:204–20.

—— 1973 Pottery sherds from Tungua, Ha'apai, *JPS* 82:218–22.

KAHLER H. 1964 Comments, *CA* 5:392–3.

KAPLAN S. 1973 *A style analysis of pottery sherds from Nissan Island*. Solomon Island Studies in Human Biogeography 2. Chicago: Field Museum.

KARIKS J. and R.J. Walsh 1968 Some physical measurements and blood groups of the Bainings in New Britain, *APAO* 3:129–42.

KARLGREN B. 1942 The date of the early Dong-Son Culture, *BMFEA* 14:1–28.

KAUDERN W. 1938 *Megalithic finds in central Celebes*. Ethnographic Studies in Celebes vol. 5. Göteborg: privately published by the author.

KEERS W. 1948 *An anthropological survey of the eastern Little Sunda Islands*. Koninklijke Vereeniging Indisch Institut, Mededeling 74.

KEESING F.M. 1962a *The ethnohistory of northern Luzon*. Stanford University Press.

—— 1962b The Isneg: shifting cultivators of the northern Philippines, *SWJA* 18:1–19.

KEESING F. and M. 1956 *Elite communication in Samoa*. Stanford Anthropology Series 3.

KELLUM-OTTINO M. 1971 *Archéologie d'une vallée des Îles Marquises: évolution des structures de l'habitat à Hane, Ua Huka*. Paris: Publication de la Société des Océanists 26.

KELLY L.G. 1951 *Marion du Fresne at the Bay of Islands*. Wellington: Reed.

KELLY M. 1967 Some problems with early descriptions of Hawaiian culture, *in* Highland G. *et al.* (eds.) 1967: 399–410.

KELLY R.C. 1968 Demographic pressure and descent group structure in the New Guinea Highlands, *Oceania* 39:36–63.

KENNEDY J. 1969 *Settlement in the Bay of Islands 1772*. OUMPA 3.

KEY C.A. 1969 The identification of New Guinea obsidians, *APAO* 4:47–55.

KEYES I.W. 1960 Cultural succession and ethnographic features of D'Urville Island, *JPS* 69:239–59.

—— 1967 The Ngatimamoe: the western Polynesian-Melanesoid sub-culture in New Zealand, *JPS* 76:47–75.

KING J. and P.J. EPLING 1972 *The dispersal of the Polynesian people*. Working Papers in Methodology 6, Institute for Research in Social Studies, University of North Carolina.

KIRCH P.V. 1971a Halawa dune site (Hawaiian Islands): a preliminary report, *JPS* 80:228–36.

—— 1971b Archaeological excavations at Palauea, southeast Maui, Hawaiian Islands, *APAO* 6:62–86.

—— 1973 Prehistoric subsistence patterns in the northern Marquesas Islands, French Polynesia, *APAO* 8:24–40.

—— 1974 The chronology of early Hawaiian settlement, *APAO* 9:110–9.

—— 1976 Ethno-archaeological investigations in Futuna and Uvea (western Polynesia): a preliminary report, *JPS* 85:27–70.

KIRCH P.V. and M. KELLY 1975 *Prehistory and ecology in a windward Hawaiian valley: Halawa Valley, Molokai*, PAR 24.

KIRCH P.V. and P.H. ROSENDAHL 1973 Archaeological investigation of Anuta, *in* Yen D.E. and J. Gordon (eds.), *Anuta: a Polynesian Outlier in the Solomon Islands*, p. 25–108. PAR 21.

KIRK R.L. 1965 Population genetic studies of indigenous peoples of Australia and New Guinea, in Steinberg A.G. and A.G. Bearn (eds.), *Progress in Medical Genetics*, vol. 4, p. 202–41. New York: Grune and Stratton.

—— 1971 Genetic evidence and its implications for Aboriginal prehistory, *in* Mulvaney D.J. and J. Golson (eds.) 1971: 326–43.

KOBAYASHI T. 1970 Microblade industries in the Japanese Archipelago, *Arctic Anthropology* 7:38–58.

KOCH G. 1961 *Die materielle Kultur der Ellice-Inseln*. Berlin: Museum für Volkerkunde.

—— 1965 *Materielle Kulture der Gilbert-Inseln*. Berlin: Museum für Volkerkunde.

—— 1966 The Polynesian-Micronesian 'culture boundary', *Abstracts of Papers, 11th Pacific Science Congress*, vol. 9, section X-2: Ethnology, p. 3.

KOENIGSWALD G.H.R. von 1952 Evidence of a prehistoric Australomelanesoid population in Malaya and Indonesia, *SWJA* 8:92–6.

—— 1956 Fossil mammals from the Philippines, *Proceedings 4th Far-Eastern Prehistory and the Anthropology Division of the 8th Pacific Science Congresses combined*, part 1, second fascicle, section 1, p. 339–70.

—— 1958a Remarks on the prehistoric fauna of the Great Cave, *SMJ* 8:620–6.

—— 1958b Preliminary report on a newly-discovered stone age culture from northern Luzon, Philippine Islands, *AP* 2:69–70.

—— 1968a Das absolute Alter des *Pithecanthropus erectus* Dubois, in Kurth G. (ed.) 1968: 195–203.

—— 1968b Classification of some stone tools from Java and New Guinea, *APAS* 2:113–39.

KOENIGSWALD G.H.R. von and A.K. GHOSH 1973 Stone implements from the Trinil beds, *Koninklijk Nederlands Akademie van Wetenschappen, Proceedings Series B*, vol. 76:1–34.

KOKOBU N. 1963 The prehistoric southern islands and east China Sea areas, *AP* 7:224–42.

KRIEGER H.W. 1943 *Island peoples of the western Pacific: Micronesia and Melanesia*. Washington: Smithsonian Institution.

KROEBER A.L. 1928 *Peoples of the Philippines*. 2nd edition. New York: American Museum of Natural History.

KRUPA V. 1973 *Polynesian languages: a survey of research*. Janua Linguarum, Series Critica 11.

KRUSKAL J.B., I. DYEN and P. BLACK 1971 The vocabulary method of reconstructing language trees: innovations and large-scale applications, *in* Hodson F.R. *et al.* (eds.), *Mathematics in the archaeological and historical sciences*, p. 361–80. Edinburgh University Press.

KRUYT A.C. 1932 L'immigration préhistorique dans les pays Toradjas occidentaux, *in Hommage du Service Archéologique des Indes Néerlandaises au Ier Congrès des Préhistoriens d'Extrême-Orient à Hanoi*, Janvier 1932. Batavia: Société Royale des Arts et des Sciences.

KUENEN Ph. H. 1950 *Marine Geology*. New York: Wiley.

KURJACK E.B., C.T. SHELDON and M.E. KELLER 1971 The urn burial caves of southern Cotobato, Mindanao, Philippines, *Silliman Journal* 18, part 2:127–53.

KURTEN B. and Y. VASARI 1960 On the date of Peking Man, *Societas Scientarum Fennica, Commentationes Biologicae* 23, no. 7:3–10. Helsinki.

KURTH G. (ed.) 1968 *Evolution und Hominisation*. 2nd edition. Stuttgart: Gustav Fischer.

KUYKENDALL R.S. 1938 *The Hawaiian kingdom 1778–1854*. University of Hawaii Press.

LADD E.J. 1969a 'Alealea temple site, Honaunau: salvage report, *APAS* 3:95–132.

—— 1969b The Great Wall stabilisation: salvage report, *APAS* 3:133–162.

—— 1969c Hale-o-Keawe temple site, Honaunau: pre-salvage report, *APAS* 3:163–90.

—— (ed.) 1973 *Makaha Valley historical project. Interim report* 4. PAR 19.

LADD E.J. and D. YEN (eds.) 1972 *Makaha Valley historical project*. Interim report 3. PAR 18.

LAFONT P.B. 1956 Note sur un site néolithique de la province de Pleiku, *BEFEO* 48:233–48.

LAMB A. 1965 Some observations on stone and glass beads in early South-east Asia, *JMBRAS* 38:87–124.

LAMBERG-KARLOVSKY C.C. 1962 Ethno-history of South China: an analysis of Han-Chinese migrations, *BIEAS* 13:65–84.

—— 1967 Ethno-history of South China: an analysis of T'ai migrations, *BIEAS* 23:129–39.

LAMONT E.H. 1867 *Wild life among the Pacific islanders*. London: Hurst and Blackett.

LAMPERT R.J. 1967 Standing stones and rock art: two sites on New Hanover, *Mankind* 6:489–92.

—— 1975 A preliminary report on some waisted blades found on Kangaroo Island, South Australia, *Australian Archaeological Association Newsletter* 2:45–8.

LANDBERG L. 1966 Tuna tagging and the extra-Oceanic distribution of curved, single-piece shell fishhooks, *American Antiquity* 31: 485–93.

LANGDON R. 1975 *The Lost Caravel*. Sydney: Pacific Publications.

LANNING E.P. 1970 South America as a source for aspects of Oceanic cultures, *in* Green R.C. and M. Kelly (eds.) 1970:175–82.

LAUER P.K. 1970a Amphlett Islands pottery trade and the Kula, *Mankind* 7:165–76.

—— 1970b *Pottery traditions in the D'Entrecasteaux Islands of Papua*. Unpublished Ph.D. thesis, Australian National University.

LAVACHERY H. 1936 Contribution a l'étude de l'archéologie de l'île de Pitcairn, *Bulletin de la Société des Américanistes de Belgique* 19:3–42.

—— 1939 *Les pétroglyphes de l'île de Pâques*. Anvers: De Sikkel.

—— 1951 Stèles et pierres levées a l'Île de Pâques, *in Südseestudien*, p. 413–22. Basel: Museum für Volkerkunde.

LAW R.G. 1969 Pits and *kumara* agriculture in the South Island, *JPS* 78:223–51.

—— 1970 The introduction of *kumara* into New Zealand, *APAO* 5:114–27.

—— 1972 Archaeology at Harataonga Bay, Great Barrier Island, *RAIM* 9:81–123.

—— 1973 Tokoroa moa-hunter site, *NZAAN* 16:150–64.

LAYCOCK D.C. 1973 *Sepik languages: checklist and preliminary classification*. Pacific Linguistics, Series B, 25.

LEACH B.F. 1969 *The concept of similarity in prehistoric studies*. OUMPA 1.

—— 1973 Obsidian in the Chatham Islands, *NZAAN* 16:104–6.

LEACH B.F. and H.M. 1971–2 Radiocarbon dates for the Wairarapa, *NZAAN* 14:199–201; 15:76, 163.

LEACH H.M. 1969 *Subsistence patterns in prehistoric New Zealand*. OUMPA 2.

—— 1972 A hundred years of Otago archaeology: a critical review, *ROMA* 6.

—— 1974 Pre-European, *New Zealand's Nature Heritage* 1:117–22, 164–9.

LEAHY A. 1970 Excavations at site N38/30, Motutapu Island, New Zealand, *RAIM* 7:61–82.

—— 1972 Further excavations at site N38/30, Motutapu Island, New Zealand, *RAIM* 9:15–26.

—— 1974 Excavations at Hot Water Beach (N44/69). Coromandel Peninsula, *RAIM* 11:23–76.

LEBAR F.M. (ed.) 1972 *Ethnic groups of insular Southeast Asia, Volume 1: Indonesia, Andaman Islands and Madagascar*. New Haven: Human Relations Area Files Press.

LEBAR F.M., G.C. HICKEY and J.K. MUSGRAVE 1965 *Ethnic groups of mainland Southeast Asia*. New Haven: Human Relations Area Files Press.

LEE I. 1920 *Captain Bligh's second voyage to the South Sea, 1791–3*, London: Longmans.

LEENHARDT M. 1930 *Notes d'ethnologie néo-calédonienne*. Paris: Institut d'Ethnologie, Travaux et Mémoirs 8.

LE GROS CLARK W. 1964 *The fossil evidence for human evolution*. University of Chicago Press.

LENORMAND M.H. 1948 Découvert d'un gisement de poteries a l'Île des Pins, *EM* 3:54–8.

LEPERVANCHE M. de 1968 Descent, residence and leadership in the New Guinea Highlands, *Oceania* 38:134–89.

LESSA W.A. 1950 Ulithi and the outer native world, *AA* 52:27–52.

—— 1962 An evaluation of early descriptions of Carolinean culture, *Ethnohistory* 9:313–403.

—— 1966 *Ulithi: a Micronesian design for living*. New York: Holt, Rinehart and Winston.

LEVISON M., R.G. WARD and J.W. WEBB 1973 *The settlement of Polynesia: a computer simulation*. Minneapolis: University of Minnesota Press.

LEVI-STRAUSS C. 1963 *Structural Anthropology*. New York: Basic Books.

LEVY P. 1943 *Recherches préhistoriques dans la région de Mlu Prei*. Publication de L'École Francaise d'Extrême-Orient 30.

LEWIS A.B. 1951 *The Melanesians*. Chicago Natural History Museum.

LEWIS D. 1972 *We, the navigators*. Canberra: Australian National University Press.

LEWTHWAITE G.R. 1949 *Human geography of Aotearoa about 1790*. Unpublished M.A. thesis, University of Auckland.

—— 1964 Man and land in Tahiti: Polynesian agriculture through European eyes, *Pacific Viewpoint* 5:11–34.

—— 1966a Man and the sea in early Tahiti: a maritime economy through European eyes, *Pacific Viewpoint* 7:28–53.

—— 1966b Tupaia's map, *Association of Pacific Coast Geographers Yearbook* 28:41–53.

—— 1967 The geographical knowledge of the Pacific peoples, *in* Friis H.R. (ed.), *The Pacific basin*, p. 57–86. New York: American Geographical Society.

LIN C.C. 1963 Geology and ecology of Taiwan prehistory, *AP* 7:203–13.

LINEHAN W. 1968 A Neolithic link between north Pahang, Malaya, and the Sino-Malayan border, *APAS* 2:97–103.

LING Shun-Sheng 1962 Stone bark cloth beaters of South China, Southeast Asia and central America, *BIEAS* 13:195–212.

LINTON R. 1923 *The material culture of the Marquesas Islands*. BPBMM 8, no. 5.

—— 1925 *Archaeology of the Marquesas Islands*. BPBMB 23.

—— 1939 Marquesan culture, *in* Kardiner A., *The individual and his society*, p. 137–250. New York: Columbia University Press.

—— 1956 *The tree of culture*. New York: Knopf.

LITTLEWOOD R.A. 1966 Isolate patterns in the Eastern Highlands of New Guinea, *JPS* 75:95–106.

—— 1972 *Physical anthropology of the Eastern Highlands of New Guinea.* Seattle: University of Washington Press.

LIVINGSTONE F.B. 1963 Blood groups and ancestry: a test case from New Guinea, *CA* 4:541–2.

LOCKERBIE L. 1959 From moa-hunter to Classic Maori in southern New Zealand, *in* Freeman J.D. and W.R. Geddes (eds.) 1959:75–109.

LOEB E.M. and J.O.M. BROEK 1947 Social organisation and the longhouse in South East Asia, *AA* 49:414–25.

LOEWENSTEIN J. 1956 The origin of the Malayan metal age, *JMBRAS* 29. part 2: 5–78.

LOOFS H.H.E. 1965 Some remarks on 'Philippine megaliths', *Asian Studies* 3:393–402.

—— 1967 *Elements of the megalithic complex in Southeast Asia: an annotated bibliography.* Canberra, Australian National University, Oriental Monograph Series 3.

—— 1970 A brief account of the Thai-British archaeological expedition, *APAO* 5:177–84.

—— 1974 Thermoluminescence dates from Thailand: comments, *Antiquity* 48:58–62.

—— 1976 Dongson drums and heavenly bodies, *in* Barnard N. (ed.) *Ancient Chinese bronzes and Southeast Asian metal and other archaeological artefacts,* p. 441–67. Melbourne: National Gallery of Victoria.

LOOMIS W.F. 1967 Skin pigment regulation of vitamin biosynthesis in man, *Science* 157:501–6.

LOVEJOY C.O. 1970 The taxonomic status of the *Meganthropus* mandibular fragments from the Djetis beds of Java, *Man* (new series) 5:228–36.

LUOMALA K. 1951 *The Menehune of Polynesia and other mythical little people of Oceania.* BPBMB 203.

—— 1973 Moving and moveable images in Easter Island custom and myth, *JPS* 82:28–46.

LUQUET G.H. 1926 *L'art néo-calédonienne.* Paris: Institut d'Ethnologie, Travaux et Mémoirs 2.

LYNCH F.X. and J.F. EWING 1968 Twelve ground stone implements from Mindanao, Philippine Islands, *APAS* 2:7–20.

LYONS A.P. 1922 Sepulchral pottery of Murua, Papua, *Man* 22:164–5.

McALISTER J.G. 1933 *Archaeology of Oahu.* BPBMB 104.

McCARTHY F.D. 1934 Norfolk Island: additional evidence of a former native occupation, *JPS* 43:267–70.

—— 1940 A comparison of the prehistory of Australia with that of Indochina, the Malay Peninsula and Archipelago, *in* Chasen F.N. and M.W.F. Tweedie (eds.) 1940:30–50.

—— 1949a Waisted hammers from the Mackay district, Queensland, *RAM* 22:151–4.

—— 1949b Some prehistoric and recent stone implements from New Guinea, *RAM* 22:155–63.

McCOY P.C. 1971 Review of Englert S. 1970, *JPS* 80: 259–60.

—— 1973 Excavation of a rectangular house on the east rim of Rano Kau volcano, Easter Island, *APAO* 8:51–67.

McCULLOCH B. 1973 A relevant radiocarbon result, *NZAAN* 16:128–32.

McELHANON K.A. 1971 Classifying New Guinea languages, *A* 66:120–44.

McELHANON K.A. and C.L. VOORHOEVE 1970 *The Trans-New Guinea phylum: explorations in deep level genetic relationships.* Pacific Linguistics, Series B, no. 16.

McFADGEN B.G. 1974 The significance of archaeological research, *NZAAN* 17:27–30.

MacINTOSH N.W.G. 1960 A preliminary note on skin colour in the Western Highland natives of New Guinea, *Oceania* 30:279–93.

—— 1972 Radiocarbon dating as a pointer in time to the arrival and history of man in Australia and islands to the north-west, *Proceedings 8th International Conference on Radiocarbon Dating,* vol. 1, p. XLIV–LVI. Wellington: Royal Society of New Zealand.

MacINTOSH N.W.G., R.J. WALSH and O. KOOPTZOFF 1958 The blood groups of the native inhabitants of the Western Highlands, New Guinea, *Oceania* 28: 173–98.

McKAY A. 1974 On the identity of the moa-hunters with the present Maori race, *TNZI* 7:98–105.

McKERN W.C. 1929 *Archaeology of Tonga.* BPBMB 60.

McKINLAY J.R. 1971 Waioneke 1968–9, *NZAAN* 14:86–9.

MacLACHLAN R.R.C. 1938 Native pottery from central and southern Melanesia and west Polynesia, *JPS* 47:64–89.

McNAB J.W. 1968 Sweet potatoes and Maori terraces in the Wellington area, *JPS* 78:83–111.

McNAB R. (ed.) 1914 *Historical records of New Zealand. Volume 2.* Wellington: Government Printer.

MAGLIONI R. 1938 Archaeological finds in Hoifung, part 1, *Hong Kong Naturalist* 3, no. 3–4:208–44.

—— 1952 Archaeology in South China, *JEAS* 2:1–20.

MAHER R.F. 1973 Archaeological investigations in central Ifugao, *AP* 16:39–70.

MALINOWSKI B. 1961 *Argonauts of the western Pacific.* New York: Dutton (first published 1922).

MALLERET L. 1958–9 Ouvrages circulaires en terre dans l'Indochine méridionale, *BEFEO* 49:409–34

—— 1959 Quelques poteries de Sa-Huynh dans leurs rapports avec divers sites du sud-est de l'Asie, *AP* 3:113–20.

—— 1960 *L'archéologie du delta du Mékong. Volume 2: La civilisation matérielle d'Oc-èo.* Publication de l'École française d'Extrême-Orient 43.

MANGELSDORF P.C., R.S. MacNEISH and G.R. WILLEY 1964 The origins of agriculture in Middle America, *in* Wauchope R. (ed.), *Handbook of Middle American Indians,* vol. 1, p. 427–44. Austin: University of Texas Press.

MANING F.E. 1948 *Old New Zealand.* New Zealand: Whitcombe and Tombs (first published 1863).

MANSUY H. 1902 *Stations préhistoriques de Somron Seng et de Longprao (Cambodge).* Hanoi: Schneider.

—— 1920 *Gisements préhistoriques des environs de Langson et de Tuyen-quang, Tonkin.* BSGI 7, fascicle 2.

—— 1923 *Résultats de nouvelles recherches effectués dans le gisement préhistorique de Somrong Sen (Cambodge).* MSGI 10, fascicle 1.

—— 1924 *Stations préhistoriques dans les cavernes du massif calcaire de Bac-Son (Tonkin).* MSGI 11, fascicle 2.

—— 1931 *Resumé de l'état de nos connaissances sur la préhistoire et l'ethnologie des races anciennes de l'Extrême-orient meridional.* Paris: Exposition Coloniale Internationale.

MANSUY H. and M. COLANI 1925 *Néolithique inférieur (Bacsonien) et néolithique supérieur dans le Haut Tonkin.* MSGI 12, fascicle 3.

MANSUY H. and J. FROMAGET 1924 *Stations néolithique de Hang-rao et de Khe-tong (Annam).* BSGI 13, fascicle 3.

MANTELL W. 1872 On moa beds, *TNZI* 5:94–7.

MARINGER J. and Th. VERHOEVEN 1970a Die Oberflächenfunde aus dem Fossilgebiet von Mengeruda und Olabula auf Flores, Indonesien, *A* 65:530–46.

—— 1970b Die Steinartefacte aus der Stegodon-Fossilschicht von Mengeruda auf Flores, Indonesien. *A* 65:229–47.

—— 1972 Steingeräte aus dem Waiklau-Trockenbett bei Maumere auf Flores, Indonesien, *A* 67:129–37.

MARSCHALL W. 1968 Metallurgie und frühe Besiedlungsgeschichte Indonesiens, *Ethnologica*, N.F. 4:31–263.

—— 1974 On the stone age of Indonesia, *Tribus* 23:71–90.

MARSHALL D.S. 1956 The settlement of Polynesia, *Scientific American* 195:58–72.

MASON L. 1959 Suprafamilial authority and economic progress in Micronesian atolls, *Humanités* 95:87–118.

—— 1968 The ethnology of Micronesia, *in* Vayda A.P. (ed.) 1969:275–98.

MASSAL E. and J. BARRAU 1956 *Food plants of the South Sea Islands*. South Pacific Commission Technical Paper 94.

MATSUMURA A. 1918 *Contributions to the ethnography of Micronesia*. Journal of the College of Science, Imperial University of Tokyo, vol. 40.

MATTHEWS J. 1964 *The Hoabinhian in South-East Asia and elsewhere*. Unpublished Ph.D. thesis, Australian National University.

—— 1966 A review of the 'Hoabinhian' in Indochina, *AP* 9:86–95.

MAUDE H.E. 1963 Discussion, *in* Fosberg F.R. (ed.) 1963:171–4.

MAYR E. 1945 Wallace's Line in the light of recent zoogeographical study, *in* Honig P. and F. Verdoorn (eds.), *Science and Scientists in the Netherlands Indies*, p. 241–50, New York.

MEACHAM W. 1973a Sham Wan: a cultural record. *Arts of Asia*, May–June 1973:36–40.

—— 1973b Notes on the early Neolithic in Hong Kong, *JHKAS* 4:45–52.

MEAD M. 1969 *Social organisation of Manu'a*. New York: Krauss. First published as BPBMB 76, 1930.

MEAD M., T. DOBZHANSKY, E. TOBACH and R.E. LIGHT (eds.) 1968 *Science and the concept of race*. New York: Columbia University Press.

MEAD S.M. 1973 *Material culture and art in the Star Harbour region, eastern Solomon Islands*. Royal Ontario Museum, Ethnographical Monograph 1.

—— 1975 The origins of Maori art: Polynesian or Chinese? *Oceania* 45:173–211.

MEAD S.M., L. BIRKS, H. BIRKS and E. SHAW 1973 *The Lapita pottery style of Fiji and its associations*. Polynesian Society Memoir 38.

MEDWAY Lord 1959 Niah animal bone II, *SMJ* 9:151–63.

—— 1969 Excavations at Gua Kechil, Pahang; IV: animal remains, *JMBRAS* 42, part 2:197–203.

—— 1972 The Quaternary mammals of Malesia: a review, *in* Ashton P. and M. (eds.) 1972:63–83.

—— 1973 The antiquity of domesticated pigs in Sarawak, *JMBRAS* 46, part 2:167–78.

MELVILLE H. 1959 *Typee*. Oxford: The World's Classics.

MERRILL E.D. 1954 The botany of Cook's voyages, *Chronica Botanica* 14:161–384.

MÉTRAUX A. 1936 Numerals from Easter Island, *Man* 36:190–1.

—— 1940 *Ethnology of Easter Island*. BPBMB 160.

—— 1957 *Easter Island*. London: Scientific Book Club.

MEYER O. 1909 Funde prähistorischer Töpferei und Steinmesser auf Vuatom, Bismarck Archipel, *A* 4:251–2, 1093–5.

—— 1910 Funde von Menschen- und Tierknochen, von prähistorischer Töpferei und Steinwerkzeugen auf Vatom, Bismarck Archipel, *A* 5:1160–1.

MILKE W. 1961 Beitrage zur ozeanischen Linguistik, *Zeitschrift für Ethnologie* 86:162–82.

—— 1965 Comparative notes on the Austronesian languages of New Guinea, *Lingua* 14:330–48.

MILLIMAN J.D. and K.O. EMERY 1969 Sea levels during the past 35,000 years, *Science* 162: 1121–3.

MILLS J.P. and J.H. HUTTON 1929 Ancient monoliths of North Cachar, *Journal and Proceedings of the Asiatic Society of Bengal* N.S. 25:285–300.

MISRA V.N. 1973 Bagor: a late Mesolithic settlement in northwest India, *WA* 5:92–110.

MOHR E.C.J. 1945 The relation between soil and population density in the Netherlands Indies, *in* Honig P. and F. Verdoorn (eds.), *Science and Scientists in the Netherlands Indies*, p. 254–62. New York.

MOLLOY B.P.J. 1969 Evidence for post-glacial climatic changes in New Zealand, *Journal of Hydrology* (New Zealand) 8:56–67.

MONTAGU M. (ed.) 1964 *The concept of race*. New York: Free Press.

MORESBY J. 1876 *Discoveries and surveys in New Guinea and the D'Entrecasteaux Islands*. London: John Murray.

MORI T. 1956 Archaeological study of jar-burials in Eneolithic Japan, *Proceedings 4th Far-Eastern Prehistory and the Anthropology Division of the 8th Pacific Science Congresses combined*, part 1, fascicle 2, section 1:225–45. Quezon City.

—— 1963 The archaeological significance of the jar-burial in Neolithic Japan, *Proceedings 9th Pacific Science Congress*, vol. 3:13.

MORLAN R. 1967 The preceramic period of Hokkaido, *Arctic Anthropology* 4:164–220.

MORLAN V.J. 1971 The preceramic period of Japan: Honshu, Shikoku and Kyushu, *Arctic Anthropology* 8:136–70.

MORRILL S. 1970 *Ponape*. San Francisco: Cadleon.

MORWOOD M.J. 1974 A functional analysis of obsidian flakes from two archaeological sites on Great Barrier Island and one at Tokoroa, *RAIM* 11:77–99.

MOURER C. and R. 1970 The prehistoric industry of Laang Spean, Province Battambang, Cambodia, *APAO* 5:128–46.

—— 1971 La coupe à pied annulaire de Laang Spean, Phnom Teak Trang, Province de Battambang, Cambodge, *Bulletin de la Société Préhistorique française, Comptes Rendues des Sciences Mensuelles* 68, part 5:156–8.

MOVIUS H.L. 1944 *Early man and Pleistocene stratigraphy in southern and eastern Asia*. Papers of the Peabody Museum 19, part 3.

—— 1948 The lower Palaeolithic cultures of southern and eastern Asia, *Transactions of the American Philosophical Society* N.S. 38, part 4:329–420.

—— 1949 Lower Palaeolithic archaeology in southern Asia and the Far East, in Howells W.W. (ed.), *Early Man in the Far East*, p. 17–81. American Association of Physical Anthropology.

—— 1955 Palaeolithic archaeology in southern and eastern Asia, exclusive of India, *Cahiers d'Histoire Mondiale* 2:157–82, 520–53.

MULLOY W. 1961 The ceremonial centre of Vinapu, *in* Heyerdahl T. and E.N. Ferdon (eds.) 1961:93–180.

—— 1970 A speculative reconstruction of techniques of carving, transporting and erecting Easter Island Statues, *APAO* 5:1–23.

—— 1973 *Preliminary report of the restoration of Ahu Huri a Urenga and two unnamed ahu at Hanga Kio'e, Easter Island*. Easter Island Committee, International Fund for Monuments Inc, Bulletin 3.

—— 1975a A solstice oriented *ahu* on Easter Island, *APAO* 10:1–37.
—— 1975b *Investigation and restoration of the ceremonial centre of Orongo, Easter Island, Part 1.* Easter Island Committee, International Fund for Monuments Inc., Bulletin 4.
MULVANEY D.J. 1970 The Patjitanian industry: Some observations, *Mankind* 7:184–7.
—— 1975 *The prehistory of Australia.* Revised edition. Penguin.
MULVANEY D.J. and R. P. SOEJONO 1970 The Australian-Indonesian expedition to Sulawesi, *AP* 13: 163–78.
—— 1971 Archaeology in Sulawesi, Indonesia, *Antiquity* 45:26–33.
MURDOCK G.P. 1960a *Social Structure.* New York: Macmillan.
—— (ed.) 1960b *Social structure in Southeast Asia.* New York: Viking Fund Publication in Anthropology 29.
—— 1964 Genetic classification of the Austronesian languages: a key to Oceanic culture history, *Ethnology* 3:117–26.
—— 1967 *Ethnographic atlas.* University of Pittsburgh Press.
MURDOCK G.P. and W.H. GOODENOUGH 1947 Social organisation of Truk, *SWJA* 3:331–43.
MURRILL R.I. 1968 *Cranial and postcranial remains from Easter Island.* University of Minnesota Press.
NASH J. and D.D. MITCHELL 1973 A note on some chipped stone objects from South Bougainville, *JPS* 82:209–12.
NAYACAKALOU R.R. 1955 The Fijian system of kinship and marriage, *JPS* 64:44–55.
—— 1957 The Fijian system of kinship and marriage, *JPS* 66:44–59.
NEEL J.V. 1967 Genetic structure of primitive human populations, *Japanese Journal of Human Genetics* 12:1–16.
NEICH R. 1971 A prehistoric stone bird from Bougainville and its relationships to northern Solomons implements, *Dominion Museum Records in Ethnology* 2:75–82. Wellington.
NELSON H.E. 1971 Disease, demography and the evolution of social structure in highland New Guinea, *JPS* 80: 204–16.
NEWMAN T.S. 1969 Cultural adaptations to the island of Hawaii ecosystem: the theory behind the 1968 Lapakahi project, *APAS* 3:3–14.
—— 1972 Two early Hawaiian field systems on Hawaii Island, *JPS* 81:87–9.
NGATA A.T. 1893 *The past and future of the Maori.* Christchurch Press.
NGUYEN P.L. 1975 Les nouvelles recherches archéologiques au Viêtnam, *Arts Asiatiques* vol. 31.
NIJENHUIS L.E., A.C. van der GUGTEN, H. den BUTTER and J.W. DOELAND 1966 Blood group frequencies in northern West New Guinea, *AJPA* 18:39–56.
NORDENSKIOLD E. 1933 (1972) Origin of the Indian civilisations in South America, *in* Jenness D. (ed.) 1933 (1972): 247–312.
OAKLEY K. 1969 *Frameworks for dating fossil man.* 3rd edition. London: Weidenfeld and Nicholson.
OBAYASHI T. 1964 Comments, *CA* 5:394–5.
O'BRIEN P.J. 1972 The sweet potato: its origin and dispersal, *AA* 74:342–65.
OLIVER D.L. 1955 *A Solomon Island society.* Harvard University Press.
—— 1961 *The Pacific Islands.* New York: American Museum of Natural History.

—— 1974 *Ancient Tahitian Society* (3 volumes). Honolulu: University of Hawaii Press.
OLIVER D.L. and W.W. HOWELLS 1957 Micro-evolution: cultural elements in physical variation, *AA* 59:965–78.
OLLIER C.D. and D.K. HOLDSWORTH 1968 Survey of a megalithic structure in the Trobriand Islands, Papua, *APAO* 3:156–8.
OLLIER C.D., D.K. HOLDSWORTH and G. HEERS 1970 Megaliths at Wagaru, Vakula, Trobriand Islands, *APAO* 5:24–6.
OOSTERWAL G. 1961 *People of the Tor.* Assen: Van Gorcum.
ORCHISTON D.W. 1967 Preserved human heads of the New Zealand Maori, *JPS* 76:297–329.
—— 1971 Buller River artefacts in the Australian Museum, Sydney, *NZAAN* 14:179–92.
ORIOL T. 1948 Découvertes récentes de sites pétroglyphiques en Nouvelle-Calédonie, *EM* 3:29–50.
OSBORNE D. 1958 The Palau Islands, *Archaeology* 11: 162–71.
—— 1966 *The archaeology of the Palau Islands.* BPBMB 230.
PAINE R.W. 1929 Some rock paintings in Fiji, *Man* 29:149–51.
PALMER J.B. 1965 Excavations at Karobo, Fiji, *NZAAN* 8:26–34.
—— 1967a *Archaeological sites of Wakaya Island.* RFM vol. 1, 2.
—— 1967b Sigatoka research project: preliminary report, *NZAAN* 10:2–15.
—— 1968a Recent results from the Sigatoka archaeological program, *in* Yawata I. and Y.H. Sinoto (eds.) 1968: 19–28.
—— 1968b Caves and shelter sites at Vatukoula, Fiji, *NZAAN* 11:150–4.
—— 1969a Adzes with triangular cross-section from Fiji, *NZAAN* 12:199–203.
—— 1969b Fijian adzes with butt modification, *APAO* 4:97–102.
—— 1969c Ring ditch fortifications on windward Viti Levu, Fiji, *APAO* 4:181–97.
—— 1971a Fijian pottery technologies, *in* Green R.C. and M. Kelly (eds.) 1971:77–103.
—— 1971b Naga ceremonial sites of Viti Levu hill country, *RFM* vol. 1, 5:92–106.
—— 1972 Pottery in the South Pacific, *in* Barnard N. (ed.) 1972, vol. 3:693–722.
PARK G.N. 1970 Palaeoclimatic change in the last 1000 years, *Tuatara* 18:114–23.
PARKE A.L. 1971–2 Some prehistoric Fijian ceremonial enclosures on the island of Vanua Levu, Fiji, *APAO* 6:243–67; 7:56–78.
PARKER R.H. 1962 Aspect and phase on Skipper's Ridge and Kumarakaiamo, *NZAAN* 5:222–32.
—— 1968 Review of Sørensen P. and T. Hatting 1967, *JPS* 77:307–13.
PARMENTIER H. 1924 Dépots de jarres à Sa Huynh (Quang-ngai, Annam), *BEFEO* 24:325–43.
—— 1928 Vestiges mégalithiques à Xuan-Loc, *BEFEO* 28:479–85.
PARSONSON G.S. 1963 The settlement of Oceania, *in* Golson J. (ed.) 1963:11–63.
—— 1965 Artificial islands in Melanesia: the role of malaria in the settlement of the Southwest Pacific, *New Zealand Geographer* 22:1–21.
—— 1968 The problem of Melanesia, *Mankind* 6:571–84.

PATTE E. 1924 Le kjökkenmödding néolithique du Bau Tro à Tam-Toa près de Dong Hoi (Annam), *BEFEO* 24:521–61.
—— 1925 *Étude anthropologique du crâne néolithique de Minh Cam (Annam)*, BSGI 13, fascicle 5.
—— 1932 *Le kjökkenmödding néolithique de Da But et ses sépultures*. BSGI 19, fascicle 3.
—— 1936 L'Indochine préhistorique, *Revue Anthropologique* 46:277–314.
—— 1965 Les ossements du kjökkenmödding de Da-But (province de Thanh Hoa), *BSEI* 40:5–201.
PAWLEY A.K. 1966 Polynesian languages: a subgrouping based on shared innovations in morphology, *JPS* 75: 37–62.
—— 1967 The relationships of Polynesian Outlier languages, *JPS* 76:259–96.
—— 1970 Grammatical reconstruction and change in Polynesia and Fiji, in Wurm S.A. and D.C. Laycock (eds.), *Pacific linguistic studies in honour of Arthur Capell*, p. 301–67. Sydney: Reed.
—— 1972 On the internal relationships of Eastern Oceanic languages, in Green R.C. and M. Kelly (eds.) 1972:1–142.
—— 1974 Austronesian languages, *Encyclopaedia Britannica*, (15th edition), Macropaedia 2:484–94.
PAWLEY A.K. and K. GREEN 1971 Lexical evidence for the Proto-Polynesian homeland, *Te Reo* 14:1–35.
PAWLEY A.K. and R.C. GREEN 1975 Dating the dispersal of the Oceanic languages, *Oceanic Linguistics* 12(1):1–67.
PAWLEY A.K. and T. SAYABA 1971 Fijian dialect divisions: Eastern and Western Fijian, *JPS* 80:405–36.
PEACOCK B.A.V. 1959 A short description of Malayan prehistoric pottery, *AP* 3:121–56.
—— 1964a The Kodiang pottery cones, *FMJ* 9:4–18.
—— 1964b A preliminary note on the Dong-son bronze drums from Kampong Sungai Lang, *FMJ* 9:1–3.
—— 1964c Recent archaeological discoveries in Malaya 1962–3, *JMBRAS* 37, part 2:201–6.
—— 1965 The prehistoric archaeology of Malayan caves, *Malayan Nature Journal* 19:40–56.
—— 1971 Early cultural development in South-East Asia with special reference to the Malay Peninsula, *APAO* 6:107–123.
PEACOCK J. 1962 Pasemah megaliths: historical, functional and conceptual interpretations, *BIEAS* 13:53–61.
PEARSON R. 1962 Dong-Son and its origins, *BIEAS* 13:27–50.
—— 1967a Recent radiocarbon dates from Ryukyu sites and their chronological significance, *APAS* 1:19–24.
—— 1967b The prehistoric cultures of East Taiwan, *APAS* 1:25–32.
—— 1969 *Archaeology of the Ryukyu Islands*. University of Hawaii Press.
PEARSON R., P.V. KIRCH and M. PIETRUSEWSKY 1971 An early prehistoric site at Bellows Beach, Waimanalo, Oahu, Hawaiian Islands, *APAO* 6:204–34.
PEI TE HURINUI 1958 Maori genealogies, *JPS* 67:162–5.
PELLETT M. and A. SPOEHR 1961 Marianas archaeology, *JPS* 70:321–5.
PELLIOT P. 1903 Le Fou-nan, *BEFEO* 3:248–303.
PERRY W.J. 1918 *The megalithic culture of Indonesia*. Manchester University Press.
PETERSON R.M. 1969 Wurm II climate at Niah Cave, *SMJ* 17:67–79.
PETERSON W. 1974 Summary report of two archaeological sites from north-eastern Luzon, *APAO* 9:26–35.

PICKERSGILL B. and A.H. BUNTING 1969 Cultivated plants and the Kon-Tiki theory, *Nature* 222:225–7.
PIDDINGTON R.O. 1939 (see Williamson R.W. 1939).
—— 1950 A note on the validity and significance of Polynesian traditions, *JPS* 65:200–3.
PIETRUSEWSKY M. 1970 An osteological view of indigenous populations in Polynesia, in Green R.C. and M. Kelly (eds.) 1970:1–12.
—— 1971 Application of distance statistics to anthroposcopic data and a comparison of results with those obtained by using discrete traits of the skull, *APAO* 6:21–33.
PILBEAM D. 1966 Notes on *Ramapithecus*, the earliest known hominid, and *Dryopithecus*, *AJPA* 25:1–5.
—— 1970 *The evolution of man*. London: Thames and Hudson.
PIRIE P. 1971–2 The effects of treponematosis and gonorrhoea on the population of the Pacific Islands, *Human Biology in Oceania* 1:187 206.
POLACH H.A., J.J. STIPP, J. GOLSON and J.A. LOVERING 1968 ANU radiocarbon date list II, *Radiocarbon* 10:179–99.
PONCET Monseigneur 1948 Notes sur un ancien village fortifié et un tombe royale de l'Ile Wallis, *EM* 3:51–3.
POOL D.I. 1964 *The Maori population of New Zealand*. Unpublished Ph.D. thesis, Australian National University.
PORTER D. 1823 *A voyage in the South Seas 1812–14*. London: Phillips.
POULSEN J. 1967 *A contribution to the prehistory of the Tongan Islands*. Unpublished Ph.D. thesis, Australian National University.
—— 1968 Archaeological excavations on Tongatapu, in Yawata I. and Y.H. Sinoto (eds.) 1968:85–92.
—— 1970 Shell artefacts in Oceania: their distribution and significance, in Green R.C. and M. Kelly (eds.) 1970: 33–46.
—— 1972 Outlier prehistory: Bellona. A preliminary report on field work and radiocarbon dates, part 1: archaeology, *APAO* 7:184–205.
POWELL J.M. 1970 The history of agriculture in the New Guinea Highlands, *Search: Journal of the Australian and New Zealand Association for the Advancement of Science* 1:199–200.
PRAEHISTORICA ASIAE ORIENTALIS 1932 *Premier Congrès des Préhistoriens d'Extrême-Orient*. Hanoi.
PRETTY G.L. 1964 Stone objects excavated in New Guinea, *Man* 64:117.
—— 1965 Two stone pestles from western Papua and their relationships to prehistoric pestles and mortars from New Guinea, *Records South Australian Museum* 15:119–30.
PURSEGLOVE J.W. 1968 *Tropical crops: dicotyledons*. 2 volumes. London: Longmans.
RAFTER T.A., H.S. JANSEN, L. LOCKERBIE and M.M. TROTTER 1972 New Zealand radiocarbon reference standards, *Proceedings 8th International Conference on Radiocarbon Dating*, vol. 2: 625–75. Wellington: Royal Society of New Zealand.
RAPPAPORT R.A. 1963 Aspects of man's influence upon island ecosystems: alteration and control, in Fosberg F.R. (ed.) 1963:155–70.
—— 1967 *Pigs for the ancestors*. New Haven: Yale University Press.
RAVEN H.C. 1926 The stone images and vats of central Celebes, *Natural History* 26:272–82. New York.
READ K.E. 1954 Cultures of the Central Highlands, New Guinea, *SWJA* 10:1–43.
REED A.H. and A.W. (ed.) 1969 *Captain Cook in New Zealand*. Wellington: Reed.

REED W.A. 1914 *Negritos of Zambales*. Manila: Bureau of Printing.

REEVES R.D. and G.C. ARMITAGE 1973 Density measurements and chemical analysis in the identification of New Zealand archaeological obsidians, *NZJS* 16:561–72.

REINMAN F. 1967 *Fishing: an aspect of Oceanic economy*. Fieldiana: Anthropology vol. 56, no. 2.

—— 1968a Guam prehistory: a preliminary report, *in* Yawata I. and Y.H. Sinoto (eds.) 1968:41–50.

—— 1968b Radiocarbon dates from Guam, Marianas Islands, *JPS* 77:80–2.

—— 1970 Fishhook variability: implications for the history and distribution of fishing gear in Oceania, *in* Green R.C. and M. Kelly (eds.) 1970:47–60.

RICHARDS R. 1972 A population distribution map of the Moriois of the Chatham Islands, circa 1790, *JPS* 81:350–74.

RIEBE I. 1967 Anthropomorphic stone carvings on Unea Island, *JPS* 76:374–8.

RIESENBERG S. 1965 Table of voyages affecting Micronesian islands, *Oceania* 36:155–70.

RIESENBERG S., and A.H. GAYTON 1952 Caroline Island belt weaving, *SWJA* 8:342–75.

RIESENFELD A. 1947 Who are the Betel People? *Internationales Archiv für Ethnographie* 45:157–215.

—— 1950a *Megalithic culture of Melanesia*. Leiden: Brill.

—— 1950b Some probable bronze age influence in Melanesian culture, *Far Eastern Quarterly* 9:227–30.

—— 1952 Was there a Palaeolithic period in Melanesia? *A* 47:405–46.

—— 1954–5 Bronze age influence in the Pacific, *Internationales Archiv für Ethnographie* 47:215–55.

—— 1955 Prehistoric stone objects from New Britain, *Man* 55:58–9.

—— 1956 Shovel-shaped incisors and a few other dental features among the native peoples of the Pacific, *AJPA* 14:505–21.

RIGG T. and J.A. BRUCE 1923 The Maori gravel soil of Waimea West, Nelson, New Zealand, *JPS* 32:85–92.

RILEY C.R., J.C. KELLEY, C.W. PENNINGTON and R.L. RANDS 1971 *Man across the sea*. University of Texas Press.

RIVERS W.H.R. 1914 *The history of Melanesian society*. 2 volumes. Cambridge University Press.

ROBEQUAIN C. 1954 *Malaya, Indonesia, Borneo and the Philippines*. London: Longmans, Green.

ROBERTON J.B.W. 1956 Genealogies as a basis for Maori chronology, *JPS* 65:45–54.

—— 1957 The role of tribal tradition in New Zealand prehistory, *JPS* 66:249–63.

—— 1958 The significance of New Zealand tribal tradition, *JPS* 67:39–57.

—— 1959 Correspondence, *JPS* 68:153.

—— 1962 The evaluation of Maori tribal tradition as history, *JPS* 71:293–309.

—— 1966 The early tradition of the Whakatane district, *JPS* 75:189–209.

—— 1969 A culture nomenclature based on tradition, *JPS* 78:252–58.

ROBINSON J.T. 1968 The origin and adaptive radiation of the Australopithecines, *in* Kurth G. (ed.) 1968:150–75.

RÖDER J. 1939 Rock pictures and prehistoric times in Dutch New Guinea, *Man* 39:175–8.

—— 1959 *Felsbilder und Vorgeschichte des MacCluer-Golfes, West-Neuguinea*. Darmstadt: Wittich.

ROGERS G. 1974 Archaeological discoveries on Niuatoputapu Island, Tonga, *JPS* 83:308–48.

ROSENDAHL P. and D.E. YEN 1971 Fossil sweet potato remains from Hawaii, *JPS* 80:379–85.

ROSENSTIEL A. 1953–4 Historical perspective and the study of Melanesian culture, *Oceania* 24:172–89.

ROTH H.L. 1891 *Crozet's voyage to Tasmania, New Zealand, the Ladrone Islands and the Philippines*. London: Truslove and Shirley.

ROUTLEDGE C.S. 1919 *The mystery of Easter Island*. 2nd edition. London: Sifton Praed.

—— 1920 Survey of the village and carved rocks of Orongo, Easter Island, by the Mana Expedition, *JAI* 50:425–51.

SAHLINS M.D. 1955 Esoteric efflorescence on Easter Island, *AA* 57:1045–52.

—— 1958 *Social stratification in Polynesia*. Seattle: University of Washington Press.

—— 1962 *Moala*. Ann Arbor: University of Michigan Press.

—— 1963 Poor man, rich man, big man, chief: political types in Melanesia and Polynesia, *Comparative Studies in Society and History* 5:285–303.

—— 1968 *Tribesmen*. Prentice-Hall.

SANGVICHIEN S., P. SIRIGAROON, J.B. JORGENSEN and T. JACOB 1969 *Archaeological excavations in Thailand, volume 3, part 2: the prehistoric Thai skeletons*. Copenhagen: Munksgaard.

SAPIR E. 1916 *Time perspective in aboriginal American culture*. Ottawa: Geological Survey, Department of Mines, Memoir 90.

SARTONO S. 1972 Discovery of another hominid skull at Sangiran, central Java, *CA* 13:124–6.

SAUER C.O. 1952 *Agricultural origins and dispersals*. New York: American Geographical Society.

SAURIN E. 1940 Stations préhistoriques du Qui-Chau et de Thuong-Xuan (Nord Annam), *in* Chasen F.N. and M.W.F. Tweedies (eds.) 1940:71–90.

—— 1951 Études géologiques et préhistorique, *BSEI* 26:525–39.

—— 1951–2 Sur un moule de hache trouvé à Nhommalat (Laos), *BEFEO* 45: 71–4.

—— 1952 Station néolithique avec outillage en silex à Nhommalat, *BEFEO* 46:297–302.

—— 1963 Stations préhistoriques à Hang-Gon près Xuan-Loc (Sud Viêt-Nam), *BEFEO* 51:433–52.

—— 1966a Cambodge, Laos, Viêt-Nam, *AP* 9:32–5.

—— 1966b Le paléolithique du Cambodge oriental, *AP* 9:96–110.

—— 1966c Le mobilier préhistorique de l'abri-sous-roche de Tam Pong (Haut Laos), *BSEI* 41:106–118.

—— 1968a Nouvelles observations préhistoriques à l'est de Saigon, *BSEI* 43:1–17.

—— 1968b Station préhistorique à ciel ouvert dans le massif du Pah Xieng Tong (Laos), *APAS* 2:87–95.

—— 1969 Les recherches préhistoriques au Cambodge, Laos et Viêt-Nam (1877–1966), *AP* 12:27–41.

—— 1971 Le paléolithique des environs de Xuan-Loc (Sud Viêt-Nam), BSEI 46:49–70.

—— 1973 La champ de jarres de Hang Gon, près Xuan-Loc (Sud Viêt-Nam) *BEFEO* 60:329–58.

SCARLETT R.J. 1972 *Bones for the New Zealand archaeologist*. CMB 4.

SCHANFIELD M.S., E. GILES and H. GERSCHOWITZ 1975 Genetic studies in the Markham Valley, northeastern Papua New Guinea, *AJPA* 42:1–7.

SCHEANS D.J., K.L. HUTTERER and R.L. CHERRY 1970 A newly discovered blade tool industry from the central Philippines, *AP* 13:179–81.

SCHEFFLER H. 1963 A further note on the Mangaian *kopu*, *AA* 65:903–8.

—— 1965a *Choiseul Island social structure.* University of California Press.

—— 1965b Review of Guiart J., *Structure de la chefferie en Mélanésie du sud, AA* 67:1574–7.

SCHMITT R.C. 1971 New estimates of the pre-censal population of Hawaii, *JPS* 80:237–43.

SCHMITZ C.A. 1961 Das problem der Austro-Melaniden Kultur, *Acta Tropica* 18:97–141.

—— 1966 Steinerne Schalenmörser, Pistille und Vogel-figuren aus Zentral-Neuguinea, *Baessler Archiv* 14:1–60.

—— 1971 *Oceanic art: myth, man and image in the South Seas.* New York: Abrams.

SCHNITGER F.W. 1964 *Forgotten kingdoms in Sumatra.* Leiden: Brill (first published 1939).

SCHOFIELD W. 1940 A protohistoric site at Shek Pek, Lantau, Hong Kong, *in* Chasen F.N. and M.W.F. Tweedie (eds.) 1940:235–305.

SCHURIG M. 1930 *Die Südseetöpferei.* Leipzig:Drückerei der Werkgemeinschaft.

SCHUSTER C. 1946 Prehistoric stone objects from New Guinea and the Solomons, *Mankind* 3:247–51.

SCHUTZ A.J. 1972 *The languages of Fiji.* Oxford: Clarendon Press.

SCHWARTZ T. 1963 Systems of areal integration: some considerations based on the Admiralty Islands of northern Melanesia. *Anthropological Forum* 1:56–97.

SCOTT S.D. 1969 Reconnaissance and some detailed site plans of major monuments of Savai'i, *in* Green R.C. and J.M. Davidson (eds.) 1969: 69–90.

—— 1970 Excavations at the 'Sunde Site', N38/24, Motu-tapu Island, New Zealand, *RAIM* 7:13–30.

SEBOEK T.E. (ed.) 1971 *Linguistics in Oceania.* 2 volumes. Current trends in linguistics volume 8. The Hague: Mouton.

SEIDENFADEN E. 1944 Review of Colani M. 1944, *Journal of the Thailand Research Society* 35:195–208.

SELIGMANN C.G. 1910 *Melanesians of British New Guinea.* Cambridge University Press.

—— 1915 Note on an obsidian axe or adze blade from Papua, *Man* 15: 161–2.

SELIGMANN C.G. ond H.C. BECK 1938 Far Eastern glass: some western origins, *BMFEA* 10:1–64.

SELIGMANN C.G. and H.C. JOYCE 1967 On prehistoric objects in British New Guinea, *in* Thomas N.W. (ed.), *Anthropological essays presented to Edward Burnett Tylor*, p. 325–41. Oxford: Clarendon Press.

SERPENTI L.M. 1965 *Cultivators in the swamps.* Assen: Van Gorcum.

SHAPIRO H. 1943 Physical differentiation in Polynesia, *in* Coon C.S. and J. Andrews (eds.) 1943:3–8.

SHARP C.A. 1956a *Ancient voyagers in the Pacific.* Wellington: Polynesian Society.

—— 1956b The prehistory of the New Zealand Maoris: some possibilities, *JPS* 65:155–60.

—— 1958 Maori genealogies and canoe traditions, *JPS* 67:37–8.

—— 1959 Maori genealogies and the Fleet, *JPS* 68:12–13.

—— 1963 *Ancient voyagers in Polynesia.* Auckland: Paul's.

SHAW E. 1967 *A re-analysis of pottery from Navatu and Vuda, Fiji.* Unpublished M.A. thesis, University of Auckland.

—— 1973 The decorative system of Natunuku, Fiji, *in* Mead S.M. *et al.* 1973:44–55.

SHAWCROSS F.W. 1964a Stone flake industries in New Zealand, *JPS* 73:7–25.

—— 1964b An archaeological assemblage of Maori combs, *JPS* 73:382–98.

—— 1967 An investigation of prehistoric diet and economy on a coastal site at Galatea Bay, New Zealand, *PPS* 33:107–31.

—— 1968 The Ngaroto site, *NZAAN* 11:2–29.

—— 1969 Archaeology with a short, isolated time-scale: New Zealand, *WA* 1:184–99.

—— 1970a Ethnographic economics and the study of population in prehistoric New Zealand: viewed through archaeology, *Mankind* 7:279–91.

—— 1970b The Cambridge University collection of Maori artefacts, made on Captain Cook's first voyage, *JPS* 79:305–48.

—— 1972 Energy and ecology: thermodynamic models in archaeology, *in* Clarke D.L. (ed.) *Models in archaeology*, p. 577–622. London: Methuen.

—— 1975 Some studies of the influence of prehistoric human predation on marine animal population dynamics, *in* Castell R.W. and G.I. Quimby (eds.), *Maritime adaptations of the Pacific*, p. 39–66. The Hague: Mouton.

SHAWCROSS F.W. and J.E. TERRELL 1966 Paterangi and Oruarangi swamp *pas*, *JPS* 75:2–27.

SHAWCROSS K. 1967 Fern root and the total scheme of 18th century Maori food production in agricultural areas, *JPS* 76:330–52.

SHEPPARD H.M. 1962 Megaliths in Malacca and Negri Sembilan, *FMJ* 7:70–85.

SHIH Chang-Ju 1963 Six types of stone celts and the pre-historic culture of China, *Proceedings 9th Pacific Science Congress,* vol. 3:20–8. Bangkok.

SHIH H.P. *et al.* 1963 *Hsi-an Pan-p'o.* Peking: Wenwu Press.

SHORTLAND E. 1868 A short sketch of the Maori race, *TNZI* 1:329–38.

SHUTLER M.E. 1971 Pottery making in Espiritu Santo, *AP* 14:81–3.

SHUTLER M.E. and R. 1966 A preliminary report of archaeological excavations in the southern New Hebrides, *AP* 9:157–66.

SHUTLER R. 1970 A radiocarbon chronology for the New Hebrides, *Proceedings 8th International Congress of Anthropological and Ethnological Sciences*, vol 3:135–7. Tokyo and Kyoto.

SHUTLER R. and C.A. KESS 1969 A lithic industry from New Britain, Territory of New Guinea, with possible areal and chronological relationships, *BIEAS* 27:129–40.

SHUTLER R. and J.C. MARCK 1975 On the dispersal of the Austronesian horticulturalists, *APAO* 10: 81–113.

SIEVEKING G. de G. 1954 Excavations at Gua Cha, Kelantan 1954, Part I, *FMJ* 1 and 2:75–143.

—— 1956a The iron age collections of Malaya, *JMBRAS* 29, part 2: 79–138.

—— 1956b The distribution of stone bark-cloth beaters in prehistoric times, *JMBRAS* 29, part 3:78–85.

—— 1962 The prehistoric cemetery at Bukit Tengku Lembu, Perlis, *FMJ* 7:25–54.

SIMMONS D.R. 1964 Chatham Island archaeological survey, *NZAAN* 7:51–69.

—— 1966 The sources of Sir George Grey's *Nga Mahi a nga Tupuna, JPS* 75:177–88.

—— 1967 *Little Papanui and Otago prehistory.* ROMA 4.

—— 1968a Man, moa and the forest, *TRSNZ* 2:115–27.

—— 1968b *The Lake Hauroko burial and the evolution of Maori clothing.* ROMA 5.

—— 1969a A New Zealand myth, *New Zealand Journal of History* 3:14–31.

—— 1969b Economic change in New Zealand prehistory, *JPS* 78:3–34.
—— 1971 Regional traditions and culture history, *NZAAN* 14:92–7.
—— 1973a Suggested periods in South Island prehistory, *RAIM* 10:1–58.
—— 1973b 'Godstick' head from Katikati, *RAIM* 10:65–7.
—— 1973c Radiocarbon dates from the Dart Valley region, *NZAAN* 16:175.
SIMMONS R.T. 1956 Report on blood group genetic surveys in eastern Asia, Indonesia, Melanesia, Micronesia. Polynesia and Australia in the study of man, *A* 51:500–12,
—— 1962 Blood group genes in Polynesians and comparisons with other Pacific peoples, *Oceania* 32:198–210.
—— 1973 Blood group genetic patterns and heterogeneity in New Guinea, *Human Biology in Oceania* 2:63–71.
SIMMONS R.T. *et al.* 1961 Studies on Kuru V: a blood group genetical survey in the Kuru region and other parts of Papua-New Guinea, *American Journal of Tropical Medicine and Hygiene* 10:639–64.
—— 1964 Blood group gene frequencies in natives of Cape Gloucester, western New Britain, and the Gazelle Peninsula, eastern New Britain, *AJPA* 22:5–15.
—— 1964–5 Blood groups genetic data from the Maprik area of the Sepik District, New Guinea, *Oceania* 35:218–32.
—— 1965–6 Blood group genetic variations in natives of the Caroline Islands and in other parts of Melanesia, *Oceania* 36:132–70.
SIMMONS R.T. and D.C. GAJDUSEK 1966 A blood group genetic survey of children of Bellona and Rennell Islands (B.S.I.P.) and certain northern New Hebridean islands, *APAO* 1:155–74.
SIMMONS R.T. and D.C. GAJDUSEK and M.K. NICHOLSON 1967 Blood group genetic variation in inhabitants of western New Guinea, *AJPA* 27:277–304.
SIMONS E.L. and P.C. ETTEL 1970 Gigantopithecus, *Scientific American* 222:76–85.
SINNETT P. *et al.* 1970 Blood, serum protein and enzyme groups among Enga speaking people of the Western Highlands, New Guinea, with an estimate of genetic distance between clans, *APAO* 5:236–52.
SINOTO Y.H. 1966a A tentative prehistoric cultural sequence in the northern Marquesas Islands, French Polynesia, *JPS* 75:287–303.
—— 1966b Polynesia, 1963–4, *AP* 9:48–61.
—— 1967 Artefacts from excavated sites in the Hawaiian, Marquesas and Society Islands: a comparative study, *in* Highland G. *et al.* (eds.) 1967:341–62.
—— 1968a Position of the Marquesas Islands in east Polynesian prehistory, *in* Yawata I. and Y.H. Sinoto (eds.) 1968:111–8.
—— 1968b Sources of New Zealand's Eastern Polynesian Culture: evidence of the cloak-pin, *APAO* 3:30–2.
—— 1969 A pendant found in Huahine, Society Islands, *NZAAN* 12:92–3.
—— 1970 An archaeologically based assessment of the Marquesas Islands as a dispersal centre in East Polynesia, *in* Green R.C. and M. Kelly (eds.) 1970:105–32.
—— 1973 Polynesia, 1970–2, *Far Eastern Prehistory Association Newsletter* 2:25.
SINOTO Y.H. and P.C. McCOY 1975 Report on the preliminary excavation of an early habitation site on Huahine, Society Islands, *JSO* 31:143–86.
SKINNER H.D. 1916 Evolution in Maori art, *JRAI* 46:184–96, 309–21.
—— 1921 Culture areas in New Zealand, *JPS* 30:71–8.

—— 1923 *The Morioris of the Chatham Islands.* BPBMM 9, no. 1.
—— 1924 Origin and relationships of Maori material culture and decorative art, *JPS* 33:229–43.
—— 1966 *The Maori Hei Tiki.* 2nd edition. Dunedin: Otago Museum.
—— 1967 Cylindrical headdresses in the Pacific region, *in* Highland G. *et al.* (eds.) 1967:167–90.
—— 1968 The north Pacific origin of some elements of Polynesian material culture, *APAS* 2:104–112.
—— 1974 *Comparatively Speaking.* Dunedin: University of Otago Press.
SKINNER H.D. and W.C. BAUCKE 1928 *The Morioris.* BPBMM 9, no. 5.
SKJÖLSVOLD A. 1961 The stone statues and quarries of Rano Raraku, *in* Heyerdahl T. and E.N. Ferdon (eds.) 1961:339–80.
—— 1965 The ceremonial enclosure of Te Rae Rae with brief notes on additional *marae*, *in* Heyerdahl T. and E.N. Ferdon (eds.) 1965:97–108.
—— 1972 *Excavations of a habitation cave, Hanapete'o, Hiva Oa, Marquesas Islands.* PAR 16.
SLEEN H.G.W. van der 1958 Ancient glass beads with special reference to the beads of east and central Africa and the Indian Ocean, *JRAI* 88:203–16.
SMART C.D. 1965 An outline of Kabara prehistory, *NZAAN* 8:43–52.
SMART C.D., R.C. GREEN and J.C. YALDWIN 1962 A stratified dune site at Tairua, Coromandel, *Dominion Museum Records in Ethnology* 1:243–66. Wellington.
SMITH C.S. 1962 An outline of Easter Island archaeology, *AP* 6:239–44.
SMITH S.P. 1898–9 *Hawaiki: the whence of the Maori.* Printed in *JPS* volumes 7–8. 3rd edition published by Whitcombe and Tombs, Wellington, 1910.
—— 1915 *Lore of the Whare Wananga. Part II: Te Kauwaeraro.* Polynesian Society Memoir 4.
—— 1921 The Polynesians in Indonesia, *JPS* 30:19–27.
SNELL C.A.R.D. 1948 Human skulls from the urn-field of Melolo, East Sumba, *Acta Neerlandica Morphologicae Normalis et Pathologicae* 6, no. 3:1–20.
SOEJONO R.P. 1961 Preliminary notes on new finds of lower Palaeolothic implements from Indonesia, *AP* 5:217–32.
—— 1962 Indonesia, *AP* 6:34–43.
—— 1969 *On prehistoric burial methods in Indonesia.* Bulletin of the Archaeological Institute of the Republic of Indonesia 7.
SOLHEIM W.G. II 1952 Oceanian pottery manufacture, *JEAS* 1, no. 2:1–40.
—— 1959a Introduction to Sa-Huynh, *AP* 3:97–108.
—— 1959b Further notes on the Kalanay pottery complex in the Philippine Islands, *AP* 3:157–65.
—— 1959c Sa-Huynh related pottery in Southeast Asia, *AP* 3:177–88.
—— 1960 Jar burial in the Babuyan and Batanes Islands and in central Philippines, and its relation to jar burial elsewhere in the Far East, *Philippine Journal of Science* 89, part 1:115–48.
—— 1962 Review of Röder J. 1959. *JPS* 71:127–9.
—— 1964a Pottery and the Malayo-Polynesians, *CA* 5:360, 376–84, 400–3.
—— 1964b *The archaeology of central Philippines.* Manila: Bureau of Printing.
—— 1964c Further relationships of the Sa-Huynh-Kalanay pottery tradition, *AP* 8:196–211.

—— 1966 Southeast Asia, *AP* 9:27–31.

—— 1967a Recent archaeological discoveries in Thailand, *APAS* 1:47–54.

—— 1967b Southeast Asia and the West, *Science* 157: 896–902.

—— 1967c Two pottery traditions of late prehistoric times in Southeast Asia, *in* Drake F.S. (ed.), *Symposium on historical, archaeological and linguistic studies on southern China, Southeast Asia, and the Hong Kong region,* p. 15–22. Hong Kong University Press.

—— 1968a Early bronze in northeastern Thailand, *CA* 9:59;62.

—— 1968b The Batungan Cave sites, Masbate, Philippines, *APAS* 2:21–62.

—— 1968c Possible routes of migration into Melanesia as shown by statistical analysis of methods of pottery manufacture, *APAS* 2:139–66.

—— 1969 Reworking Southeast Asian prehistory, *Paideuma* 15:125–39.

—— 1970 Northern Thailand, Southeast Asia, and world prehistory, *AP* 13:145–57.

—— 1972 An earlier agricultural revolution, *Scientific American* 226:34–41.

—— 1973 Remarks on the early Neolithic in South China and Southeast Asia, *JHKAS* 4:25–9.

—— 1975 Reflections on the new data of Southeast Asian prehistory: Austronesian origins and consequences, *AP* 18, part 2: 146–60.

SOLHEIM W.G. II, B. HARRISSON and L. WALL 1959 Niah 'Three Colour Ware' and related prehistoric pottery from Borneo, *AP* 3:167–76.

SØRENSEN P. 1965 The shaman grave, *in Felicitation volume of Southeast Asian studies,* volume 2:303–18. Bangkok: Siam Society.

—— 1972 The Neolithic cultures of Thailand (and north Malaysia) and their Lungshanoid relationships, *in* Barnard N. (ed.) 1972, vol. 3:459–501.

—— 1973 Prehistoric iron implements from Thailand, *AP* 16:134–73.

SØRENSEN P. and T. HATTING 1967 *Archaeological excavations in Thailand, volume 2: Ban Kao.* Copenhagen: Munksgaard.

SPECHT J. 1966 Mortars and pestles in New Britain, *JPS* 75:378–82.

—— 1967 Archaeology in Melanesia: a suggested procedure, *Mankind* 6:493–9.

—— 1968 Preliminary report of excavations on Watom Island, *JPS* 77: 117–34.

—— 1969 *Prehistoric and modern pottery industries of Buka Island, T.P.N.G.* 2 volumes. Unpublished Ph.D. thesis, Australian National University.

—— 1972 Evidence for early trade in northern Melanesia, *Mankind* 8:310–12.

—— 1974a Of menak and men: trade and the distribution of resources on Buka Island, Papua New Guinea, *Ethnology* 13:225–37.

—— 1974b Stone pestles on Buka Island, Papua New Guinea, *Mankind* 9:324–8.

SPEISER F. 1941 Art styles in the Pacific (translation of 1941 original), *in* Fraser D. (ed.), *The many faces of primitive art,* p. 165–221, Prentice Hall, 1966.

SPIEGEL H. 1971 Soul boats in Melanesia: a study in diffusion, *APAO* 6:34–43.

SPENCER J.E. 1966 *Shifting cultivation in Southeast Asia,* University of California Press.

SPENCER J.E. and G.A. HALE 1961 Origin, nature and distribution of agricultural terracing, *Pacific Viewpoint* 2:1–40.

SPOEHR A. 1952 Time perspective in Micronesia and Polynesia, *SWJA* 8:457–65.

—— 1957 *Marianas prehistory.* Fieldiana: Anthropology vol. 48.

—— 1973 *Zamboanga and Sulu.* Ethnology Monographs 1, Department of Anthropology, University of Pittsburgh.

STAIR J.B. 1895 Early Samoan voyages and settlements, *JPS* 4:99–131.

STOKES J.F.G. 1930 An evaluation of early genealogies used for Polynesian history, *JPS* 39:1–42.

STRATHERN M. 1965 Axe types and quarries (Mt. Hagen), *JPS* 74:182–91.

—— 1969 Stone axes and flake tools: evaluations from New Guinea, *PPS* 35:311–29.

SUGGS R.C. 1960a *The island civilisations of Polynesia.* New York: Mentor.

—— 1960b Historical traditions and archaeology in Polynesia, *AA* 62:764–73.

—— 1961a *The archaeology of Nuku Hiva, Marquesas Islands, French Polynesia.* APAMNH 49, part 1.

—— 1961b The derivation of Marquesan culture, *JRAI* 91:1–10.

SUKENDAR H. 1974 Catatan penggalian perbengkelan neolitik dekat Sembungan (Punung), dan berbagai temuannya, *Berita Prasejarah 1:* 27–40. Indonesian National Research Centre for Archaeology.

SULLIVAN A. 1974 Scoria mounds at Wiri, *NZAAN* 17:128–43.

SULLIVAN R. 1924 Race types in Polynesia, *AA* 26:22–6.

SUMMERS C. 1964 *Hawaiian archaeology: fishponds.* BPBMSP 52.

SUTAYASA I.M. 1972 Notes on the Buni pottery complex, northeast Java, *Mankind* 8:182–4.

—— 1973 The study of prehistoric pottery in Indonesia, *Nusantara* 4:67–82.

—— 1974 Potting the simple way, *Hemisphere* 19, part 4:34–7. Canberra.

SUZUKI M. and T. SAKAI 1964 Shovel-shaped incisors in Polynesia, *AJPA* 22:65–76.

SWADESH M. 1964a Linguistics as an instrument of prehistory, *in* Hymes D. (ed.), *Language in culture and society,* p. 575–84. New York: Harper and Row.

—— 1964b Diffusional cumulation and archaic residue as historical explanation, *in* Hymes D. (ed.), *Language in culture and society,* p. 624–37. New York: Harper and Row.

SWINDLER D.R. 1962 *A racial study of the West Nakanai.* Philadelphia: University Museum.

TAINTER J. 1973 The social correlates of mortuary patterning at Kaloko, north Kona, Hawaii, *APAO* 8:1–11.

TAKAMIYA H. 1967 Archaeological work in the Ryukyu Islands 1961–5, *APAS* 1:11–18.

TATTERSALL I. 1970 *Man's ancestors.* London: John Murray.

TAUBER H. 1973 Copenhagen radiocarbon dates X, *Radiocarbon* 15:86–112.

TAYLOR N.H. 1958 Soil science and New Zealand prehistory, *New Zealand Science Review* 16:71–9.

TAYLOR R. 1872 On New Zealand lake pas, *TNZI* 5:101–2.

TEETER K.V. 1963 Lexicostatistics and genetic relationships, *Language* 39: 638–48.

TERRELL J. 1967 Galatea Bay: the excavation of a beach-stream midden site on Ponui Island in the Hauraki Gulf, New Zealand, *TRSNZ* 2, no. 3:31–70.

TEVIOTDALE D. and H.D. SKINNER 1947 Oruarangi pa, *JPS* 56:340–56.

THOMAS D. and A. HEALEY 1962 Some Philippine language subgroupings: a lexicostatistical study, *Anthropological Linguistics* 4, no. 9:22–33.

THOMAS W.L. 1963 The variety of physical environments among Pacific Islands, *in* Fosberg F.R. (ed.) 1963:7–38.

—— 1967 The Pacific basin: an introduction, *in* Friis H.R. (ed.), *The Pacific basin: a history of its geographical exploration*, p.1–17. New York: American Geographical Society.

THOMPSON L. 1932 *The archaeology of the Marianas Islands*, BPBMB 100.

—— 1940 The function of latte in the Marianas, *JPS* 49:447–65.

THOMSON J.T. 1871 Ethnographical considerations on the whence of the Maori, *TNZI* 4:23–51.

THOMSON W.J. 1889 Te Pito te Henua, or Easter Island, *U.S. National Museum Annual Report for 1889*: 447–552.

THORNE A.G. 1971a The racial affinities and origins of the Australian Aborigines, *in* Mulvaney D.J. and J. Golson (eds.) 1971:316–25.

—— 1971b Mungo and Kow Swamp: morphological variation in Pleistocene Australians, *Mankind* 8:85–9.

THORNE A.G. and P.G. MACUMBER 1972 Discoveries of late Pleistocene man at Kow Swamp, Australia, *Nature* 238:216–9.

THURNWALD R. 1934–5. Stone monuments in Buin, *Oceania* 5:214–7.

TIPPETT A.R. 1968 *Fijian material culture*. BPBMB 232.

TITCOMB M. 1969 *Dog and man in the ancient Pacific*. BPBMSP 59.

TJIA H.D. 1973 Holocene eustatic sea levels and glacio-eustatic rebound, *Abstracts of the 9th Congress of the International Union for Quaternary Research*, p. 368. Christchurch.

TOBIAS P.V. and G.H.R. von KOENIGSWALD 1964 A comparison between the Olduvai hominines and those of Java, and some implications for hominid phylogeny, *Nature* 204:515–8.

TOLSTOY P. 1972 Diffusion: as explanation and as event, *in* Barnard N. (ed.) 1972, vol. 3:823–42.

TRAN van TOT 1969 Introduction à l'art ancien du Viêt-Nam, *BSEI* 44:5–104.

TRAVERS W.T.L. 1871 Notes upon the historical value of the 'Traditions of the New Zealanders', as collected by Sir George Grey, K.C.B., late Governor-in-Chief of New Zealand, *TNZI* 4:51–62.

TREISTMAN J.M. 1968a China at 1000 B.C.: a cultural mosaic, *Science* 161:853–6.

—— 1968b 'Ch'ü-chia-ling' and the early cultures of the Hanshui Valley, China, *AP* 11:69–92.

—— 1972 *The prehistory of China*. New York: Natural History Press.

TREVOR J.C. and D.R. BROTHWELL 1962 The human remains of Mesolithic and Neolithic date from Gua Cha, Kelantan, *FMJ* 7:6–22.

TROTTER M.M. 1971 Prehistoric rock shelter art in New Zealand, *APAO* 6:235–42.

—— 1972a Investigation of a Maori cave burial on Mary Island, Lake Hauroko, *RCM* 9:113–28.

—— 1972b A moa-hunter site near the mouth of the Rakaia River, South Island, *RCM* 9:129–50.

—— (ed.) 1974 *Prehistory of the southern Cook Islands*. CMB 6.

TROTTER M.M. and B. McCULLOCH 1971 *Prehistoric rock art of New Zealand*. Wellington: Reed.

TRYON D.T. 1971 Linguistic evidence and Aboriginal origins, *in* Mulvaney D.J. and J. Golson (eds.) 1971: 344–55.

TSUKADA M. 1966 Late Pleistocene vegetation and climate in Taiwan (Formosa), *Proceedings of the National Academy of Science* 55:543–8. Washington.

TUGGLE H.D. and P.B. GRIFFIN (eds.) 1973 *Lapakahi, Hawaii: archaeological studies*. APAS 5.

TUGGLE H.D. and K.L. HUTTERER (eds.) 1972 *Archaeology of the Sohoton area, southwestern Samar, Philippines*. Leyte-Samar Studies vol. 6, part 2.

TUREKIAN K.T. (ed.) 1971 *The late Cenozoic glacial ages*. New Haven: Yale University Press.

TURNER G. 1884 *Samoa*. London: Macmillan.

TWEEDIE M.W.F. 1953 *The stone age in Malaya*. JMBRAS 26, part 2 (no. 162).

—— 1970 *Prehistoric Malaya*. 3rd edition. Singapore: Eastern Universities Press.

UBEROI S. 1971 *Politics of the Kula Ring*. 2nd edition. Manchester University Press.

UPDIKE J. 1965 Fanning Island, *in* Updike J., *Pigeon feathers and other stories*, p. 167–9. Penguin.

URBAN M. 1961 *Die Haustiere der Polynesier*. Göttingen: Häntzschel.

USINGER R.L. 1963 Animal distribution patterns in the tropical Pacific, *in* Gressitt J.L. (ed.), *Pacific basin biogeography*, p. 255–62. Honolulu: Bishop Museum.

VANDERMEERSCH L. 1956 Bronze kettledrums of South-east Asia, *Journal of the Oriental Society* 3:291–8.

VANDERWAL R. 1973 *Prehistoric studies in central coastal Papua*. Unpublished Ph.D. thesis, Australian National University.

VAYDA A.P. 1956 Maori conquests in relation to the New Zealand environment, *JPS* 65:204–11.

—— 1959 Polynesian cultural distributions in new perspective, *AA* 61:817–28.

—— 1960 *Maori warfare*. Polynesian Society Maori Monograph 2.

—— (ed.) 1968 *Peoples and cultures of the Pacific*. New York: American Museum of Natural History.

VAYDA A.P., A. LEEDS and D.B. SMITH 1961 The place of pigs in Melanesian subsistence, *in* Garfield V.E. (ed.), *Proceedings of the 1961 annual spring meeting of the American Ethnological Society*, p. 69–77. Seattle: University of Washington Press.

VAYDA A.P. and R. A. RAPPAPORT 1963 Island cultures, *in* Fosberg F.R. (ed.) 1963:133–42.

VERHOEVEN T. 1953 Ein Mikrolithenkultur in Mittel- und West-Flores, *A* 48:597–612.

—— 1959 Der Klingenkultur der Insel Timor, *A* 54:970–2.

VERIN P. 1969 *L'ancienne civilisation de Rurutu*. Paris: Office des Recherches Scientifiques et Techniques Outre-Mer, Mémoir 33.

VERSTAPPEN H. Th. 1975 On palaeo climates and landform development in Malesia, *in* Bartstra G. and W.A. Casparie (eds.), *Modern Quaternary research in Southeast Asia*, p. 3–36. Rotterdam: Balkema.

VILLARET B. 1963 Découvertes archéologiques aux îles Wallis, *JSO* 19:205–6.

VOITOV V.I. and D.D. TUMARKIN 1967 Navigational conditions of sea routes to Polynesia, *APAS* 1:89–100.

WADDELL E. 1972 *The mound builders*. Seattle: University of Washington Press.

WALES H.G.Q. 1957 *Prehistory and religion in South-east Asia*. London: Bernard Quaritch.

WALKER D. and A. SIEVEKING 1962 The Palaeolithic industry of Kota Tampan, Perak, Malaya, *PPS* 28:103–39.

WALL L. 1962 Earthenwares: prehistoric pottery common to Malaya and Borneo, *SMJ* 10:417–27.

WALLACE B.J. 1971 *Village life in insular South East Asia*. Boston: Little, Brown.

WALLACE J.H. 1886 *Manual of New Zealand history*. Wellington: J.H. Wallace.

WALLS J.Y. 1974 Argillite quarries of the Nelson mineral belt, *NZAAN* 17:37–43.

WALSH D.S. and B.G. BIGGS 1966 *Proto-Polynesian word list I*. Auckland: Linguistic Society of New Zealand.

WARD G.K. 1973 Obsidian source localities in the North Island of New Zealand, *NZAAN* 16:85–103.

—— 1974 A paradigm for sourcing New Zealand obsidians, *JRSNZ* 4:47–62.

WARD G.K. and I.E. SMITH 1974 Characterisation of chert sources as an aid to the identification of patterns of trade, southeast Solomon Islands: a preliminary investigation, *Mankind* 9:281–6.

WATSON J.B. 1964 A previously unreported root crop from the New Guinea Highlands, *Ethnology* 3:1–5.

—— 1965a Hunting to horticulture in the New Guinea Highlands, *Ethnology* 4:295–309.

—— 1965b The significance of a recent ecological change in the Central Highlands of New Guinea, *JPS* 74:438–50.

WATSON W. 1961 *China*. London: Thames and Hudson.

—— 1965 *Early civilisation in China*. London: Thames and Hudson.

—— 1968 The Thai-British archaeological expedition, *Antiquity* 42:302–6.

—— 1970 Dongson and the kingdom of Tien, *in Readings in Asian topics*. p. 45–71. Copenhagen: Scandinavian Institute of Asian Studies Monograph 1.

—— 1971 *Cultural frontiers in ancient East Asia*. Edinburgh University Press.

—— 1972 Traditions of material culture in the territory of Ch'u, *in* Barnard N. (ed.) 1972, vol. 1:53–76.

WATSON W. and H.H.E. LOOFS 1967 The Thai-British archaeological expedition: a preliminary report on the work of the first season 1965–6, *Journal of the Siam Society* 55:237–72.

WATTERS R.F. 1960 The nature of shifting cultivation, *Pacific Viewpoint* 1:59–99.

WEIDENREICH F. 1946 *Apes, giants and man*. University of Chicago Press.

—— 1957 *Morphology of Solo Man*. APAMNH 43, part 3.

WELLMAN H.W. 1962 Maori occupation layers at D'Urville Island, New Zealand, *New Zealand Journal of Geology and Geophysics* 5:55–73.

WHEATLEY P. 1964 *Impressions of the Malay Peninsula in ancient times*. Singapore: Eastern Universities Press.

—— 1965 Agricultural terracing, *Pacific Viewpoint* 6:123–44.

WHEELER T.S. and P. MADDIN 1976 The techniques of the early Thai metalsmiths, *Expedition* 18(4):38–47.

WHITE C. 1971 Man and environment in northeast Arnhem Land, *in* Mulvaney D.J. and J. Golson (eds.) 1971: 141–57.

WHITE J. 1885 *Maori customs and superstitions*. Published as second part of Gudgeon J.W., *The history and doings of the Maoris*. Auckland: Evening Star.

WHITE J.P. 1967 Ethno-archaeology in New Guinea: two examples, *Mankind* 6:409–14.

—— 1969 Typologies for some prehistoric flaked stone artefacts of the Australian New Guinea Highlands, *APAO* 4:18–46.

—— 1971 New Guinea: the first phase in Oceanic settlement, *in* Green R.C. and M. Kelly (eds.) 1971:45–52.

—— 1972a *Ol Tumbuna*. Terra Australis 2, Department of Prehistory, Research School of Pacific Studies, Australian National University, Canberra.

—— 1972 Carbon dates for New Ireland, *Mankind* 8:309–10.

WHITE J.P., K.A.W. CROOK and B.P. BUXTON 1970 Kosipe: a late Pleistocene site in the Papuan Highlands, *PPS* 36:152–70.

WHITE J.P. and J. SPECHT 1971 Prehistoric pottery from Ambitle Island, Bismarck Archipelago, *AP* 14:88–94.

WHYTE R.O. 1972 The Gramineae, wild and cultivated, of monsoonal equatorial Asia. I: Southeast Asia, *AP* 15:127–51.

WILKES O.R. and R.J. SCARLETT 1967 Excavation of a moa-hunter site at the mouth of the Heaphy River, *RCM* 8:181–212.

WILLEMS W.J.A. 1940 Preliminary report on the excavation of an urn-burial ground at Sa'bang, central Celebes, *in* Chasen F.N. and M.W.F. Tweedie (eds.) 1940: 207–8.

WILLEY G. 1971 *An introduction to American archaeology. Volume 2: South America*. Prentice Hall.

WILLIAMS F.E. 1931 Papuan petroglyphs, *JRAI* 61: 121–56.

WILLIAMS H.W. 1937 The Maruiwi myth, *JPS* 46: 105–22.

WILLIAMS J. 1838 *A narrative of missionary enterprises in the South Sea Islands*. London: John Snow.

WILLIAMSON R.W. 1924 *The social and political systems of central Polynesia*. 3 volumes. Cambridge University Press.

—— 1939 *Essays in Polynesian ethnology*. Edited by R.O. Piddington. Cambridge University Press.

WILSON D.M. 1921 Ancient drains, Kaitaia swamp, *JPS* 30:185–8.

WILSON J. 1799 *A missionary voyage to the southern Pacific Ocean 1796–1798*. Undated reprint published by Praeger, New York.

WILSON J.A. 1866 *The story of Te Waharoa*. Reprinted by Whitcombe and Tombs, Christchurch, 1907.

—— 1894 *Sketches on ancient Maori life and history*. Auckland: Champtaloup and Cooper.

WINGERT P.S. 1965 *Primitive art*. New York: Meridian Books.

WINIATA M. 1956 Leadership in pre-European Maori society, *JPS* 65:212–31.

WINSTEDT R.O. 1941 Slab-graves and iron implements, *JMBRAS* 19:93–8.

WINTERS N.J. 1974 An application of dental anthropological analysis to the human dentition of two Early Metal Age sites, Palawan, Philippines, *AP* 17:28–35.

WIRZ P. 1951 Über die alten Steinmörser und andere Steingeräte des nordöstlichen Zentral-Neuguinea und die heilige Steinschale der Minembi, *Südseestudien*, p. 289–353. Basel: Museum für Volkerunde.

WOLTERS O.W. 1967 *Early Indonesian commerce; a study of the origins of Srivijaya*. Ithaca: Cornell University Press.

WOO Ju-Kang 1958 Tzeyang Palaeolithic man: earliest representative of modern man in China, *AJPA* 16:459–72.

—— 1966 The skull of Lantian man, *CA* 7:83–6.

WORMAN E. 1949 Somrong Sen and the reconstruction of prehistory in Indochina, *SWJA* 5:318–29.

WRIGHT A.C.S. 1962 Some terrace systems of the western hemisphere and Pacific islands, *Pacific Viewpoint* 3:97–100.

WRIGHT R.V.S. 1972 Imitative learning of a flaked stone technology – the case of an orangutan, *Mankind* 8:296–306.

WÜRM S.A. 1964 Australian New Guinea Highland languages and the distribution of their typological features, *AA* 66, no. 4, part 2:79–97.

—— 1967 Linguistics and the prehistory of the south western Pacific, *Journal of Pacific History* 2:25–38.

—— 1971 The Papuan linguistic situation, *in* Seboek T. (ed.) 1971: 541–657.

—— 1972a Linguistic research in Australia, New Guinea, and Oceania, *Linguistics* 87:87–107.

—— 1972b The classification of Papuan languages, and its problems, *Linguistic Communications* 6:118–78. Monash University, Melbourne.

WÜRM S.A. and D.C. LAYCOCK 1961 The question of language and dialect in New Guinea, *Oceania* 32:128–43.

YATE W. 1835 *An account of New Zealand*. London: Seeley and Burnside.

YAWATA I. and Y.H. SINOTO (eds.) 1968 *Prehistoric culture in Oceania*. Honolulu: Bishop Museum Press.

YEN D.E. 1960 The sweet potato in the Pacific: the propagation of the plant in relation to its distribution, *JPS* 69:368–75.

—— 1961 The adaptation of the *kumara* by the New Zealand Maori, *JPS* 70:338–48.

—— 1971 The development of agriculture in Oceania, *in* Green R.C. and M. Kelly (eds.) 1971:1–12.

—— 1973 The origins of Oceanic agriculture, *APAO* 8: 68–85.

—— 1974 *The sweet potato and Oceania*. BPBMB 236.

ZAMORA M.D. (ed.) 1967 *Studies in Philippine anthropology*. Quezon City: Phoenix Press.

ZIMMERMAN E.C. 1963 Nature of the land biota, *in* Fosberg F.R. (ed.) 1963:57–64.

Sources of Illustrations

Figures are reproduced by courtesy of the following:

2.1, photos by Geoffrey Benjamin; 2.2, photo by Ian Hughes; 2.7, Imperial University of Tokyo; 2.10, 2.13, courtesy of G. H. R. von Koenigswald and the Wenner-Gren Foundation, photos by Dragi Markovic; 2.11, Professor S. Sartono; 2.12, photos by Dragi Markovic; 2.14, Sarawak Museum; 2.15, Dr. W. Junk.

3.3, National Museum, Manila; 3.4, D. J. Mulvaney, C. Schrire, Thames and Hudson; 3.5, Trustees of Columbia University; 3.6, P. I. Boriskovsky; 3.7, photo by Dragi Markovic; 3.10, Ian Glover and the Department of Prehistory, A.N.U.; 3.11, Martinus Nijhoff.

4.2, William R. Geddes; 4.3, Anthony Forge; 4.10, Methuen.

5.5, Dr. W. Junk.

6.1, map drawn in the Department of Geography, A.N.U.; 6.2, from Prints and Proofs to Cook's First Voyage, courtesy National Library of Australia; 6.5, 6.9, photos by Nicholas Peterson; 6.6, photo by Ian Hughes.

7.2, 7.4, 7.5, 7.6, Yale University Press; 7.3, University of Hawaii Press; 7.8, 7.10, Donn Bayard; 7.9, 7.11, University of Hawaii Press; 7.12, 7.13, Munksgaard; 7.14, G. de G. Sieveking; 7.17, drawn by Wilfred Shawcross; 7.18, P. I. Boriskovsky; 7.19, Ricci Publications; 7.21, photo by Helmut Loofs; 7.22, H. A. Bernatzik; 7.23, 7.25, École Française d'Extrême-Orient; 7.26, A. and J. Picard; 7.31, 7.32, 7.33, 7.34, École Française d'Extrême-Orient.

8.2, Yale University press; 8.3, 8.4, 8.5, 8.6, 8.7, National Museum, Manila; 8.8, Wilhelm C. Solheim, II; 8.9, University of Hawaii Press; 8.10, photo by Dragi Markovic; 8.11, Sarawak Museum; 8.12, Ian Glover and the Department of Prehistory, A.N.U., 8.13, 8.14, 8.15, 8.16, 8.17, Martinus Nijhoff; 8.18, Museum of Far Eastern Antiquities, Stockholm; 8.19, Martinus Nijhoff, Helmut Loofs; 8.20, 8.23, E. J. Brill; 8.21, 8.22, W. J. Thieme; 8.24, Martinus Nijhoff (top left and right), American Museum of Natural History (middle left), Walter Kaudern (bottom left), E. J. Brill (bottom right); 8.25, photo by Visual Aids Unit, A.N.U.

9.2 9.3, Peter White and the Department of Prehistory, A.N.U.; 9.4, Trustees of the Australian Museum, photo by Gregory Millen; 9.5, Jack Golson; 9.6, 9.7, Trustees of the Australian Museum, photo by C. V. Turner; 9.8, Graeme Pretty and the South Australian Museum; 9.9, Field Museum of Natural History, Chicago; 9.10, Trustees of Columbia University; 9.12, Dr. W. Junk; 9.13, Wallace Ambrose (a–e), Jens Poulson and the Department of Prehistory, A.N.U. (f–j), Musée de l'Homme, Paris, collection O'Reilly (k–l); 9.14, Wallace Ambrose and Trustees of the Australian Museum; 9.15, Roger Green; 9.16, Fiji Museum; 9.17, Anthropological Society of New South Wales; 9.18, Jens Poulsen and the Department of Prehistory, A.N.U.; 9.19, 9.20, Ron Vanderwal and the Department of Prehistory, A.N.U.; 9.21, Trustees of the Australian Museum, photo by C. V.

Turner; 9.23, Bishop Museum Press (top), Jim Specht and the Department of Prehistory, A.N.U. (bottom); 9.24, Bishop Museum Press; 9.25, Fiji Museum; 9.26, Haagsche Drukkerij en Uitgeversmij-N.V. – Den Haag; 9.27, Brian Egloff and the Department of Prehistory, A.N.U.; 9.28, University of Hawaii Press; 9.29, Trustees of the Australian Museum, photo by Gregory Millen; 9.30, Ron Vanderwal (left), Jim Specht (right), and the Department of Prehistory, A.N.U.; 9.31, 9.32, Société des Océanistes; 9.33, Brian Egloff.

10.1, Field Museum of Natural History, Chicago; 10.3, Bishop Museum Press; 10.4, 10.5, 10.6, Douglas Osborne; 10.7, Walter de Gruyter & Co.; 10.8, 10.9, 10.10, Dr. Clifford Evans, Dr. Betty J. Meggers, Dr. Saul H. Riesenberg and the Department of Anthropology, National Museum of Natural History, Smithsonian Institution; 10.12, Methuen; 10.13, University of Hawaii Press; 10.14, Auckland Institute and Museum.

11.1, from L. Choris, *Voyage Pittoresque autour du Monde*, 1822; 11.2, from T. Williams and J. Calvert, *Fiji and the Fijians*, 1858; 11.3, National Library of Australia; 11.4, H. Kawainui Kane; 11.10, National Library of Australia; 11.11, 11.12, 11.13, Auckland Institute and Museum; 11.15, Bishop Museum Press; 11.16, 11.17, Polynesian Society; 11.18, 11.19, Yoshihiko Sinoto; 11.20, P. V. Kirch, and the Polynesian Society; 11.21, University of Hawaii Press.

12.3, Bishop Museum Press; 12.11, National Library of Australia; 12.12, Bishop Museum Press; 12.14, British Museum; 12.15, 12.16, Thor Heyerdahl; 12.17, British Museum; 12.18, University of Sydney; 12.21, drawing by Keith Mitchell; 12.22, Bishop Museum Press; 12.23, National Library of Australia; 12.24, U.S. Department of the Interior, National Park Service; 12.25, Edmund Ladd, and the Bishop Museum Press; 12.27, National Library of Australia; 12.28, 12.33, 12.35, photos by Grant McCall; 12.32, 12.34, photos by William Mulloy; 12.36, photo by Dragi Markovic; 12.38, Musee SS.CC., Roma (original), Canterbury Museum, Christchurch (cast), photo by Frank McGregor.

13.3, Auckland Institute and Museum; 13.4, Michael Trotter, Canterbury Museum, Christchurch; 13.5, Government Printer, Wellington; 13.6, Dr. W. Junk; 13.7, 13.8, photos by Dragi Markovic; 13.9, 13.10, 13.17. Michael Trotter, Beverley McCulloch, A. H. and A. W. Reed; 13.11, Methuen; 13.13, Thomas Avery and Sons, New Plymouth; 13.14, 13.15, 13.20, National Library of Australia; 13.16, Taranaki Museum; 13.19, Whites Aviation; 13.22, Wallace Ambrose; 13.23, 13.25, Prehistoric Society; 13.26, redrawn by Wilfred Shawcross.

The following maps and drawings were prepared by Joan Goodrum: 2.8, 2.9, 3.1, 3.2, 3.9, 3.12, 4.1, 4.4, 4.5, 4.8, 4.9, 4.11, 5.1, 5.2, 5.3, 5.4, 5.6, 5.7, 6.3, 7.1, 7.7, 7.15, 7.16, 7.27, 7.28, 7.35, 8.1, 9.1, 10.11, 11.5, 11.6, 11.14, 12.1, 12.7, 12.26, 13.1, 13.2, 13.12, 13.21, 13.24.

Index

References in **bold type** are to illustrations

A'a, 345
Abelam, **4.6**, 145
Acheulean industry, 56, 58
Adkin, G.L., 411
Admiralty Islands, 103, 269, 277, 286
adzes, shell, 207-8, 217, 248-50, 253, 255, 260, 264, 283, 285, 287, 290, 292, 293, **10.14**, 318
adzes, stone (see also Duff, R.), 60, 63-9, 76, 78, 153
  in Melanesia, 235, 248-56 pass., 260, 264, 266-7
  in Micronesia, 283, 287, 292, 295
  in Polynesia, 281, 309, 315, 318-26, 329-31, 352, 365, 373, 388-90, 392, 393, 398, 400, 403-4, 416
  in Southeast Asian Metal Age, 182, 194, 197, 225
  in Southeast Asian Neolithic, 155-70 pass., 170-80, 207
  terminology, 170-80
  trade, 103-4, 393
Africa, 27, 32, 34, 38, 40, 50, 53, 139, 309
ahu, 329-30, 333, 340, 343-6, 351, 353, 357, 364-77
ahupua'a, 360
Aibura, 235, 237
Ailuropoda, 55
Ainu, 32-33, 262
Aitape, 51, 137, 249
Aitutaki, **2.6**, 326, 346-52
Akerblom, K., 302
Allen, B., 147
Allen, J., 270
Alofi, 317
Alor, 119-120
Aluptaciel, 286
ambilineal descent, 84, 91, 99, 108, 112, 113
Ambitle Island, **9.13**, 247, 249, 277
Ambrose, W., 410, 414
America, American Indians, 33-5, 49, 128, 136-41, 268, 304, 306, 309-11, 336, 362-3, 373-6
Ami, 92
Amphlett Islands, 102, 266
Amphoe Mae Tha, 81
Anaa, 337
Andaman Islands, Andamanese, 26-7, 50, 78, 82, 88, 89, 121, 135, 142, 297
Andesite line, 20, 315
Aneityum, 147, 264
Anell, B., 281-2, 321
animal domestication, 135, 149-51, 162, 217-8, 247, 307, 381
Aniwa, 129, 134
Anjar, 221, 228
Anoa, 74
Anson, G., 284
Anuta, 129, 134, 250, 252, 317

Bali, 20, 49, 54, 81, 89, 124, 148, 228
Baliem Valley, 144
Balof Cave, 244
Banana, 113, 122, 127, **6.3**, 136-48 pass., 294, 311, 360, 362, 373, 381
Ban Ang, 195-8, **7.35**, 201
Banaue, **4.3**
Ban Chiang, 141, 149, 161-66, **7.11**, 200
Ban Dan Chumpol, 81
Bandung, 78, 221
Bangkinang, 225
Ban Kao Culture, 69, 166-70, **7.12**, **7.13**, 173
Banks Islands, 96, 98, 100, 104, 125-6, 130, 292, 294
Banks Peninsula, 148
Banks, Sir Joseph, 298, 306, 338-40, 363, 382, 403, 406, 409, 414-5
Bark-cloth, 92, 127, 137, 139, 168, 173, **7.16**, 175, 190, 200, 220, 309, 313, 357, 381
Barley, 136
Barrau, J., 140
Barringtonia, 139
Barthel, T., 376-7
Bataks, 30, 228
Batangas Province, 59, 207
Batari, 235
Batugajah, 227
Batungan Mountain, 213-15, 220, 247, 282
Bau, Fiji, 265
Bau-Malay ceramic complex, 214, 217, 231
Bau-Tro, 179, 201
Bayard, D., 129, 130, 164-5
Bay of Islands, 381, 383, 395, 406, **13.21**, 409, 411, 415
Bay of Plenty, 384, 392, 400, 404, 410, 415
Beads, carnelian, **7.29**, 193, 198, 211, 216, 220, 221, 225, 228, 230-2, **8.25**
Beads, glass, 60, 106, 187, 190, 193, 198, 207, 211, 214, 216, 220, 225, 228, 230, 286
Beads, shell, 162-3, 168, 175-6, 179, 187, 207, 209, 211, 217, 221, 230, **9.18**, 270-1, 283, 285, 290, **10.11**, 293
Behoa, 228, **8.24**
Bellona, 129, 130, 134, 249-50
Bellows Beach, 324-5
Bender, B., 130
Ben-Do, 194
Benedict, P., 85, 88, 123, 165
betel nut (*Areca catechu*), 71, 76, 103-4, 139, 145, 187, 207, 256, 272, 285
Beyer, O., 91, 172, 207, 213, 220
Best, E., 301, 384
Bezacier, L., 185
Biasatti, R., 25-6, 31
Bien-Hoa, 194
Biggs, B., 125, 128
Big Men, 94, 99, 100, 102-4, 112, 423

Apere Venuna, 256, **9.20**
Arahura River, 392
Arioi Society, 338, 351
Arnhem Land, 63-4, 233
aroids (taro), 71, 95, 102, 103, 113, 122, 127, 136-48 pass., 238, 265, 283, 285, 287, 327, 346, 348, 355, 360-2, 373, 381-2, 395
Asmat, 96
Assam, 173-4
Atayals, Atayalic, 91, 123, 132, 134, 203, 206
Atele, 313
Atiu, 300-1, 337, 348, 350-1
Atolls, 20, 21, 105, 109-110, 139, 147, 281-2, 293-5, 303, 308-9, 329, 343, 352
Auckland (City and Province), 399, 400, 406, 413-4
Audley-Charles, M.G., 55
Aurignacian, 59
Australia, 21-2, 31, 36, 57-8, 100, 112, 135, 393
  fauna, 54-5, 149
  fossil man, 44-6
  genetics, 32-3, 47, 50
  languages, 87, 121
  prehistory, 62-3, 67-80 pass., 113, 142, 149, 151, 172-4, 233-8 pass., 244, 258, 275, 320
Austral Islands, 128, 301-2, 308, 329-31, 335, 337-8, 344-6, 348, 386
Australoids, 21, 22, 25-50 pass., 76, 87-88, 119, 122, 170, 285, 421-2
Australopithecus, 38, 40
Austro-Asiatic languages, 87, 174
Austronesian languages and speakers, 21, 80, 95, 151, 421-3
  cultural affiliations, 87-113 pass., 136, 141-2, 168, 170, 173, 175, 180, 194, 238, 240, 244
  linguistic history, 116-34, 165, 191, 199, 203, 244, 255, 304, 421-2
  racial affiliations, 29, 33, 36, 47-9, 422
Austro-Thai languages, 85-8, 123, 165
Avias, J., 262
Awa tribes, 400, 410
Awamoa, 384
Awiden Mesa Formation, 57
axes, stone - see adzes and edge-ground axes
axes, bronze - see bronze
Axis lydekkeri, 59

Babeldoab, 286-7
Babyrousa, 74
Bacsonian industry, **3.6**, 67, 156, 173, 176, 180, 237
Bada, 288, **8.24**
Baining, 32
Baksoka River, 56

Bilateral descent, 84, 89-90, 108, 112, 113, 338, 354
Bilibili Island, 103
Binh-Ca, 180
Bipolar flaking, 58
Birdsell, J.B., 27, 47, 50
Birks, L. and H., 252
Bishop Museum, Honolulu, 83, 340, 356
Bismarck Archipelago, 20, 27, 47, 92, 147
  languages, 122, 125, 131-2
  prehistory, 238, **9.8**, 244, 249, 260
  societies, 96, 244
Bismarck Ranges, New Guinea, 144, 151
blade tools, 59, 62, 66, 69-70, 218, 220-1, 390-3, 398
  definition, 71
  flake and blade technocomplex, 71-80, **3.7, 3.9, 3.10,** 121, 123, 203, 235
Bligh, William, 340
Blust, R., 124
Boenechea, Domingo de, 301
Bollons, J., 301
Bo-Lum, 82
Bombarai Peninsula, 222
Bontoc, 30
Booth, P.B., 35
Borabora, 298, **11.14,** 227-8
Boriskovsky, P., 57, 67, 176
Borneo, 20, 30, **2.5,** 47, 54-5, 67, 76, 89, 90, 124-5, 132, 135, 145, 150, 175, 185, 191, 201, 213, 217, 226, 228, 268, 422
Boserup, E., 145, 149
Botel Tobago, 89, 173, 193, 231
Bougainville, 27, 33-5, 92, 99, 119, 144, 238, 242-3, 260, 266-7, 273
Bounty, 137, 352
bovids (cattle), 42, 54, 74, 85, 92, 135, 151, 158, 162, 170, 175, 179, 189, 217
breadfruit, 113, 122, 127, **6.2,** 138-48 pass., 316, 335, 346, 360, 362, 381
British Columbia, 268, 311, 374, 405
Bronson, B., 78
bronze, 60, 163-68, 176, 180-99 pass., 207, 210-231 pass., 242, **9.26,** 266
Brookfield, H.C., 95
Brothwell, D., 45
Brown, J.M., 305-6, 365
Brown P., 94
Buang Bep, 168
Buck, Sir Peter, 281, 307, 334, 337-8, 342, 344, 348, 353
Bui Ceri Uato, 217
Buka, 50, 242-3, 249, 259-60, **9.23, 9.30,** 270, 278
Bukit Chuping, 67
Bukit Tengku Lembu, 168
Bulakan Province, 73
Bulmer, R., 242
Bulmer, S., 235, 258
Buni, 221, 225, 232
Bunun, 92
burial practices, 60, 76, 87
  Hoabinhian, 67-9
  jar burials, 209-31 pass., 266-7, 285
  Melanesian, 249, 258, 264, 270-3
  Micronesian, 283, 285, 290
  Polynesian, 312-4, 316, 324, 334, 338, 355, 358, 363, 367-8, 373, 388-90, 404-6

South Asian Neolithic and Metal Age, 68, 153, 157-70 pass., 187-99 pass., 206-31 pass.
Burkill, I.H., 142
Burling, R., 85
Burma, 85, 87, 173-4
Burrows, E., 308-9, 317, 337
Buru, 304
Bushmen, 32

Cabenge, 59, 62, 70, 81
Cagayan Valley, 57, 63, 231
California, 320
Callenfels, P. van Stein, 73, 76, 220
Cambay, 230
Cambodia, 19, 124
  Hoabinhian, 46, 64, 70
  Metal Age, 189-90, 224
  Neolithic, 175-80
  Pleistocene industries, 57-8
  societies, 85-8
Candle-nut (*Canarium*), 71, 76, 242, 264
cannibalism, 60, 68, 92, 264, 271, 273, 331-2, 342, 384, 411
canoes, 92, 103, 113, 122, 127, 175, 255, 269, 283, 296-303, 309, 311, 318, 363, 392, 404, **13.16,** 405, 422
Canterbury, 382, 384, 387, 391, 393, **13.10**
Capell, A., 125, 267
Cape York, 297
Caroline Islands, 21, 31, 104-6, 126, 130, 132, 134, 272, 282, 285-6, 289-94, **11.1,** 302-3, 320
Carpentarian, 47
Cartailhac, E., 189
cattle — see bovids
Caucasoids, 26, 30-1, 47-8, 50, 305-7, 309, 374, 377
Celtis barbouri (hackberry), 58
Cendrawasih Peninsula, 222, 266
Cercis blackii (redbud), 58
Chalan Piao, 282
Chamorros, 105, 124, 130, 132, 283, 285
Chams (Champa, Chamic), 85-8, 113, 124, 132, 191, 194, 206
Chang, K.C., 155, 157, 159, 180-1, 200, 206
Changpinian industry, 70
Chao Phraya River, 19
Charoenwongsa, P., 163
Chatham Islands, 48, 128, 135, 148, 297-8, 383, 385, 403, 416
Chekiang Province, 141, 158, 180
Chellean industry, 56-57
Ch'en Ch'i-lu, 268
Cheng-chow, 180
chickens — see fowls
Chile, 320, 328
Chimbu, 94, 114, 144, 242
China, 19, 54, 122-3, 149, 206, 213, 226, 258, 260, 268, 286, 306, 311, 330, 405, 422
  Bronze Age, 164-5, 180-3, 187-91, 195, 198, 216, 222, 228
  fauna, 55-6, 151
  human evolution in, 38-44, **2.12,** 53, 59, 149, 421
  prehistoric cultures, 57-9, 62, 64, 70, 79,

136, 141, 149, 155-61, 166, 170-5, 179, 180, 198, 203, 206-7, 217, 220
  societies, 85-8, 91
  trade ceramics, 60, 220-1, 231
Chinchasuyo dialect, 140
Ch'ing-lien-kang culture, 158, 160
Ch'ing-yüan, 187
Ch'in Shih Huang Ti, 181
Cho-Ganh, 179
Choiseul, 99
Chopper, Chopping tool - see pebble and flake tool technocomplex
Chou Dynasty, 85, 180-3, 193, 228, 268
Chou-k'ou-tien, 40, 42, 44, 51, 58
Chowning, A., 99
Chretien, D., 125
Christian, F.W., 289-92
Christmas Island, 352
Ch'u, 181-2, 185, 190
Ch'ü-chia-ling culture, 157-8
Churchill, W., 306, 309
Churu, 88
civet cat, 218
clan, 84, 93-4, 96-7, 99, 101, 107, 112
Clarke, W.C., 144
coconut, 101, 103, 113, 122, 127, 136-7, 139, 145, 147-8, 247, 273, 281, 311, 318, 321, 324-5, 329, 335, 337, 342, 346, 350, 362, 381
Codrington, R.H., 98-9
cognatic descent, 84-115 pass.
Colani, M., 66-7, 179, 195-7
Col de Moc Drehun, 197
Colenso, W., 383
Collingwood Bay, 256, 266-7, 273
Condominas, M., 180
Cook Islands, 110, 128, 139, **6.7, 6.8,** 147, 300-3, 308, 318, 326-31, 337-8, 344, 346-53, 386, 390, 417
Cook, James, 83-4, 253, 298, 300-1, 304-6, 311-3, 331-2, 337-40, 353-4, 357-64 pass., 381-3, 385, 391-2, 403, 406-10, 414-5
Coon, C., 26, 32, 42-7, 49, 50
Cooper-Cole, F., 92
copper, 60, 91, 163-4, 198, 216
Cordy, R., 354, 361
Cordyline, 140
Coromandel Peninsula, 395, 398-9, 414-5
cotton, 141, 152, 168, 311, 362
Crook, W., 332
Cumberland, K.B., 381, 395
currencies, 179
  in Melanesia, 100, 102, 104, 112
  in Micronesia, 106, 285-6, 292

Da-But, 67, 176
Dahl, O.C. 124
Dani, A.H., 67
Danubian Cultures, 151, 175
Dart River, 392
Dau-Giay, 193-4
Da-Phuc, **3.5,** 81
Davao, 59
Davenport, W., 249
Davidson, J.M., 293, 313-4, 316
Dayaks, 89, **4.2**
Deacon, A.B., 275
De Lepervanche, M., 94

D'Entrecasteaux Islands, 266
De Surville, J.F.M., 415
Deutero-Malays, 30
diastema, 40
Dickinson, W.R., 321
Dimolit, 208-9
dingo - see dogs
Dixon, R., 301, 306
dogs, 59, 67, 75, 78, 80, 88, 100, 103,
    121-2, 127, 135, 149-50, 152-3, 157, 162,
    170, 179, 206, 217, 237, 247, 256, 258,
    260, 262, 282, 285-6, 294, 311, 321, 323,
    325-7, 332, 336-7, 346, 361-2, 382, 384,
    393, **13.10,** 396-7, 405
Dong-Dau, 191
Dong-Kohoi, 176
Don-Nai Valley, 194
Dong-Son, 161, 180-91, 193-4, 197-8, 201,
    209, 214, 222-8, 266-9
Doubtless Day, 415
Dubois, E., 40, 45, 51
Duff (mission ship), 301, 311, 332
Duff, R., adze terminology, 68, 76, 171-5,
    7.15, 176-9 pass., 194, 198, 207, 214, 216,
    220, 231, 283, 295, 330-2, **12.1,** 337, 342,
    344, 346, 348, 354, 356, 365, 390, 400,
    13.13, 416
  other work, 207, 281, 321, 385, 387-8,
    391, 395
Du Fresne, Marion, 415
Dunn, F., 168
D'Urville Island, 390, 393, 395, 398
Dutta, P.C., 78
Duyong Cave, 47, 72-3, 207-8, **8.3,** 215
Dyen, I., 119, 122, 124-6, 131-2, **5.7,** 255

ear ornaments, 176-80, **7.18,** 182, **7.20,**
    7.24, 187, **7.29,** 193-5, 198, **7.35,** 207,
    8.3, 8.5, 216, 225, 227, 363, 370, 381,
    400, **13.14**
Easter Island, 20-1, 48, 83, 110, 117, 121,
    128, 141, 147, 149, 273, 285, 289, 297,
    300-8, 311, 318-9, 325-6, 329, **12.1,** 331,
    334-6, 345-6, 352-3, 361-77, 403, 422
ecotones, 350
Ecuador, 309-11, 376
Eddystone Island, 273
edge-gloss, 74, 76, 82, 235
edge ground axes, 60, **3.4, 3.6,** 63-70, 78,
    80, 172, 198, 235
Efate, 134, 250, 259-61, 270-2
Egloff, B., 266, 273
Egypt, 136, 273, 305, 423
Elbert, S., 126, 130
Ellice Islands, 128-30, 282, 298, 301-2, 308,
    317, 320
Ellis, W., 304-5, 338, 354, 358-9
Elouae Island, 249
Ember, M., 317
Emory, K.P., 126, 325, 340, 342, 344, 352,
    356, 362, 370, 373, 376
endogamous marriage, 48, 98, 111, 338
Enga, 35, 114, 145
Engano, 124, 132, 134
epicanthic eyefold, 27, 31, 50
Erdbrink, D.P., 76
Erueti, 250, 252, 260
Espiritu Santo, 27, 270

Eua, 253
Euryceros pachyostus, 58
exogamous marriage, 49, 84, 88, 93, 96,
    98, 100-1, 105, 107, 109, 255
Eyles, J., 388
Eyraud, E., 364, 376

Fairservis, W., 78
Fakahina, 344
Fakarava, 337
Falefa Valley, 314-6
Fangatau, 344
Fanning Island, 352, 356
Fanning, E., 332
Feng-pi-t'ou, 155, 158-60
Ferdon, E., 335
Fergusson Island, 102, 256
Ferrell, R., 206
Fiji, 20, **2.4,** 128, 138-9, 144, 147, 300-2,
    304-5, 307, 312, 323
  canoes, 297-8, 327
  languages, 125-6, 133
  physical anthropology, 27-9, 31, 34, 46,
    2.15, 130
  prehistory, 248, 250-3, 255, 260-6, 269-70,
    273-5, 277, 279, 281, 316, 329
  societies, 96, 98, 100-2, 104, 112, 139
Fila, 129, 134
Finn, D.J., 183
Finney, B., 352
Finot, L., 189
Firth, R., 108
fishhooks, 76, 123, 157, 168, 176, 182, 189,
    191, 217, 249-55 pass., 260, 262, 281-3,
    287, 290, 293, 295, 309, 315-6, 318-29,
    332, 342-56 pass., 373, 383, 386, 390-1,
    396, 398, 400, 404-5, 416
Fleet, The, 383-5, 395, 400, 416
Flores, 30, 46, 55, 57, 59, 76, 80, 132, 218,
    226
Florida, 125
Fly River, 29, 104, **9.8**
Fontaine, H., 194
Forge, A., 92-3
Fornander, A., 305
Forster, George and Reinhold, 363-5
fortifications, 157, 175, 265, 275, 286
  in Polynesia, 127, 313-4, 316, 331, 335,
    344, 346, **12.15,** 385, 391, 399-400, 404,
    406-16
founder effect, 34-5, 328
fowls (chickens), 127, 135, 149-50, 158,
    179, 237, 247, 260, 264, 282, 286, 311,
    327, 346, 350, 362, 381
Fox, Lady Aileen, 409, 414
Fox, C.E., 273
Fox, R., 60, 73, 207, 209, 211-2
Frake, C.O., 113
Fraser, D., 268
Fraser, J., 305-6
Freeman, D., 89, 141, 317
Friedlaender, J.S., 35
Frost, E., 265
Fukien, 188
Fukui Cave, 153
Funan, 46, 87, 198, 224
Futuna (Hoorn Islands or East Futuna), 49,
    110, 128-30, 254, 312, 316-7

Futuna (New Hebrides), 129, 134, 264

Gabel, C., 29
Gagil District, 106
Gahuku-Gama, 94, **4.5,** 96
Gajdusek, R., 34
gammaglobulins, 33
Garanger, J., 250, 259-60, 270-2
Gawa, **9.12,** 247, 249, **9.15**
Gedeh River, 56
Geelvink Bay, 120
Geertz, C., 89, 142-3, 149
Geertz, H., 89
genealogies, genealogical ranking, 92, 94,
    98, 101, 108-112, 264, 305, 337, 354,
    376, 423
gene flow, 33-5, 44, 46, 49, 281, 285
genetic distances, 34-8
genetic drift, 25, 33-8, 48
Gerbrands, A., 96
Gifford, E.W., 101, 244, 250, 264, 285
Gigantopithecus blacki, 40
Gilbert Islands, 21, 105-6, 126, 130, 282,
    327
Gilimanuk, 228
Gill, W.W., 29, 97, 348
Gladwin, T., 303
glottochronology, 119, 124-8, 133
Glover, I.C., 74, 76, 151, 217-8, 220
goat, 135, 151, 158, 217
Gol Ba'it, 68, 200
gold, 87, 225, 228
Goldman, I., 110-111, 311, 317, 338,
    353-4, 361, 365
Goloubew, V., 185
Golson, J., 145, 238, 250, 253, 266, 366,
    385, 399-400
Go-Mun, 191
Gonzalez, Don Felipe, 363
Goodenough, W., 113
Goodenough Bay, 273, **9.34**
Gorman, C., 69, 71, 163
gourd, 71, 139, 148, 151, 238, 311, 324,
    329, 360, 362, 381, 404, 409
Grace, 124-6, 130
Graebner, F., 275
Great Barrier Island, 399
Green, K., 340
Green, R.C., 122, 126, 128-9, 249, 252,
    265, 311, 314-7, 321, 325-6, 340, 342-4,
    350, 386, 398-9, 414
Greenberg, J.H., 121
Grey, Sir George, 383
Groube, L.M., 147, 253, 400, 406, 409-10,
    415
Gua Berhala, 168
Gua Cha, 68, 82, 168, **7.14,** 170, 173, **7.16,**
    179, 182
Guadalcanal, 98, 125
Gua Kechil, 68-9, 156, 168, 170
Gua Kepah, 67-70, 220
Gua Kerbau, 68
Gua Lawa, 46, 68, 76, **3.11,** 78, 82, 221
Guam, 92, 132, 282-5
Gua Musang, 168
Gulf of Carpentaria, 121
Gulf of Guayaquil, 137
Gulf of Tonkin, 43

Gulf of Siam, 87, 214
Gulick, L.H., 289
Gunung Cantalan, 76
Guri Cave, 72-3
Guthe, C., 214

Ha'amonga-a-Maui, 312
Ha'apai, 253, 277
Haast, J. von, 384-5
Ha'atuatua, 321, 323, 328
Haddon, A.C., 297
Ha-Dong, 187, 197
Hai-feng, 158, 182
Hai-men-k'ou, 191
Hainan, 85, 87
Halawa Valley, 325, 360-1
Hale, H., 304-5, 383
Hale-o-Keawe, 358
Hallstatt Culture, 191
Halmahera, 20, 89, 119, 121, 173, 286
Hambruch, P., 288-92
Hamlin, J., 383
Hamlin's Hill, 413
Handy, E.S.C., 306-7, 332, 334, 342
Han dynasty (Han Chinese), 46, 85, 180-1,
   185, 189, 222
Hanapete'o, 332
Hanatekua, 335
hand-axes, 56-9
Hane, 321-4, 330, 332, 335, 386
Hangan, 260, 270
Hang-Gon, 191, 193-4
Hanshui Valley, 158
Hanunoo, 143-4
haptoglobins, 50
Harding, T., 103
harpoons, 159, 321, **11.17**, 323, 388, 391,
   396, 400, 416
Harris, D., 422
Harrisson, B., 216
Harrisson, T., 57, 59, 201, 216
Hauraki Plains, 410-1
Hawaiian Islands (Hawaii), 48, 102, 128,
   139, 141, 147, 150, 152, 268, 297, 300-6,
   308, 311, 337-8, 346, 363, 414, 423
   prehistory, 318-9, 323-6, 330-2, 335, 340,
   352-61, 372, 393
   society, 108-113, 338
Hawaii Island, 20, 325, 334, 336, 353-60
Hawkes Bay, 381, 406, 409, 414-5, 417
Hawksburn, 392
head-hunting, 90, 92, 104, 162, 175
Healey, A., 124
Heaphy River, 392
Hedrick, J.D., 250
Heekeren, H.R. van, 70, 73, 74, 220, 221,
   224
Heger, F., 183-5, 187, 221-2, 227
heiau, 355-60
Heine Geldern, R., 64, 92, 171, 173-5,
   190-1, 207, 224, 226, 228, 268, 308, 311
hemoglobins, 34, 170
Henderson Island, 21, 352
Heonesian languages, 132
Hesperonesian languages, 123-4, 132
Heyerdahl, T., 137, 141, 295, 302, 304,
   309-11, 335-6, 361-2, 365-8, 372-6
hibiscus, 139

Hiernaux, J., 44
Himalayas, 32, 42, 54, 58
Hiva Oa, 321, 332-3, 335
Ho, R., 149
Hoabinhian technocomplex, 46, 59, 60,
   64-71, 78, 80, 155-6, 163, 168-76 pass.,
   180, 198, 237
Hoang-Ha, 185
Hokule'a, 303, 327
Holocene epoch, 62, 421
   definition, 53-4
   fossils from, 45-47
   sea levels, 54, 70, 72, 80, 422
Hominidae, 38
Homo erectus, 38-45, 51, 55-8, 79
Homo habilis, 38, 40
Homo sapiens, 40, 43-7, 59, 60
Honan, 157, 180
Hongi Hika, 109
Hong Kong, 155, 158, 160, 168, 174,
   179-80, 182, 193
Honshu, 153
Hooijer, D., 55
Hooper, T., 110
Hornell, J., 297
horsehoof cores, 57, **3.4**, 63, 69
horticulture (see also shifting cultivation,
   terracing), 47, 88, 127, 132, 153, 247,
   323, 326
   intensification of, 93, 96, 114, 144-9, 238,
   361, 422
   and languages, 121-3, 132
   major cultigens, 136-41
   origins of, 64, 66-71, 78, 80, 136, 142, 157,
   198, 203, 220, 237-8, 385, 422-3
   systems of, 142-51, 350, 355-6, 360-1, 370,
   381-2, 390-1, 395-6, 399, 404, 414-6
Howard, A., 304
Howells, W.W., 32, 47, 281, 307, 423
Howland Island, 352
Hsien-jen-tung, 199
Hsi-hou-tu, 58
Huahine, 301, 324, 337-8, 340, **12.10**
Huangho Valley, 136, 155-8, 165, 181
Hua Pan, 195-6
Hughes, D., 44
human sacrifice, 60, 92, 100, 270-2, 331,
   338, **12.11**, 342, 353, 358
Hunan, 87, 181, 185
Huon Peninsula, 242
Hutton, J.H., 197

Iban, 89-90, 142
Ifugao, 30, 90-1, **4.3**
Ile des Pins, 101, 247, 250, 274
Incas, 311, 376-7
India, 27, 38, 54, 58, 75, 78, 82, 87, 124,
   138, 141, 151, 153, 173-4, 197-8, 217,
   220, 224, 230-1, 268, 304-6
Indianized Kingdoms (see also Funan,
   Champa, Srivijaya), 30, 47, 85, 91, 117,
   149, 151, 165, 221, 228, 231
Indochina, 166-80 pass., 183-98, 213,
   220-2, 225
Indonesia, 20, 95, 180, 185, 213, 258-61,
   266, 269, 273, 285, 294, 297, 301, 304-8,
   421-2
   horticulture in, 137-51 pass.

languages, 21, 87, 106, 117-25, 132, 255,
   281-2
Pleistocene epoch in, 53-62
Metal Age cultures, 183, 194, 222-32, 269
Neolithic cultures, 156, 170-5, 180-1, 203,
   209, 215-21
physical anthropology, 26, 29-31, 33, 42,
   46-7, 50, 71-80
societies, 83-92 pass., 97, 112, 149
stone tool industries, 60, 62, 66, 71-80
Indonesian National Research Centre for
   Archaeology, 221, 224
Indus Valley Civilization, 21, 136, 164-5,
   376
Inocarpus edulis (Tahitian chestnut), 139,
   147, 264
Irian Jaya, 95-6, 121, 124, 132, 139, 144-5,
   183, 215, 218, 222, 235, 237, 242, 266
iron, 60, 133, 149, 151, 164-5, 168, 180-99
   pass., 211-231 pass., 266, 292, 422
Irrawaddy River, 19
irrigation (see also aroids, rice), 157-8, 180,
   201, 238, 346, 350, 355, 360-1
Irwin, G.J., 261
Isabel, 125
Islamic Civilization, 85, 89-90
Isneg, 90
Isoh Kelekel, 292
Iwitini, 381-5 pass., 395-400, 406, 410,
   413-5

Jacob, T., 42, 46, 218
Jakun, 89
Jambi, 220
Jammes, L., 189-90
Janse, O., 187, 193
Japan, 20, 59, 62-3, 70-2, 78, 80, 123,
   153-6, 172-5, 203, 220, 228, 258, 268,
   281-2, 306, 321, 421
Jarai, 88
Java, 20, 30, 46, 76-8, 89, 124-5, 148-50,
   7.15, 220-8, 259, 421
   Pleistocene fossils and industries, 38-42,
   45, 53-9, 81
Java Man - see *Homo erectus*
Jetis fauna, 38, 40, 55-6, 81
Jimi Valley, 103, 277
Jomon, 78, 198, 258
Jones, R., 63

Kabara, 264
Kadavu, 126
Kafiavana, 64, **9.2**, **9.3**, 235
Kai Islands, 222, 224
Kaikoura, 384, **13.8**
Kainantu, 93
Kaipara Harbour, 410
Kaitaia, **13.17**, 405
Kalanay Culture, 193, 212, 214-7, 220-1,
   231, 247
Kalumpang, **8.13**, **8.14**, 220
Kamehameha, 353
Kampong Sungai Lang, 189, 228
Kandal, 224
Kandrian, 242, **9.10**
Kapingamarangi, 129-30, 134, 317
Karama River, 220
Karika, 348, 352

Karlgren, B., 185
Karobo, 264
Ka'u, 325
Kauai, 353-7
Kauri Point, 404, **13.2**, 410, 414
Kauvadra Mountains, 101, 264
kava, 139, 271, 290, 312
Kedah, 67-8, 168
Keesing, F., 91
Kei, 75
Kelabits, 226
Kelantan, 67-8, 168
Keleo, 87
Kellum-Ottino, M., 335
Kendeng Lembu, 221
Kenniff Cave, **3.4**
Keo Hin Tan, 195, **7.34**
Keo Tane, **7.33**, 197
Keyes, I.M., 384
Khmers - see Mon-Khmer
Kiangsi, 155, 199
Kiangsu, 141, 158
Kimam, 96, 145
King, J., 338
Kiowa, **3.5**, 235, 237, 277
Kirch, P.V., 323, 360
Kirk, R.L., 32
Klapadua, 221
Koch, G., 282
Koenigswald, R. von, 40, 42
K'o-ho, 58
Koiari, 103
Koita, 103
Kok Chaeron, 165
Kolepom Island, 96, 145
Kon-Tiki, 304, 309
Koror, 286
Kosipe, 63, **3.5**, 233, 235
Kota Kinabalu, 226
Kota Tongkat, 68
Kow Swamp, 45
Kramacati, 221
Krusenstern, A.J., 332
Kubary, J., 289, 292
Kubu, 30, 89
Kuk, 238, **9.5**
Kukuba Cave, 244
Kukukuku, 242
Kula cycle, 102-3, 106, 266
kumara - see sweet potato
Kupe, 383-5
Kusaie, 105, 130, 282, 289-90, 292, **10.12**, 295
Kusana, 224
Kwadaware, **9.26**, 266
Kwangsi, 40, 70, 87
Kwangtung, 70, 113, 155, 157-8, 182, 187
Kweichow, 87, 185
Kyushu, 153

Laang Spean, 70, 175, **7.17**, 179, 200
Lai Valley, 145
lakatoi, 102-3
Lake Hauroko, 405-6
Lake Horowhenua, 404, 410-11
Lake Kerinci, 78, 220, **8.19**
Lake Mangakaware, 404, 411-13
Lake Ngaroto, 411

Lake Paniai (Wissellakes), 27, 93, 144
Lake Sentani, **9.26**, 266
Lake Taupo, 392, 395, 399
Lake Toba, 228, **8.24**
Lake Tondano, 73
Lake Wakatipu, 392
Lal-lo, 231
Lamb, A., 230
Lamma Island, 155, 174, **7.19**, 182, **7.20**
Lamont, E.H., 353
Lanai, 353
Langsdorff, G.H., 332
Lantau Island, 182
Lan-t'ien, 40-42, 58
Lao, 87, 185
Laos, 19, 58, 64, 69-70, 85-8, 164, 175-6, 185-98 pass., 228
Lapakahi, 360-1
La Perouse, J.F., 364
Lapita Culture, 213, 215, **9.1**, 244-55, 256-64 pass., 269, 274-5, 278, 281-2, 285, 295, 303, 311, 314-6, 318, 321, 329, 405, 423
Lau (Malaita), 98
Lau Islands, 29, 102, 126, 264
Lauer, P., 266
Lavachery, H., 365
Leach, B.F., 390
lead, 164, 222
Leang Burung, 74, **3.9**
Leang Cadang, 46
Leang Tuwo Mane'e, **3.7**
Leenhardt, M., 100
Leles, 221
Lesu, 249
Leta Leta Cave, 209
Leuwiliang, 224
Levalloisian, 56, 58
Levi-Strauss, C., 268
Lewis, D., 303
Lewthwaite, G.R., 300, 381
lexicostatistics, 119, 122, 124, 130-3
Li, 87
Liang Leluat, 218
Liang Toge, 218
Lie Siri, **3.10**, 76
Line Islands, 352
lingling-o, **7.29**, 193, 207, **8.5**, 211, 213
Linton, R., 306, 332, 334
Lisiansky, U., 332
Liu-chiang, 44, 59
Lolo, 85
Lombok, 89, 124
longhouse, 88-90, **4.2**, 104
Long-Khanh, 191
Loofs, H., 189
Loomis, W.F., 34
lost-wax casting, 189, 191
Loyalty Islands, 100-1, 128, 132, 134
Luang Prabang, 69
Luangiua (Ontong Java), 109-10, 129, 134
Lautuanu'u Valley, 316
Lukunor, 105
Lungshanoid cultures, 157-61, **7.6**, 163, 166, 170, 172, 180-1, 187, 198, 200, 203-7
Luomala, D., 306-7, 342
Lutunasobasoba, 264

Luzon, 26, 54, 57, 59, 73, 80, 82, 88, 90-1, 148-9, **7.15**, 193, 207, 209, 214, 220, 225, 228

Maanyan, 124
McCoy, P., 367
MacKay, A., 385
McKern, W.C., 312-3
Madagascar, 21, 121, 124, 132, 304
Madang, 103, 240
Madura, 124, 224
Mae, 129, 134
Maeva, 340, **12.10**
Maewo, 104
Magellan, F., 92, 282
Maglioni, R., 158, 182
Mahaiatea, 339-40
Mailu, 297
Mai-Pha, 180
Makaha Valley, 147, 359-61
Makemake, 363, 365, 372, 374
Makura, 259-60, 270
Malacca, 226
malae, 314, 316-7, 330
Malagasy - see Madagascar
Malaita, 98, 125
malaria, 95, 98, 114, 423
Malayo-Polynesian languages - see Austronesian
Malayo-Polynesian linkage, 132
Malaysia, East (see also Sarawak), 21, 89-90, 141, 231
Malaysia, West (Malaya, Malays), 19, 26-7, 54, 57, 306, 309
  languages, 21, 87, 121-4, 191, 203, 228
  prehistory, 46, 64, 67-9, 70, 153, 156, 166-75, 179-80, 183, 194, 217, 220, 225-6, 228, 230
  societies, 85-9, 135, 142
Malden Island, 352
Malekula, 27, 100, 104, 270, 273
Malinowski, B., 98
Malo, 250
Maluku (Moluccas), 30, 54-5, 89, 121, 123, 131-2, 148, 150, 218, 233, 304
Mamberamo River, 121
Manahune, 305-6
Mangaasi Culture, 259-62, 265, 270
Mangaia, 110, **6.7**, 147, 337, 344, 346-52, 365
Mangareva, 110-1, 128, 147, 297-8, 300, 302, 304, 321, 326, 343-4, 363
Manihiki, 110, 352
Manis palaeojavanica, 59
Mansuy, H., 67, 176, 180, 189
Mantell, W., 384
Manton, 238
Manunggul Cave, 209, **8.4**, 211-21
Maoris - see New Zealand
Ma-pa, 59
marae (see also *ahu, heiau*), 298, 309, 316, 329-30, 333-5, 337, 339-53 pass., 357, 365, 370, 409, 411, 415-6
Maraetai, 399
Marchand, E., 332
Marianas Islands, 20, 105-6, 121, 124, 130, 132, 137, 141, 145, 214-5, 281-7, 295, 303

Marind-Anim, 145
Maring, 94, 104, 151
Markham Valley, 33, 95, 120, 262
Maros, 73-4, **3.9**, 220
Marquesas Islands, 48, 110, 127-8, 134, 141, 147, 253, 255, 268, 274-5, 302-9 pass., 315, 318, 321-6, 329-36, 338, 344-6, 348-57 pass., 365, 372, 374, 376-7, 386-90
Marschall, W., 231
Marshall Islands, 20, 31, 105-6, 126, 130, 282, 303
Masbate Island, 213-4, 247, 282
Massim District, 95, 97-8, 102, 255-6, 266, 269
Matanavat, 100
matrilineal descent, 84-115 pass., 270, 286, 290
Matthews, J.M., 64, 66
Maui (legendary figure), 305, 383
Maui (island), 303, 353, 360
Mauke, 337
Maungaroa Valley, 350-1
Maupiti, 324, 326, 330, 342, 386, 390
Mayor Island, 384, 392, 399, 416
Ma-Yüan, 187
Mead, M., 109
Mead, S.M., 405
megaliths, 92, 175-6, 194-8, 225-8, 231, 272-5, 306
Meganthropus, 38, 40, **2.10**, 42
Mejbrat, 266
Mekeo, 102
Mekong River, 19, 57-8, 87, 194
Melanesia, 14, 179, 185, 281, 286, 302, 305, 318, 342, 384-5
  canoes, 297-8, 303
  geography and climate, 19-21, 23
  horticulture in, 135-49 pass.
  languages, 21, 87, 117-32 pass., 255, 421
  physical anthropology, 21, 25-9, 32-8, 44, 47-9, 131, 285
  prehistory, 172-5, 207-8, 212-5, 220, 222, 228, 233-79, **9.1**, 295, 320-1, 423
  societies, 84-5, 92-104, 106-9, 112-3, 423
  trade networks, 102-4, 393
'Melanesoid' dentitions, 46
Mele, 129, 134
Melolo, 51, 221
Melville, H., 332-4, 356
Mengeruda, 59
Mentawei, 297
Mercury Bay, 406-9
Merir, 105
Merrill, E.D., 140
Mesopotamia, 136, 164-5, 180, 305
Metraúx, F., 365, 376
Mexico, 136, 173, 200
Meyer, O., 249
Miao-Yao languages, 21, 85, 88
microliths, 73-82 pass., **3.9**
Micronesia, 19-23, **4.8**, 179, 233, 272-3, 304, 306-9, 423
  canoes, 297-303
  horticulture in, 135-47 pass.
  languages, 121, 124, 126-7, 130-2
  physical anthropology, 26, 31-3, 47-50, 131

prehistory, 172, 220, 280-96, 318, 320-1
societies, 84-5, 92, 98, 102, 104-7, 112-3, 423
Milford Sound, 392
Milke, W., 125
millet, 89, 91-2, 133, 135-6, 141-2, 157, 159, 175
Mills, J.P., 197
Milne Bay, 125
Minahasa, 73, 123, 133, 228, **8.24**
Minanga Sipakko, 220
Mindanao, 26, 59, 73, 88, 90, 132, 215, 228, 286, 422
Mindoro, 143
Minh-Cam, 51, 179
Minot, 200
Mitiaro, 337
Mlu Prei, 190, **7.28**, 194
moa, 382-8, 390, 392-4, 396-7, 416-7
Moa Bone Point Cave, 384
Moala, 101
Mohenjo Daro, 168
Mojokerto, 38
Molokai, 325, 353, 360
Mongolia, 70
Mongoloids, 21, 25-51 pass., 59-60, 80, 87-8, 122, 132, 155, 157, 159, 173-4, 203, 209, 217, 225, 228, 255, 273, 275, 281, 306-7, 421-2
Mongols, 87
Mon-Khmer, 21, 85-9, 113-4, 124, 132, 170, 174, 194, 199
Moorea, 294, 337, 340, 342, 350, 361
Morioris - see Chatham Islands
Morlan, V.J., 71
Morobe, 103, 242
Morongo Uta, 346, **12.15**, **12.16**
Motu, 97-8, 102-3, 258, 269-70
Motupore, 269-70
Motutapu Island, 413, 417
Mount Camel, 396, **13.11**, 398
Mt. Hagen, 95, 145, 235, 242
Mousterian, 59
Movius, H., 56-8
Mu'a, 312-4
Mulifanua, 253, 314
Mulloy, W., 365, 367, 369
Mulvaney, D.J., 74, 220
Munda, 87
Mungo, 45, 62-3
Murapin, 35, **2.8**
Murdock, G.P., 84, 89, 113-4, 132
Murrayians, 47
Mururoa, 343

Naia Bay, 262
Nakanai, 133
Namonuito, 106
Nanggu, 249
Nan Madol, 288-92
Nanumea, 129
Nassau, **12.1**
Natunuku, 250-1
natural selection, 25, 33-8, 43-4, 48, 114
Nauru, 130, 132, 134
Navatu, 264
navigation (see also canoes), 300-3, 422
Ndut-Lieng-Krak, 180

Neanderthal man. 43
Nebira, 256-8
Necker Island, 353, **12.22**, 356-8, 367
Negri Sembilan, 226
Negritos, 26-7, **2.1**, 34, 44, 47, 85-9 pass., 132, 135, 292, 305, 422
Negroes, 47-8, 306-7
Negros, 26, 88
New Britain, 27, 50, 100, 103-4, 119, 132-3, 240, 242, 244, 247, 250, 287
New Caledonia, 25-6, 34, 128, 132, 336
  canoes, 297-8
  horticulture, 139-40, 144, 147, 152
  physical anthropology, 25-9, 47, 49, 262
  prehistory, 244, 247, 250, 253, 259-66, 270, 273-5, **9.34**, 320
  societies, 96, 98, 100-2, 104
New Georgia, 119
New Guinea (see also Irian Jaya, New Guinea Highlands, Papua), 20-2, 54, 64, 69, 75, 83, 286, 298, 384, 421-3
  fauna, 21, 54-5, 149, 151, 218
  horticulture in, 134-45 pass.
  languages, 21, 119-22, 125, 131-2
  physical anthropology, 27-9, 32-8, 44, 47, 50
  prehistory, 174-5, 233-44, 249, 254-8, 260, 266-70, 273, 275, 320
  societies, 92-104 pass.
New Guinea Highlands, **2.7**, 66, 422-3
  horticulture, 140-45, 288, 423
  languages - see Papuan
  physical anthropology, 27-9, 32-8, 47, 50
  prehistory, 63-4, 233-44, 273, 275
  societies, 84, 92-7, 102, 104, 112, 151
  trade, 103-4
New Hanover, 275, **9.34**
New Hebrides, 20, **2.3**, 27-9, 34, 47, 49, 100, 106, 128, 131, 147, 298
  languages, 125-34, 282
  prehistory, 250, 259-65, 270-3, 292
  societies, 96, 98, 103-4
New Ireland, 50, 119, **6.9**, 240, 242, 244, 249, 256, 269-70
New Zealand, 19-21, 34, 48, 102, 128, 172, 207, 268, 285, 287, 300-6, 308, 330
  art, 404-5
  canoes, 297-8, **11.3**, **13.6**
  horticulture, 135, 137, 141, 147-50, 381-2, 390-1, 395-6, 399, 404, 414-5
  prehistory, 315-32 pass., 352, 355, 361, 377, 381-419
  society, 108,112
Newman, T.S., 361
Ngahue, 383
Ngai Tahu, 391
Ngaju, 185
Ngandong, 42, 56, 59
Nghe-An, 179
Ngipe't Duldug, 209
Ngoc-Lu, 185, **7.23**
Nguang Chang, 82
Nguyen, P.L., 176
Nhan-Gia, 58
Niah Cave, 45-6, **2.14**, 59-64, 68, 70, 76, 173, 212-20 pass., 231, 235, 237
Nias, 30, 201, **8.20**, 226, 228, 297
Nicobar Islands, 87, 89, 297

Nihoa, 356-8
Nikiniki, **8.12**, 218
Ninh-Binh, 66, 179
Niobe, **3.5**
Niuatoputapu, 253-4
Niue, 110, 127
Niutao, 317
Nomna Bay, 283
Nong Chae Sao, 168, 170
Non Nok Tha, 141, 149, 161-70 pass., 180, 191, 194, 200, 217
Non Nong Chik, 165
non-unilineal descent, 84
Norfolk Island, 352
Northland (New Zealand), 383, 399-400, 405-6, 410, 414-5
Norwegian Expedition (see also Heyerdahl, T.), 345-6, 361, 365, 369
Normanby Island, **9.34**
North Cachar Hills, 197-8
Novaliches pottery, 214, 267
Nui-Do, 57
Nui-Nua, 187
Nuku Hiva, 110, 321, **12.2**, 333-5
Nukumanu, 134
Nukuoro, 129-30, 134, 293, 317
Nukuria, 134
Nusatenggara (Lesser Sunda Islands), 20, 30, 54, 57, 62, 79, 89, 123

Oahu, 324, 353, 359, 360
obsidian, 73, 78, 103, 218, 220-1, 225, 247, **9.14**, 248-50, 256, 258, 266, 277, 292, 325, 367, 373, 384, 392, 398-9, 404, 416, 418
Oceania, 19-21, 23, 226-8
  art history of, 268, 336, 375
  horticulture in, 135-52 pass.
  languages, 21, 117-34 pass., **5.4**, 203, 421-2
  physical anthropology, 25-38, 47-49
  prehistory - see Melanesia, Micronesia, Polynesia
  settlement of, 244, 321
  societies, 83-5, 92-115
Oc-Eo, 198, 201
Oenpelli, 63
Olduvai Gorge, 40, 57
Oliver, D., 99
Ongbah Cave, 82, 200
Ontong Java - see Luangiua
Opihi, 393
Opoa, 306, 338
Oposisi, 256-8, **9.14**
Opunohu Valley, 342-3, 350
Oro, 338, 340, 345
Orongo, 367-9, **12.34**, 372
Osborne, D., 286
Otago, 384-5, 387, 390-1, 393, **13.10**
Otakanini, 410-11, **13.23**
Oturehua, 392

pa - see fortifications
Pacitan, 76, 221
Pacitanian industry, 56-8, **3.2**, 62, 80
Pahang Province, 67-8, 168
Paiwans, Paiwanic, 91-2, 123, 203, 206-7
Pajot, M., 187

Palau Islands, 31, 105-6, 121, 124, 130, 132, 145, 281-3, 285-7, 295
Palawan (see also Tabon, Duyong), 20, 54-5, 59-61, 193, 207-13, 217
Palmer, B., 274
Palmerston Island, 352
Panama, 137
Panay, 26, 88
Pandanus, 139, 147, 238, 264, 324
Panganreang Tudea, 73
Pan-p'o-ts'un, 157
Pantar, 119-120
Papatowai, 390
paper mulberry, 127, 139, 148, 362, 381
Papua (see also New Guinea), 42, 95, 97-8, 102, 119, 125, 139, 235, 242, 244, 256-8, 266-70, 297, 303
Papuan Gulf, 102
Papuan (non-Austronesian) languages and speakers (see also Trans New Guinea Phylum)
  cultural features, 89, 92, 96-8, 103, 112-3, 238, 248, 258
  linguistic history, 117, 119-21, **5.2**, 124-5, 173-4, 244, 250, 264, 270, 272, 275, 422
  physical anthropology, 29, 33, 36, 92
Pare, 338
Parke, A., 274
Parker, R.H., 168
Parsonson, G., 98
Pasemah Plateau, 227-8
Paso, 73-4
Patrilineal descent, 84-115 pass.
Pattc, E., 176
patu, 172, 324, **13.10**, **13.13**, 403-4
Pawley, A.K., 122, 125-9
Pearson, R., 206
pebble and flake tool industries, 56-8, 60, 64-70, 79, 80, 235
Peking man - see *Homo erectus*
Pematang, 227
Penrhyn Island, 344, 352-3, 357
Perak, 67-8, 229
Perlis, 168
Perry, W., 226
Peru, 136, 140, 268, 302, 309-11, 353, 361, 363, 374-7
Pescadores Islands, 159
pestles and mortars, in Melanesia, 238-44, 260, 266
  elsewhere, 283, 309, 318, 323, 337, 346, 354, 365
Phalanger (cuscus), 54, 74, 218
Philippines, 20, 95, 150, 233, 258, 261, 273, 283, 285-6, 295, 304, 308, 321, 330, 422
  fauna, 55, 80
  horticulture in, 135-48 pass.
  languages, 21, 106, 118, 121-5, 132, 255, 281
  physical anthropology, 26-7, 46-7, 49, 57, 281-2, 422
  prehistory, 60-2, 66, 71-3, 78-9, 80, 156, 170-5, 179, 180-1, 191, 193, 198, 203, 206-21, 225, 228, 231-2, 247, 255, 266-9, 421
  societies, 84-5, 88-92
Phnom Penh, 57

Phoenix Islands, 352
Phu-Hoa, 193
Phung-Nguyen, 179
Phuoc-Tan, 194
Phu Wiang, 161
Piddington, R.O., 307
Pietrusewsky, M., 46, **2.15**
pig, 42, 54, 66, 68, 71, 73-5, 82, 94-5, 97, 100, 103-4, 113, 122, 127, 135, 144, 149-51, **6.9**, 153, 157, 162, 166, 175, 179, 217-8, 235, 247, 249, 256, 258, 260, 262, 264, 271, **9.32**, 273, 282, 285-6, 311, 321, 323, 325-7, 338, 346, 350, 352, 362, 381, 416
Pileni, 130, 134
Pinctada margaretifera (pearl oyster), 128
Pitcairn, 20, 302, 318, 352, 361
Pithecanthropus - see *Homo erectus*
Plain of Jars, 179, 189, 194-8, **7.31**, 209
Pleistocene epoch, definition in Southeast Asia, 53-4
  faunas, 38, 40, 53-5, 59, 62
  human evolution in, 38-47, 53, **3.1**
  stone industries, 55-64
Poike 'Ditch', 373
poi-pounders, 240
pollen sequences and analysis, 71, 141, 156, 159, 235, 375, 378
Polynesia, 19-23, 273-5, 303-11, 422-3
  canoes and navigation, 297-303
  horticulture in, 135-48 pass.
  linguistic history, 117-8, 124, 126-34, 255, 282, 337, 365, 374
  physical anthropology, 26-36, 47-50, **2.15**, 131, 262, 281, 373, 375
  prehistory, 172, 175, 207, 231, 240, 244-55 pass., 264, 268, 281-3, 293-5, 297-419
  societies, 83-5, 92, 98, 100-13
Polynesian outliers, 27, 100, 126-30, 249-50, 264, 293-4, 302, 317
Ponape, 105, 130, 282, 289-92, 295, 305
Pongidae, 38
Porter, D., 110, 332
Port Moresby, 97, 102, 256, 258, 269
Portuguese, 95, 141, 238
pottery, 60, 88, 95, 102-3, 113, 122-3, 153, 242
  appearance in East and Southeast Asia, 64-70, 74, 76, 78, 80, 153-7, 207-13, 217
  design features in East and Southeast Asia, 153-232 pass.
  design features in Oceania, 243-70 pass., 282-6, 312, 314-5, 318, 321, 326, 329, 373
  distribution in Melanesia and Micronesia, 237, 244, 255, 282, 295
  manufacture, 103-4, 141, 153, 159, 173-5, 206, 245, 258-60, 273, 285-6
  wheel manufacture, 158, 168, 179, 190, 193, 206, 214
Poulsen, J., 249, 253
Pounawea, 390
Proto-Malays, 30
Pseudaxis grayi, 58
Pteridium esculentum (fern rhizome), 148, 382, 404, **13.21**, 408-9, 412, 414-6
Puamau Valley, 335

Pueraria lobata, 140
Pukapuka, 108-10, 128, 139, 318, **11.14**, 352
Pulemelei, 317
Pulo Anna, 105
Pulusuk, 106
Puluwat, 105
Punans, 30, 89
Punapau, 368
Punung, 76, 221
Purea, 339
Pu'uhonua, 358-9
pygmies, 26-7

Qat society, 100
Quang-Binh, 179
Quang-Tri, 201
Quechua, 140
Queen Charlotte Sound, 148, 391-2, 415
Quiros, P.F., 332
Quynh-Van, 67, 70

rafts, 298, 309, 376
Raiatea, 298, 300-7 pass., 337-48 pass., 376
Raivavae, 335-6, 344-5
Rakahanga, 110, 352
Rakaia River, 384, 390, 392
ramage, 84, 107-112, **4.11**, 311, 317, 337, 343, 354, 365
Ramapithecus, 38
Ramu, 120
Rangiroa, 337, 352
Rano Raraku, 362, 367-8, 370, **12.33**, 372
Rapa, 21, 147, 302, 304, 344, 346
Rappaport, R., 151, 423
Raroia, 309
Rarotonga, 109, **6.8**, 147, 301, 304-5, 336-7, 346-2, 357, 361, 383
rat, 149, 283, 294, 323, 325-6, 396
Read, K.E., 96
Reao, 344
Red River, 87, 179-80, 183, 191
Reef Islands, 100, 247, 249
Reinman, F., 282, 320
Rendova, 119
Rennell, 129, 130, 134, 249-50
Retoka, 270-71
Rewa, 265, 323
Rhade, 88
rice, 51, 71, 85-92, 113, 122, 135-52 pass., 157-9, 162-3, 170, 175, 179, 198, 282-3
  wet-field cultivation, 89-91, **4.3**, 135, 142-3, 148-9, 151, 165, 231, 422
Reisenfeld, A., 272-5
Rimatara, 344
Rivers, W.H.R., 275
Rizal, 59, 73
Robarts, E., 332
Roberton, J.W., 383
rock-art, 67, 75, 265, 275, 336, 352, 361, 363, 365, 372, 376-7, 393-5, 405
Roggeveen, J., 117, 363
Romans, 230, 286
Rongo, 306
rongorongo script, 364, 372, **12.38**, 376-7
Rossell Island, 119
Rota, 282-3
Roti, 222

Rotorua, 399, 413, 415
Rotuma, 126, 133, 301, 312
Routledge, K., 365-6
Roux, J., 403, 406, 409-11
Roy Mata, 270-2
Rurutu, 344-6, 348, 352
Ryukyu Islands, 155, 172

Sa'bang, 221
sago, 89, 97, 102-3, 122, 135, 138-9, 145, **9.21**
Sahlins, M., 101, 108-11, 317, 370
Sahul Shelf, 20, 54
Sa-Huynh, 189, 191-4, 197-98, 201, 209-15, 220, 230, 247
St. Matthias Islands, 249
Saipan, 282-5
Sai Yok, **3.5**, 69, 168, 173
Sakai - see Senoi
Salayar, 223-4
Salween River, 19, 87, 170
Samar Island, 231
Samar Sea, 73
Samoa, 33, 48, 140, 147, 198, 301-2, 304-8, 321, 330, 342, 352
  language, 126-30, 352
  prehistory, 244-5, 248, **9.17**, 253-5, 281, 311-8, 320, 323, 325-6, 348
  society, 108-12, 139
Sampung Bone Industry, 76, 78
Samui Island, 214
San Agustin, 336
San Cristobal, 98, 125, 273
Sangeang, 222-3
Sangiran, 38, **2.11**, 40, 59, 62, 81
San Hin Oume, **7.32**
San Kong Phan, **7.30**, 195
Sanscrit, 85, 124, 309
Santa Ana, 249
Santa Cruz Islands, 95, 98, 100, 103-4, 119, 134, 244, **9.12**, 247-50, 275, 294, 297, 303
Sao-Dong, 66
Sapir, E., 307
Sarawak (see also Niah Cave), 45-47, 59, 89-90, 216-7, 220, 226
Sasoa'a, 314-6
Sau Deleur dynasty, 290, 292
Sauer, C., 136
Saurin, E., 57-8, 179, 193
Savai'i, 314, 316-7
Savo, 119
scapulimancy, 157
Scheffler, H., 99
Schmitz, C.A., 308
Seedik, 123
Selangor, 189
Semang (see also Negritos), 26-7, **2.1**, 85, 88, 124, 174
Senoi, 85, 87, 89, 124, 142, 174
Sepik River and District, 93, 95-7, 103, 120, 145, **9.21**, 259, 262, 268-9
Seram, 62, 75, 89
Serikan River, 56
shamanism, 166, **7.12**, 170, 185, 201
Sham Wan, 155, 158, 160, 174
Shang dynasty, 157, 180-2, 198, 268, 311
Shans, 85

Shansi, 157
Shapiro, H., 48
Sharp, A., 302, 384, 400
Shaw, E., 265
Shawcross, F.W., 396, 404
sheep, 158, 170, 217
shell middens, 54, 64-70, 73, 80, 82, 176, 206, 253, 342, 388, 392, 398, 406, 410, 413, 422
Shensi, 157
shifting cultivation, 85-91, 135, 238, 382, 414-5
  examples, 142-8
Shih-chai-shan, 183, 189, 201
Shortland Islands, 261
shovel-shaped incisors, 31, 44, 47, 50, 206
Shutler, R., 244, 250, 264, 321
Siassi Islands, 103
Sieveking, G. de G., 168
Sigatoka, **9.16**, 252, 263-4, 274
Sikaiana, 129, 134
Sikumango, 249
silkworm, 157
silver, 87, 187
Simmons, D.R., 384, 387, 390-1, 400, 406
Simmons, R.T., 33-5
Singapore, 172
Sinnett, P., 35
Sinoto, Y.H., 321, 324-6, 332, 335, 352, 386
Siuai, 99-100, 102, 144
Skinner, H.D., 321, 384-5
slab-graves, 194, **8.21**, 227-8, 232, 312-3
Smart, C., 277
Smith, S.P., 301, 305-6, 348, 382-4
Society Islands, 48, 127-8, 139, 141, 147, 298, 300-8, 315, 318, 324-5, 329-32, 335, 337-43, 348, 352, 354, 356, 385-6, 388, 390, 403
Soejono, R.P., 74, 220, 228
Sogeri, **9.34**
Sohano Island, 249, 256, 260, 262, 270
Solheim, W.G. II, 161, 213-5, 267, 282
Solo Man, 42-5, **2.13**, 51, 59
Solomon Islands, 20-1, 92, 100, 128-9, 147, 269, 297
  languages, 119, 122, 125-6, 130-1, 134
  physical anthropology, 27, 34
  prehistory, 238, 242, 248-9, 256, 259-60, 270, 273, 320
  societies, 96, 98, 103, 244
Somrong Sen, 176-9, **7.17, 7.18**, 188-90, 193-5, 198, 201, 221
Song-Ma River, 187
Sonsorol, 105
Sorensen, P., 166, 168, 170, 185
Sorgoson Province, 214-5
Southeast Asia, Island, 19, 20, 283-5, 297, 423
  faunas, 54-5
  horticulture in, 135-52 pass.
  linguistic history, 88, 117-8, 121-5, 131-2, 421
  Neolithic and Metal Age, 170-80, 203-32, 266-7, 282
  physical anthropology, 21, 25-47, 421-2
  Pleistocene and early Holocene archaeology, 56-62, 71-80

societies, 88-92, 112-3, 423
Southeast Asia, Mainland, 19
  Hoabinhian in, 60, 64-7, 80
  horticulture , 135-52 pass., 422
  linguistic history, 88, 122, 131, 203
  Neolithic and Metal Age, 153-80, 198, 225, 247
  physical anthropology, 21, 44-7, 421-2
  Pleistocene archaeology, 56, 59, 62
  societies, 85-8
South Point, Hawaii, 325, 354
Spaniards, 90-1, 95, 141, 238, 283, 300-1, 337, 354, 363, 372, 374, 377
Specht, J., 243, 249, 260, 270
Spencer, J.E., 141
spindle whorls, 153, 157-9, **7.5**, 163, 168, 173, 175-6, 188, 190, **7.29**, 193, 198, **7.35**, **8.2a**, 206
Spirit Cave, 69, 71, 76, 139, 156, **7.3**, 161, 168, 170, 172, 193
Spoehr, A., 282-3, 307
Srivijaya, 228
Stegodon, 54-5, 57, 59, 76
Stewart Island, 381
Straits of Lombok, 54
Straits of Makassar, 54
Strickland Gorge, 94
Subanun, 90
sugar cane, 122, 139, 360, 362, 373
Suggs, R.C., 311, 321, 334
Sulawesi, 20, 30, 46-7, 54-5, 59, 62, 80, 85, 89, 123, 125, 132, 139, 148, 150, **7.15**, 173, **7.16**, 197, 267, 286
  megaliths, 226, 228
  Neolithic, 203, 209, 216-21
  stone industries, 63, 72-5, 78
Sullivan, A., 414
Sullivan, L.R., 48, 306
Sulu Archipelago, 208-9
Sumatra, 20, 30, 54, 64, 70, 78, 80-1, 89, 124-5, 135, 149-50, 170, **7.15**, 197-8, 220-1, 224-8, 232, 268, 422
sumatraliths, **3.6**, 66, 68-70
Sumba, 30, 221, 226
Sumbawa, 222, 226
Sunda Shelf, 20, **2.9**, 54, 421-2
Sunglon River, 56
Suqe society, 100
Sutayasa, I.M., 73, 215, 225, 259
Suwarrow, 352
sweet potato, 95-6, **6.6**, 140-52 pass., 238, 242, 311, 356, 360, 362-3, 375, 381-2, 388, 391, 395-6, 399, 406, **13.21**, 409-16
Swindler, D.R., 47-8
Szechwan, 70, 156

Tabon Cave, Neolithic and Metal age, 193, 207-14, 220, 231
  Pleistocene, 47, 59-63, **3.3**, 70, 72, 237
Tafahi Island, 248
Tahaa, 337
Tahai, 367-8
Tahiti, Tahitians, 21, 147, 305-7, 363, 383
  canoes, 298-303, **11.4**, 327
  prehistory, 337-44, 348, 351, 356-7
  society, 102, 109-11, 149, 338-9, 353-4, 365, 423
Taipivai Valley, 333-5

Tairua, 386, 398
T'ai-tung, 70
Taiwan, 20, 49, 54-5, 70-1, 80, 268, 308, 330, 422
  languages, 121-4, 131-3
  prehistory, 155-60, 172-5, 179-81, 193, 203-7, 209, 213-4, 220, 231
  societies, 84, 88, 91-2, 141, 423
T'ai-yüan Culture, 206
Takakoto, 344
Takaroa, **12.13**
Takuu, 129, 134
Talasea, 247, 250
Talaud Islands, 73, 209, 215-7, 220, **8.25**, 230-1, **9.22**, 259
Tamate Society, 100
Tam Hang, 58, 69
Tami Islands, 103
Tam Pong, 69
Tampanian industry, 57-8
Tane, 306
Tangaloa (Tangaroa), 306-7, 338, 345
Tangi'ia, 348
Tanjong Bunga, 170
Tanjong Periuk, 221
Tanna, 29, 264
T'an-shih-shan Culture, 158, 160
Ta-p'en-k'eng, 155, **7.2**, 203-6, **8.2**
tapu, 99, 109, 113, 338
Taputapuatea, 338, 340
Taramakau River, 392
Taranaki, 381, 400, 410
taro - see aroids
Tasaday, 422
Tasmania, Tasmanians, 25-6, 45, 63, 75, 121, 262
tattooing 92, 247, 253, **9.18**, 255, 286, 318, 321, **11.17**, 368, 388, 396, **13.13**, **13.14**, 406
Taufa'ahau Tupou IV, King of Tonga, 312
Taumako, 100, 130, 134
Taveuni, 264-5
Taylor, H.W., 35
Taylor, R., 410
Tegurwangi, **8.21**
tektites, 58, 73
Teluk Berau (MacCluer Gulf), 218
Tenggarese, 30
Tepoto, 344
Te Rauparaha, 109
terracing, 144, 147-9, 227, 286-7, 312-3, 316, 329, 334-5, 342, 346, 356, 360-1, 406, 410, 414
Terrell, J., 260, 266
Tetiaroa, 338
Te Wahi Pounamu, 381, 392, 399, 417
Thai-Kadai languages, 21, 85-8, 123, 165
Thailand, 19, 80, 136, 141, 149, 151
  Hoabinhian, 41, 64, 69
  Neolithic and Metal Age, 153, 156, 161-70, 172, 175, 179, 180, 183, 185, 189, 198-9, 215
  societies, 85-8, 113, 195
Thanh-Hoa, 66, 176, 183, 187, 195
Thao Kham, 187, 197, **7.34**
Thomas, D., 124
Thompson, L., 283
Thomson, W.J., 365, 370

Tiahuanaco, 311, 374-6
Tianko Panjang, 78, 221
Tien, 189
Tikopia, 107-10, 129, 134, 217
Timor, 20, 55, 57, 62, 75, 76, **3.10**, 89, 119-120, 141, 151, 209, 216-8, 220, 235
tin, 164, 228
Tinian, 282-5
Tirimoana *pa*, 409
Toala, 30
Toalean industry, 46, 73-6, 78, 217
Tobi, 105, 130
Tobias, P., 40
tohua, 333-5
Toi, 383-5
Toiminapo, 243-4, 260
Tokelau Islands, 109-110, 113, 128, 302, 308, 317, 320
Tolai, 104
Tonga, 29, 83-4, 152, 304-5, 307-8, 423
  canoes, 298, 300-2, 330
  languages, 126-7, 134
  physical anthropology, 33-4, 48-9
  prehistory, 244, **9.13**, 247-8, 250-5, **9.17**, **9.18**, 297, 311-8, 320, 329, 352
Tongareva (Penrhyn Island), 110
Tongoa, 259-60, 270-2
Tor Valley, 96
Toraja, 30
Torres Straits, 62, 125
Touru, 101
trade, 83, 95-6, 98, 100, 183, 189, 220, 230-2
  in Melanesia, 95-100 pass., 102-4, 112, 235, 247-8, 250, 254-5, 266-9
  in Polynesia, 392-3, 398-9
Tran Ninh, 195-8, 201, 207, 227, 228
transferrins, 52
Trans New Guinea Phylum, 64, 120-1
Tran van Tot, 189
Trieng-Xen, 67
Trinil fauna, 40, 55-6, 58
Trobriand Island, 98-9, **4.7**, **6.4**, 266, 269, 273, **9.33**
Truk, **2.7**, 105-6, 130, 272, 282, 295
Tsinling mountains, 59, 70
Tsou, Tsouic, 92, 123, 203, 206
Tu (god), 306
Tu (Tahitian chief), 338
Tuamotu Archipelago, 48, 128, 298, 300-3, 308-9, **11.15**, 329-31, 337-8, 340, 343-4, 352, 356
Tubuai, 344-5
Tui Manu'a, 112
Tui Ha'a Takalaua dynasty, 312-4
Tui Kanokupolu dynasty, 312-4
Tui Tonga dynasty, 312-4
Tupaia, 300, 304, 327, 383
Turkey, 164
Tuyen-Quang, 180
Tzu-yang, 44, 51

Ua Huka, 321-3
Uai Bobo, 218
Ugi, 98
Ulawa, 98
Ulithi, 105-6, 130
Ulu Leang, 74

Ulu Tianko, 78
Unea, 287
unilineal descent, 84, 89-99 pass., 107,
    112-13, 275
Updike, J., 356
Upolu, **4.12**, 253, 314, 316
Utupua, 100
Uvea (Loyalty Islands, West Uvea), 100-1,
    128-9, 134
Uvea (Wallis Island, East Uvea), 110, 128,
    272, 312, 316-7

Vailele, 314-6, 323
Vaitootia, 324, 329, 386, 403
Vaitupu, 129
Vandermeersch, B., 189
Vanderwal, R., 244, 256, 269, 277
Van-Dien, 179
Vanua Levu, 114, 126, 264-5, 274
Varela, Andia Y., 300-1, 338
Vatcha, 250, 252, 261-2
Vava'u, 253, 313
Vayda, A.P., 308, 415
Veddoids, 30, 132
Vella Levella, 119
Venezuela, 35
Verin, P., 344-6
Viet-Khe, 183
Vietnam, 19, 54
    Hoabinhian, 46, 64-9, **3.6**
    languages, 21, 121-4, 174, 194, 203
    Neolithic and Metal Age, 168, 173,
        175-94, 198-9, 213, 229
    Pleistocene industries, 57-8
    societies, 85-8, 195
Villafranchian fauna, 53, 55
Vinapu, 366-8, 376
Vitaria, 345-6

Vitiaz Straits, 103
Viti Levu, 29, 101, 126, 250-2, **9.16**, 264-5,
    273-4, 323
Vuda, 264-5

Wabag, 94, **4.5**
Waddell, E., 145
Waenganui, 381-2, 391, 395-6, 399, 406,
    417
Wahgi Valley, 95, 103, 144, 238, 277
Waiahukini, 325
Waikato, 381-2, 395, 404, 410-13
Waioneke, 410
Wairarapa, 383, 396, 417
Wairau Bar, 324, 326, 385-6, **13.4**, 388,
    390, 392, 400
waisted tools, 63-4, **3.5**, 67, 69-70, 172, 220,
    233, 235, 237, 242-4, 266, 295
Waitaki River, 390
Wajak, 45
Wakaya, 265
Wallacea (Wallace Line), 20, 30, **2.9**, 54-5,
    57, 62, 79-80, 149
Wallanae River, 59
Wanigela, 266-7, 278
Wanlek, 64, 240
Ward, G., 398
Washington Island, 352
water buffalo, 85, 135, 149, 151, 165, 227
Watom Island, 244-52 pass.
Watson, J.B., 95
Watson, W., 189
Webber, J., 357-8
Weidenreich, F., 40, 44-5
Weishui Valley, 156-7
wheat, 136, 157
White, J.P., 95, 235, 237, 244
Whyte, R.O., 149

Willaumez Peninsula, 103, 247
Willems, W.J.A., 221
Williams, F.E., 273
Williams, H.W., 384
Williams, J., 147, 301, 304, 337, 345, 350
Williamson, R.W., 306
Wilson, J., 312-3, 338
Wilson, J.A., 383
Winters, N.J., 47
Wiri, 414
Woleai, 106
Worman, E., 189
writing, 157, 180, 363-4, 376-7
Wurm, S., 120-121, 130-1

Xuan-Loc, 191, 193, 194

yaqona - see *kava*
Yami, 89
yams, 71, 98, **4.7**, 113, 122, 136, 139-40,
    6.4, 142, 145-8, 152, 311, 362, 381, **13.21**
Yang-shao Culture, 141, 157-8, 172, 175,
    198
Yangtze River, 19, 70, 85, 157, 170, 172,
    181, 185
Yanuca Island, 252, 264
Yap, 20, 105-6, **4.9**, **4.10**, 110, 124, 130,
    132, 134, 281-6, 295, 303
Yasawa Islands, 126
Yaws, 285
Yayoi, 198
Yen, D.E., 395
Ying-p'u, 159
Yüan-shan Culture, 172, 179, 203-7, **8.2**,
    213-5, 220, 247
Yüeh, 207, 231, 268
Yuku, **3.5**, 235
Yule Island, 256-8, **9.30**, 269
Yünnan, 70, 173, 183, **7.22**, 187-91, 201